A History of the LNER:
The Age of the Streamliners, 1934–39

A History of the LNER
II. The Age of the Streamliners, 1934-39

Michael R. Bonavia, M.A., Ph.D., F.C.I.T.

GUILD PUBLISHING
LONDON

This edition published 1985 by Book Club Associates by arrangement with
George Allen & Unwin

Set in 10 on 12 point Bembo by Nene Phototypesetters Ltd, Northampton
and printed and bound in Great Britain by
Biddles Ltd, Guildford and King's Lynn

Contents

Illustrations

Maps of the 1935–40 New Works Programme

Preface and Acknowledgments

Of the three volumes planned for this history, whilst the first and last cover roughly a decade each, this book is limited to the much shorter period from 1934 to the outbreak of war, which has often been considered to contain all the LNER's finest achievements. Nostalgia, therefore, tends to concentrate attention upon it. And even if the story of the A4 streamliners and the High Speed Trains has often been told, there are interesting details to be brought out, of which most present day readers will have had no personal experience, as well as other and very important elements in a great company's history.

I am greatly in the debt of friends and former colleagues who have read and commented upon portions of the present text, especially M. A. Cameron, A. A. Harrison and R. A. Long. But, as always, responsibility for any errors is that of the author alone.

M. R. B.

I
The Second Decade Opens

At the end of the first decade of its life as an amalgamated company, the LNER had emerged with a distinct personality or corporate image, and claimed a loyalty from its managers and staff that was in general distinct from, but not competitive with, loyalties to the former constituent companies. There were several reasons for this fortunate state of affairs. First – paradoxically perhaps – was the degree of toleration shown by headquarters to the continuation of pre-Grouping practices. There was relatively little trampling upon former rivals, no paying off of old scores such as embittered so many people in the early days of the LMS.

Secondly, there was the prestige enjoyed by the Chairman and Chief General Manager, and their continuity in office, which again contrasted with the rapid changes in the LMS top echelons between 1923 and 1926. Whitelaw as Chairman, R. L. Wedgwood as Chief General Manager, Robert Bell as Assistant General Manager, and H. N. Gresley as Chief Mechanical Engineer, had all been firmly in the saddle since 1923. At Area level, there had not been quite the same continuity among the Divisional General Managers but tensions were almost confined to the Southern Area. There were occasions when this assembly of the 'Three Greats' seemed to be an awkward management unit and might have been better split into a GN/GC Area and a separate GE Area.

Oddly enough, in some ways the LNER's decentralised organisation gave the Chief General Manager a power of deciding matters which on some other railways would have been left to a chief departmental officer. Although the Divisional General Managers disposed effectively of day-to-day management questions within their own Areas, there were many matters affecting more than one Area, or in which the LNER had to speak with a single voice. These had to be dealt with by committees of the departmental officers of all three Areas. Minutes of the committees were sent to the Chief General Manager for approval before action was taken. The CGM obtained the views of the Divisional General Managers before deciding whether or not to approve proposals; and this made for delay. On the other hand, it was the CGM who settled, for instance, proposed changes in the East Coast Main Line train timetable – the sort of subject that on the GWR would have been within the prerogative of the Superintendent of the Line and not of the General Manager.

The volume of committee paper flowing into the Chief General Manager's office had to be handled in the first instance by the CGM's Heads of Sections. These people in consequence exercised considerable influence through their ability to initiate, suggest, and to draft letters for Wedgwood's approval and signature. The positions of Head of Section were often held by able young men destined for promotion in the near future; Robert Bell used them, to some extent, as posts

1 No. 1 platform at King's Cross in the 1930s.

affording training in top management for future high-fliers. The canny R.B. had an unequalled knowledge of the strengths and weaknesses of individuals, whom he moved around like pieces on a chessboard. Career progress might be halted if R.B. decided that someone was 'clerkly'. There could also be rare moments when he might say, rolling his Scottish r's: 'The time has come for you to leave the hurly-burly of the yards for the purple and fine linen of the head office.'

Salaries of the LNER were certainly much lower than those for comparable posts on the LMS. There was, however, a system of 'consolation prizes' for those for whom higher authority expected no further promotion – the appointment to stationmaster posts which included a 'coal sale'. The LNER had inherited from the North Eastern Railway and maintained the practice whereby at various stations the SM was also the merchant for retail sales of coal delivered to his station. In many, if not most cases, the proceeds of the coal sale exceeded the official salary of the SM, and some incumbents were known to refuse promotion on the ground

14

2 Liverpool Street: a quiet period in the cathedral!

that they would be seriously out of pocket if they had to move away.

There was another, if less remunerative, practice on the ex-GER Section. One or two stations also served as Post Offices. At Coldham, near Wisbech, for instance, as one retired LNER officer has recalled, the GPO paid the railway the princely sum of £20 per annum for this service, out of which the stationmaster retained £5 – his clerk, however, actually performing the duties without any supplement to his railway pay!

The welding together of the LNER was undoubtedly accelerated by R.B.'s movement of junior officers all around the system, often at short notice and, it must be said, often also with salary increments of no more than £25 a year. Sometimes the Divisional General Managers would object to an intended move, but R.B. could then always successfully invoke the authority of the Chief General Manager.

15

3 The peace of Marylebone – note the 'Wembley Stadium' platform sign.

The CGM was strongly supported by his two Assistant General Managers, Robert Bell and Kenelm Kerr, who always preserved the courtesies even though they were not on the most cordial personal terms. K.K., an expert in labour relations, hankered for a return to management which he had briefly enjoyed as Passenger Manager of the North Eastern Railway; but R.L.W. firmly kept him to his sphere of staff work – excluding, of course, managerial and career planning, reserved strictly to R.B.

The emergence of a corporate identity for the LNER was promoted by exceptionally able publicity, guided first by W. M. Teasdale and later by C. G. Dandridge. A subsidiary factor was the excellent *LNER Magazine* which in 1927 had replaced the former *Great Eastern Railway Magazine*, which it closely resembled in format.

However, the LNER's physical shape still contained a number of apparent contradictions. The glamour of the East Coast Main Line, with Gresley's handsome Pacific locomotives and modern coaching stock was one side of the picture; on the other was, for example, the fact that the LNER had by far the largest number of four and six-wheeled passenger carriages still

4 C1 Atlantic no. 4423 passing Grantham with the down 'Queen of Scots' Pullman.

trundling around, since in 1933, the total numbers of non-bogie carriages were as follows:

LNER	3,270
LMS	961
GWR	744
SR	489

Most of this stock was six-wheeled, but there were 436 four-wheelers. And that interesting Victorian phenomenon, the hot water foot-warmer, had survived into LNER days; there had been trains in the Norwich District with no heating other than foot-warmers in the winter of 1923–4! On the Great Eastern line there also survived some six-wheeled saloons lettered 'Private Carriage' which had originally been built in Victorian days for the transport of corpses, with wide central doors giving access to what had formerly been a coffin compartment.

This mixture of the glamorous new and the interesting antique was brought home to me over the period 1934–9. For two years, between 1934 and 1936, I occupied a flat in London's Northern Heights, enjoying a view to the south and east stretching to the Thames estuary. In between, at the foot of the slopes of Muswell Hill and the grounds of the Alexandra Palace, was a stretch traversed by the Great Northern main line. One of the advantages of this residence, apart from the fine view, was that at night, and especially when the wind was in the east, the sounds of the railway came clearly through the windows.

Most appreciated was the sound of the night sleeping car trains, the exhaust of an A3 clearly demonstrating the hard-won acceleration over the brief level stretch between the top of Holloway bank at 1 in 100 and the start of the long 1 in 200 from Wood Green to Potters Bar – eight miles of unremitting climb with a heavy train.

5 The non-stop 'Flying Scotsman' passing through York, headed by A3 no. 2744, 'Grand Parade'.

Equally distinctive was the sound of an up express drifting rapidly towards Finsbury Park with the engine's regulator closed, or with perhaps just a wisp of steam. Here one heard most clearly the famous 'Gresley knock' – the clanking of those loose big-ends that other engineers criticised but which Gresley stoutly defended.

Against this background of familiar sounds, in 1935 a new and thrilling one began to be heard – the melodious chime whistle of the A4s at the head of their streamlined trains. The first such train was the 'Silver Jubilee', which heralded a new era in passenger travel in Britain. One sometimes felt that the drivers enjoyed showing off their new and arresting warning of approach – certainly they pulled the whistle chains more often than their mates equipped with nothing more than the traditional British squeal, which had so amused the Americans when the LMS

'Royal Scot' (with false nameplates!) made its celebrated tour on the far side of the Atlantic!

The slopes of Muswell Hill, with visits to Hornsey station, were a favourable location for observing the LNER at its most advanced and progressive. There was another side to the LNER, however, which could be seen nearby at Cranley Gardens or Highgate Stations – the cramped suburban articulated stock, dragged up the Northern Heights by N2 tank engines, interspersed with North London trains headed by LMS 'Jinties' and composed of stock that offered 1st, 2nd and 3rd class accommodation in vehicles that were only now changing from ancient four-wheeled North London teak sets to red LMS suburban bogies. These services were a monument to the weak-kneed Great Northern desire to rid itself of the 'suburban increment' in 1875 by approaching the North London for facilities in Broad Street Station in the City – an invitation to a Trojan horse, since the GN, far

18

6 Approaching the high girders of the Tay Bridge.

John Spencer Gilks

from gaining access to a City terminus cheaply, found it had to give the North London extensive running powers on terms very favourable to the smaller railway.

However, this blunder in railway financial strategy gave commuters like myself an agreeable choice of routes to the City, either into Moorgate Street or Broad Street, with extensive interchange possibilities at Finsbury Park.

Not long afterwards, a move away from the suburbs into a remote Hertfordshire village gave an insight into another aspect of the LNER – the survival of pre-Grouping practices. I moved to Standon, which enjoyed a single-platform station on the Buntingford branch from St Margaret's, itself an offshoot of the Ware and Hertford branch from the Cambridge main line. Here a daily commuter to Liverpool Street could still appreciate Great Eastern traditional methods. Two trains up, and two trains down, over the single-line branch carried through

19

7 Typical of the GN of S Section – Aboyne station.

8 Still six-wheelers in the 1930s – D9 no. 5109 nears Grimsby with a Lincoln–Cleethorpes train.

carriages to and from the City. These were ceremoniously attached and detached at St Margaret's with much propelling and engine backing.

A remarkable train which normally took me homewards was the 6 pm from Liverpool Street, oddly enough departing from the principal main line departure platform, No. 9. This curious caravan in 1936 was hauled by a J15 0–6–0 goods locomotive. Behind the engine came three coaches for Buntingford; four for Hertford (East); three for Bishop's Stortford; and – until October 1936 – a slip carriage for Waltham Cross, the last surviving 'slip' on the Great Eastern Section. Along the Lea Valley this collection of assorted through portions would reach about 45 mph, when the locomotive would develop a curious fore-and-aft surging motion that, transmitted to the front vehicles, could induce a distinct feeling of seasickness.

But, by and large, despite these rural backwaters, the LNER by 1936 was well into the period of achievement. The management had shaken off the worst effects of post-war depression and almost every month brought news of some improvement, some evidence of a spirit of enterprise. The most tangible evidence of this was the development of Britain's first High Speed Train, the first in which speeds of 90 mph were regularly attained to meet the timetable's requirements. It seemed to proclaim that railways were not in decline after all.

2
The Age of the High Speed Trains

The period from 30 September 1935, when the 'Silver Jubilee' started to run between King's Cross and Newcastle, up to the outbreak of war four years later, when the 'Jubilee' and its later companions, the 'Coronation' and the 'West Riding Limited', were stored away, never to reappear, is often considered to be the LNER's peak of achievement. The 'streamliners' had enormous popular appeal, and in many ways represented the ultimate in passenger travel behind a steam locomotive – a fine climax to a century of development since the Rainhill trials of 1830. Their publicity value was skilfully exploited by the LNER.

The story of their origins is a fascinating one. By the early 1930s, diesel-electric traction was beginning to appear on the railways of the USA, supported by an indigenous oil industry and a powerful automobile manufacturing industry deeply involved in diesel engine development. (There was a parallel interest in high speed with steam locomotives; but the newer technology of the diesel claimed most attention.) However, the first really striking developments took place in Europe, and in a year when the world economic depression was at its worst. The Deutsche Reichsbahn, which had been interested early on in the development of diesel railcars capable of making fast inter-city services attractive to business men, in May 1933 placed in service the 'Fliegende Hamburger', an articulated diesel two-coach set carried on three bogies, the power unit being two 410 hp Maybach engines, with electric transmission. The schedule for this train's Berlin–Hamburg run of 178 miles required start-to-stop average speeds of 77.4 mph westbound, and 76.3 mph eastbound, with long stretches of continuous running at about 85 mph.

In Britain public attention was for a time chiefly attracted by the developments in America, starting with the 'Burlington Zephyr' (so-called because of its light-weight construction), which on 26 May 1934 covered the 1,015 miles from Omaha to Chicago in 13 hours 5 minutes, at an average speed of 77.6 mph, roughly halving the time of the principal steam express over the same route. The maximum speed attained was 112.5 mph.

This train's striking appearance, fully streamlined and with articulated construction as a 'triplet' unit on four bogies, seemed to foreshadow a brilliant future for diesel multiple-unit express services; certainly the enterprise of the Chicago Burlington and Quincy Railroad was quickly followed, first by the Union Pacific with a six-car diesel electric set, which made a record run in October 1934 between Los Angeles and

9 Symbolising the prosperity and confidence of the North Eastern Railway: the Royal Station Hotel, York.

New York, 3,259 miles, in 56 hours 55 minutes, and then by various other railways.

But American examples have traditionally not exerted great influence on British railway practice. Gresley had been very interested in developments nearer home especially in Germany and had obtained the speed and power output calculations of the 'Fliegende Hamburger' over the Berlin–Hamburg route. He also travelled on the train and on his return prepared a report which was submitted to the LNER Board on 29 June 1934.

He reported quite favourably on the running characteristics of the German train, but had been very impressed by the need for streamlining. He wrote: 'At a speed of 100 mph the wind resistance, notwithstanding the stream-lining, absorbs over 80% of the power of the engines, but this can probably be reduced by nearly 20% as the stream-lining can be improved.' In conclusion, he told the Board: 'The results have been so satisfactory that the German State Railways have ordered several more similar trains.'

The Board were impressed and agreed that the Chief Mechanical Engineer should continue his investigations. Gresley's next step was to translate the German diesel data into possible timings for a similar diesel unit operating between King's Cross and Newcastle. The specification was based upon the existing gradients and permanent speed restrictions of the East Coast Main Line, and with a train seating 140 passengers. With a power unit of the type used in the 'Fliegende Hamburger', the calculations yielded an estimated journey time of 4½ hours for the 268.3 miles.

10 A4 no. 2509, 'Silver Link', on the 'racing stretch' near Essendine with the up 'Silver Jubilee' on 10 May 1937.

Gresley came to the conclusion that it should be possible to obtain a sufficient power output, yielding even higher speeds, from a modified version of his A3 Pacific design, but also to provide greatly increased passenger capacity with a train of seven or eight vehicles instead of a two-coach unit.

Some years later, in his Presidential address to the Institution of Mechanical Engineers on 22 October 1936, Gresley described how he decided that, to obtain a sufficient margin of power from a modified A3 Pacific, in his own words, 'it would be essential to streamline the engine and train as effectively as possible, and at the same time to make sundry alterations to the design of cylinders and boiler which would conduce to freer running and to securing an ample reserve of power for fast uphill running.'

The 'sundry alterations' included the raising of boiler pressure from 220 lb per sq. in. to 250 lb, and a remodelling of the internal passages between boiler, steam chest, cylinders and exhaust to assist the smooth flow of steam. Springing and balancing were also attended to.

Streamlining was a new departure for British locomotive designers. Gresley was able to utilise the wind tunnel in the National Physical Laboratory for experiments which indicated that, at 80 mph, streamlining would show a saving of 97 hp compared with a standard Pacific and at 90 mph the saving would rise to 138 hp. These experiments eventually produced the characteristic shape of the A4 locomotives.

Meanwhile, tests of the speed capacity of existing Pacific locomotives had been carried out with encouraging, not to say exciting, results. On 30 November 1934 the classic A1 Pacific, no. 4472, 'Flying Scotsman', with Bill Sparshatt at the regulator, made an 'experimental run' with four coaches, including the LNER dynamometer car, from London to Leeds and back, achieving a time of 2 hours 32 minutes for the journey of 185.8 miles – 41 minutes less than the normal schedule of the fastest booked train, or an average start–to–stop average speed of 73.4 mph. The maximum speed on the up journey approached 100 mph on the Grantham–Peterborough section. On 3 January 1935 Wedgwood reported to the Board on the results of this trial run and added, 'We are still studying the improvement of our services.'

This 'record of records', as Cecil J. Allen then called it, was followed by another and even more important trial run on 5 March 1935, when a more modern engine only seven years old, the A3 'Papyrus', with higher boiler pressure and smaller cylinder diameter than the A1, made a test trip from King's Cross to Newcastle and back. This time there was a heavier load of six bogies including the dynamometer car, which would, with a normal train composition, have provided just twice as many seats as the diesel 'Fliegende Hamburger'. The average speed of the whole return journey was 68.7 mph; there were one or two delays which affected the running, but no less than 300 miles were covered at 80 mph or more and on the return journey a new record of 108 mph was recorded on the descent from Stoke Tunnel, a world record for the period. Wedgwood told the Board's Traffic Committee on 29 March 1935 that the Newcastle trial run meant that 'a definite recommendation can now be made for the inclusion in the timetable of a high-speed train between London and Newcastle, scheduled to perform the journey in four hours, compared with the present fastest time of 5 hours 6 minutes.' The Traffic Committee approved the proposal.

Once Board authority had been obtained to go ahead, in Gresley's words, 'the designs for the engines and carriages were prepared and the complete train built in the Company's works at Doncaster in the remarkably short time of five months.' All the drawings for the locomotive – the first A4, to be named 'Silver Link' – were prepared under the direct supervision of T. A. Steel, Chief Locomotive Draughtsman at Doncaster. He must have had an exciting five months. The challenge was to produce very quickly a steam locomotive that could reduce the estimated diesel timing of 4½ hours between King's Cross and Newcastle, and that with a greatly increased passenger load, to a target of four hours. The challenge was willingly accepted.

The new train set constructed simultaneously was, perhaps inevitably in the Jubilee year, named the 'Silver Jubilee', and it made a triumphant entry into passenger service on 1 October 1935, following a private run the previous day making the Newcastle–King's Cross trip with one intermediate stop only, at Darlington, in exactly four hours – 10 am from Newcastle, King's Cross arrival 2 pm; King's Cross depart 5.30 pm, Newcastle arrive 9.30 pm. Seating capacity in the seven vehicles was 198; the make-up consisted of an articulated twin brake third, a triplet articulated restaurant car set, and a twin

11 The 'beaver-tail' observation car of the 'Coronation' passing Greenwood box in 1937.

articulated first class. The interiors were luxurious, with the first-class restaurant car and open saloon having armchair seating reminiscent of Pullman practice. The silver coloured light alloy exterior was extremely attractive. The streamlining of the locomotive was continued by flexible sheathing covering the space between adjacent articulated units in order to reduce aerodynamic drag, though the last vehicle had a normal coach end without a 'spoiler'.

Before entering service on 1 October a trial run with the new train set was made behind 'Silver Link' as far as Grantham, 105.5 miles, covered in 88 minutes, despite signal checks from the preceding train between Little Bytham

and Grantham. The outstanding feature of the run, however, was the speed of 112½ miles an hour attained twice, at Arlesey and Biggleswade.

When the 'Jubilee' entered daily service such high speeds were not required for the four-hour schedule, but 90 mph was commonly and regularly attained, with a high level of punctual arrivals. In its first twelve months of operation it carried an average of 130 passengers in the Up direction and 143 in the Down. It was said that the citizens of York were accustomed to check their watches at 8.09 pm daily by the sound of the A4's chime whistle as the 'Jubilee' passed through York station at reduced speed.

The insertion of such a high-speed schedule into a timetable already congested with closely

12 Inside the 'beaver-tail'.

packed train paths was not easy. In an address to the Institute of Transport on 8 November 1937, V. M. Barrington-Ward, who had become Superintendent (Western Section) Southern Area, discussed the problem of headways and of obtaining adequate braking distances. He commented that 'a high-speed train may perform an excellent service to the public and prove a good advertisement to the railway, but from an operating point of view its effect on other trains is liable to be serious, and of course to the time-table clerk the nearer all trains run to the same speed the better.' B.-W. then discussed the disadvantages of moving distant signals further out or providing repeater distants, and explained that the solution on the LNER was to institute double-blocking for the High Speed Trains – to

signal with two, instead of one, block sections ahead clear – in semaphore areas. In colour-light areas the institution of a double-yellow aspect was considered adequate protection.

The success of the 'Silver Jubilee' led to a decision to extend the high speed principle. On 2 May 1936 Sir Ralph Wedgwood wrote to the Chairman of the Superintendents and Passenger Managers Committee saying that a high speed service from London to Edinburgh in six hours and to Aberdeen in nine hours appeared practicable. (The Aberdeen extension was soon dropped in favour of a Glasgow connection from Edinburgh.) The S and PMs Committee, on grounds of operating convenience, strongly favoured a midday train, leaving at 12.15 in each direction. The Chief General Manager demurred; if the train were to terminate at Edinburgh, a late afternoon service should meet the needs of business men most effectively. This commercial view prevailed over the operating one and, after some argument, a departure of 4 pm from King's Cross for the down train was agreed, with a call at Newcastle only (8.37–8.40 pm) and arrival at Edinburgh at 10 pm. The up train was booked to leave Edinburgh at 4.30 pm and, also calling at Newcastle, to arrive at King's Cross at 10.30 pm.

With the LNER flair for good publicity, the forthcoming coronation was adopted as the title of the new London–Edinburgh train. It was a more ambitious venture than the 'Jubilee', since it was to be a nine-coach train rather than a seven-coach one (312 tons tare instead of 220) with a through working of 393 miles instead of 268. Eight of the cars were articulated twins, the last being the celebrated 'beaver-tail' observation car. The streamlining of the train was completed by this vehicle which not merely offered a passenger amenity but reduced aerodynamic drag. The seating accommodation was 216; meals were served at every seat, except at the seats in the observation car, intended for temporary accommodation only.

In addition to the train supplementary fare a charge of 1s (5p) was made for the observation car seats. Tickets for one-hour sessions were issued by a 'lad attendant' travelling on the train. During the hours of darkness the interior lights were dimmed in the car to improve observation facilities; with a late afternoon departure this was required for most of the year.

The interior design of the 'Coronation' trains was novel: each car had central gangways but was divided by partitions into a series of alcoves. Perspex was extensively used in place of glass, especially for curved panels.

The livery of the train also differed from that of the 'Jubilee', being Garter blue below the waistline but Marlborough blue above; the lettering 'Coronation' in stainless steel was applied to the side of each coach and across the full width of the tail end.

As in the case of the 'Jubilee', before entering passenger service a trial trip was made with the 'Coronation' from King's Cross past Grantham as far as the Barkston triangle (111 miles), where the train was turned for the return to London. The time to passing Grantham ($105\frac{1}{2}$ miles) was $87\frac{1}{2}$ minutes (exactly as scheduled) and a maximum of just over 109 mph was achieved between Grantham and Peterborough.

The 'Silver Jubilee' had been worked by a set of A4s painted silver-grey and appropriately named as follows: 'Silver Link', 'Quicksilver', 'Silver King' and 'Silver Fox'. For the 'Coronation' working a further batch of five A4s was put in service, bearing names of suitably Imperial character – 'Union of South Africa', 'Dominion of Canada', 'Empire of India', 'Commonwealth of Australia' and 'Dominion of New Zealand'. These engines were painted Garter blue, with dark red wheels and stainless steel letters, numbers and mouldings. Each of them also carried the armorial bearings of the country whose name it bore, under the number. It was a nice touch that 'Dominion of Canada's' whistle was of Canadian Pacific Railway design and was specially sent over from Canada. 'Dominion of South Africa's' whistle was of the type used on the South African Railways.

Needless to say, the LNER management derived great satisfaction from the fact that the 'Coronation' with its six-hour schedule for 393 miles, was appreciably faster than its otherwise rather similar rival, the LMS 'Coronation Scot', which required 6 hours 30 minutes for the 399 miles from Euston to Glasgow.

The financial results as well as the enormous fillip to prestige produced by the 'Jubilee' and the 'Coronation' led the Board to approve the

13 Ceremonial exit from 'the Cross': the trial 'Silver Jubilee' leaves in charge of no. 2509 on 27 September 1935.

construction of another high-speed streamlined train, for the Leeds and Bradford service, called the 'West Riding Limited'. The train externally and internally was very similar to the 'Coronation' sets, using the same blue liveries and also accommodating 216 passengers. No beaver-tail observation car could be provided, however, as the 'West Riding' was obliged to reverse in Leeds (Central) station before continuing to Bradford.

The locomotives initially assigned to this service (Bradford depart 11.10 am, King's Cross arrive 2.15 pm; King's Cross depart 7.10 pm,

Bradford arrive 10.15 pm) were two more A4s, named 'Golden Fleece' and 'Golden Shuttle'. They were forerunners of the series bearing the names of birds, of which 'Mallard' was to become the most famous.

The three High Speed Trains were made up of the following five train sets:

One silver-grey eight-car set lettered 'Silver Jubilee'.

Four blue eight-car sets, two lettered 'Coronation', one lettered 'West Riding Limited', one (spare) *not* lettered.

Two beaver-tail cars lettered 'Coronation'.

29

14 Working hard, A4 no. 4495, 'Golden Fleece', sweeps over Stoke summit with the up 'West Riding' on 7 June 1938.

T. G. Hepburn – Rail Archive Stephenson

The last train to be built in the 'streamliner' series was not really in the same class, although it provided a marked improvement upon previous services. It was the 'East Anglian' train between Liverpool Street and Norwich, built at the same time as the 'West Riding Limited' but being neither articulated nor streamlined so far as the coaching stock was concerned. The streamlining was confined to the locomotives assigned to work the train, two B17 4–6–0 Sandringham class engines, formerly named 'Norwich City' and 'Manchester City' but now given a streamlined casing and renamed respectively 'East Anglian' and 'City of London'. They retained the standard LNER green livery.

LNER publicity called the above trains the 'Four Streamliners'; but only three could be classed as High Speed Trains. The 'East Anglian' set comprised six coaches with meal service at all seats and what was described as a compromise between the luxury of the 'Coronation' and that of an ordinary first class carriage. No supplement was charged, in contrast to the practice applying to the three High Speed Trains. The timing of 2 hours 10 minutes from London to Norwich required fast running by GER standards, but not in the ranges where streamlining would effectively reduce the power output re-

15 A4 no. 4489, 'Dominion of Canada', at Ganwick with the down 'Coronation' in 1937.

F. R. Hebron – Rail Archive Stephenson

quired of the locomotive, so that the casing applied to the two locomotives was little more than a cosmetic or publicity device.

Gresley claimed in his Presidential address to the Institution of Mechanical Engineers that the 'Silver Jubilee' was a great financial success – the gross receipts from the running of the train amounted to 13s 11d (69½p) per train mile, whilst the operating expenses (locomotive running, carriage expenses, wages of traffic staff, carriage cleaning, advertising, etc.) were no more than 2s 6d (12½p per mile).

Robert Bell gave some rather different figures in an address to the Institute of Transport's Metropolitan Graduate and Student Society; he claimed that, including catering receipts, the 'Jubilee' had earned 16s 2d (81p) per train mile against 'direct expenses' of 4s 2d (21p) per train mile. This he compared with average LNER passenger train receipts of 5s (25p) per mile against 2s 6d (12½p) direct expenses.

31

16 The man and his machine: Sir Nigel Gresley with A4
no. 4498 named after its designer.

Bell's comparison was not entirely valid; the overall average receipts included hundreds of trains on lightly used branch lines of the type which were eliminated under 'Beeching' in the 1960s. A more useful comparison would have been between the results of the 'Jubilee' and an ordinary King's Cross–Newcastle express of conventional rolling stock running at conventional speeds.

A comparison between the results of the four streamliners was provided in a Memorandum to the Board submitted by Wedgwood on 14 September 1938, when the trains had settled down as part of the normal Monday to Friday timetable.

For the four weeks ended 9 July 1938 the following had been the gross receipts:

	£
Silver Jubilee	8,261
Coronation	12,748
West Riding Limited	4,875
East Anglian	1,840

After deducting the direct expenses which the Chief Accountant considered attributable to the trains, the net receipts had been:

	£
Silver Jubilee	1,284
Coronation	2,018
West Riding Limited	939
East Anglian	441

Looking back after more than forty years, one can view the era of the High Speed Trains from two standpoints. From one, they represented a retreat from the real issue of the capabilities of diesel traction. In a sense they repeated the mistake which the Great Eastern Railway had made in 1920 when it dodged the insistent demand to electrify its worst suburban services by the short-term expedient of the 'Jazz Service' on the Enfield Town and Chingford branches – a skilful redeployment of resources with steam traction, but not a real long-term solution. Similarly, now Gresley showed that steam traction could, with special attention to a small stud of top link locomotives, for a time stave off the challenge of the diesel. Yet, if the LNER had followed the example of America and Germany and invested in one or more high-speed diesel trains in the 1930s, the experience thereby gained would have been invaluable after the war, when the replacement of steam eventually became inevitable,

On the other hand, given the LNER's difficult financial position, there was much to be said for exploiting known technology to the full, and gaining – as was undoubtedly the case – immense prestige and publicity value from steam trains which were an advance on anything previously available in Britain and whose romantic appeal can still affect us today when we look at illustrations of those splendid 'streamliners' of Gresley's creation.

3
Modernisation in Sight: the 1935–40 New Works Programme

At the outset of the world depression of the 1930s, most governments believed that it was necessary to adhere to financial orthodoxy – balanced budgets and strict control over public sector borrowing – in the interests of economic stability. But, eventually, what later were known as Keynesian policies became accepted in both Britain and the USA, involving 'pump priming' through government expenditure on public works which produced a double effect – immediate creation of jobs with some easement of unemployment, and secondary demand for goods and services from a wide range of businesses, filtering down through the whole economy, the so-called 'multiplier'.

The programme in Britain was less ambitious than Franklin Roosevelt's 'New Deal' schemes in the USA or Hitler's massive investment in Autobahnen in Germany; but railways were an obviously suitable organisation for starting 'public' works which would have a spin-off in increased transport efficiency, with benefits to the nation in general.

In July 1933 the necessary legislation was passed to create two government-sponsored bodies, the Railway Finance Corporation and the London Electric Transport Finance Corporation. These bodies made loans to the railways at 2½ per cent interest for schemes designed to relieve unemployment and also improve transport facilities.

The railways were willing enough to use this source of finance to carry out capital works; their main problem was to put forward suitable schemes – which incidentally had to be agreed by the government – quickly. The LNER had some very obvious candidates including main line electrification, many station and running line improvements, and drastic amelioration of both the GN and GE suburban services around London, although detailed plans did not exist and these had to be worked up quickly. They fell into two categories: those to be financed by the Railway Finance Corporation and those, confined to the London area and largely joint with London Transport, to be financed by the sister Corporation.

It is convenient to describe and discuss first the purely LNER schemes financed by the Railway Finance Corporation. These were:

17 Typical of later GER station architecture, now awaiting the handover to London Transport under the 1935–40 New Works plan: Chigwell station in 1937.

Electrification between Manchester and Sheffield, via Woodhead (and to Wath marshalling yard) at 1,500 v. d.c.
Extension of automatic train control
Station improvements at King's Cross, York and Doncaster
Improvements to running line facilities – Colchester to Clacton (doubling between Thorpe-le-Soken and Clacton); Felixstowe branch doubling; Shenfield to Southend: improvements; Ely to Newmarket: improvements
Running loops at various places
Colour-light signalling extensions
Additional rolling stock construction and conversion of gas lighting to electric
Additional steam locomotives (43)

The most important component in many ways was the Manchester–Sheffield–Wath electrification, as Britain's first main line

35

electrification scheme, covering freight as well as passenger traffic. In fact, the reasons for selecting this line now, with hindsight, seem to have been shaky. They were based upon the rather old-fashioned idea that main line electrification could be financially justified only if it could substantially reduce costs where these were high with steam traction, for instance where gradients were severe. That had been the basis for the Great Western's fruitless study of electrification between Taunton and Penzance, and the LMS Crewe–Carlisle study. The modern concept of the 'sparks effect' in stimulating traffic receipts had not yet spread from the Southern to the LNER.

It was therefore a pity that the opportunity was not taken, with cheap Government credit available, to electrify either the Great Northern or the Great Eastern main line – or perhaps York–Newcastle. No one in 1935 could foresee the changes in coal output and movement patterns that forty years later would call in question the very existence of the Manchester–Sheffield line via Woodhead.

The other purely LNER schemes for station improvements, signalling schemes, and running line improvements were mostly to prove their value, though some – like the proposed doubling of the Felixstowe branch – were never carried out.

The schemes to be financed by the London Electric Transport Finance Corporation were prepared jointly with London Transport. The LNER share was estimated to cost £7½ millions; the LPTB 'North-East London' scheme was to cost £10½ millions. The London Passenger Transport Board had come into existence on 1 July 1933, and provision had been made in the Act for a Standing Joint Committee of the LPTB and the four main line railways. This Committee had agreed that the problems of the North and East London commuter traffic could best be solved by a combination of electrification of LNER suburban lines and substantial Tube extensions, in some cases projected over LNER lines which would be handed over to LPTB operation, although in some cases with retention of LNER freight facilities. The Ministry of Transport had accepted these proposals.

The projection of Tube trains extended far beyond the built-up area. It looked to many as though history was repeating itself, with the LNER again escaping from the suburban increment on the GN lines but with London Transport replacing the old North London Railway. The High Barnet and Edgware branches were to become projections of London Transport's Northern Line, the Northern City Line, however, taking over the Finsbury Park–Highgate–Alexandra Palace route, after its electrification and connection at the south end with the existing Finsbury Park–Moorgate Northern City Line, the old Metropolitan Railway's 'Great Northern and City' line, originally built to take rolling stock of main line, not Tube, size.

The advantage to the LNER was to be a substantial reduction in steam train occupation of the busy section of line between Finsbury Park and King's Cross at peak periods, which should enable more trains to be run on the main line to, for instance, Welwyn Garden City, and on the Hertford loop. The suburbs losing LNER services would have a choice of routes to the City or to the West End, via the Northern Line.

London Transport, however, intended to push out further into what later became the 'Green Belt' after joining up the ex-LNER and Northern Lines at Edgware, as far as Elstree and Bushey Heath – an extension that was only very partially in hand when war broke out and which was subsequently abandoned, including the LNER line between Mill Hill East and Edgware.

The two new electric routes were to be Moorgate–Finsbury Park–Highgate–Alexandra

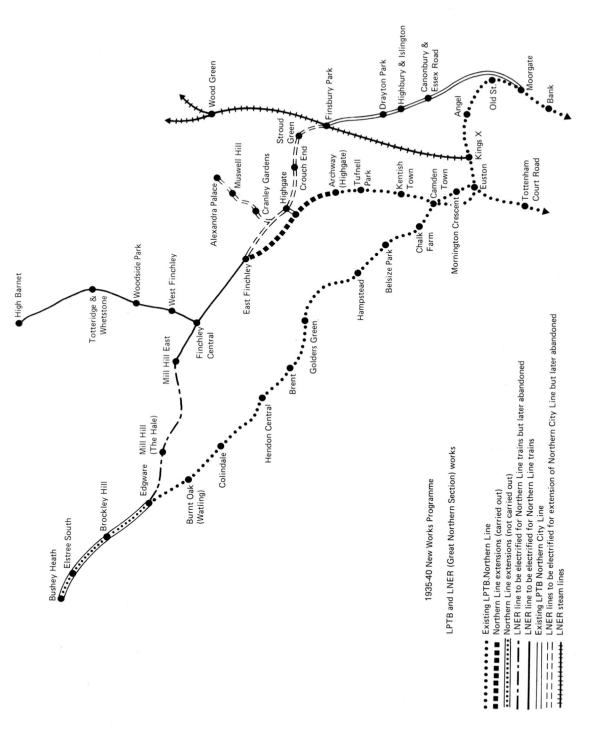

Wood Green

Finsbury Park

Drayton Park

Highbury & Islington

Canonbury & Essex Road

Moorgate

Angel

Old St.

Bank

Kings X

Stroud Green

Crouch End

Muswell Hill

Cranley Gardens

Highgate

Archway (Highgate)

Tufnell Park

Kentish Town

Camden Town

Euston

Tottenham Court Road

Alexandra Palace

East Finchley

Mornington Crescent

Chalk Farm

Belsize Park

Hampstead

High Barnet

Totteridge & Whetstone

Woodside Park

West Finchley

Finchley Central

Mill Hill East

Golders Green

Brent

Hendon Central

Mill Hill (The Hale)

Edgware

Colindale

Burnt Oak (Watling)

Brockley Hill

Elstree South

Bushey Heath

1935-40 New Works Programme

LPTB and LNER (Great Northern Section) works

Existing LPTB.Northern Line

Northern Line extensions (carried out)

Northern Line extensions (not carried out)

LNER line to be electrified for Northern Line trains but later abandoned

LNER line to be electrified for Northern Line trains

Existing LPTB Northern City Line

LNER lines to be electrified for extension of Northern City Line but later abandoned

LNER steam lines

Palace by Northern City Line trains and Arch-way–Highgate–East Finchley–High Barnet or Bushey Heath by Northern Line trains. They were to have an important interchange at High-gate, with a deep-level Tube station below the existing LNER station, connected with it by escalators.

On the Great Eastern side, equally sweeping changes were planned. Whereas in the 1920s the most serious congestion – and the most serious criticism – had existed over the Enfield and Chingford services, which served the older built-up areas such as Stoke Newington and Walthamstow, by the 1930s the pressure had shifted to the main line, in particular Ilford and the rapidly developing areas to the north and east, as far out as Shenfield, in fact. Overcrowd-ing between Ilford and Liverpool Street gave rise to strong Press and public criticism.

The plan here was for the LNER services to be electrified between Liverpool Street and Shenfield, which would ease the problem; and for the Central Line Tube to be extended, partly over existing LNER tracks to Hainault, Wood-ford and Epping but partly on a new alignment from Leytonstone to Newbury Park under an arterial road that had stimulated much develop-ment in the North Ilford area and thereby increased pressure on Ilford's LNER steam services.

The London Transport trains would not take over the LNER services as they stood; the Hainault loop trains were not replaced exactly by Tube trains, and the Epping–Ongar service was left to be operated by a steam shuttle for the time being, though ultimate electrification was in the plan.

The stock proposed for the Liverpool Street–Shenfield electric service – not delivered until after the war – was to reflect the best contem-porary practice, with open saloons and power-operated sliding doors. For a time it was intended that this electrification should in-clude Fenchurch Street to Stratford, but that was later omitted.

A number of LNER stations on the sections to be transferred to the LPTB were extensively remodelled, often in accordance with London Transport's architectural style. Loughton was an outstanding example. Others were to be given little more than a face-lift.

A London Transport scheme which affected the LNER only marginally was that for electri-fication of the Metropolitan and Great Central Joint Line beyond Rickmansworth as far as Amersham and Chesham, with four-tracking between Harrow-on-the-Hill and Watford South Junction. The planning here involved the concentration of services as far as Amersham upon London Transport, with stations beyond Amersham being served only by LNER trains. (When the works were completed after the war, however, rather more 'overlapping' of services was decided upon.)

Question marks still hang over some of the 1935 London area planning. A welcome feature was the cross-platform interchange at Stratford between LNER and London Transport trains, giving passengers a good choice of City or West End services. The other interchange at Highgate between the Northern and the Northern Line Tube trains was abandoned, unfortunately, as a post-war review of the traffic estimates con-cluded that there was insufficient justification for continuing with the Alexandra Palace line electrification.

Whether travellers have been best served by the projection of Tube trains so far into the country is uncertain. It is perhaps arguable that journeys between the West End of London or even the City to places such as Ongar (23½ miles from Liverpool Street) and Epping (16½ miles) are too long for comfort in frequently stopping Tube trains, with their cramped interiors.

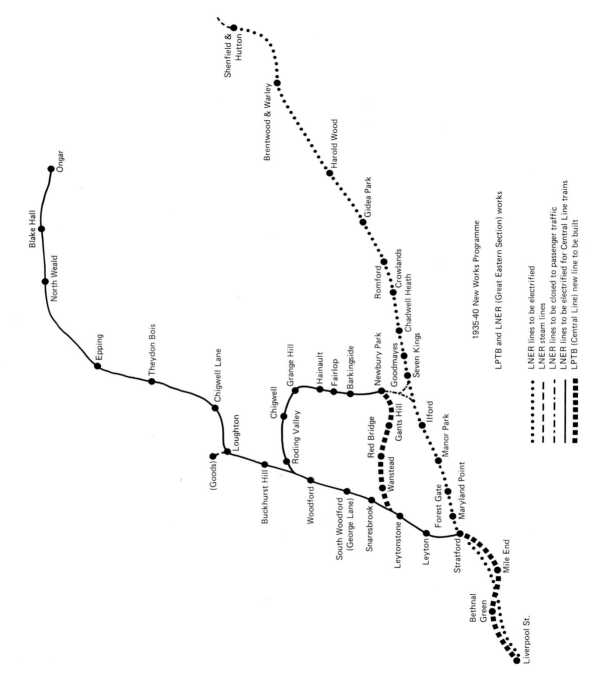

Shenfield & Hutton

Brentwood & Warley

Harold Wood

Gidea Park

Romford

Crowlands

Chadwell Heath

Seven Kings

Goodmayes

Newbury Park

Ilford

Manor Park

Maryland Point

Ongar

Blake Hall

North Weald

Epping

Theydon Bois

Chigwell Lane

Grange Hill

Hainault

Fairlop

Barkingside

Chigwell

Roding Valley

Red Bridge

Gants Hill

Wanstead

Loughton

(Goods)

Buckhurst Hill

Woodford

South Woodford
(George Lane)

Snaresbrook

Leytonstone

Forest Gate

Leyton

Stratford

Mile End

Bethnal
Green

Liverpool St.

1935-40 New Works Programme

LPTB and LNER (Great Eastern Section) works

· · · · · · ·   LNER lines to be electrified

– – – – –   LNER steam lines

–·–·–·–   LNER lines to be closed to passenger traffic

············   LNER lines to be electrified for Central Line trains

▀▀▀▀▀   LPTB (Central Line) new line to be built

18 In the heart of rural Essex, at the end of a single-line branch but eventually to be reached by Central Line 'tube' trains: Ongar station in 1935.

If the LNER seemed only too willing to hand over a large part of its traffic and its responsibility to London Transport, it must be remembered that a new situation had been created under the London Passenger Transport Act, 1933, by the establishment of a pool of receipts from passenger traffic in the London area between London Transport and the four main line companies. This removed the incentive to hang on to the provision of services which could be more efficiently and economically provided by other means.

Upon the outbreak of war most of the works in the 1935–40 Plan were brought to a rapid standstill. The whole of the GN electrification work was halted, as was the Shenfield scheme and the Met and GC line widening, and electrification to Amersham. But LPTB Northern Line trains reached High Barnet on 14 April 1940, East Finchley having already been reached on 3 July 1939. London Transport trains also reached Mill Hill East on 18 May 1941.

By and large, the 1935–40 New Works Programme was calculated to give the LNER, for so long short of capital for improvements, substantial benefits in efficiency and in popular regard. It was tragic that most of the major works were far from complete when war broke out and that so much money had been expended without any rewards accruing. When work was resumed after the war, circumstances had sometimes changed drastically – for instance, the institution of a 'Green Belt' round London inhibiting residential and other development – leading to curtailment or modification of schemes which had been so optimistically started in the late 1930s.

4
Gresley and his Last Designs

The years from 1933 until the outbreak of war saw Gresley at the summit of his career, with a knighthood, an honorary doctorate and the Presidency of the Institution of Mechanical Engineers, all in 1936. He and Stanier of the LMS were generally regarded as the two outstanding locomotive engineers of the period.

Writing years later, in 1945, Oliver Bulleid described Gresley as 'the most notable English locomotive engineer of his generation'. Certainly Gresley's place in engineering history must be a very distinguished one indeed, though his achievements are perhaps more uneven, more open to argument, than those of his contemporary Stanier, whose consistent and constructive policies so exactly fulfilled the needs of that railway. Gresley's outstanding (and always well-publicised) successful designs were accompanied by a few less satisfactory locomotive types. One thing stands out, however; he had a wonderful 'feel' for the external appearance of a locomotive, and practically never produced a design that was not a pleasure to look at, from the splendid series of Pacifics down to the Hunts and Shires, the Sandringham B17s or the more humdrum mixed traffic K3s – all were a splendid visual advertisement for the railway that owned them.

He never persisted very long with a development that failed to yield results as valuable as had been expected; he readily modified designs which showed weaknesses. His obstinacy – if it can be fairly so termed – showed up mainly over the derived motion for the inner cylinder of his three-cylinder designs – the famous 'two-to-one lever' or conjugated motion, to which he adhered although it could have been predicted that as wear developed, valve events would become imprecise and efficiency would be affected – as proved to be the case in the war years, after Gresley's death. He undoubtedly had been shaken by the relatively poor performance of his handsome A1 Pacifics in the exchange trials of 1925 with a Great Western Castle. Great Northern and indeed LNER practice had been slow to realise the virtue of running with wide regulator openings and linked-up valve motion; but Leslie Parker when Locomotive Running Superintendent of the Great Eastern Section was tireless in drumming home this lesson to his enginemen and eventually it spread all over the LNER.

The importance of streamlining the passages by which steam passes from boiler to cylinder had dawned gradually upon locomotive designers; the almost equal importance of minimising back-pressure, by assisting the passage of exhaust steam whilst maintaining the efficacy of the blast, was rather slower of realisation. When Gresley adopted the Kylchap double blastpipe the improvement in performance was marked, yet oddly enough he did not extend its use very much.

19 Pl 2–8–2 no. 2394 (with booster still fitted) leaves Potters Bar tunnel with a New England–Hornsey coal train in 1936.

F. R. Hebron – Rail Archive Stephenson

Gresley toyed (if that is the right word) with the use of ACFL feed water heaters but eventually discarded them. He tried booster engines for the trailing wheels but found the advantages less and the maintenance costs greater than had been hoped. He experimented much longer with poppet valves of the Lentz type, fitted to no less than forty-one of the Hunt and Shire class 4–4–0s. He also, like Stanier, tried out the Caprotti valve gear.

In 1934 he produced a very striking new locomotive, the first express passenger 2–8–2, 'Cock o' the North', at that time the most powerful passenger engine in Britain, also using poppet valves and the Kylchap double blastpipe and chimney. But the second engine in the series, 'Earl Marischal', was fitted with the standard Walschaerts valve gear with derived motion for the inside cylinder.

These magnificent looking machines performed well on the Edinburgh–Aberdeen service for which they were intended, with its severe gradients and service slacks, but before long there were complaints about the effect of the long rigid wheelbase on the track.

Gresley's willingness to experiment, to change and to adapt, was shown when in 1937 he rebuilt his unique high-pressure water-tube boiler 4–6–4, no. 10,000, as a conventional fire-tube boiler engine. He never persevered too long or obstinately with developments where success eluded him, as F. W. Webb had done with compounding.

43

20 Gresley's (rather pointlessly) streamlined
B17 no. 2870, 'City of London', on 21 September 1937.

T. G. Hepburn – Rail Archive Stephenson

Gresley can perhaps be criticised for building locomotives in relatively small batches to individual designs, instead of concentrating on a smaller number of designs that could be mass-produced, more akin to what Stanier was doing on the LMS. His famous Pacifics eventually numbered 119; the engines of which the largest numbers were built included the J.39 0–6–0 goods (289) and the K3 2–6–0 mixed traffic (192) both of which harked back to Ivatt and Great Northern days; the N2 0–6–2T (102, again a GNR design); the O2 2–8–0 mineral engine (66, built first in 1921). The nearest Gresley got to building a general purpose workhorse was the V2 2–6–2 class of which 184 were eventually built, and which carried the main burden of the swollen wartime traffics.

But even these very widely used types were not produced in quantities to match the 633 'Black Fives' on the LMS, for example. And against these useful and successful designs one must set the D49 Hunts and Shires – thirty-four with Walschaerts valve gear and forty-one with Lentz rotary cam valves. They were never wholly satisfactory, very rough riding at speed and far from providing the LNER answer to, say, Maunsell's splendid Schools class on the Southern or even such old stagers in the 4–4–0 class as the Midland compounds.

The B17 4–6–0 Sandringhams too, of which seventy-three were built, were rough riding and had the reputation of being rather sluggish, although in skilled hands they could put up a good performance.

The one-off examples included a couple of S

21 The first P2, no. 2001, 'Cock o' the North', on the
King's Cross turntable on 1 June 1934.

class 0–8–4T banking engines and the Beyer-
Garratt 2–8–8–2T 'Wath banker', as well as the
V4 'Bantam Cock', the lighter version of the V2
– Gresley's last design before the outbreak of
war. The V4 was intended for widespead route
availability owing to its reduced axle loading,
but only two were ever built.

A class specially designed for the West Highland line was the K4 2–6–0 type, of which five
were built, all with splendid Scottish names –
'The Great Marquess', 'Loch Long', 'Cameron
of Lochiel', 'Lord of the Isles', and 'MacLeod of
MacLeod'. They combined a light axle loading
with adequate power – 36,598 lb of tractive

effort, compared with only 30,031 of the K3
class.

Gresley was constantly rebuilding and improving engines to designs by his predecessors
on pre-Grouping railways. These changes may
not always have been personally inspired by
Gresley, but may have originated from some of
his Mechanical Engineers in the Areas, as in the
case of the ex-Great Eastern B12s which were
modified at Stratford when Edward Thompson
took office there, with excellent results.

The B12s that were sent to the GNS Section,
where they did excellent work, fitted with the
ACFL water heater were nicknamed 'Hikers'
owing to the resemblance of the heater cylinders

22 V2 no. 4830 collecting vans off the centre road at Nottingham (Victoria) on 18 June 1939, while working the 12.15 pm (Sunday) train, Manchester Central–Marylebone.

on the top of the boilers to rucksacks slung on someone's back.

When trying to assess from 'outsider' records of locomotive performance the achievements of a great locomotive designer, some inhibiting factors must be taken into account. The Locomotive Running Superintendents or Motive Power Superintendents were responsible to a CME either solely or jointly to the Operating Superintendent. To criticise a chief's designs too openly would certainly be tactless and might prejudice a career. Complaints about performance and suggestions for design changes in a new locomotive class needed to be put forward diplomatically.

Outside observers were dependent upon the goodwill of the railway officers for privileges such as footplate passes and invitations to special test runs. Cecil J. Allen, who was not a professional locomotive man although an LNER employee, would have been handicapped if he had incurred Gresley's displeasure; as it was, his skill and tact enabled him to walk the tightrope without giving offence, whilst not departing from objective observation. But in his account of A4

23 D49/1 no. 236, 'Lancashire', and D49/2 no. 357, 'The Fernie', enter York with an Edinburgh–King's Cross express in the mid-1930s.

'Mallard's' achievement of a world speed record, he wisely omitted to mention that at 126 mph the centre big end ran so hot that the engine was a casualty and could not continue from Peterborough to London as had been intended.

Gresley's flair for publicity was well rewarded, however, on this occasion – 3 July 1938 – when opportunity was taken on a Sunday to test the maximum speed of which an A4 was capable. The trial, as usual carried out between Grantham and Peterborough with a falling gradient mostly at 1 in 200, was not, like previous record runs, a test of the practicability of a proposed new train schedule; it was officially termed a 'brake test' using the spare set of coaches for the 'Coronation' plus the LNER dynamometer car; but the braking only came after a world speed record of 125 mph could be claimed, and then it was only a partial application, bringing the speed down to 70 mph but requiring some 2½ miles for this reduction. There is no doubt that speed record-breaking rather than brake testing was intended and was achieved. It demonstrated the value of 'Mallard's' Kylchap double blastpipe and chimney in assisting high speed free-running; Driver Duddington was experimenting with 40 per cent and 45 per cent cut-off on the downhill run to squeeze the last few miles an hour out of his engine, with 125 mph sustained for some distance. It was later claimed that 126 mph was touched at one point; this conveniently gave a lead, though a tiny one, over the 125 mph of a German streamlined 4–6–4 between Berlin and Hamburg, and enabled the LNER to boast of the world speed record with a steam locomotive.

24 K4 no. 3442, 'The Great Marquess', leaving Crianlarich with a Fort William–Glasgow train.

One of Gresley's many great qualities as a designer was the attention he paid to the needs and the comfort of his enginemen – forward visibility, convenience of controls, weather protection. In his cabs he followed, not the Spartan GNR practice of H. A. Ivatt so much as the excellent provision of the NER under Worsdell and Raven. And he invited and took note of the opinions of footplate staff on these matters, something many engineers did not trouble to do.

It is often emphasised that the CME of a great railway company was far from being solely a designer of new locomotives. He was also

(usually) in charge of the carriage and wagon fleets – Gresley took a close and deep interest in carriage design all his life – and the manager of a very large engineering business in which maintenance and repair work was vastly more important than new construction. Some CMEs, such as Sir Henry Fowler on the LMS, were essentially 'works' men – but not Gresley, who all his life was principally interested in performance and new.designs. He was assisted in concentrating upon this aspect of his job by the organisation of the LNER, under which there was extensive delegation by the CME to Area Mechanical Engineers – based on Doncaster and Stratford for the Southern Area, Darlington for the North Eastern and Cowlairs for the Scottish.

48

25 P2/2 no. 2003, 'Lord President', under repair in Doncaster Works, 3 April 1938.

The Mechanical Engineers – men such as R. A. Thom or Edward Thompson – were very important officers, more than just works managers or assistants to Gresley. This left the CME in his King's Cross office free to concentrate upon policy, design and relations with the Board and, of course, the Chief General Manager and Divisional General Managers. Gresley also enjoyed the support of the Locomotive Committee of the Board, who do not appear to have questioned his policy of producing frequent new designs in small numbers. Of course, with the passing of the years his prestige had become formidable.

One of Gresley's most important achievements, though not one that appeared greatly in the public eye, was his successful advocacy of a Locomotive Testing Station where scientific measurements of performance could be applied under much more strictly controlled conditions than on the line, even with the aid of a dynamometer car. As early as 1927 Gresley had made this point in his Presidential address to the Institution of Locomotive Engineers; and ten years later the directors of the LNER and the LMS – on the latter railway largely persuaded by Sir Harold Hartley, the Vice-President in charge of research – agreed to the construction of a joint Testing Station at Rugby. The GWR had long had a roller rig for static testing at Swindon; but

49

26 A replica of 'Sir Nigel Gresley' presented to the CME by the Chairman of the LNER, William Whitelaw, on 26 November 1937.

Gresley had been impressed by the much more sophisticated equipment in France, at Vitry-sur-Seine, to which he had sent his first P2 2–8–2 express engine, 'Cock o' the North', for testing, with useful results. It was sad that the war and Gresley's death came before the Rugby station was brought into use.

One might sum up with the suggestion that Gresley served the LNER well, having regard to the Company's financial position, especially in enabling it to provide a high-class express pas-senger service on the principal main lines. He did not, however, like Stanier, markedly reduce construction and maintenance costs by evolving a limited range of standard locomotives with consequent reductions in spares and works capacity. The LNER's difficult financial pos-ition might have been expected to call for stan-dardisation and economy; but in the event novelty and glamour were preferred. Half a dozen years after Gresley's death in 1941 Sir Ronald Matthews proclaimed, 'Standardisation is stagnation.' Gresley would surely have agreed with that.

5
Accidents and Safety Improvements

During the years from 1933 until the war, the LNER suffered three major accidents, all of them rear-end collisions – at Welwyn Garden City on 15 June 1935, at Castlecary on 10 December 1937, and at Hatfield on 26 January 1939. The first two accidents led to an intense review of signalling and safety procedures, with results that were intended to be far reaching, but which had not taken wide effect before war broke out.

The most serious, in terms of casualties, was the Castlecary accident, 34 passengers being killed in the collision and one dying subsequently in hospital, whilst 179 were injured or treated for shock. The Welwyn accident caused the death of 13 persons; but the toll of the Hatfield collision was comparatively light, only one passenger being killed.

The circumstances at Welwyn Garden City were that on the night of Saturday 15 June the Newcastle express leaving King's Cross at 10.45 pm ran in two portions. The second portion, departing at 10.53, had been checked by signals at Welwyn Garden City when it was run into by the 10.50 mail and parcels train for Leeds, hauled by 3-cylinder 2–6–0 no. 4009, which had left London at 10.58.

The collision occurred at the north end of the down island platform, almost opposite the signal box. The cause of the accident was an irregularity in block working on the part of the signalman, who gave 'train out of section' to Hatfield whilst the Newcastle train was still in his section, and on being offered the Leeds train immediately thereafter, accepted it.

The Inspecting Officer of Railways was of the opinion that there were two possible causes of the signalman's error. He might have given 'train out of section' for an up train passing at the time, on the wrong block instrument. In this connection it was noteworthy that the signalman had no less than eleven block bells to attend to, and sixteen block needles, Welwyn Garden City being a junction for two branches and also a point where the four tracks of the main line merge into two over the Welwyn Viaduct.

Alternatively, he might have given 'train out of section' on the correct instrument but prematurely. This the signalman denied strongly; and the Inspecting Officer concluded that the first cause was the most probable one. It was very unfortunate that the Hatfield signalman, whose suspicions were aroused by receiving 'train out of section' very quickly after the Newcastle train had passed his box and who telephoned his colleague at Welwyn, did not press the latter harder to confirm that all was in order.

A direct result of this disaster was the

27 The Welwyn Garden City accident, 15 June 1935, showing the engine of the Leeds train amid the wreckage of the Newcastle train.

introduction of what became known as the Welwyn control, involving the interlocking of track circuits, block instruments and signal levers to ensure that correct sequence of operations is maintained and that 'line clear' can only be given when a train has passed through the section; equally, a home signal must be restored to 'danger' after passage of a train and cannot be pulled off again before the correct block procedure has been followed.

Castlecary was an even more disastrous incident. The 2 pm Dundee to Glasgow express, with seven bogies and a fish van in rear, was hauled by D29 4-4-0 no. 9896, 'Dandie Dinmont', on 10 December 1937. Snow was heavy on the track, and the points at Gartshore, the next station to Castlecary, were blocked. The result was that a preceding goods train was held up at Dullatur East and signals were therefore against the train from Dundee. It was brought to a stand in Castlecary station after overrunning the home signal in poor visibility due to falling snow, despite being given a red hand signal by the signalman.

Soon afterwards the 4.03 pm Edinburgh to Glasgow express, drawn by A3 Pacific, 'Grand Parade', and comprising nine bogies, similarly overran the home signal and, in spite of another

28 A splendid display of GNR 'somersault' signals at Doncaster.

hand signal from the box, collided at an estimated 60 mph with the rear of the Dundee–Glasgow train. The damage was appalling, the three last vehicles of the train from Dundee being almost completely destroyed by 'Grand Parade' which was finally embedded in the side of a cutting, the first three coaches of the train from Edinburgh being thrown past the tender, one on each side of it, and one actually above the locomotive.

The Chief Inspecting Officer of the Ministry of Transport found that the evidence was conflicting and that no one person was to blame for the disaster, but that it almost certainly would have been prevented by a system of ATC or automatic train control such as that widely in use on the Great Western railway – more correctly described as audible cab signalling.

The Board of the LNER agreed to a trial of such a system but after reports had been studied of the comparative merits of the GWR system and the Hudd system used on the London Tilbury and Southend section of the LMS, decided in favour of the latter. The Hudd system, which obviated physical contact between the locomotive and the track apparatus through the use of permanent magnets and electro-magnets, appeared to possess advantages and it was decided to install it first on the route upon which the Castlecary accident had taken place, namely Edinburgh–Glasgow via Falkirk. On 13 August 1939 a number of track fittings were brought into use, and it was intended to extend the system to the whole route, when the outbreak of war intervened.

The last, and fortunately least serious of these accidents, was the collision at Hatfield on 26 January 1939, when, at around 10.00 am, the

53

29 King's Cross station box after modernisation, showing the miniature lever frame.

7.35 pm night sleeping car express from Aberdeen was stopped at Hatfield No. 2 box home signal on the up main line north of Hatfield station. The severe winter weather with ice and snow had put the block instruments out of order and time-interval working had been instituted. Behind the Aberdeen train, the 7.34 am from Cambridge was cautioned and brought to a stand. In turn, and further back, the 8.25 am from Cambridge was brought to a stand under similar arrangements. Lastly the 7.15 am from Peterborough, which had been stopped and cautioned at Welwyn Garden City, came up behind the three stationary trains but instead of stopping clear, ran into the 8.25 from Cambridge, demolishing the rear vehicle, and causing tele-scoping to take place over the last four units (articulated twins) of the train.

Human error, of a kind that could scarcely be prevented by any improved form of signalling, caused this accident and no important lessons could be learnt from it.

It is interesting to speculate whether, if the war had not intervened, the LNER would in fact have installed the Hudd system extensively over its main lines. The LMS was apparently satisfied with the efficiency of the system, but was in no hurry to extend its use – and the LMS enjoyed a considerably easier financial situation than did the LNER. But historically it was not always the most prosperous lines that invested most heavily in safety – the impoverished London Chatham and Dover managed to install Sykes lock-and-block very widely, whilst the lordly London and

54

North Western and the Midland adhered to simple block working. It might have been a good investment for the LNER, quite apart from the moral responsibility to ensure safety of its passengers, to find the money for cab signalling some twenty years before British Railways eventually came round to the same conclusion.

One consequence of the LNER Divisional form of organisation was that the Signal Engineers were three in number and consequently each of them enjoyed less scope than their counterparts on other railways. In the case of the brilliant A. E. Tattersall, it was his move from the North Eastern to the Southern Area that enabled him to extend the application of some of his advanced thinking on signal technology. But A. F. Bound, the ex-GCR Signal Engineer who had originally been involved with the trials of 'Reliostop' and who had installed on the LNER the pioneer three-aspect colour-light system between Marylebone and Neasden, had had to find more scope by moving (at a much higher salary) to the LMS as Chief Signal Engineer. Here there was rather more money available and Bound was successful in persuading the LMS Board to try out the Hudd Automatic Warning System, rather sooner than the LNER was similarly persuaded as a result of the Castlecary accident.

6
Passenger Services and Facilities

Next to the three streamliners, the most striking innovation among trains on the LNER in the years before the war was undoubtedly the 'Northern Belle'. It may have been the success of the week-end cruises to Belgium and Holland undertaken by the ss 'Vienna' from the Harwich–Hook of Holland service that prompted the idea of a cruising train – a bold venture that none of the other main line railways cared to copy.

It was on 16 June 1933 that the first all-rail land cruise was inaugurated. The full formation of the 'Northern Belle' required fifteen vehicles for only sixty passengers, though over part of the itinerary the train was worked as separate day and night portions. The stock included six first-class sleeping cars (equipped with shower baths – another LNER innovation); two restaurant cars; a kitchen car; two special vehicles from the 'Flying Scotsman' set, one of which incorporated a cocktail bar and hairdressing saloon; two brakes for passengers' luggage in personal lockers; and two staff cars – one a sleeping car and the other a brake first.

The train left King's Cross at 11.20 pm on Friday evening. Saturday was spent sightseeing in Edinburgh and Sunday in the Deeside and Aberdeen area. On Sunday night the train was worked back through Glasgow to Balloch, the day portion being then taken off separately for cleaning whilst the passengers enjoyed a steamer trip up Loch Lomond to Ardlui where they found the day portion awaiting them, the sleeping cars having been sent on ahead to Fort William. On Monday there was a day trip to Mallaig and back. On Tuesday the Border Counties line was reached via Edinburgh, with a coach trip from Humshaugh to Hexham. On Wednesday the Lake District was visited from Penrith; Thursday's sightseeing was concentrated on the North Yorkshire moors and Scarborough, with the evening being spent in York. The Friday return was by what was by now sometimes called the 'Cathedrals Route' – the GN and GE Joint Line – with stops at Lincoln and Ely for cathedral visits; the final return to King's Cross was via Cambridge.

Some dinners were served in LNER hotels, two being dinner dances. But, as many meals were served on the train, the LNER had instructed the Superintendent of Restaurant Car Services to pick the best chef, Chief Steward and crew he had, and gave carte blanche for the composition of appropriate menus. The result was that the quality of the meals served on the 'Northern Belle' was outstanding, something the fortunate passengers never forgot.

Motor coach and steamer trips, as well as

30 The down 'Scotsman' hauled by no. 4492, 'Dominion of New Zealand', passes under the great signal gantry at the end of Newcastle Central station on 25 August 1937.

souvenir gifts to every passenger, were included in the fare, which was £20! Whether the LNER made any real profit out of a total receipt of £1,200 is perhaps doubtful, when the haulage, staffing and catering costs, as well as the excursions and publicity are taken into account. The 'Northern Belle' had a tare weight of 550 tons and was double-headed whenever it ran over lines where a Pacific was not allowed. In parts of the North Eastern Area two Hunt class 4–4–0 engines were used; other combinations included a J39 0–6–0 piloting a K2 2–6–0.

But if the financial results were not outstandingly favourable, the popularity and prestige which the 'Northern Belle' brought the LNER were undoubtedly great. The passengers were enthusiastic and the cruise was twice repeated in the summer of 1933, several passengers making repeat reservations. On the final day of the last

31 Ex-Hull and Barnsley J28 no. 2418 waits to leave Hull (Paragon) station with a Withernsea train on 8 July 1933.

T. E. Rounthwaite

cruise in 1933 the passengers spontaneously organised and all signed a special letter of thanks to the Chief General Manager. In 1934 four cruises were made and three in 1935, the series continuing up to the war, with minor changes in the itinerary.

Perhaps cost accounting prevented the other railways from emulating LNER enterprise in pioneering train cruises; but there was a much more general participation in the 'Camping Coaches' which provided self-catering holiday accommodation, together with a certain interest for train-spotters! These were old vehicles withdrawn from traffic, modified as holiday homes with kitchen, toilet and washing facilities, and sleeping and living accommodation, stabled in a station siding in some suitably attractive area. The station master (or his wife) acted as the landlord's representative and helped with information about facilities, shopping, etc. The Camping Coaches were extremely popular and those in the most attractive areas were normally let throughout the summer.

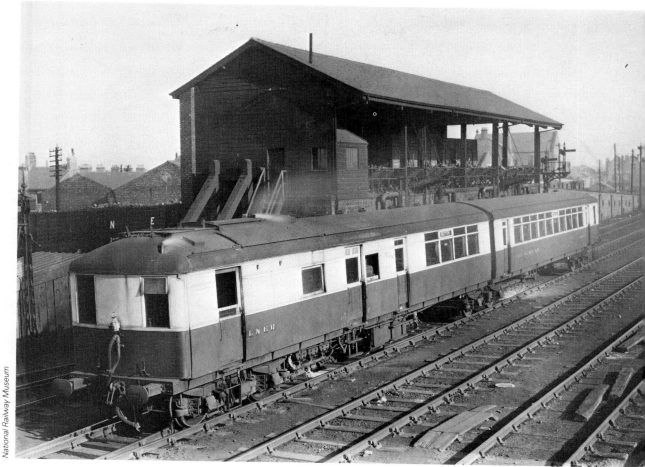

34 Sentinel railcar 'Phenomena' at Blyth.

Viaduct, the Durham Viaduct, the High Level and King Edward VII Bridges at Newcastle upon Tyne, the Royal Border Bridge and, last but far from least, the Forth and Tay Bridges. Guaranteed excursions were encouraged, and engine headboards lettered 'Eason's Special' often puzzled south-country observers who were unaware of the prevalence of these agency trips – day and half-day – to London organised by a Grimsby firm.

The LNER, in agreement with the LMS, decided in 1934 that there should be armrests and three-a-side seating in future third-class compartments of main line corridor stock. (The GWR and the Southern declined to follow suit, on the grounds that this would seriously reduce total seating accommodation at holiday peak periods.)

In 1937 more and more attention was being given to improving the standard of service on the principal express passenger trains. All East

35 A Newmarket races Pullman special hauled by two Atlantics (date uncertain).

Coast Main Line expresses, and twenty-three other booked services, had a 'Train Attendant' in addition to the guard and travelling ticket collectors, whose sole duty was to attend to passengers' comfort and deal with any complaints.

In the same year it was agreed by the Superintendents and Passenger Managers Committee that there should be women travelling cleaners (mainly to ensure cleanliness of the train lavatories) on the principal trains, fifty-three to be employed during the summer timetable and forty for the rest of the year.

A short-lived experiment was the Dictaphone typing service provided for a time for business men using the 8.15 am Newcastle–King's Cross and the return 5.30 pm from King's Cross. This was, incidentally, not a 'first' on British railways; it had been tried out as long ago as 1910 by the London and North Western Railway in the 'City to City' expresses between London (Broad Street) and Birmingham (New Street).

Marylebone and the GC line were heavily used for special occasions, such as the Wembley Cup Final in 1936 when a long procession of return excursions took tired supporters home in the night. Between 11.25 pm and 2.05 am

36 New stock for extensions of Tyneside electric lines, 1937.

sixteen trains left Marylebone for Sheffield, Pontefract, Barnsley, Manchester, Leicester, Loughborough or Mansfield – a train leaving every ten minutes between 1.05 am and 2.05 am. Marylebone could also be used to relieve both the congestion at King's Cross and the occupation of the East Coast Main Line by night sleeping car trains and freight services; in 1937 a through Marylebone–Newcastle service at 10.45 pm was instituted, with a corresponding return working.

Acceleration of individual trains was steadily taking place, although there was no move, as in 1937 on the LMS, to standardise 60 mph speeds for all main inter-city services. The 'Scarborough Flier' in 1935 was timed between King's Cross and York at 62.7 mph. In 1936 the 'Flying Scotsman' was retimed to reach Edinburgh in 7¼ hours, and in 1938 the time came down to 7 hours.

Some facilities had to be withdrawn, among them, in April 1937, the Aberdeen suburban service which had suffered heavily from tramway and bus competition. Also regretted, in 1936, was the final disappearance of LNER slip coaches – the two survivors on the GE section having been the Waltham Cross slip off the 6 pm, and the Mark's Tey slip off the 4.57 pm trains from Liverpool Street, and the two slip coaches off the 6.20 pm from Marylebone, one for Finmere, and one for Stratford upon Avon, detached at Woodford.

Liverpool Street, however, in 1937 saw non-stop buffet car services to Cambridge instituted

T. G. Hepburn – Rail Archive Stephenson

37 K3 no. 2764 stands in Nottingham (Victoria) station with a Leeds–Leicester excursion train formed of green-and-cream 'tourist' stock, on 11 July 1937.

in five-car train sets: the Cambridge line also saw the exhilarating sprint between Bishop's Stortford and Cambridge of the 11.50 pm (Thursday and Saturday nights only), known affectionately to Cambridge undergraduates returning with a late pass after an evening in the West End as the 'Flying Fornicator'.

In 1928 the LNER had agreed with the LMS and the GWR to introduce third-class sleeping cars – four berths to a compartment, but without bed linen. Pillows and rugs only were supplied, so that 'lying-down' rather than 'sleeping' accommodation would have been a more correct description. This meant that the 59 sleeping cars in the LNER stock in 1923 had increased to 129 in 1937. Restaurant and kitchen cars over the same period rose from 215 to 325. The drive to offer more facilities and attract more passengers was accelerated in 1933 when the Monthly Return ticket was introduced by all the main line railways, bringing down the cost of third-class tickets to approximately one (old) penny – less than ½p – per mile. Fares were raised by about 5 per cent in October 1937, however, to meet rising costs.

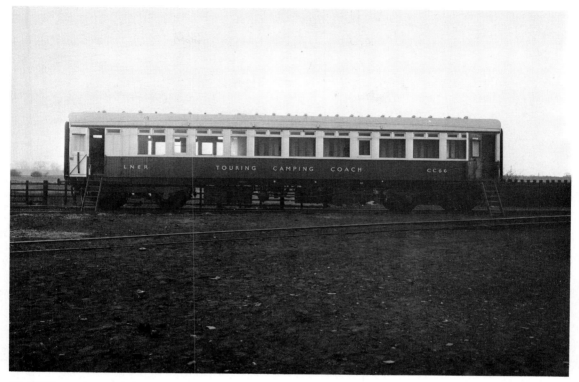

38 LNER camping coach (an ex-NER vehicle). *National Railway Museum*

Where traffic was light, the LNER tried to bring down costs and attract passengers by the use of Sentinel-Cammell railcars, a series of which was put into service between 1928 and 1933. These provided forty-eight seats; the engine and boiler compartment was situated over a motor bogie, the boilers being of a three-drum water-tube type. The engine delivered 300 hp continuously and the coaches performed well on steeply-graded lines such as the Whitby–Scarborough route.

By 1937 no less than eighty such railcars were in use; in addition there were four diesel-electric cars, of which 'Tyneside Venturer' had been the first (the cars being named as a publicity device). The Locomotive Running Superintendent of the North Eastern Area, C. M. Stedman, reported that tests had shown that, whilst the capital cost of 'Tyneside Venturer' was considerably greater than that of the steam railways, the fuel costs were 'remarkably low'. It had successfully operated between Guisborough and Middlesbrough, involving the ascent of Nunthorpe Bank, 1 in 44; and whilst working this service had been occasionally required to haul a passenger vehicle as a trailer. Stedman foresaw a bright future for diesel traction on the railway – not, however, to be realised for nearly a quarter of a century.

In chapter four the improvements financed by government loans for the 1935–40 New Works Programme were described. Apart from this source of capital, the railways had previously

39 K2 no. 4688 nears Stratford with a down Clacton
excursion on 7 August 1932 – note the ex-GER
non-corridor stock.

James R. Clarke

benefited from the Development (Loan Guarantees and Grants) Act of 1929, which helped the execution of some new works on the basis of interest charges being met by the government for a period not exceeding fifteen years; and from the remission of the obsolete Railway Passenger Duty, a tax on first-class travel dating from the earliest days of the railways which in 1928 was abolished on condition that 90 per cent

of the notional capital value of the tax would be spent on approved new works.

Most of this money was spent by the LNER on running line and engineering improvements. Station reconstruction schemes, for which direct financial justification was hard to establish, were not considerable, 'face-lifting' and modest schemes of improvement being generally preferred. 'Make do and mend' certainly applied when a new station was built at West Finchley on the High Barnet branch in 1933 – it was put together from disused buildings brought from closed stations, the footbridge coming from Wintersett and Ryhill station near Barnsley (ex-GCR).

Improvements of a minor character were carried out at King's Cross, Liverpool Street, York, and Sheffield (Victoria). But the legacy of GNR parsimony still hung around the neck of the LNER at Peterborough in particular. Schemes for remodelling the cramped and inefficient station there, like those for rebuilding King's Cross, were frighteningly costly, and nothing was done.

Money was found, however, for extending the Tyneside electric services on the south side of the river. Electrification from Newcastle to South Shields was authorised in the summer of 1935 and opened for traffic in the spring of 1938. This 11 miles of newly electrified route was associated with some modernisation of the North Tyneside lines and the construction of new rolling stock to replace the original vehicles built by the North Eastern Railway. The LNER's London commuters, who might have hoped for electrification of the GN and GE suburban lines with money provided by the 1929 Act, might feel rather jealous, since in the event they had to wait until after the war for any substantial improvement in their travelling conditions.

But, considering that the LNER in 1937 derived only 36 per cent of its gross railway receipts from passenger train traffic (against the LMS, 40 per cent; the GWR, 41 per cent; and the Southern, 77 per cent), it was perhaps remarkable that so much enterprise and managerial effort was devoted to this side of the business, especially as the general opinion among railwaymen was that freight was by far the more profitable side. The LNER's publicity was effectively directed at the passenger. Year after year, exhibitions of LNER poster art were held – in 1933 in London, opened by the Minister of Transport; in 1935 a series in the provinces starting at Hull and following at York. Exhibitions of modern rolling stock and locomotives were also arranged at various centres and attracted great public interest. Railway history was skilfully exploited in 1938 when the Patrick Stirling 'single' GNR No. 1 was restored to working order and took a replica 'Flying Scotsman' of 1888 on an excursion to Cambridge and back.

For an essentially freight line, the LNER certainly believed in trying to make friends of its passengers! It was even solicitous of their comfort on rainy days; from November 1934 it offered umbrellas for hire at both Newcastle (Central) and Hull (Paragon) stations at a charge of 2d (less than 1p) a day. A deposit was required, of 3s 6d (17½p) for a man's umbrella and 2s 6d (12½p) for a lady's umbrella. One hopes it could always be returned!

An experimental introduction of 'wireless receivers' to provide passengers with entertainment whilst travelling was tried on the midday Anglo-Scottish trains but the patronage was so small that the service had to be withdrawn, the charge made by a contractor for hire of the equipment being much more than the receipts from passengers using it.

Away from the main lines, the connoisseur of railway curiosities could find some interesting survivals. As late as 1934, four-wheeled passenger vehicles worked the Woolwich North service in sets of ten coaches with six-wheel brakes at each end, whilst second class continued until 1 January 1938 on the GN and the GE Sections in the London suburban area.

In the field of road-rail co-ordination, the LNER was well satisfied with the results of its investment in bus companies following the road powers obtained in 1928. In December 1935 the Chief General Manager reported to the Board's

40 Interior of LNER buffet car.

Suburban and Road Traffic Committee that in 1934 the total investment in fifteen bus companies had amounted to £2,434,772; dividends received had amounted to £193,999 equal to 7.97 per cent return on the outlay.

Moreover, local bus-rail co-ordination schemes had enabled passenger services on thirty-four branch lines to be withdrawn, with savings which on an annual basis amounted to £67,837. Reductions in train mileage replaced by bus services elsewhere had yielded some £6,828 per annum in addition.

Perhaps the most obvious candidate for service withdrawal was far away in Scotland, in the Great Glen, where there had survived until 30 November 1934 a passenger service on that extraordinary line, the Invergarry and Fort Augustus branch from Spean Bridge on the West Highland. It had been prompted by a local company as a competitive route to Inverness, had been worked for a time by the Highland and then handed over in disgust to the North British, who bequeathed it to the LNER. Pointing north-east along the Caledonian Canal, through a 'traffic desert' of deer forest, but stopping 30 miles short of Inverness, as it did, it was a commercial disaster. The LNER got round to withdrawing the passenger service on 1 December 1933 but owing to local protests it was kept open for one coal train a week. (It was finally closed in BR days when the reported traffic was 'one wagon of coal a week for Cameron of Lochiel'!)

7

The Battle for Freight and the 'Square Deal'

The LNER, depending more heavily on freight than any of the other main line railways, owned over 250,000 mineral and merchandise wagons in 1933, second only to the LMS, which had 267,000. Their average capacity, at 12.2 tons, was moreover the highest, due to the large number of 20-ton wagons in use on the north-east coast. And despite the attention paid to the more glamorous express passenger trains, some of the best managerial talent on the LNER was concentrated upon freight and commercial operating problems. Barrington-Ward was reported to have said that the passenger train service ran itself: the challenge lay in efficient freight operating. Jenkin Jones, his opposite number at York, considered by many as the most acute brain on the LNER, was also essentially a freight operator, though it was legendary on the LNER that these two doubled-barrelled gentlemen seldom saw eye to eye.

Many Traffic Apprentices (as management trainees were known) had to cut their teeth on freight operating, often at Whitemoor Yard or in some busy installation in the North Eastern Area. 'Fluidity', speed and reliability of movement was the objective, with the state of motive power availability and wagon supply constantly being monitored by the control organisation.

Trains which were run only if the traffic was sufficient were marked 'Q' in the working timetable (on the Great Western they were shown as 'RR' – run as required). But the framework was the 'mandatory' freight train service, especially the 'fitted' freights, fully or partially braked. Grimsby fish and Scotch meat express freights had long been familiar over the GN main line. But they began in the mid-1930s to be followed by more and more fitted freights for general merchandise, not merely perishables, in the struggle to meet competition from long distance road haulage. One of the less usual fast freights was that between Manchester (Deansgate, the ex-GNR goods station) and King's Cross Goods. This express departed nightly at 8.22 pm from Deansgate and, surprisingly, followed the Midland route via Chinley, Dore and Totley, Chesterfield, Pye Bridge, Codnor Park to Colwick (Nottingham). The corresponding down service was at 8.30 pm from King's Cross Goods which – showing what a No. 1 braked train was capable of – averaged 50.6 mph between Hitchin and Huntingdon. A more ordinary route was followed by the 'Glasgow Goods' – the 3.40 pm fitted freight from King's Cross Goods with perishable traffic for next morning's Scottish markets. There were many other such trains, some just as well known to the

41 Many years before the days of in-flight movies for airline passengers: the interior of the LNER cinema coach.

staff as the named passenger expresses. Overnight transits, with guaranteed next-day arrivals, were normal, and were publicised later in a booklet for business men issued by the railway in 1938.

Gerard Fiennes, later General Manager of the Eastern Region of British Railways, has recalled how in the 1930s the traditional 'staging' of urgent traffic from one marshalling yard to another was being replaced by through trains between principal centres. 'When I went to Whitemoor as Yardmaster in 1931, all the

42 J39 no. 2709 passing Bagthorpe junction, Nottingham, with a down goods.

T. G. Hepburn – Rail Archive Stephenson

traffics out of East Anglia – all the vegetables and the fruit, and the industrial products of North London, Norwich and Ipswich, went from Whitemoor only 55 miles to Pyewipe Yard in Lincoln, or about 100 miles to Decoy Yard in Doncaster. By the mid-1930s we were running direct trains to Edinburgh, Newcastle, Manchester, Liverpool, Leeds, Birmingham, and the whole of the freight service had been completely shaken up and reorganised to give overnight transits.'

Train service improvements were complemented by physical works such as the new Down marshalling yard at Mottram in 1935, to expedite the traffic that could not run in through trainloads, on the east-west axis connecting Yorkshire and East Anglia with Merseyside via the Cheshire Lines; the new Fish Dock at Grimsby; and the new Inward marshalling yard at Hull in 1935.

But all these efforts to improve the quality of the railway service could not avert the consequences of industrial depression and steadily increasing road competition. The total tonnage

43 K3 no. 186 with a down cattle train in the mid-1930s – a traffic that disappeared from British Rail!

of freight carried by the LNER in 1933 was only 73 per cent of that carried in the first year after Grouping, 1923; and recovery from the trough of the depression was slow, as the figures show:

	LNER: million tons of freight carried
1923	153.5
1933	114.7
1934	124.9
1935	124.3
1936	130.6
1937	136.5

This gradual recovery then suffered a setback from the mini-recession of 1938, and in 1939 the results were of course affected by the outbreak of war.

The railway companies could not do much about the economic depression; but they launched a two-pronged attack on road competition by pressing the government to regulate and tax road haulage more equitably – in the railway view – and to release the railways from the statutory restrictions on their freight charging powers which had been imposed in the days when their monopoly of inland transport was almost complete. The Railway Companies Association, a body representing the interests

73

44 A heavy down freight on the GN main line near Huntingdon in charge of an O2 2–8–0.

of the shareholders, bringing together the railway chairmen as a working group, was largely instrumental in persuading the government to pass the Road and Rail Traffic Act, 1933, which established a licensing system for road goods vehicles rather similar to that which had been set up for road passenger services by the Road

Traffic Act of 1930, administered by the Regional Traffic Commissioners.

The LNER took full advantage of the right established by the 1933 Act to object to the grant of licences for additional road haulage vehicles, often with considerable success, largely due to employing very eminent Counsel including (Sir) Walter Monckton and (Sir) David Maxwell Fyfe. Some road hauliers admitted later that the

45 LNER commercial enterprise – a road horse-box available for hire.

National Railway Museum

railway opposition, although primarily directed at preserving railway interests, had also helped to prevent a growth in cut-throat competition among haulage firms themselves.

The Act of 1933 also gave the railways one major concession, by allowing them to quote rates in the form of 'agreed charges', by which the whole of a trader's traffic could be carried by a railway company at a negotiated flat rate, usually per ton, and irrespective of distance.

The LNER took a very important part in all these negotiations. Sir Ralph Wedgwood was, of course, an experienced former Goods Manager, and he was also an admirable witness before Parliamentary Committees or Commissions. He became seriously ill during the passage of the Road and Rail Traffic Act in June 1933,

but fortunately made a good recovery and was back in harness by December of that year. He was therefore able to play a major role in the campaign launched by all four main line railways in 1938 to persuade the government to make a clean sweep of all the remaining and very complex restrictions upon their charges, and thereby allow them to compete freely and on an equal footing with road transport, whose charges were not subject to any form of control. In the preliminary discussions it was Wedgwood who suggested the slogan 'Give the Railways a Square Deal' and as the 'Square Deal Campaign' it was thereafter known.

Road competition by now was taking two distinct forms. The one the railways found most difficult to counter was the rapid expansion of 'own account' operations, which were not

46 Typical LNER 'C & D' road vehicle for country areas.

restricted by the 1933 Act. Traders built up their own fleets to carry their goods, the management of which became integrated with the main business. The advantages of instant availability, together with some 'prestige' element through advertising, were attractive.

The second was the competition from haulage firms aimed chiefly at full wagon-load consignments, the most profitable that the railway handled. The LNER, of course, did provide collection and delivery service throughout its system, but for short and medium distance movement it could not always match road haulage speed and reliability, nor did the supply of containers wholly solve the problems of the packing required for rail transit. But the real trouble was the rate. Road hauliers competed with each other without having to disclose their charges, but when competing with the railway they had no difficulty in ascertaining the railway rate and undercutting it.

The rail container business grew despite the fact that even by 1938 the average capacity was only 3.3 tons. Some were employed in the

47 Up coal train at Sandy in the mid-1930s, in charge of an O2.

household removals service operated by Pickfords, in conjunction with the railways – Pickfords having been acquired, together with Carter Paterson, the parcels firm, jointly by all four main line railways in 1930.

Even so, the process of modernising the freight service was handicapped by the layout of many goods sheds, designed for leisurely transfer of goods by hand trolley between rail wagons and horse rulleys. Here the LNER fell behind the LMS in mechanising the more important depots for handling small traffic; it had nothing comparable to the modernised goods sheds at Birmingham (Lawley Street) or Derby.

However, in common with the other railways, it invested for its collection and delivery work in 'mechanical horses' – three-wheeled motor units of low power that could 'turn on a sixpence', a considerable advantage at depots such as the ex-GNR goods station in the City of London at Farringdon Street, where the approach roadway contained a hairpin bend of acute sharpness, presenting no problem to the horse vehicle but almost impossible for a motor lorry.

The LNER also pioneered railhead concentration of its road services, later known as 'zonal

48 Q6 no. 2277 near Plawsworth with a down coal train on 28 August 1937. Note the NER-type 20-ton coal-hopper wagons.

James R. Clarke

collection and delivery' in the North Eastern Area. In that Area town cartage by 1938 was practically all by motor, largely mechanical horses.

Elsewhere on the LNER, however, advances had not been so rapid. Real horses continued to perform an appreciable proportion of the road collection and delivery work. At the beginning of 1938 the LNER still had 4,783 horse wagons and carts, drawn by 2,193 horses, even though mechanisation had progressed much further than on the LMS, which still had no less than 16,344 vehicles and 8,154 horses.

The sting of competition between the railways, which had survived the Grouping, was at last largely eliminated by the pooling arrangements for competitive traffic initiated in 1932. The LNER joined in two pools of passenger and freight traffic receipts in that year – one with the LMS alone, and one with the LMS and GWR. In 1934 parcels traffic receipts also came into the pooling.

The LNER continued to provide services which surprised some outside observers, including the hire of sacks to traders using the railway. There was a substantial organisation to cover the use and repair of wagon sheets to protect loads in open wagons, and also the ropes used to secure such loads.

In retrospect, the LNER in the 1930s seems a blend of advanced thinking coupled with the survival of some traditional methods at 'grass roots' level. But it can be said that from Sir Ralph Wedgwood, involved at the highest level with the Government over charging policy, down to the local Goods Agent, the LNER was well served by all its staff concerned with the freight business – above all in the quality of Goods Managers following in the tradition of Geddes and Wedgwood, men such as Thomas Hornsby, George Marshall, George Mills, and A. E. Sewell, to name only a few.

8
Shipping Services and Docks

The LNER's shipping interests, confined to what the company's advertising described as 'the drier side of Britain', were curiously diverse. They ranged from the premier North Sea service for passengers, maintained with the ss *Vienna*, ss *Amsterdam* and ss *Prague*, sailing nightly between Parkeston Quay and the Hook of Holland, and with the ss *Antwerp*, ss *Bruges* and ss *Malines* maintaining the Antwerp service, to the largely cargo services of the ex-GCR fleet of smallish vessels and the ex-NER half-share in Wilson's Hull-based shipping services (all cargo)

and with the ex-L & Y Hull–Zeebrugge service (mainly cargo).

In the LNER's second decade the rehabilitation of the fleet following the end of the First World War had been virtually completed and it was a period of consolidation rather than expansion. After 1930 new ship construction went through a quiet period, although up in Scotland the ex-NBR Clyde steamer fleet was reinforced by a large new paddle steamer, the P.S. *Jeanie Deans* in 1932, and in 1933 by the M.V. *Talisman* – a unique vessel, being the only known diesel-

49 'The Night Parade' – the famous LNER poster of the evening departures from Parkeston Quay.

National Railway Museum

50 The new Parkeston Quay West station on the day of its opening, 1 October 1934, with a boat train arriving.

electric paddle steamer, the engines being controlled direct from the bridge which gave the vessel excellent manoeuvrability.

Two other vessels for estuarial waters were provided, the P.S. *Wingfield Castle* and P.S. *Tattersall Castle*, both of which worked on the Hull–New Holland ferry service for many years. At the time of writing, *Tattersall Castle* is moored in the Thames awaiting a buyer, following the opening of the long-awaited Humber Bridge and the closure of the ferry.

One major development in 1933 was the purchase by the LNER of Great Eastern Train Ferries Ltd, which was joint owner with the Société Belgo-Anglaise des Ferry-Boats of three train ferry steamers named after English counties, Essex, Suffolk and Norfolk, and a stock of white-painted box wagons designed to

81

51 'Tattersall Castle' on the Hull–New Holland Humber ferry service.

run on either British or Continental railways. The ferry train terminals were at Zeebrugge and Harwich – the old port, not Parkeston Quay.

In 1932 the idea of week-end pleasure cruises from Parkeston Quay to Belgium and Holland was exploited, the ss *Vienna* being used for this purpose instead of standing by for her turn as the relief ship on the night Hook service. The cruises proved popular; 270 passengers were accommodated and entertainments on board as well as shore excursions were provided. The success of this innovation was such that a series of cruises followed yearly; from eight in 1932, the number rose to fourteen in 1933, and was maintained at

eleven in the two succeeding years. Cruising had become such an established feature that in the following year, 1936, it was considered justifiable to make some structural alterations to *Vienna* to improve amenities and weather protection. (It was a sad down-grading for *Vienna* when in the war she was used as a troop transport by the War Office. However, her more vulnerable furniture was wisely removed; some of her elegant red leather settees were transported to the LNER emergency headquarters where they helped to furnish the Officers' Mess.)

The LNER's publicity featured in a well-known poster 'The Night Parade' – the scene at Parkeston Quay when every evening three ships

52 The unique 'Talisman': the only diesel-electric paddle steamer.

J. Edgington

sailed within a few minutes of each other. On a typical evening around 10 pm one might see first *Prague* leaving for the Hook, then *Malines* for Antwerp, followed by *Archangel* (an older ex-GER steamer) for Zeebrugge.

Congestion, in fact, was forcing an enlargement at Parkeston. A new quay and terminal was constructed at Parkeston Quay West, and officially opened on 1 October 1934. Its initial use was for the Flushing service, which could now be berthed away from the older area where the night steamers were berthed by day. In all, three new berths were provided, with good immigration and customs facilities. On the first occasion upon which the 10.00 am 'Flushing Continental' from Liverpool Street used the new station, the Flushing steamer departed only sixteen minutes after the arrival of the boat train.

The LNER as the largest dock owner among

the four grouped companies, and deriving a substantial proportion of its net receipts from this source, managed to find money for some substantial dock improvements, particularly in the North Eastern Area. The Fish Dock at Hull – the St Andrew's Dock – was enlarged to make it the largest in Britain. The new Fish Dock at Grimsby was a joint enterprise with Grimsby Corporation, opened in October 1934. At Salt End, Hull, a long oil jetty was constructed.

Nevertheless, it was hard to find equal justification for much improvement to the docks inherited from the NBR, scattered along the shores of the Firth of Forth and originally constructed for the export of coal from the Fife coalfield. The export trade between the wars had dwindled relative to its booming state before 1914 and the docks were not used to capacity. They were contained in three main ports – at Methil, on the coast of Fife; Burntisland in sight of the towering Forth Bridge; and, on the south shore, Bo'ness. There was also – surprisingly – the small ex-NBR harbour at Silloth on the Solway Firth, in Cumberland, an apparent anomaly for the LNER, which traded with the Isle of Man and with Ireland.

It was a reflection of the changing pattern of overseas trade, that the LNER felt it advisable to dispose of some of its docks. Tyne Dock was sold to the Tyne Improvement Commission in 1936. The old, disused Queen's Dock in Hull had been sold to the City Corporation some years previously and it was now filled in and built over. The need for re-thinking the use of railway docks, which became acute after nationalisation, was already beginning to appear.

9
New Men at the Top

Between 1933 and the outbreak of war in 1939 many of the founding fathers of the LNER retired or died and were replaced. First to go was Lord Grey of Fallodon, whose distinguished career ended with his death on 7 September 1933. He had been Chairman of the North Eastern Railway, had resigned on becoming Foreign Secretary in 1905, but had rejoined the NER Board in 1917 and might well have become Chairman of the LNER. However, he had preferred not to be considered for this and became just an LNER Director and also Chairman of the North Eastern Area Board.

In 1934 two more links with the North Eastern Railway were severed when Sir Vincent Raven died and A. C. Stamer, who might have expected to succeed him but who on the LNER had become Mechanical Engineer, Darlington, retired.

A former doughty fighter for the Great Central, its last Chairman, Lord Faringdon, who had become Deputy Chairman of the LNER, attending particularly to financial matters, also died in 1934 and was succeeded by Sir Murrough J. Wilson. That year also saw the retirement of James Calder as General Manager (Scotland); he was succeeded by George Mills, and the opportunity was taken to bring the Scottish post into line with the others by designating Mills Divisional General Manager (Scottish Area).

Links with the old North British Railway also weakened in 1935 with the retirement of C. H. Stemp, who had been Superintendent of the Southern Scottish Area. He was succeeded by another ex-NBR man, Robert Gardiner.

In 1936 the Southern Area DGM, G. F. Thurston, retired; he had followed Alexander Wilson in the chair at Liverpool Street in 1929 and was an ex-GER man. His successor was C. H. Newton, an appointment which caused some surprise. 'C.H.N.' had been Chief Accountant since 1928 and had been regarded as a financial specialist. However, he had always had a keen interest in practical railway matters, particularly mechanical devices; he took pride in having been certificated as proficient in railway working and signalling. The Directors already regarded him as a possible successor to Wedgwood, and the Southern Area post was in the nature of a grooming for promotion.

Newton was followed as Chief Accountant by G. Sutherland, whose pre-Grouping experience had been with the Highland and North British Railways.

In the same year, 1936, T. Hornsby retired as DGM, North Eastern Area, to enter the coal industry as Chairman of the Durham Sales Control Committee. 'Thos', as he was widely known on the LNER, was a former Goods Manager and very much at home in the commercial world of the North East. He was succeeded by the incisive, quick-minded C. M. Jenkin Jones whose associations with York's civic life and the ecclesiastical establishment

53 Sir Ronald Matthews, Chairman from 1938.

National Railway Museum

Indian Railways on a more satisfactory footing. Naturally, Sir Ralph took with him two 'bright young men' from the Chief General Manager's Office, A. Forbes Smith and B. M. Strouts. The visit to India lasted from early November 1936 to early March 1937. Meanwhile Robert Bell was in charge of the LNER.

In 1937 two notable civil engineers retired. C. J. Brown from the Southern Area, was a former GNR man whose special pride lay in the excellence of the GN permanent way. C. J. Brown was succeeded by R. J. M. Inglis, who was destined for general management and who was to have a distinguished career as an administrator in post-war Germany.

John Miller, Engineer of the North Eastern Area, also retired. He was a remarkable character – born in the United Kingdom but had emigrated and become Assistant Engineer of the Pennsylvania RR, from which post Sir Henry Thornton had brought him back across the Atlantic to the GER. As Engineer of the NE Area his energy and unorthodoxy had shown to great advantage. He established a Central Reclamation Depot at Darlington which put the recovery and re-use of old permanent way material on a commercial basis. He tidied up the lineside with neat concrete edgings which gave the appearance of caring for detail so often lacking on the railway. To get his admirable schemes through he sometimes – or so it was whispered – bent the rules laid down by the Chief Accountant for charging expenditure.

John Miller had strongly supported the brilliant, diminutive A. E. Tattersall who as Signal and Telegraph Engineer, responsible to the Civil Engineer, had been responsible for planning and executing the York–Northallerton re-signalling with its pioneer route relay interlocking central control at Thirsk. Tattersall moved in 1936 to a corresponding position in the Southern Area.

were close – so close that they may have deterred him from taking up the preferment to the Chief General Managership which on sheer ability should probably have been his.

In the autumn of 1936 Sir Ralph Wedgwood was appointed, jointly with W. A. Stanier, the LMS Chief Mechanical Engineer, to constitute an Indian Railway Enquiry Committee, to seek measures designed to put the finances of the

John Miller was followed at York by F. E. Harrison who came of a famous railway family in the North East – a devoted and traditional railway engineer.

The LNER hierarchy learnt in 1937 of the death of Sir Eric Geddes, an event which in some ways closed an era. In the same year Oliver Bulleid left Sir Nigel Gresley to become CME of the Southern, where his originality was to have more scope than would have been possible on the LNER. In the next year R. A. Thom retired as Mechanical Engineer, Southern Area, and in consequence Edward Thompson came south from Darlington to Doncaster, where he was succeeded by A. H. Peppercorn. Thom's post was split between Doncaster (GN and GC) and Stratford (GE), and F. W. Carr took up the Stratford position.

The year 1938 was a momentous one for the LNER because at the end of July William Whitelaw, who had been the greatly respected Chairman since the creation of the company, announced that he wished to retire. One of his fellow-Directors, Lt-Col Arthur Murray, wrote of him that his 'act of leading and of directing has been performed with knowledge and tact, judgment and courage, vision and optimism and with infinite charm and humour, and cheeriness of spirit.' In the early days there had been a brush with the Chief General Manager, but once the boundaries of responsibility between Chairman and CGM had been settled, Whitelaw and Wedgwood had enjoyed an excellent relationship based on mutual respect.

Whitelaw's successor as Chairman was Ronald Wilfred Matthews, who had been knighted in the Birthday Honours of 1934. Sir Ronald was a Sheffield steelmaker and head of the family firm of Turton Brothers and Matthews. He had been Head Boy at Eton and after school had been educated in Switzerland and Germany. At the age of thirty-seven – the youngest man ever to hold

that office – he had been elected Master Cutler of Sheffield. He held various offices in the public life of Sheffield as well as numerous industrial and commercial directorships. Since joining the Board of the LNER in 1929 Sir Ronald had been Chairman of the Southern Area Board. His deep interest in railway matters made him a worthy successor to Mr Whitelaw.

In the next year came the retirement, on 3 March 1939, of Sir Ralph Wedgwood from the Chief General Managership. O. H. Corble, who had long been associated with the CGM, wrote an eloquent tribute to Sir Ralph in the *LNER Magazine* containing the words, 'An insatiable appetite for work, and a determination to get right to the bottom of every problem presented to him, are perhaps the characteristics by which, above all others, Sir Ralph will be best remembered by those who have had the privilege of being closely associated with him; his invariable courtesy and charm of manner have appealed to a much wider circle.' The Board minuted their 'very great appreciation of the valuable services rendered by Sir Ralph to this company.'

Wedgwood's successor, C. H. Newton, cannot have found it easy to replace a man of such distinction. Newton was a man of great sincerity and imbued with a deep love of the railway, but he was not a man of the world in the way that Wedgwood was, nor could he command quite the same respect from his fellow General Managers or carry quite the same weight in the Railway Clearing House, where Stamp of the LMS and Milne of the Great Western had sometimes agreed and sometimes argued with Wedgwood.

Sir Ralph had been appointed in 1923 at a salary of £10,000, which remained unchanged until his retirement – a fine salary for those days, even though it was appreciably less than his counterpart, the President of the LMS, was receiving. One has the impression that Wedg-

Courtesy Dame Veronica Wedgwood

wood was not greatly interested in his own remuneration; when told of the pension (half his salary) which he could expect from the LNER Superannuation Fund, he merely commented that 'it was more than he had expected', though the Board considered it inadequate and, without being asked, increased it to £6,500 a year.

Newton was appointed at a lower figure than R.L.W. had enjoyed, namely £8,000. In a way, this may have reflected the fact that his relationship with the Board, and above all with the Chairman, differed somewhat from that of his predecessor. Wedgwood's intellectual powers and his magisterial presence had established clearly that management questions should not be too much interfered with by a Chairman, whose functions ought to be confined to finance, looking after the interests of the shareholders, senior officer appointments and major policy questions. But Sir Ronald Matthews, being accustomed to take all the major managerial decisions in his own important business, could

55 The new CGM, C. H. Newton, on the footplate of no. 4901.

not refrain from raising with Newton questions that Wedgwood might have repulsed because they took the Chairman's office into a field that had previously been reserved for management. It must be said that in external relations, Matthews loyally supported Newton, though internally he sometimes gave him a rough ride.

Newton's problems were accentuated by the fact that most of his career had been spent in accountancy; and his apprenticeship in general management had lasted for only a couple of years. Some people felt in consequence that Jenkin Jones would have been a better choice of CGM. However, those who worked closely with Newton appreciated his human qualities and sympathised with the difficulties with which he was faced; these difficulties he countered, for the most part, with good humour.

An important position, although one less in the public eye, was that of the Company Secretary. James McLaren, who had originally been a Joint Secretary with G. F. Thurston, and later the sole occupant of the post, died in office on 27 January 1938 and was succeeded by P. J. Dowsett, who had been Assistant Secretary ever since the Grouping. No change took place during this period in the major post of the Chief Legal Adviser, which had been held (since Sir Francis Dunnell retired in 1928) by I. Buchanan Pritchard – a formidable lawyer. In short, the LNER continued to enjoy the loyal service of a strong management team, even though the strongly decentralised organisation created by the founding fathers occasionally showed signs of strain and some individual officers – Kenelm Kerr among them – hankered for a more departmental, centralised organisation that would lead (it was argued) to quicker decision-making. But Sir Ronald was firmly convinced that the Area structure was right and he attached great importance to the good local relationships established by the existence of Area Boards and Divisional General Managers. It was only the special needs arising from the war that were to enforce some changes in the organisation that had lasted since 1923.

10
Making Ends Meet: the Financial Struggle

Everything that has been written in the previous chapters argues that the LNER was managed, for the most part, by men of ability; dedicated railwaymen who were also commercially-minded and open to new ideas. The managerial style of the railway stimulated debate and discussion, and lively minds were not usually discouraged by over-conservative superiors. So it seems paradoxical that the LNER's financial results were the worst of any of the amalgamated companies. All the railways suffered from road competition, general economic depression in the 1930s, and the aftermath of the General Strike and prolonged coal strike of 1926; but none of the other companies suffered such a severe drop in net revenue as the LNER, from £13.1 million in 1929 to £7.2 million in 1932, a year in which the Preferred and Deferred Ordinary stock holders received no dividend at all and even the holders of the Preference stocks failed to obtain their full dividend.

Two factors contributed to this depressing picture. The LNER drew much if not most of its traffic receipts from the areas of heavy industry which were hardest hit by the recession – the North East Coast and Central Scotland, as well as the steel and textile centres of Yorkshire. Secondly, there was little doubt that the com-

pany's capital structure was top-heavy – the total burden of debentures and fixed-dividend prior charges was excessive, leading to what financiers term high 'gearing', in which a small fluctuation in net revenues can have a disproportionately great effect upon the dividend available for the Ordinary shareholders.

This, of course, made it difficult if not impossible to raise much-needed new capital for major improvements such as electrification. It was necessary, therefore, to rely upon internal financing (renewal funds, superannuation fund balances, etc.) or else upon Government-assisted finance such as the Railway Finance Corporation loans, for major investments.

It was not the fault of the Board that the LNER was over-capitalised, that, in other words, the capital obligations were greater than the net revenues could adequately support. The capital structure was a direct result of the Railways Act, 1921, which created the company. Under that Act, stock in the new LNER was issued to the stockholders of the former constituent and subsidiary companies based on the assumed earning capacity of the new group, in relation to the earnings record of the absorbed railways. The LNER was to be assigned a 'standard revenue' (basically, the 1913 revenues of the absorbed railways, with an allowance

56 Ex-NBR J37 no. 9296 with an up goods near Shandon on the West Highland line in 1936.

F. R. Hebron – Rail Archive Stephenson

for any subsequent capital expenditure); and 'standard revenue' was supposed, under the Act, to be provided by manipulating charges. If any railway failed to earn its 'standard revenue', it was entitled to apply to the Railway Rates Tribunal, a body created by the Act with semi-judicial functions and powers, for authority to increase its charges to an extent calculated to bring the net revenue up to the 'standard'. Contrariwise, if in any year, 'standard revenue' was exceeded, the Rates Tribunal had power to order the railways to reduce charges to an extent calculated to absorb 80 per cent of the excess.

These provisions of the Act were quite unrealistic. They could only have worked as intended if, on the one hand, economic conditions had remained stable from year to year, and on the other, if the railways had retained a virtual monopoly of inland transport and the demand for their services had been, in economic terms, 'fully inelastic'. Neither circumstance existed in the 1920s and 1930s.

The actual 'standard revenue' allocated to the LNER in 1928 was £14,787,733. (The significance of 1928 is that it was the year in which the intended linking of charges and revenues by the machinery of the Railway Rates Tribunal began to operate.) In the case of the LNER the 'standard revenue' was equal to 4.52 per cent upon that company's capital receipts. After paying interest and dividends on the 'prior charges' – i.e. the Debentures, Preference and Preferred Ordinary stocks – there would have been left an amount sufficient to pay 4.18 per cent on the LNER 'equity' – the Deferred Ordinary stock.

But this happy result was never achieved. The LNER never earned its 'standard revenue'; in its worst year it earned less than half the target figure. There was accordingly an unremitting struggle to make ends meet. The unfortunate holders of Deferred Ordinary stock, and even the holders of the Preferred Ordinary and the Junior Preference stocks, felt cheated, particularly if they had been stockholders since the creation of the group in 1923. An LNER Stockholders Association was formed as early as 1927 and it regularly challenged the Board at Annual General Meetings, though it was unable to secure election of its own nominees as Directors despite several attempts.

Until 1932 there were several occasions when reserves were drawn upon to maintain a payment on the Preferred Ordinary stock. The reason was that, by doing so, the prior stocks remained available, by law, for investment by trustees. However, in 1932 Mr Whitelaw announced that there could no longer be any question of this course being followed, in view of the insufficiency of net revenue.

In fact, the auditors in issuing their certificate upon the accounts had withheld their endorsement of the adequacy of the provisions for renewals, and no doubt this influenced the Board in deciding that no further transfers from reserve could be made for the purpose of paying dividends, if the railway was to be properly maintained.

To meet these financial stringencies, the management made numerous economies. In common with the other main line companies, wages and salaries were reduced by a flat 2½ per cent between August 1929 and May 1930, when the cut was temporarily restored. But less than a year later, in May 1931, the overall 2½ per cent reduction was again imposed with a further 2½ per cent deduction where wages were in excess of £2 a week or salaries were over £100 per annum. This remained in force until 1934 when the financial results had improved somewhat from the all-time 'low' of 1932; the second 2½ per cent was no longer deducted, but the basic 2½ per cent remained longer in force, being restored in two instalments of 1¼ per cent each in 1936 and 1937.

Many economies were sought from a steady improvement in operating efficiency. The total train-miles operated in 1937 were 111 per cent of those in 1923, but railway operating expenditure was only 84 per cent of the 1923 figure. The character of the freight business, and the ratio of expenditure to receipts from this source, were affected by the fall in coal class traffic (from 98.5 million tons in 1923 to 86.6 million in 1937) and the reduction in size of the average consignment of general merchandise, which increased handling costs. The drop in average size of consignment was largely a consequence of the competition from road hauliers, who could offer attractive rates for a lorry-load (often equating to a railway wagon-load) but who left most of the smaller stuff, less economic to handle, to the railways.

The LNER did manage to achieve some improvement in the classic statistic of operating efficiency, 'net ton-miles per total engine-hour', which rose from 476 in 1923 to 501 in 1937; but it did not widely introduce such methods as cyclic diagramming of locomotives, akin to what was practised on the LMS, in the search for higher utilisation: it was still often the case that locomotives would be handled by only two crews and would return to the home shed daily after completing a 'diagram' of duties. This probably had advantages in that locomotives were more carefully handled by their regular drivers; but whereas engine-miles per day per engine in use (weekdays) rose on the LMS from an average of 97.53 in 1923 to 117.42 in 1937, on the LNER they only rose from 98.99 to 104.78 over the same period.

The LNER Board was constantly on the lookout for economies. Total staff employed fell from 207,528 in March 1924 to 175,849 in March 1937. This indicated the effect of Grouping in rationalisation of services; the fall in traffic; and various measures to improve productivity. Wages and the clerical staff salaries up to Special Class were, of course, fixed by national agreements with the unions and were not within one railway's power to determine. But salaries and grading of management posts were a different matter. The LNER officers' salaries were certainly the lowest of the four groups and the grading of junior management and supervisory posts was generally at a lower level than that which prevailed on, say, the LMS. There was, however, a slightly less inquisitorial attitude to expenses and travel privileges, due to the integration of staff work with management and its less centralised and authoritarian procedures, compared with the LMS. If you were an LNER officer, you felt trusted by your superiors and by the Board, in a way that made for loyalty even if the pay was not brilliant.

It must be said, though, that the low LNER salaries tempted a number of able people to resign and seek more highly paid posts outside. G. F. Thurston's move has already been mentioned. But W. M. Teasdale, who had been brilliantly successful in charge of publicity and risen to be an Assistant General Manager, left to become Head of Advertising in the Allied Newspapers group; C. A. Lambert (then Passenger Manager, NE Area) became General Manager of the Bolsover Colliery Co.; and F. C. C. Stanley (then District Passenger Manager, Newcastle) became Managing Director of the B & N Line.

Looking back over the LNER's financial history, with hindsight one can see that a drastic reconstruction of the capital structure, bringing it into line with the reduced earning capacity of the business, would have been a wise piece of surgery. But the whole legal constitution of the company, based on the Railways Act 1921 and the various Acts governing the form of railway accounts, made this difficult if not impossible even to contemplate. One can therefore only sympathise with the LNER Board in their difficult task of answering criticism from the stockholders deprived of what they considered a proper return on their investment, and simultaneously meeting the demands for more and more improvements in the quality of service from the customers of the railway. On the whole, one may say that the Board walked this tightrope without falling off, despite a few perilous lurches.

11
The Last Summer of Peace

There can be no doubt that the summer timetable of 1939 offered passengers on all four main line railways a better service than they had ever enjoyed before. There had certainly been a long delay, in the inter-war years, in restoring let alone excelling the standards of 1914; but now speed, frequency and comfort had reached a new peak. So far as the LNER was concerned, the best average journey times on the GN Section were now 16 per cent better than in 1914 and on the East Coast services 13 per cent better. The Great Eastern Section was 8 per cent, but the Great Central only 1 per cent better.

A train-spotter standing at the end of No. 10 platform at King's Cross that summer could witness a majestic procession of restaurant car expresses departing throughout the day. At 10.00 the 'Flying Scotsman' left for Edinburgh, to be followed five minutes later by the Aberdeen and Glasgow coaches as a separate train. At 10.15 came a train for Leeds, at 11.20 the 'Queen of Scots' Pullman, at 1.05 a Newcastle express followed by the midday Edinburgh train at 1.20 and a Leeds train at 1.30. Ten minutes later the 1.40 departed for Harrogate and Scarborough.

There would be excitement at 4 pm when a Newcastle express left simultaneously with the down 'Coronation', running on the slow line until the streamliner had drawn well ahead. At 4.45 the 'Yorkshire Pullman' drew out, and at 5.30 the 'Silver Jubilee' left for Newcastle, followed by an express for Hull at 5.45 and one for Leeds at 5.50. The 'West Riding Limited' departed at 7.10 followed by a Hull express at 7.15. The first sleeping car train was the 7.30 'Aberdonian' with its tail-end dining car (detached at York). More East Coast sleeper trains left at 10.25, 10.45 and 1.05 am.

Of course on Saturdays there were numerous extra expresses, as well as the daily semi-fasts sandwiched in between the principal trains. Today's diesel Inter-City 125 and locomotive-hauled expresses offer faster and more frequent services, usually at standardised departure times, but they cannot offer the visual pleasure of trains headed by Gresley's splendid Pacifics in green, silver or Garter blue. Nor do they offer anything like the number of through coaches to destinations other than the principal one. Nor can the simplified restaurant car meals or buffet snacks of today match the solid comfort of the pre-war 'diner' and its equally solid menus!

The principal train services out of Marylebone and Liverpool Street retained respectively a strong GCR and GER flavour, despite the Doncaster character of the locomotives and of the more modern rolling stock. And along the Joint Line (no longer truly joint, since the GNR and GER had become part of the LNER, but always still so called) trains padded steadily across the Lincolnshire flats without undue exertion.

Up in the North Eastern Area the 'smack of firm government' emanating from York was still felt, and standards were kept up even if

57 An antique survivor: Beyer Peacock ex-Midland and Great Northern Joint Railway class 'A' no. 025 at Spalding, after the LNER became responsible for M & GN motive power, around 1938.

revenue was inadequate to generate funds for investment in new stations and rolling stock for the secondary services.

In the Chief General Manager's office there was a massive file entitled 'Good Housekeeping at Stations'. Making the best of what the railway had got, instead of letting it deteriorate and then blaming this upon lack of investment, was a very sensible practice of the LNER, dear to Newton's heart. Station Improvement Committees, which he had first instituted when DGM Southern Area, toured the system, noting minor shortcomings and arranging for attention to be paid to repairs and modifications that could usually be effected through Small Works Orders.

Standards on the principal expresses were monitored by East Coast Inspectors who regularly travelled on the trains to report any difficulties – such as a need for strengthening vehicles, inadequacy of cleaning arrangements, or problems of maintaining advertised connections.

Train catering, whether by LNER Hotels Departments or the Pullman Car Company, was generally maintained to quite a high standard, although the traditional set menus continued to be served on most trains and there were

58 P2 no. 2005, 'Thane of Fife', leaving Stonehaven with an evening Edinburgh–Aberdeen express in 1937.

occasional complaints of the lack of choice such as an à la carte service would offer. Sir Ralph Wedgwood once told a public meeting that he had little sympathy with those delicate stomachs that could not enjoy a straightforward British table d'hôte!

The refreshment rooms, however, still mostly retained their Victorian atmosphere; they were the Cinderellas of the Hotels Departments, of which there were three, the Hotels Superintendents in each Area reporting to the Divisional General Manager.

The railway hotels were in fact closely integrated with the passenger business, still geared

97

"THE CORONATION"
CROSSING THE ROYAL BORDER BRIDGE BERWICK-upon-TWEED
IT'S QUICKER BY RAIL
FULL INFORMATION FROM ANY L·N·E·R OFFICE OR AGENCY

59 The pride of the LNER, expressed in a poster.

primarily to serve the railway traveller, even though both the 'business' and the 'resort' hotels enjoyed a large non–railway custom. The principal hotels in each Area were used for hospitality by the Area Boards, as a means of getting to know their principal officers and to make contact with local notabilities and important customers of the railway.

The hotels were also widely used for meetings and conferences of railway officers, which the decentralised organisation of the LNER tended to proliferate. Any shortcomings in the standard of service would therefore, unless quickly rectified, be reported back to the Divisional General Manager through the grapevine.

In the Southern Area the Great Eastern Hotel at Liverpool Street was, since the closure of the Cannon Street Hotel, quite unchallenged as the premier hotel in the City of London. It was particularly favoured by visitors using the Parkeston Quay boat trains – a lift from the station's Platform 10 took guests direct into the hotel – as well as providing very large banqueting facilities for business purposes in the Abercorn Rooms. The Great Northern Hotel at

60 Very 'North Eastern' still. C6 no. 698 leaves
Scarborough with the 11.00 am to Leeds on 16 April 1938.

T. G. Hepburn – Rail Archive Stephenson

King's Cross was a more modest establishment, though very popular with north-country visitors.

In fact, all the ex-GNR hotels were rather unpretentious – like the GNR stations – whereas the NER had built the impressive Royal Station Hotel in a commanding position in York, and an almost equally imposing edifice at Newcastle. The North British Station Hotel at Edinburgh dominated the east end of Princes Street as though to challenge the Caledonian Hotel at the other end. Its endless corridors and acres of tiled wall suggesting a Turkish bath or a public lavatory could be forgiven by travellers arriving by the night sleeper trains from London and

99

F. R. Hebron – Rail Archive Stephenson

61 Ex-GCR C4 no. 6083 with a Cambridge and Garden Cities Buffet Car Express (one of the 'beer trains') near Brookmans Park in 1936.

sampling a splendid Scottish breakfast in the restaurant.

The little GNSR had had two major ventures into hotel keeping, both disastrous. At Aberdeen the Palace Hotel, the premier hotel in the city, was to be burnt down in LNER days and never re-opened; whilst at Cruden Bay, twenty miles north of Aberdeen, a grand resort hotel and golf course were established, designed to compete with the Gleneagles Hotel, but destined to financial failure. The main interest of the Cruden Bay Hotel venture lay in the electric tramway linking the railway station with the hotel, with two electric tramcars built in the GNSR works at Kittybrewster in 1899. The trams carried not merely visitors to and from the hotel but also freight – coal in particular – in trailer wagons. All the washing on the GNSR was done in the hotel laundry, so the tramway handled a considerable traffic in dirty and clean linen.

The LNER closed the Boddam branch, serving Cruden Bay, to passenger traffic in 1932, after which the tramway also became a 'freight-only' line, hotel passengers using a bus service to and from Aberdeen. (The tramway was finally closed and the tramcars scrapped in 1941.)

On the commercial field the railways might have seemed to have entered a more hopeful stage in their history by 1939. In that summer the Minister of Transport made a statement to the effect that there appeared to be a strong case for granting the railways the freedom from statutory restraints upon their charges which they had asked for in the 'Square Deal' campaign. They had reached some understanding with both the road haulage industry and trade associations representing the major consignors of goods by rail, which suggested that a *modus vivendi* could be found to replace the savage competition previously experienced, and probably also to permit the railways to invest more heavily in road goods transport themselves.

Recovery from the trough of the depression had been continuous until it was interrupted by the 'mini-recession' of 1938 – a quite serious set-back for the railway. Now in 1939, however, traffic seemed to have recovered the upward trend.

But behind these encouraging features there was the sinister development of the international scene which even busy railwaymen could not ignore. Until the 1938 Munich crisis there had been little evidence on the LNER of any planning for war conditions, although as early as 1937 the railway General Managers had discussed with the Ministry of Transport the problems that would arise if there was another European war. The Government then appointed the Railway Executive Committee, composed of three general managers, with the President of the LMS and the Vice-Chairman of the London Passenger Transport Board as, at this stage, an advisory body, in September 1938.

Sir Ralph Wedgwood was elected Chairman at the outset; and when he retired in March 1939 as CGM of the LNER, he was asked to continue as Chairman of the REC.

The planning work of that Committee continued at an increasing tempo until war broke out and the REC overnight became a truly executive body acting as agents of the Minister for the purpose of giving effect to Directions which he was now empowered to issue under the Emergency (Railway Control) Order 1939.

Railway staffs had seen a number of changes in the twelve months between Munich and the declaration of war. A priority task was to protect the Control Offices as far as possible from bomb damage. At Gerrards Cross in Buckinghamshire the evacuated Control Office for the GN and GC Sections of the Southern Area was established, whilst King's Cross District Control was moved to Knebworth. The Southern Area (Eastern) Control was re-located at Shenfield in Essex; Doncaster District Control at Bawtry, eight miles south of that town; and Manchester District Control at Godley. Other Control Offices just dug themselves in; York found an underground site below the city wall (in the process uncovering some foundations of a Roman bath-house); both Norwich and Cambridge District Controls went to basement level.

In Edinburgh, both the Scottish Central Control and the Edinburgh District Control retired into the Scotland Street tunnel, now disused but originally built for a direct Waverley Station –

62 Heartland of the LNER: a Raven Atlantic with ex-NER clerestory coaches in York station.

Leith railway, to be operated with rope haulage. They displaced the mushroom growing industry located in the tunnel.

In the summer, the LNER rented 'The Hoo', near Welwyn, a large red-brick country mansion, given the intriguing address of 'H.Q.1, via Hitchin, Herts' – to baffle German spies and bomber pilots! H.Q.2 was Sir Nigel Gresley's private house at Watton, near Stevenage, not far away. The Chief General Manager and the Divisional General Manager, Southern Area, together with some 'All-Line Officers', were to move into H.Q.1; the CME's office to H.Q.2.

In the world outside railways, events were moving rapidly. Some may have remembered, on 3 September, when the blackout was suddenly – and effectively – imposed, that it had been a former LNER and NER Director who, whilst Foreign Secretary, had sadly remarked on 4 August 1914, 'The lamps are going out all over Europe.' This time the lamps were extinguished less figuratively and more literally.

For a few days after war had been declared trains continued to run in the summer timetable; but on 10 September the whole era of the High Speed Trains came to an abrupt end. In the new wartime timetable the 6 hour London–Edinburgh journey by the 'Coronation' became, overnight, 9 hours 25 minutes. Another volume must tell how the LNER coped with wartime problems, survived, planned for the post-war world, but was finally, after a struggle, merged in British Railways.

Index

EVERYMAN, I will go with thee,

and be thy guide,

In thy most need to go by thy side

SAMUEL RICHARDSON

Born at Derby in 1689, the son of a joiner.
Came to London at seventeen, and entered
the printing trade, eventually purchasing
the moiety of the patent of King's Printer.
Died in London in 1761.

SAMUEL RICHARDSON

Clarissa

OR, THE HISTORY OF A YOUNG LADY

IN FOUR VOLUMES · VOLUME FOUR

Introduction by

JOHN BUTT, M.A., B.LITT., F.B.A.

*Regius Professor of Rhetoric and English Literature
in the University of Edinburgh*

DENT: LONDON
EVERYMAN'S LIBRARY
DUTTON: NEW YORK

NO. *885*

SBN: 460 00885 4

THE HISTORY OF CLARISSA HARLOWE

Letter I—Miss Clarissa Harlowe to Mrs. Norton

Monday Night, July 24.

MY DEAR MRS. NORTON,—Had I not fallen into fresh troubles, which disabled me for several days from holding a pen, I should not have forborne inquiring after your health, and that of your son; for I should have been but too ready to impute your silence to the cause to which, to my very great concern, I find it was owing. I pray to Heaven, my dear good friend, to give you comfort in the way most desirable to yourself.

I am exceedingly concerned at Miss Howe's writing about me to my friends. I do assure you, that I was as ignorant of her intention so to do, as of the contents of her letter. Nor has she yet let me know (discouraged, I suppose, by her ill-success) that she *did* write. It is impossible to share the delight which such charming spirits give, without the inconvenience that will attend their volatility. So mixed are our best enjoyments!

It was but yesterday that I wrote to chide the dear creature for freedoms of that nature, which her unseasonably-expressed love for me had made her take, as you wrote me word in your former. I was afraid that all such freedoms would be attributed to *me*. And I am sure that nothing but my own application to my friends, and a full conviction of my contrition, will procure me favour. Least of all can I expect that either your mediation or hers (both of whose fond and partial love of me is so well known) will avail me.

She then gives a brief account of the arrest: of her dejection under it: of her apprehensions of being carried to her former lodgings: of Mr. Lovelace's avowed innocence as to that insult: of her release by Mr. Belford: of Mr. Lovelace's promise not to molest her: of her clothes being sent her: of the earnest desire of all his friends, and of himself, to marry her: of Miss Howe's advice to comply with their requests: and of her declared resolution rather to die than be his, sent to Miss Howe, to be given to his relations, but as the day before. After which she thus proceeds:

I

Now, my dear Mrs. Norton, you will be surprised, perhaps, that I should have returned such an answer: but, when you have everything before you, you, who know me so well, will not think me wrong. And, besides, I am upon a *better preparation* than for an earthly husband.

Nor let it be imagined, my dear and ever-venerable friend, that my present turn of mind proceeds from gloominess or melancholy: for although it was *brought on* by disappointment (the world showing me early, even at my first *rushing* into it, its true and ugly face), yet I hope that it has obtained a better root, and will every day more and more, by its fruits, demonstrate to me, and to all my friends, that it has.

I have written to my sister. Last Friday I wrote. So the die is thrown. I hope for a gentle answer. But perhaps they will not vouchsafe me *any*. It is my *first* direct application, you know. I wish Miss Howe had left me to my own workings in this tender point.

It will be a great satisfaction to me to hear of your perfect recovery; and that my foster-brother is out of danger. But why said I, *out of danger*? When can *this* be justly said of creatures who hold by so uncertain a tenure? This is one of those forms of common speech that proves the *frailty* and the *presumption* of poor mortals at the same time.

Don't be uneasy you cannot answer your wishes to be with me. I am happier than I could have expected to be among mere strangers. It was grievous at first; but use reconciles everything to us. The people of the house where I am are courteous and honest. There is a widow who lodges in it [have I not said so formerly?], a good woman; who is the better for having been a proficient in the school of affliction.

An excellent school! my dear Mrs. Norton, in which we are taught to know ourselves, to be able to compassionate and bear with one another, and to look up to a better hope.

I have as humane a physician (whose fees are his least regard), and as worthy an apothecary, as ever patient was visited by. My nurse is diligent, obliging, silent, and sober. So I am not unhappy *without*: and *within*—I hope, my dear Mrs. Norton, that I shall be every day more and more happy *within*.

No doubt it would be one of the greatest comforts I could know, to have you with me: you, who love me so dearly: who have been the watchful sustainer of my helpless infancy: you, by whose precepts I have been so much benefited! In your dear bosom could I repose all my griefs: and by your piety and experience in the ways of Heaven, should I be strengthened in what I am still to go through.

But, as it must not be, I will acquiesce; and so, I hope, will you: for you see in what respects I am *not* unhappy; and in those that I *am*, they lie not in your power to remedy.

Then, as I have told you, I have all my clothes in my own possession. So I am rich enough, as to this world, and in common conveniences.

So you see, my venerable and dear friend, that I am not always turning the dark side of my prospects, in order to move compassion; a trick imputed to me, too often, by my hard-hearted sister; when, if I know my own heart, it is above all trick or artifice. Yet I hope at last I shall be so happy as to receive *benefit* rather than *reproach* from this talent, if it *be* my talent. At *last*, I say; for whose heart have I *hitherto* moved? Not one, I am sure, that was not *predetermined* in my favour.

As to the day—I have passed it, as I ought to pass it. It has been a very heavy day to me! More for my friends' sake, too, than for my own! How did *they* use to pass it! What a festivity! How have they now passed it! To *imagine* it, how grievous! Say not that those are cruel, who suffer so much for my fault; and who, for eighteen years together, rejoiced in me, and rejoiced me, by their indulgent goodness! But I will think the rest! Adieu, my dearest Mrs. Norton!

Adieu!

Letter II—Miss Clarissa Harlowe to Miss Arabella Harlowe

Friday, July 21.

IF, my dearest sister, I did not think the state of my health very precarious, and that it was my duty to take this step, I should hardly have dared to approach you, although but with my pen, after having found your censures so dreadfully justified as they have been.

I have not the courage to write to my father himself; nor yet to my mother. And it is with trembling that I address myself to you, to beg of you to intercede for me, that my father will have the goodness to revoke that heaviest part of the very heavy curse he laid upon me, which relates to HEREAFTER: for, as to the HERE, *I have* indeed *met with my punishment from the very wretch in whom I was supposed to place my confidence.*

As I hope not for restoration to favour, I may be allowed to be very earnest on this head: yet will I not use any arguments in support of my request, because I am sure my father, were it in his power, would not have his poor child miserable for ever.

I have the most grateful sense of my mother's goodness in sending me up my clothes. I would have acknowledged the favour the moment I received them, with the most thankful duty, but that I feared any line from me would be unacceptable.

I would not give fresh offence: so will decline all other commendations of duty and love; appealing to my heart for both, where *both* are flaming with an ardour that nothing but death can extinguish: therefore only subscribe myself, without so much as a name,

My dear and happy sister,
Your afflicted servant.

A letter directed for me, at Mr. Smith's, a glover, in King Street, Covent Garden, will come to hand.

Letter III—Mr. Belford to Robert Lovelace, Esq.

[*In answer to Letters CXIX and CXXII of vol. iii.*]

Edgware, Monday, July 24.

WHAT pains thou takest to persuade thyself that the lady's ill-health is owing to the vile arrest, and to the implacableness of her friends!   Both primarily (if they were) to be laid at thy door. What poor excuses will good heads make for the evils they are put upon by bad hearts!   But 'tis no wonder that he who can sit down premeditatedly to do a bad action, will content himself with a bad excuse: and yet, what fools must he suppose the rest of the world to be, if he imagines them as easy to be imposed upon as he can impose upon himself?

In vain dost thou impute to pride or wilfulness the necessity to which thou hast reduced this lady of parting with her clothes: for can she do otherwise, and be the noble-minded creature she is?

Her implacable friends have refused her the current cash she left behind her; and wished, as her sister wrote to her, to see her reduced to want: probably, therefore, they will not be sorry that she is reduced to such straits; and will take it for a justification from Heaven of their wicked hard-heartedness.   Thou canst not suppose she would take supplies from thee: to take them from me would, in her opinion, be taking them from thee.   Miss Howe's mother is an avaricious woman; and, perhaps, the daughter can do nothing of that sort unknown to her; and, if she *could*, is too noble a girl to deny it, if charged.   And then Miss Harlowe is firmly of opinion that she shall never want nor wear the things she disposes of.

Having heard nothing from town that obliges me to go thither, I shall gratify poor Belton with my company till to-morrow, or perhaps till Wednesday: for the unhappy man is more and more loath to part with me. I shall soon set out for Epsom, to endeavour to serve him there, and reinstate him in his own house. Poor fellow! he is most horribly low-spirited; mopes about; and nothing diverts him. I pity him at my heart; but can do him no good. What consolation can I give him, either from his past life, or from his future prospects?

Our friendships and intimacies, Lovelace, are only calculated for strong life and health. When sickness comes, we look round us, and upon one another, like frighted birds at the sight of a kite ready to souse upon them. Then, with all our bravery, what miserable wretches are we!

Thou tellest me that thou seest reformation is coming swiftly upon me. I hope it is. I see so much difference in the behaviour of this admirable woman in *her* illness, and that of poor Belton in *his*, that it is plain to me the sinner is the real coward, and the saint the true hero; and, sooner or later, we shall all find it to be so, if we are not cut off suddenly.

The lady shut herself up at six o'clock yesterday afternoon; and intends not to see company till seven or eight this; not even her nurse—imposing upon herself a severe fast. And why? *It is her* BIRTHDAY! Blooming—yet declining in her very blossom! Every birthday till this, no doubt, happy! What must be her reflections! What ought to be thine!

What sport dost thou make with my aspirations, and my prostrations, as thou callest them; and with my dropping of the bank-note behind her chair! I had too much awe of her at the time, and too much apprehended her displeasure at the offer, to make it with the grace that would better have become my intention. But the action, if awkward, was modest. Indeed, the fitter subject for ridicule with thee; who canst no more taste the beauty and delicacy of modest obligingness than of modest love. For the same may be said of inviolable respect that the poet says of unfeigned affection:

> I *speak*, I know not what!—
> Speak ever so; and if I *answer* you
> I know not what, it shows the more of Love.
> Love is a child that talks in broken language;
> Yet then it speaks most plain.

The like may be pleaded in behalf of that modest respect which made the humble offerer afraid to invade the awful eye, or the revered hand; but awkwardly to drop its incense beside the altar it should have been laid upon. But how should that soul, which could treat delicacy itself brutally, know anything of this?

But I am still more amazed at thy courage, to think of throwing thyself in the way of Miss Howe, and Miss Arabella Harlowe! Thou wilt not dare, surely, to carry this thought into execution!

As to *my* dress, and *thy* dress, I have only to say that the sum total of thy observation is this: that *my* outside is the *worst* of me; and *thine* the *best* of thee: and what gettest thou by the comparison? Do thou reform the one, and I'll try to mend the other. I challenge thee to begin.

Mrs. Lovick gave me, at my request, the copy of a meditation she showed me, which was extracted by the lady from the Scriptures, while under arrest at Rowland's, as appears by the date. The lady is not to know that I have taken a copy.

You and I always admired the noble simplicity, and natural ease and dignity of style, which are the distinguishing characteristics of these books, whenever any passages from them, by way of quotation in the works of other authors, popped upon us. And once I remember you, even *you,* observed that those passages always appeared to you like a rich vein of golden ore, which runs through baser metals; embellishing the work they were brought to authenticate.

Try, Lovelace, if thou canst relish a divine beauty. I think it must strike transient (if not permanent) remorse into thy heart. Thou boastest of thy ingenuousness: let this be the test of it; and whether thou canst be serious on a subject so deep, the occasion of it resulting from thyself.

MEDITATION

Saturday, July 15

O that my grief were thoroughly weighed, and my calamity laid in the balance together!

For now it would be heavier than the sand of the sea: therefore my words are swallowed up.

For the arrows of the Almighty are within me; the poison whereof drinketh up my spirit. The terrors of God do set themselves in array against me.

When I lie down, I say, When shall I arise? When will the night be gone? And I am full of tossings to and fro, unto the dawning of the day.

My days are swifter than a weaver's shuttle, and are spent without hope—mine eye shall no more see good.

Wherefore is light given to *her* that *is* in misery: and life unto the bitter in soul?

Who longeth for death; but it cometh not; and diggeth for it more than for hid treasures?

Why is light given to *one* whose way is hid; and whom God hath hedged in?

For the thing which I greatly feared is come upon me!

I was not in safety; neither had I rest; neither was I quiet: yet trouble came.

But behold God is mighty, and despiseth not any.

He giveth right to the poor—and if they be bound in fetters, and holden in cords of affliction, then He showeth them their work and their transgressions.

I have a little leisure, and am in a scribbling vein: indulge me, Lovelace, a few reflections on these sacred books.

We are taught to read the Bible when children, and as a rudiment only; and, as far as I know, this may be the reason why we think ourselves above it when at a maturer age. For you know that our parents, as well as we, *wisely* rate our proficiency by the books we are advanced to, and not by our understanding of those we have passed through. But, in my uncle's illness, I had the curiosity, in some of my dull hours (lighting upon one in his closet), to dip into it: and then I found, wherever I turned, that there were *admirable things in it.* I have borrowed one, on receiving from Mrs. Lovick the above meditation; for I had a mind to compare the passages contained in it by the book, hardly believing they could be so exceedingly apposite as I find they are. And one time or other, it is very likely that I shall make a resolution to give the whole Bible a perusal, by way of *course,* as I may say.

This, meantime, I will venture to repeat, is certain, that the style is that truly easy, simple, and natural one, which we should admire in other authors excessively. Then all the world join in an opinion of the antiquity, and authenticity too, of the book; and the learned are fond of strengthening their different arguments by its sanctions. Indeed, I was so much taken with it at my uncle's, that I was half ashamed that it appeared so *new* to me. And yet, I cannot but say that I have some of the Old Testament history, as it is called, in my head: but, perhaps, am more obliged for it to Josephus than to the Bible itself.

Odd enough, with all our pride of learning, that we choose to derive the little we know from the undercurrents, perhaps muddy ones too, when the clear, the pellucid fountain-head is much nearer at hand, and easier to be come at. Slighted the more, possibly, for that very reason!

But man is a pragmatical, foolish creature; and the more we look into him the more we must despise him. Lords of the creation! Who can forbear indignant laughter! When we see not one of the individuals of that creation (his perpetually eccentric self excepted) but acts within its own natural and original appointments: and all the time, proud and vain as the conceited wretch is of fancied and self-dependent excellence, he is obliged not only for the ornaments, but for the necessaries of life (that is to say, for food as well as raiment), to all the other creatures; strutting with their blood and spirits in his veins, and with their plumage on his back: for what has he of his own, but a very mischievous, monkey-like, bad nature? Yet thinks himself at liberty to kick, and cuff, and elbow out every worthier creature: and when he has none of the animal creation to hunt down and abuse, will make use of his power, his strength, or his wealth, to oppress the less powerful and weaker of his own species!

When you and I meet next, let us enter more largely into this subject: and I dare say we shall take it by turns, in imitation of the two sages of antiquity, to laugh and to weep at the thoughts of what miserable yet conceited beings men in general, but we libertines in particular, are.

I fell upon a piece at Dorrell's this very evening, entitled *The Sacred Classics*, written by one Blackwall.

I took it home with me; and had not read a dozen pages, when I was convinced that I ought to be ashamed of myself to think how greatly I have admired less noble and less natural beauties in pagan authors; while I have known nothing of this all-excelling collection of beauties, the Bible! By my faith, Lovelace, I shall for the future have a better opinion of the good sense and taste of half a score of parsons whom I have fallen in with in my time, and despised for *magnifying*, as I thought they did, the language and the sentiments to be found in it, in preference to all the ancient poets and philosophers. And this is now a convincing proof to me, and shames as much an infidel's presumption as his ignorance, that those who know least are the greatest scoffers. A pretty pack of would-be wits of us, who censure without knowledge, laugh without reason, and are most noisy and loud against things we know least of!

Letter IV—Mr. Belford to Robert Lovelace, Esq.

Wednesday, July 26.

I CAME not to town till this morning early; poor Belton clinging to me, as a man destitute of all other hold.

I hastened to Smith's; and had but a very indifferent account of the lady's health. I sent up my compliments; and she desired to see me in the afternoon.

Mrs. Lovick told me, that after I went away on Saturday, she actually parted with one of her best suits of clothes to a gentle-woman who is her [Mrs. Lovick's] benefactress, and who bought them for a niece who is very speedily to be married, and whom she fits out and portions as her intended heiress. The lady was so jealous that the money might come from you or me, that she would see the purchaser: who owned to Mrs. Lovick that she bought them for half their worth: but yet, though her conscience permitted her to take them at such an under-rate, the widow says her friend admired the lady, as one of the loveliest of her sex: and having been let into a little of her story, could not help tears at taking away her purchase.

She may be a good sort of a woman: Mrs. Lovick says she *is*: but SELF is an odious devil, that reconciles to some people the most cruel and dishonest actions. But, nevertheless, it is my opinion, that those who can suffer themselves to take advantage of the necessities of their fellow-creatures, in order to buy anything at a less rate than would allow them the legal interest of their purchase-money (supposing they purchase *before they want*), are no better than robbers for the difference. To plunder a wreck, and to rob at a fire, are indeed higher degrees of wicked-ness: but do not those as well as these heighten the distresses of the distressed, and heap misery on the miserable, whom it is the duty of every one to relieve?

About three o'clock I went again to Smith's. The lady was writing when I sent up my name; but admitted of my visit. I saw a visible alteration in her countenance for the worse; and Mrs. Lovick respectfully accusing her of too great assiduity to her pen, early and late, and of her abstinence the day before, I took notice of the alteration; and told her that her physician had greater hopes of her than she had of herself; and I would take the liberty to say that despair of recovery allowed not room for cure.

She said she neither despaired nor hoped. Then stepping to the glass, with great composure, My countenance, said she, is indeed an honest picture of my heart.   But the mind will run away with the body at any time.

Writing is all my diversion, continued she; and I have subjects that cannot be dispensed with.   As to my hours, I have always been an early riser: but now rest is less in my power than ever: sleep has a long time ago quarrelled with me, and will not be friends, although I have made the first advances.   What *will* be, *must*.

She then stepped to her closet, and brought to me a parcel sealed up with three seals: Be so kind, said she, as to give this to your friend.   A very grateful present it ought to be to him: for, sir, this packet contains all his letters to me.   Such letters they are, as, compared with his actions, would reflect dishonour upon all his sex, were they to fall into other hands.

As to my letters to him, they are not many.   He may either keep or destroy them, as he pleases.

I thought, Lovelace, I ought not to forego this opportunity to plead for you: I therefore, with the packet in my hand, urged all the arguments I could think of in your favour.

She heard me out with more attention than I could have promised myself, considering her determined resolution.

I would not interrupt you, Mr. Belford, said she, though I am far from being pleased with the subject of your discourse.   The motives for your pleas in his favour are generous.   I love to see instances of generous friendship in either sex.   But I have written my full mind on this subject to Miss Howe, who will communicate it to the ladies of his family.   No more, therefore, I pray you, upon a topic that may lead to disagreeable recriminations.

Her apothecary came in.   He advised her to the air, and blamed her for so great an application, as he was told she made, to her pen; and he gave it as the doctor's opinion, as well as his own, that she would recover, if she herself desired to recover, and would use the means.

She may possibly write too much for her health: but I have observed on several occasions, that when the physical men are at a loss what to prescribe, they inquire what their patients best like, or are most diverted with, and forbid them that.

But, noble-minded as they see this lady is, they know not half her nobleness of mind, nor how deeply she is wounded; and depend too much upon her *youth*, which I doubt will not do in this case, and upon *time*, which will not alleviate the woes of such a mind: for, having been bent upon doing good, and upon reclaiming a libertine whom she loved, she is disappointed in all her darling views, and will never be able, I fear, to look up with satisfaction enough in herself to make life desirable to her. For this lady had *other* views in living, than the common ones of eating, sleeping, dressing, visiting, and those other fashionable amusements which fill up the time of most of her sex, especially of those of it who think themselves fitted to shine in and adorn polite assemblies. Her grief, in short, seems to me to be of such a nature, that *time*, which alleviates most other persons' afflictions, will, as the poet says, *give increase to hers.*

Thou, Lovelace, mightest have seen all this superior excellence, as thou wentest along. In every word, in every sentiment, in every action, is it visible. But thy cursed inventions and intriguing spirit ran away with thee. 'Tis fit that the subject of thy wicked boast, and thy reflections on talents so egregiously misapplied, should be *thy* punishment and thy curse.

Mr. Goddard took his leave; and I was going to do so too, when the maid came up, and told her a gentleman was below, who very earnestly inquired after her health, and desired to see her: his name Hickman.

She was overjoyed; and bid the maid desire the gentleman to walk up.

I would have withdrawn; but I suppose she thought it was likely I should have met him upon the stairs; and so she forbid it.

She shot to the stairs-head to receive him, and, taking his hand, asked half a dozen questions (without waiting for any answer) in relation to Miss Howe's health; acknowledging, in high terms, her goodness in sending him to see her, before she set out upon her little journey.

He gave her a letter from that young lady, which she put into her bosom, saying she would read it by and by.

He was visibly shocked to see how ill she looked.

You look at me with concern, Mr. Hickman, said she. O sir! times are strangely altered with me since I saw you last at my dear Miss Howe's! What a cheerful creature was I then!— my heart at rest! my prospects charming! and beloved by everybody!—but I will not pain you!

Indeed, madam, said he, I am grieved for you at my soul.

He turned away his face with visible grief in it.

Her own eyes glistened: but she turned to each of us, pre-senting one to the other—him to me, as a gentleman *truly* deserving to be *called so*—me to him, as *your* friend, indeed [how was I, at that instant, ashamed of myself!]; but, nevertheless, as a man of humanity; detesting my friend's baseness; and desirous of doing her all manner of good offices.

Mr. Hickman received my civilities with a coldness, which, however, was rather to be expected on your account, than that it deserved exception on mine. And the lady invited us both to breakfast with her in the morning; he being obliged to return the next day.

I left them together, and called upon Mr. Dorrell, my attorney, to consult him upon poor Belton's affairs; and then went home, and wrote thus far, preparative to what may occur in my breakfasting visit in the morning.

Letter V—Mr. Belford to Robert Lovelace, Esq.

Thursday, July 27.

I WENT this morning, according to the lady's invitation, to breakfast, and found Mr. Hickman with her.

A good deal of heaviness and concern hung upon his countenance; but he received me with more respect than he did yesterday; which, I presume, was owing to the lady's favourable character of me.

He spoke very little; for I suppose they had all their talk out yesterday and before I came this morning.

By the hints that dropped, I perceived that Miss Howe's letter gave an account of your interview with her at Col. Ambrose's— of your professions to Miss Howe; and Miss Howe's opinion, that marrying you was the only way now left to repair her wrongs.

Mr. Hickman, as I also gathered, had pressed her, in Miss Howe's name, to let her, on her return from the Isle of Wight, find her at a neighbouring farm-house, where neat apartments would be made ready to receive her. She asked how long it would be before they returned? And he told her it was proposed to be no more than a fortnight out and in. Upon which, she said she should then perhaps have time to consider of that kind proposal.

He had tendered her money from Miss Howe; but could not induce her to take any. No wonder I was refused! She only said that, if she had occasion, she would be obliged to nobody but Miss Howe.

Mr. Goddard, her apothecary, came in before breakfast was over. At her desire he sat down with us. Mr. Hickman asked him if he could give him any consolation in relation to Miss

Harlowe's recovery, to carry down to a friend who loved her as she loved her own life?

The lady, said he, will do very well, if she will resolve upon it herself. Indeed you *will*, madam. The doctor is entirely of this opinion; and has ordered nothing for you but weak jellies and innocent cordials, lest you should starve yourself. And let me tell you, madam, that so much watching, so little nourishment, and so much grief, as you seem to indulge, is enough to impair the most vigorous health, and to wear out the strongest constitution.

What, sir, said she, can I do? I have no appetite. Nothing you call nourishing will stay on my stomach. I do what I can: and have such kind directors in Dr. H. and you, that I should be inexcusable if I did not.

I 'll give you a regimen, madam, replied he; which, I am sure, the doctor will approve of, and will make physic unnecessary in your case. And that is, "Go to rest at ten at night. Rise not till seven in the morning. Let your breakfast be water-gruel, or milk-pottage, or weak broths: your dinner anything you like, so you will *but* eat: a dish of tea, with milk, in the afternoon; and sago for your supper: and, my life for yours, this diet, and a month's country air, will set you up."

We were much pleased with the worthy gentleman's disinterested regimen: and she said, referring to her nurse (who vouched for her), Pray, Mr. Hickman, let Miss Howe know the good hands I am in: and as to the kind charge of the gentleman, assure her, that all I promised to her, in the longest of my two last letters, on the subject of my health, I do and will, to the utmost of my power, observe. I have engaged, sir [to Mr. Goddard], I have engaged, sir [to me], to Miss Howe, to avoid all wilful neglects. It would be an unpardonable fault, and very ill become the character I would be glad to deserve, or the temper of mind I wish my friends hereafter to think me mistress of, if I did not.

Mr. Hickman and I went afterwards to a neighbouring coffee-house; and he gave me some account of your behaviour at the ball on Monday night, and of your treatment of him in the conference he had with you before that; which he represented in a more favourable light than you had done yourself: and yet he gave his sentiments of you with great freedom, but with the politeness of a gentleman.

He told me how very determined the lady was against marrying you; that she had, early this morning, set herself to write a letter to Miss Howe, in answer to one he brought her, which he was to call for at twelve, it being almost finished before he saw her at breakfast; and that at three he proposed to set out on his return.

He told me that Miss Howe, and her mother, and himself, were to begin their little journey for the Isle of Wight on Monday next: but that he must make the most favourable representation of Miss Harlowe's bad health, or they should have a very uneasy absence. He expressed the pleasure he had in finding the lady in such good hands. He proposed to call on Dr. H. to take his opinion whether it were likely she would recover; and hoped he should find it favourable.

As he was resolved to make the best of the matter, and as the lady had refused to accept of money offered by Mr. Hickman, I said nothing of her parting with her clothes. I thought it would serve no other end to mention it, but to shock Miss Howe: for it has such a sound with it, that a woman of her rank and fortune should be so reduced, that I cannot myself think of it with patience; nor know I but *one* man in the world who can.

This gentleman is a little finical and formal. Modest or diffident men wear not soon off those little preciseness, which the confident presently, if ever they had them, get above. And why? Because they are too confident to doubt anything. But I think Mr. Hickman is an agreeable, sensible man, and not at all deserving of the treatment or the character you give him.

But you are really a strange mortal: because you have advantages in your person, in your air, and intellect, above all the men I know, and a face that would deceive the devil, you can't think any man else tolerable.

It is upon this *modest* principle that thou deridest some of us, who, not having thy confidence in their outside appearance, seek to hide their defects by the tailor's and peruke-maker's assistance [mistakenly enough, if it be really done so absurdly as to expose them more]; and sayst that we do but hang out a sign, in our dress, of what we have in the shop of our minds. This, no doubt, thou thinkest, is smartly observed: but prithee, Lovelace, tell me, if thou canst, what sort of a sign must thou hang out, wert thou obliged to give us a clear idea by it of the furniture of *thy* mind?

Mr. Hickman tells me he should have been happy with Miss Howe some weeks ago (for all the settlements have been some time engrossed); but that she will not marry, she declares, while her dear friend is so unhappy.

This is truly a charming instance of the force of *female friend-*

ship; which you and I, and our brother rakes, have constantly ridiculed as a chimerical thing in women of equal age, rank, and perfections.

But really, Lovelace, I see more and more that there are not in the world, with all our conceited pride, narrower-souled wretches than we rakes and libertines are. And I'll tell thee how it comes about.

Our early love of roguery makes us generally run away from instruction; and so we become mere smatterers in the sciences we are put to learn; and, because we *will* know no more, think there is no more to *be* known.

With an infinite deal of vanity, unreined imaginations, and no judgments at all, we next commence *half-wits*; and then think we have the whole field of knowledge in possession, and despise every one who takes more pains, and is more serious, than ourselves, as phlegmatic, stupid fellows, who have no taste for the most poignant pleasures of life.

This makes us insufferable to men of modesty and merit, and obliges us to herd with those of our own cast; and by this means we have no *opportunities* of seeing or conversing with anybody who could or would show us what we are; and so we conclude that we are the cleverest fellows in the world, and the only men of spirit in it; and, looking down with supercilious eyes on all who give not themselves the liberties we take, imagine the world made for us, and for us only.

Thus, as to useful knowledge, while others go to the bottom, we only skim the surface; are despised by people of solid sense, of true honour, and superior talents; and, shutting our eyes, move round and round (like so many blind mill-horses) in one narrow circle, while we imagine we have all the world to range in.

.   .   .   .

I threw myself in Mr. Hickman's way, on his return from the lady.

He was excessively moved at taking leave of her; being afraid, as he said to me (though he would not tell her so), that he should never see her again. She charged him to represent everything to Miss Howe in the most favourable light that the truth would bear.

He told me of a tender passage at parting; which was, that having saluted her at her closet door, he could not help once more taking the same liberty, in a more fervent manner, at the stairs-head, whither she accompanied him; and this in the thought, that it was the last time he should ever have that honour; and offering to apologize for his freedom (for he had pressed her to his heart with a vehemence that he could neither account for nor resist). "Excuse you, Mr. Hickman! that I will: you are my brother, and my friend: and to show you that the good man, who is to be happy with my beloved Miss Howe, is very dear to me, you shall carry to her this token of my love" [offering her sweet face to his salute, and pressing his hand between hers]: "and perhaps her love of *me* will make it more agreeable to her, than her punctilio would otherwise allow it to be: and tell her, said she, dropping on one knee, with clasped hands, and uplifted eyes, that in this posture you see me, in the last moment of our parting, begging a blessing upon you both, and that you may be the delight and comfort of each other, for many, very many, happy years!"

Tears, said he, fell from my eyes: I even sobbed with mingled joy and sorrow; and she retreating as soon as I raised her, I went downstairs, highly dissatisfied with myself for going; yet unable to stay, my eyes fixed the contrary way to my feet, as long as I could behold the skirts of her raiment.

I went into the back shop, continued the worthy man, and recommended the angelic lady to the best care of Mrs. Smith; and, when I was in the street, cast my eye up at her window: there, for the last time, I doubt, said he, that I shall ever behold her, I saw her; and she waved her charming hand to me, and with such a look of smiling goodness, and mingled concern, as I cannot describe.

Prithee tell me, thou vile Lovelace, if thou hast not a notion, even from these jejune descriptions of mine, that there must be a more exalted pleasure in intellectual friendship, than ever thou couldst taste in the gross fumes of sensuality? And whether it may not be possible for thee, in time, to give that preference to the *infinitely* preferable, which I hope, now, that I shall always give?

I will leave thee to make the most of this reflection, from

Thy true friend,

J. BELFORD.

Letter VI—Miss Howe to Miss Clarissa Harlowe

Tuesday, July 25.

YOUR two affecting letters were brought to me (as I had directed any letter from you should be) to the colonel's, about an hour before we broke up. I could not forbear dipping into them there; and shedding more tears over them than I will tell you of;

although I dried my eyes as well as I could, that the company I was obliged to return to, and my mother, should see as little of my concern as possible.

I am yet (and was then still more) excessively fluttered. The occasion I will communicate to you by and by: for nothing but the flutters given by the stroke of death could divert my *first* attention from the sad and solemn contents of your last favour. These therefore I must begin with.

How can I bear the thoughts of losing so dear a friend! I will not so much as suppose it. Indeed I *cannot*! Such a mind as yours was not vested in humanity to be snatched away from us so soon. There must be still a great deal for you to do for the good of all who have the happiness to know you.

You enumerate in your letter of Thursday last,[1] the particulars in which your situation is already mended: let me see by effects that you are in earnest in that enumeration; and that you really have the courage to resolve to get above the sense of injuries you could not avoid; and then will I trust to Providence and my humble prayers for your perfect recovery: and glad at my heart shall I be, on my return from the little island, to find you well enough to be near us, according to the proposal Mr. Hickman has to make to you.

You chide me in yours of Sunday on the freedom I take with your friends.[2]

I *may* be warm. I know I *am*—too warm. Yet warmth in friendship, surely, cannot be a crime; especially when our friend has great merit, labours under oppression, and is struggling with undeserved calamity.

I have no notion of coolness in friendship, be it dignified or distinguished by the name of *prudence*, or what it will.

You may excuse your relations. It was ever your way to do so. But, my dear, other people must be allowed to judge as they please. I am not *their* daughter, nor the sister of your brother and sister—I thank Heaven I am not.

But if you are displeased with me for the freedoms I took so long ago as you mention, I am afraid, if you knew what passed upon an application I made to your sister very lately (in hopes to procure you the absolution your heart is so much set upon), that you would be still *more* concerned. But they have been even with me—but I must not tell you all. I hope, however, that these *unforgivers* [my mother is among them] were always good, dutiful, passive children to *their* parents.

[1] See vol. iii, Letter cxv.   [2] Ibid., pp. 523–4.

Once more, forgive me. I owned I was too warm. But I have no example to the contrary but from you: and the treatment you meet with is very little encouragement to me to endeavour to imitate you in your dutiful meekness.

You leave it to me to give a negative to the hopes of the noble family, whose only disgrace is that so very vile a man is so nearly related to them. But yet—alas! my dear, I am so fearful of consequences, so *selfishly* fearful, if this negative must be given—I don't know what I should say—but give me leave to suspend, however, this negative, till I hear from you again.

This earnest courtship of you into their splendid family is so *very* honourable to you—they *so justly* admire you—you must have had such a *noble triumph* over the base man—he is so *much* in earnest—the world knows so *much* of the unhappy affair—you may do *still* so *much* good—your will is *so* inviolate—your relations are *so* implacable—think, my dear, and *re*-think.

And let me leave you to do so, while I give you the occasion of the flutter I mentioned at the beginning of this letter; in the conclusion of which you will find the obligation I have consented to lay myself under, to refer this important point once more to your discussion, before I give, in your name the negative that cannot, when given, be with honour to yourself repented of or recalled.

.   .   .   .

Know then, my dear, that I accompanied my mother to Colonel Ambrose's, on the occasion I mentioned to you in my former. Many ladies and gentlemen were there whom you know; particularly Miss Kitty D'Oily, Miss Lloyd, Miss Biddy D'Ollyffe, Miss Biddulph, and their respective admirers, with the colonel's two nieces, fine women both; besides many whom you know not; for they were strangers to me but by name. A splendid company, and all pleased with one another, till Colonel Ambrose introduced one who, the moment he was brought into the great hall, set the whole assembly into a kind of agitation.

It was your villain.

I thought I should have sunk as soon as I set my eyes upon him. My mother was also affected; and, coming to me, Nancy, whispered she, can you bear the sight of that wretch without too much emotion? If not, withdraw into the next apartment.

I could not remove. Everybody's eyes were glanced from him to me. I sat down, and fanned myself, and was forced to order a glass of water. Oh, that I had the eye the basilisk is reported to have, thought I, and that his life were within the power of it!—directly would I kill him.

He entered with an air so hateful to me, but so agreeable to every other eye, that I could have looked him dead for that too.

After the general salutations, he singled out Mr. Hickman, and told him he had recollected some parts of his behaviour to him when he saw him last, which had made him think himself under obligation to his patience and politeness.

And so, indeed, he was.

Miss D'Oily, upon his complimenting her, among a knot of ladies, asked him, in their hearing, how Miss Clarissa Harlowe did?

He heard, he said, you were not so well as he wished you to be, and as you deserved to be.

O Mr. Lovelace, said she, what have you to answer for on that young lady's account, if all be true that I have heard?

I have a great deal to answer for, said the unblushing villain: but that dear lady has so many excellences, and so much delicacy, that little sins are great ones in her eye.

Little sins! replied Miss D'Oily: Mr. Lovelace's character is so well known that nobody believes he can commit *little* sins.

You are very good to me, Miss D'Oily.

Indeed I am not.

Then I am the only person to whom you are *not* very good: and so I am the less obliged to you.

He turned, with an unconcerned air, to Miss Playford, and made her some genteel compliments. I believe you know her not. She visits his Cousins Montague. Indeed, he had something in his specious manner to say to everybody: and this too soon quieted the disgust each person had at his entrance.

I still kept my seat, and he either saw me not or would not yet see me; and addressing himself to my mother, taking her unwilling hand, with an air of high assurance, I am glad to see you here, madam. I hope Miss Howe is well. I have reason to complain greatly of her: but hope to owe to her the highest obligation that can be laid on man.

My daughter, sir, is accustomed to be too warm and too zealous in her friendships for either my tranquillity or her own.

There had indeed been some late occasion given for mutual displeasure between my mother and me: but I think she might have spared this to *him*; though nobody heard it, I believe, but the person to whom it was spoken, and the lady who told it to me; for my mother spoke it low.

We are not wholly, madam, to live for ourselves, said the vile hypocrite. It is not every one who has a soul capable of friendship: and what a heart must that be, which can be insensible to the interests of a suffering friend?

This sentiment from Mr. Lovelace's mouth! said my mother. Forgive me, sir; but you can have no end, surely, in endeavouring to make *me* think as well of you as some innocent creatures have thought of you, to their cost.

She would have flung from him. But, detaining her hand— Less severe, dear madam, said he, be less severe in *this* place, I beseech you. You will allow that a very faulty person may see his errors; and when he does, and owns them, and repents, should he not be treated mercifully?

Your air, sir, seems not to be that of a penitent. But the place may as properly excuse this subject, as what you call my severity.

But, dearest madam, permit me to say, that I hope for your interest with your *charming* daughter (was his sycophant word) to have it put into my power to convince all the world that there never was a truer penitent. And why, why this anger, dear madam (for she struggled to get her hand out of his), these violent airs—so *maidenly*! [impudent fellow!]—May I not ask if Miss Howe be here?

She would not have been here, replied my mother, had she known whom she had been to see.

And is she here, then? Thank Heaven! He disengaged her hand, and stepped forward into company.

Dear Miss Lloyd, said he, with an air (taking her hand as he quitted my mother's), tell me, tell me, is Miss Arabella Harlowe here? Or will she be here? I was informed she would—and this, and the opportunity of paying my compliments to your friend Miss Howe, were great inducements with me to attend the colonel.

Superlative assurance! Was it not, my dear?

Miss Arabella Harlowe, excuse me, sir, said Miss Lloyd, would be very little inclined to meet you here, or anywhere else.

Perhaps so, my dear Miss Lloyd: but, perhaps, for that very reason, I am more desirous to see *her*.

Miss Harlowe, sir, said Miss Biddulph, with a threatening air, will hardly be here without her *brother*. I imagine, if one come, both will come.

Heaven grant they both may! said the wretch. Nothing, Miss Biddulph, shall *begin* from me to disturb this assembly, I assure you, if they do. One calm half-hour's conversation with that brother and sister would be a most fortunate opportunity to me, in presence of the colonel and his lady, or whom else they should choose.

Then turning round, as if desirous to find out the one or the other, or both, he 'spied me, and, with a very low bow, approached me.

I was all in a flutter, you may suppose. He would have taken my hand. I refused it, all glowing with indignation: everybody's eyes upon us.

I went from him to the other end of the room, and sat down, as I thought, out of his hated sight: but presently I heard his odious voice, whispering, behind my chair (he leaning upon the back of it, with impudent unconcern), *Charming Miss Howe!* looking over my shoulder: *one request*—[I started up from my seat; but could hardly stand neither, for very indignation]—Oh, this sweet, but becoming disdain! whispered on the insufferable creature. I am sorry to give you all this emotion: but either here, or at your own house, let me entreat from you one quarter of an hour's audience. I beseech you, madam, but one quarter of an hour, in any of the adjoining apartments.

Not for a *kingdom*, fluttering my fan. I knew not what I did. But I could have killed him.

We are so much observed — else on my knees, my dear Miss Howe, would I beg your interest with your charming friend.

She 'll have nothing to say to you.

I had not then your letters, my dear.

Killing words! But indeed I have deserved them, and a dagger in my heart besides. I am so conscious of my demerits, that I have no hope but in *your* interposition. Could I owe that favour to Miss Howe's mediation which I cannot hope for on any other account——

My mediation, vilest of men!—*my* mediation!—I abhor you! —from my *soul*, I abhor you, vilest of men! Three or four times I repeated these words, stammering too. I was excessively fluttered.

You can call me nothing, madam, so bad as I will call myself. I *have* been, indeed, the vilest of men: but now I am not so. Permit me—everybody's eyes are upon us!—but one moment's audience—to exchange but ten words with you, dearest Miss Howe—in whose presence you please—for your dear friend's sake —but ten words with you in the next apartment.

It is an insult upon me, to presume that I would exchange

one with you, if I could help it! Out of my way! Out of my sight—fellow!

And away I would have flung: but he took my hand. I was excessively disordered — everybody's eyes more and more intent upon us.

Mr. Hickman, whom my mother had drawn on one side, to enjoin him a patience which perhaps needed not to have been enforced, came up just then with my mother, who had him by his leading-strings—by his sleeve, I should say.

Mr. Hickman, said the bold wretch, be my advocate but for ten words in the next apartment with Miss Howe, in your presence, and in yours, madam, to my mother.

Hear, Nancy, what he has to say to you. To get rid of him, hear his *ten words*.

Excuse me, madam! his very breath—Unhand me, sir!

He sighed, and looked—Oh, how the practised villain sighed and looked! He then let go my hand, with such a reverence in his manner, as brought blame upon me from some, that I would not hear him. And this incensed me the more. O my dear, this man is a devil! This man is *indeed* a devil! So much patience when he pleases! So much gentleness! Yet so resolute, so persisting, so audacious!

I was going out of the assembly in great disorder. He was at the door as soon as I.

How kind this is! said the wretch; and, ready to follow me, opened the door for me.

I turned back upon this, and, not knowing what I did, snapped my fan just in his face, as he turned short upon me; and the powder flew from his wig.

Everybody seemed as much pleased as I was vexed.

He turned to Mr. Hickman, nettled at the powder flying, and at the smiles of the company upon him; Mr. Hickman, you will be one of the happiest men in the world, because you are a *good* man, and will do nothing to provoke this passionate lady; and because she has too much good sense to be provoked without reason: but else, the Lord have mercy upon you!

This man, this Mr. Hickman, my dear, is too meek for a man. Indeed he is. But my patient mother twits me, that her passionate daughter ought to like him *the better* for that. But meek men abroad are not always meek men at home. I have observed that, in more instances than one: and if they *were,* I should not, I verily think, like them the better for being so.

He then turned to my mother, resolved to be even with *her* too: Where, good madam, could miss get all this spirit?

The company round smiled; for I need not tell you that my mother's high-spiritedness is pretty well known; and she, sadly vexed, said, Sir, you treat me as you do the rest of the world—but——

I beg pardon, madam, interrupted he: I might have spared my question; and instantly (I retiring to the other end of the hall) he turned to Miss Playford: What would I give, miss, to hear you sing that song you obliged us with at Lord M.'s?

He then, as if nothing had happened, fell into a conversation with her and Miss D'Ollyffe, upon music; and whisperingly sung to Miss Playford, holding her two hands, with such airs of genteel unconcern, that it vexed me not a little to look round, and see how pleased half the giddy fools of our sex were with him, notwithstanding his notorious wicked character. To this it is that such vile fellows owe much of their vileness; whereas, if they found themselves shunned, and despised, and treated as beasts of prey, as they are, they would run to their caverns; there howl by themselves; and none but such as sad accident, or unpitiable presumption, threw in their way, would suffer by them.

He afterwards talked very seriously, at times, to Mr. Hickman: at *times*, I say; for it was with such breaks and starts of gaiety, turning to this lady, and to that, and then to Mr. Hickman again, resuming a serious or a gay air at pleasure, that he took everybody's eye, the women's especially; who were full of their whispering admirations of him, qualified with *if's*, and *but's*, and *what pity's*, and such sort of stuff, that showed in their very dispraises too much liking.

Well may our sex be the sport and ridicule of such libertines! Unthinking eye-governed creatures! Would not a little reflection teach us that a man of merit must be a man of modesty, because a diffident one? And that such a wretch as this must have taken his degrees in wickedness, and gone through a course of vileness, before he could arrive at this impenetrable effrontery? an effrontery which can proceed only from the light opinion he has of us, and the high one of himself.

But our sex are generally modest and bashful themselves, and are too apt to consider that which in the main is their principal grace, as a defect: and *finely* do they judge, when they think of supplying that defect by choosing a man who cannot be ashamed.

His discourse to Mr. Hickman turned upon you, and his

acknowledged injuries of you, though he could so lightly start from the subject, and return to it.

I have no patience with such a devil—*man* he cannot be called. To be sure he would behave in the same manner anywhere, or in any presence, even at the altar itself, if a woman were with him there.

It shall ever be a rule with me, that he who does not regard a woman with some degree of reverence, will look upon her and occasionally *treat* her with contempt.

He had the confidence to offer to take me out; but I absolutely refused him, and shunned him all I could, putting on the most contemptuous airs: but noth' ig could mortify him.

I wished twenty times I had not been there.

The gentlemen were as ready as I to wish he had broken his neck, rather than been present, I believe: for nobody was regarded but he. So little of the fop; yet so elegant and rich in his dress: his person so specious: his air so intrepid: so much meaning and penetration in his face: so much gaiety, yet so little of the monkey: though a travelled gentleman, yet no affectation; no mere toupet-man; but all manly; and his courage and wit, the one so known, the other so dreaded, you must think the *petits-maîtres* (of which there were four or five present) were most deplorably off in his company: and one grave gentleman observed to me (pleased to see me shun him as I did) that the poet's observation was too true, that the generality of ladies were *rakes in their hearts*, or they could not be so much taken with a man who had so notorious a character.

I told him the reflection both of the poet and applier was much too general, and made with more ill-nature than good manners.

When the wretch saw how industriously I avoided him (shifting from one part of the hall to another), he at last boldly stepped up to me, as my mother and Mr. Hickman were talking to me; and thus before them accosted me:

I beg your pardon, madam; but, by your mother's leave, I must have a few moments' conversation with you, either here, or at your own house; and I beg you will give me the opportunity.

Nancy, said my mother, hear what he has to say to you. In my presence you may: and better in the adjoining apartment, if it must be, than to come to you at our own house.

I retired to one corner of the hall, my mother following me, and he, taking Mr. Hickman under the arm, following her— Well, sir, said I, what have you to say? Tell me *here*.

I have been telling Mr. Hickman, said he, how much I am

concerned for the injuries I have done to the most excellent woman in the world: and yet, that she obtained such a glorious triumph over me the last time I had the honour to see her, as, with my penitence, ought to have qualified her former resentments: but that I will, with all my soul, enter into any measures to obtain her forgiveness of me. My Cousins Montague have told you this. Lady Betty, and Lady Sarah, and my Lord M. are engaged for my honour. I know your power with the dear creature. My cousins told me you gave them hopes you would use it in my behalf. My Lord M. and his two sisters are impatiently expecting the fruits of it. You must have heard from her before now: I hope you have. And will you be so good as to tell me, if I may have any hopes?

If I must speak on this subject, let me tell you that you have broken her heart. You know not the value of the lady you have injured. You deserve her not. And she despises you as she ought.

Dear Miss Howe, mingle not passion with denunciations so severe. I must know my fate. I will go abroad once more, if I find her absolutely irreconcilable. But I hope she will give me leave to attend upon her, to know my doom from her own mouth.

It would be death immediate for her to see you. And what must *you* be, to be able to look her in the face?

I then reproached him (with vehemence enough you may believe) on his baseness, and the evils he had made you suffer: the distress he had reduced you to: all your friends made your enemies: the vile house he had carried you to: hinted at his villainous arts; the dreadful arrest: and told him of your present deplorable illness, and resolution to die rather than to have him.

He vindicated not any part of his conduct, but that of the arrest; and so solemnly protested his sorrow for his usage of you, accusing himself in the freest manner, and by *deserved* appellations, that I promised to lay before you this part of our conversation. And now you have it.

My mother, as well as Mr. Hickman, believes, from what passed on this occasion, that he is touched in conscience for the wrongs he has done you: but, by his whole behaviour, I must own, it seems to me that nothing can touch him for half an hour together. Yet I have no doubt that he would willingly marry you; and it piques his pride, I could see, that he should be denied: as it did mine, that such a wretch had dared to think it in his power to have such a woman whenever he pleased; and that it must be accounted a condescension, and matter of obligation (by all his own family at least), that he would vouchsafe to think of marriage.

Now, my dear, you have before you the reason why I suspend the decisive negative to the ladies of his family: my mother, Miss Lloyd, and Miss Biddulph, who were inquisitive after the subject of our retired conversation, and whose curiosity I thought it was right, in some degree, to gratify (especially as those young ladies are of our select acquaintance), are all of opinion that you should be his.

You will let Mr. Hickman know your whole mind; and when he acquaints me with it, I will tell you all my own.

Meantime, may the news he will bring me of the state of your health be favourable! prays, with the utmost fervency,

Your ever faithful and affectionate

ANNA HOWE.

Letter VII—Miss Clarissa Harlowe to Miss Howe

Thursday, July 27.

MY DEAREST MISS HOWE,—After I have thankfully acknowledged your favour in sending Mr. Hickman to visit me before you set out upon your intended journey, I must chide you (in the sincerity of that faithful love, which could not be the love it is if it would not admit of that *cementing* freedom) for suspending the decisive negative, which, upon such full deliberation, I had entreated you to give to Mr. Lovelace's relations.

I am sorry that I am obliged to *repeat* to you, my dear, who know me so well, that, were I sure I should live *many years*, I would not have Mr. Lovelace: much less can I think of him, as it is probable I may not live *one*.

As to the *world* and its *censures*, you know, my dear, that however desirous I always was of a fair fame, yet I never thought it right to give more than a *second place* to the world's opinion. The challenges made to Mr. Lovelace by Miss D'Oily, in public company, are a fresh proof that I have lost my reputation: and what advantage would it be to me, were it retrievable, and were I to live long, if I could not acquit myself to *myself*?

Having in my former said so much on the freedoms you have taken with my friends, I shall say the less now: but *your hint*, that something else has newly passed between some of them and you, gives me great concern, and that as well for *my own* sake as for *theirs*; since it must necessarily incense them against me.   I wish, my dear, that I had been left to my own course on an occasion so *very* interesting to myself. But since what is done cannot be helped, I must abide the consequences: yet I dread, *more than before,* what may be my sister's answer, if an answer be at all vouchsafed.

Will you give me leave, my dear, to close this subject with one remark? It is this: that my beloved friend, in points where her own laudable *zeal* is concerned, has ever seemed more ready to fly from the *rebuke,* than from the *fault.* If you will excuse this freedom, I will acknowledge thus far in favour of your way of thinking, as to the conduct of some parents in these nice cases, that *indiscreet* opposition does frequently as much mischief as *giddy* love.

As to the invitation you are so kind as to give me, to remove privately into your neighbourhood, I have told Mr. Hickman that I will consider of it: but believe, if you will be so good as to excuse me, that I shall not accept of it, even should I be *able* to remove. I will give you my reasons for declining it; and so I ought, when both my love and my gratitude would make a visit now and then from my dear Miss Howe the most consolatory thing in the world to me.

You must know then, that this great town, wicked as it is, wants not opportunities of being better; having daily prayers at several churches in it; and I am desirous, as my strength will permit, to embrace those opportunities. The method I have proposed to myself (and was beginning to practise when that cruel arrest deprived me both of freedom and strength) is this: when I was disposed to gentle exercise, I took a chair to St. Dunstan's Church in Fleet Street, where are prayers at seven in the morning: I proposed, *if the weather favoured,* to walk (*if not,* to take chair) to Lincoln's Inn Chapel; where, at eleven in the morning, and at five in the afternoon, are the same desirable opportunities; and at other times to go no farther than Covent Garden Church, where are early morning prayers likewise.

This method pursued, I doubt not, will greatly help, as it has already done, to calm my disturbed thoughts, and to bring me to that perfect resignation after which I aspire: for I must own, my dear, that sometimes still my griefs and my reflections are too heavy for me; and all the aid I can draw from *religious duties* is hardly sufficient to support my staggering reason. I am a very young creature, you know, my dear, to be left to my own conduct in such circumstances as I am in.

Another reason why I choose not to go down into your

neighbourhood, is the displeasure that might arise on my account between your mother and you.

If indeed you were actually married, and the worthy man (who would then have a title to all your regard) were earnestly desirous of my near neighbourhood, I know not what I might do: for although I might not perhaps intend to give up my other important reasons at the *time* I should make you a congratulatory visit, yet I might not know how to deny myself the pleasure of continuing near you when there.

I send you enclosed the copy of my letter to my sister. I hope it will be thought to be written with a true penitent spirit; for indeed it is. I desire that you will not think I stoop too low in it; since there can be no such thing as *that* in a child to parents whom she has unhappily offended.

But if still (perhaps more disgusted than before at your freedom with them) they should pass it by with the contempt of silence (for I have not yet been favoured with an answer), I must learn to think it right in them so to do; especially as it is my first direct application: for I have often censured the boldness of those, who, applying for a favour, which it is in a person's option to grant or to refuse, take the liberty of being offended, if they are not gratified; as if the *petitioned* had not as good a right to reject, as the *petitioner* to ask.

But if my letter should be answered, and that in such terms as will make me loath to communicate it to so warm a friend—you must not, my dear, take upon you to censure my relations; but allow for them, as they know not what I have suffered; as being filled with *just* resentments against me (*just* to them, if they *think* them just); and as not being able to judge of the reality of my penitence.

And after all, what can they do for me? They can only pity me: and what will that do, but augment their own *grief*; to which at present their *resentment* is an alleviation? For can they by their pity restore to me my lost reputation? Can they by it purchase a sponge that will wipe out from the year the past fatal five months of my life? [1]

Your account of the gay unconcerned behaviour of Mr. Lovelace at the colonel's, does not surprise me at all, after I am told that he had the intrepidity to go thither, knowing who were *invited* and *expected*. Only this, my dear, I really wonder at, that Miss Howe could imagine that I could have a thought of such a man for a husband.

[1] She takes in the time that she appointed to meet Mr. Lovelace.

Poor wretch! I pity him, to see him fluttering about; abusing talents that were given him for excellent purposes; taking inconsideration for courage; and dancing, fearless of danger, on the edge of a precipice!

But indeed his threatening to see me most sensibly alarms and shocks me. I cannot but hope that I never, never more shall see him in this world.

Since you are so loath, my dear, to send the desired negative to the ladies of his family, I will only trouble you to transmit the letter I shall enclose for that purpose; directed indeed to yourself, because it was to you that those ladies applied themselves on this occasion; but to be sent by you to any one of the ladies at your own choice.

I commend myself, my dearest Miss Howe, to your prayers; and conclude with repeated thanks for sending Mr. Hickman to me; and with wishes for your health and happiness, and for the speedy celebration of your nuptials.

Your ever affectionate and obliged
CLARISSA HARLOWE.

Letter VIII—Miss Clarissa Harlowe to Miss Howe
[Enclosed in the preceding]

Thursday, July 27.

MY DEAREST MISS HOWE,—Since you seem loath to acquiesce in my determined resolution, signified to you as soon as I was able to hold a pen, I beg the favour of you, by this, or by any other way you think most proper, to acquaint the worthy ladies who have applied to you in behalf of their relation, that, although I am infinitely obliged to their generous opinion of me, yet I cannot consent to *sanctify*, as I may say, Mr. Lovelace's repeated breaches of all moral sanctions, and hazard my *future* happiness by an union with a man, through whose premeditated injuries, in a long train of the basest contrivances, I have forfeited my *temporal* hopes.

He himself, when he reflects upon his own actions, must surely bear testimony to the justice as well as fitness of my determination. The ladies, I dare say, would, were they to know the whole of my unhappy story.

Be pleased to acquaint them that I deceive myself, if my resolution on this head (however ungratefully, and even inhumanly, he has treated me) be not owing more to *principle* than *passion*. Nor can I give a stronger proof of the truth of this assurance, than by declaring that I *can* and *will* forgive him, on this one easy condition, *that he will never molest me more.*

In whatever way you choose to make this declaration, be pleased to let my most respectful compliments to the ladies of the noble family, and to my Lord M., accompany it. And do you, my dear, believe that I shall be, to the last moment of my life,

Your ever obliged and affectionate
CLARISSA HARLOWE.

Letter IX—Mr. Lovelace to John Belford, Esq.

Friday, July 28.

I HAVE three letters of thine to take notice of [1]: but am divided in my mind, whether to quarrel with thee on thy unmerciful reflections, or to thank thee for thy acceptable particularity and diligence. But several of my sweet dears have I, indeed, in my time made to cry and laugh in a breath; nay, one side of their pretty faces laugh, before the cry could go off the other: why may I not, therefore, curse and applaud thee in the same moment? So take both in one: and what follows, as it shall rise from my pen.

How often have I ingenuously confessed my sins against this excellent creature? Yet thou never sparest me, although as bad a man as myself. Since then I get so little by my confessions, I had a good mind to try to defend myself; and that not only from ancient and modern story, but from common practice; and yet avoid repeating anything I have suggested before in my own behalf.

I am in a humour to play the fool with my pen: briefly then, from ancient story first: Dost thou not think that I am as much entitled to forgiveness on Miss Harlowe's account, as Virgil's hero was on Queen Dido's? For what an ungrateful varlet was that vagabond to the *hospitable* princess, who had *willingly* conferred upon him the last favour? Stealing away (whence, I suppose, the ironical phrase of *trusty Trojan* to this day) like a thief—pretendedly indeed at the command of the gods; but could that be, when the errand he went upon was to rob other princes, not only of their dominions, but of their lives? Yet this fellow is, at every word, the *pious* Æneas with the immortal bard who celebrates him.

Should Miss Harlowe even break her heart (which Heaven

<hr>

[1] Letters iii, iv, v.

forbid!) for the usage she has received (to say nothing of her disappointed pride, to which her death would be attributable, more than to reason), what comparison will *her* fate hold to Queen Dido's? And have I half the obligation to her, that Æneas had to the Queen of Carthage? The latter placing a confidence, the former none, in her man? Then, whom *else* have I robbed? Whom *else* have I injured? Her brother's worthless life I gave him, instead of taking any man's; while the Trojan vagabond destroyed his thousands. Why then should it not be the *pious* Lovelace, as well as the *pious* Æneas? For, dost thou think, had a conflagration happened, and had it been in my power, that I would not have saved my old Anchises (as he did his from the Ilion bonfire), even at the expense of my Creüsa, had I had a wife of that name?

But for a more modern instance in my favour. Have I used Miss Harlowe, as our famous maiden-queen, as she was called, used one of her own blood, a sister-queen; who threw herself into her protection from her rebel subjects; and whom she detained prisoner eighteen years, and at last cut off her head? Yet do not honest Protestants pronounce *her* pious too? And call her particularly *their* queen?

As to *common practice*. Who, let me ask, that has it in his power to gratify a predominant passion, be it what it will, denies himself the gratification? Leaving it to cooler deliberation (and, if he be a great man, to his flatterers) to find a reason for it afterwards?

Then, as to the worst part of my treatment of this lady. How many men are there, who, as well as I, have sought, by intoxicating liquors, first to inebriate, then to subdue? What signifies what the *potations* were, when the same end was in view?

Let me tell thee, upon the whole, that neither the Queen of Carthage, nor the Queen of Scots, would have thought they had any reason to complain of cruelty, had they been used no worse than I have used the queen of my heart: and then do I not aspire with my whole soul to repair by marriage? Would the *pious* Æneas, thinkest thou, have done such a piece of justice by Dido, had she lived?

Come, come, Belford, let people run away with notions as they will, I am *comparatively* a very innocent man. And if by these, and other like reasonings, I have quieted my own conscience, a great end is answered. What have I to do with the world?

And now I sit me peaceably down to consider thy letters.

I hope thy pleas in my favour,[1] when she gave thee (so generously gave thee) for me my letters, were urged with an honest energy. But I suspect thee much for being too ready to give up thy client. Then thou hast such a misgiving aspect; an aspect rather inviting rejection than carrying persuasion with it; and art such a hesitating, such a humming and hawing caitiff; that I shall attribute my failure, if I do fail, rather to the inability and ill-looks of my advocate, than to my cause. Again, thou art deprived of the force men of our cast give to arguments; for she won't let thee *swear*! Art moreover a very heavy thoughtless fellow; tolerable only at a second rebound; a horrid dunce at the *impromptu*. These, encountering with such a lady, are great disadvantages. And still a greater is thy balancing (as thou dost at present) between old rakery and new reformation: since this puts thee into the same situation with her, as they told me at Leipzig Martin Luther was in, at the first public dispute which he held, in defence of his supposed *new* doctrines with Eckius. For Martin was then but a linsey-wolsey reformer. He retained some dogmas, which, by natural consequence, made others that he held untenable. So that Eckius, in some points, had the better of him. But, from that time, he made clear work, renouncing all that stood in his way: and then his doctrines ran upon all fours. He was never puzzled afterwards; and could boldly declare that he would defend them in the face of angels and men; and to his friends, who would have dissuaded him from venturing to appear before the Emperor Charles the Fifth at Spires, *That, were there as many devils at Spires as tiles upon the houses, he would go.* An answer that is admired by every Protestant Saxon to this day.

Since then thy unhappy awkwardness destroys the force of thy arguments, I think thou hadst better (for the present, however) forbear to urge her on the subject of accepting the reparation I offer; lest the continual teasing of her to forgive me should but strengthen her in her denials of forgiveness; till, for *consistency* sake, she 'll be forced to adhere to a resolution so often avowed. Whereas, if left to herself, a little time, and better health, which will bring on better spirits, will give her quicker resentments; those quicker resentments will lead her into vehemence; that vehemence will subside, and turn into expostulation and parley: my friends will then interpose, and guarantee for me: and all our trouble on both sides will be over. Such is the natural course of things.

[1] See p. 10.

I cannot endure thee for thy hopelessness in the lady's recovery[1]; and that in contradiction to the doctor and apothecary.

Time, in the words of Congreve, thou sayst, *will give increase to her afflictions.* But why so? Knowest thou not that those words (so contrary to common experience) were applied to the case of a person while passion was in its full vigour? At such a time, every one in a heavy grief *thinks* the same: but as enthusiasts do by Scripture, so dost thou by the poets thou hast read: anything that carries the most distant allusion from *either* to the case in hand, is put down by both for gospel, however incongruous to the general scope of either, and to *that case.* So once, in a pulpit, I heard one of the former very vehemently declare himself to be a *dead dog*; when every man, woman, and child, were convinced to the contrary by his howling.

I can tell thee that, if nothing else will do, I am determined, in spite of thy buskin-airs, and of thy engagements for me to the contrary, to see her myself.

Face to face have I known many a quarrel made up, which distance would have kept alive and widened. Thou wilt be a madder Jack than he in the *Tale of a Tub*, if thou givest an *active* opposition to this interview.

In short, I cannot bear the thought that a woman whom once I had bound to me in the silken cords of love, should slip through my fingers, and be able, while *my* heart flames out with a violent passion for her, to despise me, and to set both love and me at defiance. Thou canst not imagine how much I envy *thee*, and her *doctor*, and her *apothecary*, and every one who I hear are admitted to her presence and conversation; and wish to be the *one* or the *other* in turn.

Wherefore, if nothing else will do, I *will* see her. I'll tell thee of an admirable expedient, just come across me, to save *thy* promise, and *my own*.

Mrs. Lovick, you say, is a good woman: if the lady be worse, she shall advise her to send for a parson to pray by her: unknown to her, unknown to the lady, unknown to *thee* (for so it may pass), I will contrive to be the man, *petticoated out*, and vested in a gown and cassock. I once, for a certain purpose, did assume the canonicals; and I was thought to make a fine sleek appearance; my broad rose-bound beaver became me *mightily*; and I was much admired upon the whole by all who saw me.

Methinks it must be charmingly apropos to see me kneeling down by her bedside (I am sure I shall pray heartily), beginning

[1] See pp. 10–11.

out of the Common Prayer Book the Sick Office for the restoration of the languishing lady, and concluding with an exhortation to charity and forgiveness for myself.

I will consider of this matter. But, in whatever shape I shall choose to appear, of this thou mayst assure thyself, I will apprise thee beforehand of my visit, that thou mayst contrive to be out of the way, and to know nothing of the matter. This will save *thy* word; and, as to *mine*, can she think worse of me than she does at present?

An indispensable of true love and profound respect, in thy wise opinion,[1] is absurdity or awkwardness. 'Tis surprising that *thou* shouldst be one of those partial mortals who take their measures of right and wrong from what they find *themselves to be*, and cannot *help being*! So awkwardness is a perfection in the awkward! At this rate, no man ever can be in the wrong. But I insist upon it, that an awkward fellow will do everything awkwardly: and if he be like thee, will, when he has done foolishly, rack his unmeaning brain for excuses as awkward as his first fault. Respectful love is an inspirer of actions worthy of itself; and he who cannot show it, where he most means it, manifests that he is an unpolite, rough creature, a perfect Belford, and has it not in him.

But here thou 'lt throw out that notable witticism, that my outside is the best of *me*, thine the worst of *thee*; and that, if I set about mending my mind, thou wilt mend thy appearance.

But prithee, Jack, don't stay for *that*; but set about thy amendment in dress when thou leavest off thy mourning; for why shouldst thou prepossess in thy disfavour all those who never saw thee before? It is hard to remove early-taken prejudices, whether of liking or distaste: people will *hunt*, as I may say, for reasons to confirm first impressions, in compliment to their own sagacity: nor is it every mind that has the ingenuousness to confess itself mistaken, when it finds itself to be wrong. Thou thyself art an adept in the pretended science of reading men; and whenever thou art out, wilt study to find some reasons why it was more probable that thou shouldst have been right; and wilt watch every motion and action, and every word and sentiment, in the person thou hast once censured, for proofs, in order to help thee to revive and maintain thy first opinion. And, indeed, as thou seldom errest on the *favourable side*, human nature is so vile a thing, that thou art likely to be right five times in six, on the *other*: and perhaps it is but guessing of others, by what thou

[1] See p. 6.

findest in thy own heart, to have reason to compliment thyself
on thy penetration.

Here is preachment for thy preachment: and I hope, if thou
likest thy own, thou wilt thank me for mine; the rather, as thou
mayest be the better for it, if thou wilt: since it is calculated for
thy own meridian.

Well, but the lady refers my destiny to the letter she has
written, *actually written,* to Miss Howe; to whom it seems she has
given her reasons why she will not have me.   I long to know the
contents of this letter: but am in great hopes that she has so
expressed her denials, as shall give room to think she only wants
to be persuaded to the contrary, in order to reconcile herself
to herself.

I could make some pretty observations upon one or two places
of the lady's meditation: but, wicked as I am thought to be, I
never was so abandoned as to turn into ridicule, or even to treat
with levity, things sacred.   I think it the highest degree of ill
manners to jest upon those subjects which the world in general
look upon with veneration, and call divine.   I would not even
treat the mythology of the heathen to a heathen, with the
ridicule that perhaps would fairly lie from some of the absurdities
that strike every common observer.   Nor, when at Rome, and
in other popish countries, did I ever behave shockingly at those
ceremonies which I thought very extraordinary: for I saw some
people affected, and seemingly edified, by them; and I contented
myself to think, though they were beyond my comprehension,
that if they answered any good end to the *many*, there was
religion enough in them, or civil policy at least, to exempt them
from the ridicule of even a *bad* man who had common sense and
good manners.

For the like reason I have never given noisy or tumultuous
instances of dislike to a new play, if I thought it ever so indifferent: for I concluded, first, that every one was entitled to see
quietly what he paid for: and, next, as the theatre (the epitome
of the world) consisted of pit, boxes, and gallery, it was hard, I
thought, if there could be such a performance exhibited as would
not please somebody in that mixed multitude: and, if it did, those
somebodies had as much right to enjoy their own judgments
undisturbedly as I had to enjoy mine.

This was *my* way of showing my disapprobation; I never went
again.   And as a man is at his option, whether he will go to a
play or not, he has not the same excuse for expressing his dislike
clamorously as if he were *compelled* to see it.

I have ever, thou knowest, declared against those shallow libertines who could not make out their pretensions to wit, but on two subjects, to which every man of *true* wit will scorn to be beholden: PROFANENESS and OBSCENITY, I mean; which must shock the ears of every man or woman of sense, without answering any end, but of showing a very low and abandoned nature. And, till I came acquainted with the brutal Mowbray [no great praise to myself from such a tutor], I was far from making so free, as I now do, with oaths and curses; for then I was forced to out-swear him sometimes in order to keep him in his allegiance to me his general: nay, I often check myself to myself, for this empty unprofitable liberty of speech; in which we are outdone by the sons of the common sewer.

All my vice is women, and the love of plots and intrigues; and I cannot but wonder how I fell into those shocking freedoms of speech; since, generally speaking, they are far from helping forward my main end: only, now and then, indeed, a little novice rises to one's notice, who seems to think dress, and oaths, and curses, the diagnostics of the rakish spirit she is inclined to favour: and indeed they are the only qualifications that some who are called rakes and pretty fellows have to boast of. But what must the women be, who can be attracted by such *empty-souled* profligates?—since wickedness *with* wit is hardly tolerable but, *without* it, is equally shocking and contemptible.

There again is preachment for thy preachment; and thou wilt be apt to think that I am reforming too: but no such matter. If this were *new light* darting in upon me, as thy morality seems to be to thee, something of this kind might be apprehended: but this was *always* my way of thinking; and I defy thee, or any of thy brethren, to name a time when I have either ridiculed religion, or talked obscenely. On the contrary, thou knowest how often I have checked that bear in love matters, Mowbray, and the finical Tourville, and thyself too, for what ye have called the double entendre. In *love*, as in points that required a *manly resentment*, it has always been my maxim, to *act*, rather than *talk*; and I do assure thee, as to the first, the women themselves will excuse the one sooner than the other.

As to the admiration thou expressest for the books of Scripture, thou art certainly right in it. But 'tis strange to me that thou wert ignorant of their beauty, and noble simplicity, till now. Their antiquity always made me reverence them: and how was it possible that thou couldest not, for that reason, if for no other, give them a perusal?

I 'll tell thee a short story, which I had from my tutor, admonishing me against exposing myself by *ignorant wonder*, when I should quit college, to go to town, or travel.

"The first time Dryden's *Alexander's Feast* fell into his hands, he told me he was prodigiously charmed with it: and, having never heard anybody speak of it before, thought, as thou dost of the Bible, that he had made a new discovery.

"He hastened to an appointment which he had with several wits (for he was then in town), one of whom was a noted critic, who, according to him, had more merit than good fortune; for all the little nibblers in wit, whose writings would not stand the test of criticism, made it, he said, a common cause to run him down, as men would a mad dog.

"The young gentleman (for young he then was) set forth magnificently in the praises of that inimitable performance; and gave himself airs of *second-hand* merit, for finding out its beauties.

"The old bard heard him out with a smile, which the collegian took for approbation, till he spoke; and then it was in these mortifying words: 'Sdeath, sir, where have you lived till now, or with what sort of company have you conversed, young as you are, that you have never before heard of the finest piece in the English language?"

This story had such an effect upon *me*, who had ever a proud heart, and wanted to be thought a clever fellow, that, in order to avoid the like disgrace, I laid down two rules to myself. The first, whenever I went into company where there were strangers, to hear every one of them speak, before I gave myself liberty to prate: the other, if I found any of them above my match, to give up all title to new discoveries, contenting myself to praise what they praised, as beauties familiar to me, though I had never heard of them before. And so, by degrees, I got the reputation of a wit myself: and when I threw off all restraint, and books, and learned conversation, and fell in with some of our brethren who are now wandering in Erebus, and with such others as Belton, Mowbray, Tourville, and thyself, I set up on my own stock; and, like what we have been told of Sir Richard, in his latter days, valued myself on being the emperor of the company; for, having fathomed the depth of them all, and afraid of no rival but thee, whom also I had got a little under (by my gaiety and promptitude at least), I proudly, like Addison's Cato, delighted to give laws to my little senate.

Proceed with thee by and by.

Letter X—Mr. Lovelace to John Belford, Esq.

BUT now I have cleared myself of any *intentional* levity on occasion of my beloved's meditation; which, as you observe, is finely suited to her case (that is to say, as she and you have drawn her case); I cannot help expressing my pleasure that by one or two verses of it [the *arrow*, Jack, and *what she feared being come upon her*!], I am encouraged to hope, what it will be very surprising to me if it do not happen; that is, in plain English, that the dear creature is in the way to be a mamma.

This cursed arrest, because of the ill effects the terror might have had upon her, in that hoped-for circumstance, has concerned me more than on any other account. It would be the pride of my life to prove, in this charming frost-piece, the triumph of nature over principle, and to have a young Lovelace by such an angel; and then, for its sake, I am confident she will live and will legitimate it. And what a meritorious little cherub would it be, that should lay an obligation upon both parents before it was born, which neither of them would be able to repay! Could I be sure it is so, I should be out of all pain for her recovery; *pain*, I say, since were she to *die* [*die*! abominable word! how I hate it!] I verily think I should be the most miserable man in the world.

As for the earnestness she expresses for death, she has found the words ready to her hand in honest Job; else she would not have delivered herself with such strength and vehemence.

Her innate piety (as I have more than once observed) will not permit her to shorten her own life, either by violence or neglect. She has a mind too noble for that, and would have done it before now had she designed any such thing; for to do it, like the Roman matron, when the mischief is over, and it can serve no end; and when the man, however a Tarquin, as some may think me in this action, is not a Tarquin in power, so that no *national point* can be made of it; is what she has too much good sense to think of.

Then, as I observed in a like case a little while ago, the distress when this was written was strong upon her, and she saw no end of it; but all was darkness and apprehension before her. Moreover, has she it not in her power to *disappoint* as much as she has been *disappointed*? Revenge, Jack, has induced many a woman to cherish a life to which grief and despair would otherwise have put an end.

And after all, death is no such eligible thing as Job in his *calamities* makes it. And a death desired merely from worldly disappointment shows not a right mind, let me tell this lady, whatever she may think of it.[1]   You and I, Jack, although not afraid, in the height of passion or resentment, to rush into those dangers which might be followed by a sudden and violent death, whenever a point of honour calls upon us, would shudder at his cool and deliberate approach in a lingering sickness which had debilitated the spirits.

So we read of a French general in the reign of Harry the IVth [I forget his name, if it were not Mareschal Biron] who, having faced with intrepidity the ghastly varlet on an hundred occasions in the field, was the most dejected of wretches when, having forfeited his life for treason, he was led with all the cruel parade of preparation and surrounding guards to the scaffold.

The poet says well:

> 'Tis not the Stoic lesson, got by rote,
> The pomp of words, and pedant dissertation,
> That can support us in the hour of terror.
> Books have taught cowards to talk nobly of it:
> But when the *trial* comes, they start, and stand aghast.

Very true; for then it is the old man in the fable with his bundle of sticks.

The lady is well read in Shakespeare, our English pride and glory; and must sometimes reason with herself in his words, so greatly expressed, that the subject, affecting as it is, cannot produce anything greater.

> Ay, but to die, and go we know not where;
> To lie in cold obstruction, and to rot;
> *This* sensible, warm motion to become
> A kneaded clod; and the delighted spirit
> To bathe in fiery floods, or to reside
> In thrilling regions of thick-ribbed ice:
> To be imprison'd in the viewless winds,
> Or blown, with restless violence, about
> The pendent worlds; or to be worse than worst
> Of those that lawless and uncertain thought

[1] Mr. Lovelace could not know that the lady was *so* thoroughly sensible of the solidity of this doctrine, as she really was; for, in Letter i to Mrs. Norton (p. 2 of this volume) she says: "Nor let it be imagined, that my present turn of mind proceeds from gloominess or melancholy; for although it was brought on by disappointment (the world showing me early, even at my first *rushing* into it, its true and ugly face), yet I hope that it has obtained a better root, and will every day more and more, by its fruits, demonstrate to me, and to all my friends, that it has."

Imagines howling: 'tis too horrible!
The weariest and most loaded worldly life,
That pain, age, penury, and *imprisonment*,
Can lay on nature, is a paradise
To what we fear of death.

I find, by one of thy three letters, that my beloved had some
account from Hickman of my interview with Miss Howe at
Col. Ambrose's. I had a very agreeable time of it there,
although severely rallied by several of the assembly. It concerns
me, however, not a little, to find our affair so generally known
among the *flippanti* of both sexes. It is all her own fault.
There never, surely, was such an odd little soul as this. Not to
keep her own secret, when the revealing of it could answer no
possible good end; and when she wants not (one would think) to
raise to herself either pity or friends, or to me enemies, by the
proclamation!—Why, Jack, must not all her own sex laugh in
their sleeves at her weakness? What would become of the peace
of the world, if all women should take it into their heads to
follow her example? What a fine time of it would the heads of
families have! Their wives always filling their ears with *their*
confessions, their daughters with *theirs*; sisters would be every
day setting their brothers about cutting of throats, if the
brothers had at heart *the honour of their families*, as it is called,
and the whole world would either be a scene of confusion, or
cuckoldom as much the fashion as it is in Lithuania.[1]

I am glad, however, that Miss Howe (as much as she hates me)
kept her word with my cousins on their visit to her, and with me
at the colonel's, to endeavour to persuade her friend to make
up all matters by matrimony; which no doubt is the best, nay,
the *only* method she can take, for her own honour and that of
her family.

I had once thoughts of revenging myself on that vixen, and
particularly, as thou mayst[2] remember, had planned something
to this purpose on the journey she is going to take, which had
been talked of some time. But I think—let me see—yes, I
think I will let this Hickman have her safe and entire, as thou
believest the fellow to be a tolerable sort of a mortal, and that
I had made *the worst of him*; and I am glad, for his own sake, he
has not launched out too virulently against me to thee.

But thou seest, Jack, by her refusal of money from him or

---

[1] In Lithuania, the women are said to have *so allowedly* their gallants,
called *adjutores*, that the husbands hardly ever enter upon any party of
pleasure without them.

[2] See vol. ii, pp. 418 et seq.

Miss Howe,[1] that the dear extravagant takes a delight in oddnesses, choosing to part with her clothes, though for a song Dost think she is not a little touched at times? I am afraid she is. A little spice of that insanity, I doubt, runs through her, that she had in a stronger degree in the first week of my operations. Her contempt of life; her proclamations; her refusal of matrimony; and now of money from her most intimate friends, are sprinklings of this kind, and no other way, I think, to be accounted for.

Her apothecary is a good honest fellow. I like him much. But the silly dear's harping so continually upon one string, dying, dying, dying, is what I have no patience with. I hope all this melancholy jargon is owing entirely to the way I would have her to be in. And it being as new to her, as the Bible beauties to thee,[2] no wonder she knows not what to make of herself; and so fancies she is breeding death, when the event will turn out quite the contrary.

Thou art a sorry fellow in thy remarks on the education and qualification of smarts and beaux of the rakish order, if by thy *we's* and *us's* thou meanest thyself or me [3]; for I pretend to say that the picture has no resemblance of us, who have read and conversed as we have done. It may indeed, and I believe it does, resemble the generality of the fops and coxcombs about town. But that let them look to; for, if it affects not me, to what purpose thy random shot? If indeed thou findest, by the new light darted in upon thee, since thou hast had the honour of conversing with this admirable creature, that the cap fits thy own head, why then, according to the *qui capit* rule, e'en take and clap it on; and I will add a string of bells to it, to complete thee for the fore-horse of the idiot team.

Although I just now said a kind thing or two for this fellow Hickman, yet I can tell thee, I could (to use one of my noble peer's humble phrases) *eat him up without a corn of salt,* when I think of his impudence to salute my charmer *twice* at parting [4]; and have still less patience with the lady herself for presuming to offer her cheek or lip (thou sayest not which) to him, and to press his clumsy fist between her charming hands. An honour worth a king's ransom; and what I would give—what would I not give? to have!—And then he in return to press her, as thou sayest he did, to his stupid heart; at that time, no doubt, more sensible than ever it was before!

---

[1] See p. 12 of this volume.　　　[2] Ibid. p. 7.
[3] Ibid. pp. 7, 15.　　　[4] Ibid. p. 15.

By thy description of their parting, I see thou wilt be a delicate fellow in time. My mortification in this lady's displeasure will be thy exaltation from her conversation. I envy thee as well for thy opportunities as for thy improvements; and such an impression has thy concluding paragraph [1] made upon me, that I wish I do not get into a reformation humour as well as thou; and then what a couple of lamentable puppies shall we make, howling in recitative to each other's discordant music!

Let me improve upon the thought, and imagine that, turned hermits, we have opened the two old caves at Hornsey, or dug new ones; and in each of our cells set up a death's head and an hour-glass for objects of contemplation—I have seen such a picture; but then, Jack, had not the old penitent fornicator a suffocating long grey beard? What figures would a couple of brocaded or laced-waistcoated toupets make with their sour screwed-up half-cocked faces, and more than half-shut eyes, in a kneeling attitude, recapitulating their respective rogueries? This scheme, were we only to make trial of it and return afterwards to our old ways, might serve to better purpose by far, than Horner's in the *Country Wife*, to bring the pretty wenches to us.

Let me see; the author of *Hudibras* has somewhere a description that would suit us, when met in one of our caves, and comparing our dismal notes together. This is it. Suppose *me* described:

> ——He sat upon his rump,
> His head like one in doleful dump;
> Betwixt his knees his hands apply'd
> Unto his cheeks, on either side:
> And by him, in another hole,
> Sat stupid *Belford*, cheek by jowl.

I know thou wilt think me too ludicrous. I think myself so. It is truly, to be ingenuous, a forced put; for my passions are so wound up that I am obliged either to laugh or cry. Like honest drunken Jack Daventry [poor fellow! what an unhappy end was his!]. Thou knowest I used to observe that whenever he rose from an entertainment, which he never did sober, it was his way, as soon as he got to the door, to look round him like a carrier-pigeon just thrown up, in order to spy out his course; and then, taking to his heels, he would run all the way home, though it were a mile or two, when he could hardly stand, and must have tumbled on his nose if he had attempted to walk moderately.

[1] See p. 16.

This then be my excuse, in this my unconverted estate, for a conclusion so unworthy of the conclusion to thy third letter.

What a length have I run! Thou wilt own, that if I pay thee not in quality, I do in quantity; and yet I leave a multitude of things unobserved upon. Indeed I hardly at this present know what to do with myself but scribble. Tired with Lord M., who, in his recovery, has played upon me the fable of the nurse, the crying child, and the wolf; tired with my Cousins Montague, though charming girls, were they not so near of kin; tired with Mowbray and Tourville, and their everlasting identity; tired with the country; tired of myself—longing for what I have not—I must go to town, and there have an interview with the charmer of my soul; for desperate diseases must have desperate remedies; and I only wait to know my doom from Miss Howe; and then, if it be rejection, I will try my fate, and receive my sentence at her feet. But I will apprise thee of it beforehand, as I told thee, that thou mayst keep thy parole with the lady in the best manner thou canst.

Letter XI—Miss Howe to Miss Clarissa Harlowe
[*In answer to hers of July* 27, *p.* 26]

Friday Night, July 28.

I WILL now, my dearest friend, write to you all my mind, without reserve, on your resolution not to have this vilest of men. You gave me, in yours of Sunday the 23rd, reasons so worthy of the pure mind of my Clarissa, in support of this your resolution, that nothing but self-love, lest I should lose my ever-amiable friend, could have prevailed upon me to wish you to alter it.

Indeed, I thought it was impossible there could be (however desirable) so noble an instance given by any of our sex, of a passion conquered, when there were so many inducements to give way to it. And, therefore, I was willing to urge you once more to overcome your just indignation, and to be prevailed upon by the solicitations of *his* friends, before you carried your resentments to so great a height, that it would be more difficult for you, and less to your honour to comply, than if you had complied at first.

But now, my dear, that I see you fixed in your noble resolution, and that it is impossible for your pure mind to join itself with that of so perjured a miscreant; I congratulate you most heartily upon it; and beg your pardon for but seeming to doubt that *theory* and *practice* were not the same thing with my beloved Clarissa Harlowe.

I have only one thing that saddens my heart on this occasion; and that is, the bad state of health Mr. Hickman (unwillingly) owns you are in; for, although you so well observe the doctrine you always laid down to me, that a censured person should first seek to be justified to *herself*, and give but a *second* place to the world's opinion of her; and in all cases where the two could not be reconciled, to prefer the *first* to the *last*; and though you *are* so well justified to your own heart, and to your Anna Howe; yet, my dear, let me beseech you to endeavour, by all possible means, to recover your health and spirits; and this, as what, if it *can* be effected, will crown the work, and show the world that you were *indeed* got above the base wretch; and though put out of your course for a little while, could resume it again, and go on blessing all within your knowledge, as well by your example as by your precepts.

For Heaven's sake, then, for the world's sake, for the honour of our sex, and for *my* sake, once more I beseech you, try to overcome this shock; and if you *can* overcome it, I shall then be as happy as I wish to be; for I cannot, indeed I cannot, think of parting with you for many, many years to come.

The reasons you give for discouraging my wishes to have you near us are so convincing, that I ought at present to acquiesce in them; but, my dear, when your mind is fully settled, as (now you are so absolutely determined in it, with regard to this wretch) I hope it will soon be, I shall expect you with us, or near us; and then you shall chalk out every path that I will set my foot in; nor will I turn aside either to the right hand or to the left.

You wish I had not mediated for you to your friends. I wish so too; because my mediation was ineffectual; because it may give new ground for the malice of some of them to work upon; and because you are angry with me for doing so. But how, as I said in my former, could I sit down in quiet, when I knew how uneasy their implacableness made you?—But I will tear myself from the subject; for I see I shall be warm again, and displease you—and there is not one thing in the world that I would do, however agreeable to myself, if I thought it would disoblige you; nor any one that I would omit to do, if I knew it would give you pleasure. And indeed, my dear half-severe friend, I will try if I cannot avoid the *fault* as willingly as I would the *rebuke*.

For this reason, I forbear saying anything on so nice a subject as your letter to your sister. It *must* be right, because you think

it so—and if it be taken as it ought, that will show you that it *is*.
But if it beget insults and revilings, as it is but too likely—I find
you don't intend to let me know it.

You was always so ready to accuse *yourself* for *other people's
faults*, and to suspect your own conduct, rather than the
judgment of your relations, that I have often told you I cannot
imitate you in this. It is not a necessary point of belief with
me, that all people in *years* are *therefore* wise; or that all *young
people* are *therefore* rash and headstrong; it may be *generally* the
case, as far as I know: and possibly it may be so in the case of *my*
mother and *her* girl; but I will venture to say that it has not
yet appeared to be so between the principals of Harlowe Place
and their second daughter.

You are for excusing them beforehand for their expected
cruelty, as not knowing what you have suffered, nor how ill
you are: they have *heard* of the former, and are not sorry for
it: of the latter they have been *told*, and *I* have most reason to
know how they have taken it—but I shall be far from avoiding
the *fault*, and as surely shall incur the *rebuke*, if I say any more
upon this subject. I will therefore only add at present, that
your reasonings in their behalf show *you* to be all excellence;
their returns to you, that *they* are all—— Do, my dear, let me
end with a little bit of spiteful justice—but you won't, I know—
so I have done, quite done, however reluctantly: yet if you think
of the word I would have said, don't doubt the justice of it, and
fill up the blank with it.

You intimate that were I actually married, and Mr. Hickman
to *desire* it, you would think of obliging me with a visit on the
occasion; and that perhaps, when with me, it would be difficult
for you to remove far from me.

Lord, my dear, what a stress do you seem to lay upon Mr.
Hickman's *desiring* it! To be sure he does and would of all
things desire to have you *near* us, and *with* us, if we might be so
favoured. Policy, as well as veneration for *you*, would undoubtedly make the man, if not a fool, *desire* this. But let me
tell you, that if Mr. Hickman, after marriage, should pretend to
dispute with me my friendships, as I hope I am not quite a fool,
I should let him know how far his own quiet was concerned in
such an impertinence; especially if they were such friendships as
were contracted before I knew him.

I know I always differed from you on this subject; for you
think more highly of a *husband's* prerogative than most people
do of the *royal* one. These notions, my dear, from a person of

your sense and judgment, are noway advantageous to us; inasmuch as they justify that assuming sex in their insolence; when hardly one out of ten of them, their opportunities considered, deserves any prerogative at all. Look through all the families we know; and we shall not find one-third of them have half the sense of their wives. And yet these are to be vested with prerogatives! And a woman of twice their sense has nothing to do but hear, tremble, and obey—and for *conscience* sake too, I warrant!

But Mr. Hickman and I may perhaps have a little discourse upon these sort of subjects, before I suffer him to talk of the day: and then I shall let him know what he has to trust to; as he will me, if he be a sincere man, what he pretends to expect from me. But let me tell you, my dear, that it is more in *your* power than perhaps you think it, to hasten the day so much pressed for by my mother, as well as wished for by you—for the very day that you can assure me that you are in a tolerable state of health, and have discharged your doctor and apothecary, at their own motions, on that account—some day in a month from that desirable news shall be it. So, my dear, make haste and be well; and then this matter will be brought to effect in a manner more agreeable to your Anna Howe than it otherwise ever can.

I send this day, by a particular hand, to the Misses Montague, your letter of just reprobation of the greatest profligate in the kingdom; and hope I shall not have done amiss that I transcribe some of the paragraphs of your letter of the 23rd, and send them with it, as you at first intended should be done.

You are, it seems (and that too much for your health), employed in writing. I hope it is in penning down the particulars of your tragical story. And my mother has put me in mind to press you to it, with a view that one day, if it might be published under feigned names, it would be of as much use as honour to the sex. My mother says she cannot help admiring you for the propriety of your resentment in your refusal of the wretch; and she would be extremely glad to have her advice of penning your sad story complied with. And then, she says, your noble conduct throughout your trials and calamities will afford not only a shining example to your sex, but at the same time (those calamities befalling SUCH a person) a fearful warning to the inconsiderate young creatures of it.

On Monday we shall set out on our journey; and I hope to be back in a fortnight, and on my return will have one pull more with my mother for a London journey: and if the *pretence must*

be the buying of clothes, the *principal motive* will be that of
seeing once more my dear friend, *while* I can say I have not finally
given consent to the change of a visitor into a relation; and so I
can call myself MY OWN, as well as

YOUR
ANNA HOWE.

Letter XII—*Miss Howe to the two Misses Montague*

Sat., July 29.

DEAR LADIES,—I have not been wanting to use all my interest
with my beloved friend, to induce her to forgive and be reconciled
to your kinsman (though he has so ill deserved it); and have
even *repeated* my earnest advice to her on this head. This
repetition, and the waiting for her answer, having taking up
time, have been the cause that I could not sooner do myself
the honour of writing to you on this subject.

You will see, by the enclosed, her immovable resolution,
grounded on noble and high-souled motives, which I cannot
but *regret* and *applaud* at the same time: *applaud,* for the justice
of her determination, which will confirm all your worthy house in
the opinion you had conceived of her unequalled merit; and
regret, because I have but too much reason to apprehend, as well
by that, as by the report of a gentleman just come from her, that
she is in such a declining way as to her health, that her thoughts
are very differently employed than on a continuance here.

The enclosed letter she thought fit to send to me unsealed,
that, after I had perused it, I might forward it to you: and this
is the reason it is superscribed by myself and sealed with my seal.
It is very full and peremptory; but as she had been pleased, in a
letter to me, dated the 23rd instant (as soon as she could hold a
pen), to give me more ample reasons why she could not comply
with your pressing requests, as well as mine, I will transcribe
some of the passages in that letter, which will give one of the
wickedest men in the world (if he sees them) reason to think
himself one of the most unhappy, in the loss of so incomparable
a wife as he might have gloried in, had he not been so *superlatively* wicked. These are the passages:

[*See, for these passages, Miss Harlowe's Letter No. cxxxi of
vol. iii, dated July 23, marked with turned comma's thus* "]

And now, ladies, you have before you my beloved friend's
reasons for her refusal of a man unworthy of the relation he
bears to so many excellent persons: and I will add (for I cannot

help it), that the merit and rank of the person considered, and the vile manner of his proceedings, there never was a greater villainy committed: and since she thinks her first and *only* fault cannot be expiated but by death, I pray to God *daily*, and will *hourly* from the moment I shall hear of that sad catastrophe, that He will be pleased to make him the subject of His vengeance, in some such way, as that all who know of his perfidious crime, may see the hand of Heaven in the punishment of it!

You will forgive me, ladies: I love not mine own soul better than I do Miss Clarissa Harlowe. And the distresses she has gone through; the persecutions she suffers from all her friends; the curse she lies under, for his sake, from her implacable father; her reduced health and circumstances, from high health and affluence; and that execrable arrest and confinement, which have deepened all her other calamities (and which must be laid at his door, as it was the act of his vile agents, that, whether from his immediate orders or not, naturally flowed from his preceding baseness); the sex dishonoured in the eye of the world, in the person of one of the greatest ornaments of it; the unmanly methods, whatever they were (for I know not all as yet), by which he compassed her ruin—all these considerations join to justify my warmth, and my execrations of a man whom I think excluded by his crimes from the benefit even of Christian forgiveness—and were you to see all she writes, and to know the admirable talents she is mistress of, you yourselves would join with me to admire her and execrate him.

Believe me to be, with a high sense of your merits,

Dear ladies,

Your most obedient humble servant,

ANNA HOWE.

Letter XIII—*Mrs. Norton to Miss Clarissa Harlowe*

Friday, July 28.

MY DEAREST YOUNG LADY,—I have the consolation to tell you that my son is once again in an hopeful way, as to his health. He desires his duty to you. He is very low and weak. And so am I. But this is the first time that I have been able, for several days past, to sit up to write, or I would not have been so long silent.

Your letter to your sister is received and answered. You have the answer by this time, I suppose. I wish it may be to your satisfaction: but am afraid it will not: for, by Betty

Barnes, I find they were in a great ferment on receiving yours, and much divided whether it should be answered or not. They will not yet believe that you are so ill as (to my infinite concern) I find you are. What passed between Miss Harlowe and Miss Howe has been, as I feared it would be, an aggravation.

I showed Betty two or three passages in your letter to me; and she seemed moved, and said she would report them favourably, and would procure me a visit from Miss Harlowe, if I would promise to show the same to *her*. But I have heard no more of that.

Methinks I am sorry you refuse the wicked man: but doubt not, nevertheless, that your motives for doing so are more commendable than my wishes that you would not. But as you would be resolved, as I may say, on life, if you gave way to such a thought; and as I have so much interest in your recovery, I cannot forbear showing this regard to myself; and to ask you if you cannot get over your just resentments?—But I dare say no more on this subject.

What a dreadful thing indeed was it for my dearest tender young lady to be arrested in the streets of London! How does my heart go over again for you, what yours must have suffered at that time! Yet this, to such a mind as yours, must be light, compared to what you had suffered before.

O my dearest Miss Clary, how shall we know what to pray for, when we pray, but that *God's will may be done*, and that we may be *resigned to it*! When at nine years old, and afterwards at eleven, you had a dangerous fever, how incessantly did we all grieve and pray, and put up our vows to the Throne of Grace for your recovery! For all our lives were bound up in your life—yet *now*, my dear, as it has proved (especially if we are *soon* to lose you), what a much more desirable event, both for you and for us, would it have been had we *then* lost you!

A sad thing to say! But as it is in pure love to you that I say it, and in full conviction that we are not always fit to be our own choosers, I hope it may be excusable; and the rather, as the same reflection will naturally lead both you and me to acquiesce under the present dispensation; since we are assured that nothing happens by chance; and that the greatest good may, for aught we know, be produced from the heaviest evils.

I am glad you are with such honest people; and that you have all your effects restored. How dreadfully have you been used, that one should be glad of such a poor piece of justice as that!

Your talent at moving the passions is always hinted at; and

this Betty of your sister never comes near me that she is not full of it. But as you say, whom has it moved that you *wished* to move? Yet were it not for this unhappy notion, I am sure your mother would relent. Forgive me, my dear Miss Clary; for I must try one way to be convinced if my opinion be not just. But I will not tell you what that is, unless it succeeds. I will try, in pure duty and love to *them*, as well as to *you*.

May Heaven be your support in all your trials, is the constant prayer, my dearest young lady, of

Your ever affectionate friend and servant,

JUDITH NORTON.

Letter XIV—Mrs. Norton to Mrs. Harlowe

Friday, July 28.

HONOURED MADAM,—Being forbidden (without leave) to send you anything I might happen to receive from my beloved Miss Clary, and so ill, that I cannot attend to *ask* your leave, I give you this trouble, to let you know that I have received a letter from her; which, I think, I should hereafter be held inexcusable, as things may happen, if I did not desire permission to communicate to you, and that as soon as possible.

Applications have been made to the dear young lady from Lord M., from the two ladies his sisters, and from both his nieces, and from the wicked man himself, to forgive and marry him. This, in noble indignation for the usage she has received from him, she has absolutely refused. And perhaps, madam, if you and the honoured family should be of opinion that to comply with their wishes is *now* the properest measure that *can* be taken, the circumstances of things may require your authority or advice to induce her to change her mind.

I have reason to believe that one motive for her refusal is her full conviction that she shall not long be a trouble to anybody; and so she would not give a husband a right to interfere with her family in relation to the estate her grandfather devised to her. But of this, however, I have not the least intimation from her. Nor would she, I dare say, mention it *as* a reason, having still stronger reasons, from his vile treatment of her, to refuse him.

The letter I have received will show how truly penitent the dear creature is; and if I have your permission, I will send it sealed up, with a copy of mine, to which it is an answer. But as I resolve upon this step without her knowledge [and indeed I do],

I will not acquaint her with it unless it, be attended with desirable effects: because, otherwise, besides making me incur her displeasure, it might quite break her already half-broken heart. I am,

Honoured madam,
Your dutiful and ever obliged servant,
JUDITH NORTON.

Letter XV—Mrs. Harlowe to Mrs. Judith Norton

Sunday, July 30.

WE all know your virtuous prudence, worthy woman: we all do. But your partiality to this your rash favourite is likewise known. And we are no less acquainted with the unhappy body's power of painting her distresses so as to pierce a stone.

Every one is of opinion that the dear naughty creature is working about to be forgiven and received; and for this reason it is that Betty has been forbidden [not by *me*, you may be sure!] to mention any more of her letters; for she did speak to my Bella of some moving passages you read to her.

This will convince you that nothing will be heard in her favour. To what purpose, then, should I mention anything about her? But you may be sure that I *will*, if I can have but one second. However, that is not at all likely, until we see what the *consequences* of her crime will be: and who can tell that?—She may —How can I speak it, and my once darling daughter unmarried! —She may be with child! This would perpetuate her stain. Her brother may come to some harm; which God forbid! One child's ruin, I hope, will not be followed by another's murder!

As to her grief and her present misery, whatever it be, she must bear with it; and it must be short of what I hourly bear for her! Indeed I am afraid nothing but her being at the last extremity of all will make her father, and her uncles, and her other friends, forgive her.

The easy pardon perverse children meet with, when they have done the rashest and most rebellious thing they can do, is the reason (*as is pleaded to us every day*) that so *many* follow their example. They depend upon the indulgent weakness of their parents' tempers, and, in *that* dependence, harden their own hearts: and a little humiliation, when they have brought themselves into the foretold misery, is to be a sufficient atonement for the greatest perverseness.

But for such a child as this [*I mention what others hourly say, but what I must sorrowfully subscribe to*] to lay plots and stratagems to deceive her parents, as well as herself; and to run away with a libertine; can there be any atonement for her crime? And is she not answerable to God, to us, to you, and to all the world who knew her, for the abuse of such talents as *she* has abused?

You say her heart is half broken: is it to be wondered at? Was not her sin committed equally against warning and the light of her own knowledge?

That *he* would now marry her, or that *she* would refuse him, if she believed him in earnest, as she has circumstanced herself, is not at all probable; and were *I* inclined to believe it, *nobody else* here would. He values not his relations; and would deceive them as soon as any others: his aversion to marriage he has always openly declared; and still occasionally declares it. But if he be now in earnest; which every one who knows him must doubt; which do you think (hating us too as he professes to hate and despise us all) would be most eligible here, to hear of her death, or of her marriage with such a vile man?

To all of us, yet I cannot say! For, O my good Mrs. Norton, you know what a mother's tenderness for the child of her heart would make her choose, notwithstanding all that child's faults, rather than lose her for ever!

But I must sail with the tide; my own judgment also joining with the general resentment; or I should make the unhappiness of the more worthy still greater [my dear Mr. Harlowe's particularly]; which is already more than enough to make them unhappy for the remainder of their days. This I know: if I were to oppose the rest, our son would fly out to find this libertine; and who could tell what would be the issue of *that* with such a man of violence and blood as that Lovelace is known to be?

All I can expect to prevail for her is, that in a week or so Mr. Brand may be sent up to inquire privately about her present state and way of life, and to see she is not altogether destitute: for nothing she writes herself will be regarded.

Her father indeed has, at her earnest request, withdrawn the curse, which, in a passion, he laid upon her, at her first wicked flight from us. But Miss Howe [*it is a sad thing, Mrs. Norton, to suffer so many ways at once!*] had made matters so difficult by her undue liberties with us all, as well by speech in all companies, as by letters written to my Bella, that we could hardly prevail upon him to hear her letter read.

These liberties of Miss Howe with us; the general cry against us abroad wherever we are spoken of; and the *visible*, and not seldom *audible*, disrespectfulness which high and low treat us with to our faces, as we go to and from church, and even *at* church (for nowhere else have we the heart to go), as if none of us had been regarded but upon her account; and as if she were innocent, we all in fault; are constant aggravations, you must needs think, to the whole family.

She has made my lot heavy, I am sure, that was far from being light before! To tell you truth, I am enjoined not to receive anything of hers, from any hand, without leave. Should I therefore gratify my yearnings after her, so far as to receive privately the letter you mention, what would the case be, but to torment myself, without being able to do her good?—And were it to be known—Mr. Harlowe is *so* passionate. And should it throw his gout into his stomach, as her rash flight did— Indeed, indeed, I am very unhappy! For, O my good woman, she is my child still! But unless it were more in my power—Yet do I long to see the letter—you say it tells of her present way and circumstances. The poor child, who ought to be in possession of thousands!—and *will*!—For her father will be a faithful steward for her. But it must be in his own way, and at his own time.

And is she *really* ill?—so *very* ill?—But she *ought* to sorrow. She has given a double measure of it.

But does she *really* believe she shall not *long* trouble us?— But O my Norton!—she must, she *will* long trouble us—for can she think her death, if we should be deprived of her, will put an end to our afflictions? Can it be thought that the fall of such a child will not be regretted by us to the last hour of our lives?

But in the letter you have, does she, without *reserve*, express her contrition? Has she in it no reflecting hints? Does she not aim at extenuations? If I *were* to see it, will it not shock me so much that my *apparent* grief may expose me to harshnesses? Can it be contrived——

But to what purpose? Don't send it—I charge you don't—I dare not see it——

Yet——

But, alas!——

O forgive the almost distracted mother! You *can*. You know how to allow for all this. So I will let it go. I will not write over again this part of my letter.

But I choose not to know more of her than is communicated

to us all—no more than I dare *own* I have seen—and what some
of them may rather communicate *to* me, than receive *from* me:
and this for the sake of my outward quiet: although my inward
peace suffers more and more by the compelled reserve.

.   .   .   .   .

I was forced to break off.   But I will now try to conclude my
long letter.

I am sorry you are ill.   But if you were well, I could not, for
your own sake, wish you to go up, as Betty tells us you long to
do.   If you *went*, nothing would be minded that came from you.
As they already think you too partial in her favour, your going
up would confirm it, and do yourself prejudice, and her no good.
And as everybody values you here, I advise you not to interest
yourself too warmly in her favour, especially before my Bella's
Betty, till I can let you know a *proper* time.   Yet to forbid you
to love the dear naughty creature, who can?   O my Norton!
you *must* love her!—And so must I!

I send you five guineas to help you in your present illness
and your son's; for it must have lain heavy upon you.   What a
sad, sad thing, my dear good woman, that all *your* pains and all
my pains for eighteen or nineteen years together, have, in so few
months, been rendered thus deplorably vain!   Yet I must be
always your friend, and pity you, for the very reason that I
myself deserve every one's pity.

Perhaps I may find an opportunity to pay you a visit, as in
your illness, and then may weep over the letter you mention,
with you.   But, for the future, write nothing to me about the
poor girl that you think may not be communicated to us all.

And I charge you, as you value my friendship, as you wish
my peace, not to say anything of a letter you have from me,
either to the naughty one or to anybody else.   It was some
little relief (the occasion given) to write to you, who must, in so
particular a manner, share my affliction.   A mother, Mrs.
Norton, cannot forget her child, though that child could abandon
her mother; and in so doing, run away with all her mother's
comforts!—As I can truly say, is the case of

Your unhappy friend,

CHARLOTTE HARLOWE.

Letter XVI—Miss Clarissa Harlowe to Mrs. Judith Norton

Sat., July 29.

I CONGRATULATE you, my dear Mrs. Norton, with all my heart, on your son's recovery; which I pray to God, with your own health, to perfect.

I write in some hurry, being apprehensive of the consequence of the hints you give of some method you propose to try in my favour [with my relations, I presume you mean]: but you will not tell me what, you say, if it prove unsuccessful.

Now I must beg of you that you will not take any step in my favour with which you do not first acquaint me.

I have but one request to make to them, besides what is contained in my letter to my sister; and I would not, methinks, for the sake of their own future peace of mind, that they should be teased so, by your well-meant kindness and that of Miss Howe, as to be put upon denying me that. And why should more be asked for me than I can partake of? More than is absolutely necessary for my own peace?

You suppose I should have my sister's answer to my letter by the time yours reached my hand. I have it; and a severe one, a very severe one, it is. Yet, considering my fault in their eyes, and the provocations I am to suppose they so newly had from my dear Miss Howe, I am to look upon it as a favour that it was answered at all. I will send you a copy of it soon; as also of mine, to which it is an answer.

I have reason to be very thankful that my father has withdrawn that heavy malediction which affected me so much—a parent's curse, my dear Mrs. Norton! What child could die in peace under a parent's curse? so literally fulfilled too as this has been in what relates to this life!

My heart is too full to touch upon the particulars of my sister's letter. I can make but *one* atonement for my fault. May *that* be accepted! And may it soon be forgotten by *every* dear relation that there was such an unhappy daughter, sister, or niece, as Clarissa Harlowe!

My Cousin Morden was one of those who was so earnest in prayers for my recovery, at nine and eleven years of age, as you mention. My sister thinks he will be one of those who will wish I never had had a being. But pray, when he does come, let me hear of it with the first.

You think that, were it not for that unhappy notion of my moving talent, my mother would relent. What would I give to see her once more, and, although unknown to her, to kiss but the hem of her garment!

Could I have thought that the last time I saw her would *have been the last*, with what difficulty should I have been torn from her embraced feet! And when, screened behind the yew hedge on the 5th of April last,[1] I saw my father, and my Uncle Antony, and my brother and sister, how little did I think that that would be the last time I should ever see them; and in so short a space, that so many dreadful evils would befall me!

But I can write nothing but what must give you trouble. I will therefore, after repeating my desire that you will not intercede for me but with my previous consent, conclude with the assurance, that I am, and ever will be,

Your most affectionate and dutiful
CLARISSA HARLOWE.

Letter XVII—Miss Arab. Harlowe to Miss Cl. Harlowe
[*In answer to hers of Friday, July* 21, *p.* 3]

Thursday, July 27.

O MY UNHAPPY LOST SISTER!—What a miserable hand have you made of your romantic and giddy expedition!—I pity you at my heart.

You may *well* grieve and repent! Lovelace has left you!—In what way or circumstances you know best.

I wish your conduct had made your case more pitiable. But 'tis your own seeking!

God help you!—for you have not a friend will look upon you! Poor, wicked, undone creature!—fallen, as you are, against warning, against expostulation, against duty!

But it signifies nothing to reproach you. I weep over you.

My poor mother!—your rashness and folly have made *her* more miserable than *you* can be. Yet she has besought my father to grant your request.

My uncles joined with her; for they thought there was a little more modesty in your letter than in the letters of your pert advocate: and my father is pleased to give me leave to write; but only these words for *him*, and no more: "That he withdraws the curse he laid upon you, at the first hearing of your wicked flight, so far as it is in his power to do it; and hopes that your present punishment may be all that you will meet with. For

[1] See vol. i. p. 411.

the rest, he will never own you, nor forgive you; and grieves he has such a daughter in the world."

All this, and more, you have deserved from him and from all of *us*: but what have you done to this abandoned libertine, to deserve what you have met with at *his* hands?—I fear, I fear, sister!—But no more! A blessed four months' work have you made of it.

My brother is now at Edinburgh, sent thither by my father [though he knows not this to be the motive], that he may not meet your triumphant deluder.

We are told he would be glad to marry you: but why then did he abandon you? He had kept you till he was tired of you, no question; and it is not likely he would wish to have you but upon the terms you have already without all doubt been *his*.

You ought to advise your friend Miss Howe to concern herself less in your matters than she does, except she could do it with more decency. She has written three letters to me: very insolent ones. Your favourer, poor Mrs. Norton, thinks you know of the pert creature's writing. I hope you don't. But then the more impertinent the writer. But, believing the fond woman, I sat down the more readily to answer your letter; and I write with less severity, I can tell you, than otherwise I should have done if I had answered it at all.

Monday last was your birthday. Think, poor ungrateful wretch, as you are! how we all used to keep it; and you will not wonder to be told that we ran away from one another that day. But God give you true penitence, if you have it not already! And it *will* be true, if it be equal to the shame and the sorrow you have given us all.

Your afflicted sister,
ARABELLA HARLOWE.

Your Cousin Morden is every day expected in England. He, as well as others of the family, when he comes to hear what a blessed piece of work you have made of it, will wish you never had had a being.

Letter XVIII—Miss Clarissa Harlowe to Miss Howe

Sunday, July 30.

YOU have given me great pleasure, my dearest friend, by your approbation of my reasonings, and of my resolution founded upon them, never to have Mr. Lovelace. This approbation is so *right* a thing, give me leave to say, from the nature of the case, and from the strict honour and true dignity of mind, which I always admired in my Anna Howe, that I could hardly tell to what, but to my evil destiny, which of late would not let me please anybody, to attribute the advice you gave me to the contrary.

But let not the ill state of my health, and what that may naturally tend to, sadden you. I have told you that I will not run away from life, nor avoid the means that may continue it, if God see fit: and if He do *not*, who shall repine at His will?

If it shall be found that I have not acted unworthy of your love, and of my own character, in my greater trials, that will be a happiness to both on reflection.

The shock which you so earnestly advise me to try to get above, was a shock the greatest that I could receive. But, my dear, as it was not occasioned by my *fault*, I hope I am already got above it. I hope I am.

I am more grieved (at times, however) for *others*, than for *myself*. And so I *ought*. For as to *myself*, I cannot but reflect that I have had an escape, rather than a loss, in missing Mr. Lovelace for a husband—even had he *not* committed the vilest of all outrages.

Let any one, who knows my story, collect his character from his behaviour to *me before* that outrage; and then judge whether it was in the least probable that such a man should make me happy. But to collect his character from his principles with regard to the *sex in general*, and from his enterprises upon many of them, and to consider the *cruelty of his nature*, and the *sportiveness of his invention*, together with the *high opinion he has of himself*, it will not be doubted that a wife of his must have been miserable; and more miserable if she loved him, than she could have been were she to be indifferent to him.

A *twelvemonth* might very probably have put a period to my life; situated as I was with my friends; persecuted and harassed as I had been by my brother and sister; and my very heart torn in pieces by the *wilful*, and (as it is now apparent) *premeditated* suspenses of the man, whose gratitude I wished to engage, and whose protection I was the more entitled to expect, as he had robbed me of every other, and reduced me to an absolute dependence upon himself. Indeed I once thought that it was *all* his view to bring me to this (as he hated my family); and uncomfortable enough for me, if it had been all.

Can it be thought, my dear, that my heart was not more than

half broken (happy as I was before I knew Mr. Lovelace) by such a grievous change in my circumstances?—Indeed it was. Nor perhaps was the wicked violence *wanting* to have cut short, though possibly not so *very* short, a life that he has sported with.

Had I been his but a *month*, he must have possessed the estate on which my relations had set their hearts; the more to their regret, as they hated *him* as much as he hated *them*.

Have I not reason, these things considered, to think myself happier without Mr. Lovelace than I could have been with him? My *will too unviolated*; and very little, nay, not anything as to him, to reproach myself with?

But with my *relations* it is *otherwise*. They indeed deserve to be pitied. They are, and no doubt will long be, unhappy.

To judge of their resentments, and of their conduct, we must put ourselves in their situation: and while *they* think me more in fault than themselves (whether my favourers are of their opinion, or not), and have a right to judge for themselves, they ought to have great allowances made for them; my parents especially. They stand at least *self*-acquitted (that cannot I); and the rather, as they can recollect, to their pain, their past indulgences to me, and their unquestionable love.

Your partiality for the friend you so much value will not easily let you come into this way of thinking. But only, my dear, be pleased to consider the matter in the following light.

"Here was my MOTHER, one of the most prudent persons of her sex, married into a family, not perhaps so happily tempered as herself; but every one of which she had the address, for a great while, absolutely to govern as she pleased by her directing wisdom, at the same time that they knew not but her pre-scriptions were the dictates of their own hearts; such a sweet art had she of conquering by seeming to yield. Think, my dear, what must be the pride and the pleasure of such a mother, that in my brother she could give a *son* to the family she distinguished with her love, not unworthy of their wishes; a *daughter*, in my *sister*, of whom she had no reason to be ashamed; and in *me* a *second* daughter, whom everybody complimented (such was their partial favour to me) as being the still more immediate likeness of herself? How, self-pleased, could she smile round upon a family she had so blessed! What compliments were paid her upon the example she had given us, which was followed with such hopeful effects! With what a noble confidence could she look upon her dear Mr. Harlowe, as a person made happy by her; and be delighted to think that nothing but purity streamed from a fountain so pure!

"Now, my dear, reverse, as I daily do, this charming prospect. See my dear *mother*, sorrowing in her closet; endeavouring to suppress her sorrow at her table, and in those retirements where sorrow was before a stranger: hanging down her pensive head: smiles no more beaming over her benign aspect: her virtue made to suffer for faults she could not be guilty of: her patience continually tried (because she has more of it than any other) with repetitions of faults she is as much wounded by, as those can be from whom she so often hears of them: taking to herself, as the fountain-head, a taint which only had infected one of the under-currents: afraid to open her lips (were she willing) in my favour, lest it should be thought she has any bias in her own mind to failings that never could have been suspected in her: robbed of that pleasing merit which the mother of well-nurtured and hopeful children may glory in: every one who visits her, or is visited by her, by dumb-show, and looks that mean more than words can express, condoling where they used to congratulate: the affected silence wounding: the compassionating look reminding: the half-suppressed sigh in *them* calling up deeper sighs from *her*; and their averted eyes, while they endeavour to restrain the rising tear, provoking tears from *her*, that will not be restrained.

"When I consider these things, and, added to these, the pangs that tear in pieces the stronger heart of my FATHER, because it cannot relieve itself by those tears which carry the torturing grief to the eyes of softer spirits: the overboiling tumults of my impatient and uncontrollable BROTHER, piqued to the heart of his honour, in the fall of a sister in whom he once gloried: the pride of an ELDER SISTER, who had given unwilling way to the honours paid over her head to one born after her: and, lastly, the dishonour I have brought upon TWO UNCLES, who each contended which should most favour their then happy niece:— When, I say, I reflect upon my fault in these strong, yet just lights, what room can there be to censure anybody but my unhappy self? And how much reason have I to say, *If I justify myself, mine own heart shall condemn me; if I say I am perfect, it shall also prove me perverse?*"

Here permit me to lay down my pen for a few moments.

. . . .

You are very obliging to me, *intentionally*, I know, when you tell me it is in my power to hasten the day of Mr. Hickman's happiness. But yet, give me leave to say that I admire this kind assurance less than any other paragraph of your letter.

In the first place, you know it is *not* in my power to say *when* I can dismiss my physician; and you should not put the cele- bration of a marriage *intended* by *yourself*, and so *desirable* to your *mother*, upon so precarious an issue. Nor will I accept of a compliment which must mean a slight to *her*.

If anything could give me a relish for life, after what I have suffered, it would be the hopes of the continuance of the more than sisterly love, which has for years uninterruptedly bound us together as one mind. And why, my dear, should you defer giving (by a tie still stronger) another friend to one who has so few?

I am glad you have sent my letter to Miss Montague. I hope I shall hear no more of this unhappy man.

I had begun the particulars of my tragical story: but it is so painful a task, and I have so many more important things to do, and, as I apprehend, so little time to do them in, that could I avoid it, I would go no further in it.

Then, to this hour, I know not by what means several of his machinations to ruin me were brought about; so that some material parts of my sad story must be defective, if I were to sit down to write it. But I have been thinking of a way that will answer the end wished for by your mother and you full as well; perhaps better.

Mr. Lovelace, it seems, has communicated to his friend Mr. Belford all that has passed between himself and me, as he went on. Mr. Belford has not been able to deny it. So that (as we may observe by the way) a poor young creature, whose indis- cretion has given a libertine power over her, has a reason *she little thinks of*, to regret her folly; since these wretches, who have no more honour in one point than in another, scruple not to make her weakness a part of their triumph to their brother- libertines.

I have nothing to apprehend of this sort, if I have the justice done me in his letters which Mr. Belford assures me I have: and therefore the particulars of my story, and the base arts of this vile man, will, I think, be best collected from those very letters of his (if Mr. Belford can be prevailed upon to communicate them); to which I dare appeal with the same truth and fervour as he did, who says: *O that one would hear me! and that mine adversary had written a book! Surely I would take it upon my shoulders, and bind it to me as a crown! For I covered not*

*my transgressions as Adam, by hiding mine iniquity in my
bosom.*

There is one way which may be fallen upon to induce Mr.
Belford to communicate these letters; since he seems to have
(and declares he always had) a sincere abhorrence of his friend's
baseness to me: but that, you 'll say when you hear it, is a
strange one. Nevertheless, I am very earnest upon it at present.

It is no other than this:

I think to make Mr. Belford the executor of my last will
[don't be surprised]: and with this view I permit his visits with
the less scruple: and every time I see him, from his concern for
me, am more and more inclined to do so. If I hold in the same
mind, and if he accept the trust, and will communicate the
materials in his power, those, joined with what you can furnish,
will answer the whole end.

I know you will start at my notion of such an executor: but
pray, my dear, consider, in my present circumstances, what I
can do better, as I am empowered to make a will, and have
considerable matters in my own disposal.

Your mother, I am sure, would not consent that *you* should
take this office upon you. It might subject *Mr. Hickman* to the
insults of that violent man. *Mrs. Norton* cannot, for several
reasons respecting herself. My *brother* looks upon what I
ought to have as his right: my *Uncle Harlowe* is already one of
my trustees (as my Cousin Morden is the other) for the estate
my grandfather left me: but you see I could not get from my
own family the few guineas I left behind me at Harlowe Place;
and my *Uncle Antony* once threatened to have my grandfather's
will controverted. My *father!*—To be sure, my dear, I could
not expect that my *father* would do all I wish should be done:
and a *will* to be executed by a father for a daughter (parts of it,
perhaps, absolutely against his own judgment), carries somewhat
daring and prescriptive in the very *word*.

If indeed my *Cousin Morden* were to come in time, and would
undertake this trust—but even *him* it might subject to hazards;
and the more, as he is a man of great spirit; and as the other man
(of *as* great) looks upon me (unprotected as I have long been) as
his property.

Now Mr. Belford, as I have already mentioned, knows everything that has passed. He is a man of spirit, and, it seems, as
fearless as the other, with more humane qualities. You don't
know, my dear, what instances of sincere humanity this Mr.
Belford has shown, not only on occasion of the cruel arrest, but

on several occasions since. And Mrs. Lovick has taken pains to inquire after his general character; and hears a very good one of him, for justice and generosity in all his concerns of *meum* and *tuum*, as they are called: he has a knowledge of law matters; and has two executorships upon him at this time, in the discharge of which his honour is unquestioned.

All these reasons have already in a manner *determined* me to ask this favour of him; although it will have an odd sound with it to make an intimate friend of Mr. Lovelace my executor.

This is certain: my brother will be more acquiescent a great deal in such a case with the articles of my will, as he will see that it will be to no purpose to controvert some of them, which else, I dare say, he would controvert, or persuade my other friends to do so.   And who would involve an executor in a lawsuit, if they could help it?—which would be the case, if anybody were left whom my brother could hope to awe or control; since my father has possession of all, and is absolutely governed by him. [Angry spirits, my dear, as I have often seen, will be overcome by more angry ones, as well as sometimes be disarmed by the meek.] Nor would I *wish*, you may believe, to have effects torn out of my father's hands: while Mr. Belford, who is a man of fortune (and a good economist in his own affairs), would have no interest but to do justice.

Then he exceedingly presses for some occasion to show his readiness to serve me: and he would be able to manage his violent friend, over whom he has more influence than any other person.

But, after all, I know not if it were not more eligible by far, that my story, *and myself too*, should be forgotten as soon as possible. And of this I shall have the less doubt, if the character of my parents [you will forgive me, my dear] cannot be guarded against the unqualified bitterness which, from your affectionate zeal for me, has sometimes mingled with your ink—a point that *ought*, and (I insist upon it) *must* be well considered of, if anything be done which your mother and you are desirous to have done. The generality of the world is too apt to oppose a duty—and general duties, my dear, ought not to be weakened by the justification of a single person, however unhappily circumstanced.

My father has been so good as to take off the heavy malediction he laid me under. I must be now solicitous for a last blessing; and that is all I shall presume to petition for. My sister's letter, communicating this grace, is a severe one: but as she writes to me as *from everybody*, how could I expect it to be otherwise?

If you set out to-morrow, this letter cannot reach you till you get to your Aunt Harman's. I shall therefore direct it thither, as Mr. Hickman instructed me.

I hope you will have met with no inconveniences in your little journey and voyage; and that you will have found in good health all whom you wish to see well.

If your relations in the little island join their solicitations with your mother's commands, to have your nuptials celebrated before you leave them, let me beg of you, my dear, to oblige them. How grateful will the notification that you have done so, be to

Your ever faithful and affectionate
CL. HARLOWE!

Letter XIX—*Miss Clarissa Harlowe to Miss Harlowe*

Saturday, July 29.

I REPINE not, my dear sister, at the severity you have been pleased to express in the letter you favoured me with; because that severity was accompanied with the grace I had petitioned for; and because the reproaches of mine own heart are stronger than any other person's reproaches can be: and yet I am not half so culpable as I am imagined to be: as would be allowed, if all the circumstances of my unhappy story were known; and which I shall be ready to communicate to Mrs. Norton, if she be commissioned to inquire into them; or to you, my sister, if you can have patience to hear them.

I remembered with a bleeding heart what day the 24th of July was. I began with the eve of it; and I passed the day itself—*as it was fit I should pass it.* Nor have I any comfort to give to my dear and ever honoured father and mother, and to you, my Bella, but this—that, as it was the first *unhappy* anniversary of my birth, in all probability it will be the *last.*

Believe me, my dear sister, I say not this merely to move compassion; but from the *best* grounds. And as, on that account, I think it of the highest importance to my peace of mind to obtain one further favour, I would choose to owe to your intercession, *as my sister*, the leave I beg, to address half a dozen lines (with the hope of having them answered as I wish) to either or to both my honoured parents, to beg their *last blessing.*

This blessing is all the favour I have now to ask: it is all I *dare* to ask: yet am I afraid to rush at once, though by *letter,* into the presence of either. And if I did not ask it, it might seem to be owing to stubbornness and want of duty, when my heart is all humility and penitence. Only, be so good as to embolden me to attempt this task — write but this one line, "Clary Harlowe, you are at liberty to write as you desire." This will be enough—and shall to my last hour be acknowledged as the greatest favour by

Your truly penitent sister,
CLARISSA HARLOWE.

Letter XX—Mrs. Norton to Miss Clarissa Harlowe

Monday, July 31.

MY DEAREST YOUNG LADY,—I must indeed own that I took the liberty to write to your mother, offering to enclose to her, if she gave me leave, yours of the 24th: by which I thought she would see what was the state of your mind; what the nature of your last troubles was, from the wicked arrest; and what the people are where you lodge; what proposals were made you from Lord M.'s family; also your sincere penitence; and how much Miss Howe's writing to them, in the terms she wrote in, disturbed you —but, as you have taken the matter into your own hands, and forbid me, in your last, to act in this nice affair unknown to you, I am glad the letter was *not required of me*—and indeed it may be better that the matter lie wholly between you and them; since my affection for you is thought to proceed from partiality.

They would choose, no doubt, that you should owe to *themselves,* and not to my humble mediation, the favour for which you so earnestly sue, and of which I would not have you despair: for I will venture to assure you that your mother is ready to take the first opportunity to show her maternal tenderness: and this I gather from several hints I am not at liberty to explain myself upon.

I long to be with you, now I am better, and now my son is in a fine way of recovery. But is it not hard to have it signified to me, that at present it will not be taken well if I go?—I suppose, while the reconciliation, which I hope will take place, is negotiating by means of the correspondence so newly opened between you and your sister. But if you would have me come, I will rely on my good intentions, and risk every one's displeasure.

Mr. Brand has business in town; to solicit for a benefice which it is expected the incumbent will be obliged to quit for a better preferment: and when there, he is to inquire privately after your way of life, and of your health.

He is a very officious young man; and, but that your Uncle Harlowe (who has chosen him for this errand) regards him as an oracle, your mother had rather anybody else had been sent.

He is one of those puzzling, over-doing gentlemen who think they see farther into matters than anybody else, and are fond of discovering mysteries where there are none, in order to be thought shrewd men.

I can't say I like him, either in the pulpit, or out of it: I who had a father one of the soundest divines and finest scholars in the kingdom; who never made an ostentation of what he knew; but loved and venerated the Gospel he taught, preferring it to all other learning; to be obliged to hear a young man depart from his text as soon as he has named it (so contrary, too, to the example set him by his learned and worthy principal,[1] when his health permits him to preach); and throwing about, to a Christian and country audience, scraps of Latin and Greek from the pagan classics; and not always brought in with great propriety neither (if I am to judge by the only way given me to judge of them, by the English he puts them into); is an indication of something wrong, either in his head, or his heart, or both; for, otherwise, his education at the university must have taught him better. You know, my dear Miss Clary, the honour I have for the cloth: it is owing to *that* that I say what I do.

I know not the day he is to set out; and as his inquiries are to be private, be pleased to take no notice of this intelligence. I have no doubt that your life and conversation are such as may defy the scrutinies of the most officious inquirer.

I am just now told that you have written a second letter to your sister: but am afraid they will wait for Mr. Brand's report before further favour will be obtained from them; for they will not yet believe you are so ill as I fear you are.

But you would soon find that you have an indulgent mother, were she at liberty to act according to her own inclination. And this gives me great hopes that all will end well at last: for I verily think you are in the right way to a reconciliation. God give a blessing to it, and restore your health, and you to all your friends, prays

Your ever affectionate
JUDITH NORTON.

---

[1] Dr. Lewen.

Your good mother has privately sent me five guineas: she is pleased to say, to help us in the illness we have been afflicted with; but, more likely, that I might send them to you as from myself. I hope, therefore, I may send them up, with ten more I have still left.

I will send you word of Mr. Morden's arrival the moment I know it.

If agreeable, I should be glad to know all that passes between your relations and you.

Letter XXI—Miss Clarissa Harlowe to Mrs. Norton

Wednesday, Aug. 2.

You give me, my dear Mrs. Norton, great pleasure in hearing of yours and your son's recovery. May you continue, for many, many years, a blessing to each other!

You tell me that you did actually write to my mother, *offering* to enclose to her mine of the 24th past: and you say it was not *required* of you. That is to say, although you cover it over as gently as you could, that your offer was rejected; which makes it evident that no plea will be heard for me. Yet you bid me hope that the grace I sued for would, *in time*, be granted.

The grace I then sued for was indeed granted: but you are afraid, you say, that they will wait for Mr. Brand's report before favour will be obtained in return to the second letter which I wrote to my sister: and you add that I have an indulgent mother, were she at liberty to act according to her own inclination; and that all will end well at last.

But what, my dear Mrs. Norton, what is the grace I sue for in my second letter? It is not that they will receive me into favour—if they think it is, they are mistaken. I do not, I cannot expect that: nor, as I have often said, should I, if they *would* receive me, bear to live in the eye of those dear friends whom I have so grievously offended. 'Tis only, simply, a blessing I ask: a blessing to *die* with; not to *live* with. Do they know that? And do they know that their unkindness will perhaps shorten my date? So that their favour, if ever they intend to grant it, may come too late?

Once more, I desire you not to think of coming to me. I have no uneasiness now, but what proceeds from the apprehension of seeing a man I would not see for the world, if I could help it; and from the severity of my nearest and dearest relations: a severity *entirely their own*, I doubt; for you tell me that my *brother is at Edinburgh*! You would therefore heighten their severity, and make yourself enemies besides, if you were to come to me—don't you see that you would?

Mr. Brand may come, if he will. He is a clergyman, and *must mean well*; or I must think so, let him say of me what he will. All my fear is, that, as he knows I am in disgrace with a family whose esteem he is desirous to cultivate; and as he has obligations to my Uncle Harlowe and to my father; he will be but a languid acquitter—not that I am afraid of what he, or anybody in the world, can hear as to my conduct. You may, my reverend and dear friend, indeed you may rest satisfied that that is such as may warrant me to challenge the inquiries of the most officious.

I will send you copies of what passes, as you desire, when I have an answer to my second letter. I now begin to wish that I had taken the heart to write to my father himself; or to my mother, at least; instead of to my sister; and yet I doubt my poor mother can do nothing for me of *herself*. A strong confederacy, my dear Mrs. Norton (a strong confederacy indeed!), against a poor girl, their daughter, sister, niece!—My brother, perhaps, got it renewed before he left them. He needed not—his work is done; and more than done.

Don't afflict yourself about money matters on my account. I have no occasion for money. I am glad my mother was so considerate to you. I was in pain for you on the same subject. But Heaven will not permit so good a woman to want the humble blessings she was always satisfied with. I wish every individual of our family were but as rich as you!—O my mamma Norton, you are rich! You are rich indeed! The true riches are such content as you are blessed with. And I hope in God that I am in the way to be rich too.

Adieu, my ever indulgent friend. You say all will be at last happy—and I *know* it will—I confide that it will, with as much security, as you may, that I will be to my last hour

Your ever grateful and affectionate
CL. HARLOWE.

Letter XXII—Mr. Lovelace to John Belford, Esq.
Tuesday, Aug. 1.

I AM most confoundedly chagrined and disappointed: for here, on Saturday, arrived a messenger from Miss Howe with a letter to my cousins[1]; which I knew nothing of till yesterday;

[1] See Letter xii.

when Lady Sarah and Lady Betty were procured to be here, to sit in judgment upon it with the old peer and my two kins-women. And never was bear so miserably baited as thy poor friend!—And for what?—Why, for the cruelty of Miss Harlowe: for have I committed any *new* offence? And would I not have succeeded in her favour upon her own terms, if I could? And is it fair to punish me for what is my misfortune, and not my fault? Such *event-judging* fools as I have for my relations! I am ashamed of them all.

In that of Miss Howe was enclosed one to *her* from Miss Harlowe,[1] to be transmitted to my cousins, containing a final rejection of me; and that in very vehement and positive terms; yet she pretends that in this rejection she is governed more by *principle* than *passion* [damned lie, as ever was told!]. And, as a proof that she is, says that she *can* forgive me, and *does*, on this one condition, That I will never molest her more—the whole letter so written as to make *herself* more admired, *me* more detested.

What we have been told of the agitations and workings, and sighings and sobbings, of the French prophets among us formerly, was nothing at all to the scene exhibited by these maudlin souls, at the reading of these letters; and of some affecting passages extracted from another of my fair implacable's to Miss Howe. Such lamentations for the loss of so charming a relation! Such applaudings of her virtue, of her exaltedness of soul and senti-ment! Such menaces of disinherisons! I, not needing *their* reproaches to be stung to the heart with my own reflections, and with the rage of disappointment; and as sincerely as any of them admiring her—"What the devil, cried I, is all this for? Is it not enough to be despised and rejected? Can I help her implacable spirit? Would I not repair the evils I have made her suffer?" Then was I ready to curse them all, herself and Miss Howe for company: and heartily I swore that she should yet be mine.

I now swear it over again to thee. "Were her death to follow in a week after the knot is tied, by the Lord of Heaven, it *shall* be tied, and she shall die a Lovelace." Tell her so, if thou wilt: but at the same time, tell her that I have no *view of her fortune*; and that I will solemnly resign that, and all pretensions to it, in whose favour she pleases, if she resign life issueless. I am not so low-minded a wretch as to be *guilty* of any sordid views to her fortune. Let her judge for herself, then, whether it be not

[1] See Letter viii.

for her honour rather to leave this world a Lovelace than a Harlowe.

But do not think I will entirely rest a cause so near my heart, upon an advocate who so much more admires his client's adversary than his client. I will go to town in a few days, in order to throw myself at her feet: and I will carry with me, or have at hand, a *resolute, well-prepared* parson; and the ceremony shall be performed, let what will be the consequence.

But if she will permit me to attend her for this purpose at either of the churches mentioned in the licence (which she has by her, and, thank Heaven! has not returned me with my letters), then will I not disturb her; but meet her at the altar in either church, and will engage to bring my two cousins to attend her, and even Lady Sarah and Lady Betty; and my Lord M. in person shall give her to me.

Or, if it will be still more agreeable to her, I will undertake that either Lady Sarah or Lady Betty, or both, shall go to town, and attend her down; and the marriage shall be celebrated in their presence, and in that of Lord M., either here or elsewhere, at her own choice.

Do not play me booty, Belford; but sincerely and warmly use all the eloquence thou art master of, to prevail upon her to choose one of these three methods. One of them she *must* choose—by my soul, she must.

Here is Charlotte tapping at my closet door for admittance. What a devil wants Charlotte? I will bear no more reproaches! —Come in, girl!

. . . . . .

My Cousin Charlotte, finding me writing on with too much earnestness to have any regard for politeness to her, and guessing at my subject, besought me to let her see what I had written.

I obliged her. And she was so highly pleased on seeing me so much in earnest, that *she* offered, and I accepted her offer, to write a letter to Miss Harlowe; with permission to treat me in it as she thought fit.

I shall enclose a copy of her letter.

When she *had* written it, she brought it to me, with apologies for the freedom taken with me in it: but I excused it; and she was ready to give me a kiss for joy of my approbation: and I gave her two for writing it; telling her I had hopes of success from it; and that I thought she had luckily hit it off.

Every one approves of it as well as I; and is pleased with me for so patiently submitting to be abused, and undertaken for.

If it do not succeed, all the blame will be thrown upon the dear creature's perverseness: her charitable or forgiving disposition, about which she makes such a parade, will be justly questioned; and the pity of which she is now in full possession, will be transferred to me.

Putting, therefore, my whole confidence in this letter, I postpone all my other alternatives, as also my going to town, till my empress send an answer to my Cousin Montague.

But if she persist, and will not promise to take time to *consider* of the matter, thou mayest communicate to her what I had written, as above, before my cousin entered; and, if she be still perverse, assure her that I *must* and *will* see her—but this with all honour, all humility: and if I cannot move her in my favour, I will then go abroad, and perhaps never more return to England.

I am sorry thou art, at *this critical time*, so busily employed, as thou informest me thou art, in thy Watford affairs, and in preparing to do Belton justice. If thou wantest my assistance in the latter, command me. Though engrossed by this perverse beauty, and plagued as I am, I will obey thy first summons.

I have great dependence upon thy zeal and thy friendship: hasten back to her, therefore, and resume a task *so* interesting to me, that it is equally the subject of my dreams as of my waking hours.

Letter XXIII—*Miss Montague to Miss Clarissa Harlowe*

Tuesday, Aug. 1.

DEAREST MADAM,—All our family is deeply sensible of the injuries you have received at the hands of one of it, whom you only can render in any manner worthy of the relation he stands in to us all: and if, as an act of mercy and charity, the greatest your pious heart can show, you will be pleased to look over his past wickedness and ingratitude, and suffer yourself to be our kinswoman, you will make us the happiest family in the world: and I can engage that Lord M., and Lady Sarah Sadleir, and Lady Betty Lawrance, and my sister, who are all admirers of your virtues and of your nobleness of mind, will for ever love and reverence you, and do everything in all their powers to make you amends for what you have suffered from Mr. Lovelace. This, madam, we should not, however, dare to petition for, were we not assured that Mr. Lovelace is most sincerely sorry for his past vileness to you; and that he will, on his knees, beg your pardon, and vow eternal love and honour to you.

Wherefore, *my dearest cousin* [how you will charm us all, if this agreeable style may be permitted!], for *all* our sakes, for his *soul's* sake [you must, I am sure, be so good a lady as to wish to save a soul!], and allow me to say, for *your own fame's* sake, condescend to our joint request: and if, by way of encouragement, you will but say you will be glad to see, and to be as much known personally as you are by fame to Charlotte Montague, I will, in two days' time from the receipt of your permission, wait upon you, *with* or *without* my sister, and receive your further commands.

Let me, *our dearest cousin* [we cannot deny ourselves the pleasure of calling you so; let me] entreat you to give me your permission for my journey to London; and put it in the power of Lord M., and of the ladies of the family, to make you what reparation they *can* make you, for the injuries which a person of the greatest merit in the world has received from one of the most audacious men in it; and you will infinitely oblige us all; and particularly her who repeatedly presumes to style herself

Your affectionate cousin and obliged servant,

CHARLOTTE MONTAGUE.

Letter XXIV—Mr. Belford to Robert Lovelace, Esq.

Thursday Morning, Aug. 3, Six o'clock.

I HAVE been so much employed in my own and Belton's affairs, that I could not come to town till last night; having contented myself with sending to Mrs. Lovick, to know from time to time the state of the lady's health; of which I received but very indifferent accounts, owing, in a great measure, to letters or advices brought her from her implacable family.

I have now completed my own affairs; and next week shall go to Epsom, to endeavour to put Belton's sister into possession of his own house for him: after which I shall devote myself wholly to your service, and to that of the lady.

I was admitted to her presence last night; and found her visibly altered for the worse. When I went home, I had your letter of Tuesday last put into my hands. Let me tell thee, Lovelace, that I insist upon the performance of thy engagement to me that thou wilt not personally molest her.

Mr. Belford dates again on Thursday morning ten o'clock; and gives an account of a conversation which he had just held with the lady upon the subject of Miss Montague's letter to her, preceding, and upon Mr. Lovelace's alternatives, as mentioned

*in Letter No. xxii which Mr. Belford supported with the
utmost earnestness. But, as the result of this conversation
will be found in the subsequent letters, Mr. Belford's pleas and
arguments in favour of his friend, and the lady's answers, are
omitted.*

Letter XXV—Miss Clarissa Harlowe to Miss Montague

Thursday, Aug. 3.

DEAR MADAM,—I am infinitely obliged to you for your kind and
condescending letter. A letter, however, which heightens my
regrets, as it gives me a new instance of what a happy creature
I might have been in an alliance so much approved of by such
worthy ladies; and which, on their accounts, and on that of
Lord M., would have been so reputable to myself, and was once
so desirable.

But indeed, indeed, madam, my heart sincerely repulses the
man, who, descended from such a family, could be guilty, *first*, of
such premeditated violence as he has been guilty of; and, as *he*
knows, *further* intended me, on the night previous to the day he
set out for Berkshire; and *next*, pretending to spirit, could be so
mean as to wish to lift into that family a person he was capable
of abasing into a companionship with the most abandoned of
her sex.

Allow me then, dear madam, to declare with fervour that I
think I never could deserve to be ranked with the ladies of a
family so splendid and so noble, if, by vowing love and honour
at the altar to such a violator, I could *sanctify*, as I may say, his
unprecedented and elaborate wickedness.

Permit me, however, to make one request to my good Lord M.,
and to Lady Betty and Lady Sarah, and to your kind self and
your sister. It is, that you will all be pleased to join your
authority and interests to prevail upon Mr. Lovelace not to
molest me further.

Be pleased to tell him, that if I am designed for *life*, it will be
very cruel in him to attempt to hunt me out of it; for I am determined never to see him more, if I can help it. The more
cruel, because he knows that I have nobody to defend me from
him: nor do I wish to engage anybody to *his* hurt, or to their own.

If I am, on the other hand, destined for *death*, it will be no less
cruel, if he will not permit me to die in peace—since a peaceable
and happy end I wish him. Indeed I do.

Every worldly good attend you, dear madam, and every

branch of the honourable family, is the wish of one whose misfortune it is, that she is obliged to disclaim any other title than that of, dear madam,

Your and their obliged and faithful servant,

CLARISSA HARLOWE.

Letter XXVI—Mr. Belford to Robert Lovelace, Esq.

Thursday Afternoon, Aug. 3.

I AM just now agreeably surprised by the following letter, delivered into my hands by a messenger from the lady. The letter she mentions, as enclosed,[1] I have returned, without taking a copy of it. The contents of it will soon be communicated to you, I presume, by other hands. They are an absolute rejection of thee—*Poor Lovelace*!

To John Belford, Esq.

Aug. 3.

SIR,—You have frequently offered to oblige me in anything that shall be within your power: and I have such an opinion of you, as to be willing to hope that at the times you made these offers you meant more than mere compliment.

I have, therefore, two requests to make to you: the first I will now mention; the other, if this shall be complied with, otherwise not.

It behoves me to leave behind me such an account as may clear up my conduct to several of my friends who will not at present concern themselves about me: and Miss Howe, and her mother, are very solicitous that I will do so.

I am apprehensive that I shall not have time to do this; and you will not wonder that I have less and less inclination to set about such a painful task; especially as I find myself unable to look back with patience on what I have suffered; and shall be too much discomposed by the retrospection, were I obliged to make it, to proceed with the requisite temper in a task of *still greater* importance which I have before me.

It is very evident to me that your wicked friend has given you, from time to time, a circumstantial account of all his behaviour *to* me, and devices *against* me; and you have more than once assured me that he has done my character all the justice I could wish for, both by writing and speech.

Now, sir, if I may have a fair, a faithful specimen from his letters or accounts to you, written upon some of the most

---

[1] See Miss Montague's letter No. xxxiii.

interesting occasions, I shall be able to judge whether there will or will not be a necessity for me, for my honour's sake, to enter upon the solicited task.

You may be assured, from my *enclosed* answer to the letter which Miss Montague has honoured me with (and which you 'll be pleased to return me as soon as read), that it is impossible for me ever to think of your friend in the way I am importuned to think of him: he cannot, therefore, receive any detriment from the requested specimen: and I give you my honour that no use shall be made of it to his prejudice, in law or otherwise. And that it may *not*, after I am no more, I assure you that it is a *main part of my view* that the passages you shall oblige me with shall be always in your own power, and not in that of any other person.

If, sir, you think fit to comply with my request, the passages I would wish to be transcribed (making neither better nor worse of the matter) are those which he has written to you on or about the 7th and 8th of June, when I was alarmed by the wicked pretence of a fire; and what he has written from Sunday, June 11, to the 19th. And in doing this you will much oblige

Your humble servant,
CL. HARLOWE.

Now, Lovelace, since there are no hopes for thee of her returning favour—since some praise may lie for thy ingenuousness, having never offered [*as more diminutive-minded libertines would have done*] to palliate thy crimes, by aspersing the lady, or her sex—since she may be made easier by it—since thou must fare better from thine own pen than from hers—and finally, since thy actions have manifested that thy letters are not the most guilty part of what she *knows* of thee, I see not why I may not oblige her, upon her honour, and under the restrictions, and for the reasons she has given; and this without breach of the confidence due to friendly communications; especially, as I might have added, *since thou gloriest in thy pen, and in thy wickedness, and canst not be ashamed.*

But, be this as it may, she *will* be obliged before thy remonstrances or clamours against it can come; so, prithee now, make the best of it, and rave not; except for the sake of a pretence against me, and to exercise thy talent of execration! And, if thou likest to do so for these reasons, rave and welcome.

I long to know what the second request is: but this I know, that if it be anything less than cutting *thy* throat, or endangering *my* own neck, I will certainly comply; and be proud of having it in my power to oblige her.

And now I am actually going to be busy in the extracts.

Letter XXVII—Mr. Belford to Miss Clarissa Harlowe

Aug. 3, 4.

MADAM,—You have engaged me to communicate to you, upon honour (making neither better nor worse of the matter), what Mr. Lovelace has written to me in relation to yourself, in the period preceding your going to Hampstead, and in that between the 11th and 19th of June: and you assure me you have no view in this request but to see if it be necessary for you, from the account he gives, to touch the painful subjects yourself, for the sake of your own character.

Your commands, madam, are of a very delicate nature, as they may seem to affect the *secrets of private friendship*: but as I know you are not capable of a view, the motives to which you will not own; and as I think the communication may do some credit to my unhappy friend's character, as an *ingenuous* man; though his actions by the most excellent woman in the world have lost him all title to that of an *honourable* one; I obey you with the greater cheerfulness.

He then proceeds with his extracts, and concludes them with an address to her in his friend's behalf, in the following words :

"And now, madam, I have fulfilled your commands; and, I hope, have not disserved my friend with you; since you will hereby see the justice he does to your virtue in every line he writes. He does the same in all his letters, though to his own condemnation: and give me leave to add, that if this ever-amiable sufferer can think it in any manner consistent with her honour to receive his vows at the altar, on his truly penitent turn of mind, I have not the least doubt but that he will make her the best and tenderest of husbands. What obligation will not the admirable lady hereby lay upon all *his* noble family, who so greatly admire her! and, I will presume to say, upon *her own*, when the unhappy family aversion (which certainly has been carried to an unreasonable height against him) shall be got over, and a general reconciliation takes place! For who is it that would not give these two admirable persons to each other, were not his morals an objection?"

However this be, I would humbly refer to you, madam, whether, as you will be mistress of very delicate particulars from *me* his friend, you should not in honour think yourself concerned to pass them by as if you had never seen them; and not to take any advantage of the communication, not even in argument, as some perhaps might lie, with respect to the *pre-meditated* design he seems to have had, not against you, *as* you; but as against the *sex*; over whom (I am sorry I can bear witness myself) it is the villainous aim of all libertines to triumph: and I would not, if any misunderstanding should arise between him and me, give him room to reproach me, that his losing of you, and (through his usage of you) of his own friends, were owing to what perhaps he would call breach of trust, were he to judge rather by the event than by my intention.

I am, madam, with the most profound veneration,
Your most faithful humble servant,
J. BELFORD.

Letter XXVIII—Miss Clarissa Harlowe to John Belford, Esq.

Friday, Aug. 4.

SIR,—I hold myself extremely obliged to you for your communications. I will make no use of them that you shall have reason to reproach either yourself or me with. I wanted no new lights to make the unhappy man's premeditated baseness to me unquestionable, as my answer to Miss Montague's letter might convince you.[1]

I must own in his favour that he has observed some decency in his accounts to you of the most indecent and shocking actions. And if all his strangely communicative narrations are equally decent, nothing will be rendered criminally odious by them, but the vile heart that could meditate such contrivances as were much stronger evidences of his inhumanity than of his wit: since men of very contemptible parts and understanding may succeed in the vilest attempts, if they can once bring themselves to trample on the sanctions which bind man to man; and sooner upon an innocent person than upon any other; because such a one is apt to judge of the integrity of others' hearts by its own.

I find I have had great reason to think myself obliged to your intention in the whole progress of my sufferings. It is, however, impossible, sir, to miss the natural inference on this occasion, that lies against his predetermined baseness. But I say the less, because you shall not think I borrow, from what you have communicated, aggravations that are not needed.

[1] See Letter xxv.

And now, sir, that I may spare you the trouble of offering any future arguments in his favour, let me tell you that I have weighed everything throughly — all that human vanity could suggest—all that a desirable reconciliation with my friends, and the kind respects of his own, could bid me hope for—the enjoyment of Miss Howe's friendship, the dearest consideration to me now of all worldly ones—all these I have weighed: and the result is, and *was* before you favoured me with these communications, that I have more satisfaction in the hope that, in one month, there will be an end of all with me, than in the most agreeable things that could happen from an alliance with Mr. Lovelace, although I were to be assured he would make the best and tenderest of husbands. But as to the rest; if, satisfied with the evils he has brought upon me, he will forbear all further persecutions of me, I will, to my last hour, wish him good: although *he hath overwhelmed the fatherless, and digged a pit for his friend*: fatherless may *she* well be called, and motherless too, who has been denied all paternal protection and motherly forgiveness.

.   .   .   .

And now, sir, acknowledging gratefully your favour in the extracts, I come to the second request I had to make you; which requires a great deal of courage to mention: and which courage nothing but a great deal of distress, and a very destitute condition, can give. But, if improper, I can but be denied; and dare to say I shall be at least excused. Thus, then, I preface it:

"You see, sir, that I am thrown absolutely into the hands of strangers, who, although as kind and compassionate as strangers can be wished to be, are nevertheless persons from whom I cannot expect anything more than pity and good wishes; nor can my memory receive from them any more protection than my person, if either should need it.

"If then I request it of the *only* person possessed of materials that will enable him to do my character justice;

"And who has courage, independence, and ability to oblige me;

"To be the protector of my memory, as I may say;

"And to be my *executor*; and to see some of my dying requests performed;

"And if I leave it to him to do the whole in his own way, manner, and time; consulting, however, in requisite cases, my dear Miss Howe;

"I presume to hope that this my second request may be granted."

And if it may, these satisfactions will accrue to me from the favour done me, and the office undertaken:

"It will be an honour to my memory, with all those who shall know, that I was so well satisfied of my innocence that, having not time to write my own story, I could entrust it to the relation which the destroyer of my fame and fortunes has given of it.

"I shall not be apprehensive of involving any one in troubles or hazards by this task, either with my own relations or with your friend; having dispositions to make which perhaps my own friends will not be so well pleased with as it were to be *wished* they would be"; as I intend not unreasonable ones: but you know, sir, where *self* is judge, matters, even with *good people*, will not always be rightly judged of.

"I shall also be freed from the pain of recollecting things that my soul is vexed at; and this at a time when its tumults should be allayed, in order to make way for the most important preparation.

"And who knows, but that Mr. Belford, who already, from a principle of humanity, is touched at my misfortunes, when he comes to revolve the whole story, placed before him in one strong light, and when he shall have the catastrophe likewise before him; and shall become in a manner interested in it: who knows but that, *from a still higher principle*, he may so regulate his future actions as to find his own reward in the everlasting welfare which is wished him by his

Obliged servant,
CLARISSA HARLOWE?

Letter XXIX—Mr. Belford to Miss Clarissa Harlowe

Friday, Aug. 4.

MADAM,—I am so sensible of the honour done me in yours of this day, that I would not delay for one moment the answering of it. I hope you will live to see many happy years; and to be your own executrix in those points which your heart is most set upon. But, in case of survivorship, I most cheerfully accept of the sacred office you are pleased to offer me; and you may absolutely rely upon my fidelity, and, if possible, upon the literal perform-ance of every article you shall enjoin me.

The effect of the kind wish you conclude with has been my concern ever since I have been admitted to the honour of your conversation. It shall be my whole endeavour that it be not vain. The happiness of approaching you, which this trust, as I presume, will give me frequent opportunities of doing, must necessarily promote the desirable end; since it will be impossible to be a witness of your piety, equanimity, and other virtues, and not aspire to emulate you. All I beg is that you will not suffer any future candidate or event to displace me; unless some new instances of unworthiness appear either in the morals or behaviour of,

Madam,
Your most obliged and faithful servant,
J. BELFORD.

Letter XXX—*Mr. Belford to Robert Lovelace, Esq.*

Friday Night, Aug. 4.

I HAVE actually delivered to the lady the extracts she requested me to give her from your letters. I do assure you that I have made the very best of the matter for you, *not* that conscience, but that friendship, could oblige me to make. I have changed or omitted some free words. The warm description of her person in the *fire scene*, as I may call it, I have omitted. I have told her that I have done justice to you, in the justice you have done to her unexampled virtue. But take the very words which I wrote to her immediately following the extracts:

"And now, madam,"—*see the paragraph marked with inverted commas* ["thus], p. 76.

The lady is extremely uneasy at the thoughts of your attempting to visit her. For Heaven's sake (your word being given), and for pity's sake (for she is really in a very weak and languishing way), let me beg of you not to think of it.

Yesterday afternoon she received a cruel letter (as Mrs. Lovick supposes it to be, by the effect it had upon her) from her sister, in answer to one written last Saturday, entreating a blessing and forgiveness from her parents.

She acknowledges that if the same decency and justice are observed in all your letters, as in the extracts I have obliged her with (as I have assured her they are), she shall think herself freed from the necessity of writing her own story: and this is an advantage to thee which thou oughtest to thank me for.

But what thinkest thou is the second request she had to make to me? No other than that I would be her *executor*! Her motives will appear before thee in proper time; and then, I dare to answer, will be satisfactory.

You cannot imagine how proud I am of this trust. I am afraid I shall too soon come into the execution of it. As she is always writing, what a melancholy pleasure will the perusal and disposition of her papers afford me! Such a sweetness of temper, so much patience and resignation, as she seems to be mistress of; yet writing of and in the midst of *present* distresses! How *much more* lively and affecting, for that reason, must her style be, her mind tortured by the pangs of uncertainty (the events then hidden in the womb of fate), *than* the dry narrative, unanimated style of a person relating difficulties and dangers surmounted; the relater perfectly at ease; and if himself unmoved by his own story, not likely greatly to affect the reader.

Saturday Morning, Aug. 5.

I am just returned from visiting the lady, and thanking her in person for the honour she has done me; and assuring her, if called to the sacred trust, of the utmost fidelity and exactness.

I found her very ill. I took notice of it. She said she had received a second hard-hearted letter from her sister; and she had been writing a letter (and that on her knees) directly to her mother; which, *before*, she had not had the courage to do. It was for a last blessing and forgiveness. No wonder, she said, that I saw her affected. Now that I had accepted of the last charitable office for her (for which, as well as for complying with her other request, she thanked me), I should one day have all these letters before me: and could she have *a kind one* in return to that she had been now writing, to *counterbalance* the unkind one she had from her sister, she might be induced to show me both together—otherwise, for her sister's sake, it were no matter how few saw the poor Bella's letter.

I knew she would be displeased if I had censured the cruelty of her relations: I therefore only said that surely she must have enemies who hoped to find their account in keeping up the resentments of her friends against her.

It may be so, Mr. Belford, said she: the unhappy never want enemies. One fault, wilfully committed, authorizes the imputation of many more. Where the ear is opened to accusations, accusers will not be wanting; and every one will officiously come with stories against a disgraced child, where nothing dare be said in her favour. I should have been wise in time, and not have needed to be convinced by my own misfortunes of the truth of what common experience daily demonstrates. Mr. Lovelace's baseness, my father's inflexibility, my sister's reproaches, are the natural consequences of my own rashness; so I must make the best of my hard lot. Only, as these consequences follow one another so closely, while they are *new*, how can I help being anew affected?

I asked if a letter written by myself, by her doctor or apothecary, to any of her friends, representing her low state of health and great humility, would be acceptable? Or if a journey to any of them would be of service, I would gladly undertake it in person, and strictly conform to her orders, to whomsoever she would direct me to apply.

She earnestly desired that nothing of this sort might be attempted, especially without her knowledge and consent. Miss Howe, she said, had done harm by her kindly intended zeal; and if there were room to expect favour by mediation, she had ready at hand a kind friend, Mrs. Norton, who for piety and prudence had few equals; and who would let slip no opportunity to endeavour to do her service.

I let her know that I was going out of town till Monday: she wished me pleasure; and said she should be glad to see me on my return.

Adieu!

Letter XXXI—*Miss Arab. Harlowe to Miss Cl. Harlowe*

[In answer to hers of July 29. See No. XIX]

Thursday Morn., Aug. 3.

SISTER CLARY,—I wish you would not trouble me with any more of your letters. You had always a knack at writing; and depended upon making every one do what you would when you wrote. But your wit and your folly have undone you. And now, as all naughty creatures do, when they can't help themselves, you come begging and praying, and make others as uneasy as yourself.

When I wrote last to you, I *expected* that I should not be at rest.

And so you 'd creep on, by little and little, till you 'll want to be received again.

But you only hope for *forgiveness* and a *blessing*, you say. A blessing for what, Sister Clary? Think for what! However, I read your letter to my father and mother.

I won't tell you what my father said—one who has the true sense you boast to have of your misdeeds may guess, without my telling you, what a justly incensed father would say on such an occasion.

My poor mother—O wretch! what has not your ungrateful folly cost my poor mother! Had you been less a darling, you would not, perhaps, have been so graceless: but I never in my life saw a cockered favourite come to good.

My heart is full, and I can't help writing my mind; for your crimes have disgraced us all; and I am afraid and ashamed to go to any public or private assembly or diversion: and why?—I *need* not say why, when your actions are the subjects either of the open talk or of the affronting whispers of both sexes at all such places.

Upon the whole, I am sorry I have no more comfort to send you: but I find nobody willing to forgive you.

I don't know what *time* may do for you; and when it is seen that your penitence is not owing more to disappointment than to true conviction: for it is too probable, Miss Clary, that, had you gone on as swimmingly as you expected, and had not your feather-headed villain abandoned you, we should have heard nothing of these moving supplications; nor of anything but defiances from *him*, and a guilt gloried in from *you*. And this is every one's opinion, as well as that of

Your grieved sister,
ARABELLA HARLOWE.

I send this by a particular hand, who undertakes to give it you or leave it for you by to-morrow night.

Letter XXXII—Miss Clarissa Harlowe to her Mother

Sat. Aug. 5.

HONOURED MADAM,—No self-convicted criminal ever approached her angry and just judge with greater awe, nor with a truer contrition, than I do you by these lines.

Indeed I must say, that if the matter of my humble prayer had not respected my future welfare, I had not dared to take this liberty. But my heart is set upon it, as upon a thing next to God Almighty's forgiveness necessary for me.

Had my happy sister known my distresses, she would not have wrung my heart, as she has done, by a severity which I must needs think unkind and unsisterly.

But complaint of any unkindness from her belongs not to me: yet, as she is pleased to write that it must be seen that my penitence is less owing to disappointment than to true conviction, permit me, madam, to insist upon it, that, if such a plea can be allowed me, I am actually *entitled* to the blessing I sue for; since my humble prayer is founded upon a true and unfeigned repentance: and this you will the readier believe, if the creature who never, to the best of her remembrance, told her mamma a wilful falsehood, may be credited, when she declares, as she does, in the most solemn manner, that she met the seducer with a determination not to go off with him: that the rash step was owing more to compulsion than to infatuation: and that her heart was so little in it, that she repented and grieved from the moment she found herself in his power; and for every moment after, for several weeks *before* she had any cause from him to apprehend the usage she met with.

Wherefore, on my knees, my ever-honoured mamma (for on my knees I write this letter), I do most humbly beg your blessing; say but, in so many words (I ask you not, madam, to call me your daughter): *Lost, unhappy wretch, I forgive you! and may God bless you!* This is all! Let me, on a blessed scrap of paper, but see one sentence to this effect under your dear hand, that I may hold it to my heart in my most trying struggles, and I shall think it a passport to Heaven. And, if I do not too much presume, and it were WE instead of I, and both your honoured names subjoined to it, I should then have nothing more to wish. Then would I say: "Great and merciful God! Thou seest here in this paper Thy poor unworthy creature absolved by her justly offended parents: O join, for my Redeemer's sake, Thy all-gracious *fiat,* and receive a repentant sinner to the arms of Thy mercy!"

I can conjure you, madam, by no subject of motherly tenderness, that will not, in the opinion of my severe censurers (before whom this humble address must appear), add to my reproach: let me therefore, for God's sake, prevail upon you to pronounce me blessed and forgiven, since you will thereby sprinkle comfort through the last hours of

Your

CLARISSA HARLOWE.

Letter XXXIII—Miss Montague to Miss Clarissa Harlowe
[In answer to hers of Aug. 3.   See No. XXV]

Monday, *Aug. 7.*

DEAR MADAM,—We were all of opinion *before* your letter came, that Mr. Lovelace was utterly unworthy of you, and deserved condign punishment, rather than to be blessed with such a wife: and hoped far *more* from your kind consideration for *us* than any we supposed you could have for so base an *injurer.*   For we were all determined to love you, and admire you, let *his* behaviour to you be what it would.

But, after your letter, what can be said?

I am, however, commanded to write in all the subscribing names, to let you know how greatly your sufferings have affected us: to tell you that my Lord M. has forbid him ever more to enter the doors of the apartments where he shall be: and as you labour under the unhappy effects of your friends' displeasure, which may subject you to inconveniences, his lordship, and Lady Sarah, and Lady Betty, beg of you to accept, for your life, or, at least, till you are admitted to enjoy your own estate, of one hundred guineas per quarter, which will be regularly brought you by an especial hand, and of the enclosed bank bill for a beginning.   And do not, dearest madam, we all beseech you, do not think you are beholden (for this token of Lord M.'s and Lady Sarah's and Lady Betty's love to you) to the *friends of this vile man*; for he has not one friend left among us.

We each of us desire to be favoured with a place in your esteem; and to be considered upon the same foot of relationship, as if what once was so much our pleasure to hope *would* be, *had* been.   And it shall be our united prayer that you may recover health and spirits, and live to see many happy years: and, since this wretch can no more be pleaded for, that, when he is gone abroad, as he now is preparing to do, we may be permitted the honour of a personal acquaintance with a lady who has no equal. These are the earnest requests, dearest young lady, of

Your affectionate friends,
and most faithful servants,
M.
SARAH SADLEIR.
ELIZ. LAWRANCE.
CHARL. MONTAGUE.
MARTH. MONTAGUE.

You will break the hearts of the three first-named more particularly, if you refuse them your acceptance. Dearest young lady, punish not *them* for *his* crimes. We send by a particular hand, which will bring us, we hope, your accepting favour.

Mr. Lovelace writes by the same hand; but he knows nothing of our letter, nor we of his: for we shun each other; and one part of the house holds *us*, another *him*, the remotest from each other.

Letter XXXIV—Mr. Lovelace to John Belford, Esq.

Sat. Aug. 5.

I AM so excessively disturbed at the contents of Miss Harlowe's answer to my Cousin Charlotte's letter of Tuesday last (which was given her by the same fellow that gave me yours), that I have hardly patience or consideration enough to weigh what you write.

She had need indeed to cry out for mercy herself from *her* friends, who knows not how to show any! She is a true daughter of the Harlowes—by my soul, Jack, she is a true daughter of the Harlowes! Yet has she so many excellences that I must love her; and, fool that I am, love her the more for her despising me.

Thou runnest on with thy cursed nonsensical *reformado*-rote of dying, dying, dying! and, having once got the word by the end, canst not help foisting it in at every period! The devil take me if I don't think thou wouldst give her poison with thy own hands, rather than she should recover and rob thee of the merit of being a conjurer!

But no more of thy cursed knell; thy changes upon death's candlestick turned bottom upwards: she 'll live to bury me; I see that: for, by my soul, I can neither eat, drink, nor sleep; nor, what is still worse, love any woman in the world but her. Nor care I to look upon a woman now: on the contrary, I turn my head from every one I meet; except by chance an eye, an air, a feature, strikes me resembling hers in some glancing-by face; and then I cannot forbear looking again; though the second look recovers me; for there can be nobody like her.

But surely, Belford, the devil 's in this woman! The more I think of her nonsense and obstinacy, the less patience I have with her. Is it possible she can do herself, her family, her friends, so much justice any *other* way as by marrying me? Were she sure she should live but a day, she ought to die a wife. If her *Christian revenge* will not let her wish to do so for her *own* sake, ought she not for the sake of her family, and of her sex, which she pretends sometimes to have so much concern for? And if no *sake* is dear enough to move her Harlowe-spirit in my favour, has she any title to the pity thou so pitifully art always bespeaking for her?

As to the difference which her letter has made between me and the stupid family here [and I must tell thee we are all broke in pieces], I value not that of a button. They are fools to anathematize and curse me, who can give them ten curses for one, were they to hold it for a day together.

I have one half of the house to myself; and that the best; for the great enjoy that least which costs them most: *grandeur* and *use* are two things: the common part is theirs; the state part is mine: and here I lord it, and *will* lord it as long as I please; while the two pursy sisters, the old gouty brother, and the two musty nieces, are stived up in the other half, and dare not stir for fear of meeting me: whom (that's the jest of it) they have forbidden coming into their apartments, as I have them into mine. And so I have them all prisoners, while I range about as I please. Pretty dogs and *doggesses*, to quarrel and bark at me, and yet, whenever I appear, afraid to pop out of their kennels; or if out before they see me, at the sight of me run growling in again, with their flapped ears, their sweeping dewlaps, and their quivering tails curling inwards.

And here, while I am thus worthily waging war with beetles, drones, wasps, and hornets, and am all on fire with the rage of slighted love, thou art regaling thyself with phlegm and rock-water, and art going on with thy reformation scheme, and thy exultations in my misfortunes!

The devil take thee for an insensible dough-baked varlet: I have no more patience with thee than with the lady; for thou knowest nothing either of love or friendship, but art as unworthy of the one as incapable of the other; else wouldst thou not rejoice, as thou dost under the *grimace of pity*, in my disappointments.

And thou art a pretty fellow, art thou not? to engage to transcribe for her some parts of my letters written to thee in confidence? Letters that thou shouldst sooner have parted with thy cursed tongue, than have owned thou ever hadst received such: yet these are now to be communicated to *her*! But I charge thee, and woe be to thee if it be too late! that thou do not oblige her with a line of mine.

If thou *hast* done it, the least vengeance I will take is to break through *my* honour given to thee not to visit her, as thou wilt have broken through *thine* to me in communicating letters written under the seal of friendship.

I am now convinced, too sadly for my hopes, by her letter to my Cousin Charlotte, that she is determined never to have me.

Unprecedented wickedness, she calls mine to her. But how does *she* know what the ardour of flaming love will stimulate men to do? How does *she* know the requisite distinctions of the words she uses in this case? To think the *worst,* and to be able to *make comparisons* in these *very* delicate situations, must she not be less delicate than I had imagined her to be? But she has heard that the devil is black; and having a mind to make one of me, brays together, in the mortar of her wild fancy, twenty chimney-sweepers, in order to make one sootier than ordinary rise out of the dirty mass.

But what a whirlwind does she raise in my soul by her proud contempts of me! Never, never was mortal man's pride so mortified! How does she sink me, even in my own eyes! "*Her heart* sincerely repulses me, she says, for my MEANNESS." Yet she intends to reap the benefit of what she calls so! Curse upon her *haughtiness,* and her *meanness,* at the same time!— Her haughtiness to *me,* and her meanness to *her own relations*; more unworthy of kindred with her than I can be, or I am *mean* indeed.

Yet who but must admire, who but must adore her? O that cursed, cursed house! But for the women of that!—Then their damned potions! But for *those,* had her *unimpaired* intellects and the *majesty of her virtue* saved her, as once it did by her humble eloquence,[1] another time by her terrifying menaces against her own life.[2]

Yet in both these to find her power over me, and my love for her, and to hate, to despise, and to refuse me! She might have done this with some show of justice had the last intended violation been perpetrated:—But to go away conqueress and triumphant in every light! Well may she despise me for suffering her to do so.

She left me *low* and *mean* indeed!—and the impression holds with her. I could tear my flesh, that I gave her not cause— that I humbled her not *indeed*—or that I stayed not in town to attend her motions instead of Lord M.'s, till I could have exalted myself by giving to myself a wife superior to all trial, to all temptation.

[1] In the fire scene vol. ii, pp. 503–4.
[2] Vol. iii, pp. 288 et seq. in the penknife scene.

I will venture one more letter to her, however; and if that don't do, or procure me an answer, then will I endeavour to see her, let what *will* be the consequence. If she get out of my way, I will do some noble mischief to the vixen girl whom she most loves and then quit the kingdom for ever.

And now, Jack, since thy hand is in at communicating the contents of private letters, tell her this, if thou wilt. And add to it, that if SHE abandon me, GOD will: and what then will be the fate of

Her

LOVELACE!

Letter XXXV—Mr. Lovelace to John Belford, Esq.
[*In answer to his of Aug. 4. See No. XXX*]

Monday, Aug. 7.

AND so you have actually delivered to the fair implacable extracts of letters written in the confidence of friendship! Take care—take care, Belford—I do indeed love you better than I love any man in the world: but this is a very delicate point. The matter is grown very serious to me. My heart is bent upon having her. And have her I will, though I marry her in the agonies of death.

She is very earnest, you say, that I will not offer to molest her. *That*, let me tell her, will absolutely depend upon herself, and the answer she returns, whether by pen and ink, or the contemptuous one of silence, which she bestowed upon my last four to her: and I will write it in such humble, and in such reasonable terms, that, if she be not a true Harlowe, she *shall* forgive me. But as to the *executorship* which she is for conferring upon thee—thou shalt not be her *executor*: let me perish if thou shalt. Nor shall she die. Nobody shall be anything, nobody shall *dare* to be anything to her but I—thy happiness is already too great, to be admitted daily to her presence; to look upon her, to talk to her, to hear her talk, while I am forbid to come within view of her window. What a reprobation is this of the man who was once more dear to her than all the men in the world! And now to be able to look down upon me, while her exalted head is hid from me among the stars, sometimes with scorn, at other times with pity, I cannot bear it.

This I tell thee, that if I have not success in my effort by letter, I will overcome the creeping folly that has found its way to my heart, or I will tear it out in her presence, and throw it at hers, that she may see how much more tender than her own that organ is, which she, and you, and every one else, have taken the liberty to call callous.

Give notice to the people who live back and edge, and on either hand, of the cursed mother, to remove their best effects, if I am rejected: for the first vengeance I shall take will be to set fire to that den of serpents. Nor will there be any fear of taking them when they are in any act that has *the relish of salvation in it,* as Shakespeare says—so that my revenge, if they perish in the flames I shall light up, will be complete as to them.

Letter XXXVI—*Mr. Lovelace to Miss Clarissa Harlowe*

Monday, Aug. 7.

LITTLE as I have reason to expect either your patient ear, or forgiving heart, yet cannot I forbear to write to you once more (as a more pardonable intrusion, perhaps, than a visit would be), to beg of you to put it in my power to atone, as far as it is possible to atone, for the injuries I have done you.

Your angelic purity, and my awakened conscience, are standing records of your exalted merit and of my detestable baseness: but your forgiveness will lay me under an eternal obligation to you—forgive me, then, my dearest life, my earthly good, the visible anchor of my future hope! As you (who believe you have something to be forgiven for) hope for pardon yourself, forgive me, and consent to meet me, upon your own conditions, and in whose company you please, at the holy altar, and to give yourself a title to the most repentant and affectionate heart that ever beat in a human bosom.

But perhaps a time of probation may be required. It may be impossible for you, as well from *indisposition* as *doubt,* so soon to receive me to absolute favour as my heart wishes to be received. In this case I will submit to your pleasure; and there shall be no penance which you can impose that I will not cheerfully undergo, if you will be pleased to give me hope that, after an expiation, suppose of months, wherein the regularity of my future life and actions shall convince you of my reformation, you will at last be mine.

Let me beg the favour then of a few lines, encouraging me in this *conditional* hope, if it must not be a still *nearer* hope, and a more generous encouragement.

If you refuse me this, you will make me desperate. But even then I must, at all events, throw myself at your feet, that I may not charge myself with the omission of any earnest, any humble effort, to move you in my favour: for in YOU, madam, in YOUR *forgiveness*, are centred my hopes as to *both worlds*: since to be reprobated finally by *you* will leave me without expectation of mercy from *above*! For I am now awakened enough to think that to be forgiven by injured innocents is *necessary* to the Divine pardon; the Almighty putting into the power of such (as is reasonable to believe) the wretch who causelessly and capitally offends them. And *who* can be entitled to this power if YOU are not?

Your cause, madam, in a word, I look upon to be the *cause of virtue*, and, as such, the *cause of God*. And may I not expect that He will assert it in the perdition of a man, who has acted by a person of the most spotless purity as I have done, if *you*, by rejecting me, show that I have offended beyond the possibility of forgiveness?

I do most solemnly assure you that no temporal or worldly views induce me to this earnest address. I deserve not forgiveness from *you*. Nor do my Lord M. and his sisters from *me*. I despise them from my heart for presuming to imagine that I will be controlled by the prospect of any benefits in their power to confer. There is not a person breathing but yourself who shall prescribe to me. Your whole conduct, madam, has been so nobly principled, and your resentments are so admirably just, that you appear to me even in a divine light; and in an infinitely more amiable one at the same time, than you could have appeared in, had you not suffered the barbarous wrongs that now fill my mind with anguish and horror at my own recollected villainy to the most excellent of women.

I *repeat* that all I beg for the present is a few lines, to guide my doubtful steps; and (if possible for you so far to condescend) to encourage me to hope that, if I can justify my present vows by my future conduct, I may be permitted the honour to style myself

Eternally yours,

R. LOVELACE.

*Letter XXXVII—Miss Clarissa Harlowe to Lord M. and to
the Ladies of his House*

[*In reply to Miss Montague's of Aug.* 7.   *See No. XXXIII*]

Tuesday, Aug 8.

EXCUSE me, my good lord, and my ever-honoured ladies, from accepting of your noble quarterly bounty; and allow me to return, with all grateful acknowledgment and true humility, the enclosed earnest of your goodness to me. Indeed I have no need of the one, and cannot possibly want the other: but, nevertheless, have such a sense of your generous favour that, to my last hour, I shall have pleasure in contemplating upon it, and be proud of the place I hold in the esteem of such venerable personages, to whom I once had the ambition to hope to be related.

But give me leave to express my concern that you have banished your kinsman from your presence and favour: since now, perhaps, he will be under less restraint than ever; and since I in particular, who had hoped by your influences to remain unmolested for the remainder of my days, may be again subjected to his persecutions.

He has not, my good lord, and my dear ladies, offended against *you* as he has against *me*; and yet you could all very generously intercede for him with *me*: and shall I be *very* improper if I desire, for my own peace sake; for the sake of other poor creatures who may be still injured by him, if he be made quite desperate; and for the sake of all your worthy family; that you will extend to *him* that forgiveness which you hoped for from *me*? and this the rather, as I presume to think that his daring and impetuous spirit will not be subdued by violent methods; since I have no doubt that the gratifying of a present passion will be always more prevalent with him than any future prospects, however unwarrantable the one, or beneficial the other.

Your resentments on my account are extremely generous, as your goodness to me is truly noble: but I am not without hope that he will be properly affected by the evils he has made me suffer; and that, when I am laid low and forgotten, your whole honourable family will be enabled to rejoice in his reformation; and see many of those happy years together which, my good lord, and my dear ladies, you so kindly wish to

Your ever grateful and obliged

CLARISSA HARLOWE.

Letter XXXVIII—Mr. Belford to Robert Lovelace, Esq.

Thursday Night, Aug. 10.

YOU have been informed by Tourville how much Belton's illness and affairs have engaged *me*, as well as Mowbray and him, since my former. I called at Smith's on Monday, in my way to Epsom.

The lady was gone to chapel: but I had the satisfaction to hear she was not worse; and left my compliments, and an intimation that I should be out of town for three or four days.

I refer myself to Tourville, who will let you know the difficulty we had to drive out this *meek* mistress and *frugal* manager, with her cubs, and to give the poor fellow's sister possession for him of his own house; he skulking meanwhile at an inn at Croydon, too dispirited to appear in his own cause.

But I must observe that we were probably but just in time to save the shattered remains of his fortune from this rapacious woman and her accomplices: for, as he cannot live long, and she thinks so, we found she had certainly taken measures to set up a marriage, and keep possession of all for herself and her sons.

Tourville will tell you how I was forced to chastise the quondam hostler in her sight, before I could drive him out of the house. He had the insolence to lay hands on me: and I made him take but one step from the top to the bottom of a pair of stairs. I thought his neck and all his bones had been broken. And then, he being carried out neck-and-heels, Thomasine thought fit to walk out after him.

Charming consequences of *keeping*; the state we have been so fond of extolling! Whatever it may be thought of in strong health, *sickness* and *declining spirits* in the keeper will bring him to see the difference.

She should soon have him, she told a confidant, in the space of six foot by five; meaning his bed: and then she would let nobody come near him but whom she pleased. The hostler-fellow, I suppose, would then have been his physician; his will ready made for him; and widow's weeds probably ready provided; who knows but she to appear in them in his own sight? as once I knew an instance in a wicked wife, insulting a husband she hated, when she thought him past recovery: though it gave the man such spirits, and such a turn, that he got over it, and lived to see *her* in her coffin, dressed out in the very weeds she had insulted him in.

So much, for the present, for Belton and his Thomasine.

. . . .

I begin to pity thee heartily, now I see thee in earnest, in the fruitless love thou expressest to this angel of a woman; and the rather as, say what thou wilt, it is impossible she should get over her illness and her friends' implacableness, of which she has had fresh instances.

I hope thou art not indeed displeased with the extracts I have made from thy letters for her. The letting her know the justice thou hast done to her virtue in them, is so much in favour of thy ingenuousness (a quality, let me repeat, that gives thee a superiority over common libertines), that I think in my heart I was right; though to any other woman, and to one who had not known the worst of thee that she could know, it might have been wrong.

If the *end* will justify the *means*, it is plain that I have done well with regard to ye both; since I have made *her* easier, and *thee* appear in a better light to her than otherwise thou wouldst have done.

But if, nevertheless, thou art dissatisfied with my having obliged her in a point, which I acknowledge *to be delicate*, let us canvass this matter at our first meeting: and then I will show thee what the extracts *were*, and in what connexions I gave them in thy favour.

But surely thou dost not pretend to say what I shall, or shall not do, as to the executorship.

I am my own man, I hope. I think thou shouldst be glad to have the justification of her memory left to one who at the same time, thou mayst be assured, will treat thee and thy actions with all the lenity the case will admit.

I cannot help expressing my surprise at one instance of thy self-partiality; and that is where thou sayst: She had need, indeed, to cry out for mercy herself from *her* friends, who knows not how to show any.

Surely thou canst not think the cases alike. For she, as I understand, desires but a last blessing, and a last forgiveness, for a fault in a manner *involuntary*, if a fault at all; and does not so much as *hope* to be *received*; thou, to be forgiven *premeditated* wrongs (which, nevertheless, she forgives, on condition to be no more molested by thee); and hopest to be *received into favour*, and to make the finest jewel in the world thy absolute property in consequence of that forgiveness.

I will now briefly proceed to relate what has passed since my last, as to the excellent lady. By the account I shall give thee, thou wilt see that she has troubles enough upon her, all springing originally from thyself, without needing to add more to them by new vexations. And as long as thou canst exert thyself so very cavalierly at M. Hall, where every one is thy prisoner, I see not but the bravery of thy spirit may be as well gratified in domineering there over half a dozen persons of rank and distinction, as it could be over a helpless orphan, as I may call this lady, since she has not a single friend to stand by her if I do not; and who will think herself happy if she can refuge herself from thee, and from all the world, in the arms of death.

My last was dated on Saturday.

On Sunday, in compliance with her doctor's advice, she took a little airing. Mrs. Lovick, and Mr. Smith and his wife, were with her. After being at Highgate Chapel at divine service, she treated them with a little repast; and in the afternoon was at Islington Church, in her way home; returning tolerably cheerful.

She had received several letters in my absence, as Mrs. Lovick acquainted me, besides yours. Yours, it seems, much distressed her; but she ordered the messenger, who pressed for an answer, to be told that it did not require an immediate one.

On Wednesday she received a letter from her Uncle Harlowe,[1] in answer to one she had written to her mother on Saturday on her knees. It must be a very cruel one, Mrs. Lovick says, by the effects it had upon her: for, when she received it, she was intending to take an afternoon airing in a coach; but was thrown into so violent a fit of hysterics upon it, that she was forced to lie down; and (being not recovered by it) to go to bed about eight o'clock.

On Thursday morning she was up very early; and had recourse to the Scriptures to calm her mind, as she told Mrs Lovick: and, weak as she was, would go in a chair to Lincoln's Inn Chapel, about eleven. She was brought home a little better; and then sat down to write to her uncle. But was obliged to leave off several times—to struggle, as she told Mrs. Lovick, for a humble temper. "My heart, said she to the good woman, is a proud heart, and not yet, I find, enough mortified to my condition; but, do what I can, will be for prescribing resenting things to my pen."

I arrived in town from Belton's this Thursday evening; and went directly to Smith's. She was too ill to receive my visit.

[1] See Letter xli.

But on sending up my compliments, she sent me down word that she should be glad to see me in the morning.

Mrs. Lovick obliged me with the copy of a Meditation collected by the lady from the Scriptures. She has entitled it, *Poor mortals the cause of their own misery*; so entitled, I presume, with intention to take off the edge of her repinings at hardships so disproportioned to her fault, were her fault even as great as she is inclined to think it. We may see by this the method she takes to fortify her mind, and to which she owes, in a great measure, the magnanimity with which she bears her undeserved persecutions.

MEDITATION

Poor mortals the cause of their own misery

Say not thou, It is through the Lord that I fell away; for thou oughtest not to do the thing that He hateth.

Say not thou, He hath caused me to err; for He hath no need of the sinful man.

He Himself made man from the beginning, and left him in the hand of his own counsel;

If thou wilt, to keep the Commandments, and to perform acceptable faithfulness.

He hath set fire and water before thee: stretch forth thine hand to whether thou wilt.

He hath commanded no man to do wickedly; neither hath He given any man licence to sin.

And now, Lord, what is my hope? Truly my hope is *only* in Thee.

Deliver me from all my offences; and make me not a rebuke unto the foolish.

When Thou with rebuke dost chasten man for sin, Thou makest his beauty to consume away, like as it were a moth fretting a garment: every man therefore is vanity.

Turn Thee unto me, and have mercy upon me; for I am desolate and afflicted.

The troubles of my heart are enlarged. O bring Thou me out of my distresses!

·   ·   ·   ·   ·

Mrs. Smith gave me the following particulars of a conversation that passed between herself and a young clergyman on Tuesday afternoon, who, as it appears, was employed to make inquiries about the lady by her friends.

He came into the shop in a riding-habit, and asked for some Spanish snuff; and finding only Mrs. Smith there, he desired to have a little talk with her in the back shop.

He beat about the bush in several distant questions, and at last began to talk more directly about Miss Harlowe.

He said he knew her before her *fall* [that was his impudent word]; and gave the substance of the following account of her, as I collected it from Mrs. Smith.

"She was then, he said, the admiration and delight of everybody: he lamented, with great solemnity, her *backsliding*; another of his phrases. Mrs. Smith said he was a fine scholar; for he spoke several things *she understood not*; and either in Latin or Greek, she could not tell which; but was so good as to give her the English of them without asking. A fine thing, she said, for a scholar to be so condescending!"

He said, "Her going off with so vile a rake had given great scandal and offence to all the neighbouring ladies, as well as to her friends."

He told Mrs. Smith "how much she used to be followed by every one's eye whenever she went abroad, or to church; and praised and blessed by every tongue as she passed; especially by the poor: that she gave the fashion to the fashionable, without seeming herself to intend it, or to know she did: that, however, it was pleasant to see ladies imitate her in dress and behaviour, who, being unable to come up to her in grace and ease, exposed but their own affectation and awkwardness, at the time that they thought themselves secure of a general approbation, because they wore the same things, and put them on in the same manner that *she* did, who had everybody's admiration; little considering that were *her* person like *theirs*, or if she had had *their* defects, she would have brought up a very different fashion; for that *nature* was her guide in everything, and *ease* her study; which, joined with a mingled dignity and condescension in her air and manner, whether she received or paid a compliment, distinguished her above all her sex.

"He spoke not, he said, his own sentiments only on this occasion, but those of everybody: for that the praises of Miss Clarissa Harlowe were such a favourite topic, that a person who could not speak well upon any other subject was sure to speak well upon that; because he could say nothing but what he had heard repeated and applauded twenty times over."

Hence it was, perhaps, that this novice accounted for the best things he said himself; though I must own that the personal knowledge of the lady which I am favoured with, made it easy to me to lick into shape what the good woman reported to me, as the character given her by the young Levite: for who, even now, in her decline of health, sees not that all these attributes belong to her?

I suppose he has not been long come from college, and now thinks he has nothing to do but to blaze away for a scholar among the *ignorant*; as such young fellows are apt to think those who cannot cap verses with them, and tell us how an ancient author expressed himself in Latin on a point which, however, they may know how, as well as that author, to express in English.

Mrs. Smith was so taken with him that she would fain have introduced him to the lady, not questioning but it would be very acceptable to her to see one who knew her and her friends so well. But this he declined for several *reasons*, as he called them; which he gave. One was that persons of his cloth should be very cautious of the *company they were in*, especially where *sex* was concerned, and where a woman had *slurred her reputation*. [I wish I had been there when he gave himself these airs.] Another, that he was desired to inform himself of her present way of life, and who her visitors were; for, as to the praises Mrs. Smith gave the lady, he hinted that *she* seemed to be a good-natured woman, and might (though for the lady's sake he hoped not) be too partial and short-sighted to be trusted to absolutely in a concern of so high a nature as he intimated the task was which he had undertaken; nodding out words of doubtful import, and assuming airs of great significance (as I could gather), throughout the whole conversation. And when Mrs. Smith told him that the lady was in a very bad state of health, he gave a careless shrug. She may be very ill, says he: her disappointments must have touched her to the quick: but she is not bad enough, I dare say, yet, to atone for her very great lapse, and to expect to be forgiven by those whom she has so much disgraced.

A starched, conceited coxcomb! What would I give he had fallen in my way!

He departed highly satisfied with himself, no doubt, and assured of Mrs. Smith's great opinion of his sagacity and learning: but bid her not say anything to the lady about him or his inquiries. And I, for very different reasons, enjoined the same thing.

I am glad, however, for her peace of mind's sake, that they begin to think it behoves them to inquire about her.

Letter XXXIX—Mr. Belford to Robert Lovelace, Esq.

Friday, Aug. 11.

Mr. Belford acquaints his friend with the generosity of Lord M. and the ladies of his family ; and with the lady's grateful sentiments upon the occasion.

He says that in hopes to avoid the pain of seeing him [Mr. Lovelace], she intends to answer his letter of the 7th, though much against her inclination.

"She took great notice, *says Mr. Belford,* of that passage in yours which makes necessary to the *Divine* pardon the forgiveness of a person causelessly injured.

"Her grandfather, I find, has enabled her at eighteen years of age to make her will, and to devise great part of his estate to whom she pleases of the family, and the rest out of it (if she die single) at her own discretion; and this to create respect to her; as he apprehended that she would be envied: and she now resolves to set about making her will out of hand."

Mr. Belford insists upon the promise he had made him not to molest the lady: and gives him the contents of her answer to Lord M. and the ladies of his lordship's family, declining their generous offers. See Letter xxxvii.

Letter XL—Miss Clarissa Harlowe to Robert Lovelace, Esq.

Friday, Aug. 11.

IT is a cruel alternative to be either forced to see you or to write to you. But a will of my own has been long denied me; and to avoid a greater evil, nay, now I may say, the greatest, I write.

Were I capable of disguising or concealing my real sentiments, I might safely, I dare say, give you the remote hope you request, and yet keep all my resolutions. But I must tell you, sir (it becomes my character to tell you), that, were I to live more years than perhaps I may weeks, and there were not another man in the world, I could not, I would not, be yours.

There is no *merit* in performing a *duty*.

Religion enjoins me not only to forgive injuries, but to return good for evil. It is all my consolation, and I bless God for giving me that, that I am now in such a state of mind with regard to you that I can cheerfully obey its dictates. And accordingly I tell you that, wherever you go, I wish you happy. And in this I mean to include every good wish.

And now having, with great reluctance I own, complied with one of your compulsatory alternatives, I expect the fruits of it.

CLARISSA HARLOWE.

Letter XLI—Mr. John Harlowe to Miss Clarissa Harlowe
[*In answer to hers to her mother.   See No. XXXII*]

Monday, Aug. 7.

POOR UNGRATEFUL, NAUGHTY KINSWOMAN, — Your mother neither caring, nor being *permitted* to write, I am desired to set pen to paper, though I had resolved against it.

And so I am to tell you that your letters, joined to the occasion of them, almost break the hearts of us all.

Were we sure you had seen your folly, and were *truly* penitent, and, at the same time, that you were so very ill as you pretend, I know not what might be done for you. But we are all acquainted with your moving ways when you want to carry a point.

Unhappy girl! how miserable have you made us all! We, who used to visit with so much pleasure, now cannot endure to look upon one another.

If you had not known, upon a hundred occasions, how dear you once was to us, you might judge of it now, were you to know how much your folly has unhinged us all.

Naughty, naughty girl! You see the fruits of preferring a rake and libertine to a man of sobriety and morals. Against full warning, against better knowledge. And such a modest creature, too, as you were! How could you think of such an unworthy preference?

Your mother *can't* ask, and your sister knows not in modesty *how* to ask; and so *I* ask you, If you have any reason to think yourself with child by this villain? You *must* answer this, and answer it truly, before anything can be resolved upon about you.

You may well be touched with a deep remorse for your misdeeds. Could I ever have thought that my doting-piece, as every one called you, would have done thus? To be sure I loved you too well. But that is over now. Yet, though I will not pretend to answer for anybody but myself, for my own part I say, God forgive you! And this is all from

Your afflicted uncle,

JOHN HARLOWE.

The following MEDITATION *was stitched to the bottom of this letter with black silk:*

MEDITATION

O that Thou wouldst hide me in the grave! That Thou wouldst keep me secret, till Thy wrath be past!

My face is foul with weeping; and on my eyelid is the shadow of death.

My friends scorn me; but mine eye poureth out tears unto God.

A dreadful sound is in my ears; in prosperity the destroyer came upon me!

I have sinned! What shall I do unto Thee, O Thou Preserver of men! Why hast Thou set me as a mark against Thee; so that I am a burden to myself!

When I say, My bed shall comfort me; My couch shall ease my complaint;

Then Thou scarest me with dreams, and terrifiest me through visions.

So that my soul chooseth strangling and death rather than life.

I loathe it! I would not live alway!—Let me alone; for my days are vanity!

He hath made me a byword of the people; and aforetime I was as a tabret.

My days are past, my purposes are broken off, even the thoughts of my heart.

When I looked for good, then evil came unto me; and when I waited for light, then came darkness.

And where now is my hope?—

Yet all the days of my appointed time will I wait, till my change come.

Letter XLII—Miss Clarissa Harlowe to John Harlowe, Esq.

Thursday, Aug. 10.

HONOURED SIR,—It was an act of charity I begged: only for a last blessing, that I might die in peace. I ask not to be received again, as my severe sister [O that I had not written to her!] is pleased to say is my view. Let that grace be denied me when I do.

I could not look forward to my last scene with comfort, without seeking at least to obtain the blessing I petitioned for; and that with a contrition so deep, that I deserved not, were it known, to be turned over from the tender nature of a mother to the upbraiding pen of an uncle; and to be wounded by a cruel question, put by him in a shocking manner; and which a little, a very little time, will better answer than I can: for I am not either a hardened or shameless creature: if I were, I should not have been so solicitous to obtain the favour I sued for.

And permit me to say that I asked it as well for my father and mother's sake as for my own; for I am sure *they* at least will be uneasy, after I am gone, that they refused it to me.

I should still be glad to have theirs, and yours, sir, and all your blessings and your prayers; but, denied in such a manner, I will not presume again to ask it: relying entirely on the Almighty's; which is never denied when supplicated for with such true penitence as I hope mine is.

God preserve my dear uncle, and all my honoured friends! prays

Your unhappy

CLARISSA HARLOWE.

Letter XLIII—Miss Howe to Miss Clarissa Harlowe

Yarmouth, Isle of Wight, Monday, Aug. 7.

MY DEAREST CREATURE,—I can write just now but a few lines. I cannot tell how to bear the *sound* of that Mr. Belford for your executor, cogent as your reasons for that measure are: and yet I am firmly of opinion that none of your relations should be named for the trust. But I dwell the less upon this subject, as I hope (and cannot bear to apprehend the contrary) that you will still live many, many years.

Mr. Hickman, indeed, speaks very handsomely of Mr. Belford. But he, poor man! has not much penetration. If he had, he would hardly think so well of *me* as he does.

I have a particular opportunity of sending this by a friend of my Aunt Harman's; who is ready to set out for London (and this occasions my hurry) and is to return out of hand. I expect therefore by him a large packet from you; and hope and long for news of your amended health: which Heaven grant to the prayers of

Your ever affectionate

ANNA HOWE.

Letter XLIV—Miss Clarissa Harlowe to Miss Howe

Friday, Aug. 11.

I WILL send you a large packet, as you desire and expect; since I can do it by so safe a conveyance: but not all that is come to my hand. For I must own that my friends are very severe; too severe for anybody who loves them not to see their letters. You, my dear, would not call them my *friends*, you said, long ago; but my *relations*: indeed I cannot call them my *relations*,

I think! But I am ill; and therefore perhaps more peevish than I should be. It is difficult to go out of ourselves to give a judgment against ourselves; and yet, oftentimes, to pass a *just* judgment, we ought.

I thought I should alarm you in the choice of my executor. But the sad necessity I am reduced to must excuse me.

I shall not repeat anything I have said before on that subject: but if your objections will not be answered to your satisfaction by the papers and letters I shall enclose, marked 1, 2, 3, 4, to 9, I must think myself in another instance unhappy; since I am engaged too far (and with my own judgment too) to recede.

As Mr. Belford has transcribed for me in confidence from his friend's letters the passages which accompany this, I must insist that you suffer no soul but yourself to peruse them; and that you return them by the very first opportunity; that so no use may be made of them that may do hurt either to the original writer or to the communicator. You 'll observe I am bound by promise to this care. If through *my* means any mischief should arise between this *humane* and that *inhuman* libertine, I should think myself utterly inexcusable.

I subjoin a list of the papers or letters I shall enclose. You must return them all when perused.[1]

I am very much tired and fatigued—with—I don't know what —with writing, I think—but most with myself, and with a situation I cannot help aspiring to get out of, and above!

O my dear, 'tis a sad, a very sad world! While under our parents' protecting wings we know nothing at all of it. Book-learned and a scribbler, and looking at people as I saw them as

---

[1] 1. A letter from Miss Montague, dated Aug. 1.

2. A copy of my answer. Aug. 3.

3. Mr. Belford's letter to me, which will show you what my request was to him, and his compliance with it; and the desired extracts from his friend's letters. Aug. 3, 4.

4. A copy of my answer, with thanks; and requesting him to undertake the executorship. Aug. 4.

5. Mr. Belford's acceptance of the trust. Aug. 4.

6. Miss Montague's letter, with a generous offer from Lord M. and the ladies of that family. Aug. 7.

7. Mr. Lovelace's to me. Aug. 7.

8. Copy of mine to Miss Montague, in answer to hers of the day before. Aug. 8.

9. Copy of my answer to Mr. Lovelace. Aug. 11.

You will see by these several letters, written and received in so little a space of time (to say nothing of what I have received and written which I *cannot* show you), how little opportunity or leisure I can have for writing my own story.

visitors or visiting, I thought I knew a great deal of it.   Pitiable ignorance!   Alas! I knew nothing at all!

With zealous wishes for your happiness, and the happiness of every one dear to you, I am, and will ever be,

Your gratefully affectionate

CL. HARLOWE.

Letter XLV—Mr. Antony Harlowe to Miss Cl. Harlowe

[*In reply to hers to her Uncle Harlowe of Thursday, Aug.* 10]

Aug. 12.

UNHAPPY GIRL!—As your Uncle Harlowe chooses not to answer your pert letter to him; and as mine written to you before [1] was written as if it were in the spirit of prophecy, as you have found to your sorrow; and as you are now making yourself worse than you are in your health, and better than you are in your penitence, *as we are very well assured,* in order to move compassion; which you do not deserve, having had so much warning: for all these reasons I take up my pen once more; though I had told your *brother, at his going to Edinburgh,* that I would not write to you, even were you to write to me, without letting him know.   So indeed *had we all*; for he prognosticated what would happen, as to your applying to us, when you knew not how to help it.

Brother John has hurt your niceness, it seems, by asking you a plain question, which your mother's heart is too full of grief to let her ask; and modesty will not let your sister ask, though but the consequence of your actions.   And yet it *must* be answered before you'll obtain from your father and mother, and us, the notice you hope for, I can tell you that.

You lived several guilty weeks with one of the vilest fellows that ever drew breath, at bed as well as board, no doubt (for is not his character known?); and pray don't be ashamed to be asked after what may naturally come of such free living. This modesty indeed would have become you for eighteen years of your life—you'll be pleased to mark that—but makes no good figure compared with your behaviour since the beginning of April last.   So pray don't take it up, and wipe your mouth upon it, as if nothing had happened.

But maybe I likewise am too shocking to your niceness!   O girl, girl! your modesty had better been shown at the right time and place!   Everybody but you believed what the rake was:

[1] Vol. i, p. 159 et seq.

but you would believe nothing bad of him. What think you now?

Your folly has ruined all our peace. And who knows where it may yet end? Your poor father but yesterday showed me this text: with bitter grief he showed it me, poor man! And do you lay it to your heart:

"A father waketh for his daughter when no man knoweth; and the care for her taketh away his sleep—When she is young, lest she pass away the flower of her age [*and you know what proposals were made to you at different times*]: and, being married, lest she should be hated: in her virginity, lest she should be defiled, and gotten with child in her father's house [*I don't make the words, mind that*]: and, having an husband, lest she should misbehave herself." *And what follows?* "Keep a sure watch over a shameless daughter [*yet no watch could hold you!*], lest she make thee a laughing-stock to thine enemies [*as you have made us all to this cursed Lovelace*], and a byword in the city, and a reproach among the people, and make thee ashamed before the multitude."—Ecclus. xlii, 9, 10, etc.

Now will you wish you had not written pertly. Your sister's severities! Never, girl, say that is *severe* that is *deserved*. You know the meaning of words. Nobody better. Would to the Lord you had acted up but to one half of what you know. Then had we not been disappointed and grieved, as we all have been: and nobody more than him who was

Your loving uncle,
ANTONY HARLOWE.

This will be with you to-morrow. Perhaps you may be suffered to have some part of your estate, after you have smarted a little more. Your pertly answered Uncle John, who is your trustee, will not have you be destitute. But we hope all is not true *that we hear of you*. Only take care, I advise you, that, bad as you have acted, you act not still worse, if it be possible to act worse. *Improve upon the hint.*

Letter XLVI—Miss Clarissa Harlowe to Antony Harlowe, Esq.

Sunday, Aug. 13.

HONOURED SIR,—I am very sorry for my pert letter to my Uncle Harlowe. Yet I did not intend it to be pert. People *new* to misfortune may be too easily moved to impatience.

The fall of a regular person, no doubt, is dreadful and inexcusable. It is like the sin of apostasy. Would to Heaven, however, that I had had the circumstances of mine inquired into!

If, sir, I make myself worse than I am in my health, and better than I am in my penitence, it is fit I should be punished for my double dissimulation: and *you* have the pleasure of being one of my punishers. My sincerity in both respects will, however, be best justified by the event. To *that* I refer. May Heaven give you always as much comfort in reflecting upon the reprobation I have met with, as you seem to have pleasure in mortifying a poor creature, *extremely* mortified; and that from a *right* sense, as she presumes to hope, of her own fault!

What you have *heard of me* I cannot tell. When the nearest and dearest relations give up an unhappy wretch, it is not to be wondered at that those who are *not* related to her are ready to take up and propagate slanders against her. Yet I think I may defy calumny itself, and (excepting the fatal, though involuntary, step of *April* 10) wrap myself in my own innocence, and be easy. I thank you, sir, nevertheless, for your *caution,* mean it what it will.

As to the question required of me to answer, and which is allowed to be too shocking either for a mother to put to a daughter, or a sister to a sister; and which, however, *you* say I *must* answer:—O sir!—And *must* I answer? This then be my answer: "A *little* time, a much *less* time than is imagined, will afford a more satisfactory answer to my whole family, and even to my *brother* and *sister*, than I can give in words."

Nevertheless, be pleased to let it be remembered that I did not petition for a restoration to favour. I could not hope for that. Nor yet to be put in possession of any part of my own estate. Nor even for means of necessary subsistence from the produce of that estate—but only for a blessing; for a *last* blessing!

And this I will further add, because it is *true*, that I have no wilful crime to charge against myself: no free living at bed and at board, as you phrase it!

Why, why, sir, were not *other* inquiries made of me, as well as this shocking one?—Inquiries that modesty *would* have permitted a mother or a sister to make; and which, if I may be excused to say so, would have been still *less* improper, and *more* charitable, to have been made by *uncles* (were the mother *forbidden*, or the sister *not inclined* to make them) than those they have made.

Although my humble application has brought upon me so much severe reproach, I repent not that I have written to my mother (although I cannot but wish that I had not written to my sister); because I have satisfied a dutiful consciousness by it, however unanswered by the wished-for success. Nevertheless, I cannot help saying that mine is indeed a hard fate, that I cannot beg pardon for my capital error without doing it in such terms as shall be an aggravation of the offence.

But I had best leave off, lest, as my full mind, I find, is rising to my pen, I have other pardons to beg, as I multiply lines, where none at all will be given.

God Almighty bless, preserve, and comfort my dear sorrowing and grievously offended father and mother!—And continue in honour, favour, and merit, my happy sister! May God forgive my brother, and protect him from the violence of his own temper, as well as from the destroyer of his sister's honour! And may you, my dear uncle, and your no less now than ever dear brother, my second papa, as he used to bid me call him, be blessed and happy in them, and in each other! And, in order to this, may you all speedily banish from your remembrance for ever

The unhappy
CLARISSA HARLOWE.

Letter XLVII—Mrs. Norton to Miss Clarissa Harlowe

Monday, Aug. 14.

ALL your friends here, my dear young lady, now seem set upon proposing to you to go to one of the plantations. This, I believe, is owing to some misrepresentations of Mr. Brand; from whom they have received a letter.

I wish with all my heart that you could, consistently with your own notions of honour, yield to the pressing requests of all Mr. Lovelace's family in his behalf. This, I think, would stop every mouth; and, in time, reconcile everybody to you. For your own friends will not believe that he is in earnest to marry you; and the hatred between the families is such that they will not condescend to inform themselves better; nor would believe *him* if he were ever so solemnly to avow that he is.

I should be very glad to have in readiness, upon occasion, some brief particulars of your sad story under your own hand. But let me tell you at the same time, that no misrepresentations, nor even your own confession, shall lessen my opinion either of your piety or of your prudence in essential points; because I know it was always your humble way to make light **faults** heavy against yourself: and well might you, my dearest young lady, aggravate your own failings, who have ever had so few; and those few so slight that your ingenuousness has turned most of them into excellences.

Nevertheless, let me advise you, my dear Miss Clary, to discountenance any visits which, with the censorious, may affect your character. As *that* has not hitherto suffered by your *wilful* default, I hope you will not, in a desponding negligence (satisfying yourself with a consciousness of your own innocence), permit it to suffer. Difficult situations, you know, my dear young lady, are the tests not only of prudence but of virtue.

I think I *must* own to you that, since Mr. Brand's letter has been received, I have a renewed prohibition to attend you. However, if you will give me leave, that shall not detain me from you. Nor would I stay for that leave, if I were not in hopes that, in this critical situation, I may be able to do you service here.

I have often had messages and inquiries after your health from the truly reverend Dr. Lewen, who has always expressed, and still expresses, infinite concern for you. He entirely disapproves of the measures of the family with regard to you. He is too much indisposed to go abroad. But, were he in good health, he would not, as I understand, visit at Harlowe Place; having some time since been unhandsomely treated by your brother, on his offering to mediate for you with your family.

.   .   .   .

I am just now informed that your Cousin Morden is arrived in England. He is at Canterbury, it seems, looking after some concerns he has there; and is soon expected in these parts. Who knows what may arise from his arrival? God be with you, my dearest Miss Clary, and be your comforter and sustainer. And never fear but He will; for I am sure, I am very sure, that you put your whole trust in Him.

And what, after all, is this world, on which we so much depend for durable good, poor creatures that we are!—When all the joys of it, and (what is a balancing comfort) all the *troubles* of it, are but momentary, and vanish like a morning dream?

And be this remembered, my dearest young lady, that worldly joy claims no kindred with the joys we are bid to aspire after. These latter we must be fitted for by affliction and disappointment. You are therefore in the direct road to glory, however thorny the path you are in. And I had almost said that it depends upon yourself, by your patience, and by your resignedness to the dispensation (God enabling you, who never fails the true penitent and sincere invoker), to be an heir of a blessed immortality.

But this glory I humbly pray that you may not be permitted to enter into, ripe as you are so soon likely to be for it, till with your gentle hand (a pleasure I have so often, as you know, promised to myself) you have closed the eyes of

Your maternally affectionate

JUDITH NORTON.

Letter XLVIII—Miss Clarissa Harlowe to Mrs. Norton

Thursday, Aug. 17.

WHAT Mr. Brand, or anybody, can have written or said to my prejudice I cannot imagine; and yet some evil reports have gone out against me; as I find by some hints in a very severe letter written to me by my Uncle Antony. Such a letter as I believe was never written to any poor creature who, by ill-health of body as well as of mind, was before tottering on the brink of the grave. But my friends may possibly be better justified than the reporters—for who knows what they may have heard?

You give me a kind caution, which seems to imply *more* than you express, when you advise me against countenancing visitors that may discredit me. You should, in so tender a point, my dear Mrs. Norton, have spoken quite out. Surely I have had afflictions enough to strengthen my mind, and to enable it to bear the worst that can now happen. But I will not puzzle myself by *conjectural evils*; as I *might* perhaps do, if I had not enough that were *certain*. I shall hear all when it is thought proper that I should. Meantime let me say, for *your* satisfaction, that I know not that I have anything criminal or disreputable to answer for, either in word or deed, since the fatal 10th of April last.

You desire an account of what passes between me and my friends; and also particulars or brief heads of my sad story, in order to serve me as occasions shall offer. My dear, good Mrs. Norton, you shall have a whole packet of papers, which I have sent to my Miss Howe, when she returns them; and you shall have likewise another packet (and that with this letter) which I cannot at present think of sending to that dear friend for the sake of my *own relations*; whom, without seeing that packet, she is but too ready to censure heavily. From these you will be able to collect a great deal of my story. But for what is previous to these papers, and which more particularly relates to what I have suffered from Mr. Lovelace, you must have patience; for at present I have neither head nor heart for such subjects. The papers I send you with this will be those mentioned in the margin.[1] You must restore them to me as soon as perused: and upon your honour make no use of them, or of any intelligence you have from me, but by my previous consent.

These communications you must not, my good Mrs. Norton, look upon as appeals against my relations. On the contrary, I am heartily sorry that they have incurred the displeasure of so excellent a divine as Dr. Lewen. But you desire to have everything before you; and I think you *ought*; for who knows, as you say, but you may be applied to at last to administer comfort from their conceding hearts to one that wants it; and who sometimes, judging by what she knows of her own heart, thinks herself entitled to it?

I know that I have a most indulgent and sweet-tempered mother; but, having to deal with violent spirits, she has too often forfeited that peace of mind which she so much prefers by her over-concern to preserve it.

I am sure she would not have turned me over for an answer to a letter written with so contrite and fervent a spirit, as was mine to her, to a *masculine* spirit, had she been left to herself.

But, my dear Mrs. Norton, might not, think you, the revered lady have favoured me with one *private* line?—If not, might not *you* have written by her order, or connivance, one softening, one *motherly* line, when she saw her poor girl whom once she dearly loved, borne so hard upon?

O no, she might not!—because her heart, to be sure, is in their measures!—and if *she* think them right, perhaps they *must be right!*—at least, knowing only what *they* know, they must!

---

[1] 1. A copy of mine to my sister, begging off my father's malediction, dated July 21.
2. My sister's answer, dated July 27.
3. Copy of my second letter to my sister, dated July 29.
4. My sister's answer, dated Aug. 3.
5. Copy of my letter to my mother, dated Aug. 5.
6. My Uncle Harlowe's letter, dated Aug. 7.
7. Copy of my answer to it, dated the 10th.
8. Letter from my Uncle Antony, dated the 12th.
9. And, lastly, the copy of my answer to it, dated the 13th.

—and yet they *might* know all, if they would!—and possibly, in their own good time, they think to make proper inquiry. My application was made to them but *lately*. Yet how deeply will it afflict them, if *their* time should be *out of time*!

When you have before you the letters I have sent to Miss Howe, you will see that Lord M. and the ladies of his family, jealous as they are of the honour of *their house* (to express myself in their language), think better of me than my own relations do. You will see an instance of their generosity to me which at the time extremely affected me, and indeed still affects me. Unhappy man! gay, inconsiderate, and cruel! What has been his gain by making unhappy a creature who hoped to make him happy! and who was determined to deserve the love of all to whom he is related! Poor man!—But you will mistake a compassionate and placable nature for love! He took care, great care, that I should rein in betimes any passion that I might have had for him, had he known how to be but commonly grateful or generous! But the Almighty knows what is best for His poor creatures.

Some of the letters in the same packet will also let you into the knowledge of a strange step which I have taken (strange you will think it); and, at the same time, give you my reasons for taking it.[1]

It must be expected that situations uncommonly difficult will make necessary some extraordinary steps, which but for those situations would be hardly excusable. It will be very happy indeed, and somewhat wonderful, if all the measures I have been driven to take should be right. A pure intention, void of all undutiful resentment, is what must be my consolation, whatever others may think of those measures when they come to know them: which, however, will hardly be till it is out of my power to justify them, or to answer for myself.

I am glad to hear of my Cousin Morden's safe arrival. I should wish to see him, methinks: but I am afraid that he will sail with the stream; as it must be expected that he will hear what they have to say first. But what I most fear is that he will take upon himself to avenge me. Rather than he should do so, I would have him look upon me as a creature utterly unworthy of his concern; at least of his *vindictive* concern.

How soothing to the wounded heart of your Clarissa, how balmy, are the assurances of your continued love and favour! Love me, my dear Mamma Norton, continue to love me to the

[1] She means that of making Mr. Belford her executor.

end! I now think that I may, without presumption, promise to *deserve* your love to the end. And when I am gone, cherish my memory in your worthy heart; for in so doing you will cherish the memory of one who loves and honours you more than she can express.

But when I am no more, get over, I charge you, as soon as you can, the smarting pangs of grief that will attend a recent loss; and let all be early turned into that sweetly melancholy regard to MEMORY which, engaging us to forget all faults, and to remember nothing but what was thought amiable, gives more pleasure than pain to survivors—especially if they can comfort themselves with the humble hope that the Divine mercy has taken the dear departed to itself.

And what is the space of time to look backward upon, between an early departure and the longest survivance? And what the consolation attending the sweet hope of meeting again, never more to be separated, never more to be pained, grieved, or aspersed!—But mutually blessing, and being blessed, to all eternity!

In the contemplation of this happy state, in which I hope, in God's good time, to rejoice with you, my beloved Mrs. Norton, and also with my dear relations, all reconciled to and blessing the child against whom they are now so much incensed, I conclude myself

Your ever dutiful and affectionate

CLARISSA HARLOWE.

Letter XLIX—Mr. Lovelace to John Belford, Esq.

Sunday, Aug. 13.

I DON'T know what a devil ails me; but I never was so much indisposed in my life. At first I thought some of my blessed relations here had got a dose administered to me, in order to get the whole house to themselves. But, as I am the hopes of the family, I believe they would not be so wicked.

I must lay down my pen. I cannot write with any spirit at all. What a plague can be the matter with me!

.   .   .   .

Lord M. paid me just now a cursed gloomy visit, to ask me how I do after bleeding. His sisters both drove away yesterday, God be thanked. But they asked not my leave; and hardly bid me good-bye. My lord was more tender, and more dutiful.

than I expected. Men are less unforgiving than women. I have reason to say so, I am sure. For besides implacable Miss Harlowe and the old ladies, the two Montague apes haven't been near me yet.

.   .   .   .

Neither eat, drink, nor sleep! A piteous case, Jack! If I should die like a fool now, people would say Miss Harlowe had broken my heart. That she *vexes* me to the heart is certain.

Confounded squeamish! I would fain write it off. But must lay down my pen again. It won't do. Poor Lovelace! What a devil ails thee?

.   .   .   .

Well, but now let's try for't. Hoy—hoy—hoy! Confound me for a gaping puppy, how I yawn! Where shall I begin? At thy executorship? Thou shalt have a double office of it: for I really think thou mayst send me a coffin and a shroud. I shall be ready for them by the time they can come down.

What a little fool is this Miss Harlowe! I warrant she'll now repent that she refused me. Such a lovely young widow—what a charming widow would she have made! How would she have adorned the weeds! To be a widow in the first twelve months is one of the greatest felicities that can befall a fine woman. Such pretty employment in *new dismals*, when she had hardly worn round her *blazing joyfuls*! Such lights and such shades! how would they set off one another, and be adorned by the wearer!

Go to the devil! I *will* write! Can I do anything else?

They would not have me write, Belford. I must be ill indeed when I can't write.

.   .   .   .

But thou seemest nettled, Jack! Is it because I was stung? It is not for two friends, any more than for man and wife, to be out of patience at one time. What must be the consequence if they are? I am in no fighting mood just now: but as patient and passive as the chickens that are brought me in broth—for I am come to that already.

But I can tell thee, for all this, be *thy own man*, if thou wilt, as to the executorship, I will never suffer thee to expose my letters. They are too ingenuous by half to be seen. And I absolutely insist upon it, that on receipt of this thou burn them all.

I will never forgive thee that impudent and unfriendly

reflection, of my *cavaliering* it here over half a dozen persons of distinction: remember, too, thy words poor *helpless orphan*—these reflections are too serious, and thou art also too serious, for me to let these things go off as jesting; notwithstanding the Roman style is preserved; and, indeed, but just preserved. By my soul, Jack, if I had not been taken thus egregiously cropsick, I would have been up with thee, and the lady too, before now.

But write on, however: and send me copies, if thou canst, of all that passes between our Charlotte and Miss Harlowe. I'll take no notice of what thou communicatest of that sort. I like not the *people here* the worse for their generous offer to the lady. But you see she is as proud as implacable. There's no obliging her. She'd rather sell her clothes than be beholden to anybody, although she would oblige by permitting the obligation.

O Lord! O Lord! Mortal ill! Adieu, Jack!

.   .   .   .

I was forced to leave off, I was so ill, at this place. And what dost think? Why, Lord M. brought the parson of the parish to pray by me; for his chaplain is at Oxford. I was lain down in my night-gown over my waistcoat, and in a doze: and, when I opened my eyes, who should I see but the parson kneeling on one side the bed; Lord M. on the other; Mrs. Greme, who had been sent for to *tend me*, as they call it, at the feet: God be thanked, my lord! said I, in an ecstasy. Where's Miss? For I supposed they were going to marry me.

They thought me delirious at first; and prayed louder and louder.

This roused me: off the bed I started; slid my feet into my slippers; put my hand in my waistcoat pocket, and pulled out thy letter with my beloved's meditation in it: My lord, Dr. Wright, Mrs. Greme, you have thought me a very wicked fellow: but, see! I can read you as good as you can read me.

They stared at one another. I gaped, and read, Poor mo—or—tals the cau—o—ause of their own—their own mis—ser—ry.

It is as suitable to my case as to the lady's, as thou 'lt observe if thou readest it again.[1] At the passage where it is said, that *when a man is chastened for sin, his beauty consumes away*, I stepped to the glass: A poor figure, by Jupiter! cried I. And they all praised and admired me; lifted up their hands and their eyes; and the doctor said he always thought it impossible that

[1] See p. 96.

a man of my sense could be so wild as the world said I was. My lord chuckled for joy; congratulated me; and, thank my dear Miss Harlowe, I got high reputation among good, bad, and indifferent. In short, I have established myself for ever with all here.—But, O Belford, even this will not do! I must leave off again.

A visit from the Montague sisters, led in by the hobbling peer, to congratulate my amendment and reformation both in one. What a lucky event this illness with this meditation in my pocket; for we were all to pieces before! Thus, when a boy, have I joined with a crowd coming out of church, and have been thought to have been there myself.

I am incensed at the insolence of the young Levite. Thou wilt highly oblige me, if thou 'lt find him out, and send me his ears in thy next letter.

My beloved mistakes me if she thinks I proposed her writing to me as an alternative that should dispense with my attendance upon her. That it shall *not* do, nor did I intend it should, unless she had pleased me better in the contents of her letter than she has done. Bid her read again. I gave no such hopes. I would have been with her, in spite of you both, by to-morrow at furthest, had I not been laid by the heels thus, like a helpless miscreant.

But I grow better and better every hour, *I* say: the *doctor* says not: but I am sure I know best: and I will soon be in London, depend on 't. But say nothing of this to my dear, cruel, and implacable Miss Harlowe.

A—dieu—u, Ja—aack—what a gaping puppy (yaw—n! yaw—n! yaw—n!)

Thy LOVELACE.

Letter L—Mr. Belford to Robert Lovelace, Esq.

Monday, Aug. 14.

I AM extremely concerned for thy illness. I should be very sorry to lose thee. Yet, if thou diest so soon, I could wish from my soul it had been before the beginning of last April: and this as well for thy sake as for the sake of the most excellent woman in the world: for then thou wouldst not have had the most crying sin of thy life to answer for.

I was told on Saturday that thou wert very much out of order; and this made me forbear writing till I heard further. Harry, on his return from thee, confirmed the bad way thou art in.

But I hope Lord M., in his unmerited tenderness for thee, thinks the worst of thee. What can it be, Bob? A violent fever, they say; but attended with odd and severe symptoms.

I will not trouble thee, in the way thou art in, with what passes here with Miss Harlowe. I wish thy repentance as swift as thy illness; and as efficacious, if thou diest; for it is else to be feared that she and you will never meet in one place.

I told her how ill you are. Poor man! said she. *Dangerously* ill, say you?

Dangerously *indeed*, madam! So Lord M. sends me word!

God be merciful to him, if he die! said the admirable creature. Then, after a pause, Poor wretch! May he meet with the mercy he has not shown!

I send this by a special messenger: for I am impatient to hear how it goes with thee. If I have received thy *last* letter, what melancholy reflections will *that last*, so full of shocking levity, give to

Thy true friend,

JOHN BELFORD!

Letter LI—Mr. Lovelace to John Belford, Esq.

Tuesday, Aug. 15.

THANK thee, Jack; most heartily I thank thee, for the sober conclusion of thy last! I have a good mind, for the sake of it, to forgive thy till now absolutely unpardonable extracts.

But dost think I will lose such an angel, such a *forgiving* angel as this? By my soul I will not! To pray for mercy for such an ungrateful miscreant! How she wounds me, how she cuts me to the soul, by her exalted generosity! But SHE must have mercy upon me first! Then will she teach me a reliance for the sake of which her prayer for me will be answered.

But hasten, hasten to me, particulars of her health, of her employments, of her conversation.

I am sick only of love! O that I could have called her mine! It would then have been worth while to be sick! To have sent for her down to me from town; and to have had her, with healing in her dove-like wings, flying to my comfort; her duty and her choice to pray for me, and to bid me live for her sake! O Jack! what an angel have I——

But I *have not* lost her!—I *will not* lose her! I am almost well;

should be quite well but for these prescribing rascals who, to do credit to their skill, will make the disease of importance. And I will make her mine! And be sick again, to entitle myself to her *dutiful* tenderness, and *pious* as well as *personal* concern!

God for ever bless her! Hasten, hasten particulars of her! I am sick of love! Such generous goodness! By all that's great and good, I will not lose her! So tell her! She says that she could not pity me if she thought of being mine! This, according to Miss Howe's transcriptions to Charlotte. But bid her hate me, and have me: and my behaviour to her shall soon turn that hate to love! For, body and mind, I will be wholly hers.

Letter LII—*Mr. Belford to Robert Lovelace, Esq.*

Thursday, Aug. 17.

I AM sincerely rejoiced to hear that thou art already so much amended, as thy servant tells me thou art. Thy letter looks as if thy morals were mending with thy health. This was a letter I *could* show, as I *did*, to the lady.

She is very ill (cursed letters received from her implacable family!): so I could not have much conversation with her, in thy favour, upon it. But what passed will make thee more and more adore her.

She was very attentive to me as I read it; and when I had done, Poor man! said she; what a letter is this! He had timely instances that my temper was not ungenerous, if generosity could have obliged him! But his remorse, and that for *his own* sake, is all the punishment I wish him. Yet I must be more reserved, if you write to him everything I say!

I extolled her unbounded goodness—how could I help it, though to her face!

No goodness in it! she said. It was a frame of mind she had endeavoured after for *her own sake*. She suffered too much in want of mercy not to wish it to a penitent heart. He *seems* to be penitent, said she; and it is not for me to judge beyond appearances. If he be not, he deceives himself more than anybody else.

She was so ill that this was all that passed on the occasion.

What a fine subject for tragedy would the injuries of this lady, and her behaviour under them, both with regard to her implacable friends, and to her persecutor, make! With a grand objection as to the moral, nevertheless [1]; for here virtue is punished! Except indeed we look forward to the rewards of HEREAFTER, which, morally, *she* must be sure of, or who can? Yet, after all, I know not, so sad a fellow art thou, and so vile a husband mightest thou have made, whether her virtue is not rewarded in missing thee: for things the most grievous to human nature, when they happen, as this charming creature once observed, are often the happiest for us in the event.

I have frequently thought, in my attendance on this lady, that if Belton's admired author, Nic Rowe, had had such a character before him, he would have drawn another sort of a penitent than he *has* done, or given his play, which he calls *The Fair Penitent,* a fitter title. Miss Harlowe is a penitent indeed! I think, if I am not guilty of a contradiction in terms; a penitent without a fault; her parents' conduct towards her from the first considered.

The whole story of the other is a pack of damned stuff. Lothario, 'tis true, seems such another wicked, ungenerous varlet as thou knowest who: the author knew how to draw a rake; but not to paint a penitent. Calista is a desiring luscious wench, and her penitence is nothing else but rage, insolence, and scorn. Her passions are all storm and tumult; nothing of the finer passions of the sex, which, if naturally drawn, will distinguish themselves from the masculine passions by a softness that will even shine through rage and despair. Her character is made up of deceit and disguise. She has no virtue; is all pride; and her devil is as much *within* her as *without* her.

How then can the fall of such a one create a proper distress, when all the circumstances of it are considered? For does she not brazen out her crime even after detection? Knowing her own guilt, she calls for Altamont's vengeance on his best friend, as if he had traduced her; yields to marry Altamont, though criminal with another; and actually beds that whining puppy, when she had given up herself body and soul to Lothario; who, nevertheless, refused to marry her.

---

[1] Mr. Belford's objection, that virtue ought not to suffer in a tragedy, is not well considered; Monimia in the *Orphan*, Belvidera in *Venice Preserved*, Athenais in *Theodosius*, Cordelia in Shakespeare's *King Lear*, Desdemona in *Othello*, Hamlet (to name no more), are instances that a tragedy could hardly be justly called a tragedy, if virtue did not temporarily suffer, and vice for a while triumph. But he recovers himself in the same paragraph, and leads us to look up to the FUTURE for the reward of virtue, and for the punishment of guilt, and observes not amiss when he says: He knows not but that the virtue of such a woman as Clarissa is rewarded in missing such a man as Lovelace.

Her penitence, when begun, she justly styles *the frenzy of her soul*; and, as I said, after having, as long as she could, most audaciously brazened out her crime, and done all the mischief she could do (occasioning the death of Lothario, of her father, and others), she stabs herself.

And can this be an act of penitence?

But, indeed, our poets hardly know how to create a distress without horror, murder, and suicide; and must shock your soul to bring tears from your eyes.

Altamont, indeed, who is an amorous blockhead, a credulous cuckold, and (though painted as a brave fellow and a soldier) a mere Tom Essence, and a quarreller with his best friend, dies like a fool (as we are led to suppose at the conclusion of the play), without either sword or pop-gun, of mere grief and non-sense, for one of the vilest of her sex: but the *fair penitent*, as she is called, perishes by her own hand; and, having no title by her past crimes to *laudable* pity, forfeits all claim to *true* penitence, and, in all probability, to future mercy.

But here is Miss CLARISSA HARLOWE, a virtuous, noble, wise, and pious young lady; who being ill-used by her friends, and unhappily ensnared by a vile libertine, whom she believes to be a man of honour, is in a manner *forced* to throw herself upon his protection. And he, in order to obtain her confidence, never scruples the deepest and most solemn protestations of honour.

After a series of plots and contrivances, all baffled by her virtue and vigilance, he basely has recourse to the vilest of arts, and, to rob her of her honour, is forced first to rob her of her senses.

Unable to bring her, notwithstanding, to his ungenerous views of cohabitation, she overawes him in the very entrance of a fresh act of premeditated guilt, in presence of the most abandoned of women assembled to assist his devilish purpose; triumphs over them all by virtue only of her innocence; and escapes from the vile hands he had put her into.

She nobly, not frantically, resents: refuses to see or to marry the wretch; who, repenting his usage of so divine a creature, would fain move her to forgive his baseness and make him her husband: and this though persecuted by all her friends, and abandoned to the deepest distress, being obliged, from ample fortunes, to make away with her apparel for subsistence, sur-rounded also by strangers; and forced (in want of others) to make a friend of the friend of her seducer.

Though longing for death, and making all proper preparations for it, convinced that grief and ill-usage have broken her noble heart, she abhors the impious thought of shortening her allotted period; and, as much a stranger to revenge as despair, is able to forgive the author of her ruin; wishes his repentance, and that she may be the last victim to his barbarous perfidy: and is solicitous for nothing so much in this life as to prevent vindictive mischief *to* and *from* the man who has used her so basely.

This is penitence! This is piety! And hence a distress naturally arises that must *worthily* affect every heart.

Whatever the ill-usage of this excellent woman is from her relations, she breaks not out into excesses: she strives, on the contrary, to find reason to justify them at her own expense; and seems more concerned for their cruelty to her for their sakes hereafter, when she shall be no more, than for her own: for, as to herself, she is sure, she says, God will forgive her, though no one on earth will.

On every extraordinary provocation she has recourse to the Scriptures, and endeavours to regulate her vehemence by sacred precedents. "Better people, she says, have been more afflicted than she, grievous as she sometimes thinks her afflictions: and shall she not bear what less faulty persons have borne?" On the very occasion I have mentioned (some new instances of implacableness from her friends) the enclosed meditation will show how mildly and yet how forcibly she complains. See if thou, in the wicked levity of thy heart, canst apply it to thy case, as thou didst the other. If thou canst not, give way to thy conscience, and that will make the properest application.

MEDITATION

How long will ye vex my soul, and break me in pieces with words!
Be it indeed that I have erred, mine error remaineth with myself.
To *her* that is afflicted, pity should be shown from her friend.
But she that is ready to slip with *her* feet, is as a lamp despised in the thought of *them* that *are* at ease.
There is a shame which bringeth sin, and there is a shame which bringeth glory and grace.
Have pity upon me, have pity upon me, O ye, my friends! for the hand of God hath touched me.
If your soul were in my soul's stead, I also could speak as ye do: I could heap up words against you——
But I would strengthen you with my mouth, and the moving of my lips should assuage your grief.

Why will ye break a leaf driven to and fro? *Why will ye* pursue the dry stubble? *Why will ye* write bitter words against me, and make me possess the iniquities of my youth?

Mercy is seasonable in the time of affliction, as clouds of rain in the time of drought.

Are not my days few? Cease then, and let me alone, that I may take comfort a little—before I go whence I shall not return; even to the land of darkness, and shadow of death!

Let me add that the excellent lady is informed, by a letter from Mrs. Norton, that Colonel Morden is just arrived in England. He is now the only person she wishes to see.

I expressed some jealousy upon it, lest he should have place given over me in the executorship. She said that she had no thoughts to do so now; because such a trust, were he to accept of it (which she doubted), might, from the nature of some of the papers which in that case would necessarily pass through his hands, occasion mischiefs between my friend and him, that would be worse than death for her to think of.

Poor Belton, I hear, is at death's door. A messenger is just come from him, who tells me he cannot die till he sees me. I hope the poor fellow will not go off yet; since neither his affairs in this world nor for the other are in tolerable order. I cannot avoid going to the poor man. Yet am unwilling to stir till I have an assurance from you that you will not disturb the lady: for I know he will be very loath to part with me when he gets me to him.

Tourville tells me how fast thou mendest: let me conjure thee not to think of molesting this incomparable woman. For thy own sake I request this, as well as for hers, and for the sake of thy given promise: for, should she die within a few weeks, as I fear she will, it will be said, and perhaps too justly, that thy visit has hastened her end.

In hopes thou wilt not, I wish thy perfect recovery: else, that thou mayst relapse, and be confined to thy bed.

Letter LIII—*Mr. Belford to Miss Clarissa Harlowe*

Sat. Morn. Aug. 19.

MADAM,—I think myself obliged in honour to acquaint you that I am afraid Mr. Lovelace will try his fate by an interview with you.

I wish to Heaven you could prevail upon yourself to receive his visit. All that is respectful, even to veneration, and all that is penitent, will you see in his behaviour, if you can admit of it. But as I am obliged to set out directly for Epsom (to perform, as I apprehend, the last friendly offices for poor Mr. Belton, whom once you saw), and as I think it more likely that Mr. Lovelace will *not* be prevailed upon than that he *will*, I thought fit to give you this intimation, lest, if he should come, you should be too much surprised.

He flatters himself that you are not so ill as I represent you to be. When he sees you, he will be convinced that the most obliging things he can do will be as proper to be done for the sake of his own future peace of mind as for your health's sake; and, I dare say, in fear of hurting the latter, he will forbear the thoughts of any further intrusion; at least while you are so much indisposed: so that *one half-hour's shock*, if it *will* be a shock to see the unhappy man (but just got up himself from a dangerous fever), will be all you will have occasion to stand.

I beg you will not too much hurry and discompose yourself. It is impossible he can be in town till Monday at soonest. And if he resolve to come, I hope to be at Mr. Smith's before him.

I am, madam, with the profoundest veneration,
Your most faithful and most obedient servant,
J. BELFORD.

Letter LIV—Mr. Lovelace to John Belford, Esq.
[In answer to his of Aug 17. See Letter LII]

Sunday, Aug. 20.

WHAT an unmerciful fellow art thou! A man has no need of a conscience who has such an impertinent monitor. But if Nic. Rowe wrote a play that answers not his title, am I to be reflected upon for that? I have sinned; I repent; I would repair—she forgives my sin: she accepts my repentance: but she won't let me repair. What wouldst have me do?

But get thee gone to Belton as soon as thou canst. Yet whether thou goest or not, up I *must* go, and see what I can do with the sweet oddity myself. The moment these *prescribing* varlets will let me, depend upon it, I go. Nay, Lord M. thinks she ought to permit me one interview. His opinion has great authority with me—when it squares with my own: and I have assured him, and my two cousins, that I will behave with all the decency and respect that man can behave with to the person whom he *most* respects. And so I will. Of this, if thou choosest not to go to Belton meantime, thou shalt be witness.

Colonel Morden, thou hast heard me say, is a man of honour and bravery: but Colonel Morden has had his girls as well as you and I. And indeed, either openly or secretly, who has not? The devil always baits with a pretty wench when he angles for a man, be his age, rank, or degree what it will.

I have often heard my beloved speak of the colonel with great distinction and esteem. I wish he could make matters a little easier, for her mind's sake, between the rest of the implacables and herself.

Methinks I am sorry for honest Belton. But a man cannot be ill, or vapourish, but thou liftest up thy shriek-owl note and killest him immediately. None but a fellow who is fit for a drummer in death's forlorn hope could take so much delight as thou dost in beating a dead march with thy goose-quills.

Whereas, didst thou but know thine own talents, thou art formed to give mirth by thy very appearance; and wouldst make a better figure by half, leading up thy brother-bears at Hockley-in-the-Hole to the music of a Scots bagpipe. Methinks I see thy clumsy sides (shaking and shaking the sides of all beholders) in these very attitudes; thy fat head archly beating time on thy porterly shoulders, right and left by turns, as I once beheld thee practising to the hornpipe at Preston. Thou rememberest the frolic, as I have done a hundred times; for I never before saw thee appear so much in character.

But I know what I shall get by this—only that notable observation repeated, That thy outside is the worst of thee, and mine the best of me. And so let it be. Nothing thou writest of *this sort* can I take amiss.

But I shall call thee seriously to account, when I see thee, for the extracts thou hast given the lady from my letters, notwithstanding what I said in my last; especially if she continue to refuse me. A hundred times have I myself known a woman deny, yet comply at last: but, by these extracts, thou hast, I doubt, made her bar up the door of her heart, as she used to do her chamber door, against me. This, therefore, is a disloyalty that friendship cannot bear, nor honour allow me to forgive.

Letter LV—Mr. Lovelace to John Belford, Esq.

London, Aug. 21, Monday.

I BELIEVE I am bound to curse thee, Jack. Nevertheless I won't anticipate, but proceed to write thee a longer letter than thou hast had from me for some time past. So here goes.

That thou mightest have as little notice as possible of the time I was resolved to be in town, I set out in my lord's chariot and six yesterday, as soon as I had dispatched my letter to thee, and arrived in town last night: for I knew I could have no dependence on thy friendship where Miss Harlowe's humour was concerned.

I had no other place so ready, and so was forced to go to my old lodgings, where also my wardrobe is; and there I poured out millions of curses upon the whole crew, and refused to see either Sally or Polly; and this not only for suffering the lady to escape, but for the villainous arrest, and for their detestable insolence to her at the officer's house.

I dressed myself in a never worn suit, which I had intended for one of my wedding suits; and liked myself so well that I began to think with thee, that my outside was the best of me.

I took a chair to Smith's, my heart bounding in almost audible thumps to my throat, with the assured expectation of seeing my beloved. I clasped my fingers, as I was danced along: I charged my eyes to languish and sparkle by turns: I talked to my knees, telling them how they must bend; and, in the language of a charming describer, acted my part in fancy, as well as spoke it to myself:

> Tenderly kneeling, *thus* will I complain:
> *Thus* court her pity; and *thus* plead my pain:
> *Thus* sigh for fancy'd frowns, if frowns should rise;
> And *thus* meet favour in her soft'ning eyes.

In this manner entertained I myself till I arrived at Smith's; and there the fellows set down their gay burden. Off went their hats; Will ready at hand in a new livery; up went the head; out rushed my honour; the woman behind the counter all in flutters; respect and fear giving due solemnity to her features; and her knees, I doubt not, knocking against the inside of her wainscot fence.

Your servant, madam.—Will, let the fellows move to some distance, and wait.

You have a young lady lodges here; Miss Harlowe, madam: is she above?

Sir, sir, and please your honour [the woman is struck with my figure, thought I]: Miss Harlowe, sir! There is, indeed, such a young lady lodges here—but, but——

But what, madam? I must see her. One pair of stairs, is it not? Don't trouble yourself—I shall find her apartment. And was making towards the stairs.

Sir, sir, the lady—the lady is not at home. She is abroad—she is in the country——

In the country! Not at home! Impossible! You will not pass this story upon me, good woman. I *must* see her. I have business of life and death with her.

Indeed, sir, the lady is not at home! Indeed, sir, she is abroad!——

She then rung a bell: John, cried she, pray step down!—Indeed, sir, the lady is not at home.

Down came John, the good man of the house, when I expected one of his journeymen, by her saucy familiarity.

My dear, said she, the gentleman will not believe Miss Harlowe is abroad.

John bowed to my fine clothes: Your servant, sir. Indeed the lady is abroad. She went out of town this morning by six o'clock—into the country—by the doctor's advice.

Still I would not believe either John or his wife. I am sure, said I, she cannot be abroad. I heard she was very ill—she is not able to go out in a coach. Do you know Mr. Belford, friend?

Yes, sir; I have the honour to know 'Squire Belford. He is gone into the country to visit a sick friend. He went on Saturday, sir.

This had also been told from thy lodgings to Will, whom I sent to desire to see thee on my first coming to town.

Well, and Mr. Belford wrote me word that she was exceeding ill. How then can she be gone out?

O sir, she is very ill very ill, indeed—she could hardly walk to the coach.

Belford, thought I, *himself* knew nothing of the time of my coming; neither can he have received my letter of yesterday: and so ill, 'tis impossible she would go out.

Where is her servant? Call her servant to me.

Her servant, sir, is her nurse: she has no other. And *she* is gone with her.

Well, friend, I must not believe you. You 'll excuse me; but I must go upstairs myself. And was stepping up.

John hereupon put on a serious and a less respectful face: Sir, this house is mine; and——

And what, friend? not doubting then but she was above. I must and will see her. I have authority for it. I am a justice of peace. I have a search-warrant.

And up I went; they following me, muttering, and in a plaguy flutter.

The first door I came to was locked. I tapped at it.

The lady, sir, has the key of her own apartment.

On the inside, I question not, my honest friend; tapping again. And being assured, if she heard my voice, that her timorous and soft temper would make her betray herself, by some flutters, to my listening ear, I said aloud, I am confident Miss Harlowe is here. Dearest madam, open the door: admit me but for one moment to your presence.

But neither answer nor fluttering saluted my ear; and, the people being very quiet, I led on to the next apartment; and, the key being on the outside, I opened it, and looked all round it and into the closet.

The man said he never saw so uncivil a gentleman in his life.

Hark thee, friend, said I; let me advise thee to be a little decent; or I shall teach thee a lesson thou never learnedst in all thy life.

Sir, said he, 'tis not like a gentleman to affront a man in his own house.

Then prithee, man, replied I, don't crow upon thine own dunghill.

I stepped back to the locked door: My dear Miss Harlowe, I beg of you to open the door, or I 'll break it open; pushing hard against it, that it cracked again.

The man looked pale; and, trembling with his fright, made a plaguy long face; and called to one of his bodice-makers above: *Joseph, come down quickly.*

Joseph came down: a lion's-face, grinning fellow; thick, and short, and bushy-headed, like an old oak pollard. Then did Master John put on a sturdier look. But I only hummed a tune, traversed all the other apartments, sounded the passages with my knuckles, to find whether there were private doors, and walked up the next pair of stairs, singing all the way; John, and Joseph, and Mrs. Smith, following me trembling.

I looked round me there, and went into two open-door bedchambers; searched the closets, the passages, and peeped through the keyhole of another: No Miss Harlowe, by Jupiter! What shall I do! What shall I do! as the girls say. Now will she be grieved that she is out of the way.

I said this on purpose to find out whether these people knew the lady's story; and had the answer I expected from Mrs. Smith: I believe not, sir.

Why so, Mrs. Smith? Do you know who I am?

I can guess, sir.

Whom do you guess me to be?

Your name is Mr. Lovelace, sir, I make no doubt.

The very same. But how came you to guess so well, Dame Smith? You never saw me before, did you?

Here, Jack, I laid out for a compliment, and missed it.

'Tis easy to guess, sir; for there cannot be two such gentlemen as you.

Well said, Dame Smith—but mean you *good* or *bad*? *Handsome* was the least I thought she would have said.

I leave you to guess, sir.

Condemned, thought I, by myself, on this appeal.

Why, Father Smith, thy wife is a wit, man! Didst thou ever find that out before? But where is Widow Lovick, Dame Smith? My cousin John Belford says she is a very good woman. Is she within? Or is *she* gone with Miss Harlowe too?

She will be within by and by, sir. She is not with the lady.

Well, but my good, dear Mrs. Smith, whither is the lady gone? And when will she return?

I can't tell, sir.

Don't tell fibs, Dame Smith; don't tell fibs; chucking her under the chin: which made John's upper lip, with chin shortened, rise to his nose. I am sure you know! But here 's another pair of stairs: let us see; who lives up there? But hold, here 's another room locked up, tapping at the door: Who 's at home? cried I.

That 's Mrs. Lovick's apartment. She is gone out, and has the key with her.

Widow Lovick! rapping again, I believe you are at home: pray open the door.

John and Joseph muttered and whispered together.

No whispering, honest friends: 'tis not manners to whisper. Joseph, what said John to thee?

JOHN, sir! disdainfully repeated the good woman.

I beg pardon, Mrs. Smith: but you see the force of example.

Had *you* showed your honest man more respect, *I* should. Let me give you a piece of advice: Women who treat their husbands irreverently teach strangers to use them with contempt. There, honest Master John; why dost not pull off thy hat to me? Oh, so thou wouldst, if thou hadst it on: but thou never wearest thy hat in thy wife's presence, I believe; dost thou?

None of your fleers and your jeers, sir, cried John. I wish every married pair lived as happily as we do.

I wish so too, honest friend. But I'll be hanged if thou hast any children.

Why so, sir?

Hast thou? Answer me, man: hast thou, or not?

Perhaps not, sir. But what of that?

What of that? Why, I'll tell thee: the man who has no children by his wife must put up with plain John. Hadst thou a child or two, thou'dst be called Mr. Smith, with a curtsy, or a smile at least, at every word.

You are very pleasant, sir, replied my dame. I fancy, if either my husband or I had as much to answer for as I know whom, we should not be so merry.

Why then, Dame Smith, so much the worse for those who were obliged to keep you company. But I am not merry—I am sad! Heigh-ho! Where shall I find my dear Miss Harlowe?

My beloved Miss Harlowe! [calling at the foot of the third pair of stairs] if you are above, for Heaven's sake answer me. I am coming up.

Sir, said the good man, I wish you'd walk down. The servants' rooms, and the working-rooms, are up those stairs, and another pair; and nobody's there that you want.

Shall I go up, and see if Miss Harlowe be there, Mrs. Smith?

You may, sir, if you please.

Then I won't; for if she was, you would not be so obliging.

I am ashamed to give you all this attendance: you are the politest traders I ever knew. Honest Joseph, slapping him upon the shoulders on a sudden, which made him jump, didst ever grin for a wager, man? For the rascal seemed not displeased with me; and, cracking his flat face from ear to ear, with a distended mouth, showed his teeth, as broad and as black as his thumbnails. But don't I hinder thee? What canst earn a day, man?

Half a crown I can earn a day; with an air of pride and petulance at being startled.

There, then, is a day's wages for thee. But thou needest not attend me further.

Come, Mrs. Smith, come, John (Master Smith, I should say), let's walk down, and give me an account where the lady is gone, and when she will return.

So downstairs led I; John and Joseph (though I had discharged the latter) and my dame following me, to show their complaisance to a stranger.

I re-entered one of the first-floor rooms. I have a great mind to be your lodger: for I never saw such obliging folks in my life. What rooms have you to let?

None at all, sir.

I am sorry for that. But whose is this?

Mine, sir, chuffily said John.

Thine, man! Why, then, I will take it of thee. This, and a bedchamber, and a garret for one servant, will content me. I will give thee thy own price, and half a guinea a day over, for those conveniences.

For ten guineas a day, sir——

Hold, John! (Master Smith, I should say)—before thou speakest, consider. I won't be affronted, man.

Sir, I wish you'd walk down, said the good woman. Really, sir, you take——

Great liberties, I hope you would not say, Mrs. Smith?

Indeed, sir, I was going to say something like it.

Well, then, I am glad I prevented you; for such words better become my mouth than yours. But I must lodge with you till the lady returns. I *believe* I must. However, you may be wanted in the shop; so we'll talk that over there.

Down I went, they paying diligent attendance on my steps.

When I came into the shop, seeing no chair or stool, I went behind the counter, and sat down under an arched kind of canopy of carved work, which these proud traders, emulating the *royal niche-fillers*, often give themselves, while a joint-stool, perhaps, serves those by whom they get their bread: such is the dignity of trade in this mercantile nation!

I looked about me, and above me, and told them I was very proud of my seat; asking if John were ever permitted to fill this superb niche?

Perhaps he was, he said very surlily.

That is it that makes thee look so like a statue, man.

John looked plaguy glum upon me. But his man Joseph

and my man Will turned round with their backs to us to hide their grinning, with each his fist in his mouth.

I asked what it was they sold?

Powder, and washballs, and snuff, they said; and gloves and stockings.

Oh, come, I 'll be your customer. Will, do I want washballs?

Yes, and please your honour, you can dispense with one or two.

Give him half a dozen, Dame Smith.

She told me she must come where I was to serve them. Pray, sir, walk from behind the counter.

Indeed, but I won't. The shop shall be mine. Where are they, if a customer should come in?

She pointed over my head, with a purse-mouth, as if she would not have simpered could she have helped it. I reached down the glass and gave Will six. There—put 'em up, sirrah.

He did, grinning with his teeth out before; which touching my conscience, as the loss of them was owing to me: Joseph, said I, come hither. Come hither, man, when I bid thee.

He stalked towards me, his hands behind him, half willing, and half unwilling.

I suddenly wrapped my arm round his neck. Will, thy penknife, this moment. D—n the fellow, where's thy penknife?

O Lord! said the pollard-headed dog, struggling to get his head loose from under my arm, while my other hand was muzzling about his cursed chaps, as if I would take his teeth out.

I will pay thee a good price, man: don't struggle thus! The penknife, Will!

O Lord! cried Joseph, struggling still more and more: and out comes Will's pruning-knife; for the rascal is a gardener in the country. I have only this, sir.

The best in the world to launch a gum. D—n the fellow, why dost struggle thus?

Master and Mistress Smith being afraid, I suppose, that I had a design upon Joseph's throat, because he was their champion (and this, indeed, made me take the more notice of him), coming towards me with countenances tragi-comical, I let him go.

I only wanted, said I, to take out two or three of this rascal's broad teeth, to put them into my servant's jaws—and I would have paid him his price for them. I would, by my soul, Joseph.

Joseph shook his ears; and with both hands stroked down, smooth as it would lie, his bushy hair; and looked at me as if he knew not whether he should laugh or be angry: but, after a stupid stare or two, stalked off to the other end of the shop, nodding his head at me as he went, still stroking down his hair; and took his stand by his master, facing about, and muttering that I was plaguy strong in the arms, and he thought would have throttled him. Then folding his arms, and shaking his bristled head, added, 'Twas well I was a gentleman, or he would not have taken such an affront.

I demanded where their rappee was? The good woman pointed to the place; and I took up a scallop-shell of it, refusing to let her weigh it, and filled my box. And now, Mrs. Smith, said I, where are your gloves?

She showed me; and I chose four pair of them, and set Joseph, who looked as if he wanted to be taken notice of again, to open the fingers.

A female customer, who had been gaping at the door, came in for some Scots snuff; and I would serve her. The wench was plaguy homely; and I told her so; or else, I said, I would have treated her. She in anger [no woman is homely in her own opinion] threw down her penny; and I put it in my pocket.

Just then, turning my eye to the door, I saw a pretty genteel lady, with a footman after her, peeping in with a What's the matter, good folks? to the starers; and I ran to her from behind the counter, and, as she was making off, took her hand, and drew her into the shop, begging that she would be my customer; for that I had but just begun trade.

What do you sell, sir? said she, smiling; but a little surprised.

Tapes, ribbons, silk laces, pins, and needles; for I am a pedlar: powder, patches, washballs, stockings, garters, snuffs, and pincushions—don't we, Goody Smith?

So in I gently drew her to the counter, running behind it myself, with an air of great diligence and obligingness. I have excellent gloves and washballs, madam; rappee, Scots, Portugal, and all sorts of snuff.

Well, said she, in very good humour, I'll encourage a young beginner for once. Here, Andrew [to her footman], you want a pair of gloves, don't you?

I took down a parcel of gloves, which Mrs. Smith pointed to, and came round to the fellow to fit them on myself.

No matter for opening them, said I: thy fingers, friend, are as stiff as drumsticks. Push—thou'rt an awkward dog! I wonder such a pretty lady will be followed by such a clumsy varlet.

The fellow had no strength for laughing: and Joseph was mightily pleased, in hopes, I suppose, I would borrow a few of

Andrew's teeth, to keep him in countenance: and Father and Mother Smith, like all the world, as the jest was turned from themselves, seemed diverted with the humour.

The fellow said the gloves were too little.

Thrust, and be d—ned to thee, said I: why, fellow, thou hast not the strength of a cat.

Sir, sir, said he, laughing, I shall hurt your honour's side.

D—n thee, thrust, I say.

He did; and burst out the sides of the glove.

Will, said I, where's thy pruning-knife? By my soul, friend, I had a good mind to pare thy cursed paws. But come, here's a larger pair: try them when thou gettest home; and let thy sweetheart, if thou hast one, mend the other; and so take both.

The lady laughed at the humour; as did my fellow, and Mrs. Smith, and Joseph: even John laughed, though he seemed by the force put upon his countenance to be but half pleased with me neither.

Madam, said I, and stepped behind the counter, bowing over it, now I hope you will buy something for yourself. Nobody shall use you better, nor sell you cheaper.

Come, said she, give me sixpennyworth of Portugal snuff.

They showed me where it was, and I served her; and said, when she would have paid me, I took nothing at my opening.

If I treated her footman, she told me, I should not treat her.

Well, with all my heart, said I: 'tis not for us tradesmen to be saucy—is it, Mrs. Smith?

I put her sixpence in my pocket; and, seizing her hand, took notice to her of the crowd that had gathered about the door, and besought her to walk into the back shop with me.

She struggled her hand out of mine, and would stay no longer.

So I bowed, and bid her kindly welcome, and thanked her, and hoped I should have her custom another time.

She went away smiling; and Andrew after her; who made me a fine bow.

I began to be out of countenance at the crowd, which thickened apace; and bid Will order the chair to the door.

Well, Mrs. Smith, with a grave air, I am heartily sorry Miss Harlowe is abroad. You don't tell me where she is?

Indeed, sir, I cannot.

You *will* not, you mean. She could have no notion of my coming. I came to town but last night. I have been very ill. She has almost broken my heart by her cruelty. You know my story, I doubt not. Tell her I must go out of town to-morrow morning. But I will send my servant to know if she will favour me with one half-hour's conversation; for, as soon as I get down, I shall set out for Dover in my way to France, if I have not a countermand from *her* who has the sole disposal of my fate.

And so, flinging down a Portugal six-and-thirty, I took Mr. Smith by the hand, telling him I was sorry we had not more time to be better acquainted; and bidding farewell to honest Joseph (who pursed up his mouth as I passed by him, as if he thought his teeth still in jeopardy), and Mrs. Smith adieu, and to recommend me to her fair lodger, hummed an air, and, the chair being come, whipped into it; the people about the door seeming to be in good humour with me; one crying, A pleasant gentleman, I warrant him! And away I was carried to White's, according to direction.

As soon as I came thither, I ordered Will to go and change his clothes, and to disguise himself by putting on his black wig and keeping his mouth shut; and then to dodge about Smith's, to inform himself of the lady's motions.

.   .   .   .

I give thee this impudent account of myself that thou mayst rave at me, and call me hardened, and what thou wilt. For, in the first place, I, who had been so lately ill, was glad I was alive; and then I was so balked by my charmer's unexpected absence, and so ruffled by that, and by the bluff treatment of Father John, that I had no other way to avoid being out of humour with all I met with. Moreover I was rejoiced to find, by the lady's absence, and by her going out at six in the morning, that it was impossible she should be so ill as thou representest her to be; and this gave me still higher spirits. Then I know the sex always love cheerful and humorous fellows. The dear creature herself used to be pleased with my gay temper and lively manner; and had she been told that I was blubbering for her in the back shop, she would have despised me still more than she does.

Furthermore, I was sensible that the people of the house must needs have a terrible notion of me, as a savage, bloody-minded, obdurate fellow; a perfect woman-eater; and, no doubt, expected to see me with the claws of a lion and the fangs of a tiger; and it was but policy to show them what a harmless, pleasant fellow I am, in order to familiarize the Johns and the Josephs to me. For it was evident to me, by the good woman's calling them down, that she thought me a dangerous man.

Whereas now, John and I having shaken hands together, and Dame Smith having seen that I have the face, and hands, and looks of a man, and walk upright, and prate, and laugh, and joke, like other people; and Joseph, that I can talk of taking his teeth out of his head without doing him the least hurt; they will all, at my next visit, be much more easy and pleasant with me than Andrew's gloves were to him; and we shall be as thoroughly acquainted as if we had known one another a twelvemonth.

When I returned to our mother's, I again cursed her and all her nymphs together; and still refused to see either Sally or Polly. I raved at the horrid arrest; and told the old dragon that it was owing to her and hers that the fairest virtue in the world was ruined; my reputation for ever blasted; and that I was not married, and happy in the love of the most excellent of her sex.

She, to pacify me, said she would show me a new face that would please me; since I would not see my Sally, who was dying for grief.

Where is this new face, cried I? Let me see her, though I shall never see any face with pleasure but Miss Harlowe's.

She won't come down, replied she. She will not be at the word of command yet. She is but just in the trammels; and must be waited upon, I 'll assure you; and courted much besides.

Ay! said I, that looks well. Lead me to her this instant.

I followed her up: and who should she be but that little toad Sally!

O curse you, said I, for a devil, is it you? Is yours the new face?

O my dear, dear Mr. Lovelace! cried she, I am glad anything will bring you to me! And so the little beast threw herself about my neck, and there clung like a cat. Come, said she, what will you give me, and I 'll be virtuous for a quarter of an hour, and mimic your Clarissa to the life?

I was *Belforded* all over. I could not bear such an insult upon the dear creature (for I have a soft and generous nature in the main, whatever thou thinkest); and cursed her most devoutly for taking my beloved's name in her mouth in such a way. But the little devil was not to be balked; but fell a crying, sobbing, praying, begging, exclaiming, fainting, that I never saw my lovely girl so well aped. Indeed I was almost taken in; for I could have fancied I had her before me once more.

O this sex! this artful sex! There's no minding them. At first, indeed, their grief and their concern may be real: but give way to the hurricane, and it will soon die away in soft murmurs, trilling upon your ears like the notes of a well-tuned viol. And, by Sally, one sees that art will generally so well supply the place of nature that you shall not easily know the difference. Miss Clarissa Harlowe, indeed, is the only woman in the world, I believe, that can say, in the words of her favourite Job (for I can quote a text as well as she): *But it is not so with me.*

They were very inquisitive about my fair one. They told me that you seldom came near them; that, when you did, you put on plaguy grave airs; would hardly stay five minutes; and did nothing but praise Miss Harlowe and lament her hard fate. In short, that you despised them; was full of sentences; and they doubted not, in a little while, would be a lost man, and marry.

A pretty character for thee, is it not? Thou art in a blessed way, yet hast nothing to do but to *go on in it*; and then what a work hast thou to go through! If thou turnest back, these sorceresses will be like the Tsar's Cossacks [at Pultowa, I think it was], who were planted with ready primed and cocked pieces behind the regulars, in order to shoot them dead if they did not push on and conquer; and then wilt thou be most lamentably despised by every harlot thou hast made—and, O Jack! how formidable, in that case, will be the number of thy enemies!

I intend to regulate my motions by Will's intelligence; for see this dear creature I must and will. Yet I have promised Lord M. to be down in two or three days at farthest; for he is grown plaguy fond of me since I was ill.

I am in hopes that the word I left, that I am to go out of town to-morrow morning, will soon bring the lady back again.

Meantime I thought I would write to divert thee, while thou art of such importance about the dying; and as thy servant, it seems, comes backward and forward every day, perhaps I may send thee another letter to-morrow, with the particulars of the interview between the dear creature and me; after which my soul thirsteth.

Letter LVI—Mr. Lovelace to John Belford, Esq.

Tuesday, Aug. 22.

I MUST write on to divert myself: for I can get no rest; no refreshing rest. I awaked just now in a cursed fright. How a man may be affected by dreams!

"Methought I had an interview with my beloved. I found her all goodness, condescension, and forgiveness. She suffered herself to be overcome in my favour by the joint intercessions of Lord M., Lady Sarah, Lady Betty, and my two Cousins Montague, who waited upon her in deep mourning; the ladies in long trains sweeping after them; Lord M. in a long black mantle trailing after *him*. They told her they came in these robes to express their sorrow for my sins against her, and to implore her to forgive me.

"I myself, I thought, was upon my knees, with a sword in my hand, offering either to put it up in the scabbard, or to thrust it into my heart, as she should command the one or the other.

"At that moment her Cousin Morden, I thought, all of a sudden, flashed in through a window with his drawn sword. Die, Lovelace! said he, this instant die, and be damned, if in earnest thou repairest not by marriage my cousin's wrongs!

"I was rising to resent this insult, I thought, when Lord M. ran between us with his great black mantle, and threw it over my face: and instantly my charmer, with that sweet voice which has so often played upon my ravished ears, wrapped her arms round me, muffled as I was in my lord's mantle: O spare, spare my Lovelace! and spare, O Lovelace, my beloved Cousin Morden! Let me not have my distresses augmented by the fall of either or both of those who are so dear to me!

"At this, charmed with her sweet mediation, I thought I would have clasped her in my arms: when immediately the most angelic form I had ever beheld, all clad in transparent white, descended in a cloud, which, opening, discovered a firmament above it, crowded with golden cherubs and glittering seraphs, all address-ing her with: Welcome, welcome, welcome! and, encircling my charmer, ascended with her to the region of seraphims; and instantly, the opened cloud closing, I lost sight of *her*, and of the *bright form* together, and found wrapped in my arms her azure robe (all stuck thick with stars of embossed silver), which I had caught hold of in hopes of detaining her; but was all that was left me of my beloved Clarissa. And then (horrid to relate!) the floor sinking under *me*, as the firmament had opened for *her*, I dropped into a hole more frightful than that of Elden; and, tumbling over and over down it, without view of a bottom, I awaked in a panic; and was as effectually disordered for half an hour, as if my dream had been a reality."

Wilt thou forgive me troubling thee with such visionary stuff? Thou wilt see by it only that, sleeping or waking, my Clarissa is always present with me.

But here this moment is Will, come running hither to tell me that his lady actually returned to her lodgings last night between eleven and twelve; and is now there, though very ill.

I hasten to her. But, that I may not add to her indisposition by any rough or boisterous behaviour, I will be as soft and gentle as the dove herself in my addresses to her.

> That I do love her, O all ye host of heaven,
> Be witness!—That she is dear to me!
> Dearer than day, to one whom sight must leave;
> Dearer than life, to one who fears to die!

The chair is come. I fly to my beloved.

Letter LVII—Mr. Lovelace to John Belford, Esq.

CURSE upon my stars! Disappointed again! It was about eight when I arrived at Smith's. The woman was in the shop.

So, old acquaintance, how do you now? I know my love is above. Let her be acquainted that I am here, waiting for admission to her presence, and can take no denial. Tell her that I will approach her with the most respectful duty, and in whose company she pleases; and I will not touch the hem of her garment without her leave.

Indeed, sir, you are mistaken. The lady is not in this house, nor near it.

I'll see that.—Will! beckoning him to me, and whispering, See if thou canst any way find out (without losing sight of the door, lest she should be below stairs) if she be in the neighbourhood, if not within.

Will bowed and went off. Up went I without further ceremony; attended now only by the good woman.

I went into each apartment, except that which was locked before, and was now also locked: and I called to my Clarissa in the voice of love: but by the still silence was convinced she was not there. Yet, on the strength of my intelligence, I doubted not but she was in the house.

I then went up two pair of stairs, and looked round the first room: but no Miss Harlowe.

And who, pray, is in this room? stopping at the door of another.

A widow gentlewoman, sir—Mrs. Lovick

Oh, my dear Mrs. Lovick! said I. I am intimately acquainted with Mrs. Lovick's character from my cousin John Belford.

I must see Mrs. Lovick by all means.   Good Mrs. Lovick, open the door.

She did.

Your servant, madam.   Be so good as to excuse me.   You have heard my story.   You are an admirer of the most excellent woman in the world.   Dear Mrs. Lovick, tell me what is become of her?

The poor lady, sir, went out yesterday on purpose to avoid you.

How so?   She knew not that I would be here.

She was afraid you would come, when she heard you were recovered from your illness.   Ah! sir, what pity it is that so fine a gentleman should make such ill returns for God's goodness to him!

You are an excellent woman, Mrs. Lovick: I know that, by my cousin John Belford's account of you: and Miss Clarissa Harlowe is an angel.

Miss Harlowe is indeed an angel, replied she; and soon will be company for angels.

No jesting with such a woman as this, Jack.

Tell me of a truth, good Mrs. Lovick, where I may see this dear lady.   Upon my soul, I will neither frighten nor offend her. I will only beg of her to hear me speak for one half-quarter of an hour; and, if she will have it so, I will never trouble her more.

Sir, said the widow, it would be death for her to see you. She was at home last night; I'll tell you truth: but fitter to be in bed all day.   She came home, she said, to die; and, if she could not avoid your visit, she was unable to fly from you; and believed she should die in your presence.

And yet go out again this morning early?   How can that be, widow?

Why, sir, she rested not two hours, for fear of you.   Her fear gave her strength, which she'll suffer for when that fear is over. And finding herself, the more she thought of your visit, the less able to stay to receive it, she took chair, and is gone nobody knows whither.   But I believe she intended to be carried to the water-side, in order to take boat; for she cannot bear a coach. It extremely incommoded her yesterday.

But before we talk any further, said I, if she be gone abroad, you can have no objection to my looking into every apartment above and below; because I am told she is actually in the house.

Indeed, sir, she is *not*.   You may satisfy yourself, if you please: but Mrs. Smith and I waited on her to her chair.   We were forced to support her, she was so weak.   She said: Whither *can* I go, Mrs. Lovick? Whither *can* I go, Mrs. Smith? Cruel, cruel man! Tell him I called him so, if he come again! God give him that peace which he denies me!

Sweet creature! cried I, and looked down, and took out my handkerchief.

The widow wept. I wish, said she, I had never known so excellent a lady, and so great a sufferer! I love her as my own child!

Mrs. Smith wept.

I then gave over the hope of seeing her for this time. I was extremely chagrined at my disappointment, and at the account they gave of her ill-health.

Would to Heaven, said I, she would put it in my power to repair her wrongs! I have been an ungrateful wretch to her. I need not tell you, Mrs. Lovick, how much I have injured her, nor how much she suffers by her relations' implacableness. 'Tis that, Mrs. Lovick, 'tis that implacableness, Mrs. Smith, that cuts her to the heart. Her family is the most implacable family on earth; and the dear creature, in refusing to see me, and to be reconciled to me, shows her relation to them a little too plainly.

O sir, said the widow, not one syllable of what you say belongs to this lady. I never saw so sweet a creature! so edifying a piety! and one of so forgiving a temper! She is always accusing herself, and excusing her relations. And, as to you, sir, she forgives you: she wishes you well; and happier than you will let her be. Why will you not, sir, why will you not let her die in peace? 'Tis all she wishes for. You don't look like a hard-hearted gentleman! How can you thus hunt and persecute a poor lady, whom none of her relations will look upon? It makes my heart bleed for her.

And then she wept again. Mrs. Smith wept also. My seat grew uneasy to me. I shifted to another several times; and what Mrs. Lovick further said and showed me made me still more uneasy.

Bad as the poor lady was last night, said she, she transcribed into her book a meditation on your persecuting her thus. I have a copy of it. If I thought it would have any effect I would read it to you.

Let me read it myself, Mrs. Lovick.

She gave it to me. It has a Harlowe-spirited title: and from a forgiving spirit, intolerable. I desired to take it with me. She consented, on condition that I showed it to 'Squire Belford. So here, Mr. 'Squire Belford, thou mayst read it, if thou wilt.

On being hunted after by the enemy of my soul

Monday, Aug. 21.

Deliver me, O Lord, from the evil man.   Preserve me from the violent man.

Who imagines mischief in *his* heart.

He hath sharpened *his* tongue like a serpent.   Adder's poison is under *his* lips.

Keep me, O Lord, from the hands of the wicked.   Preserve me from the violent man; *who hath* purposed to overthrow my goings.

He hath hid a snare for me.   *He hath* spread a net by the wayside. *He hath* set gins for me in the way wherein I walked.

Keep me from the snares which *he hath* laid for me, and the gins of *this* worker of iniquity.

The enemy hath persecuted my soul.   He hath smitten my life down to the ground.   *He* hath made me dwell in darkness, as those that have been long dead.

Therefore is my spirit overwhelmed within me.   My heart within me is desolate.

Hide not Thy face from me in the day when I am in trouble.

For my days are consumed like smoke; and my bones are burnt as the hearth.

My heart is smitten and withered like grass; so that I forget to eat my bread.

By reason of the voice of my groaning, my bones cleave to my skin.

I am like a pelican of the wilderness.   I am like an owl of the desert.

I watch; and am as a sparrow alone upon the house-top.

I have eaten ashes like bread; and mingled my drink with weeping: Because of Thine indignation and Thy wrath; for Thou hast lifted me up, and cast me down.

My days are like a shadow that declineth, and I am withered like grass.

Grant not, O Lord, the desires of the wicked; further not his devices, lest he exalt himself.

Why now, Mrs. Lovick, said I, when I had read this meditation, as she called it, I think I am very severely treated by the lady, if she mean *me* in all this.   For how is it that I am the *enemy of her soul*, when I love her both soul and body?

She says that I am a *violent* man, and a *wicked* man.   That I have been so I own: but I repent, and only wish to have it in my power to repair the injuries I have done her.

The *gin*, the *snare*, the *net*, mean matrimony, I suppose—but is it a crime in me to wish to marry her?   Would any other woman think it so? and choose to become a *pelican in the wilderness*, or a *lonely sparrow on the house-top*, rather than have a mate that would chirp about her all day and all night?

She says she *has eaten ashes like bread*—a sad mistake, to be sure!—and *mingled her drink with weeping*—sweet, maudlin soul! should I say of anybody confessing this but Miss Harlowe.

She concludes with praying that *the desires of the wicked* (meaning poor me, I doubt) *may not be granted*; that m*y devices may not be furthered, lest I exalt myself.* I should undoubtedly exalt myself, and with reason, could I have the honour and the blessing of such a wife. And if my *desires* have so honourable an end, I know not why I should be called *wicked*, and why I should not be allowed to hope, that my honest *devices* may be *furthered*, that I MAY exalt myself.

But here, Mrs. Lovick, let me ask, as something is undoubtedly meant by the *lonely sparrow on the house-top*, is not the dear creature at this very instant (tell me truly) concealed in Mrs. Smith's cockloft? What say you, Mrs. Lovick: what say you, Mrs. Smith, to this?

They assured me to the contrary; and that she was actually abroad, and they knew not where.

Thou seest, Jack, that I would fain have diverted the chagrin given me not only by the women's talk, but by this collection of Scripture texts drawn up in array against me. Several *other* whimsical and light things I said [all I had for it!] with the same view: but the widow would not let me come off so. She stuck to me; and gave me, as I told thee, a good deal of uneasiness, by her sensible and serious expostulations. Mrs. Smith put in now and then; and the two jack-pudding fellows, John and Joseph, not being present, I had no provocation to turn the conversation into a farce; and, at last, they both joined warmly to endeavour to prevail upon me to give up all thoughts of seeing the lady. But I could not hear of that. On the contrary, I besought Mrs. Smith to let me have one of her rooms but till I could see her; and were it but for one, two, or three days I would pay a year's rent for it; and quit it the moment the interview was over. But they desired to be excused; and were sure the lady would not come to the house till I was gone, were it for a *month*.

This pleased me; for I found they did not think her so very ill as they would have me believe her to be; but I took no notice of the slip, because I would not guard them against more of the like.

In short, I told them I *must* and *would* see her: but that it should be with all the respect and veneration that heart could pay to excellence like hers: and that I would go round to all the churches in London and Westminster, where there were prayers or service, from sunrise to sunset, and haunt their house like a ghost, till I had the opportunity my soul panted after.

This I bid them tell her. And thus ended our serious conversation.

I took leave of them, and went down; and, stepping into my chair, caused myself to be carried to Lincoln's Inn; and walked in the gardens till chapel was opened; and then I went in, and stayed prayers, in hopes of seeing the dear creature enter: but to no purpose; and yet I prayed most devoutly that she might be conducted thither, either by my good angel or her own. And indeed I burn more than ever with impatience to be once more permitted to kneel at the feet of this adorable woman. And had I met her, or espied her in the chapel, it is my firm belief that I should not have been able (though it had been in the midst of the sacred office and in the presence of thousands) to have forborne prostration to her, and even clamorous supplication for her *forgiveness*: a Christian act; the exercise of it therefore worthy of the place.

After service was over I stepped into my chair again, and once more was carried to Smith's, in hopes I might have surprised her there: but no such happiness for thy friend. I stayed in the back shop an hour and a half by my watch; and again underwent a good deal of preachment from the women. John was mainly civil to me now; won over a little by my serious talk and the honour I professed for the lady. They all three wished matters could be made up between us: but still insisted that she could never get over her illness; and that her heart was broken. A cue, I suppose, they had from you.

While I was there, a letter was brought by a particular hand. They seemed very solicitous to hide it from me; which made me suspect it was for her. I desired to be suffered to cast an eye upon the seal and the superscription; promising to give it back to them unopened.

Looking upon it, I told them I knew the hand and seal. It was from her sister.[1] And I hoped it would bring her news that she would be pleased with.

They joined most heartily in the same hope: and giving the letter to them again, I civilly took my leave, and went away.

But I will be there again presently; for I fancy my courteous behaviour to these women will, on their report of it, procure me the favour I so earnestly covet. And so I will leave my letter unsealed, to tell thee the event of my next visit at Smith's.

[1] See Letter lxviii.

Thy servant just calling, I send thee this. And will soon follow it by another. Meantime, I long to hear how poor Belton is. To whom my best wishes.

Letter LVIII—Mr. Belford to Robert Lovelace, Esq.

Tuesday, Aug. 22.

I HAVE been under such concern for the poor man, whose exit I almost hourly expect, and at the shocking scenes his illness and his agonies exhibit, that I have been only able to make memoranda of the melancholy passages, from which to draw up a more perfect account, for the instruction of us all, when the writing appetite shall return.

.   .   .   .

It is returned! Indignation has revived it, on receipt of thy letters of Sunday and yesterday; by which I have reason to reproach thee in very serious terms, that thou hast not kept thy honour with me: and if thy breach of it be attended with such effects as I fear it will be, I shall let thee know more of my mind on this head.

If thou wouldst be thought in earnest in thy wishes to move the poor lady in thy favour, thy ludicrous behaviour at Smith's, when it comes to be represented to her, will have a very *consistent* appearance; will it not? It will, indeed, confirm her in her opinion that the *grave* is more to be wished for, by one of her serious and pious turn, than a *husband* incapable either of reflection or remorse; just recovered, as thou art, from a dangerous, at least a sharp, illness.

I am extremely concerned for the poor, unprotected lady; she was so excessively low and weak on Saturday that I could not be admitted to her speech: and to be driven out of her lodgings, when it was fitter for her to be in bed, is such a piece of cruelty as he only could be guilty of, who could act as thou hast done by such an angel.

Canst thou thyself say, on reflection, that it has not the look of a wicked and hardened sportiveness in thee, for the sake of a wanton humour only (since it can answer no end that thou proposest to thyself, but the direct contrary), to hunt from place to place a poor lady, who, like a harmless deer that has already a barbed shaft in her breast, seeks only a refuge from thee, in the shades of death?

But I will leave this matter upon thy own conscience, to paint thee such a scene from my memoranda as thou perhaps wilt be moved by more effectually than by any other: because it is such a one as thou thyself must one day be a principal actor in, and, as I thought, hadst very lately in apprehension: and is the last scene of one of thy most intimate friends, who has been for the four past days labouring in the agonies of death. For, Lovelace, let this truth, this undoubted truth, be engraven on thy memory in all thy gaieties, That the life we are so fond of, is hardly life; a mere breathing-space only; and that at the end of its longest date,

THOU MUST DIE, AS WELL AS BELTON.

Thou knowest by Tourville what we had done as to the poor man's worldly affairs; and that we had got his unhappy sister to come and live with him (little did we think him so very near his end): and so I will proceed to tell thee that when I arrived at his house on Saturday night, I found him excessively ill: but just raised, and in his elbow-chair, held up by his nurse and Mowbray (the roughest and most untouched creature that ever entered a sick man's chamber); while the maidservants were trying to make that bed easier for him which he was to return to; his mind ten times uneasier than that could be, and the true cause that the down was no softer to him.

He had so much longed to see me, as I was told by his sister (whom I sent for down to inquire how he was), that they all rejoiced when I entered: Here, said Mowbray, here, Tommy, is honest Jack Belford!

Where, where? said the poor man.

I hear his voice, cried Mowbray: he is coming upstairs.

In a transport of joy, he would have raised himself at my entrance, but had like to have pitched out of the chair: and when recovered, called me his best friend! his *kindest* friend! but burst out into a flood of tears: O Jack! O Belford! said he, see the way I am in! See how weak! So *much*, and so *soon* reduced! Do you know me? Do you know your poor friend Belton?

You are not so much altered, my dear Belton, as you think you are. But I see you are weak; very weak—and I am sorry for it.

Weak, weak, indeed, my dearest Belford, said he, and weaker in mind, if possible, than in body; and wept bitterly—or I should not thus unman myself. I, who never feared *anything*, to be forced to show myself such a *nursling*! I am quite ashamed of myself! But don't despise me; dear Belford, don't despise me, I beseech thee.

I ever honoured a man that could weep for the distresses of *others*; and ever shall, said I; and such a one cannot be insensible of *his own*.

However, I could not help being *visibly* moved at the poor fellow's emotion.

Now, said the brutal Mowbray, do I think thee insufferable, Jack. Our poor friend is already a peg too low; and here thou art letting him down lower and lower still. This soothing of him in his dejected moments, and joining thy womanish tears with his, is not the way; I am sure it is not. If our Lovelace were here, he'd tell thee so.

Thou art an impenetrable creature, replied I; unfit to be present at a scene, the terrors of which thou wilt not be able to feel till thou feelest them in thyself; and then, if thou hast *time for feeling*, my life for thine, thou behavest as pitifully as those thou thinkest *most* pitiful.

Then turning to the poor sick man: Tears, my dear Belton, are no signs of an *unmanly*, but, contrarily, of a humane nature; they ease the overcharged heart, which would burst but for that kindly and natural relief.

> Give sorrow *words* (says Shakespeare);
> —The grief that does not speak,
> Whispers the o'er-fraught heart, and bids it break.

I know, my dear Belton, thou used to take pleasure in repetitions from the poets; but thou must be tasteless of their beauties now: yet be not discountenanced by this uncouth and unreflecting Mowbray, for, as Juvenal says, *Tears are the prerogative of manhood.*

'Tis at least seasonably said, my dear Belford. It is kind to keep me in countenance for this *womanish weakness*, as Mowbray has been upbraidingly calling it, ever since he has been with me. And in so doing (whatever I might have thought in such high health as he enjoys) has convinced me that bottle-friends feel nothing but what moves in that little circle.

Well, well, proceed in your own way, Jack. I love my friend Belton as well as you can do; yet for the blood of me, I cannot but think that soothing a man's weakness is increasing it.

If it be weakness to be touched at great and concerning events in which our humanity is concerned, said I, thou mayest be right.

I have seen many a man, said the rough creature, going up

Holborn Hill, that has behaved more like a man than either
of you.

Ay, but, Mowbray, replied the poor man, those wretches have
not had their minds enervated by such infirmities of body as
I have long laboured under.   Thou art a shocking fellow, and
ever wert.   But to be able to remember nothing in these moments
but what reproaches me, and to know that I cannot hold it
long, and what may *then* be my lot, if——But interrupting
himself, and turning to me: Give me thy pity, Jack; 'tis balm to
my wounded soul; and let Mowbray sit indifferent enough to
the pangs of a dying friend to laugh at us both.

The hardened fellow then retired, with the air of a Lovelace;
only more stupid; yawning and stretching, instead of humming
a tune as thou didst at Smith's.

I assisted to get the poor man into bed.   He was so weak and
low that he could not bear the fatigue, and fainted away; and I
verily thought was quite gone.   But recovering, and his doctor
coming, and advising to keep him quiet, I retired, and joined
Mowbray in the garden; who took more delight to talk of the
living Lovelace and his levities, than of the dying Belton and
his repentance.

I just saw him again on Saturday night before I went to bed;
which I did early; for I was surfeited with Mowbray's frothy
insensibility, and could not bear him.

It is such a horrid thing to think of, that a man who had lived
in such strict terms of—what shall I call it?—with another; the
proof does not come out so as to say *friendship*; who had pretended so much love for him; could not bear to be out of his
company; would ride a hundred miles on end to enjoy it; and
would fight for him, be the cause right or wrong: yet now could
be so little moved to see him in such misery of body and mind
as to be able to rebuke him, and rather ridicule than pity him,
because he was more affected by what he felt, than he had seen
a malefactor (hardened perhaps by liquor, and not softened by
previous sickness) on his going to execution.

This put me strongly in mind of what the divine Miss HARLOWE
once said to me, talking of friendship, and what my friendship
to *you* required of me: "Depend upon it, Mr. Belford," said she,
"that one day you will be convinced that what *you* call friendship is chaff and stubble; and that nothing is worthy of that
sacred name,

THAT HAS NOT VIRTUE FOR ITS BASE."

Sunday morning, I was called up at six o'clock, at the poor man's earnest request, and found him in a terrible agony. O Jack! Jack! said he, looking wildly, as if he had seen a spectre. Come nearer me! reaching out both arms. Come nearer me! Dear, dear Belford, save me! Then clasping my arm with both his hands, and rearing up his head towards me, his eyes strangely rolling: Save me! dear Belford, save me! repeated he.

I put my other arm about him. Save you from what, my dear Belton? said I. Save you from what? Nothing shall hurt you. What must I save you from?

Recovering from his terror, he sank down again: O save me from myself! said he; save me from my own reflections. O dear Jack! what a thing it is to die, and not to have one comfortable reflection to revolve! What would I give for one year of my past life?—only *one* year—and to have the same sense of things that I now have!

I tried to comfort him as well as I could: but free-livers to free-livers are sorry death-bed comforters. And he broke in upon me: O my dear Belford, said he, I am told (and I have heard you ridiculed for it) that the excellent Miss Harlowe has wrought a conversion in you. May it be so! You are a man of sense; O may it be so! Now is your time! Now that you are in full vigour of mind and body! But your poor Belton, alas! your poor Belton kept his vices till they left him—and see the miserable effects in debility of mind and despondency! Were Mowbray here, and were he to *laugh* at me, I would own that this is the cause of my despair—that God's *justice* cannot let His *mercy* operate for my comfort: for, oh! I have been very, *very* wicked; and have despised the offers of His grace, till He has withdrawn it from me for ever.

I used all the arguments I could think of to give him consolation: and what I said had such an effect upon him as to quiet his mind for the greatest part of the day; and in a lucid hour his memory served him to repeat these lines of Dryden, grasping my hand, and looking wistfully upon me:

> O that I less could fear to lose this Being,
> Which, like a snowball, in my coward-hand,
> The more 'tis grasp'd, the faster melts away!

In the afternoon of Sunday, he was inquisitive after you and your present behaviour to Miss Harlowe. I told him how you had been, and how light you made of it. Mowbray was pleased with your impenetrable hardness of heart, and said Bob

Lovelace was a good edge-tool, and steel to the back: and such coarse but hearty praises he gave you as an abandoned man might *give*, and only an abandoned man could wish to *deserve*.

But hadst thou heard what the poor dying Belton said on this occasion, perhaps it would have made thee serious an *hour or two* at least.

"When poor Lovelace is brought, said he, to a sick-bed, as I am now, and his mind forebodes that it is impossible he should recover (which *his* could not do in his late illness: if it had, he could not have behaved so lightly in it); when he revolves his past misspent life; his actions of offence to helpless innocents; in Miss Harlowe's case particularly: what then will he think of himself or of his past actions? His mind debilitated; his strength turned into weakness; unable to stir or to move without help; not one ray of hope darting in upon his benighted soul; his conscience standing in the place of a thousand witnesses; his pains excruciating; weary of the poor remnant of life he drags, yet dreading that in a few short hours his bad will be changed to worse, nay, to worst of all; and that worst of all to last beyond time and to all eternity; O Jack! what will he then think of the poor transitory gratifications of sense which now engage all his attention? Tell him, dear Belford, tell him how happy he is if he know his own happiness; how happy compared to his poor dying friend, that he has recovered from his illness, and has still an opportunity lent him for which I would give a thousand worlds, had I them to give!"

I approved exceedingly of his reflections, as suited to his present circumstances; and inferred consolations to him from a mind so properly touched.

He proceeded in the like penitent strain: I have lived a very wicked life; so have we all. We have never made a conscience of doing whatever mischief either force or fraud enabled us to do. We have laid snares for the innocent heart; and have not scrupled by the too ready sword to extend, as occasions offered, the wrongs we did to the persons whom we had before injured in their dearest relations. But yet I think in my heart that I have less to answer for than either Lovelace or Mowbray; for I, by taking to myself that accursed deceiver from whom thou hast freed me (and who for years, unknown to me, was *retaliating upon my own head* some of the evils I had brought upon others), and retiring, and living with her as a wife, was not party to half the mischiefs that I doubt they, and Tourville, and even you, Belford, committed. As to the ungrateful Thomasine, I hope I have met with my punishment in her. But notwithstanding this, dost thou not think that *such* an action—and *such* an action—and *such* an action [and then he recapitulated several enormities, in the perpetration of which (led on by false bravery and the heat of youth and wine) we have all been concerned]; dost thou not think that these villainies (let me call them *now* by their proper name), joined to the wilful and gloried-in neglect of every duty that our better sense and education gave us to know were required of us as men and Christians, are not enough to weigh down my soul into despondency? Indeed, indeed they are! And now to hope for *mercy*; and to depend upon the efficacy of that gracious attribute when that no less shining one of *justice* forbids me to hope; how can I!—I, who have despised all warnings, and taken no advantage of the benefit I might have reaped from the lingering consumptive illness I have laboured under, but left all to the last stake; hoping for recovery against hope, and driving off repentance, till that grace is denied me; for oh! my dear Belford! I can neither repent nor pray as I ought; my heart is hardened, and I can do nothing but despair!

More he would have said; but, overwhelmed with grief and infirmity, he bowed his head upon his pangful bosom, endeavouring to hide from the sight of the hardened Mowbray, who just then entered the room, those tears which he could not restrain.

Prefaced by a phlegmatic hem: Sad, very sad, truly! cried Mowbray; who sat himself down on one side of the bed, as I sat on the other: his eyes half closed, and his lips pouting out to his turned-up nose, his chin curdled [to use one of thy descriptions], leaving one at a loss to know whether stupid drowsiness or intense contemplation had got most hold of him.

An excellent, however uneasy lesson, Mowbray! said I. By my faith it is! It may one day, who knows how soon? be our own case!

I thought of thy yawning fit, as described in thy letter of Aug. 13. For up started Mowbray, writhing and shaking himself as in an ague-fit; his hands stretched over his head—with thy hoy! hoy! hoy! yawning. And then recovering himself, with another stretch and a shake, What 's o'clock? cried he, pulling out his watch—and stalking by long tiptoe strides through the room, downstairs he went; and meeting the maid in the passage, I heard him say: Betty, bring me a bumper of claret; thy poor master and this damned Belford are enough to throw a Hercules into the vapours.

Mowbray, after this, amusing himself in our friend's library, which is, as thou knowest, chiefly classical and dramatical, found out a passage in Lee's *Œdipus*, which he would needs have to be extremely apt, and in he came full fraught with the notion of the courage it would give the dying man, and read it to him. 'Tis poetical and pretty. This is it:

> When the *Sun sets,* shadows that show'd at *noon*
> But small, appear most long and terrible:
> So when we think fate hovers o'er our heads,
> Our apprehensions shoot beyond all bounds:
> Owls, ravens, crickets seem the watch of death:
> Nature's worst vermin scare her godlike sons:
> Echoes, the very leavings of a voice,
> Grow babbling ghosts, and call us to our graves.
> Each mole-hill thought swells to a huge Olympus;
> While we, fantastic dreamers, heave and puff,
> And sweat with our imagination's weight.

He expected praises for finding this out. But Belton, turning his head from him: Ah, Dick! (said he) these are not the reflections of a dying man! What thou wilt one day feel, if it be what I now feel, will convince thee that the evils *before* thee, and *with* thee, are more than the effects of imagination.

I was called twice on Sunday night to him; for the poor fellow, when his reflections on his past life annoy him most, is afraid of being left with the women; and his eyes, they tell me, hunt and roll about for me. Where's Mr. Belford? But I shall tire him out, cries he—yet beg of him to step to me—yet don't— yet do; were once the doubting and changeful orders he gave: and they called me accordingly.

But, alas! what could Belford do for him? Belford, who had been but too often the companion of his guilty hours, who wants mercy as much as he does; and is unable to promise it to himself, though 'tis all he can bid his poor friend *rely* upon!

What miscreants are we! What figures shall we make in these terrible hours!

If Miss HARLOWE's glorious *example*, on one hand, and the terrors of this poor man's *last scene* on the other, affect me not, I must be abandoned to perdition; as I fear thou wilt be if thou benefitest not thyself from both.

Among the consolatory things I urged, when I was called up the last time on Sunday night, I told him that he must not absolutely give himself up to despair: that many of the apprehensions he was under were such as the best men must have, on

the dreadful uncertainty of what was to succeed to this life.
'Tis well observed, said I, by a poetical divine, who was an
excellent Christian,[1] that

> Death could not a more sad retinue find,
> Sickness and Pain before, and Darkness all behind.

About eight o'clock yesterday (Monday) morning, I found him
a little calmer. He asked me who was the author of the two
lines I had repeated to him; and made me speak them over
again. A *sad retinue* indeed! said the poor man. And then
expressing his hopelessness of life, and his terrors at the thoughts
of dying; and drawing from thence terrible conclusions with
regard to his future state; There is, said I, such a *natural* aversion
to death in human nature, that you are not to imagine that you,
my dear Belton, are singular in the fear of it, and in the apprehensions that fill the thoughtful mind upon its approach; but
you ought, as much as possible, to separate those *natural* fears
which all men must have on so solemn an occasion, from those
particular ones which your justly-apprehended unfitness fills
you with.   Mr. Pomfret, in his *Prospect of Death*, which I dipped
into last night from a collection in your closet, and which I put
into my pocket, says [and I turned to the place]:

> Merely to die, no man of reason fears;
>   For certainly we must,
>   As we are born, return to dust;
> 'Tis the last point of many ling'ring years:
>   But whither then we go,
>   Whither, we fain would know;
> But human understanding cannot show.
>   This makes us tremble——

Mr. Pomfret, therefore, proceeded I, had such apprehensions
of this dark state as you have: and the excellent divine I hinted
at last night, who had very little else but human frailties to
reproach himself with, and whose *Miscellanies* fell into my hands
among my uncle's books in my attendance upon him in his last
hours, says:

> It must be done, my soul: but 'tis a strange,
>   A dismal and mysterious change,
> When thou shalt leave this tenement of clay,
>   And to an unknown—somewhere—wing away;
> When Time shall be Eternity, and thou
>   Shalt be—thou know'st not what—and live—
>   Thou know'st not how!

[1] The Rev. Mr. Norris of Bemerton.

> Amazing state! no wonder that we dread
>   To think of death, or view the dead;
> Thou 'rt all wrapt up in clouds, as if to thee
>   Our very knowledge had antipathy.

Then follows what I repeated:

> Death could not a more sad retinue find,
> Sickness and Pain before, and Darkness all behind.

Alas! my dear Belford (inferred the unhappy deep-thinker), what poor creatures does this convince me we mortals are *at best*! But what then must be the case of such a profligate as I, who by a past wicked life have added greater force to these natural terrors? If death be so repugnant a thing to human nature that *good* men will be startled at it, what must it be to one who has lived a life of sense and appetite; nor ever reflected upon the end which I now am within view of?

What could I say to an inference so fairly drawn? Mercy, mercy, *unbounded* mercy, was still my plea, though his repeated opposition of *justice* to it in a manner silenced that plea: and what would I have given to have had rise in my mind one good, one eminently good action to have remembered him of, in order to combat his fears with it?

I believe, Lovelace, I shall tire thee, and that more with the subject of my letter than even with the length of it. But, really, I think thy spirits are so offensively up since thy recovery that I ought, as the melancholy subjects offer, to endeavour to reduce thee to the standard of humanity by expatiating upon them. And then thou canst not but be curious to know everything that concerns the poor man, for whom thou hast always expressed a great regard. I will therefore proceed as I have begun. If thou likest not to read it now, lay it by, if thou wilt, till the like circumstances befall thee, till like reflections from those circumstances seize thee; and then take it up, and compare the two cases together.

.   .   .   .

At his earnest request I sat up with him last night; and, poor man! it is impossible to tell thee how easy and safe he thought himself in my company for the first part of the night: *A drowning man will catch at a straw*, the proverb well says: and a straw was I with respect to any real help I could give him. He often awaked in terrors, and once calling out for me: Dear Belford, said he, where are you! Oh! there you are! Give me your friendly hand! Then grasping it, and putting his clammy, half-cold lips to it: How kind! I fear everything when you are absent. But the presence of a friend, a sympathizing friend—oh! how comfortable!

But about four in the morning he frighted me much: he waked with three terrible groans; and endeavoured to speak, but could not presently; and when he did: Jack, Jack, Jack, five or six times repeated he as quick as thought, now, now, now, save me, save me, save me—I am going—going indeed!

I threw my arms about him, and raised him upon his pillow, as he was sinking (as if to hide himself) in the bedclothes—and staring wildly: Where am I! said he, a little recovering. Did you not see him? turning his head this way and that; horror in his countenance; Did you not see him?

See whom, see what, my dear Belton?

Oh, lay me upon the bed again! cried he. Let me not die upon the floor! Lay me down gently; and stand by me! Leave me not! All, all will soon be over!

You are already, my dear Belton, upon the bed. You have not been upon the floor. This is a strong delirium; you are faint for want of refreshment [for he had refused several times to take anything]: let me persuade you to take some of this cordial julep. I will leave you, if you will not oblige me.

He then readily took it; but said he could have sworn that Tom Metcalfe had been in the room, and had drawn him out of bed by the throat, upbraiding him with the injuries he had first done his sister, and then him, in the duel to which he owed that fever which cost him his life.

Thou knowest the story, Lovelace, too well to need my repeating it: but, mercy on us, if in these terrible moments all the evils we do rise to our frightened imaginations! If so, what shocking scenes have I, but still what more shocking ones hast thou to go through, if, as the noble poet says:

　　　　If any sense at that sad time remains!

The doctor ordered him an opiate this morning early, which operated so well that he dozed and slept several hours more quietly than he had done for the two past days and nights, though he had sleeping-draughts given him before. But it is more and more evident every hour that nature is almost worn out in him.

　　·　　　·　　　·　　　·　　　·　　　·　　　·

Mowbray, quite tired with this house of mourning, intends to

set out in the morning to find you. He was not a little rejoiced
to hear you were in town; I believe to have a pretence to leave us.

.   .   .   .

He has just taken leave of his poor friend, intending to go
away early: an everlasting leave, I may venture to say; for I
think he will hardly live till to-morrow night.

I believe the poor man would not have been sorry had he left
him when I arrived; for 'tis a shocking creature, and enjoys too
strong health to know how to pity the sick. Then (to borrow an
observation from thee) he has, by nature, strong bodily organs,
which those of his soul are not likely to whet out; and he, as
well as the wicked friend he is going to, may last a great while
from the strength of their constitutions, though so greatly
different in their talents; if neither the sword nor the halter
interpose.

I must *repeat* that I cannot but be very uneasy for the poor
lady whom you so cruelly persecute; and that I do not think
you have kept your honour with me. I was apprehensive,
indeed, that you would attempt to see her as soon as you got
well enough to come up; and I told her as much, making use of
it as an argument to prepare her for your visit, and to induce
her to stand it. But she could not, it is plain, bear the shock of
it: and indeed she told me that she would not see you, though
but for one half-hour, for the world.

Could she have prevailed upon herself, I know that the sight
of her would have been as affecting to you as your visit could
have been to her; when you had seen to what a lovely skeleton
(for she is really lovely still, nor can she, with such a form and
features, be otherwise) you have, in a few weeks, reduced one of
the most charming women in the world; and that in the full
bloom of her youth and beauty.

Mowbray undertakes to carry this, that he may be more
welcome to you, he says. Were it to be sent unsealed, the
characters we write in would be Hebrew to the dunce. I desire
you to return it; and I 'll give you a copy of it upon demand;
for I intend to keep it by me as a guard against the infection
of your company, which might otherwise, perhaps, some time
hence, be apt to weaken the impressions I always desire to have
of the awful scene before me. God convert us both!

Letter LIX—Mr. Belford to Robert Lovelace, Esq.

Wednesday Morn. 11 *o'clock.*

I BELIEVE no man has two such servants as I have. Because I treat them with kindness, and do not lord it over my inferiors, and damn and curse them by looks and words like Mowbray; or beat their teeth out like Lovelace; but cry, Prithee, Harry, do this, and Prithee, Jonathan, do that; the fellows pursue their own devices, and regard nothing I say but what falls in with these.

Here, this vile Harry, who might have brought your letter of yesterday in good time, came not in with it till past eleven last night (drunk, I suppose); and concluding that I was in bed, as he pretends (because he was told I sat up the preceding night), brought it not to me; and having overslept himself, just as I had sealed up my letter, in comes the villain with the forgotten one, shaking his ears, and looking as if he himself did not believe the excuses he was going to make. I questioned him about it, and heard his pitiful pleas; and though I never think it becomes a gentleman to treat people insolently who by their stations are humbled beneath his feet, yet could I not forbear to *Lovelace* and *Mowbray* him most cordially.

And this detaining Mowbray (who was ready to set out to you before) while I write a few lines upon it, the fierce fellow, who is impatient to exchange the company of a dying Belton for that of a too lively Lovelace, affixed a *supplement* of curses upon the staring fellow that was larger than my *book*—nor did I offer to take off the bear from such a mongrel, since on this occasion he deserved not of me the protection which every master owes to a good servant.

He has not done cursing him yet; for stalking about the courtyard with his boots on (the poor fellow dressing his horse, and unable to get from him), he is at him without mercy; and I will heighten his impatience (since being just under the window where I am writing, he will not let me attend to my pen) by telling you how he fills my ears as well as the fellow's with his Hey, sir! and G—d damn ye, sir! and Were you my servant, ye dog ye! and Must I stay here till the midday sun scorches me to a parchment, for such a mangy dog's drunken neglect? Ye lie, sirrah! Ye lie, I tell you—[I hear the fellow's voice in a humble excusatory tone, though not articulately]. Ye lie, ye dog! I'd a good mind to thrust my whip down your drunken throat. Damn me, if I would not flay the skin from the back of such a rascal, if thou wert mine, and have dogskin gloves made of it, for thy brother scoundrels to wear in remembrance of thy abuses of such a master.

The poor horse suffers for this, I doubt not; for, What now! and, Stand still, and be damned to ye! cries the fellow, with a kick, I suppose, which he better deserves himself. For these varlets, where they can, are Mowbrays and Lovelaces to man or beast; and, not daring to answer *him*, is flaying the poor *horse*.

I hear the fellow is just escaped, the horse (better curried than ordinary, I suppose, in half the usual time) by his clanking shoes, and Mowbray's silence, letting me know that I may now write on: and so I will tell thee that in the first place (little as I, as well as you, regard dreams) I would have thee lay thine to heart; for I could give thee such an interpretation of it as would shock thee, perhaps: and if thou askest me for it, I will.

Mowbray calls to me from the courtyard that 'tis a cursed hot day, and he shall be fried by riding in the noon of it: and that poor Belton longs to see me. So I will only add my earnest desire that you will give over all thoughts of seeing the lady, if, when this comes to your hand, you have not seen her: and that it would be kind if you 'd come and, for the last time you will ever see your poor friend, share my concern for him; and in him see what, in a little time, will be your fate and mine, and that of Mowbray, Tourville, and the rest of us—for what are ten, fifteen, twenty, or thirty years to look back to; in the longest of which periods forward we shall all perhaps be mingled with the dust from which we sprung?

Letter LX—*Mr. Lovelace to John Belford, Esq.*

Wednesday Morn. Aug. 23.

ALL alive, dear Jack, and in ecstasy! Likely to be once more a happy man! For I have received a letter from my beloved Miss HARLOWE; in consequence, I suppose, of that which I mentioned in my last to be left for her from her sister. And I am setting out for Berks directly, to show the contents to my Lord M., and to receive the congratulations of all my kindred upon it.

I went last night, as I intended, to Smith's: but the dear creature was not returned at near ten o'clock. And, lighting upon Tourville, I took him home with me, and made him sing me out of my megrims. I went to bed tolerably easy at two; had bright and pleasant dreams (not such a frightful one as that I gave thee an account of); and at eight this morning, as

I was dressing, to be in readiness against the return of my fellow, whom I had sent to inquire after the lady, I had this letter brought me by a chairman.

To Robert Lovelace, Esq.

Tuesday Night, 11 o'clock (Aug. 22).

SIR,—I have good news to tell you. I am setting out with all diligence for my father's house. I am bid to hope that he will receive his poor penitent with a goodness peculiar to himself; for I am overjoyed with the assurance of a thorough reconciliation, through the interposition of a dear, blessed friend whom I always loved and honoured. I am so taken up with my preparation for this joyful and long-wished-for journey that I cannot spare one moment for any other business, having several matters of the last importance to settle first. So pray, sir, don't disturb or interrupt me—I beseech you, don't. You may possibly in time see me at my father's; at least, if it be not your own fault.

I will write a letter, which shall be sent you when I am got thither and received: till when, I am, etc.

CLARISSA HARLOWE.

I dispatched instantly a letter to the dear creature, assuring her, with the most thankful joy, "that I would directly set out for Berks, and wait the issue of the happy reconciliation and the charming hopes she had filled me with. I poured out upon her a thousand blessings. I declared that it should be the study of my whole life to merit such transcendent goodness: and that there was nothing which her father or friends should require at my hands that I would not for *her* sake comply with, in order to promote and complete so desirable a reconciliation."

I hurried it away without taking a copy of it; and I have ordered the chariot and six to be got ready; and hey for M. Hall! Let me but know how Belton does. I hope a letter from thee is on the road. And if the poor fellow can spare thee, make haste, I command thee, to attend this truly divine lady. Thou mayest not else see her of months perhaps; at least, not while she is Miss HARLOWE. And oblige me, if possible, with one letter before she sets out, confirming to me and accounting for this generous change.

But what accounting for it is necessary? The dear creature cannot receive consolation herself but she must communicate it to others. How noble! She would not see me in her adversity; but no sooner does the sun of prosperity begin to shine upon her than she forgives me.

I know to whose mediation all this is owing. It is to Colonel Morden's. She always, as she says, loved and honoured him: and he loved her above all his relations.

I shall now be convinced that there is something in dreams. The opening cloud is the reconciliation in view. The bright form, lifting up my charmer through it to a firmament stuck round with golden cherubims and seraphims, indicates the charming little boys and girls that will be the fruits of this happy reconciliation. The welcomes, thrice repeated, are those of her family, now no more to be deemed implacable. Yet are they a family, too, that my soul cannot mingle with.

But then what is my tumbling over and over through the floor into a frightful hole, *descending* as she *ascends*? Ho! only this: it alludes to my disrelish to matrimony: which is a bottomless pit, a gulf, and I know not what. And I suppose, had I not awoke in such a plaguy fright, I had been soused into some river at the bottom of the hole, and then been carried (mundified or purified from my past iniquities) by the same bright form (waiting for me upon the mossy banks) to my beloved girl; and we should have gone on cherubiming of it and carolling to the end of the chapter.

But what are the black, sweeping mantles and robes of Lord M. thrown over my face, and what are those of the ladies? O Jack! I have these too: they indicate nothing in the world but that my lord will be so good as to die and leave me all he has. So, rest to thy good-natured soul, honest Lord M.

Lady Sarah Sadleir and Lady Betty Lawrance will also die, and leave me swingding legacies.

Miss Charlotte and her sister—what will become of them? Oh! they will be in mourning, of course, for their uncle and aunts. That's right!

As to Morden's flashing through the window, and crying: Die, Lovelace, and be damned, if thou wilt not repair my cousin's wrongs! That is only that he would have sent me a challenge had I not been disposed to do the lady justice.

All I dislike is this part of the dream: for, even in a dream, I would not be thought to be threatened into any measure, though I liked it ever so well.

And so much for my prophetic dream.

Dear, charming creature! What a meeting will there be

between her and her father and mother and uncles! What transports, what pleasure, will this happy, long-wished-for reconciliation give her dutiful heart!   And indeed now methinks I am glad she *is* so dutiful to them; for her duty to parents is a conviction to me that she will be *as* dutiful to her husband: since duty upon principle is a uniform thing.

Why, prithee now, Jack, I have not been so much to blame as thou thinkest: for had it not been for me, who have led her into so much distress, she could neither have *received* nor *given* the joy that will now overwhelm them all.   So here rises great and durable good out of temporary evil!

I knew they loved her (the pride and glory of their family) too well to hold out long!

I wish I could have seen Arabella's letter.   She has always been so much eclipsed by her sister that, I dare say, she has signified this reconciliation to her with intermingled phlegm and wormwood; and her invitation most certainly runs all in the rock-water style.

I shall long to see the promised letter too when she is got to her father's, which I hope will give an account of the reception she will meet with.

There is a solemnity, however, I think, in the style of her letter, which pleases and affects me at the same time.   But as it is evident she loves me still, and hopes soon to see me at her father's, she could not help being a little solemn, and half-ashamed [dear blushing, pretty rogue!] to own her love, after my usage of her.

And then her subscription: *Till when, I am,* CLARISSA HAR-LOWE: as much as to say, *after that,* I shall be, if not *your own fault,* CLARISSA LOVELACE!

O my best love!   My ever-generous and adorable creature! How much does this thy forgiving goodness exalt us both!   Me, for the occasion given thee!   Thee, for turning it so gloriously to thy advantage, and to the honour of both!

And if, my beloved creature, you will but connive at the imperfections of your adorer, and not play the *wife* upon me: if, while the charms of novelty have their force with me, I should happen to be drawn aside by the love of intrigue, and of plots that my soul delights to form and pursue; and if thou wilt not be open-eyed to the follies of my youth [a transitory state!], every excursion shall serve but the more to endear thee to me, till in time, and in a very little time too, I shall get above sense; and then, charmed by thy soul-attracting converse, and brought to despise my former courses, what I now, at distance, consider as a painful duty, will be my joyful choice, and all my delight will centre in thee!

.   .   .   .

Mowbray is just arrived with thy letters. I therefore close my agreeable subject, to attend to one which I doubt will be very shocking.

I have engaged the rough varlet to bear me company in the morning to Berks; where I shall file off the rust he has contracted in his attendance upon the poor fellow.

He tells me that, between the dying Belton and the preaching Belford, he shan't be his own man these three days. And says that thou addest to the unhappy fellow's weakness instead of giving him courage to help him to bear his destiny.

I am sorry he takes the unavoidable lot so heavily. But he has been long ill; and sickness enervates the mind as well as the body; as he himself very significantly observed to thee.

Letter LXI—Mr. Lovelace to John Belford, Esq.

Wedn. Evening.

I have been reading thy shocking letter. Poor Belton! what a multitude of lively hours have we passed together! He was a fearless, cheerful fellow: who 'd have thought that all should end in such dejected whimpering and terror?

But why didst thou not comfort the poor man about the rencounter between him and that poltroon Metcalfe? He acted in that affair like a man of true honour, and as I should have acted in the same circumstances. Tell him I say so, and that what happened he could neither help nor foresee.

Some people are as sensible of a scratch from a pin's point as others from a push of a sword: and who can say anything for the sensibility of such fellows? Metcalfe would resent for his sister, when his sister resented not for herself. Had she demanded her brother's protection and resentment, that would have been *another man's matter*, to speak in Lord M.'s phrase: but she herself thought her brother a coxcomb to busy himself undesired in her affairs, and wished for nothing but to be provided for decently and privately in her lying-in; and was willing to take the chance of *Maintenon-ing* his conscience in her favour,[1] and getting him to marry when the little stranger came; for she knew what an easy, good-natured fellow he was. And indeed, if she *had* prevailed upon him, it might have been happy for both; as then he would not have fallen in with his cursed Thomasine. But truly this officious brother of hers must interpose. This made a trifling affair important: and what was the issue? Metcalfe challenged; Belton met him; disarmed him; gave him his life: but the fellow, more sensible in his *skin* than in his *head*, having received a scratch, was frighted; it gave him first a puke, then a fever, and then he died. *That was all.* And how could Belton help that? But sickness, a long, tedious sickness, will make a bugbear of anything to a languishing heart, I see that. And so far was Mowbray *apropos* in the verses from *Nat Lee* which thou hast transcribed.

Merely to die, no man of reason fears, is a mistake, say thou, or say thy author, what ye will. And thy solemn parading about the natural repugnance between life and death is a proof that it is.

Let me tell thee, Jack, that so much am I pleased with this world, in the main; though in some points, too, the world (to make a *person* of it) has been a rascal to me; so delighted am I with the joys of youth; with my worldly prospects as to fortune; and now, newly, with the charming hopes given me by my dear, thrice dear, and for ever dear CLARISSA; that were I even sure that nothing bad would come hereafter, I should be very loath (very much *afraid*, if thou wilt have it so) to lay down my life and them together; and yet upon a call of honour no man fears death less than myself.

But I have not either inclination or leisure to weigh thy *leaden* arguments, except in the *pig*, or, as thou wouldst say, in the *lump*.

If I return thy letters, let me have them again some time hence, that is to say, when I am married, or when poor Belton is half forgotten; or when *time* has enrolled the honest fellow among those whom we have *so long* lost, that we may remember them with more pleasure than pain; and then I may give them a serious perusal, and enter with thee as deeply as thou wilt into the subject.

When I am married, said I? What a sound has that!

I must wait with patience for a sight of this charming creature till she is at her father's. And yet, as the but blossoming beauty,

[1] Madam Maintenon was reported to have prevailed upon Lewis XIV of France, in his old age (sunk, as he was, by ill-success in the field), to marry her, by way of compounding with his conscience for the freedoms of his past life, to which she attributed his public losses.

as thou tellest me, is reduced to a shadow, I should have been exceedingly delighted to see her now, and every day till the happy one; that I might have the pleasure of beholding how sweetly, hour by hour, she will rise to her pristine glories, by means of that state of ease and contentment which will take place of the stormy *past*, upon her reconciliation with her friends and our happy nuptials.

Letter LXII—Mr. Lovelace to John Belford, Esq.

WELL, but now my heart is a little at ease, I will condescend to take brief notice of some other passages in thy letters.

I find I am to thank *thee* that the dear creature has avoided my visit. Things are now in so good a train that I must forgive thee; else thou shouldst have heard more of this new instance of disloyalty to thy general.

Thou art continually giving thyself high praise, by way of *opposition*, as I may say, to others; gently and artfully blaming thyself for qualities thou wouldst at the same time have to be thought, and which generally are thought, praiseworthy.

Thus, in the airs thou assumest about thy servants, thou wouldst pass for a mighty humane mortal, and that at the expense of Mowbray and me: whom thou representest as kings and emperors to our menials. Yet art thou always unhappy in thy attempts of this kind, and never canst make us who know thee believe that to be a virtue in thee which is but the effect of constitutional phlegm and absurdity.

Knowest thou not that some men have a native dignity in manner that makes them more regarded by a look than either thou canst be in thy low style or Mowbray in his high?

I am fit to be a prince, I can tell thee; for I reward well, and I punish seasonably and properly; and I am generally as well served as any man.

The art of governing these underbred varlets lies more in the dignity of looks than in words, and thou art a sorry fellow, to think humanity consists in acting by thy servants as men must act who are not able to pay them their wages; or had made them masters of secrets which, if divulged, would lay them at the mercy of such wretches.

Now to me, who never did anything I was ashamed to own, and who have more ingenuousness than ever man had; who can call a villainy by its right name, though practised by myself,

and (by my own readiness to reproach myself) anticipate all
reproach from others; who am not such a hypocrite as to wish
the world to think me other or better than I am—It is my part
to *look* a servant into his duty, if I can: nor will I keep one who
knows not how to take me by a nod or a wink; and who, when
I smile, shall not be all transport; when I frown, all terror. If,
indeed, I am out of the way a little, I always take care to reward
the varlets for patiently bearing my displeasure. But this
I hardly ever am but when a fellow is egregiously stupid in any
plain point of duty, or will be wiser than his master; and when
he shall tell me that he thought acting contrary to my orders
was the way to serve me best.

One time or other I will enter the lists with thee upon thy
conduct and mine to servants; and I will convince thee that
what thou wouldst have pass for humanity, if it be indiscrimi-
nately practised to all tempers, will perpetually subject thee to
the evils thou complainest of; and *justly* too; and that *he* only
is fit to be a master of servants who can command their attention
as much by a *nod* as if he were to *prithee* a fellow to do his
duty on one hand, or to talk of *flaying* and *horse-whipping*, like
Mowbray, on the other: for the servant who, being *used* to
expect thy creeping style, will always be master of his master,
and he who deserves to be treated as the other, is not fit to be
any man's servant; nor would I keep such a fellow to rub my
horse's heels.

I shall be the readier to enter the lists with thee upon this
argument, because I have presumption enough to think that
we have not, in any of our dramatic poets that I can at present
call to mind, one character of a servant of either sex that is
justly hit off. So absurdly wise *some*, and so sottishly foolish
others; and *both* sometimes in the *same* person. *Foils* drawn
from the lees or dregs of the people to set off the characters of
their masters and mistresses; nay, sometimes, which is still more
absurd, introduced with more wit than the poet has to bestow
upon their principals. Mere *flints* and *steels* to strike fire with;
or, to vary the metaphor, to serve for whetstones to wit which
otherwise could not be made apparent: or for engines to be made
use of like the *machinery* of the ancient poets (or the still *more*
unnatural soliloquy), to help on a sorry plot, or to bring about a
necessary *éclaircissement*, to save the poet the trouble of thinking
deeply for a better way to wind up his bottoms.

Of this I am persuaded (whatever my *practice* be to my own
servants): that thou wilt be benefited by my *theory* when we

come to controvert the point. For then I shall convince thee that the *dramatic* as well as *natural* characteristics of a good servant ought to be fidelity, common sense, cheerful obedience, and silent respect: that wit in his station, except to his companions, would be sauciness: that he should never presume to give his advice: that if he ventured to expostulate upon any unreasonable command, or such a one as appeared to him to be so, he should do it with humility and respect, and take a proper season for it. But such lessons do most of the dramatic performances I have seen give, where servants are introduced as characters essential to the play, or to act very significant or long parts in it (which, of itself, I think a fault); such lessons, I say, do they give to the footmen's gallery, that I have not wondered we have so few modest or good menservants among those who often attend their masters or mistresses to plays. Then how miserably evident must that poet's conscious want of genius be who can stoop to raise or give force to a clap by the indiscriminate roar of the parti-coloured gallery!

But this subject I will suspend to a better opportunity; that is to say, to the happy one when my nuptials with my Clarissa will oblige me to increase the number of my servants, and of consequence to enter more nicely into their qualifications.

.   .   .   .

Although I have the highest opinion that man can have of the generosity of my dear Miss Harlowe, yet I cannot for the heart of me account for this agreeable change in her temper, but one way. Faith and troth, Belford, I verily believe, laying all circumstances together, that the dear creature unexpectedly finds herself in the way I have so ardently wished her to be in; and that this makes her, at last, incline to favour me, that she may set the better face upon her gestation when at her father's.

If this be the case, all her falling away, and her fainting fits, are charmingly accounted for. Nor is it surprising that such a sweet novice in these matters should not, for some time, have known to what to attribute her frequent indispositions. If this should be the case, how shall I laugh at *thee*! and (when I am sure of her) at the dear novice *herself*, that all her grievous distresses shall end in a man-child: which I shall love better than all the cherubims and seraphims that may come after; though there were to be as many of them as I beheld in my dream; in which a vast expanse of firmament was stuck as full of them as it could hold.

I shall be afraid to open thy next, lest it bring me the account of poor Belton's death. Yet, as there are no hopes of his recovery—but what should I say, unless the poor man were better fitted—but thy heavy sermon shall not affect me too much neither.

I enclose thy papers: and do thou transcribe them for me, or return them; for there are some things in them which, at a proper season, a *mortal* man should not avoid attending to: and thou seemest to have entered deeply into the shocking subject— but here I will end, lest I grow too serious.

.   .   .   .

Thy servant called here about an hour ago, to know if I had any commands: I therefore hope that thou wilt have this early in the morning. And if thou *canst* let me hear from thee, do. I 'll stretch an hour or two in expectation of it. Yet I must be at Lord M.'s to-morrow night if possible, though ever so late.

Thy fellow tells me the poor man is much as he was when Mowbray left him.

Wouldst thou think that this varlet Mowbray is sorry that I am so near being happy with Miss Harlowe? And, egad, Jack, I know not what to say to it, now the fruit seems to be within my reach—but let what will come, I 'll stand to 't: for I find I can't live without her.

Letter LXIII—Mr. Belford to Robert Lovelace, Esq.

Wednesday, Three o'clock.

I WILL proceed where I left off in my last.

As soon as I had seen Mowbray mounted, I went to attend upon poor Belton; whom I found in dreadful agonies, in which he awoke, as he generally does.

The doctor came in presently after; and I was concerned at the scene that passed between them.

It opened with the dying man's asking him, with melancholy earnestness, if nothing, if nothing at all, could be done for him?

The doctor shook his head, and told him he doubted not.

I *cannot* die, said the poor man; I cannot *think* of dying. I am very desirous of living a little longer, if I could but be free from these horrible pains in my stomach and head. Can you give me nothing to make me pass one week, but *one* week, in tolerable ease, that I may die like a man?—if I *must* die!

But, doctor, I am *yet* a young man; in the prime of my years.

Youth is a good subject for a physician to work upon: can you do nothing, nothing *at all* for me, doctor?

Alas! sir, replied his physician, you have been long in a bad way. I fear, I fear nothing in physic can help you.

He was then out of all patience: What, then, is your art, sir? I have been a passive machine for a whole twelvemonth, to be wrought upon at the pleasure of you people of the faculty. I verily believe, had I not taken such doses of nasty stuff, I had been now a well man—but who the plague would regard physicians, whose art is to cheat us with hopes while they help to destroy us? and who, not one of you, know anything but by guess?

Sir, continued he fiercely (and with more strength of voice, and coherence, than he had shown for several hours before), if you give *me* over, I give *you* over. The only honest and certain part of the art of healing is surgery. A good surgeon is worth a thousand of you. I have been in surgeons' hands often, and have always found reason to depend upon their skill: but *your* art, sir, what is it? but to daub, daub, daub; load, load, load; plaster, plaster, plaster; till ye utterly destroy the appetite first, and the constitution afterwards, which you are called in to help. I had a companion once—my dear Belford, thou knewest honest Blomer—as pretty a physician he would have made as any in England, had he kept himself from excess in wine and women; and he always used to say there was nothing at all but pick-pocket parade in the physician's art; and that the best guesser was the best physician. And I used to believe him too; and yet, fond of life, and fearful of death, what do we do when we are taken ill but call *ye* in? And what do *ye* do, when called in, but nurse our distempers, till from pygmies you make giants of them? And then ye come creeping with solemn faces, when ye are ashamed to prescribe, or when the stomach won't bear its natural food, by reason of your poisonous potions: *Alas! I am afraid physic can do no more for him!* Nor need it, when it has brought to the brink of the grave the poor wretch who placed all his reliance in your cursed slops and the flattering hopes you gave him.

The doctor was out of countenance; but said: If we could make mortal men *immortal*, and *would not*, all this might be just.

I blamed the poor man; yet excused him to the physician. To die, dear doctor, when, like my poor friend, we are so desirous of life, is a melancholy thing. We are apt to hope too much, not considering that the seeds of death are sown in us when we begin to live, and grow up, till, like rampant weeds, they choke the tender flower of life; which declines in us as those weeds flourish. We ought therefore to begin early to study what our constitutions will bear, in order to root out, by temperance, the weeds which the soil is most apt to produce; or at least to keep them down as they rise; and not, when the flower or plant is withered at the root, and the weed in its full vigour, expect that the medical art will restore the one or destroy the other; when that other, as I hinted, has been rooting itself in the habit from the time of our birth.

This speech, Bob, thou wilt call a *prettiness*; but the allegory is just; and thou hast not quite cured me of the metaphorical.

Very true, said the doctor, you have brought a good metaphor to illustrate the thing. I am sorry I can do nothing for the gentleman; and can only recommend patience and a better frame of mind.

Well, sir, said the poor angry man, vexed at the doctor, but more at death; you will perhaps recommend the next in succession to the physician, when *he* can do no more; and, I suppose, will send your brother to pray by me for those virtues which you wish me.

It seems the physician's brother is a clergyman in the neighbourhood.

I was greatly concerned to see the gentleman thus treated; and so I told poor Belton when he was gone: but he continued impatient, and would not be denied, he said, the liberty of talking to a man who had taken so many guineas of him for doing nothing, or worse than nothing, and never declined one, though he knew all the time he could do him no good.

It seems the gentleman, though rich, is noted for being greedy after fees; and poor Belton went on raving at the extravagant fees of English physicians, compared with those of the most eminent foreign ones. But, poor man! he, like the Turks, who judge of a general by his success (out of patience to think he must die), would have worshipped the doctor, and not grudged three times the sum, could he have given him hopes of recovery.

But nevertheless I must needs say that gentlemen of the faculty should be more moderate in their fees, or take more pains to deserve them; for generally they only come into a room, feel the sick man's pulse, ask the nurse a few questions, inspect the patient's tongue, and perhaps his water; then sit down, look plaguy wise, and *write*. The golden fee finds the ready hand, and they hurry away, as if the sick man's room were infectious.

So to the next they troll, and to the next, if men of great practice; valuing themselves upon the number of visits they make in a morning, and the little time they make them in. They go to dinner, and unload their pockets; and sally out again to refill them. And thus, in a little time, they raise vast estates; for, as Ratcliffe said, when first told of a great loss which befell him: It was only going up and down a hundred pair of stairs to fetch it up.

Mrs. Sambre (Belton's sister) had several times proposed to him a minister to pray by him; but the poor man could not, he said, bear the thoughts of one; for that he should certainly die in an hour or two after: and he was willing to hope still, against all probability, that he might recover; and was often asking his sister if she had not seen people as bad as he was who, almost to a miracle, when everybody gave them over, had got up again?

She, shaking her head, told him she had: but, once saying that *their* disorders were of an acute kind, and such as had a crisis in them, he called her *Small-hopes*, and *Job's comforter*; and bid her say *nothing*, if she could not say more to the purpose, and what was *fitter* for a sick man to hear. And yet, poor fellow! he has no hopes himself, as is plain by his desponding terrors; one of which he fell into, and a very dreadful one, soon after the doctor went.

Wednesday, 9 o'clock at night.

The poor man has been in convulsions, terrible convulsions! for an hour past. O Lord! Lovelace, death is a shocking thing! by my faith it is! I wish thou wert present on this occasion. It is not merely the concern a man has for his friend; but, as death is the common lot, we see, in *his* agonies, how it will be one day with ourselves. I am all over as if cold water were poured down my back, or as if I had a strong ague fit upon me. I was obliged to come away. And I write, hardly knowing what. I wish *thou* wert here.

.   .   .   .

Though I left him because I could stay no longer, I can't be easy by myself, but must go to him again.

Eleven o'clock.

Poor Belton! Drawing on apace! Yet was he sensible when I went in—too sensible, poor man! He has something upon his mind to reveal, he tells me, that is the worst action of his life; worse than ever you or I knew of him, he says. It *must* be then very bad!

He ordered everybody out; but was seized with another convulsion fit before he could reveal it: and in it he lies struggling between life and death.   But I 'll go in again.

One o'clock in the morning.

All now must soon be over with him: poor! poor fellow! He has given me some hints of what he wanted to say; but all incoherent, interrupted by dying hiccoughs and convulsions.

Bad enough it must be, Heaven knows, by what I can gather! Alas! Lovelace, I fear, I fear he came *too soon* into his uncle's estate.

If a man were to live always, he might have some temptation to do base things in order to procure to himself, as it would then be, *everlasting* ease, plenty, or affluence: but, for the sake of ten, twenty, thirty years of poor life, to be a villain—can that be worth while? with a conscience stinging him all the time too! And when he comes to wind up all, such agonizing reflections upon his past guilt! all then appearing as nothing! What he most valued, most disgustful! and not one thing to think of, as the poor fellow says twenty and twenty times over, but what is attended with anguish and reproach!

To hear the poor man wish he had never been born! To hear him pray to be nothing after death! Good God! how shocking!

By his incoherent hints, I am afraid 'tis very bad with him. No pardon, no mercy, he repeats, can lie for him!

I hope I shall make a proper use of this lesson.   Laugh at me if thou wilt, but never, never more will I take the liberties I have taken; but whenever I am tempted, will think of Belton's dying agonies, and what my own may be.

Thursday, Three in the morning.

He is now at the last gasp—rattles in the throat—has a new convulsion every minute almost! What horror is he in! His eyes look like breath-stained glass! They roll ghastly no more; are quite set: his face distorted and drawn out by his sinking jaws, and erected staring eyebrows, with his lengthened furrowed forehead, to double its usual length, as it seems. It is not, it cannot be, the face of Belton, thy Belton and my Belton, whom we have beheld with so much delight over the social bottle, comparing notes, that one day may be brought against us and make *us* groan, as they very lately did *him*—that is to say, while he had strength to groan; for now his voice is not to be heard; all inward, lost; not so much as speaking by his eyes: yet, strange! how can it be? the bed rocking under him like a cradle.

Four o'clock.

> Alas! he 's gone! That groan, that *dreadful* groan,
> Was the last farewell of the parting mind!
> The struggling soul has bid a long adieu
> To its late mansion—Fled!—Ah! whither fled?

Now is all indeed over! Poor, poor Belton! By this time thou knowest if thy crimes were above the size of God's mercies! Now are every one's cares and attendance at an end! Now do we, thy friends—poor Belton!—know the worst of thee as to this life! Thou art released from insufferable tortures both of body and mind! May those tortures, and thy repentance, expiate for thy offences, and mayst thou be happy to all eternity!

We are told that God desires not the death, the *spiritual* death, of a sinner: and 'tis certain that thou didst deeply repent! I hope therefore, as thou wert not cut off in the midst of thy sins by the sword of injured friendship, which more than once thou hadst braved [the dreadfullest of all deaths, next to suicide, because it gives no opportunity for repentance], that this is a merciful earnest that thy penitence is accepted; and that thy long illness, and dreadful agonies in the last stages of it, were thy only punishment.

I wish indeed, I *heartily* wish, we could have seen one ray of comfort darting in upon his benighted mind before he departed. But all, alas! to the very last gasp, was horror and confusion. And my only fear arises from this, that, till within the four last days of his life, he could not be brought to think he should die, though in a visible decline for months; and, in that presumption, was too little inclined to set about a serious preparation for a journey which he hoped he should not be obliged to take; and when he began to apprehend that he could not put it off, his impatience, and terror, and apprehension showed too little of that reliance and resignation which afford the most comfortable reflections to the *friends* of the dying, as well as to the *dying* themselves.

But we must leave poor Belton to that mercy of which we have all so much need; and for my own part (do you, Lovelace, and the rest of the fraternity, as ye will), I am resolved I will endeavour to begin to repent of my follies while my health is sound, my intellects untouched, and while it is in my power to make some atonement, as near to restitution or reparation as is possible, to those I have wronged or misled. And do ye *outwardly*, and from a point of *false bravery*, make as light as ye will of my resolution, as ye are none of ye of the class of abandoned and stupid sots who endeavour to disbelieve the future existence of which ye are afraid, I am sure you will justify me in your *hearts*, if not by your *practices*; and one day you will wish you had joined with me in the same resolution, and will confess there is more good sense in it than now perhaps you will own.

Seven o'clock, Thursday morning.

You are very earnest, by your last letter (just given me), to hear again from me before you set out for Berks. I will therefore close with a few words upon the *only* subject in your letter which I can at present touch upon: and this is the letter of which you give me a copy from the lady.

Want of rest, and the sad scene I have before my eyes, have rendered me altogether incapable of accounting for the contents of it in any shape. You are in ecstasies upon it. You have reason to be so, if it be as you think. Nor would I rob you of your joy: but I must say that I am amazed at it.

Surely, Lovelace, this surprising letter cannot be a forgery of thy own, in order to carry on some view and to impose upon me. Yet by the style of it, it cannot; though thou art a perfect Proteus, too.

I will not, however, add another word, after I have desired the return of this, and have told you that I am

Your true friend and well-wisher,

J. BELFORD.

Letter LXIV—Mr. Lovelace to John Belford, Esq.

Aug. 24, Thursday Morn.

I RECEIVED thy letter in such good time, by thy fellow's dispatch, that it gives me an opportunity of throwing in a few paragraphs upon it. I read a passage or two of it to Mowbray; and we both agree that thou art an absolute master of the lamentable.

Poor Belton! what terrible conflicts were thy last conflicts! I hope, however, that he is happy: and I have the more hope, because the hardness of his death is likely to be such a warning to *thee*. If it have the effect thou declarest it shall have, what a world of mischief will it prevent! How much good will it do! How many poor wretches will rejoice at the *occasion* (if they know it), however melancholy in itself, which shall bring them in a compensation for injuries they had been forced to sit down contented with! But, Jack, though thy uncle's death has made thee a rich fellow, art thou sure that the making good of such a vow will not totally bankrupt thee?

Thou sayest I may laugh at thee, if I will. Not I, Jack: I do not take it to be a laughing subject: and I am heartily concerned at the loss we all have in poor Belton: and when I get a little settled, and have leisure to contemplate the vanity of all sublunary things (a subject that will now and then, in my gayest hours, obtrude itself upon me), it is very likely that I may talk seriously with thee upon these topics; and, if thou hast not got too much the start of me in the repentance thou art entering upon, will go hand-in-hand with thee in it. If thou hast, thou wilt let me just keep thee in my eye; for it is an uphill work; and I shall see thee, at setting out, at a great distance; but as thou art a much heavier and clumsier fellow than myself, I hope that without much puffing and sweating, only keeping on a good round dog-trot, I shall be able to overtake thee.

Meantime, take back thy letter, as thou desirest. I would not have it in my pocket upon any account at present; nor read it once more.

I am going down without seeing my beloved. I was a hasty fool to write her a letter, promising that I would not come near her till I saw her at her father's. For as she is now actually at Smith's, and I so near her, one short visit could have done no harm.

I sent Will two hours ago with my grateful compliments, and to know how she does.

How must I adore this charming creature! For I am ready to think my servant a happier fellow than myself, for having been within a pair of stairs and an apartment of her.

Mowbray and I will drop a tear apiece, as we ride along, to the memory of poor Belton—*as we ride along,* I say: for we shall have so much joy when we arrive at Lord M.'s, and when I communicate to him and my cousins the dear creature's letter, that we shall forget everything grievous: since now their family hopes in my reformation (the point which lies so near their hearts) will all revive; it being an article of their faith, that if I marry, repentance and mortification will follow of course.

Neither Mowbray nor I shall accept of thy *verbal* invitation to the funeral. We like not these dismal formalities. And as to

the respect that is supposed to be shown to the memory of a
deceased friend in such an attendance, why should we do anything to reflect upon those who have made it a fashion to leave
this parade to people whom they *hire for that purpose*?

Adieu, and be cheerful.   Thou canst now do no more for poor
Belton, wert thou to howl for him to the end of thy life.

Letter LXV—Mr. Belford to Robert Lovelace, Esq.

Sat. Aug. 26.

ON Thursday afternoon I assisted at the opening of poor Belton's
will, in which he has left me his sole executor, and bequeathed me
a legacy of a hundred guineas; which I shall present to his
unfortunate sister, to whom he has not been so kind as I think
he ought to have been.   He has also left twenty pounds apiece
to Mowbray, Tourville, thyself, and me, for a ring to be worn in
remembrance of him.

After I had given some particular orders about the preparations to be made for his funeral, I went to town; but having
made it late before I got in on Thursday night, and being
fatigued for want of rest several nights before, and low in my
spirits [I could not help it, Lovelace!], I contented myself to
send my compliments to the innocent sufferer, to inquire after
her health.

My servant saw Mrs. Smith, who told him she was very glad
I was come to town; for that the lady was worse than she had
yet been.

It is impossible to account for the contents of her letter to you;
or to reconcile those contents to the facts I have to communicate.

I was at Smith's by seven yesterday (Friday) morning; and
found that the lady was just gone in a chair to St. Dunstan's to
prayers: she was too ill to get out by six to Covent Garden
Church; and was forced to be supported to her chair by
Mrs. Lovick.   They would have persuaded her against going;
but she said she knew not but it would be her last opportunity.
Mrs. Lovick, dreading that she would be taken worse at church,
walked thither before her.

Mrs. Smith told me she was so ill on Wednesday night, that
she had desired to receive the Sacrament; and accordingly it
was administered to her by the parson of the parish: whom she
besought to take all opportunities of assisting her in her solemn
preparation.

This the gentleman promised: and called in the morning to

inquire after her health; and was admitted at the first word. He stayed with her about half an hour; and when he came down, with his face turned aside, and a faltering accent: "Mrs. Smith, said he, you have an angel in your house. I will attend her again in the evening, as she desires, and as often as I think it will be agreeable to her."

Her increased weakness she attributed to the fatigues she had undergone by your means; and to a letter she had received from her sister, which she answered the same day.

Mrs. Smith told me that two different persons had called there, one on Thursday morning, one in the evening, to inquire after her state of health; and seemed as if commissioned from her relations for that purpose; but asked not to see her, only were very inquisitive after her visitors (particularly, it seems, after *me*: what could they mean by that?), after her way of life, and expenses; and one of them inquired after her manner of supporting them; to the latter of which Mrs. Smith said she had answered, as the truth was, that she had been obliged to sell some of her clothes, and was actually about parting with more; at which the inquirist (a grave old farmer-looking man) held up his hands, and said: Good God! this will be sad, sad news to somebody! I believe I must not mention it. But Mrs. Smith says she desired he *would*, let him come from whom he would. He shook his head, and said, if she died, the flower of the world would be gone, and the family she belonged to would be no more than a common family.[1] I was pleased with the man's expression.

You may be curious to know how she passed her time when she was obliged to leave her lodging to avoid you.

Mrs. Smith tells me "that she was very ill when she went out on Monday morning, and sighed as if her heart would break as she came downstairs, and as she went through the shop into the coach, her nurse with her, as you had informed me before: that she ordered the coachman (whom she hired for the day) to drive anywhither, so it was into the air: he accordingly drove her to Hampstead, and thence to Highgate. There, at the Bowling Green House, she alighted, extremely ill, and having break-fasted, ordered the coachman to drive very slowly anywhither. He crept along to Muswell Hill, and put up at a public-house there; where she employed herself two hours in writing, though exceedingly weak and low; till the dinner she had ordered was

---

[1] This man came from her Cousin Morden; as will be seen hereafter. Letters xciv, xcviii.

brought in: she endeavoured to eat; but could not; her appetite was gone, quite gone, she said. And then she wrote on for three hours more: after which, being heavy, she dozed a little in an elbow-chair. When she awoke, she ordered the coachman to drive her very slowly to town, to the house of a friend of Mrs. Lovick; whom, as agreed upon, she met there: but, being extremely ill, she would venture home at a late hour, although she heard from the widow that you had been there; and had reason to be shocked at your behaviour. She said she found there was no avoiding you: she was apprehensive she should not live many hours, and it was not impossible but the shock the sight of you must give her would determine her fate in your presence.

"She accordingly went home. She heard the relation of your astonishing vagaries, with hands and eyes often lifted up; and with these words intermingled: Shocking creature! Incorrigible wretch! and, Will nothing make him serious! And not being able to bear the thoughts of an interview with a man so hardened, she took to her usual chair early in the morning, and was carried to the Temple Stairs, whither she had ordered her nurse before her, to get a pair of oars in readiness (for her fatigues the day before made her unable to bear a coach); and then she was rowed to Chelsea, where she breakfasted; and after rowing about, put in at the Swan at Brentford-Ait, where she dined; and would have written, but had no convenience either of tolerable pens, or ink, or private room; and then proceeding to Richmond, they rowed her back to Mortlake; where she put in, and drank tea at a house her waterman recommended to her. She wrote there for an hour; and returned to the Temple; and, when she landed, made one of the watermen get her a chair, and so was carried to the widow's friend, as the night before; where she again met the widow, who informed her that you had been after her twice that day.

"Mrs. Lovick gave her there her sister's letter[1]; and she was so much affected with the contents of it that she was twice very nigh fainting away; and wept bitterly, as Mrs. Lovick told Mrs. Smith; dropping some warmer expressions than ever they had heard proceed from her lips, in relation to her friends; calling them cruel, and complaining of ill offices done her, and of vile reports raised against her.

"While she was thus disturbed, Mrs. Smith came to her, and told her that you had been there a third time, and was just gone (at half an hour after nine), having left word how civil and

[1] See Letter lxvii.

respectful you would be; but that you was determined to see her at all events.

"She said it was hard she could not be permitted to die in peace: that her lot was a severe one: that she began to be afraid she should not forbear repining, and to think her punishment greater than her fault: but recalling herself immediately, she comforted herself that her life would be short, and with the assurance of a better."

By what I have mentioned, you will conclude with me that the letter brought her by Mrs. Lovick (the superscription of which you saw to be written in her sister's hand) could not be the letter on the contents of which she grounded *that* she wrote to you on her return home. And yet neither Mrs. Lovick, nor Mrs. Smith, nor the servant of the latter, know of any other brought her. But as the women assured me that she actually *did* write to you, I was eased of a suspicion which I had begun to entertain, that you (for some purpose I could not guess at) had forged the letter from her of which you sent me a copy.

On Wednesday morning, when she received your letter in answer to hers, she said: Necessity may well be called the mother of invention—but calamity is the test of integrity. I hope I have not taken an inexcusable step——And there she stopped a minute or two; and then said: I shall now, perhaps, be allowed to die in peace.

I stayed till she came in. She was glad to see me; but, being very weak, said she must sit down before she could go upstairs; and so went into the back shop; leaning upon Mrs. Lovick: and when she had sat down, "I am glad to see you, Mr. Belford, said she; I *must* say so—let misreporters say what they will."

I wondered at this expression [1]; but would not interrupt her.

Oh! sir, said she, I have been grievously harassed. Your friend, who would not let me live with reputation, will not permit me to die in peace. You see how I am. Is there not a great alteration in me within this week? But 'tis all for the better. Yet were I to wish for life, I must say that your friend, your barbarous friend, has *hurt* me greatly.

She was so very weak, so short-breathed, and her words and action so very moving, that I was forced to walk from her; the two women and her nurse turning away their faces also, weeping.

I have had, madam, said I, since I saw you, a most shocking scene before my eyes for days together. My poor friend Belton is no more. He quitted the world yesterday morning in such

[1] Explained in Letter lxx.

dreadful agonies that the impression they have left upon me have *so weakened* my mind——

I was loath to have her think that my grief was owing to the weak state I saw her in, for fear of dispiriting her.

That is only, Mr. Belford, interrupted she, in order to *strengthen* it, if a proper use be made of the impression. But I should be glad, since you are so humanely affected with the solemn circumstance, that you could have written an account of it to your gay friend, in the style and manner you are master of. Who knows, as it would have come *from* an associate and *of* an associate, how it might have affected him?

That I *had* done, I told her, in such a manner as had, I believed, some effect upon you.

His behaviour in this honest family so lately, said she, and his cruel pursuit of me, give but little hope that anything serious or solemn will affect him.

We had some talk about Belton's dying behaviour, and I gave her several particulars of the poor man's impatience and despair; to which she was very attentive; and made fine observations upon the subject of procrastination.

A letter and packet were brought her by a man on horseback from Miss Howe, while we were talking. She retired upstairs to read it; and while I was in discourse with Mrs. Smith and Mrs. Lovick, the doctor and apothecary both came in together. They confirmed to me my fears as to the dangerous way she is in. They had both been apprised of the new instances of implacableness in her friends, and of your persecutions: and the doctor said he would not for the world be either the unforgiving father of that lady, or the man who had brought her to this distress. Her heart's broken: she'll die, said he: there is no saving her. But how, were I either the one or the other of the people I have named, I should support myself afterwards, I cannot tell.

When she was told we were all three together, she desired us to walk up. She arose to receive us, and after answering two or three general questions relating to her health, she addressed herself to us to the following effect.

As I may not, said she, see you three gentlemen together again, let me take this opportunity to acknowledge my obligations to you all. I am inexpressibly obliged to you, sir, and to you, sir [curtsying to the doctor and to Mr. Goddard], for your *more* than friendly, your *paternal* care and concern for me. Humanity in your profession, I dare say, is far from being a rare qualification, because you are gentlemen *by* your profession: but so much kindness, so much humanity, did never desolate creature meet with, as I have met with from you both.   But indeed I have always observed, that where a person relies upon Providence, it never fails to raise up a new friend for every old one that falls off.

This gentleman [bowing to me], who, some people think, should have been one of the last I should have thought of for my executor, is nevertheless (such is the strange turn that things have taken!) the only one I can choose; and therefore I have chosen him for that charitable office, and he has been so good as to accept of it: for, rich as I may boast myself to be, I am rather so in *right* than in *fact*, at this present.   I repeat therefore my humble thanks to you all three, and beg of God to return to you and yours [looking to each] a hundredfold the kindness and favour you have shown me; and that it may be in the power of you and of yours, to the end of time, to *confer* benefits, rather than to be obliged to *receive* them.   This is a godlike power, gentlemen: I once rejoiced in it, in some little degree; and much more in the prospect I had of its being enlarged to me; though I have had the mortification to experience the reverse, and to be obliged almost to everybody I have seen or met with—but all, originally, through my own fault; so I ought to bear the punishment without repining: and I hope I do.   Forgive these impertinences: a grateful heart, that wants the power it wishes for, to express itself suitably to its own impulses, will be at a loss what properly to dictate to the tongue; and yet, unable to restrain its overflowings, will force the tongue to say weak and silly things, rather than appear ungratefully silent.   Once more, then, I thank ye all three for your kindness to me: and God Almighty make you that amends which at present I cannot!

She retired from us to her closet with her eyes full; and left us looking upon one another.

We had hardly recovered ourselves when she, quite easy, cheerful, and smiling, returned to us.   Doctor, said she (seeing we had been moved), you will excuse me for the concern I give you; and so will you, Mr. Goddard, and you, Mr. Belford; for 'tis a concern that only generous natures can show; and to such natures *sweet* is the pain, if I may so say, that attends such a concern.   But as I have some few preparations still to make, and would not (though in ease of Mr. Belford's future cares, which is, and ought to be, part of my study) undertake more than it is likely I shall have time lent me to perform, I would beg of you to give me your opinions [you see my way of living; and you may be assured that I will do nothing wilfully to shorten my life] how long it may possibly be before I may hope to be released from all my troubles.

They both hesitated, and looked upon each other. Don't be afraid to answer me, said she, each sweet hand pressing upon the arm of each gentleman, with that mingled freedom and reserve which virgin modesty, mixed with conscious dignity, can only express, and with a look serenely earnest: Tell me how long you think I may hold it? And believe me, gentlemen, the shorter you tell me my time is likely to be, the more comfort you will give me.

With what pleasing woe, said the doctor, do you fill the minds of those who have the happiness to converse with you, and see the happy frame you are in! What you have undergone within a few days past has much hurt you: and should you have fresh troubles of those kinds, I could not be answerable for your holding it——And there he paused.

How long, doctor? I believe I *shall* have a little more ruffling —I am afraid I shall—but there can happen only one thing that I shall not be tolerably easy under——How long then, sir?

He was silent.

A fortnight, sir?

He was still silent.

Ten days? A week? How long, sir? with smiling earnestness.

If I *must* speak, madam: if you have not better treatment than you have lately met with, I am afraid——There again he stopped.

Afraid of what, doctor? Don't be afraid. How long, sir?

That a fortnight or three weeks may deprive the world of the finest flower in it.

A fortnight or three weeks yet, doctor? But God's will be done! I shall, however, by this means, have full time, if I have but strength and intellect, to do all that is now upon my mind to do. And so, sirs, I can but once more thank you [turning to each of us] for all your goodness to me; and, having letters to write, will take up no more of your time. Only, doctor, be pleased to order me some more of those drops: they cheer me a little when I am low; and, putting a fee into his unwilling hand: You know the terms, sir! Then, turning to Mr. Goddard: You 'll be so good, sir, as to look in upon me to-night, or to-morrow, as you have opportunity: and you, Mr. Belford, I know, will be desirous to set out to prepare for the last office for your late friend: so I wish you a good journey, and hope to see you when that is performed.

She then retired, with a cheerful and serene air. The two gentlemen went away together. I went down to the women, and, inquiring, found that Mrs. Lovick was this day to bring her twenty guineas more, for some other of her apparel.

The widow told me that she had taken the liberty to expostulate with her upon the *occasion* she had for raising this money to such great disadvantage; and it produced the following short and affecting conversation between them.

None of my friends will wear anything of mine, said she. I shall leave a great many good things behind me. And as to what I want the money for—don't be surprised: but suppose I want it to purchase a house?

You are all mystery, madam. I don't comprehend you.

Why then, Mrs. Lovick, I will explain myself. I have a man, not a woman, for my executor: and think you that I will leave to his care anything that concerns my own person? Now, Mrs. Lovick, smiling, do you comprehend me?

Mrs. Lovick wept.

O fie! proceeded the lady, drying up her tears with her own handkerchief, and giving her a kiss. Why this kind weakness for one with whom you have been so little a while acquainted? Dear, good Mrs. Lovick, don't be concerned for me on a prospect with which I have occasion to be pleased; but go to-morrow to your friends, and bring me the money they have agreed to give you.

Thus, Lovelace, it is plain that she means to bespeak her *last* house! Here's presence of mind; here's tranquillity of heart, on the most affecting occasion! This is magnanimity indeed! Couldst thou, or could I, with all our boisterous bravery, and offensive false courage, act thus? Poor Belton! how unlike was thy behaviour!

Mrs. Lovick tells me that the lady spoke of a letter she had received from her favourite divine, Dr. Lewen, in the time of my absence; and of an answer she had returned to it. But Mrs. Lovick knows not the contents of either.

When thou receivest the letter I am now writing, thou wilt see what will soon be the end of all thy injuries to this divine lady. I say, *when thou receivest* it; for I will delay it for some little time, lest thou shouldst take it into thy head (under pretence of resenting the disappointment her letter must give thee) to molest her again.

This letter having detained me by its length, I shall not now set out for Epsom till to-morrow.

I should have mentioned that the lady explained to me what the *one thing* was that she was afraid might happen to ruffle her. It was the apprehension of what may result from a visit which Col. Morden, as she is informed, designs to make *you*.

Letter LXVI—*The Rev. Dr. Lewen to Miss Clarissa Harlowe*

Friday, Aug. 18.

PRESUMING, dearest and ever-respectable young lady, upon your former favour, and upon your opinion of my judgment and sincerity, I cannot help addressing you by a few lines, on your present unhappy situation.

I will not look back upon the measures into which you have either been *led* or *driven*: but will only say as to *those*, that I think you are the least to blame of any young lady that was ever reduced from happy to unhappy circumstances; and I have not been wanting to say as much, where I hoped my freedom would have been better received than I have had the mortification to find it to be.

What I principally write for now is, to put you upon doing a piece of justice to yourself, and to your sex, in the prosecuting for his life (I am assured his life is in your power) the most profligate and abandoned of men, as *he* must be who could act so basely as I understand Mr. Lovelace has acted by you.

I am very ill; and am now forced to write upon my pillow; my thoughts confused; and incapable of method: I shall not therefore aim at method: but to give you in general my opinion. And that is, that your religion, your duty to your family, the duty you owe to your honour, and even charity to your sex, oblige you to give public evidence against this very wicked man.

And let me add another consideration: the prevention, by this means, of the mischiefs that may otherwise happen between your brother and Mr. Lovelace, or between the latter and your Cousin Morden, who is now, I hear, arrived, and resolves to have justice done you.

A consideration which ought to affect your conscience (forgive me, dearest young lady, I think I am now in the way of my duty); and to be of more concern to you than that hard pressure upon your modesty which I know the appearance against him in an open court must be of to such a lady as you; and which, I conceive, will be your great difficulty. But I know, madam, that you have dignity enough to *become* the blushes of the most naked truth, when necessity, justice, and honour exact it from you. Rakes and ravishers would meet with encouragement *indeed*, and most from those who had the greatest abhorrence of their actions, if violated modesty were never to complain of the injury it received from the villainous attempters of it.

In a word, the reparation of your family dishonour now rests in your own bosom: and which only one of these two alternatives *can* repair; to wit, either to marry the offender, or to prosecute him at law. Bitter expedients for a soul so delicate as yours!

He, and all his friends, I understand, solicit you to the first: and it is certainly, now, all the amends within his power to make. But I am assured that you have rejected *their* solicitations, and *his*, with the indignation and contempt that his foul actions have deserved: but yet that you refuse not to extend to him the Christian forgiveness he has so little reason to expect, provided he will not disturb you further.

But, madam, the prosecution I advise will not let your present and future exemption from fresh disturbance from so vile a molester depend upon his *courtesy*: I should think so noble and so rightly guided a spirit as yours would not permit that it should, if you could help it.

And can indignities of any kind be *properly pardoned* till we have it in *our power to punish them*? To pretend to pardon, while we are labouring under the pain or dishonour of them, will be thought by some to be but the vaunted mercy of a pusillanimous heart trembling to resent them. The remedy I propose is a severe one; but what pain can be more severe than the injury? or how will injuries be believed to grieve us that are never honourably complained of?

I am sure Miss Clarissa Harlowe, however injured and oppressed, remains unshaken in her sentiments of honour and virtue: and although she would sooner die than *deserve* that her modesty should be drawn into question, yet she will think no truth immodest that is to be uttered in the vindicated cause of innocence and chastity. Little, very little difference is there, my dear young lady, between a *suppressed* evidence and a *false* one.

It is a terrible circumstance, I once more own, for a young lady of your delicacy to be under the obligation of telling so shocking a story in public court: but it is still a worse imputation that she should pass over so mortal an injury unresented.

Conscience, honour, justice, and the cares of Heaven are on

your side: and modesty would, by some, be thought but an empty name, should *you* refuse to obey their dictates.

I have been consulted, I own, on this subject. I have given it as my opinion that you ought to prosecute the abandoned man — but without my reasons. These I reserved, with a resolution to lay them before you, unknown to anybody, that the result, if what I wish, may be *your own*.

I will only add, that the misfortunes which have befallen you, had they been the lot of a child of my own, could not have affected me *more* than yours have done. My own child I love: but I both love and honour you: since to love you is to love virtue, good sense, prudence, and everything that is good and noble in woman.

Wounded as I think all these are by the injuries you have received, you will believe that the knowledge of your distresses must have afflicted beyond what I am able to express,

Your sincere admirer and humble servant,

Arthur Lewen.

I just now understand that your sister will, by proper authority, propose this prosecution to you. I humbly presume that the reason why you resolved not upon this step *from the first*, was that you did not know that it would have the *countenance and support of your relations*.

Letter LXVII—Miss Clarissa Harlowe to the Rev. Dr. Lewen

Sat. Aug. 19.

Reverend and dear Sir,—I thought, till I received your affectionate and welcome letter, that I had neither father, uncle, brother left; nor hardly a friend among my former favourers of your sex. Yet, knowing *you* so well, and having no reason to upbraid myself with a faulty will, I was to blame (even although I had doubted the continuance of your good opinion) to decline the trial whether I had forfeited it or not; and if I had, whether I could not *honourably* reinstate myself in it.

But, sir, it was owing to different causes that I did not; partly to *shame*, to think how high, in my happier days, I stood in your esteem, and how much I must be sunk in it, since those so much nearer in relation to me gave me up; partly to *deep distress*, which makes the humbled heart diffident; and made mine afraid to claim the kindred mind in yours, which would have supplied to me in some measure all the dear and lost relations I have named.

Then, so loath, as I sometimes was, to be thought to want to make a *party* against those whom both duty and inclination bid me reverence: so long *trailed* on between *hope and doubt*: so *little my own mistress* at one time; so fearful of *making or causing mischief* at another; and not being encouraged to hope, by *your kind notice*, that my application to you would be acceptable; apprehending that my relations had engaged your *silence* at least [1]—

THESE—but why these unavailing retrospections now? I *was* to be unhappy—in order to *be* happy; that is my hope! Resigning therefore to that hope, I will, without any further preamble, write a few lines (if, writing to *you*, I can write *but* a few) in answer to the subject of your kind letter.

Permit me, then, to say that I believe your arguments would have been unanswerable in almost every *other* case of this nature but in that of the unhappy *Clarissa Harlowe*.

It is certain that creatures who cannot stand the shock of *public shame* should be doubly careful how they expose themselves to the danger of incurring *private guilt*, which may possibly bring them to it. But as to *myself*, suppose there were no objections from the declining way I am in as to my health; and supposing I could have prevailed upon myself to appear against this man; were there not room to apprehend that the end so much wished for by my friends (to wit, his condign punishment) would not have been obtained, when it came to be seen that I had consented to give him a clandestine meeting; and, in consequence of that, had been weakly tricked out of myself; and further still, had not been able to avoid living under one roof with him for several weeks; which I did (not only without complaint, but) without *cause* of complaint?

Little advantage *in a court* (perhaps bandied about, and jested profligately with) would some of those pleas in my favour have been, which *out of court*, and to a *private* and *serious* audience, would have carried the greatest weight against him — such, particularly, as the infamous methods to which he had recourse.

It would, no doubt, have been a ready retort from *every* mouth, that I ought not to have thrown myself into the power of such

---

[1] The stiff visit this good divine was prevailed upon to make her, as mentioned in vol. i, pp. 362-4 (of which, however, she was too generous to remind him), might warrant the lady to think that he had rather inclined to their party, as to the *parental side*, than to hers.

a man, and that I ought to take for my pains what had befallen me.

But had the prosecution been carried on to *effect*, and had he even been *sentenced to death*, can it be thought that his family would not have had interest enough to obtain his pardon for a crime thought too lightly of, though one of the greatest that can be committed against a creature valuing her honour above her life?—While I had been censured as pursuing with sanguinary views a man who offered me early all the reparation in his power to make?

And had he been *pardoned*, would he not then have been at liberty to do as much mischief as ever?

I dare say, sir, such is the assurance of the man upon whom my unhappy destiny threw me, and such his inveteracy to my family (which would then have appeared to be justified by their known inveteracy to *him*, and by their earnest endeavours to take away his life), that he would not have been sorry to have had an opportunity to confront me and my father, uncles, and brother, at the bar of a court of justice on such an occasion. In which case, would not (on his acquittal, or pardon) resentments have been reciprocally heightened? And then would my brother, or my Cousin Morden, have been more secure than now?

How do these considerations aggravate my fault! My motives, at first, were not indeed blamable: but I had forgotten the excellent caution, which yet I was not ignorant of, *that we ought not to do evil that good may come of it.*

In full conviction of the purity of my heart, and of the firmness of my principles [why may I not, thus called upon, say what I am conscious of, and yet without the imputation of faulty pride; since all is but a *duty*, and I should be utterly inexcusable could I not justly say what I do?—In this full conviction] he has offered me marriage. He has avowed his penitence: a *sincere* penitence I have reason to think it, though perhaps not a *Christian* one. And his noble relations (kinder to the poor sufferer than her own), on the same conviction, and his own not ungenerous acknowledgments, have joined to intercede with me to *forgive* and *accept* of him. Although I cannot comply with the latter part of their intercession, have you not, sir, from the *best* rules, and from the *divinest* example, taught me to forgive injuries?

The injury I have received from him is indeed of the highest nature, and it was attended with circumstances of unmanly baseness and premeditation; yet, I bless God, it has not tainted my mind; it has not hurt my morals.   No thanks indeed to the wicked man that it has not.   No vile courses have followed it. My will is unviolated.   The evil (respecting *myself*, and not my *friends*) is merely personal.   No credulity, no weakness, no want of vigilance, have I to reproach myself with.   I have, through grace, triumphed over the deepest machinations.   I have escaped from him.   I have renounced him.   The man whom once I could have loved, I have been enabled to despise: and shall not *charity* complete my triumph?   And shall I not *enjoy* it?   And where would be my triumph if he *deserved* my forgiveness?   Poor man!   He has had a loss in losing me!   I have the pride to think so, because I think I know my own heart.   I have had none in losing him!

But I have *another* plea to make, which alone would have been enough (as I presume) to answer the contents of your very kind and friendly letter.

I know, my dear and reverend friend, the spiritual guide and director of my happier days!   I know that you will allow of my endeavour to bring myself to this charitable disposition, when I tell you how near I think myself to that great and awful moment *in* which, and even in the ardent preparation *to* which, every sense of indignity or injury that concerns not the immortal soul ought to be absorbed in higher and more important contemplations.

Thus much for *myself*.

And for the satisfaction of my *friends* and *favourers*, Miss Howe is solicitous to have all those letters and materials preserved which will set my whole story in a true light.   The good Dr. Lewen is one of the principal of those friends and favourers.

The warning that may be given from those papers to all such young creatures as may have known or heard of me, may be of more efficacy to the end wished for, as I humbly presume to think, than my appearance could have been in a court of justice, pursuing a doubtful event under the disadvantages I have mentioned.   And if, my dear and good sir, you are now, on considering everything, of *this* opinion, and I could *know* it, I should consider it as a particular felicity; being as solicitous as ever to be justified in what I may in your eyes.

I am sorry, sir, that your indisposition has reduced you to the necessity of writing upon your pillow.   But how much am I obliged to that kind and generous concern for me which has *impelled* you, as I may say, to write a letter containing so many paternal lines, with such inconvenience to yourself!

May the Almighty bless you, dear and reverend sir, for all your goodness to me of long time past, as well as for that which engages my present gratitude! Continue to esteem me to the last, as I do and will venerate you! And let me bespeak your prayers; the *continuance*, I should say, of your prayers; for I doubt not that I have always had them: and to them, perhaps, has in part been owing (as well as to your pious precepts instilled through my earlier youth) that I have been able to make the stand I have made; although everything that you prayed for has not been granted to me by that Divine wisdom, which knows what is best for its poor creatures.

My prayers for *you* are, that it will please God to restore you to your affectionate flock; and after as many years of life as shall be for *His* service, and to *your own* comfort, give us a happy meeting in those regions of blessedness which you have taught me, as well by *example* as by *precept*, to aspire to!

Clarissa Harlowe.

Letter LXVIII—Miss Arab. Harlowe to Miss Cl. Harlowe
[In answer to hers to her Uncle Antony of Aug. 13 [1]]

Monday, Aug. 21.

Sister Clary,—I find by your letters to my uncles, that they, as well as I, are in great disgrace with you for writing our minds to you.

We can't help it, Sister Clary.

You don't think it worth your while, I find, a second time to press for the blessing you pretend to be so earnest about. You think, no doubt, that you have done your duty in asking for it: so you 'll sit down satisfied with that, I suppose, and leave it to your wounded parents to repent hereafter that they have not done *theirs*, in giving it to you, at the *first* word; and in making such inquiries about you as you think ought to have been made. Fine encouragement to inquire after a runaway daughter! living with her fellow as long as he would live with her! You repent also (with your *full mind*, as you modestly call it) that you wrote to me.

So we are not likely to be applied to any more, I find, in this way.

Well then, since this is the case, Sister Clary, let me, *with all humility*, address myself with a proposal or two to you; to which you will be *graciously* pleased to give an answer.

[1] See pp. 105–7.

Now you must know that we have had hints given us from several quarters, that you have been used in such a manner by the villain you ran away with, that his life would be answerable for his crime if it were fairly to be proved. And, by your own hints, something like it appears to us.

If, Clary, there be anything but jingle and affected period in what proceeds from your *full mind*, and your *dutiful consciousness*; and if there be truth in what Mrs. Norton and Mrs. Howe have acquainted us with; you may yet justify your character to us, and to the world, in everything but your scandalous elopement; and the law may reach the villain: and, could we but bring him to the gallows, what a meritorious revenge would that be to our whole injured family, and to the innocents he has deluded, as well as the saving from ruin many others!

Let me, therefore, know (*if you please*) whether you are willing to appear to do *yourself*, and *us*, and your *sex*, this justice? If *not*, Sister Clary, we shall know what to think of you; for neither *you* nor *we* can suffer more than we have done from the scandal of your fall: and, if *you will*, Mr. Ackland and Counsellor Derham will both attend you to make *proper inquiries*, and to take minutes of your story, to found a process upon, if it will bear one with as great a probability of success as we are told it may be prosecuted with.

But, by what Mrs. Howe intimates, this is not likely to be complied with; for it is what she hinted to you, it seems, by her lively daughter, but without effect [1]; and then, again, possibly, you may not at present behave so prudently in some certain points as to entitle yourself to public justice; which, if true, the Lord have mercy upon you!

One word only more as to the above proposal: your admirer, Dr. Lewen, is clear in his opinion that you should prosecute the villain.

But if you will not agree to this, I have another proposal to make to you, and that in the name of every one in the family; which is, that you will think of going to Pennsylvania to reside there for some few years till all is blown over; and, if it please God to spare you, and your unhappy parents, till they can be satisfied that you behave like a true and uniform penitent; at least till you are one-and-twenty: you may then come back to your own estate, or have the produce of it sent you thither, as you shall choose. A period which my father fixes, because it is the *custom*; and because he thinks your *grandfather* should have

[1] See vol. iii, pp. 378–80.

fixed it; and because, let *me* add, you have fully proved by your fine conduct, that you were not at years of discretion at *eighteen*. Poor, doting, though good old man!—your grandfather, he thought——But I would not be too severe.

Mr. Hartley has a widow sister at Pennsylvania, with whom he will undertake you may board, and who is a sober, sensible, and well-read woman. And if you were once well there, it would rid your father and mother of a world of cares, and fears, and scandal; and I think is what you should wish for of all things.

Mr. Hartley will engage for all accommodations in your passage suitable to your rank and fortune; and he has a concern in a ship, which will sail in a month; and you may take your secret-keeping Hannah with you, or whom you will of your *newer* acquaintance. 'Tis presumed that your companions will be of your own sex.

These are what I had to communicate to you; and if you'll oblige me with an answer (which the hand that conveys this will call for on Wednesday morning), it will be very condescending.

ARABELLA HARLOWE.

Letter LXIX—*Miss Cl. Harlowe to Miss Arab. Harlowe*

Tuesday, Aug. 22.

WRITE to me, my hard-hearted sister, in what manner you please, I shall always be thankful to you for your notice. But (think what you will of me) I cannot see Mr. Ackland and the counsellor on such a business as you mention.

The Lord have mercy upon me indeed! For none else will.

Surely I am believed to be a creature past all shame, or it could not be thought of sending two *gentlemen* to me on such an errand.

Had my *mother* required of me (or would *modesty* have permitted *you* to inquire into) the particulars of my sad story, or had *Mrs. Norton* been directed to receive them from me, methinks it had been more fit: and I presume to think that it would have been more in every one's character, too, had they been required of me before such heavy judgment had been passed upon me as has been passed.

I *know* that this is Dr. Lewen's opinion. He has been so good as to enforce it in a kind letter to me. I have answered his letter; and given such reasons as I hope will satisfy *him*. I could wish it were thought worth while to request of him a sight of my answer.[1]

To your other proposal, of going to Pennsylvania, this is my answer: If nothing happen within a month which may full as effectually rid my parents and friends of that world of cares, and fears, and scandals, which you mention, and if I am *then* able to be carried on board of ship, I will cheerfully obey my father and mother, although I were sure to die in the passage. And, if I may be forgiven for saying so (for indeed it proceeds not from a spirit of reprisal), you shall set over me, instead of my poor, obliging, but really inculpable Hannah, your Betty Barnes; to whom I will be answerable for all my conduct. And I will make it worth her while to accompany me.

I am equally surprised and concerned at the hints which both you and my Uncle Antony give of *new* points of misbehaviour in me! What can be meant by them?

I will not tell you, Miss Harlowe, how much I am afflicted at your severity, and how much I suffer by it, and by your hard-hearted levity of style, because what I shall say may be construed into *jingle* and *period*, and because I know it is *intended*, very possibly for *kind* ends, to mortify me. All I will therefore say is, that it does not lose its end, if that be it.

But, nevertheless (divesting myself as much as possible of all resentment), I will only pray that Heaven will give you, for *your own* sake, a kinder heart than at present you seem to have; since a kind heart, I am convinced, is a greater blessing to its possessor than it can be to any other person. Under this conviction I subscribe myself, my dear Bella,

Your ever affectionate sister,
CL. HARLOWE.

Letter LXX—Mrs. Norton to Miss Clarissa Harlowe
[*In answer to hers of Thursday, Aug.* 17 [2]]

Tuesday, Aug. 22.

MY DEAREST YOUNG LADY,—The letters you sent me I now return by the hand that brings you this.

It is impossible for me to express how much I have been affected by them, and by your last of the 17th. Indeed, my

---

[1] Her letter containing the reasons she refers to, was not asked for; and Dr. Lewen's death, which fell out soon after he had received it, was the reason that it was not communicated to the family till it was too late to do the service that might have been hoped for from it.

[2] See pp. 109 et seq.

dear Miss Clary, you are very harshly used; indeed you are! And if you should be taken from us, what grief and what punishment are they not treasuring up against themselves in the heavy reflections which their rash censures and unforgivingness will occasion them!

But I find to what your Uncle Antony's cruel letter is owing, as well as one you will be still more afflicted by [God help you, my poor dear child!], when it comes to your hand, written by your sister, with proposals to you.[1]

It was finished to send you yesterday, I know; and I apprise you of it, that you should fortify your heart against the contents of it.

The motives which incline them all to this severity, if well grounded, would authorize any severity they could express, and which, while they believe them to be so, both they and you are to be equally pitied.

They are owing to the information of that officious Mr. Brand, who has acquainted them (from some enemy of yours in the neighbourhood about you) that visits are made you, highly censurable, by a man of a free character, and an intimate of Mr. Lovelace; who is often in private with you; sometimes twice or thrice a day.

Betty gives herself great liberties of speech upon this occasion, and all your friends are too ready to believe that things are not as they should be; which makes me wish that, let the gentleman's views be ever so honourable, you could entirely drop acquaintance with him.

Something of this nature was hinted at by Betty to me before, but so darkly that I could not tell what to make of it; and this made me mention it to you so *generally* as I did in my last.

Your Cousin Morden has been among them. He is exceedingly concerned for your misfortunes; and as they will not believe Mr. Lovelace would marry you, he is determined to go to Lord M.'s, in order to inform himself from Mr. Lovelace's own mouth whether he intends to do you that justice or not.

He was extremely caressed by every one at his first arrival; but I am told there is some little coldness between them and him at present.

I was in hopes of getting a sight of this letter of Mr. Brand (a rash officious man!): but it seems Mr. Morden had it given him yesterday to read, and he took it away with him.

God be your comfort, my dear miss! But indeed I am exceed-

[1] See Letter lxviii.

ingly disturbed at the thoughts of what may still be the issue of all these things. I am, my beloved young lady,

Your most affectionate and faithful

JUDITH NORTON.

Letter LXXI—Mrs. Norton to Miss Clarissa Harlowe

Tuesday, Aug. 22.

AFTER I had sealed up the enclosed, I had the honour of a private visit from your Aunt Hervey; who has been in a very low-spirited way, and kept her chamber for several weeks past; and is but just got abroad.

She longed, she said, to see me, and to weep with me, on the hard fate that had befallen her beloved niece.

I will give you a faithful account of what passed between us; as I expect that it will, upon the whole, administer hope and comfort to you.

"She pitied very much your good mother, who, she assured me, is obliged to act a part entirely contrary to her inclinations; as she herself, she owns, had been in a great measure.

"She said that the poor lady was with great difficulty withheld from answering your letter to her; which had (as was your aunt's expression) almost broken the heart of every one: that she had reason to think that she was neither consenting to your two uncles writing, nor approving of what they wrote.

"She is sure they all love you dearly; but have gone so far that they know not how to recede.

"That, but for the *abominable league* which your brother had got everybody into (he refusing to set out for Scotland till it was renewed, and till they had all promised to take no step towards a reconciliation in his absence but by his consent; and to which your sister's resentments kept them up), all would before now have happily subsided.

"That nobody knew the pangs which their inflexible behaviour gave them, ever since you had begun to write to them in so affecting and humble a style.

"That, however, they were not inclined to believe that you were either so ill, or so penitent, as you really are; and still less that Mr. Lovelace is in earnest in his offers of marriage.

"She is sure, however, she says, that all will soon be well: and the sooner for Mr. Morden's arrival: who is very zealous in your behalf.

"She wished to Heaven that you would accept of Mr. Lovelace, wicked as he has been, if he were now in earnest.

"It had always, she said, been matter of astonishment to her, that so weak a pride in her Cousin James, of making himself the *whole family*, should induce them all to refuse an alliance with such a family as Mr. Lovelace's was.

"She would have it that your going off with Mr. Lovelace was the unhappiest step for your honour and your interest that could have been taken; for that although you would have had a severe trial the next day, yet it would probably have been the *last*; and your pathetic powers must have drawn you off some friends—hinting at your mother, at your Uncle Harlowe, at your Uncle Hervey, and herself."

But here (that the regret that you did not trust to the event of that meeting may not, in your present low way, too much afflict you) I must observe that it seems a little too evident, even from this opinion of your aunt's, that it was not so absolutely determined that all compulsion was designed to be avoided, since your freedom from it must have been owing to the party to be made among them by your persuasive eloquence and dutiful expostulation.

"She owned that some of them were as much afraid of meeting you, as you could be of meeting them": but why so, if they designed, in the last instance, to give you your way?

Your aunt told me "that Mrs. Williams [1] had been with her, and asked her opinion, if it would be taken amiss if she desired leave to go up to attend her *dearest young lady in her calamity*. Your aunt referred her to your mother: but had heard no more of it.

"Her daughter (Miss Dolly), she said, had been frequently earnest with her on the same subject; and renewed her request with the greatest fervour when your first letter came to hand."

Your aunt says, "that she being then very ill, wrote to your mother upon it, hoping it would not be taken amiss if she permitted Miss Dolly to go; but that your sister, as from your mother, answered her, that now you seemed to be coming to, and to have a due sense of your faults, you must be left entirely to their own management.

"Miss Dolly, she said, had pined ever since she had heard of Mr. Lovelace's baseness; being doubly mortified by it: first, on account of your sufferings; next, because she was one who rejoiced in your getting off, and vindicated you for it: and had

[1] The former housekeeper at Harlowe Place.

incurred censure and ill-will on that account; especially from your brother and sister; so that she seldom went to Harlowe Place."

Make the best use of these intelligences, my dearest young lady, for your consolation.

I will only add that I am, with the most fervent prayers for your recovery and restoration to favour,

Your ever faithful

JUDITH NORTON.

Letter LXXII—Miss Cl. Harlowe to Mrs. Judith Norton

Thursday, Aug. 24.

THE relation of such a conversation as passed between my aunt and you, would have given me pleasure had it come some time ago; because it would have met with a spirit more industrious than mine *now* is, to pick out remote comfort in the hope of a favourable turn that might one day have rewarded my patient duty.

I did not doubt my aunt's good will to me. Her affection I did not doubt. But shall we wonder that kings and princes meet with so little control in their passions, be they ever so violent, when in a private family an aunt, nay, even a mother in that family, shall choose to give up a once favoured child against their own inclinations, rather than oppose an aspiring young man, who had armed himself with the authority of a father, who, when once determined, never would be expostulated with?

And will you not *blame* me if I say that good sense, that kindred indulgence, must be a little offended at the treatment I have met with; and if I own that I think that great rigour has been exercised towards me? And yet I am now authorized to call it *rigour* by the judgment of two excellent sisters, my mother and my aunt, who acknowledge (as you tell me from my aunt) that they have been obliged to join against me, contrary to their inclinations; and that, even in a point which might seem to concern my eternal welfare.

But I must not go on at this rate. For may not the inclination my mother has given up be the effect of a too fond indulgence, rather than that I merit the indulgence? And yet so petulantly perverse am I that I must tear myself from the subject.

All then that I will say further to it, at this time, is, that were the intended goodness to be granted to me but a week hence, it would possibly be too late—too late, I mean, to be of the consolation to me that I would wish from it: for what an inefficacious preparation must I have been making, if it has not, by this time, carried me above—but above what? Poor mistaken creature! Unhappy self-deluder! that finds herself above nothing! Nor able to subdue her own faulty impatience!

But in*deed* to have done with a subject that I dare not trust myself with; if it come in your way, let my Aunt Hervey, let my dear Cousin Dolly, let the worthy Mrs. Williams, know how exceedingly grateful to me their kind intentions and concern for me are: and, as the best warrant or justification of their good opinions (since I know that their favour for me is founded on the belief that I loved virtue), tell them that I *continued* to love virtue to my last hour, as I presume to hope it may be said; and assure them that I never made the least *wilful* deviation, however unhappy I became for one faulty step; which nevertheless was not owing to unworthy or perverse motives.

I am very sorry that my Cousin Morden has taken a resolution to see Mr. Lovelace.

My apprehensions on this intelligence are a great abatement to the pleasure I have in knowing that he still loves me.

My sister's letter to me is a most afflicting one—so *needlessly*, so *ludicrously* taunting. But for that part of it that is so, I ought rather to pity her than to be so much concerned at it as I am.

I wonder what I have done to Mr. Brand. I pray God to forgive both him and his informants, whoever they be. But if the scandal arise solely from Mr. Belford's visits, a very little time will confute it. Meanwhile, the packet I shall send you, which I sent to Miss Howe, will I hope satisfy *you*, my dear Mrs. Norton, as to my reasons for admitting his visits.

My sister's taunting letter, and the inflexibleness of my dearer friends——But how do remoter-begun subjects tend to the point which lies nearest the heart!—as new-caught bodily disorders all crowd to a fractured or distempered part.

I will break off, with requesting your prayers that I may be blessed with patience and due resignation; and with assuring you that I am, and will be to the last hour of my life,

Your equally grateful and affectionate

CL. HARLOWE

Letter LXXIII—Miss Howe to Miss Clarissa Harlowe
[*In reply to hers of Friday, Aug.* 11 [1]]

Yarmouth, Isle of Wight, Aug. 23.

MY DEAREST FRIEND,—I have read the letters and copies of letters you favoured me with: and I return them by a particular hand.

I am extremely concerned at your indifferent state of health: but I approve of all your proceedings and precautions in relation to the appointment of Mr. Belford for an office in which I hope neither he nor anybody else will be wanted to act for many, very many years.

I admire, and so we do all, that greatness of mind which can make you so steadfastly despise (through such inducements as no other woman could resist, and in such desolate circumstances as you have been reduced to) the wretch that ought to be so heartily despised and detested.

What must the contents of those letters from your relations be which you will not communicate to me! Fie upon them! How my heart rises! But I dare say no more—though you yourself now begin to think they use you with great severity.

Everybody here is so taken with Mr. Hickman (and the more from the horror they conceive at the character of the detestable Lovelace) that I have been teased to death almost to name a day. This has given him airs; and, did I not keep him to it, he would behave as carelessly and as insolently as if he were sure of me. I have been forced to mortify him no less than four times since we have been here.

I made him lately undergo a severe penance for some negligences that were not to be passed over: not *designed* ones, he said: but that was a poor excuse, as I told him: for, had they been *designed*, he should never have come into my presence more: that they were *not*, showed his want of thought and attention; and those were inexcusable in a man only in his probatory state.

He hoped he had been more than in a *probatory* state, he said.

And therefore, sir, might be more *careless*! So you add *ingratitude* to *negligence*, and make what you plead as *accident*, that *itself* wants an excuse, *design*, which deserves none.

I would not see him for two days, and he was so penitent, and so humble, that I had like to have lost myself, to make him amends: for, as you have said, a resentment carried too high often ends in an amends too humble.

I long to be nearer to you: but that must not yet be it seems. Pray, my dear, let me hear from you as often as you can.

May Heaven increase your comforts, and restore your health, are the prayers of

> Your ever faithful and affectionate
>
> ANNA HOWE.

P.S. Excuse me that I did not write before: it was owing to a little coasting voyage I was obliged to give in to.

Letter LXXIV—Miss Clarissa Harlowe to Miss Howe

Friday, Aug. 25.

YOU are very obliging, my dear Miss Howe, to account to me for your silence. I was easy in it, as I doubted not, that among such near and dear friends as you are with, you was diverted from writing by some such agreeable excursion as that you mention.

I was in hopes that you had given over, at this time of day, those very sprightly airs which I have taken the liberty to blame you for as often as you have given me occasion to do so; and that has been *very* often.

I was always very grave with you upon this subject: and while your own and a worthy man's future happiness are in the question, I must enter into it whenever you forget yourself, although I had not a day to live: and indeed I am very ill.

I am sure it was not your intention to take your future husband with you to the little island to make him look weak and silly among those of your relations who never before had seen him. Yet do you think it possible for them (however prepared and resolved they may be to like him) to forbear smiling at him when they see him suffering under your whimsical penances? A modest man should no more be made little in *his own eyes* than in the eyes of *others*. If he be, he will have a diffidence which will give an awkwardness to everything he says or does: and this will be no more to the credit of your choice than to that of the approbation he meets with from your friends, or to his own credit.

I love an obliging and even an *humble* deportment in a man to the woman he addresses. It is a mark of his politeness, and tends to give her that opinion of herself which it may be supposed bashful merit wants to be inspired with. But if the woman exacts it with a high hand, she shows not either her own politeness or gratitude; although I must confess she does her courage. I gave you expectation that I would be very serious with you.

O my dear, that it had been my lot (as I was not permitted to live single) to have met with a man by whom I could have acted generously and unreservedly!

Mr. Lovelace, it is now plain, in order to have a pretence against me, taxed my behaviour to him with stiffness and distance. You, at one time, thought me guilty of some degree of prudery. Difficult situations should be allowed for; which often make occasions for censure unavoidable. I deserved not blame from *him* who made mine difficult. And you, my dear, if I had had any other man to deal with, or had he had but half the merit which Mr. Hickman has, should have found that my doctrine on this subject should have governed my practice.

But to put myself out of the question—I 'll tell you what I should think, were I an indifferent bystander, of these high airs of yours, in return for Mr. Hickman's humble demeanour. "The lady thinks of having the gentleman, I see plainly, would I say. But I see, *as* plainly, that she has a very great indifference to him. And to what may this indifference be owing? To one or all of these considerations, no doubt: That she receives his addresses rather from motives of convenience than choice: that she thinks meanly of *his* endowments and intellects; at least more highly of *her own*: or, she has not the generosity to use that power with moderation, which his great affection for her puts into her hands."

How would you like, my dear, to have any of these things said?

Then to give but the shadow of a reason for free-livers and free-speakers to say, or to imagine, that Miss Howe gives her hand to a man who has no reason to expect any share in her heart, I am sure you would not wish that such a thing should be so much as supposed. Then, all the regard from you to come *afterwards*; none to be shown *before*; must, I should think, be capable of being construed as a compliment to the *husband* made at the expense of the *wife's delicacy*.

There is no fear that attempts could be formed by the most audacious [two Lovelaces there cannot be!] upon a character so revered for virtue, and so charmingly spirited, as Miss Howe's: yet to have any man encouraged to despise a husband by the example of one who is most concerned to do him honour—what, my dear, think you of that? It is but too natural for envious men (and who that knows Miss Howe will not envy Mr. Hickman?) to scoff at, and to jest upon, those who are treated with or will bear indignity from a woman.

If a man so treated have a true and ardent love for the woman he addresses, he will be easily overawed by her displeasure: and this will put him upon acts of submission which will be called *meanness*. And what woman of true spirit would like to have it said that she would impose anything upon the man from whom she one day expects protection and defence, that should be capable of being construed as a meanness, or unmanly abjectness in his behaviour, even to herself? Nay, I am not sure, and I ask it of you, my dear, to resolve me, whether in your own opinion it is not likely that a woman of spirit will *despise* rather than *value* more the man who will take patiently an insult at her hands; especially *before company*.

I have always observed that prejudices in *disfavour* of a person at his first appearance, fix deeper, and are much more difficult to be removed *when* fixed, than prejudices in *favour*: whether owing to envy, or to that malignant principle so eminently visible in little minds, which makes them wish to bring down the more worthy characters to their own low level, I pretend not to determine. When once, therefore, a woman of your good sense gives room to the world to think she has not a high opinion of the *lover* whom, nevertheless, she *entertains*, it will be very difficult for her afterwards to make that world think so well as she would have it, of the *husband* she has chosen.

Give me leave to observe, that to condescend with *dignity*, and to command with such *kindness*, and *sweetness of manners*, as should let the condescension, while single, be seen and acknowledged, are points which a wise woman, *knowing her man*, should aim at: and a wise woman, I should think, would choose to live single all her life rather than give herself to a man whom she thinks unworthy of a treatment so noble.

But when a woman lets her lover see that she has the generosity to approve of and reward a well-meant service; that she has a mind that lifts her above the little captious follies which some (too licentiously, I hope) attribute to the sex in general: that she resents not (if ever she thinks she has reason to be displeased) with petulance, or through pride: nor thinks it necessary to insist upon little points, to come at or secure great ones, perhaps not proper to be aimed at: nor leaves room to suppose she has so much cause to doubt her own merit, as to put the love of the man she intends to favour upon disagreeable or arrogant trials: but lets reason be the principal guide of her actions—she will then never fail of that true respect, of that sincere veneration, which she wishes to meet with; and which will make her judgment after marriage consulted, sometimes with a *preference* to a man's own, at other times as a delightful *confirmation* of his.

And so much, my beloved Miss Howe, for this subject *now*, and I dare say *for ever*!

I will begin another letter by and by, and send both together. Meantime, I am, etc.

Letter LXXV—*Miss Clarissa Harlowe to Miss Howe*

In this letter the lady acquaints Miss Howe with Mr. Brand's report ; with her sister's proposals either that she will go abroad, or prosecute Mr. Lovelace. She complains of the severe letters of her Uncle Antony and her sister ; but in milder terms than they deserved.

She sends her Dr. Lewen's letter, and the copy of her answer to it.

She tells her of the difficulties she had been under to avoid seeing Mr. Lovelace. She gives her the contents of the letter she wrote to him to divert him from his proposed visit : she is afraid, she says, that it is a step that is not strictly right, if allegory or metaphor be not allowable to one in her circumstances.

She informs her of her Cousin Morden's arrival and readiness to take her part with her relations ; of his designed interview with Mr. Lovelace ; and tells her what her apprehensions are upon it.

She gives her the purport of the conversation between her Aunt Hervey and Mrs. Norton. And then adds :

But were they ever so favourably inclined to me now, what can they do for me? I wish, and that for their sakes more than for my own, that they would yet relent. But I am very ill— I must drop my pen—a sudden faintness overspreads my heart. Excuse my crooked writing! Adieu, my dear! Adieu!

Three o'clock, Friday.

Once more I resume my pen. I thought I had taken my last farewell of you. I never was so very oddly affected: something that seemed totally to overwhelm my faculties—I don't know how to describe it—I believe I do amiss in writing so much, and taking too much upon me: but an active mind, though clouded by bodily illness, cannot be idle.

I 'll see if the air, and a discontinued attention, will help me. But if it will not, don't be concerned for me, my dear. I shall be happy. Nay, I am more so already than of late I thought

I could ever be in this life. Yet how this *body* clings! How it encumbers!

Seven o'clock.

I could not send this letter away with so melancholy an ending, as *you* would have thought it. So I deferred closing it till I saw how I should be on my return from my airing: and now I must say I am quite another thing: so alert!—that I could proceed with as much spirit as I began, and add more preachment to your lively subject, if I had not written more than enough upon it already.

I wish you would let me give you and Mr. Hickman joy. Do, my dear. I should take some to *myself*, if you would.

My respectful compliments to all your friends, as well to those I have the honour to know, as to those I do not know.

. . . .

I have just now been surprised with a letter from one whom I long ago gave up all thoughts of hearing from. From Mr. Wyerley. I will enclose it. You'll be surprised at it as much as I was. This seems to be a man whom I *might* have reclaimed. But I could not love him. Yet I hope I never treated him with arrogance. Indeed, my dear, if I am not too partial to myself, I think I refused him with more gentleness than you retain somebody else. And this recollection gives me less pain than I should have had in the other case, on receiving this instance of a generosity that affects me. I will also enclose the rough draft of my answer, as soon as I have transcribed it.

If I begin another sheet, I shall write to the end of it: wherefore I will only add my prayers for your honour and prosperity, and for a long, long, happy life; and that, when it comes to be wound up, you may be as calm and as easy at quitting it, as I hope in God I shall be. I am, and will be, to the latest moment,

Your truly affectionate and obliged servant,

CL. HARLOWE.

Letter LXXVI—Mr. Wyerley to Miss Clarissa Harlowe

Wednesday, Aug. 23.

DEAREST MADAM,—You will be surprised to find renewed, at this distance of time, an address so positively though so politely discouraged: but, however it be received, I *must* renew it. Everybody has heard that you have been vilely treated by a man who, to treat *you* ill, must be the vilest of men. Every-body knows your just resentment of his base treatment: that you are determined never to be reconciled to him: and that you persist in these sentiments against all the entreaties of his noble relations, against all the prayers and repentance of his ignoble self. And all the world that have the honour to know *you,* or have heard of *him,* applaud your resolution, as worthy of yourself; worthy of your virtue, and of that strict honour which was always attributed to you by every one who spoke of you.

But, madam, were all the world to have been of a different opinion, it could never have altered mine. I ever loved you; I ever *must* love you. Yet have I endeavoured to resign to my hard fate. When I had so many ways, in vain, sought to move you in my favour, I sat down, seemingly contented. I even wrote to you that I *would* sit down contented. And I endeavoured to make all my friends and companions think I was. But nobody knows what pangs this self-denial cost me! In vain did the chase, in vain did travel, in vain did lively company, offer themselves, and were embraced in their turn. With redoubled force did my passion for you renew my unhappiness, when I looked into myself, into my own heart; for there did your charming image sit enthroned; and you engrossed me all.

I truly deplore those misfortunes, and those sufferings, for your *own* sake; which, nevertheless, encourage *me* to renew my bold hope. I know not particulars. I dare not inquire after them; because *my* sufferings would be increased with the knowledge of what *yours* have been. I therefore desire not to know more than what common report wounds my ears with; and what is given me to know, by your absence from your cruel family, and from the sacred place where I, among numbers of your rejected admirers, used to be twice a week sure to behold you doing credit to that service of which your example gave me the highest notions. But whatever be those misfortunes, of whatsoever nature those sufferings, I shall bless the occasion for *my own* sake (though for *yours* curse the author of them) if they may give me the happiness to know that this my renewed address may not be absolutely rejected. Only give me hope that it may one day meet with encouragement, if in the interim nothing happen, either in my morals or behaviour, to give you fresh offence. Give me but hope of this—not absolutely to *reject* me is all the hope I ask for; and I will love you, if possible, still more than I ever loved you—and that for your sufferings;

for well you deserve to be loved, even to adoration, who can, for honour's and for virtue's sake, subdue a passion which common spirits [I speak by cruel experience] find invincible; and this at a time when the black offender kneels and supplicates, as I am well assured he does (all his friends likewise supplicating for him), to be forgiven.

That you cannot forgive him, not forgive him so as to receive him again to favour, is no wonder. His offence is against virtue: that is a part of your essence. What magnanimity is this! How just to yourself, and to your spotless character! Is it any merit to admire more than ever a lady who can so exaltedly distinguish? It is not. I cannot plead it.

What hope have I left, may it be said, when my address was *before* rejected, now that your sufferings, so *nobly borne*, have, with all *good judges*, exalted your character? Yet, madam, I have to pride myself in this, that while your friends (not looking upon you in the just light I do) persecute and banish you; while your estate is withheld from you, and threatened (as I *know*) to *be* withheld, as long as the chicaning law, or rather the chicaneries of its practisers, can keep it from you: while you are destitute of protection; everybody standing aloof, either through fear of the injurer of one family, or of the hard-hearted of the other; I pride myself, I say, to stand forth, and offer my fortune, and my life, at your devotion. With a *selfish* hope indeed: I should be too great a hypocrite not to own this! And I know how much you abhor insincerity.

But, whether you encourage that hope or not, accept my best services, I beseech you, madam: and be pleased to excuse me for a piece of honest art, which the nature of the case (doubting the honour of your notice otherwise) makes me choose to conclude with. It is this:

If I am to be still the most unhappy of men, let your pen, by *one line*, tell me so. If I am permitted to indulge a hope, however distant, your *silence* shall be deemed by me the happiest indication of it that you can give—except that *still* happier (the happiest that *can* befall me)—a signification that you will accept the tender of that life and fortune which it would be my pride and my glory to sacrifice in your service, leaving the reward to *yourself*.

Be your determination as it may, I must for ever admire and love you. Nor will I ever change my condition while you live, whether you change yours or not: for, having once had the presumption to address *you*, I cannot stoop to think of any other woman: and this I solemnly declare in the presence of that God whom I daily pray to bless and protect you, be your determination what it will with regard to, dearest madam,

Your most devoted and ever affectionate
and faithful servant,
ALEXANDER WYERLEY.

Letter LXXVII—Miss Clarissa Harlowe to Alex. Wyerley, Esq.

Sat. Aug. 26.

SIR,—The generosity of your purpose would have commanded not only my notice, but my thanks, although you had *not* given me the alternative you are pleased to call *artful*. And I do therefore give you my thanks for your kind letter.

At the time you distinguished me by your favourable opinion, I told you, sir, that my choice was the single life. And most *truly* did I tell you so.

When that was not permitted me, and I looked round upon the several gentlemen who had been proposed to me, and had reason to believe that there was not one of them against whose morals or principles there lay not *some* exception, it would not have been *much* to be wondered at, if FANCY *had* been allowed to give a preference where JUDGMENT was at a loss to determine.

Far be it from me to say this with a design to upbraid you, sir, or to reflect upon you. I always wished you well. You had reason to think I did. You had the generosity to be pleased with the frankness of my behaviour to you; as I had with that of yours to me: and I am sorry, very sorry, to be now told that the acquiescence you obliged me with gave you so much pain.

Had the option I have mentioned been allowed me *afterwards* (as I not only wished but proposed), things had not happened that did happen. But there was a kind of fatality by which our whole family was impelled, as I may say; and which none of us were permitted to avoid. But this is a subject that cannot be dwelt upon.

As matters are, I have only to wish, for your own sake, that you will encourage and cultivate those good motions in your mind, to which many passages in your kind and generous letter now before me must be owing. Depend upon it, sir, that such motions wrought into habit will yield you pleasure at a *time* when nothing else can. And at *present*, shining out in your actions and conversation, will commend you to the worthiest of our sex. For, sir, the man who is good upon *choice*, as well as by *education*,

has that quality in himself which ennobles the human race, and
without which the most dignified by birth or rank are ignoble.

As to the resolution you so solemnly make not to marry while
I live, I should be concerned at it, were I not morally sure that
you may keep it, and yet not be detrimented by it.   Since a few,
a very few days, will convince you that I am got above all human
dependence; and that there is no need of that protection and
favour which you so generously offer to, sir,

Your obliged well-wisher and humble servant,

CL. HARLOWE.

Letter LXXVIII—Mr. Lovelace to John Belford, Esq.

Monday Noon, Aug. 28.

ABOUT the time of poor Belton's interment last night, as near as
we could guess, Lord M., Mowbray, and myself toasted once, *To
the memory of honest Tom Belton*; and, by a quick transition to the
living, *Health to Miss Harlowe*; which Lord M. obligingly began,
and, *To the happy reconciliation*; and then we stuck in a remembrance *To honest Jack Belford*, who, of late, we all agreed, is
become a useful and humane man; and one who prefers his
friends' service to his own.

But what is the meaning I hear nothing from thee?[1]   And
why dost thou not let me into the grounds of the sudden reconciliation between my beloved and her friends, and the cause of
the generous invitation which she gives me of attending her at
her father's some time hence?

Thou must certainly have been let into the secret by this time;
and I can tell thee I shall be plaguy jealous if there be any one
thing pass between my angel and thee that is to be concealed
from me.   For either I am a principal in this cause, or I am
nothing.

I have dispatched Will to know the reason of thy neglect.

But let me whisper a word or two in thy ear.   I begin to be
afraid, after all, that this letter was a stratagem to get me out
of town, and for nothing else: for, in the first place, Tourville, in a
letter I received this morning, tells me that the lady is actually
very ill [I am sorry for it with all my soul!].   This, thou 'lt say,
I may think a reason why she cannot *set out as yet*: but then,
I have heard on the other hand but last night, that the family
is as implacable as ever; and my lord and I expect this very

---

[1] Mr. Belford had **not yet** sent him his last-written letter.   His reason
for which see p. 180.

afternoon a visit from Colonel Morden; who undertakes, it seems, to question me as to my intention with regard to his cousin.

This convinces me that if she *has* apprised her friends of my offers to her, they will not believe me to be in earnest till they are assured that I am so from my own mouth. But then I understand that the intended visit is an officiousness of Morden's own, without the desire of any of her friends.

Now, Jack, what can a man make of all this? My intelligence as to the continuance of her family's implacableness is not to be doubted; and yet when I read her letter, what can one say? Surely the dear little rogue will not lie!

I never knew her dispense with her word but once: and that was when she promised to forgive me after the dreadful fire that had like to have happened at our mother's, and yet would not see me next day, and afterwards made her escape to Hampstead, in order to avoid forgiving me: and as she severely smarted for this departure from her honour given (for it is a sad thing for good people to break their word when it is in their power to keep it), one would not expect that she should set about deceiving again; more especially by the *premeditation of writing*. Thou, perhaps, wilt ask: What honest man is obliged to keep his promise with a highwayman? for well I know thy unmannerly way of making comparisons: but I say, *every* honest man is. And I will give thee an illustration.

Here is a marauding varlet who demands your money, with his pistol at your breast. You have neither money nor valuable effects about you; and promise solemnly, if he will spare your life, that you will send him an agreed upon sum, by such a day, to such a place.

The question is, If your life is not in the fellow's power?

How he came by the power is another question; for which he must answer with *his* life when caught—so he runs risk for risk.

Now, if he give you *your* life, does he not give, think you, a valuable consideration for the money you engage your honour to send him? If not, the sum must be exorbitant, or your life is a very paltry one, even in your own opinion.

I need not make the application; and I am sure that even thou thyself, who never sparest me, and thinkest thou knowest *my* heart by *thy own*, canst not possibly put the case in a stronger light against me.

Then why do good people take upon themselves to censure, as they do, persons *less* scrupulous than themselves? Is it not because the latter allow themselves in *any* liberty, in order to carry a point? And can my not doing *my* duty warrant another for not doing *his*? Thou wilt not say it can.

And how would it sound, to put the case as strongly once more, as my greatest enemy would put it, both as to *fact* and in *words*: Here has that profligate wretch Lovelace broken his vow with and deceived Miss Clarissa Harlowe. A vile fellow! would an enemy say: but it is *like* him. But when it comes to be said that the pious Clarissa has broken her word with and deceived Lovelace; Good Lord! would every one say. Sure it cannot be!

Upon my soul, Jack, such is the veneration I have for this admirable woman, that I am shocked barely at putting the case. And so wilt thou, if thou respectest her as thou oughtest: for thou knowest that men and women all the world over form their opinions of one another by each person's professions and known practices. In this lady, therefore, it would be as unpardonable to tell a wilful untruth, as it would be strange if I kept my word—in love-cases, I mean; for as to the rest I am an honest moral man, as all who know me can testify.

And what, after all, would this lady deserve if she has deceived me in this case? For did she not set me prancing away upon Lord M.'s best nag, to Lady Sarah's, and to Lady Betty's, with an erect and triumphing countenance, to show them her letter to me?

And let me tell thee that I have received their congratulations upon it: Well, and now, Cousin Lovelace, cries one; Well, and now, Cousin Lovelace, cries t' other; I hope you 'll make the best of husbands to so excellent and so forgiving a lady!—And now we shall soon have the pleasure of looking upon you as a reformed man! added one. And now we shall see you in the way we have so long wished you to be in! cried out the other.

My Cousins Montague also have been ever since rejoicing in the new relationship. Their charming cousin, and their lovely cousin, at every word! And how dearly they will love her! What lessons they will take from her! And yet Charlotte, who pretends to have the eye of an eagle, was for finding out some mystery in the style and manner, till I overbore her, and laughed her out of it.

As for Lord M., he has been in hourly expectation of being sent to with proposals of one sort or other from the Harlowes: and still will have it that such proposals will be made by Colonel Morden when he comes; and that the Harlowes only put on a face of irreconcilableness till they know the issue of Morden's visit, in order to make the better terms with us.

Indeed, if I had not undoubted reason, as I said, to believe the continuance of their antipathy to *me*, and implacableness to *her*, I should be apt to think there might be some foundation for my lord's conjecture; for there is a cursed deal of low cunning in all that family, except in the angel of it; who has so much generosity of soul that she despises cunning, both name and thing.

What I mean by all this, is to let thee see what a stupid figure I shall make to all my own family, if my Clarissa has been capable, as Gulliver in his abominable Yahoo story phrases it, of saying the *thing that is not*. By my soul, Jack, if it were only that I should be *outwitted* by such a novice at plotting, and that it would make me look silly to my kinswomen here, who know I value myself upon my contrivances, it would vex me to the heart; and I would instantly clap a feather bed into a coach and six, and fetch her away, sick or well, and marry her at my leisure.

But Colonel Morden is come, and I must break off.

Letter LXXIX—Mr. Belford to Robert Lovelace, Esq.

Monday Night, Aug. 28.

I DOUBT you will be all impatience that you have not heard from me since mine of Thursday last. You would be still more so, if you knew that I had by me a letter ready written.

I went early yesterday morning to Epsom; and found everything disposed according to the directions I had left on Friday; and at night the solemn office was performed. Tourville was there; and behaved very decently, and with greater concern than I thought he would ever have expressed for anybody.

Thomasine, they told me, in a kind of disguise, was in an obscure pew, out of curiosity (for it seems she was far from showing any tokens of grief) to see the last office performed for the man whose heart she had so largely contributed to break.

I was obliged to stay till this afternoon, to settle several necessary matters, and to direct inventories to be taken, in order for appraisement; for everything is to be turned into money, by his will. I presented his sister with the hundred guineas the poor man left me as his executor, and desired her to continue in the house, and take the direction of everything, till I could hear from his nephew at Antigua, who is *heir at law*. He had left her but fifty pounds, although he knew her indigence;

and that it was owing to a vile husband, and not to herself, that she *was* indigent.

The poor man left about two hundred pounds in money, and two hundred pounds in two East India bonds; and I will contrive, if I can, to make up the poor woman's fifty pounds, and my hundred guineas, two hundred pounds to her; and then she will have some little matter coming in certain, which I will oblige her to keep out of the hands of a son who has completed the ruin which his father had very near effected.

I gave Tourville his twenty pounds, and will send you and Mowbray yours by the first order.

And so much for poor Belton's affairs till I see you.

I got to town in the evening, and went directly to Smith's. I found Mrs. Lovick and Mrs. Smith in the back shop, and I saw they had been both in tears. They rejoiced to see me, however; and told me that the doctor and Mr. Goddard were but just gone; as was also the worthy clergyman who often comes to pray by her; and all three were of opinion that she would hardly live to see the entrance of another week. I was not so much surprised as grieved; for I had feared as much when I left her on Saturday.

I sent up my compliments; and she returned that she would take it for a favour if I would call upon her in the morning, by eight o'clock. Mrs. Lovick told me that she had fainted away on Saturday, while she was writing, as she had done likewise the day before; and having received benefit then by a little turn in a chair, she was carried abroad again. She returned somewhat better; and wrote till late; yet had a pretty good night; and went to Covent Garden Church in the morning: but came home so ill that she was obliged to lie down.

When she arose, seeing how much grieved Mrs. Lovick and Mrs. Smith were for her, she made apologies for the trouble she gave them. You were happy, said she, before I came hither. It was a cruel thing in me to come among honest strangers, and to be sick, and die with you.

When they touched upon the irreconcilableness of her friends, I have had ill offices done me to them, said she, and they do not know how ill I am; nor will they believe anything I should write. But yet I cannot sometimes forbear thinking it a little hard, that out of so many near and dear friends as I have living, not one of them will vouchsafe to look upon me. No old servant, no old friend, proceeded she, to be permitted to come near me, without being sure of incurring displeasure! And to have such a great work to go through by myself, a young creature as I am, and to have everything to think of as to my temporal matters, and to order, to my very interment! No dear mother, said the sweet sufferer, to pray by me and bless me! No kind sister to soothe and comfort me! But come, recollected she, how do I know but all is for the best—if I can but make a right use of my discomforts? Pray for me, Mrs. Lovick—pray for me, Mrs. Smith, that I may—I have great need of your prayers. This cruel man has discomposed me. His persecutions have given me a pain just here [putting her hand to her heart]. What a step has he made me take to avoid him! Who can *touch pitch and not be defiled*? He has made a bad spirit take possession of me, I think—broken in upon all my duties. And will not yet, I doubt, let me be at rest. Indeed he is very cruel. But this is one of my trials, I believe. By God's grace I shall be easier to-morrow, and especially if I have no more of his tormentings, and if I can get a tolerable night. And I will sit up till eleven, that I may.

She said that though this was so heavy a day with her, she was at other times, within these few days past especially, blessed with bright hours; and particularly that she had now and then such joyful assurances (which she hoped were not presumptuous ones) that God would receive her to His mercy, that she could hardly contain herself, and was ready to think herself above this earth while she was in it: and what, inferred she to Mrs. Lovick, must be the state itself, the very aspirations after which have often cast a beamy light through the thickest darkness, and when I have been at the lowest ebb, have dispelled the black clouds of despondency?—As I hope they soon will this spirit of repining.

She had a pretty good night, it seems; and this morning went in a chair to St. Dunstan's Church.

The chairmen told Mrs. Smith that after prayers (for she did not return till between nine and ten) they carried her to a house in Fleet Street, whither they never waited on her before. And where dost think this was? Why, to an undertaker's! Good Heaven! what a woman is this! She went into the back shop, and talked with the master of it about half an hour, and came from him with great serenity; he waiting upon her to her chair with a respectful countenance, but full of curiosity and seriousness.

'Tis evident that she then went to bespeak her *house* that she talked of.[1] *As soon as you can, sir*, were her words to him as she

[1] See p. 180.

got into the chair. Mrs. Smith told me this with the same surprise and grief that I heard it.

She was very ill in the afternoon, having got cold either at St. Dunstan's or at chapel, and sent for the clergyman to pray by her; and the women, unknown to her, sent both for Dr. H. and Mr. Goddard: who were just gone, as I told you, when I came to pay my respects to her this evening.

And thus have I recounted from the good women what passed to this night since my absence.

I long for to-morrow, that I may see her: and yet 'tis such a melancholy longing as I never experienced, and know not how to describe.

Tuesday, Aug. 29.

I was at Smith's at half an hour after seven. They told me that the lady was gone in a chair to St. Dunstan's; but was better than she had been in either of the two preceding days; and that she said to Mrs. Lovick and Mrs. Smith, as she went into the chair: I have a good deal to answer for to you, my good friends, for my vapourish conversation of last night.

If, Mrs. Lovick, said she, smiling, I have no new matters to discompose me, I believe my spirits will hold out purely.

She returned immediately after prayers.

Mr. Belford, said she, as she entered the back shop where I was, and upon my approaching her, I am very glad to see you. You have been performing for your poor friend a kind last office. 'Tis not long ago since you did the same for a near relation. Is it not a little hard upon you that these troubles should fall so thick to your lot? But they are charitable offices: and it is a praise to your humanity that poor dying people know not where to choose so well.

I told her I was sorry to hear she had been so ill since I had the honour to attend her; but rejoiced to find that now she seemed a good deal better.

It will be sometimes better, and sometimes worse, replied she, with poor creatures, when they are balancing between life and death. But no more of these matters just now. I hope, sir, you'll breakfast with me. I was quite vapourish yesterday. I had a very bad spirit upon me. Had I not, Mrs. Smith? But I hope I shall be no more so. And to-day I am perfectly serene. This day rises upon me as if it would be a bright one.

She desired me to walk up, and invited Mr. Smith and his wife, and Mrs. Lovick also, to breakfast with her. I was better pleased with her liveliness than with her looks.

The good people retiring after breakfast, the following conversation passed between us.

Pray, sir, let me ask you, said she, if you think I may promise myself that I shall be no more molested by your friend?

I hesitated: for how could I answer for such a man?

What shall I do if he comes again? You see how I am. I cannot fly from him now. If he has any pity left for the poor creature whom he has thus reduced, let him not come. But have you heard from him lately? And will he come?

I hope not, madam; I have not heard from him since Thursday last, that he went out of town, rejoicing in the hopes your letter gave him of a reconciliation between your friends and you, and that he might in good time see you at your father's; and he is gone down to give all his friends joy of the news, and is in high spirits upon it.

Alas for me! I shall then surely have him come up to persecute me again! As soon as he discovers that that was only a stratagem to keep him away, he will come up; and who knows but even *now* he is upon the road? I thought I was so bad that I should have been out of his and everybody's way before now; for I expected not that this contrivance would serve me above two or three days; and by this time he must have found out that I am not so happy as to have any hope of a reconciliation with my family; and then he will come, if it be only in revenge for what he will think a deceit; but is not, I hope, a wicked one.

I believe I looked surprised to hear her confess that her letter was a stratagem only; for she said: You wonder, Mr. Belford, I observe, that I could be *guilty of such an artifice. I doubt it is not right*: it was done in a hurry of spirits. How could I see a man who had so mortally injured me; yet, pretending sorrow for his crimes (and wanting to see me), could behave with so much shocking levity as he did to the honest people of the house? Yet, 'tis strange too, that neither you nor he found out my meaning on perusal of my letter. You have seen what I wrote, no doubt?

I have, madam. And then I began to account for it as an *innocent* artifice.

Thus far indeed, sir, it is *innocent*, that I meant him no hurt, and had a *right* to the effect I hoped for from it; and he had *none* to invade me. But have you, sir, that letter of his in which he gives you (as I suppose he does) the copy of mine?

I have, madam. And pulled it out of my letter-case: but hesitating, Nay, sir, said she, be pleased to read my letter to yourself—I desire not to see *his*—and see if you can be longer a stranger to a meaning so obvious.

I read it to myself. Indeed, madam, I can find nothing but that you are going down to Harlowe Place to be reconciled to your father and other friends: and Mr. Lovelace presumed that a letter from your sister, which he saw brought when he was at Mr. Smith's, gave you the welcome news of it.

She then explained all to me, and that, as I may say, in six words. A *religious* meaning is couched under it, and that 's the reason that neither you nor I could find it out.

"Read but for my *father's house, heaven*, said she, and for the interposition of my dear blessed friend, suppose the *mediation* of my *Saviour* (which I humbly rely upon); and all the rest of the letter will be accounted for." I hope (repeated she) that it is a pardonable artifice. But I am afraid it is not strictly right.

I read it so, and stood astonished for a minute at her invention, her piety, her charity, and at thine and mine own stupidity, to be thus taken in.

And now, thou vile Lovelace, what hast thou to do (the lady all consistent with herself, and no hopes left for thee) but to hang, drown, or shoot thyself, for an outwitted boaster?

My surprise being a little over, she proceeded: As to the letter that came from my sister while your friend was here, you will *soon* see, sir, that it is the cruellest letter she ever wrote me.

And then she expressed a deep concern for what might be the consequence of Colonel Morden's intended visit to you; and besought me, that if now, or at any time hereafter, I had opportunity prevent any further mischief, without detriment or danger to myself, I would do it.

I assured her of the most particular attention to this and to all her commands; and that in a manner so agreeable to her that she invoked a blessing upon me for my goodness, as she called it, to a desolate creature who suffered under the *worst of orphanage*; those were her words.

She then went back to her first subject, her uneasiness for fear of your molesting her again; and said: If you have any influence over him, Mr. Belford, prevail upon him, that he will give me the assurance that the short remainder of my time shall be all my own. I have *need* of it. Indeed I have. Why will he wish to interrupt me in my duty? Has he not punished me enough for my preference of him to all his sex? Has he not destroyed my fame and my fortune? And will not his causeless vengeance upon me be complete, unless he ruin my soul too?

Excuse me, sir, for this vehemence! But indeed it greatly imports me to know that I shall be no more disturbed by him. And yet, with all this aversion, I would sooner give way to his visit, though I were to expire the moment I saw him, than to be the cause of any fatal misunderstanding between you and him.

I assured her that I would make such a representation of the matter to you, and of the state of her health, that I would undertake to *answer for you*, that you would not attempt to come near her.

And for this reason, Lovelace, do I lay the whole matter before you, and desire you will authorize me, as soon as this and mine of Saturday last come to your hands, to dissipate her fears.

This gave her a little satisfaction; and then she said, that had I not told her that I *could* promise for you, she was determined, ill as she is, to remove somewhere out of my knowledge as well as out of yours. And yet, to have been obliged to leave people I am but just got acquainted with, said the poor lady, and to have died among perfect strangers, would have completed my hardships.

This conversation, I found, as well from the length as the nature of it, had fatigued her; and seeing her change colour once or twice, I made that my excuse, and took leave of her: desiring her permission, however, to attend her in the evening; and as often as possible; for I could not help telling her, that every time I saw her I more and more considered her as a beatified spirit; and as one sent from Heaven to draw me after her out of the miry gulf in which I had been so long immersed.

And laugh at me if thou wilt; but it is true, that every time I approach her I cannot but look upon her as one just entering into a companionship with saints and angels. This thought so wholly possessed me, that I could not help begging, as I went away, her prayers and her blessing; with the reverence due to an angel.

In the evening, she was so low and weak that I took my leave of her in less than a quarter of an hour. I went directly home; where, to the pleasure and wonder of my cousin and her family, I now pass many honest evenings: which they impute to your being out of town.

I shall dispatch my packet to-morrow morning early by my own servant, to make thee amends for the suspense I must have kept thee in: thou 'lt thank me for that, I hope; but wilt not, I am sure, for sending thy servant back without a letter.

I long for the particulars of the conversation between you and Mr. Morden: the lady, as I have hinted, is full of apprehensions about it. Send me back this packet when perused: for I have not had either time or patience to take a copy of it. And I beseech you enable me to make good my engagements to the poor lady that you will not invade her again.

Letter LXXX—Mr. Belford to Robert Lovelace, Esq.

Wednesday, Aug. 30.

I HAVE a conversation to give you that passed between this admirable lady and Dr. H. which will furnish a new instance of the calmness and serenity with which she can talk of death, and prepare for it, as if it were an occurrence as familiar to her as dressing and undressing.

As soon as I had dispatched my servant to you with my letters of the 26th, 28th, and yesterday the 29th, I went to pay my duty to her, and had the pleasure to find her, after a tolerable night, pretty lively and cheerful. She was but just returned from her usual devotions. And Doctor H. alighted as she entered the door.

After inquiring how she did, and hearing her complaints of shortness of breath (which she attributed to inward decay, precipitated by her late harasses, as well from her friends as from you), he was for advising her to go into the air.

What will that do for me? said she. Tell me truly, good sir, with a cheerful aspect (you know you cannot disturb me by it), whether now you do not put on the *true* physician; and, despairing that anything in medicine will help me, advise me to the air as the last resource? Can you think the air will avail in such a malady as mine?

He was silent.

I ask, said she, because my friends (who will possibly some time hence inquire after the means I used for my recovery) may be satisfied that I omitted nothing which so worthy and so skilful a physician prescribed.

The air, madam, may possibly help the difficulty of breathing which has so lately attacked you.

But, sir, you see how weak I am. You must see that I have been consuming from day to day; and now, if I can judge by what I feel in myself, putting her hand to her heart, I cannot continue long. If the air would very probably add to my days though I am far from being *desirous* to have them lengthened,

I would go into it; and the rather as I know Mrs. Lovick would kindly accompany me. But if I were to be at the trouble of removing into new lodgings (a trouble which I think now would be too much for me), and this only to *die* in the country, I had rather the scene were to be shut up here. For here have I meditated the spot, and the manner, and everything, as well of the minutest as of the highest consequence, that can attend the solemn moments. So, doctor, tell me truly, may I stay here, and be clear of any imputations of curtailing, through wilfulness or impatience, or through resentments which I hope I am got above, a life that might otherwise be prolonged? Tell me, sir; you are not talking to a coward in this respect; indeed you are not!—unaffectedly smiling.

The doctor, turning to me, was at a loss what to say, lifting up his eyes only in admiration of her.

Never had any patient, said she, a more indulgent and more humane physician. But since you are loath to answer my question directly, I will put it in other words: You don't *enjoin* me to go into the air, doctor, do you?

I do *not*, madam. Nor do I now visit you as a physician; but as a person whose conversation I admire, and whose sufferings I condole. And to explain myself more directly, as to the occasion of this day's visit in particular, I must tell you, madam, that, understanding how much you suffer by the displeasure of your friends; and having no doubt but that if they knew the way you are in, they would alter their conduct to you; and believing it must cut them to the heart when, too late, they shall be informed of everything; I have resolved to apprise them by letter (stranger as I am to their persons) how necessary it is for some of them to attend you very speedily. For *their* sakes, madam, let me press for your approbation of this measure.

She paused, and at last said: This is kind, very kind in you, sir. But I hope that you do not think me so perverse, and so obstinate, as to have left till now any means unessayed which I thought likely to move my friends in my favour. But now, doctor, said she, I should be too much disturbed at their grief, if they were any of them to come or to send to me: and perhaps, if I found they still loved me, wish to live; and so should quit unwillingly that life which I am now really fond of quitting, and hope to quit, as becomes a person who has had such a weaning-time as I have been favoured with.

I hope, madam, said I, we are not so near as you apprehend to that deplorable catastrophe you hint at with such an amazing presence of mind. And therefore I presume to second the doctor's motion, if it were only for the sake of your father and mother, that they may have the satisfaction, if they *must* lose you, to think they were first reconciled to you.

It is very kindly, very humanely considered, said she. But, if you think me not so *very* near my last hour, let me desire this may be postponed till I see what effect my Cousin Morden's mediation may have. Perhaps he may vouchsafe to make me a visit yet, after his intended interview with Mr. Lovelace is over; of which, who knows, Mr. Belford, but your next letters may give an account? I hope it will not be a fatal one to *any-body*. Will you promise me, doctor, to forbear writing for two days only, and I will communicate to you anything that occurs in that time; and then you shall take your own way? Meantime, I repeat my thanks for your goodness to me. Nay, dear doctor, hurry not away from me so precipitately [for he was going for fear of an offered fee], I will no more affront you with tenders that have pained you for some time past: and since I must now, from this kindly offered favour, look upon you only as a friend, I will assure you henceforth that I will give you no more uneasiness on that head: and now, sir, I know I shall have the pleasure of seeing you oftener than heretofore.

The worthy gentleman was pleased with this assurance, telling her that he had always come to see her with great pleasure, but parted with her, on the account she hinted at, with as much pain; and that he should not have forborne to double his visits could he have had this kind assurance as early as he wished for it.

There are few instances of like disinterestedness, I doubt, in this tribe. Till now I always held it for gospel that *friendship* and *physician* were incompatible things; and little imagined that a man of medicine, when he had given over his patient to death, would think of any visits but those of ceremony, that he might stand well with the family, against it came to their turns to go through his turnpike.

After the doctor was gone, she fell into a very serious discourse of the vanity of life, and the wisdom of preparing for death while health and strength remained, and before the infirmities of body impaired the faculties of the mind, and disabled them from acting with the necessary efficacy and clearness: the whole calculated for every one's meridian, but particularly, as it was easy to observe, for thine and mine.

She was very curious to know further particulars of the behaviour of poor Belton in his last moments. You must not wonder at my inquiries, Mr. Belford, said she; for who is it that is to undertake a journey into a country they never travelled to before, that inquires not into the difficulties of the road, and what accommodations are to be expected in the way?

I gave her a brief account of the poor man's terrors, and unwillingness to die; and when I had done: Thus, Mr. Belford, said she, must it always be with poor souls who have never thought of their long voyage till the moment they are to embark for it.

She made such other observations upon this subject as, coming from the mouth of a person who will so soon be a companion for angels, I shall never forget. And indeed, when I went home, that I might engraft them the better on my memory, I entered them down in writing: but I will not let you see them until you are in a frame more proper to benefit by them than you are likely to be in one while.

Thus far I had written, when the unexpected early return of my servant with your packet (yours and he meeting at Slough, and exchanging letters) obliged me to leave off to give its contents a reading. Here, therefore, I close this letter.

Letter LXXXI—Mr. Lovelace to John Belford, Esq.

Tuesday Morn. Aug. 29.

Now, Jack, will I give thee an account of what passed on occasion of the visit made us by Colonel Morden.

He came on horseback, attended by one servant; and Lord M. received him as a relation of Miss Harlowe's, with the highest marks of civility and respect.

After some general talk of the times, and of the weather, and such nonsense as Englishmen generally make their introductory topics to conversation, the colonel addressed himself to Lord M. and to me, as follows:

I need not, my lord, and Mr. Lovelace, as you know the relation I bear to the Harlowe family, make any apology for entering upon a subject which, on account of that relation, you must think is the principal reason of the honour I have done myself in this visit.

Miss Harlowe, Miss Clarissa Harlowe's affair, said Lord M., with his usual forward bluntness. That, sir, is what you mean. She is, by all accounts, the most excellent woman in the world.

I am glad to hear that is your lordship's opinion of her. It is every one's.

It is not only my opinion, Colonel Morden (proceeded the prating peer), but it is the opinion of all my family. Of my sisters, of my nieces, and of Mr. Lovelace himself.

Col. Would to Heaven it had been always Mr. Lovelace's opinion of her!

Lovel. You have been out of England, colonel, a good many years. Perhaps you are not yet fully apprised of all the particulars of this case.

Col. I have been out of England, sir, about seven years. My Cousin Clary was then about *twelve* years of age: but never was there at *twenty* so discreet, so prudent, and so excellent a creature. All that knew her, or saw her, admired her. Mind and person, never did I see such promises of perfection in any young lady: and I am told, nor is it to be wondered at, that as she advanced to maturity, she more than justified and made good those promises. Then, as to fortune—what her father, what her uncles, and what I myself intended to do for her, besides what her grandfather had done—there is not a finer fortune in the county.

Lovel. All this, colonel, and more than this, is Miss Clarissa Harlowe; and had it not been for the implacableness and violence of her family (all resolved to push her upon a match as unworthy *of* her as hateful *to* her), she had still been happy.

Col. I own, Mr. Lovelace, the truth of what you observed just now, that I am not thoroughly acquainted with all that has passed between you and my cousin. But permit me to say that when I first heard that you made your addresses to her, I knew but of one objection against you. That, indeed, a very great one: and upon a letter sent me, I gave her my free opinion upon the subject.[1] But had it not been for that, I own that, in my private mind, there could not have been a more suitable match: for you are a gallant gentleman, graceful in your person, easy and genteel in your deportment, and in your family, fortunes, and expectations, happy as a man can wish to be. Then the knowledge I had of you in Italy (although, give me leave to say, your conduct there was not wholly unexceptionable) convinces me that you are brave: and few gentlemen come up to you in wit and vivacity. Your education has given you great advantages; your manners are engaging, and you have travelled; and I know, if you'll excuse me, you make better observations than you are governed by. All these qualifications make it not at all surprising that a young lady should love you: and that this

---

[1] See vol. ii, pp. 256 et seq.

love, joined to that indiscreet warmth wherewith my cousin's friends would have forced her inclinations in favour of men who are far your inferiors in the qualities I have named, should throw her upon your protection: but then, if there were these two strong motives, the one to *induce*, the other to *impel* her, let me ask you, sir, if she were not doubly entitled to generous usage from a man whom she chose for her protector; and whom, let me take the liberty to say, she could so amply reward for the protection he was to afford her?

Lovel. Miss Clarissa Harlowe was entitled, sir, to the best usage that man could give her. I have no scruple to own it. I will always do her the justice she so well deserves. I know what will be your inference; and have only to say that time past cannot be recalled. Perhaps I wish it could.

The colonel then in a very manly strain set forth the wickedness of attempting a woman of virtue and character. He said that men had generally too many advantages from the weakness, credulity, and inexperience of the fair sex: that their early learning, which chiefly consisted in inflaming novels, and idle and improbable romances, contributed to enervate and weaken their minds: that his cousin, however, he was sure, was above the reach of common seduction, or to be influenced by weaker motives than *their* violence, and the most solemn promises on *my part*: but, nevertheless, *having* those motives, and her prudence (eminent as it was) being rather the effect of *constitution* than *experience* (a fine advantage, however, he said, to ground an unblamable future life upon), she might not be apprehensive of bad designs in a man she loved: it was, therefore, a very heinous thing to abuse the confidence of such a woman.

He was going on in this trite manner, when, interrupting him, I said: These general observations, colonel, suit not perhaps this particular case. But you yourself are a man of gallantry; and, possibly, were you to be put to the question, might not be able to vindicate every action of your life any more than I.

Col. You are welcome, sir, to put what questions you please to me. And, I thank God, I can both *own* and be *ashamed* of my errors.

Lord M. looked at *me*; but as the colonel did not by his manner seem to intend a reflection, I had no occasion to take it for one; especially as I can as readily *own* my errors, as he or any man can his, whether *ashamed* of them or not.

He proceeded: As you seem to call upon me, Mr. Lovelace,

I will tell you (without boasting of it) what has been my general practice, till lately, that I hope I have reformed it a good deal.

I have taken liberties which the laws of morality will by no means justify; and once I should have thought myself warranted to cut the throat of any young fellow who should make as free with a sister of mine as I have made with the sisters and daughters of others. But then I took care never to promise anything I intended not to perform. A modest ear should as soon have heard downright obscenity from my lips as matrimony, if I had not intended it. Young ladies are generally ready enough to believe we mean honourably, if they love us; and it would look like a strange affront to their virtue and charms that it should be supposed *needful* to put the question whether in your address you mean a wife. But when once a man makes a promise, I think it ought to be performed; and a woman is well warranted to appeal to every one against the perfidy of a deceiver; and is always sure to have the world of her side.

Now, sir, continued he, I believe you have so much honour as to own that you could not have made way to so eminent a virtue without promising marriage; and that very explicitly and solemnly——

I know very well, colonel, interrupted I, all you would say. You will excuse me, I am sure, that I break in upon you, when you find it is to answer the end you drive at.

I own it to you, then, that I have acted very unworthily by Miss Clarissa Harlowe; and I 'll tell you further, that I heartily repent of my ingratitude and baseness to her. Nay, I will say *still* further, that I am so grossly culpable *as to her,* that even to plead that the abuses and affronts I daily received from her implacable relations were in any manner a provocation to me to act vilely by her, would be a mean and low attempt to excuse myself—so low and so mean that it would doubly condemn me. And if you can say worse, speak it.

He looked upon Lord M., and then upon me, two or three times. And my lord said: My kinsman speaks what he thinks, I 'll answer for him.

Lovel. I do, sir; and what can I say more? And what further, in your opinion, can be done?

Col. Done! sir? Why, sir [in a haughty tone he spoke], I need not tell you that reparation follows repentance. And I hope you make no scruple of justifying your sincerity as to the one by the other.

I hesitated (for I relished not the manner of his speech and his haughty accent), as undetermined whether to take proper notice of it or not.

Col. Let me put this question to you, Mr. Lovelace: Is it true, as I have heard it is, that you would marry my cousin if she would have you? What say you, sir?

This wound me up a peg higher.

Lovel. Some questions, as they may be put, imply *commands*, colonel. I would be glad to know how I am to take yours? And what is to be the end of your interrogatories?

Col. My questions are not meant by me as commands, Mr. Lovelace. The *end* is, to prevail upon a gentleman to act *like* a gentleman, and a man of honour.

Lovel. (*briskly*) And by what arguments, sir, do you propose to prevail upon me?

Col. By what arguments, sir, prevail upon a gentleman to act like a gentleman! I am surprised at that question from Mr. Lovelace.

Lovel. Why so, sir?

Col. WHY so, sir (*angrily*)—Let me——

Lovel. (*interrupting*) I don't choose, colonel, to be repeated upon in that accent.

Lord M. Come, come, gentlemen, I beg of you to be willing to understand one another. You young gentlemen are so warm——

Col. Not I, my lord—I am neither very young nor unduly warm. Your nephew, my lord, can make me be everything he would have me to be.

Lovel. And that shall be whatever you please to be, colonel.

Col. (*fiercely*) The choice be yours, Mr. Lovelace. Friend or foe! as you do or are willing to do justice to one of the finest women in the world.

Lord M. I guessed from both your characters what would be the case when you met. Let me interpose, gentlemen, and beg you but to understand one another. You *both shoot at one mark*; and if you are patient, will both *hit it*. Let me beg of you, colonel, to give no challenges——

Col. Challenges, my lord! They are things I ever was readier to accept than to offer. But does your lordship think that a man so nearly related as I have the honour to be to the most accomplished woman on earth——

Lord M. (*interrupting*) We all allow the excellences of the lady—and we shall all take it as the greatest honour to be allied to her that can be conferred upon us.

Col. So you ought, my lord!

A perfect *Chamont*! thought I.[1]

Lord M. So we *ought*, colonel! And so we *do*! And pray let *every one* do as he ought!—and no *more* than he *ought*; and you, colonel, let me tell you, will not be so hasty.

Lovel. (*coolly*) Come, come, Colonel Morden, don't let this dispute, whatever you intend to make of it, go farther than with you and me. You deliver yourself in very high terms. Higher than ever I was talked to in my life. But here, beneath this roof, 'twould be inexcusable for me to take that notice of it which perhaps it would become me to take elsewhere.

Col. This is spoken as I wish the man to speak whom I should be pleased to call my friend, if all his actions were of a piece; and as I would have the man speak whom I would think it worth my while to call my foe. I love a man of spirit as I love my soul. But, Mr. Lovelace, as my lord thinks we aim at *one mark*, let me say that, were we permitted to be alone for six minutes, I dare say we should soon understand one another perfectly well. And he moved to the door.

Lovel. I am entirely of your opinion, sir, and will attend you.

My lord rang, and stepped between us: Colonel, return, I beseech you, return, said he; for he had stepped out of the room, while my lord held me. Nephew, you shall not go out.

The bell and my lord's raised voice brought in Mowbray, and Clements, my lord's gentleman; the former in his careless way, with his hands behind him: What's the matter, Bobby? What's the matter, my lord?

Only—only—only, stammered the agitated peer, these young gentlemen are—are—are—*are* young gentlemen, that's all. Pray, Colonel Morden [who again entered the room with a sedater aspect], let this cause have a fair trial, I beseech you.

Col. With all my heart, my lord.

Mowbray whispered me: What is the cause, Bobby? Shall I take the gentleman to task for thee, my boy?

Not for the world, whispered I. The colonel is a gentleman, and I desire you'll not say one word.

Well, well, well, Bobby, I have done. I can turn thee loose to the best man upon God's earth; that's all, Bobby; strutting off to the other end of the room.

Col. I am sorry, my lord, I should give your lordship the least uneasiness. I came not with such a design.

Lord M. Indeed, colonel, I thought you did, by your taking

---

[1] See Otway's *Orphan*.

fire so quickly. I am glad to hear you say you did not. How soon a little *spark kindles into a flame*; especially when it meets with such combustible spirits!

Col. If I had had the least thought of proceeding to extremities, I am sure Mr. Lovelace would have given me the honour of a meeting where I should have been less an intruder: but I came with an amicable intention—to reconcile differences rather than to widen them.

Lovel. Well, then, Colonel Morden, let us enter upon the subject in your own way. I don't know the man I should sooner choose to be upon terms with than one whom Miss Clarissa Harlowe so much respects. But I cannot bear to be treated, either in word or accent, in a menacing way.

Lord M. Well, well, well, well, gentlemen, this is somewhat like. *Angry men make to themselves beds of nettles,* and when they lie down in them are uneasy with everybody. But I hope you are friends. Let me hear you say you are. I am persuaded, colonel, that you don't know all this unhappy story. You don't know how desirous my kinsman is, as well as all of us, to have this matter end happily. You don't know, do you, colonel, that Mr. Lovelace, at all our requests, is disposed to marry the lady?

Col. *At all your requests,* my lord? I should have hoped that Mr. Lovelace was disposed to do justice for the *sake* of justice; and when at the same time the doing of justice was doing himself the highest honour.

Mowbray lifted up his before half-closed eyes to the colonel, and glanced them upon me.

Lovel. This is in very high language, colonel.

Mowbr. By my soul, I thought so.

Col. *High* language, Mr. Lovelace? Is it not *just* language?

Lovel. It is, colonel. And I think the man that does honour to Miss Clarissa Harlowe does me honour. But, nevertheless, there is a manner in speaking that may be liable to exception, where the words, without that manner, can bear none.

Col. Your observation in the general is undoubtedly just: but *if* you have the value for my cousin that you say you have, you must needs think——

Lovel. You must allow me, sir, to interrupt you—IF I have the value *I say* I have. I hope, sir, when *I say I have* that value, there is no room for that *if*, pronounced as you pronounced it with an emphasis.

Col. You have broken in upon me twice, Mr. Lovelace. I am

as little accustomed to be broken in upon as you are to be *repeated* upon.

Lord M. Two barrels of gunpowder, by my conscience! What a devil will it signify talking, if thus you are to blow one another up at every wry word?

Lovel. No man of honour, my lord, will be easy to have his veracity called in question, though but by implication.

Col. Had you heard me out, Mr. Lovelace, you would have found that my *if* was rather an *if* of *inference* than of *doubt*. But 'tis really a strange liberty gentlemen of free principles take; who at the same time that they would resent unto death the imputation of being capable of telling an untruth to a man, will not scruple to break through the most solemn oaths and promises to a woman. I must assure you, Mr. Lovelace, that I always made a conscience of my vows and promises.

Lovel. You did right, colonel. But let me tell you, sir, that you know not the man you talk to, if you imagine he is not able to rise to a proper resentment, when he sees his generous confessions taken for a mark of base-spiritedness.

Col. (*warmly, and with a sneer*) Far be it from me, Mr. Lovelace, to impute to you the baseness of spirit you speak of; for what would that be, but to imagine that a man who has done a very flagrant injury, is not ready to show his *bravery* in defending it——

Mowbr. This is damned severe, colonel. It is, by Jove! I could not take so much at the hands of any man breathing as Mr. Lovelace before this took at yours.

Col. Who are you, sir? What pretence have you to interpose in a cause where there is an acknowledged guilt on one side, and the honour of a considerable family wounded in the tenderest part by that guilt on the other?

Mowbr. (*whispering to the colonel*) My dear child, you will oblige me highly if you will give me the opportunity of answering your question. And was going out.

The colonel was held in by my lord. And I brought in Mowbray.

Col. Pray, my good lord, let me attend this officious gentleman, I beseech you do. I will wait upon your lordship in three minutes, depend upon it.

Lovel. Mowbray, is this acting like a friend by me, to suppose me incapable of answering for myself? And shall a man of honour and bravery, as I know Colonel Morden to be (rash as perhaps in this visit he has shown himself), have it to say that he comes to my Lord M.'s house, in a manner naked as to attendants and friends, and shall not for that reason be rather borne with than insulted? This moment, my dear Mowbray, leave us. You have really no concern in this business; and if you are my friend, I desire you 'll ask the colonel pardon for interfering in it in the manner you have done.

Mowbr. Well, well, Bob; thou shalt be arbiter in this matter. I know I have no business in it. And, colonel (*holding out his hand*), I leave you to one who knows how to defend his own cause as well as any man in England.

Col. (*taking Mowbray's hand, at Lord M.'s request*) You need not tell me *that*, Mr. Mowbray. I have no doubt of Mr. Lovelace's ability to defend his own cause, were it a cause to be defended. And let me tell you, Mr. Lovelace, that I am astonished to think that a brave man, and a generous man, as you have appeared to be in two or three instances that you have given in the little knowledge I have of you, should be capable of acting as you have done by the most excellent of her sex.

Lord M. Well, but, gentlemen, now Mr. Mowbray is gone, and you have both shown instances of courage and generosity to boot, let me desire you to lay your heads together amicably, and think whether there be anything to be done to make all end happily for the lady?

Lovel. But hold, my lord, let me say one thing, now Mowbray *is* gone; and that is, that I think a gentleman ought not to put up tamely one or two severe things that the colonel has said.

Lord M. What the devil canst thou mean? I thought all had been over. Why, thou hast nothing to do but to confirm to the colonel that thou art willing to marry Miss Harlowe, if she will have thee.

Col. Mr. Lovelace will not scruple to say *that*, I suppose, notwithstanding all that has passed: but if you think, Mr. Lovelace, I have said anything I should *not* have said, I suppose it is this: that the man who has shown so little of the *thing* honour to a defenceless unprotected woman, ought not to stand so nicely upon the *empty name* of it with a man who is expostulating with him upon it. I am sorry to have cause to say this, Mr. Lovelace; but I would on the same occasion repeat it to a king upon his throne, and surrounded by all his guards.

Lord M. But what is all this, but more *sacks upon the mill?* more *coals upon the fire?* You have a mind to quarrel both of you, I see that. Are you not willing, nephew, are you not *most*

willing, to marry this lady, if she can be prevailed upon to
have you?

Lovel. Damn me, my lord, if I 'd marry an empress upon
such treatment as this.

Lord M. Why now, Bob, thou art more choleric than the
colonel. It was *his* turn just now. And now you see he is
cool, you are all gunpowder.

Lovel. I own the colonel has many advantages over me; but,
perhaps, there is one advantage he has not, if it were put to
the trial.

Col. I came not hither, as I said before, to seek the occasion:
but if it be offered me, I won't refuse it. And since we find we
disturb my good Lord M., I 'll take my leave, and will go home
by the way of St. Albans.

Lovel. I 'll see you part of the way, with all my heart, colonel.

Col. I accept your civility very cheerfully, Mr. Lovelace.

Lord M. (*interposing again, as we were both for going out*) And
what will this do, gentlemen? Suppose you kill one another,
will the matter be bettered or worsted by that? Will the lady
be made happier or unhappier, do you think, by either or both
of your deaths? Your characters are too well known to make
fresh instances of the courage of either needful. And I think,
if the honour of the lady is your view, colonel, it can be no other
way so effectually promoted as by marriage. And, sir, if *you*
would use your interest with her, it is very probable that *you*
may succeed, though nobody else can.

Lovel. I think, my lord, I have said all that a man can say
(since what is passed cannot be recalled); and you see Colonel
Morden rises in proportion to my coolness, till it is necessary
for me to assert myself, or even *he* would despise me.

Lord M. Let me ask you, colonel: Have you any way, any
method, that you think reasonable and honourable to propose,
to bring about a reconciliation with the lady? That is what we
all wish for. And I can tell you, sir, it is not a little owing to
her family, and to their implacable usage of her, that her
resentments are heightened against my kinsman; who, however,
has used her viiely; but is willing to repair her wrongs.

Lovel. Not, my lord, for the sake of her family; nor for this
gentleman's haughty behaviour; but for *her own sake*, and in full
sense of the wrongs I have done her.

Col. As to my haughty behaviour, as you call it, sir, I am
mistaken if you would not have gone beyond it in the like case
of a relation so meritorious, and so unworthily injured. And,

sir, let me tell you, that if your motives are not love, honour, and justice, and if they have the least tincture of mean compassion for *her*, or of an uncheerful assent on *your part*, I am sure it will neither be desired nor accepted by a person of my cousin's merit and sense; nor shall I wish that it should.

Lovel. Don't think, colonel, that I am meanly compounding off a debate, that I should as willingly go through with you as to eat or drink, if I have the occasion given me for it: but thus much I will tell you, that my lord, that Lady Sarah Sadleir, Lady Betty Lawrance, my two Cousins Montague, and myself, have written to her in the most solemn and sincere manner, to offer her such terms as no one but herself would refuse, and this long enough before Colonel Morden's arrival was dreamt of.

Col. What reason, sir, may I ask, does she give against listening to so powerful a mediation, and to such offers?

Lovel. It looks like capitulating, or else——

Col. It looks not like any such thing to *me*, Mr. Lovelace, who have as good an opinion of your spirit as man can have. And what, pray, is the part I act, and my motives for it? Are they not, in desiring that justice may be done to my Cousin Clarissa Harlowe, that I seek to establish the honour of *Mrs. Lovelace*, if matters can once be brought to bear?

Lovel. Were she to honour me with her acceptance of that name, Mr. Morden, I should not want you or any man to assert the honour of Mrs. Lovelace.

Col. I believe it. But till she *has* honoured you with that acceptance, she is nearer to me than to you, Mr. Lovelace. And I speak this only to show you that in the part I take I mean rather to deserve your thanks than your displeasure, though against *yourself*, were there occasion. Nor ought you to take it amiss, if you rightly weigh the matter: for, sir, whom does a lady want protection against but her injurers? And who has been her *greatest* injurer? Till, therefore, she becomes entitled to your protection, as *your wife*, you yourself cannot refuse me ;ome merit in wishing to have justice done *my cousin*. But, sir, you was going to say, that if it were not to look like capitulating, you would hint the reasons my cousin gives against accepting such an honourable mediation?

I then told him of my sincere offers of marriage; "I made no difficulty, I said, to own my apprehensions that my unhappy behaviour to her had greatly affected her: but that it was the implacableness of her friends that had thrown her into despair, and given her a contempt for life." I told him "that she had

been so good as to send me a letter to divert me from a visit my
heart was set upon making her: a letter on which I built great
hopes, because she assured me in it that she was *going to her
father's*; and that *I might see her there, when she was received, if it
were not my own fault.*"

Col. Is it possible? And were you, sir, thus earnest? And
did she send you such a letter?

Lord M. confirmed both; and also that, in obedience to her
desires, and that intimation, I had come down without the
satisfaction I had proposed to myself in seeing her.

It is very true, colonel, said I: and I should have told you this
before: but your heat made me decline it; for, as I said, it had
an appearance of meanly capitulating with you. An abjectness
of heart, of which had I been capable, I should have despised
myself as much as I might have expected *you* would despise me.

Lord M. proposed to enter into the proof of all this: he said,
in his phraseological way, *That one story was good till another was
heard*: that the Harlowe family and I, 'twas true, had behaved
like so many *Orsons* to one another; and that they had been very
free with all our family besides: that nevertheless, for the lady's
sake more than for theirs, or even for *mine* (he could tell me),
he would do greater things for me than they could ask, if she
could be brought to have me: and that this he *wanted* to declare,
and would *sooner* have declared, if he could have brought us
sooner to patience and a good understanding.

The colonel made excuses for his warmth on the score of his
affection to his cousin.

My regard for her made me readily admit them: and so a fresh
bottle of burgundy, and another of champagne, being put upon
the table, we sat down in good humour, after all this blustering,
in order to enter closer into the particulars of the case: which
I undertook, at both their desires, to do.

But these things must be the subject of another letter, which
shall immediately follow this, if it do not accompany it.

Meantime you will observe that a bad cause gives a man great
disadvantages: for I myself think that the interrogatories put
to me with so much spirit by the colonel made me look cursedly
mean; at the same time that it gave him a superiority which
I know not how to allow to the best man in Europe. So that,
literally speaking, as a *good man* would infer, guilt is its own
punisher; in that it makes the most lofty spirit look like the
miscreant he is.—A *good man*, I say: so, Jack, *proleptically* I add,
thou hast no right to make the observation.

Letter LXXXII—Mr. Lovelace. [*in Continuation*]

Tuesday Afternoon, Aug. 29.

I WENT back in this part of our conversation to the day that I was obliged to come down to attend my lord, in the dangerous illness which *some* feared would have been his last.

I told the colonel "what earnest letters I had written to a particular friend, to engage him to prevail upon the lady not to slip a day that had been proposed for the private celebration of our nuptials; and of my letters [1] written to herself on that subject"; for I had stepped to my closet, and fetched down all the letters and drafts and copies of letters relating to this affair.

I read to him "several passages in the copies of those letters, which thou wilt remember make not a little to my honour." And I told him "that I wished I had kept copies of those to my friend on the same occasion; by which he would have seen how much in earnest I was in my professions to her, although she would not answer one of them." And thou mayst remember that one of those four letters accounted to herself why I was desirous she should remain where I had left her. [2]

I then proceeded to give him an account "of the visit made by Lady Sarah and Lady Betty to Lord M. and me, in order to induce me to do her justice: of my readiness to comply with their desires; and of their high opinion of her merit: of the visit made to Miss Howe by my Cousins Montague, in the name of us all, to engage her interest with her friend in my behalf: of my conversation with Miss Howe at a private assembly, to whom I gave the same assurances, and besought her interest with her friend."

I then read the copy of the letter (though so much to my disadvantage) which was written to her by Miss Charlotte Montague, Aug. 1, [3] entreating her alliance in the names of all our family.

This made him ready to think that his fair cousin carried her resentment against me too far. He did not imagine, he said, that either myself or our family had been so much in earnest.

So thou seest, Belford, that it is but glossing over *one* part of a story, and omitting *another*, that will make a bad cause a good one at any time. What an admirable lawyer should I have made! And what a poor hand would this charming creature, with all her innocence, have made of it in a court of justice

---

[1] See vol. iii, pp. 293-8.   [2] Ibid. p. 293.
[3] See pp. 71-2, of this volume.

against a man who had so much to *say* and to *show* for himself!

I then hinted at the generous annual tender which Lord M. and his sisters made to his fair cousin, in apprehension that she might suffer by her friends' implacableness.

And this also the colonel highly applauded, and was pleased to lament the unhappy misunderstanding between the two families, which had made the Harlowes less fond of an alliance with a family of so much honour as this instance showed ours to be.

I then told him, "That having, by my friend [meaning thee], who was admitted into her presence (and who had always been an admirer of her virtues, and had given me such advice from time to time in relation to her as I wished I had followed), been assured that a visit from me would be very disagreeable to her, I once more resolved to try what a letter would do; and that, accordingly, on the 7th of August I wrote her one.

"This, colonel, is the copy of it. I was then out of humour with my Lord M. and the ladies of my family. You will therefore read it to yourself." [1]

This letter gave him high satisfaction. You write here, Mr. Lovelace, from your heart. 'Tis a letter full of penitence and acknowledgment. Your request is reasonable—to be forgiven only as you shall appear to deserve it after a time of probation, which you leave to her to fix. Pray, sir, did she return an answer to this letter?

She did, but with *reluctance*, I own, and not till I had declared by my friend, that if I could not procure one, I would go up to town and throw myself at her feet.

I wish I might be permitted to see it, sir, or to hear such parts of it read as you shall think proper.

Turning over my papers, Here it is, sir. [2] I will make no scruple to put it into your hands.

This is very obliging, Mr. Lovelace.

He read it. My charming cousin! How strong her resentments! Yet how charitable her wishes! Good Heaven! that such an excellent creature——But, Mr. Lovelace, it is to your regret, as much as to mine, I doubt not——

Interrupting him, I swore that it was.

So it ought, said he. Nor do I wonder that it should be so. I shall tell you by and by, proceeded he, how much she suffers with her friends by false and villainous reports. But, sir, will

[1] See pp. 90–1.   [2] See pp. 99–100.

you permit me to take with me these two letters? I shall make use of them to the advantage of you both.

I told him I would oblige him with all my heart. And this he took very kindly (as he had reason) and put them in his pocket-book, promising to return them in a few days.

I then told him, "That upon this her refusal, I took upon myself to go to town, in hopes to move her in my favour; and that, though I went without giving her notice of my intention, yet had she got some notion of my coming, and so contrived to be out of the way: and at last, when she found I was fully determined at all events to see her, before I went abroad (which I *shall* do, said I, if I cannot prevail upon her), she sent me the letter I have already mentioned to you, desiring me to suspend my purposed visit: and that for a reason which amazes and confounds me, because I don't find there is anything in it: and yet I never knew her once dispense with her word; for she always made it a maxim, that *it was not lawful to do evil, that good might come of it*: and yet in this letter, for no reason in the world but to avoid seeing me (to gratify a humour only), has she sent me out of town, depending upon the assurance she had given me."

Col. This is indeed surprising. But I cannot believe that my cousin, for such an end *only*, or indeed for *any* end, according to the character I hear of her, should stoop to make use of such an artifice.

Lovel. This, colonel, is the thing that astonishes me; and yet, see here! This is the letter she wrote me — nay, sir, 'tis her own hand.

Col. I see it is; and a charming hand it is.

Lovel. You observe, colonel, that all her hopes of reconciliation with her parents are from you. You are her *dear blessed friend*! She always talked of you with delight.

Col. Would to Heaven I had come to England before she left Harlowe Place! Nothing of this had then happened. Not a man of those whom I have heard that her friends proposed for her should have had her. Nor you, Mr. Lovelace, unless I had found you to be the man every one who sees you must wish you to be: and if you *had* been that man, no one living should I have preferred to you for such an excellence.

My lord and I both joined in the wish: and 'faith I wished it most cordially.

The colonel read the letter twice over, and then returned it to me. 'Tis all a mystery, said he. I can make nothing of it. For, alas! her friends are as averse to reconciliation as ever.

Lord M. I could not have thought it.   But don't you think there is something very favourable to my nephew in this letter— something that looks as if the lady would comply at last?

Col. Let me die if I know what to make of it.   This letter is very different from her preceding one!   You returned an answer to it, Mr. Lovelace?

Lovel. An answer, colonel!   No doubt of it.   And an answer full of transport.   I told her "I would directly set out for Lord M.'s in obedience to her will.   I told her that I would consent to anything she should command, in order to promote this happy reconciliation.   I told her that it should be my hourly study to the end of my life, to deserve a goodness so transcendent."   But I cannot forbear saying that I am not a little shocked and surprised, if nothing more be meant by it than to get me into the country without seeing her.

Col. That can't be the thing, depend upon it, sir.   There must be more in it than that.   For were that all, she must think you would soon be undeceived, and that you would then most probably resume your intention—unless, indeed, she depended upon seeing *me* in the interim, as she knew I was arrived.   But I own I know not what to make of it.   Only that she does me a great deal of honour, if it be me that she calls her *blessed friend, whom she always loved and honoured*.   Indeed, I ever loved her: and if I die unmarried and without children, shall be as kind to her as her grandfather was: and the rather, as I fear that there is too much of envy and self-love in the resentments her brother and sister endeavour to keep up in her father and mother against her.   But I shall know better how to judge of this when my Cousin James comes from Edinburgh; and he is every hour expected.

But let me ask you, Mr. Lovelace, What is the name of your friend, who is admitted so easily into my cousin's presence? Is it not Belford, pray?

Lovel. It is, sir; and Mr. Belford's a man of honour; and a great admirer of your fair cousin.

Was I right as to the *first*, Jack?   The *last* I have such strong proof of, that it makes me question the *first*; since she would not have been out of the way of my intended visit but for thee.

Col. Are you sure, sir, that Mr. Belford is a man of honour?

Lovel. I can swear for him, colonel.   What makes you put this question?

Col. Only this: that an officious pragmatical novice has been sent up to inquire into my cousin's life and conversation: and, would you believe it? the frequent visits of this gentleman have been interpreted basely to her disreputation. Read that letter, Mr. Lovelace, and you will be shocked at every part of it.

This cursed letter, no doubt, is from the young Levite whom thou, Jack, describedst as making inquiry of Mrs. Smith about Miss Harlowe's character and visitors.[1]

I believe I was a quarter of an hour in reading it: for I made it, though not a short one, six times as long as it is, by the additions of oaths and curses to every pedantic line. Lord M. too helped to lengthen it by the like execrations. And thou, Jack, wilt have as much reason to curse it as we.

You cannot but see, said the colonel, when I had done reading it, that this fellow has been *officious* in his malevolence; for what he says is mere hearsay, and that hearsay conjectural scandal without fact, or the appearance of fact, to support it; so that an unprejudiced eye, upon the face of the letter, would condemn the writer of it, as I did, and acquit my cousin. But yet, such is the spirit by which the rest of my relations are governed, that they run away with the belief of the worst it insinuates, and the dear creature has had shocking letters upon it; the pedant's hints are taken; and a voyage to one of the colonies has been proposed to her, as the only way to avoid Mr. Belford and you. I have not seen these letters indeed; but they took a pride in repeating some of their contents, which must have cut the poor soul to the heart; and these, joined to her former sufferings——What have you not, Mr. Lovelace, to answer for?

Lovel. Who the devil could have expected such consequences as these? Who could have believed there could be parents so implacable? Brother and sister so envious? And, give me leave to say, a lady so immovably fixed against the only means that could be taken to put all right with everybody? And what now can be done?

Lord M. I have great hopes that Colonel Morden may yet prevail upon his cousin. And by her last letter, it runs in my mind that she has some thoughts of forgiving all that's past. Do you think, colonel, if there should *not* be such a thing as a reconciliation going forward at present, that her letter may not imply, that if we *could* bring such a thing to bear with her friends, she would be reconciled to Mr. Lovelace?

Col. Such an artifice would better become the Italian subtlety than the English simplicity. Your lordship has been in Italy, I presume?

¹ See p. 96.

Lovel. My lord has read Boccaccio, perhaps; and that's as well, as to the hint he gives, which may be borrowed from one of that author's stories. But Miss Clarissa Harlowe is above all artifice. She must have some meaning I cannot fathom.

Col. Well, my lord, I can only say that I will make some use of the letters Mr. Lovelace has obliged me with: and after I have had some talk with my Cousin James, who is hourly expected; and when I have dispatched two or three affairs that press upon me, I will pay my respects to my dear cousin; and shall then be able to form a better judgment of things. Meantime I will write to her; for I have sent to inquire about her, and find she wants consolation.

Lovel. If you favour me, colonel, with the damned letter of that fellow Brand for a day or two, you will oblige me.

Col. I will. But remember, the man is a parson, Mr. Lovelace; an innocent one too, they say. Else I had been at him before now. And these college novices, who think they know everything in their cloisters, and that all learning lies in *books,* make dismal figures when they come into the world among *men* and *women.*

Lord M. Brand! Brand! It should have been *Firebrand,* I think in my conscience!

Thus ended this doughty conference.

I cannot say, Jack, but I am greatly taken with Colonel Morden. He is brave and generous, and knows the world; and then his contempt of the parsons is a certain sign that he is one of *us.*

We parted with great civility; Lord M. (not a little pleased that we did, and as greatly taken with the colonel) repeated his wish, after the colonel was gone, that he had arrived in time to save the lady; if that would have done it.

I wish so too. For by my soul, Jack, I am every day more and more uneasy about her. But I hope she is not so ill as I am told she is.

I have made Charlotte transcribe the letter of this *Firebrand,* as my lord calls him; and will enclose her copy of it. All thy phlegm I know will be roused into vengeance when thou readest it.

I know not what to advise as to showing it to the lady. Yet, perhaps, she will be able to reap more satisfaction than concern from it, knowing her own innocence; in that it will give her to hope that her friends' treatment of her is owing as much to misrepresentation as to their own natural implacableness Such a mind as hers, I know, would be glad to find out the shadow of a reason for the shocking letters the colonel says they have sent her, and for their proposal to her of going to some one of the colonies [confound them all—but if I begin to curse, I shall never have done].   Then it may put her upon such a defence as she might be glad of an opportunity to make, and to shame them for their monstrous credulity.   But this I leave to thy own fat-headed prudence.   Only it vexes me to the heart that even scandal and calumny should dare to surmise the bare possibility of any man's sharing the favours of a woman whom now methinks I could worship with a veneration due only to a divinity.

Charlotte and her sister could not help weeping at the base aspersion: When, when, said Patty, lifting up her hands, will this sweet lady's sufferings be at an end?   O Cousin Lovelace!

And thus am I blamed for every one's faults!   When her brutal father curses her, it is I.   I upbraid her with her severe mother.   The implacableness of her stupid uncles is all mine. The virulence of her brother, and the spite and envy of her sister, are entirely owing to me.   The letter of this rascal Brand is of my writing.   O Jack, what a wretch is thy Lovelace!

.   .   .   .

Returned without a letter!   This damned fellow Will is returned without a letter!   Yet the rascal tells me that he hears you have been writing to me these two days!

Plague confound thee, who must know my impatience, and the reason for it!

To send a man and horse on purpose, as I did!   My imagination chained to the belly of the beast, in order to keep pace with him!   Now he is got to this place; now to that; now to London; now to thee!

Now [a letter given him] whip and spur upon the return.   This town just entered, not staying to bait: that village passed by: leaves the wind behind him; in a foaming sweat man and horse.

And in this way did he actually enter Lord M.'s courtyard.

The reverberating pavement brought me down.   The letter, Will!   The letter, dog!   The letter, sirrah!

No letter, sir!   Then wildly staring round me, fists clenched, and grinning like a maniac, Confound thee for a dog, and him that sent thee without one!   This moment out of my sight, or I'll scatter thy stupid brains through the air.   I snatched from his holsters a pistol, while the rascal threw himself from the foaming beast, and ran to avoid the fate which I wished with all

my soul thou hadst been within the reach of me to have met
with.

But, to be as meek as a lamb to one who has me at his mercy,
and can wring and torture my soul as he pleases, *What canst thou
mean* to send back my varlet without a latter? I will send away
by day-dawn another fellow upon another beast for what thou
hast written; and I charge thee on thy allegiance that thou
dispatch him not back empty-handed.

Postscript

Charlotte, in a whim of delicacy, is displeased that I send the
enclosed letter to you—that her handwriting, forsooth! should
go into the hands of a single man!

There's encouragement for thee, Belford! This is a certain
sign that thou mayst have her if thou wilt. And yet, till she had
given me this unerring demonstration of her glancing towards
thee, I could not have thought it. Indeed I have often in
pleasantry told her that I would bring such an affair to bear.
But I never intended it; because she really is a dainty girl. And
thou art such a clumsy fellow in thy person, that I should have
as soon wished her a rhinoceros for a husband as thee. But,
poor little dears! they must stay till their time's come! They
won't have this man, and they won't have that man, from
seventeen to twenty-five: but then afraid, as the saying is, that
God has forgot them, and finding their bloom departing, they are
glad of whom they can get, and verify the fable of the parson
and the pears.

Letter LXXXIII—Mr. Brand to John Harlowe, Esq.

[Enclosed in the preceding]

WORTHY SIR, MY VERY GOOD FRIEND AND PATRON,—I arrived
in town yesterday, after a tolerable pleasant journey (considering
the hot weather and dusty roads). I put up at the Bull and Gate
in Holborn, and hastened to Covent Garden. I soon found the
house where the unhappy lady lodgeth. And, in the back shop,
had a good deal of discourse [1] with Mrs. Smith (her landlady),
whom I found to be so *highly prepossessed* in her *favour*, that I saw
it would not answer your desires to take my informations

[1] See pp. 96–7.

altogether from her, and being obliged to attend my patron (who, to my sorrow,

(Miserum est aliena vivere quadra)

I find wanteth much waiting upon, and is *another* sort of man than he was at college: for, sir, *inter nos, honours change manners.* For the *aforesaid causes*) I thought it would best answer all the ends of the commission with which you honoured me, to engage, in the desired scrutiny, the wife of a *particular friend,* who liveth almost over against the house where she lodgeth, and who is a gentlewoman of *character* and *sobriety,* a *mother of children,* and one who *knoweth* the *world* well.

To her I applied myself therefore, and gave her a short history of the case, and desired she would very particularly inquire into the *conduct* of the unhappy young lady; her *present way of life* and *subsistence*; her *visitors,* her *employments,* and such-like; for these, sir, you know, are the things whereof you wished to be informed.

Accordingly, sir, I waited upon the gentlewoman aforesaid this day; and, to *my* very great trouble (because I know it will be to *yours,* and likewise to all your worthy family's), I must say that I do find things look a little more *darkly* than I hoped they would. For, alas! sir, the gentlewoman's report turneth not out so *favourable* for miss's reputation as *I* wished, as *you* wished, and as *every one* of her friends wished. But so it is throughout the world, that *one false step* generally brings on *another*; and peradventure *a worse,* and *a still worse*; till the poor *limed soul* (a very fit epithet of the divine Quarles's!) is quite *entangled,* and (without infinite *mercy*) lost for ever.

It seemeth, sir, she is, notwithstanding, in a very *ill state of health.* In this, *both* gentlewomen (that is to say, Mrs. Smith, her landlady, and my friend's wife) agree. Yet she goeth often out in a chair, to *prayers* (as it is said). But my friend's wife told me that nothing is more common in London than that the frequenting of the church at morning prayers is made the *pretence* and *cover* for *private assignations.* What a sad thing is this! that what was designed for *wholesome nourishment* to the *poor soul* should be turned into *rank poison*! But as Mr. Daniel de Foe (an ingenious man, though a *Dissenter*) observeth (but indeed it is an old proverb; only I think he was the first that put it into verse):

God never had a House of Pray'r,
But Satan had a Chapel there.

Yet to do the lady *justice*, nobody cometh home with her: nor indeed *can* they, because she goeth forward and backward in a *sedan*, or *chair* (as they call it). But then there is a gentleman of *no good character* (an *intimado* of Mr. Lovelace) who is a *constant* visitor of her, and of the people of the house, whom he *regales* and *treats*, and hath (of consequence) their *high good words*.

I have hereupon taken the trouble (for I love to be *exact* in any *commission* I undertake) to inquire *particularly* about this *gentleman*, as he is called (albeit I hold no man so but by his actions: for, as Juvenal saith,

—Nobilitas sola est, atque unica virtus).

And this I did *before* I would sit down to write to you.

His name is Belford. He hath a paternal estate of upwards of one thousand pounds by the year; and is now in mourning for an uncle who left him very considerably besides. He beareth a very profligate character as to *women* (for I inquired *particularly* about *that*), and is Mr. Lovelace's more especial *privado*, with whom he holdeth a *regular correspondence*; and hath been often seen with miss (*tête-à-tête*) at the *window*—in no *bad way*, indeed: but my friend's wife is of opinion that all is not *as it should be*. And, indeed, it is mighty strange to me, if Miss be so *notable a penitent* (as is represented), and if she have such an *aversion* to Mr. Lovelace, that she will admit his *privado* into *her retirements*, and see *no other company*.

I understand, from Mrs. Smith, that Mr. Hickman was to see her some time ago, from Miss Howe; and I am told, by *another* hand (you see, sir, how diligent I have been to execute the *commissions* you gave me), that he had no *extraordinary opinion* of this Belford at first; though they were seen together one morning by the opposite neighbour, at *breakfast*: and another time this Belford was observed to *watch* Mr. Hickman's coming from her; so that, as it should seem, he was mighty zealous to *ingratiate* himself with Mr. Hickman; no doubt, to engage him to make a *favourable report to Miss Howe* of the *intimacy* he was admitted into by her unhappy friend; who (*as she is very ill*) may *mean no harm* in allowing his visits (for he, it seemeth, brought to her, or recommended, at least, the doctor and apothecary that attend her): but I think (upon the whole) *it looketh not well*.

I am sorry, sir, I cannot give you a better account of the young lady's *prudence*. But what shall we say?

Uvaque conspectâ livorem ducit ab uvâ,

as Juvenal observeth.

One thing I am afraid of; which is that Miss may be under *necessities*; and that this Belford (who, as Mrs. Smith owns, hath *offered her money*, which she, *at the time*, refused) may find an opportunity to *take advantage* of those *necessities*: and it is well observed by the poet, that

> Ægrè formosam poteris servare puellam:
> Nunc prece, nunc pretio, forma petita ruit.

And this Belford (who is a *bold man*, and hath, as they say, the *look* of one) may make good that of Horace (with whose writings you are so well acquainted; nobody better):

> Audax omnia perpeti,
> Gens humana ruit per vetitum nefas.

Forgive me, sir, for what I am going to write: but if you could prevail upon the rest of your family to join in the scheme which *you*, and her *virtuous sister*, Miss Arabella, and the archdeacon, and I, once talked of (which is to persuade the unhappy young lady to go, in some *creditable* manner, to some one of the foreign colonies), it might save not only her *own credit* and *reputation*, but the *reputation* and *credit* of all her *family*, and a great deal of *vexation* moreover. For it is my humble opinion that you will hardly (any of you) enjoy yourselves while this (*once* innocent) young lady is in the way of being so frequently heard of by you: and this would put her *out of the way* both of *this Belford* and of *that Lovelace*, and it might, peradventure, prevent as much *evil* as *scandal*.

You will forgive me, sir, for this my *plainness*. Ovid pleadeth for me,

> —Adulator nullus amicus erit.

And I have no view but that of approving myself a *zealous well-wisher* to *all* your worthy family (whereto I owe a great number of obligations), and very particularly, sir,

Your obliged and humble servant,

ELIAS BRAND.

Wedn. Aug. 9.

P.S. I shall give you *further hints* when I come down (which will be in a few days); and who my *informants* were; but by *these* you will see that I have been very assiduous (for the time) in the task you set me upon.

The *length* of my letter you will excuse; for I need not tell you, sir, what *narrative, complex*, and *conversation* letters (such a one as *mine*) require. Every one to his *talent*. *Letter-writing* is mine, I will be bold to say; and that my *correspondence* was much coveted at the university, on that account, by *tyros*, and even by *sophs*, when I was hardly a *soph* myself. But this I should not have taken upon me to mention, but only in defence of the *length* of my letter; for nobody writeth *shorter*, or *pithier*, when the subject requireth *common forms* only—but in apologizing for my *prolixity*, I am *adding* to the *fault* (if it were one, which, how-ever, I cannot think it to be, the *subject* considered: but this I have said before in other words): so, sir, if you will excuse my *postscript*, I am sure you will not find fault with my *letter*.

One word more, as to a matter of *erudition*, which you greatly love to hear me *start* and *dwell upon*. Dr. Lewen once, in your presence (as you, *my good patron*, cannot but remember) in a *smartish* kind of debate between *him* and *me*, took upon him to censure the *parenthetical* style, as I call it. He was a very learned and judicious man, to be sure, and an ornament to *our function*: but yet I must needs say that it is a style which I greatly like; and the good doctor was then past his *youth*, and that time of life, of consequence, when a *fertile imagination*, and *rich fancy*, pour in ideas so fast upon a writer, that parentheses are often wanted (and that for the sake of *brevity*, as well as *perspicuity*) to save the reader the trouble of reading a passage *more than once*. Every man to his talent (as I said before). We are all so apt to set up our *natural biases* for *general standards*, that I wondered *the less* at the worthy doctor's *stiffness* on this occasion. He *smiled at me*, you may remember, sir—and, whether I was right or not, I am sure I *smiled at him*. And *you*, my *worthy patron* (as I had the satisfaction to observe), seemed to be of *my party*. But was it not strange that the *old gentleman* and *I* should so widely differ, when the *end* with *both* (that is to say, *perspicuity* or *clearness*) was the same? But what shall we say?—

Errare est hominis, sed non persistere.

I think I have nothing to add until I have the honour of attending you in *person*; but that I am (as above) etc. etc. etc.

E. B.

Letter LXXXIV—Mr. Belford to Robert Lovelace, Esq.

Wednesday Night, Aug. 30.

IT was lucky enough that our two servants met at Hannah's,[1] which gave them so good an opportunity of exchanging their letters time enough for each to return to his master early in the day.

Thou dost well to boast of thy capacity for managing servants, and to set up for correcting our poets in their characters of this class of people,[2] when, like a madman, thou canst beat their teeth out, and attempt to shoot them through the head, for not bringing to thee what they had no power to obtain.

You well observe [3] that you would have made a thorough-paced lawyer. The whole of the conversation-piece between you and the colonel affords a convincing proof that there is a black and a white side to every cause: but what must the conscience of a partial whitener of his *own* cause, or blackener of *another's*, tell him, while he is throwing dust in the eyes of his judges, and all the time knows his own guilt?

The colonel, I see, is far from being a faultless man; but while he sought not to carry his point by breach of faith, he has an excuse which thou hast not. But with respect to him, and to us all, I can now, with detestation of some of my own actions, see that the taking advantage of another person's good opinion of us, to injure (perhaps to ruin) that other, is the most ungenerous wickedness that can be committed.

Man acting thus by *man*, we should not be at a loss to give such actions a name: but is it not doubly and trebly aggravated, when such advantage is taken of an inexperienced and innocent young creature, whom we pretend to love above all the women in the world; and when we seal our pretences by the most solemn vows and protestations of inviolable honour that we can invent?

I see that this gentleman is the best match thou ever couldst have had, upon all accounts: his spirit such another impetuous one as thy own; soon taking fire; vindictive; and only differing in this, that the cause he engages in is a just one. But, commend me to honest brutal Mowbray, who, before he *knew* the cause, offers his sword in thy behalf against a man who had taken the injured side, and whom he had never seen before.

As soon as I had run through your letters, and the copy of that of the incendiary Brand's (by the latter of which I saw to

---

[1] The Windmill, near Slough.   [2] See pp. 162–4.   [3] See p. 230.

what cause a great deal of this last implacableness of the
Harlowe family is owing), I took coach to Smith's, although
I had been come from thence but about an hour, and had taken
leave of the lady for the night.

I sent down for Mrs. Lovick, and desired her, in the first place,
to acquaint the lady (who was busied in her closet) that I had
letters from Berks: in which I was informed that the interview
between Colonel Morden and Mr. Lovelace had ended without
ill consequences; that the colonel intended to write to her very
soon, and was interesting himself meanwhile in her favour, with
her relations; that I hoped that this agreeable news would be
a means of giving her good rest; and I would wait upon her in
the morning by the time she should return from prayers with
all the particulars.

She sent me word that she should be glad to see me in the
morning; and was highly obliged to me for the good news I had
sent her up.

I then, in the back shop, read to Mrs. Lovick and to Mrs. Smith
the copy of Brand's letter, and asked them if they could guess at
the man's informant? They were not at a loss; Mrs. Smith
having seen the same fellow Brand who had talked with her, as
I mentioned in a former,[1] come out of a milliner's shop over
against them; which milliner, she said, had also been lately very
inquisitive about the lady.

I wanted no further hint; but, bidding them take no notice
to the lady of what I had read, I shot over the way, and asking
for the mistress of the house, she came to me.

Retiring with her, at her invitation, into her parlour, I desired
to know if she were acquainted with a young country clergyman
of the name of *Brand*. She hesitatingly, seeing me in some
emotion, owned that she had some small knowledge of the
gentleman. Just then came in her husband, who is, it seems, a
petty officer in the excise (and not an ill-behaved man), who
owned a fuller knowledge of him.

I have the copy of a letter, said I, from this Brand, in which
he has taken great liberties with my character, and with that of
the most unblamable lady in the world, which he grounds upon
informations that you, madam, have given him. And then
I read to them several passages in his letter; and asked what
foundation she had for giving that fellow such impressions of
either of us?

They knew not what to answer: but at last said that he had

[1] See p. 96.

told them how wickedly the young lady had run away from her parents: what worthy and rich people they were: in what favour *he* stood with them; and that they had employed him to inquire after her behaviour, visitors, etc.

They said, "That indeed they knew very little of the young lady; but that [curse upon their censoriousness!] it was but too natural to think that where a lady had given way to a delusion, and taken so wrong a step, she would not stop there: that the most sacred places and things were but too often made cloaks for bad actions. That Mr. Brand had been informed (perhaps by some enemy of mine) that I was a man of very free principles, and an *intimado*, as he calls it, of the man who had ruined her. And that their cousin Barker, a mantua-maker, who lodged up one pair of stairs" (and who, at their desire, came down and confirmed what they said), "had often from her window seen me with the lady in her chamber, and both talking very earnestly together: and that Mr. Brand being unable to account for her admitting my visits, and knowing I was but a new acquaintance of hers, and an old one of Mr. Lovelace, thought himself obliged to lay these matters before her friends."

This was the sum and substance of their tale. O how I cursed the censoriousness of this plaguy triumvirate! A parson, a milliner, and a mantua-maker! The two latter, not more by *business* led to adorn the person, than generally by *scandal* to destroy the *reputations* of those they have a mind to exercise their talents upon!

The two women took great pains to persuade me that they themselves were people of conscience:—of consequence, I told them, too much addicted, I feared, to censure other people who pretended not to their strictness; for that I had ever found censoriousness, narrowness, and uncharitableness to prevail too much with those who affected to be thought more pious than their neighbours.

They answered that that was not their case; and that they had since inquired into the lady's character and manner of life, and were very much concerned to think anything they had said should be made use of against her: and as they heard from Mrs. Smith that she was not likely to live long, they should be sorry she should go out of the world a sufferer by their means, or with an ill opinion of them, though strangers to her. The husband offered to write, if I pleased, to Mr. Brand, in vindication of the lady; and the two women said they should be glad to wait upon her in person, to beg her pardon for anything she had reason to take amiss from them; because they were now convinced that there was not such another young lady in the world.

I told them that the least said of the affair to the lady, in her present circumstances, was best. That she was a heavenly creature, and fond of taking all occasions to find excuses for her relations on their implacableness to her; that therefore I should take some notice to her of the uncharitable and weak surmises which gave birth to so vile a scandal; but that I would have him, Mr. Walton (for that is the husband's name), write to his acquaintance Brand as soon as possible, as he had offered—and so I left them.

As to what thou sayest of thy charming cousin, let me know if thou hast any meaning in it. I have not the vanity to think myself deserving of such a lady as Miss Montague: and should not therefore care to expose myself to her scorn, and to thy derision. But were I assured I might avoid both these, I would soon acquaint thee that I should think no pains nor assiduity too much to obtain a share in the good graces of such a lady.

But I know thee too well to depend upon anything thou sayest on this subject. Thou lovest to make thy friends the object of ridicule to ladies; and imaginest, from the vanity (and in this respect, I will say, littleness) of thine own heart, that thou shinest the brighter for the foil.

Thus didst thou once play off the rough Mowbray with Miss Hatton, till the poor fellow knew not how to go either backward or forward.

Letter LXXXV—Mr. Belford to Robert Lovelace, Esq.

Thursday, 11 o'clock, Aug. 31.

I AM just come from the lady, whom I left cheerful and serene.

She thanked me for my communication of the preceding night. I read to her such parts of your letters as I *could* read to her; and I thought it was a good test to distinguish the froth and whipped-syllabub in them from the cream, in what one *could* and could *not* read to a woman of so fine a mind; since four parts out of six of thy letters, which I thought entertaining as I read them to myself, appeared to me, when I would have read them to her, most abominable stuff, and gave me a very contemptible idea of thy talents and of my own judgment.

She was far from rejoicing, as I had done, at the disappointment her letter gave you when explained.

She said she meant only an innocent allegory, which might carry instruction and warning to you, when the meaning was taken, as well as answer her own hopes for the time. It was run off in a hurry. She was afraid it was not quite right in *her*. But hoped the end would excuse (if it could not justify) the means. And then she again expressed a good deal of apprehension lest you should still take it into your head to molest her, when her time, she said, was so short that she wanted every moment of it; repeating what she had once said before, that when she wrote she was so ill that she believed she should not have lived till now: if she had thought she should, she must have studied for an expedient that would have better answered her intentions; hinting at a removal out of the knowledge of us both.

But she was much pleased that the conference between you and Colonel Morden, after two or three such violent sallies, as I acquainted her you had had between you, ended so amicably; and said she must absolutely depend upon the promise I had given her to use my utmost endeavours to prevent further mischief on her account.

She was pleased with the justice you did her character to her cousin.

She was glad to hear that he had so kind an opinion of her, and that he would write to her.

I was under an unnecessary concern how to break to her that I had the copy of Brand's vile letter: *unnecessary*, I say; for she took it just as you thought she would, as an excuse she wished to have for the implacableness of her friends; and begged I would let her read it herself; for, said she, the contents cannot disturb me, be they what they will.

I gave it to her, and she read it to herself; a tear now and then being ready to start, and a sigh sometimes interposing.

She gave me back the letter with great and surprising calmness, considering the subject.

There was a time, said she, and that not long since, when such a letter as this would have greatly pained me. But I hope I have now got above all these things: and I can refer to your kind offices, and to those of Miss Howe, the justice that will be done to my memory among my friends. There is a good and a bad light in which everything that befalls us may be taken. If the human mind will busy itself to make the worst of every disagreeable occurrence, it will never want woe. This letter, affecting as the subject of it is to my reputation, gives me more pleasure than pain, because I can gather from it, that had not my friends been prepossessed by misinformed or rash and officious persons, who are always at hand to flatter or soothe the passions of the affluent, they could not have been so immovably determined against me. But now they are sufficiently cleared from every imputation of unforgivingness; for, while I appeared to them in the character of a vile hypocrite, pretending to true penitence, yet giving up myself to profligate courses, how could I expect either their pardon or blessing?

But, madam, said I, you'll see by the date of this letter, *August* 9, that their severity, *previous* to that, cannot be excused by it.

It imports me much, replied she, on account of my present wishes, as to the office you are so kind to undertake, that you should not think harshly of my friends. I must own to you that I have been apt sometimes myself to think them not only severe but cruel. Suffering minds will be partial to their own cause and merits. Knowing their own hearts, if sincere, they are apt to murmur when harshly treated: but if they are not *believed* to be innocent, by persons who have a right to decide upon their conduct according to their own judgments, how can it be helped? Besides, sir, how do you know that there are not about my friends as well-meaning misrepresenters as Mr. Brand really seems to be? But be this as it will, there is no doubt that there are and have been multitudes of persons, as innocent as myself, who have suffered upon surmises as little probable as those on which Mr. Brand founds his judgment. Your intimacy, sir, with Mr. Lovelace, and (may I say?) a character which, it seems, you have been less solicitous formerly to justify than perhaps you will be for the future, and your frequent visits to me, may well be thought to be questionable circumstances in my conduct.

I could only admire her in silence.

But you see, sir, proceeded she, how necessary it is for young people of our sex to be careful of our company: and how much, at the same time, it behoves young persons of yours to be chary of their own reputation, were it only for the sake of such of ours as they may mean honourably by; and who otherwise may suffer in their good names for being seen in their company.

As to Mr. Brand, continued she, he is to be pitied; and let me enjoin you, Mr. Belford, not to take up any resentments against him which may be detrimental either to his person or his fortunes. Let his function and his good meaning plead for him. He will have concern enough, when he finds everybody whose displeasure

I now labour under, acquitting my memory of perverse guilt, and joining in a general pity for me.

This, Lovelace, is the woman whose life thou hast curtailed in the blossom of it! How many opportunities must thou have had of admiring her inestimable worth, yet couldst have thy senses so much absorbed in the WOMAN in her charming person, as to be blind to the ANGEL that shines out in such full glory in her mind! Indeed, I have ever thought myself, when blest with her conversation, in the company of a real angel: and I am sure it would be impossible for me, were she to be as beautiful, and as crimsoned over with health as I have seen her, to have the least thought of sex, when I heard her talk.

Thursday, Three o'clock, Aug. 31.

On my revisit to the lady I found her almost as much a sufferer from joy as she had sometimes been from grief: for she had just received a very kind letter from her Cousin Morden; which she was so good as to communicate to me. As she had already begun to answer it, I begged leave to attend her in the evening, that I might not interrupt her in it.

The letter is a very tender one. . . .

Here Mr. Belford gives the substance of it upon his memory ; but that is omitted ; as the letter is given at length [*see the next letter*]. *And then adds :*

But, alas! all will be now too late. For the decree is certainly gone out. The world is unworthy of her!

Letter LXXXVI—Colonel Morden to Miss Clarissa Harlowe

Tuesday, Aug. 29.

I SHOULD not, my dearest cousin, have been a fortnight in England, without either doing myself the honour of waiting upon you in person, or of writing to you, if I had not been busying myself almost all the time in your service, in hopes of making my visit or letter still more acceptable to you—acceptable as I have reason to presume either will be from the unquestionable love I ever bore you, and from the esteem you always honoured me with.

Little did I think that so many days would have been required to effect my well-intended purpose, where there used to be a love so ardent on one side, and where there still is, as I am thoroughly convinced, the most exalted merit on the other!

I was yesterday with Mr. Lovelace and Lord M. I need not

tell *you*, it seems, how very desirous the whole family and all the relations of that nobleman are of the honour of an alliance with you; nor how exceedingly earnest the ungrateful man is to make you all the reparation in his power.

I think, my dear cousin, that you cannot now do better than to give him the honour of your hand. He says such just and great things of your virtue, and so heartily condemns himself, that I think there is honourable room for you to forgive him: and the more room, as it seems you are determined against a legal prosecution.

Your effectual forgiveness of Mr. Lovelace, it is evident to me, will accelerate a general reconciliation: for, at present, my other cousins cannot persuade themselves that he is in earnest to do you justice; or that you would refuse him, if you believed he was.

But, my dear cousin, there may possibly be something in this affair to which I may be a stranger. If there be, and you will acquaint me with it, all that a *naturally* warm heart can do in your behalf shall be done.

I hope I shall be able, in my next visits to my several cousins, to set all right with them. Haughty spirits, when convinced that they have carried resentments too high, want but a good excuse to condescend: and parents must *always* love the child they *once* loved.

But if I find them inflexible, I will set out, and attend you without delay; for I long to see you, after so many years' absence.

Meanwhile I beg the favour of a few lines, to know if you have reason to doubt Mr. Lovelace's sincerity. For my part, I can have none, if I am to judge from the conversation that passed between us yesterday, in presence of Lord M.

You will be pleased to direct for me at your Uncle Antony's.

Permit me, my dearest cousin, till I can procure a happy reconciliation between you and your father, and brother, and uncles, to supply the place to you of all those near relations, as well as that of

> Your affectionate kinsman, and humble servant,
> WM. MORDEN.

Letter LXXXVII—Miss Cl. Harlowe to Wm. Morden, Esq.

Thursday, Aug. 31.

I MOST heartily congratulate you, dear sir, on your return to your native country.

I heard with much pleasure that you were come; but I was

both afraid and ashamed, till you encouraged me by a first notice, to address myself to you.

How consoling is it to my wounded heart to find that you have not been carried away by that tide of resentment and displeasure with which I have been so unhappily overwhelmed; but that, while my still nearer relations have not thought fit to examine into the truth of vile reports raised against me, you have informed yourself of my innocence, and generously *credited* the information!

I have not the least reason to doubt Mr. Lovelace's sincerity in his offers of marriage: nor that all his relations are heartily desirous of ranking me among them. I have had noble instances of their esteem for me, on their apprehending that my father's displeasure must have subjected me to difficulties: and this, after I had absolutely refused *their* pressing solicitations in their kinsman's favour, as well as *his own*.

Nor think me, my dear cousin, blamable for refusing him. I had given Mr. Lovelace no reason to think me a weak creature. If I *had,* a man of his character might have thought himself warranted to endeavour to take ungenerous advantage of the weakness he had been able to inspire. The consciousness of *my own* weakness (in that case) might have brought me to a composition with *his* wickedness.

I can indeed forgive him. But that is because I think his crimes have set me above him. Can I be above the man, sir, to whom I shall give my hand and my vows, and with them a sanction to the most premeditated baseness? No, sir, let me say that your Cousin Clarissa, were she likely to live many years, and *that* (if she married not this man) in penury or want, despised and forsaken by all her friends, puts not so high a value upon the conveniences of life, nor upon life itself, as to seek to re-obtain the one, or to preserve the other, by giving *such* a sanction: a sanction which (*were she to perform her duty*) would reward the violator.

Nor is it so much from pride, as from principle, that I say this. What, sir! when virtue, when chastity, is the crown of a woman, and particularly of a wife, shall your cousin stoop to marry the man who could not form an attempt upon *hers* but upon a presumption that she was capable of receiving his offered hand, when he had found himself mistaken in the vile opinion he had conceived of her? Hitherto he has not had reason to think me weak. Nor will I give him an instance so flagrant, that weak I am in a point in which it would be criminal to be *found* weak.

One day, sir, you will perhaps know all my story. But, whenever it is known, I beg that the author of my calamities may not be vindictively sought after. He could not have been the author of them but for a strange concurrence of unhappy causes. As the law will not be able to reach him when I am gone, the apprehension of any other sort of vengeance terrifies me. Since, in such a case, should my friends be *safe*, what honour would his death bring to my memory? If any of them should come to misfortune, how would my fault be aggravated!

God long preserve you, my dearest cousin, and bless you but in *proportion* to the consolation you have given me, in letting me know that you still love me; and that I have one near and dear relation who can pity and forgive me (and then will you be *greatly* blessed); is the prayer of

Your ever grateful and affectionate
CLARISSA HARLOWE.

Letter LXXXVIII—Mr. Lovelace to John Belford, Esq.
[*In answer to his Letters LXV, LXXIX*]

Thursday, Aug. 31.

I CANNOT but own that I am cut to the heart by *this* Miss Harlowe's interpretation of her letter. She ought never to be forgiven. *She*, a meek person, and a penitent, and innocent, and pious, and I know not what, who can deceive with a foot in the grave!

'Tis evident that she sat down to write this letter with a design to mislead and deceive. And if she be capable of that, at such a crisis, she has as much need of *Heaven's* forgiveness as I have of *hers*: and, with all her cant of *charity* and *charity*, if she be not more sure of it than I am of her *real pardon*, and if she take the thing in the light she ought to take it in, she will have a few darker moments yet to come than she seems to expect.

Lord M. himself, who is not one of those (to speak in his own phrase) *who can penetrate a millstone*, sees the deceit, and thinks it unworthy of her; though my Cousins Montague vindicate her. And no wonder: this cursed partial sex [I hate 'em all—by my soul, I hate 'em all!] will never allow anything against an individual of it, where ours is concerned. And why? Because, if they censure deceit in another, they must condemn their own hearts.

She is to send me a letter after she is in heaven, is she? The devil take such *allegories*; and the devil take thee for calling this absurdity an *innocent* artifice!

I insist upon it, that if a woman of her character, at such a critical time, is to be justified in such a deception, a man in full health and vigour of body and mind, as I am, may be excused for all his stratagems and attempts against her. And, thank my stars, I can now sit me down with a quiet conscience on that score. By my soul, I can, Jack. Nor has anybody, who can acquit *her*, a right to blame *me*. But with some, indeed, everything *she* does must be good, everything *I* do must be bad. And why? Because she has always taken care to coax the stupid misjudging world, like a *woman*: while I have constantly defied and despised its censures, like a *man*.

But, notwithstanding all, you may let her know from me that I will *not* molest her, since my visits would be so shocking to her: and I hope she will take this into her consideration as a piece of generosity which she could hardly expect after the deception she has put upon me. And let her further know, that if there be anything in my power, that will contribute either to her ease or honour, I will obey her, at the very first intimation, however disgraceful or detrimental to myself. All this to make her unapprehensive, and that she may have nothing to pull her back.

If her cursed relations could be brought as cheerfully to perform *their* parts, I'd answer life for life for her recovery.

But who, that has so many ludicrous images raised in his mind by thy awkward penitence, can forbear laughing at thee? Spare, I beseech thee, dear Belford, for the future, all thine own aspirations, if thou wouldst not dishonour those of an angel indeed.

When I came to that passage where thou sayest that thou considerest her[1] as one sent from heaven to draw thee after her—for the heart of me, I could not for an hour put thee out of my head, in the attitude of Dame Elizabeth Carteret, on her monument in Westminster Abbey. If thou never observedst it, go thither on purpose; and there wilt thou see this dame in effigy, with uplifted head and hand, the latter taken hold of by a Cupid every inch of stone, one clumsy foot lifted up also, aiming, as the sculptor designed it, to ascend; but so executed as would rather make one imagine that the figure (without shoe or stocking, as it is, though the rest of the body is robed) was looking up to its corn-cutter: the other riveted to its native earth, bemired, like thee (*immersed* thou callest it), beyond the

[1] See p. 214.

possibility of unsticking itself. Both figures, thou wilt find, seem to be in a contention, the bigger, whether it should pull down the lesser about its ears—the lesser (a chubby fat little varlet, of a fourth part of the other's bigness, with wings not much larger than those of a butterfly), whether it should raise the larger to a heaven it points to, hardly big enough to contain the great toes of either.

Thou wilt say, perhaps, that the dame's figure in *stone* may do credit, in the comparison, to thine, both in grain and shape, *wooden* as thou art all over; but that the lady, who, in everything but in the trick she has played me so lately, is truly an angel, is but sorrily represented by the fat-flanked Cupid. This I allow thee. But yet there is enough in thy aspirations to strike my mind with a resemblance of thee and the lady to the figures on the wretched monument; for thou oughtest to remember that, prepared as she may be to mount to her native skies, it is impossible for her to draw after her a heavy fellow who has so much to repent of as thou hast.

But now, to be serious once more, let me tell you, Belford, that, if the lady be really so ill as you write she is, it will become you [*no Roman style here!*], in a case so very affecting, to be a little less pointed and sarcastic in your reflections. For, upon my soul, the matter begins to grate me most confoundedly.

I am now so impatient to hear oftener of her, that I take the hint accidentally given me by our two fellows meeting at Slough, and resolve to go to our friend Doleman's at Uxbridge; whose wife and sister, as well as he, have so frequently pressed me to give them my company for a week or two. There shall I be within two hours' ride, if anything should happen to induce her to see me: for it will well become her piety, and avowed charity, should the worst happen [the Lord of Heaven and Earth, however, avert that worst!], to give me that pardon from her *lips*, which she has not denied me by *pen and ink*. And as she wishes my reformation, she knows not what good effects such an interview may have upon me.

I shall accordingly be at Doleman's to-morrow morning, by eleven at furthest. My fellow will find me there at his return from you (with a letter, I hope). I shall have Joel with me likewise, that I may send the oftener, as matters fall out. Were I to be *still nearer*, or in town, it would be impossible to withhold myself from seeing her.

But, if the worst happen!—as, by your continual knelling, I know not what to think of it!—[Yet, once more, Heaven avert that worst! How natural is it to pray, when one cannot help oneself!]—THEN say not, in so many dreadful words, what the event is—only, that you advise me to take a trip to Paris—and that will stab me to the heart.

. . . .

I so well approve of your generosity to poor Belton's sister, that I have made Mowbray give up his legacy, as I do mine, towards her India bonds. When I come to town, Tourville shall do the like; and we will buy each a ring, to wear in memory of the honest fellow, with our own money, that we may perform *his* will as well as our *own*.

My fellow rides the rest of the night. I charge you, Jack, if you would save his life, that you send him not back empty-handed.

Letter LXXXIX—*Mr. Belford to Robert Lovelace, Esq.*

Thursday Night, Aug. 31.

WHEN I concluded my last, I hoped that my next attendance upon this *surprising* lady would furnish me with some particulars as agreeable as now could be hoped for from the declining way she is in, by reason of the welcome letter she had received from her Cousin Morden. But it proved quite otherwise to *me*, though not to *herself*; for I think I never was more shocked in my life than on the occasion I shall mention presently.

When I attended her about seven in the evening, she told me that she found herself in a very petulant way after I had left her. Strange, said she, that the pleasure I received from my cousin's letter should have such an effect upon me! But I could not help giving way to a *comparative* humour, as I may call it, and to think it very hard that my nearer relations did not take the methods which my Cousin Morden kindly took, by inquiring into my merit or demerit, and giving my cause a fair audit before they proceeded to condemnation.

She had hardly said this, when she started, and a blush over-spread her sweet face, on hearing, as I also did, a sort of lumbering noise upon the stairs, as if a large trunk were bringing up between two people: and, looking upon me with an eye of concern, Blunderers! said she, they have brought in *something* two hours before the time. Don't be surprised, sir—it is all to save *you* trouble.

Before I could speak, in came Mrs. Smith: O madam, said she, what have you done? Mrs. Lovick, entering, made the same exclamation. Lord have mercy upon me, madam, cried I, what have you done! For, she stepping at the instant to the door, the women told me it was a coffin. O Lovelace! that thou hadst been there at the moment! Thou, the causer of all these shocking scenes! Surely thou couldst not have been less affected than I, who have no guilt, as to *her*, to answer for.

With an intrepidity of a piece with the preparation, having directed them to carry it into her bedchamber, she returned to us: They were not to have brought it in till after dark, said she. Pray excuse me, Mr. Belford: and don't you, Mrs. Lovick, be concerned: nor you, Mrs. Smith. Why should you? There is nothing more in it than the unusualness of the thing. Why may we not be as reasonably shocked at going to the church where are the monuments of our ancestors, with whose dust we even *hope* our dust shall be one day mingled, as to be moved at such a sight as this?

We all remaining silent, the women having their aprons at their eyes, Why this concern for nothing at all? said she: if I am to be blamed for anything, it is for showing too much solicitude, as it may be thought, for this earthly part. I love to do everything for myself that I can do. I ever did. Every other material point is so far done and taken care of, that I have had *leisure* for things of lesser moment. Minutenesses may be observed, where greater articles are not neglected for them. I might have had this to order, perhaps, when less fit to order it. I have no mother, no sister, no Mrs. Norton, no Miss Howe, near me. Some of you must have seen *this* in a few days, if not now; perhaps have had the friendly trouble of directing it. And what is the difference of a few days to *you*, when *I* am gratified rather than discomposed by it? I shall not die the sooner for such a preparation. Should not everybody that has anything to bequeath make their will? And who, that makes a will, should be afraid of a coffin? My dear friends [to the women], I have considered these things; do not, with such an object before you as you have had in *me* for weeks, give me reason to think you have not.

How reasonable was all this! It showed, indeed, that she herself had well considered it. But yet we could not help being shocked at the thoughts of the coffin thus brought in; the lovely person before our eyes who is in all likelihood so soon to fill it.

We were all silent still, the women in grief, I in a manner

stunned. She would not ask *me*, she said; but would be glad, since it had thus earlier than she had intended been brought in, that her two good friends would walk in and look upon it. They would be less shocked when it was made more familiar to their eye: don't you lead back, said she, a starting steed to the object he is apt to start at, in order to familiarize him to it, and cure his starting? The same reason will hold in this case. Come, my good friends, I will lead you in.

I took my leave; telling her she had done wrong, very wrong; and ought not, by any means, to have such an object before her.

The women followed her in. 'Tis a strange sex! Nothing is too shocking for them to look upon, or see acted, that has but novelty and curiosity in it.

Down I posted; got a chair; and was carried home, extremely shocked and discomposed: yet, weighing the lady's arguments, I know not why I was so affected—except, as she said, at the unusualness of the thing.

While I waited for a chair, Mrs. Smith came down, and told me that there were devices and inscriptions upon the lid. Lord bless me! Is a coffin a proper subject to display fancy upon? But these great minds cannot avoid doing extraordinary things!

Letter XC—Mr. Belford to Robert Lovelace, Esq.

Friday Morn. Sept. 1.

IT is surprising that I, a *man*, should be so much affected as I was, at such an object as is the subject of my former letter; who also, in my late uncle's case, and poor Belton's, had the like before me, and the directing of it: when she, a *woman*, of so weak and tender a frame, who was to fill it (so soon perhaps to fill it!), could give orders about it, and draw out the devices upon it, and explain them with so little concern as the women tell me she did to them last night after I was gone.

I really was ill and restless all night. Thou wert the subject of my execration, as she of my admiration, all the time I was quite awake: and, when I dozed, I dreamt of nothing but of flying hour-glasses, death's-heads, spades, mattocks, and eternity; the hint of her devices (as given me by Mrs. Smith) running in my head.

However, not being able to keep away from Smith's, I went thither about seven. The lady was just gone out: she had slept better, I found, than I, though her solemn repository was under her window not far from her bedside.

I was prevailed upon by Mrs. Smith and her nurse Shelburne (Mrs. Lovick being abroad with her) to go up and look at the devices. Mrs. Lovick has since shown me a copy of the draft by which all was ordered. And I will give thee a sketch of the symbols.

The principal device, neatly etched on a plate of white metal, is a crowned serpent, with its tail in its mouth, forming a ring, the emblem of eternity; and in the circle made by it is this inscription:

CLARISSA HARLOWE
April x
[Then the year]
ÆTAT. XIX.

For ornaments: at top, an hour-glass winged. At bottom, an urn.

Under the hour-glass, on another plate, this inscription:

HERE the wicked cease from troubling: and HERE the weary be at rest. Job iii, 17.

Over the urn, near the bottom:

Turn again unto thy rest, O my soul! for the Lord hath rewarded thee. And why? Thou hast delivered my soul from death; mine eyes from tears; and my feet from falling. Ps. cxvi, 7, 8.

Over this text is the head of a white lily snapped short off, and just falling from the stalk; and this inscription over that, between the principal plate and the lily:

The days of man are but as grass. For he flourisheth as a flower of the field: for, as soon as the wind goeth over it, it is gone; and the place thereof shall know it no more. Ps. ciii, 15, 16.

She excused herself to the women, on the score of her youth, and being used to draw for her needleworks, for having shown more fancy than would perhaps be thought suitable on so solemn an occasion.

The date, April 10, she accounted for, as not being able to tell what her *closing-day* would be; and as that was the fatal day of her leaving her father's house.

She discharged the undertaker's bill after I went away, with as much cheerfulness as she could ever have paid for the clothes she sold to purchase this her *palace*: for such she called it; reflecting upon herself for the expensiveness of it, saying that they might observe in *her* that pride left not poor mortals to the last: but indeed she did not know but her father would permit it, *when furnished*, to be carried down to be deposited with her ancestors; and, in that case, she ought not to discredit those ancestors in her *appearance amongst them.*

It is covered with fine black cloth, and lined with white satin; soon, she said, to be tarnished by viler earth than any it could be covered by.

The burial-dress was brought home with it. The women had curiosity enough, I suppose, to see her open that, if she did open it. And perhaps thou wouldst have been glad to have been present, to have admired it too!

Mrs. Lovick said she took the liberty to blame her; and wished the removal of such an object — from her *bedchamber* at least: and was so affected with the noble answer she made upon it, that she entered it down the moment she left her.

"To persons in health, said she, this sight may be shocking; and the preparation, and my unconcernedness in it, may appear affected: but to me, who have had so gradual a weaning-time from the world, and so much reason not to love it, I must say I dwell on, I indulge (and, strictly speaking, I enjoy) the thoughts of death. For, believe me [looking steadfastly at the awful receptacle], believe what at this instant I feel to be most true, that there is such a vast superiority of weight and importance in the thought of death, and its hoped-for happy consequences, that it in a manner annihilates all other considerations and concerns. Believe me, my good friends, it does what nothing else can do: it teaches me, by strengthening in me the force of the divinest example, to forgive the injuries I have received; and shuts out the remembrance of past evils from my soul."

And now let me ask thee, Lovelace, Dost thou think that, when the time shall come that thou shalt be obliged to launch into the boundless ocean of eternity, thou wilt be able (any more than poor Belton) to act thy part with such true heroism, as this sweet and tender blossom of a woman has manifested, and continues to manifest!

O no! it cannot be! And why cannot it be? The reason is evident: she has no *wilful* errors to look back upon with self-reproach—and her mind is strengthened by the consolations which flow from that *religious rectitude* which has been the guide of all her actions; and which has taught her rather to choose to be a sufferer than an aggressor!

This was the support of the divine Socrates, as thou hast read.

When led to execution, his wife lamenting that he should suffer being innocent, Thou fool, said he, wouldst thou wish me to be guilty?

Letter XCI—Mr. Belford to Robert Lovelace, Esq.

Friday, Sept. 1.

How astonishing, in the midst of such affecting scenes, is thy mirth on what thou callest my *own aspirations*! Never, surely, was there such another man in this world, thy talents and thy levity taken together! Surely, what I shall send thee with this will affect thee. If not, nothing can, till *thy own hour* come: and heavy will then thy reflections be!

I am glad, however, that thou enablest me to assure the lady that thou wilt no more molest her; that is to say, in other words, that, after having ruined her fortunes, and all her worldly prospects, thou wilt be so gracious as to let her lie down and die in peace.

Thy giving up to poor Belton's sister the little legacy, and thy undertaking to make Mowbray and Tourville follow thy example, is, I must say, to thy honour, of a piece with thy generosity to thy Rosebud and her Johnny; and to a number of other good actions in pecuniary matters; although thy Rosebud's is, I believe, the only instance, where a pretty woman was concerned, of such a disinterested bounty.

Upon my faith, Lovelace, I love to praise thee; and often and often, as thou knowest, have I *studied* for occasions to do it: insomuch that when for the life of me I could not think of any-thing done by thee that deserved it, I have taken pains to applaud the not ungraceful manner in which thou hast performed actions that merited the gallows.

Now thou art so near, I will dispatch *my* servant to thee, if occasion requires. But I fear I shall soon give thee the news thou apprehendest. For I am just now sent for by Mrs. Smith; who has ordered the messenger to tell me that she knew not if the lady will be alive when I come.

Friday, Sept. 1, Two o'clock, at Smith's.

I could not close my letter in such an uncertainty as must have added to your impatience. For you have, on several occasions, convinced me that the suspense you love to *give* would be the greatest torment to you that you could *receive*. A common case with all aggressive and violent spirits, I believe. I will just mention then (your servant waiting here till I have written) that the lady has had two very severe fits: in the last of which, whilst she lay, they sent to the doctor and Mr. Goddard, who both advised that a messenger should be dispatched for me, as her executor; being doubtful whether, if she had a third, it would not carry her off.

She was tolerably recovered by the time I came; and the doctor made her promise before me, that, while she was so weak, she would not attempt any more to go abroad; for, by Mrs. Lovick's description, who attended her, the shortness of her breath, her extreme weakness, and the fervour of her devotions when at church, were contraries which, pulling different ways (the soul aspiring, the body sinking), tore her tender frame in pieces.

So much for the present. I shall detain Will no longer than just to beg that you will send me back this packet and the last. Your memory is so good, that once reading is all you ever give, or need to give, to anything. And who but ourselves can make out our characters, were you inclined to let anybody see what passes between us? If I cannot be obliged, I shall be tempted to withhold what I write till I have time to take a copy of it.[1]

A letter from Miss Howe is just now brought by a particular messenger, who says he must carry back a few lines in return. But, as the lady is just retired to lie down, the man is to call again by and by.

Letter XCII—Mr. Lovelace to John Belford, Esq.

Uxbridge, Sept. 1, Twelve o'clock at Night.

I SEND you the papers with this. You must account to me honestly and fairly when I see you for the earnestness with which you write for them. And then also will we talk about the contents of your last dispatch, and about some of your severe and unfriendly reflections.

Meantime, whatever thou dost, don't let the wonderful creature leave us! Set before her the sin of her preparation, as if she thought she could depart when she pleased. She 'll persuade herself, at this rate, that she has nothing to do, when all is ready, but to lie down and go to sleep: and such a lively fancy as hers will make a reality of a jest at any time.

[1] It may not be amiss to observe, that Mr. Belford's solicitude to get back his letters was owing to his desire of fulfilling the lady's wishes that he would furnish Miss Howe with materials to vindicate her memory.

A *jest*, I call all that has passed between her and me; a mere jest to die for—for has not her triumph over me, from first to last, been infinitely greater than her sufferings from me?

Would the sacred regard I have for her purity, even for her *personal* as well as *intellectual* purity, permit, I could prove this as clear as the sun. Tell, therefore, the dear creature that she must not be wicked in her piety. There is a *too much*, as well as a *too little*, even in righteousness. Perhaps she does not think of that. O that she would have permitted my attendance, as obligingly as she does of thine! The dear soul used to love humour. I remember the time that she knew how to smile at a piece of apropos humour. And, let me tell thee, a smile upon the lips, or a sparkling in the eye, must have had its correspondent cheerfulness in a heart so sincere as hers.

Tell the doctor I will make over all my possessions, and all my reversions, to him, if he will but prolong her life for one twelvemonth to come. But for one twelvemonth, Jack! He will lose all his reputation with me, and I shall treat him as Belton did his doctor, if he cannot do this for me, on so young a subject. But *nineteen*, Belford!—*nineteen* cannot so soon die of grief, if the doctor deserve that name; and so blooming and so fine a constitution as she had but three or four months ago!

But what need the doctor to ask her leave to write to her friends? Could he not have done it without letting her know anything of the matter? That was one of the likeliest means that could be thought of to bring some of them about her, since she is so desirous to see them. At least, it would have induced them to send up her favourite Norton. But these plaguy solemn fellows are great traders in parade. They'll cram down your throat their poisonous drugs by wholesale, without asking you a question; and have the assurance to *own* it to be *prescribing*: but, when they are to do good, they are to require your consent.

How the dear creature's character rises in every line of thy letters! But it is owing to the uncommon occasions she has met with that she blazes out upon us with such a meridian lustre. How, but for those occasions, could her noble sentiments, her prudent consideration, her forgiving spirit, her exalted benevolence, and her equanimity in view of the most shocking prospects (which set her in a light so superior to all her sex, and even to the philosophers of antiquity), have been manifested?

I know thou wilt think I am going to claim some merit to myself for having given her such opportunities of signalizing her virtues. But I am not; for, if I did, I must share that merit with her implacable relations, who would justly be entitled to *two-thirds* of it, at least: and my soul disdains a partnership in anything with such a family.

But this I mention as an answer to thy reproaches, that I could be so little edified by perfections to which, thou supposest, I was for so long together daily and hourly a personal witness— when, admirable as she was in all she said, and in all she did, occasion had not at that time ripened, and called forth, those amazing perfections which now astonish and confound me.

Hence it is that I admire her more than ever; and that my love for her is less *personal*, as I may say, more *intellectual*, than ever I thought it could be to woman.

Hence also it is that I am confident (would it please the Fates to spare her, and make her mine) I could love her with a purity that would draw on *my own* FUTURE, as well as ensure *her* TEMPORAL, happiness. And hence, by necessary consequence, shall I be the most miserable of all men, if I am deprived of her.

Thou severely reflectest upon me for my levity: the Abbey instance in thine eye, I suppose. And I will be ingenuous enough to own, that as thou seest not my heart, there may be passages in every one of my letters which (the melancholy occasion considered) deserve thy most pointed rebukes. But, faith, Jack, thou art such a tragi-comical mortal, with thy leaden aspirations at one time, and thy flying hour-glasses and dreaming terrors at another, that, as Prior says, *What serious is, thou turn'st to farce*; and it is impossible to keep within the bounds of decorum or gravity when one reads what thou writest.

But to restrain myself (for my constitutional gaiety was ready to run away with me again), I will repeat, I must *ever* repeat, that I am most egregiously affected with the circumstances of the case: and, were this paragon actually to quit the world, should never enjoy myself one hour together, though I were to live to the age of Methusalem.

Indeed it is to this *deep concern* that my *levity* is owing: for I struggle and struggle, and try to buffet down my cruel reflections as they rise: and when I cannot, I am forced, as I have often said, to try to make myself laugh, that I may not cry; for one or other I must do: and is it not philosophy carried to the highest pitch, for a man to conquer such tumults of soul as I am sometimes agitated by, and, in the very height of the storm, to be able to quaver out a horse-laugh?

Your Senecas, your Epictetuses, and the rest of your stoical tribe, with all their apathy nonsense, could not come up to this. They could forbear wry faces: bodily pains they could well enough *seem* to support; and that was all: but the pangs of their own smitten-down souls they could not *laugh* over, though they could at the follies of others. They read grave lectures; but they *were* grave. This high point of philosophy, to laugh and be merry in the midst of the most soul-harrowing woes, when the heartstrings are just bursting asunder, was reserved for thy Lovelace.

There is something owing to constitution, I own; and that this is the laughing-time of my life. For what a woe that must be, which for an hour together can mortify a man of six or seven and twenty, in high blood and spirits, of a naturally gay disposition, who can sing, dance, and scribble, and take and give delight in them all? But then my grief, as my joy, is sharper-pointed than most other men's; and, like what Dolly Welby once told me, describing the parturient throes, if there were not lucid intervals, if they did not come and go, there would be no bearing them.

.   .   .   .   .   .

After all, as I am so little distant from the dear creature, and as she is so very ill, I think I cannot excuse myself from making her *one* visit. Nevertheless, if I thought her so near—[what word shall I use that my soul is not shocked at!], and that she would be *too much discomposed* by a visit, I would not think of it. Yet how can I bear the recollection, that when she last went from me (her innocence so triumphant over my premeditated guilt, as was enough to reconcile her to life, and to set her above the sense of injuries so nobly sustained, that) she should then depart with an incurable fracture in her heart; and that *that* should be the last time I should ever see her! How, how, can I bear this reflection!

O Jack! how my conscience, that gives edge even to thy blunt reflections, tears me! Even this moment would I give the world to push the cruel reproacher from me by one ray of my usual gaiety! Sick of myself! Sick of the remembrance of my vile plots; and of my *light*, my momentary ecstasy [villainous burglar, felon, thief, that I was!], which has brought upon me such *durable* and such *heavy* remorse! what would I give that I had not been guilty of such barbarous and ungrateful perfidy to the most excellent of God's creatures!

I would end, methinks, with one sprightlier line! But it will not be. Let me tell thee then, and rejoice at it if thou wilt, that I am

Inexpressibly miserable !

Letter XCIII—Mr. Belford to Robert Lovelace, Esq.

Sat. Morning, Sept. 2.

I HAVE some little pleasure given me by thine, just now brought me. I see now that thou hast a little humanity left. Would to Heaven, for the dear lady's sake, as well as for thy own, that thou hadst rummaged it up from all the dark forgotten corners of thy soul a little sooner!

The lady is alive, and serene, and calm, and has all her noble intellects clear and strong: but *nineteen* will not, however, save her. She says she will now content herself with her closet duties and the visits of the parish minister; and will not attempt to go out. Nor, indeed, will she, I am afraid, ever walk up or down a pair of stairs again.

I am sorry at my soul to have this to say: but it would be a folly to flatter thee.

As to thy seeing her, I believe the least hint of that sort, now, would cut off some hours of her life.

What has contributed to her serenity, it seems, is that, taking the alarm her fits gave her, she has entirely finished, and signed and sealed, her last will: which she had deferred doing till this time, in hopes, as she said, of some good news from Harlowe Place; which would have induced her to alter some passages in it.

Miss Howe's letter was not given her till four in the afternoon yesterday; at what time the messenger returned for an answer. She admitted him into her presence in the dining-room, ill as she then was; and she would have written a few lines, as desired by Miss Howe; but, not being able to hold a pen, she bid the messenger tell her that she hoped to be well enough to write a long letter by the next day's post; and would not now detain him.

Saturday, Six in the afternoon.

I called just now, and found the lady writing to Miss Howe. She made me a melancholy compliment, that she showed me not Miss Howe's letter, because I should soon have that and all her papers before me. But she told me that Miss Howe had very considerately obviated to Colonel Morden several things which might have occasioned misapprehensions between him and me;

and had likewise put a lighter construction, for the sake of peace, on some of your actions than they deserved.

She added that her Cousin Morden was warmly engaged in her favour with her friends: and one good piece of news Miss Howe's letter contained; that her father would give up some matters, which (appertaining to her of right) would make my executorship the easier in some particulars that had given her a little pain.

She owned she had been obliged to leave off (in the letter she was writing) through weakness.

Will says he shall reach you to-night. I shall send in the morning; and if I find her not worse, will ride to Edgware, and return in the afternoon.

Letter XCIV—Miss Howe to Miss Clarissa Harlowe
Tuesday, Aug. 29.

MY DEAREST FRIEND,—We are at length returned to our own home. I had intended to wait on you in London: but my mother is very ill. Alas! my dear, she is very ill indeed. And you are likewise very ill—I see *that* by yours of the 25th. What shall I do if I lose two such near, and dear, and tender friends? She was taken ill yesterday at our last stage in our return home, and has a violent surfeit and fever, and the doctors are doubtful about her.

If she should die, how will all my pertnesses to her fly in my face! Why, why did I ever vex her? She says I have been all duty and obedience! She kindly forgets all my faults, and remembers everything I have been so happy as to oblige her in. And this cuts me to the heart.

I see, I see, my dear, you are very bad—and I cannot bear it. Do, my beloved Miss Harlowe, if you *can* be better, do, for *my* sake, *be* better; and send me word of it. Let the bearer bring me a line. Be sure you send me a line. If I lose you, my more than sister, and lose my mother, I shall distrust my own conduct, and will not marry. And why should I? Creeping, cringing in courtship! O my dear, these men are a vile race of *reptiles* in *our day*, and mere *bears* in *their own*. See in Lovelace all that is desirable in figure, in birth, and in fortune: but in his heart a devil! See in Hickman—indeed, my dear, I cannot tell what anybody can see in Hickman, to be always preaching in his favour. And is it to be expected that I, who could hardly bear control from a mother, should take it from a husband?—from one, too, who has neither more wit, nor more understanding, than myself? Yet he to be my instructor! So he will, I suppose; but more by the insolence of his will than by the merit of his counsel. It is in vain to think of it. I cannot be a wife to any man breathing whom I at present know. This I the rather mention now, because, on my mother's danger, I know you will be for pressing me the sooner to throw myself into another sort of protection, should I be deprived of her. But no more of this subject, or indeed of any other; for I am obliged to attend my mamma, who cannot bear me out of her sight.

Wednesday, Aug. 30.

My mother, Heaven be praised! has had a fine night, and is much better. Her fever has yielded to medicine! And now I can write once more with freedom and ease to you, in hopes that *you* also are better. If this be granted to my prayers, I shall again be happy. I write with still the more alacrity, as I have an opportunity given me to touch upon a subject in which you are nearly concerned.

You must know then, my dear, that your Cousin Morden has been here with me. He told me of an interview he had on Monday at Lord M.'s with Lovelace; and asked me abundance of questions about you, and about that villainous man.

I could have raised a fine flame between them if I would: but, observing that he is a man of very lively passions, and believing you would be miserable if anything should happen to him from a quarrel with a man who is known to have so many advantages at his sword, I made not the worst of the subjects we talked of. But, as I could not tell untruths in his favour, you must think I said enough to make him curse the wretch.

I don't find, well as they all used to respect Colonel Morden, that he has influence enough upon them to bring them to any terms of reconciliation.

What can they mean by it! But your brother is come home, it seems: so, the honour of the house, the reputation of the family, is all the cry!

The colonel is exceedingly out of humour with them all. Yet has he not hitherto, it seems, seen your brutal brother. I told him how ill you were, and communicated to him some of the contents of your letter. He admired *you,* cursed *Lovelace,* and raved against all your *family.* He declared that they were all unworthy of you.

At his earnest request, I permitted him to take some brief notes of such of the contents of your letter to me as I thought

I *could* read to him; and, particularly, of your melancholy conclusion.[1]

He says that none of your friends think you so ill as you are; nor will believe it. He is sure they all love you, and that dearly too.

If they do, their present hardness of heart will be the subject of everlasting remorse to them should you be taken from us. But now it seems [barbarous wretches!] you are to *suffer within an inch of your life.*

He asked me questions about Mr. Belford: and when he had heard what I had to say of that gentleman, and his disinterested services to you, he raved at some villainous surmises thrown out against you by that officious pedant, Brand: who, but for his gown, I find, would come off poorly enough between your cousin and Lovelace.

He was so uneasy about you himself, that on Thursday the 24th he sent up an honest serious man,[2] one Alston, a gentleman farmer, to inquire of your condition, your visitors, and the like; who brought him word that you was very ill, and was put to great straits to support yourself: but as this was told him by the gentlewoman of the house where you lodge, who it seems mingled with it some tart, though deserved, reflections upon your relations' cruelty, it was not credited by them: and I myself hope it cannot be true; for surely you could not be so *unjust,* I will say, to my friendship, as to suffer any inconveniences for want of money. I think I could not forgive you if it were so.

The colonel (as one of your trustees) is resolved to see you put into possession of your estate: and, in the meantime, he has actually engaged them to remit to him for you the produce of it accrued since your grandfather's death (a very considerable sum); and proposes himself to attend you with it. But, by a hint he dropped, I find you had disappointed some people's littleness, by not writing to them for money and supplies; since they were determined to distress you, and to put you at defiance.

Like all the rest!—I hope I may say *that* without offence.

Your cousin imagines that, before a reconciliation takes place, they will insist that you shall make such a will as to that estate as they shall approve of: but he declares he will not go out of England till he has seen justice done you by *everybody*; and that you shall not be imposed on either by friend or foe——

By *relation* or foe, should he not have said?—for a friend will not impose upon a friend.

So, my dear, you are to *buy your peace*, if some people are to have their wills!

Your cousin [not *I*, my dear, though it was always my opinion [1]] says that the whole family is *too rich* to be either *humble, considerate,* or *contented*. And as for himself, he has an ample fortune, he says, and thinks of leaving it wholly to you.

Had this villain Lovelace consulted his worldly interest *only*, what a fortune would he have had in you, even although your marrying him had deprived you of a paternal share?

I am obliged to leave off here. But having a good deal still to write, and my mother better, I will pursue the subject in another letter, although I send both together. I need not say how much I am, and will ever be,

Your affectionate, etc.
ANNA HOWE.

Letter XCV—*Miss Howe to Miss Clarissa Harlowe*

Thursday, Aug. 31.

THE colonel thought fit once, in praise of Lovelace's *generosity,* to say, that (*as a man of honour ought*) he took to himself all the blame, and acquitted you of the consequences of the precipitate step you had taken; since, he said, as you loved him, and was in his power, he *must* have had advantages, which he would *not* have had, if you had continued at your father's, or at any friend's.

Mighty generous, I said (were it as he *supposed*), in such insolent reflectors, the best of them; who pretend to *clear* reputations which never had been *sullied* but by falling into their dirty acquaintance! But in this case, I averred that there was no need of anything but the strictest truth to demonstrate Lovelace to be the blackest of villains, you the brightest of innocents.

This he caught at; and swore that if anything uncommon or barbarous in the seduction were to come out, as indeed one of the letters you had written to your friends, and which had been shown him, very strongly implied; that is to say, my dear, if anything *worse* than perjury, breach of faith, and abuse of a generous confidence were to appear! [sorry fellows!] he would avenge his cousin to the utmost.

I urged your apprehensions on this head from your last letter to me: but he seemed capable of taking what I know to be real

<hr>

[1] See vol. i, p. 41.

greatness of soul in an unworthy sense: for he mentioned directly upon it the expectation your friends had that you should (previous to any reconciliation with them) appear in a court of justice against the villain—IF you could do it with the advantage to yourself that I hinted might be done.

And truly, if I would have heard him, he had indelicacy enough to have gone into the nature of the proof of the crime upon which they wanted to have Lovelace arraigned. Yet this is a man improved by travel and learning! Upon my word, my dear, I, who have been accustomed to the most delicate conversation ever since I had the honour to know you, despise this sex from the gentleman down to the peasant.

Upon the whole, I find that Mr. Morden has a very slender notion of women's virtue, in particular cases: for which reason I put him down, though your favourite, as one who is not entitled *to cast the first stone.*

I never knew a man who deserved to be well thought of himself for his morals, who had a slight opinion of the virtue of our sex in general. For if, from the *difference* of *temperament* and *education,* modesty, chastity, and piety too, are not to be found in our sex preferably to the other, I should think it a sign of a much worse nature in *ours.*

He even hinted (as from your relations indeed) that it is impossible but there must be some *will* where there is much *love.*

These sort of reflections are enough to make a woman, who has at heart her own honour and the honour of her sex, to look about her, and consider what she is doing when she enters into an intimacy with these wretches; since it is plain that, whenever she throws herself into the power of a man, and leaves for him her parents or guardians, everybody will believe it to be owing more to her good luck than to her discretion, if there be not an end of her virtue: and let the man be ever such a villain to her, she must take into her own bosom a share of his guilty baseness.

I am writing to *general cases.* You, my dear, are out of the question. Your story, as I have heretofore said, will afford a warning, as well as an example [1]: for who is it that will not infer, that if a person of your fortune, character, and merit could not escape ruin, after she had put herself into the power of her *hyæna,* what can a thoughtless, fond, giddy creature expect?

Every man, they will say, is not a LOVELACE—true: but then, neither is every woman a CLARISSA. And allow for the one and for the other, the example must be of general use.

[1] See vol. ii, p. 280.

I prepared Mr. Morden to expect your appointment of Mr. Belford for an office that we both hope he will have no occasion to act in (nor anybody else) for many, very many years to come. He was at first startled at it: but, upon hearing such of your reasons as had satisfied me, he only said that such an appointment, were it to take place, would exceedingly affect his other cousins.

He told me he had a copy of Lovelace's letter to you, imploring your pardon, and offering to undergo any penance to procure it;[1] and also of your answer to it.[2]

I find he is willing to hope that a marriage between you may still take place; which, he says, will heal up all breaches.

I would have written much more—on the following particulars especially; to wit, of the wretched man's hunting you out of your lodgings: of your relations' strange *implacableness* [I am in haste, and cannot think of a word you would like better *just now*]: of your last letter to Lovelace, to divert him from pursuing you: of your Aunt Hervey's penitential conversation with Mrs. Norton: of Mr. Wyerley's renewed address: of your lessons to me in Hickman's behalf, so approvable, were the man *more so* than he is; but indeed I am offended with him at this instant, and have been for these two days: of your sister's transportation project: and of twenty and twenty other things—but am obliged to leave off, to attend my two Cousins Spilsworth, and my Cousin Herbert, who are come to visit us on account of my mother's illness. I will therefore dispatch these by Rogers; and if my mother gets well soon (as I hope she will), I am resolved to see you in town, and tell you everything that now is upon my mind; and particularly, mingling my soul with yours, how much I am, and will ever be, my dearest, dear friend,

Your affectionate
ANNA HOWE.

Let Rogers bring one line, I pray you. I thought to have sent him this afternoon; but he cannot set out till to-morrow morning early.

I cannot express how much your staggering lines, and your conclusion, affect me!

[1] See p. 90 of this volume.   [2] Ibid. p. 99.

Letter XCVI—Mr. Belford to Robert Lovelace, Esq.

Sunday Evening, Sept. 3.

I WONDER not at the impatience your servant tells me you express to hear from me. I was designing to write you a long letter, and was just returned from Smith's for that purpose; but, since you are so urgent, you must be contented with a short one.

I attended the lady this morning, just before I set out for Edgware. She was so ill overnight, that she was obliged to leave unfinished her letter to Miss Howe. But early this morning she made an end of it, and had just sealed it up as I came. She was so fatigued with writing, that she told me she would lie down after I was gone, and endeavour to recruit her spirits.

They had sent for Mr. Goddard when she was so ill last night; and not being able to see him out of her own chamber, he, for the first time, saw her *house*, as she calls it. He was extremely shocked and concerned at it; and chid Mrs. Smith and Mrs. Lovick for not persuading her to have such an object removed from her bedchamber: and when they excused themselves on the *little authority* it was reasonable to suppose they must have with a lady so much their superior, he reflected warmly on those who had *more* authority, and who left her to proceed with such a shocking and solemn whimsy, as he called it.

It is placed near the window, like a harpsichord, though covered over to the ground: and when she is so ill that she cannot well go to her closet, she writes and reads upon it, as others would upon a desk or table. But (only as she was so ill last night) she chooses not to see anybody in that apartment.

I went to Edgware; and, returning in the evening, attended her again. She had a letter brought her from Mrs. Norton (a long one, as it seems by its bulk) just before I came. But she had not opened it; and said, that as she was pretty calm and composed, she was afraid to look into the contents, lest she should be ruffled; expecting now to hear of nothing that could do her good or give her pleasure from that good woman's *dear hard-hearted neighbours*, as she called her own relations.

Seeing her so weak and ill, I withdrew; nor did she desire me to tarry, as sometimes she does, when I make a motion to depart.

I had some hints, as I went away, from Mrs. Smith, that she had appropriated that evening to some offices, that were to save trouble, as she called it, after her departure; and had been giving orders to her nurse, and to Mrs. Lovick, and Mrs. Smith, about what she would have done when she *was gone*; and I believe they were of a very delicate and affecting nature; but Mrs. Smith descended not to particulars.

The doctor had been with her, as well as Mr. Goddard; and they both joined with great earnestness to persuade her to have her *house* removed out of her sight: but she assured them that it gave her pleasure and spirits; and, being a necessary preparation, she wondered they should be surprised at it, when she had not any of her family about her, or any old acquaintance, on whose care and exactness in these *punctilios*, as she called them, she could rely.

The doctor told Mrs. Smith that he believed she would hold out long enough for any of her friends to have notice of her state, and to see her, and hardly longer; and since he could not find that she had any certainty of seeing her Cousin Morden (which made it plain that her relations continued inflexible), he would go home and write a letter to her father, take it as she would.

She had spent great part of the day in intense devotions; and to-morrow morning she is to have with her the same clergyman who has often attended her; from whose hands she will again receive the Sacrament.

Thou seest, Lovelace, that all is preparing, that all will be ready; and I am to attend her to-morrow afternoon, to take some instructions from her in relation to my part in the office to be performed for her. And thus, omitting the particulars of a fine conversation between her and Mrs. Lovick, which the latter acquainted me with, as well as another between her and the doctor and apothecary, which I had a design this evening to give you, they being of a very affecting nature, I have yielded to your impatience.

I shall dispatch Harry to-morrow morning early with her letter to Miss Howe: an offer she took very kindly; as she is extremely solicitous to lessen that young lady's apprehensions for her on not hearing from her by Saturday's post: and yet, if she write truth, as no doubt but she will, how can her apprehensions be lessened?

Letter XCVII—Miss Clarissa Harlowe to Miss Howe

Saturday, Sept. 2.

I WRITE, my beloved Miss Howe, though very ill still: but I could not by the return of your messenger; for I was then unable to hold a pen.

Your mother's illness (as mentioned in the first part of your letter) gave me great distress for you, till I read farther. You bewailed it as became a daughter so sensible. May you be blessed in each other for many, very many, happy years to come! I doubt not that even this sudden and grievous indisposition, by the frame it has put you in, and the apprehension it has given you of losing so dear a mother, will contribute to the happiness I wish you: for, alas! my dear, we seldom know how to value the blessings we enjoy, till we are in danger of losing them, or have actually lost them: and then, what would we give to have them restored to us?

What, I wonder, has again happened between you and Mr. Hickman? Although I know it not, I dare say it is owing to some pretty petulance, to some half-ungenerous advantage taken of his obligingness and assiduity. Will you never, my dear, give the weight you and all our sex ought to give to the qualities of sobriety and regularity of life and manners in that sex? Must bold creatures, and forward spirits, for ever, and by the best and wisest of us, as well as by the indiscreetest, be the most kindly treated?

My dear friends know not that I *have* actually suffered within *less* than *an inch of my life*.

Poor Mr. Brand! He meant well, I believe. I am afraid all will turn heavily upon him, when he probably imagined that he was taking the best method to oblige. But were he *not* to have been so light of belief, and so weakly officious; and had given a more favourable and, it would be strange if I could not say, a *juster* report; things would have been, nevertheless, exactly as they are.

I must lay down my pen. I am very ill. I believe I shall be better by and by. The bad writing would betray me, although I had a mind to keep from you what the event must soon——

.   .   .   .

Now I resume my trembling pen. Excuse the unsteady writing. It *will* be so——

I have wanted no money: so don't be angry about such a trifle as money. Yet am I glad of what you inclined me to hope, that my friends will give up the produce of my grandfather's estate since it has been in their hands: because, knowing it to be my right, and that *they* could not want it, I had already disposed of a good part of it; and could only hope they would be willing to give it up at my last request. And now how rich shall I think myself in this my last stage! And yet I did not want before — indeed I did not — for who, that has many *superfluities*, can be said to want?

Do not, my dear friend, be concerned that I call it my *last stage*; for what is even the long life which in high health we wish for? What, but, as we go along, a life of apprehension, sometimes for our friends, oftener for ourselves? And at last, when arrived at the old age we covet, one heavy loss or deprivation having succeeded another, we see ourselves stripped, as I may say, of every one we loved; and find ourselves exposed, as uncompanionable poor creatures, to the slights, to the contempts, of jostling youth, who want to push us off the stage, in hopes to possess what we have—and, superadded to all, our own infirmities every day increasing: of themselves enough to make the life we wished for the greatest disease of all! Don't you remember the lines of Howard which once you read to me in my ivy-bower?[1]

In the disposition of what belongs to me, I have endeavoured to do everything in the justest and best manner I could think of; putting myself in my relations' places, and, in the greater points, ordering my matters as if no misunderstanding had happened.

I hope they will not think much of some bequests where wanted, and where due from my gratitude: but if they should, what is done, is done; and I cannot now help it. Yet I must repeat, that I hope, I *hope*, I have pleased every one of them. For I would not, on any account, have it thought that, in my last disposition, anything undaughterly, unsisterly, or unlike a kinswoman, should have had place in a mind that is *so* truly free (as I will presume to say) from all resentment, that it now overflows with gratitude and blessings for the good I *have* received, although it be not all that my heart wished to receive. Were it even a *hardship* that I was not favoured with more, what is it but a hardship of half a year, against the *most* indulgent

---

[1] These are the lines the lady refers to:

> "From Death we rose to Life: 'Tis but the same,
> Through Life to pass again from whence we came.
> With shame we see our PASSIONS can prevail,
> Where *Reason, Certainty*, and *Virtue* fail.
> HONOUR, that empty name! can Death despise:⎞
> SCORN'D LOVE, to Death, as to a *refuge*, flies; ⎬
> And SORROW waits for Death with longing eyes. ⎠
> HOPE triumphs o'er the thoughts of Death; and FATE
> Cheats fools, and flatters the unfortunate.
> We fear to lose, what a *small time* must waste,
> Till Life itself grows the *disease* at last.
> Begging for Life, we beg for *more decay*,
> And to be *long a dying* only pray.

goodness of eighteen years and a half, that ever was shown to a daughter?

My cousin, you tell me, thinks I was off my guard, and that I was taken at some advantage. Indeed, my dear, I was not. Indeed I gave no room for advantage to be taken of me. I hope, one day, that will be seen, if I have the justice done me which Mr. Belford assures me of.

I should hope that my cousin has not taken the liberties which you, by an observation (not, in general, unjust), seem to charge him with. For it is sad to think that the generality of that sex should make so light of crimes, which they justly hold so unpardonable in their own most intimate relations of ours— yet cannot commit them without doing such injuries to other families as they think themselves obliged to resent unto death when offered to their own.

But we women are too often to blame on this head; since the most virtuous among us seldom make *virtue* the test of their approbation of the other sex: insomuch that a man may glory in his wickedness of this sort without being rejected on that account, even to the faces of women of unquestionable virtue. Hence it is that a libertine seldom thinks himself concerned so much as to save appearances: and what is it not that our sex suffers in their opinions on this very score? And what have I, more than many others, to answer for on this account in the world's eye?

May my story be a warning to all, how they prefer a libertine to a man of true honour; and how they permit themselves to be misled (where they mean the *best*) by the specious, yet foolish hope of subduing riveted habits, and, as I may say, of altering natures! The *more* foolish, as constant experience might convince us that there is hardly one in ten of even tolerably happy marriages in which the wife keeps the hold in the *husband's* affections which she had in the *lover's*. What influence then can she hope to have over the morals of an avowed libertine, who marries perhaps for conveniency, who despises the tie, and whom, it is too probable, nothing but old age, or sickness, or disease (the consequence of ruinous riot) can reclaim?

I am very glad you gave my cous——

Sunday Morning (Sept. 3), Six o'clock.

Hitner I had written, and was forced to quit my pen. And so much weaker and worse I grew, that had I resumed it, to have closed here, it must have been with such trembling unsteadiness that it would have given you more concern for me, than the delay of sending it away by last night's post can do. I deferred it, therefore, to see how it would please God to deal with me. And I find myself, after a better night than I expected, lively and clear; and hope to give you a proof that I do, in the continuation of my letter, which I will pursue as currently as if I had not left off.

I am glad you so considerately gave my Cousin Morden favourable impressions of Mr. Belford; since, otherwise, some misunderstanding might have happened between *them*: for although I hope this Mr. Belford is an altered man, and in time will be a reformed one, yet is he one of those high spirits that has been accustomed to resent *imaginary indignities* to *himself*, when, I believe, he has not been studious to avoid giving *real offences* to *others*; men of this cast acting as if they thought all the world was made to bear with them, and they with nobody in it.

Mr. Lovelace, you tell me, thought fit to entrust my cousin with the copy of his letter of penitence to me, and with my answer to it, rejecting him and his suit: and Mr. Belford moreover acquaints me how much concerned Mr. Lovelace is for his baseness, and how freely he accused himself to my cousin. This shows that the *true* bravery of spirit is to be above doing a vile action; and that nothing subjects the human mind to so much meanness as the consciousness of having done wilful wrong to our fellow-creatures. How low, how sordid, are the submissions which elaborate baseness compels! that that wretch could treat me as he did, and then could so poorly creep to me for forgiveness of crimes so wilful, so black, and so premeditated! How my soul despised him for his meanness on a certain occasion, of which you will one day be informed![1] And him whose actions one's heart despises, it is far from being difficult to reject, had one ever so partially favoured him once.

Yet am I glad this violent spirit *can* thus creep; that, like a poisonous serpent, he *can* thus coil himself, and hide his head in his own narrow circlets; because this stooping, this abasement, gives me hope that no further mischief will ensue.

All my apprehension is what may happen when I am gone; lest then my cousin, or any other of my family, should endeavour to avenge me, and risk their own more precious lives on that account.

---

[1] Meaning his meditated second violence (see vol. iii, Letter liii) and his succeeding letters to her, supplicating for her pardon.

If that part of Cain's curse were Mr. Lovelace's, *to be a fugitive and vagabond in the earth*; that is to say, if it meant no more harm to him than that he should be obliged to travel, as it seems he intends (though I wish him no ill in his travels), and I could know it; then should I be easy in the hoped-for safety of my friends from his skilful violence. O that I could hear he was a thousand miles off!

When I began this letter, I did not think I could have run to such a length. But 'tis to YOU, my dearest friend, and *you* have a title to the spirits you raise and support; for they are no longer mine, and will subside the moment I cease writing to you.

But what do you bid me hope for, when you tell me that, if your mother's health will permit, you will see me in town? I *hope* your mother's health will be perfected as you wish; but I dare not promise myself so great a favour; so great a *blessing*, I will call it—and indeed I know not if I should be able to bear it now!

Yet one comfort it is in your power to give me; and that is, let me know, and very speedily it must, be if you wish to oblige me, that all matters are made up between you and Mr. Hickman; to whom, I see, you are resolved, with all your bravery of spirit, to owe a multitude of obligations for his patience with your flightiness. Think of this, my dear proud friend! and think, likewise, of what I have often told you, that PRIDE, in man or woman, is an extreme that hardly ever fails, sooner or later, to bring forth its mortifying CONTRARY.

May you, my dear Miss Howe, have no discomforts but what you make to yourself! As it will be in your own power to lessen such as these, they ought to be your punishment if you do not. There is no such thing as *perfect happiness* here, since the busy mind will *make* to itself evils, were it to *find* none. You will therefore pardon this limited wish, strange as it may appear till you consider it: for to wish you no infelicities, either within or without you, were to wish you what can never happen in this world; and what perhaps ought not to be wished for, if *by a wish* one could give one's friend such an exemption; since we are not to live here always.

We must not, in short, expect that our roses will grow without thorns: but then they are useful and instructive thorns; which, by pricking the fingers of the too hasty plucker, teach future caution. And who knows not that difficulty gives poignancy to our enjoyments; which are apt to lose their relish with us when they are over-easily obtained?

I *must* conclude—

God for ever bless you, and all you love and honour, and reward you here and hereafter for your kindness to

Your ever obliged and affectionate

CLARISSA HARLOWE.

Letter XCVIII—Mrs. Norton to Miss Clarissa Harlowe

[*In answer to hers of Thursday, August 24. See Letter LXXII*]

Thursday, Aug. 31.

I HAD written sooner, my dearest young lady, but that I have been endeavouring ever since the receipt of your last letter to obtain a private audience of your mother, in hopes of leave to communicate it to her. But last night I was surprised by an invitation to breakfast at Harlowe Place this morning: and the chariot came early to fetch me: an honour I did not expect.

When I came, I found there was to be a meeting of all your family with Colonel Morden at Harlowe Place; and it was proposed by your mother, and consented to, that I should be present. Your cousin, I understand, had with difficulty brought this meeting to bear; for your brother had before industriously avoided all conversation with him on the affecting subject; urging that it was not necessary to talk to Mr. Morden upon it, who, being a remoter relation than themselves, had no business to make himself a judge of their conduct to their daughter, their niece, and their sister; especially as he had declared himself in her favour; adding that he should hardly have patience to be questioned by Mr. Morden on that head.

I was in hopes that your mother would have given me an opportunity of talking with her alone before the company met; but she seemed studiously to avoid it: I dare say, however, not with her inclination.

I was ordered in just before Mr. Morden came; and was bid to sit down—which I did by the window.

The colonel, when he came, began the discourse by *renewing*, as he called it, his solicitations in your favour. He set before them your penitence; your ill-health; your virtue, though once betrayed and basely used: he then read to them Mr. Lovelace's letter, a most contrite one indeed [1]; and your *high-souled* answer [2]; for that was what he justly called it; and he treated as it deserved Mr. Brand's officious information (of which I had

<hr>

[1] See p. 90.   [2] See p. 99.

before heard he had made them ashamed), by representations founded upon inquiries made by Mr. Alston,[1] whom he had procured to go up on purpose to acquaint himself with your manner of life, and what was meant by the visits of that Mr. Belford.

He then told them that he had the day before waited upon Miss Howe, and had been shown a letter from you to her,[2] and permitted to take some memorandums from it, in which you appeared, both by handwriting and the contents, to be so very ill that it seemed doubtful to him if it were possible for you to get over it. And when he read to them that passage where you ask Miss Howe, "What can be done for you now, were your friends to be ever so favourable? and wish, for *their* sakes more than for your *own*, that they would still relent"; and then say, "You are very ill—you must drop your pen—and ask excuse for your crooked writing; and take, as it were, a last farewell of Miss Howe: *Adieu, my dear, adieu*," are your words—

O my child! my child! said your mamma, weeping, and clasping her hands.

Dear madam, said your brother, be so good as to think you have more children than this ungrateful one.

Yet your sister seemed affected.

Your Uncle Harlowe, wiping his eyes, O cousin, said he, if one thought the poor girl was really so ill——

She *must*, said your Uncle Antony. This is written to her private friend. God forbid she should be quite lost!

Your Uncle Harlowe wished they did not carry their resentments too far.

I begged for God's sake, wringing my hands, and with a bended knee, that they would permit me to go up to you; engaging to give them a faithful account of the way you were in. But I was chidden by your brother; and this occasioned some angry words between him and Mr. Morden.

I believe, sir, I believe, madam, said your sister to her father and mother, we need not trouble my cousin to read any more. It does but grieve and disturb you. My sister Clary seems to be ill: I think, if Mrs. Norton were permitted to go up to her, it would be right. Wickedly as she has acted, if she be truly penitent——

Here she stopped; and every one being silent, I stood up once more, and besought them to let me go: and then I offered to read a passage or two in your letter to me of the 24th. But

I was taken up again by your brother; and this occasioned still higher words between the colonel and him.

Your mother, hoping to gain upon your inflexible brother, and to divert the anger of the two gentlemen from each other, proposed that the colonel should proceed in reading the minutes he had taken from your letter.

He accordingly read "of your resuming your pen: that you thought you had taken your last farewell; and the rest of that very affecting passage in which you are obliged to break off more than once, and afterwards to take an airing in a chair." Your brother and sister were affected at this; and he had recourse to his snuff-box. And where you comfort Miss Howe, and say, "You shall be happy"; It is more, said he, than she will let anybody else be.

Your sister called you sweet soul; but with a low voice: then grew hard-hearted again; yet said nobody could help being affected by your pathetic grief—but that it was your talent.

The colonel then went on to the good effect your airing had upon you; to your good wishes to Miss Howe and Mr. Hickman; and to your concluding sentence, that when the happy life you wish to *her* comes to be wound up, she may be as calm and as easy at quitting it as you hope in God you shall be. Your mother could not stand this, but retired to a corner of the room, and sobbed and wept. Your father for a few minutes could not speak, though he seemed inclined to say something.

Your uncles were also both affected: but your brother went round to each; and again reminded your mother that she had other children: What was there, he said, in what was read, but the result of the talent you had of moving the passions? And he blamed them for choosing to hear read what they knew their abused indulgence could not be proof against.

This set Mr. Morden up again: Fie upon you, Cousin Harlowe! said he. I see plainly to whom it is owing that all relationship and ties of blood with regard to this sweet sufferer are laid aside. Such rigours as these make it difficult for a sliding virtue ever to recover itself.

Your brother pretended the honour of the family; and declared that no child ought to be forgiven who abandoned the most indulgent of parents against warning, against the light of knowledge, as you had done.

But, sir, and ladies, said I, rising from my seat in the window, and humbly turning round to each, if I may be permitted to speak, my dear miss asks only for a blessing. She does not beg to be received to favour: she is very ill, and asks only for a last blessing.

Come, come, goody Norton [I need not tell you who said this], you are up again with your lamentables! A good woman, as you are, to forgive so readily a crime that has been as disgraceful to your part in her education as to her family, is a weakness that would induce one to suspect your virtue if you were to be encountered by a temptation *properly adapted*.

By some such charitable logic, said Mr. Morden, as this is my Cousin Arabella captivated, I doubt not. If to be uncharitable and unforgiving is to give a proof of virtue, you, Mr. James Harlowe, are the most virtuous young man in the world.

I knew how it would be, replied your brother in a passion, if I met Mr. Morden upon this business. I would have declined it: but you, sir, to his father, would not permit me so to do.

But, sir, turning to the colonel, in no other presence——

Then, Cousin James, interrupted the other gentleman, that which is *your* protection, it seems, is *mine*. I am not used to bear defiances thus. You are my cousin, sir—and the son and nephew of persons as dear as near to me——There he paused.

Are we, said your father, to be made still more unhappy among ourselves, when the villain lives that ought to be the object of every one's resentment who has either a value for the family or for this ungrateful girl?

That's the man, said your cousin, whom last Monday, as you know, I went purposely to make the object of mine. But what could I say when I found him so willing to repair his crime? And I give it as my opinion, and have written accordingly to my poor cousin, that it is best for all round that his offer should be accepted: and let me tell you——

Tell me nothing, said your father, quite enraged, of that very vile fellow! I have a riveted hatred to him. I would rather see the rebel die a hundred deaths, were it possible, than that she should give such a villain as him a relation to my family.

Well, but there is no room to think, said your mother, that she *will* give us such a relation, my dear. The poor girl will lessen, I fear, the number of our relations; not increase it. If she be so ill as we are told she is, let us send Mrs. Norton up to her. That's the *least* we can do. Let us take her, however, out of the hands of that Belford.

Both your uncles supported this motion; the latter part of it especially.

Your brother observed, in his ill-natured way, what a fine

piece of consistency it was in you, to refuse the vile injurer and the amends he offered; yet to throw yourself upon the protection of his fast friend.

Miss Harlowe was apprehensive, she said, that you would leave all you *could* leave to that pert creature Miss Howe [so she called her] if you should die.

Oh, do not, do not suppose *that*, my Bella, said your poor mother. I cannot think of parting with my Clary. With all her faults, she is my child. Her reasons for her conduct are not heard. It would break my heart to lose her. I think, my dear, to your father, none so fit as I to go up, if you will give me leave: and Mrs. Norton shall accompany me.

This was a sweet motion; and your father paused upon it. Mr. Morden offered his service to escort her. Your uncles seemed to approve of it. But your brother dashed all. I hope, sir, said he to his father; I hope, madam, to his mother, that you will not endeavour to recover a faulty daughter by losing an inculpable son. I do declare, that if ever my Sister Clary darkens these doors again, I never will. I will set out, madam, the same hour you go to London (on such an errand), to Edinburgh; and there I will reside; and try to forget that I have relations in England so near and so dear as you are now all to me.

Good God! said the colonel, what a declaration is this! And suppose, sir, and suppose, madam [turning to your father and mother], this *should* be the case, whether is it better, think you, that you should lose for ever such a daughter as my Cousin Clary, or that your son should go to Edinburgh, and reside there upon an estate which will be the better for his residence upon it?

Your brother's passionate behaviour hereupon is hardly to be described. He resented it, as promoting an alienation of the affection of the family to him. And to such a height were resentments carried, every one siding with him, that the colonel, with hands and eyes lifted up, cried out: What hearts of flint am I related to! O Cousin Harlowe, to your father, are you resolved to have had but one daughter? Are you, madam, to be taught, by a son who has no bowels, to forget that you are a mother?

The colonel turned from them to draw out his handkerchief, and could not for a minute speak. The eyes of every one but the hard-hearted brother caught tears from his.

But then turning to them (with the more indignation, as it seemed, as he had been obliged to show a humanity which, however, no brave heart should be ashamed of), I leave ye all, said he, fit company for one another. I will never open my lips to any of you more upon this subject. I will instantly make my will, and in me shall the dear creature have the father, uncle, brother she has lost. I will prevail upon her to take the tour of France and Italy with me; nor shall she return till ye know the value of *such* a daughter.

And saying this he hurried out of the room, went into the courtyard, and ordered his horse.

Mr. Antony Harlowe went to him there, just as he was mounting; and said he hoped he should find him cooler in the evening (for he till then had lodged at his house), and that then they would converse calmly; and every one, meantime, would weigh all matters well. But the angry gentleman said: Cousin Harlowe, I shall endeavour to discharge the obligations I owe to your civility since I have been in England: but I have been so treated by that hot-headed young man (who, as far as I know, has done more to ruin his sister than Lovelace himself, and *this* with the approbation of you all), that I will not again enter into *your* doors or *theirs*. My servants shall have orders whither to bring what belongs to me from your house. I will see my dear Cousin Clary as soon as I can. And so God bless you all together! Only this one word to your nephew, if you please: That he wants to be taught the difference between courage and bluster; and it is happy for him, perhaps, that I am *his* kinsman; though I am sorry he is *mine*.

I wondered to hear your uncle, on his return to them all, repeat this; because of the consequences it may be attended with, though I hope it will not have bad ones: yet it was considered as a sort of challenge, and so it confirmed everybody in your brother's favour; and Miss Harlowe forgot not to inveigh against that error which had brought on all these evils.

I took the liberty again, but with fear and trembling, to desire leave to attend you.

Before any other person could answer, your brother said: I suppose you look upon yourself, Mrs. Norton, to be your own mistress. Pray do you want our consents and *courtship* to go up? If I may speak my mind, you and my Sister Clary are the *fittest* to be together. Yet I wish you would not trouble your head about our family matters till you are desired to do so.

But don't you know, brother, said Miss Harlowe, that the error of any branch of a family splits that family into two parties, and makes not only every common friend and acquaintance, but even *servants*, judges over both? This is one of the blessed effects of my Sister Clary's fault!

There never was a creature so criminal, said your father, looking with displeasure at me, who had not some weak heads to pity and side with her.

I wept. Your mother was so good as to take me by the hand: Come, good woman, said she, come along with me. You have too much reason to be afflicted with what afflicts us, to want additions to your grief.

But, my dearest young lady, I was more touched for your sake than for my own: for I have been low in the world for a great number of years; and, of consequence, must have been accustomed to snubs and rebuffs from the affluent. But I hope that patience is written as legibly on my forehead as haughtiness on that of any of my obligers.

Your mother led me to her chamber; and there we sat and wept together for several minutes without being able to speak either of us one word to the other. At last she broke silence; asking me if you were really and indeed so ill as it was said you were?

I answered in the affirmative; and would have shown her your last letter; but she declined seeing it.

I would fain have procured from her the favour of a line to you, with her blessing. I asked what was *intended* by your brother and sister? Would nothing satisfy them but your final reprobation? I insinuated how easy it would be, did not your duty and humility govern you, to make yourself independent as to circumstances; but that nothing but a blessing, a *last* blessing, was requested by you. And many other things I urged in your behalf. The following brief repetition of what she was pleased to say in answer to my pleas will give you a notion of it all; and of the present situation of things.

She said: "She was very unhappy! She had lost the little authority she once had over her other children, through one child's failing; and all influence over Mr. Harlowe and his brothers. Your father, she said, had besought her to leave it to him to take his own methods with you; and (as she valued him) to take no step in your favour unknown to him and your uncles: yet she owned that they were too much governed by your brother. They would, however, give way in time, she knew, to a reconciliation: they designed no other; for they all still loved you.

"Your brother and sister, she owned, were very jealous of

your coming into favour again: yet, could but Mr. Morden have kept his temper, and stood her son's first sallies, who (having always had the family grandeur in view) had carried his resentment so high that he knew not how to descend, the conferences, so abruptly broken off just now, would have ended more happily; for that she had reason to think that a few concessions on your part with regard to your grandfather's estate, and your cousin's engaging for your submission as from *proper* motives, would have softened them all.

"Mr. Brand's account of your intimacy with the friend of the obnoxious man, she said, had, for the time, very unhappy effects; for before that she had gained some ground: but afterwards dared not, nor indeed had inclination, to open her lips in your behalf.   Your continued intimacy with that Mr. Belford was wholly unaccountable, and as wholly inexcusable.

"What made the wished-for reconciliation, she said, more difficult was, first, that you yourself acknowledged yourself dishonoured (and it was too well known that it was your own fault that you ever were in the power of so great a profligate); of consequence, that their and your disgrace could not be greater than it was: yet that you refused to prosecute the wretch.   Next, that the pardon and blessing hoped for must probably be attended with your marriage to the man they hate, and who hates them as much: very disagreeable circumstances, she said, I must allow, to found a reconciliation upon.

"As to her own part, she needs must say that if there were any hope that Mr. Lovelace would become a reformed man, the letter her Cousin Morden had read to them from him to you, and the justice (as she hoped it was) he did your character, though to his own condemnation (his family and fortunes being unexceptionable), and all his relations earnest to be related to you, were arguments that would have weight with her, could they have any with your father and uncles."

To my plea of your illness: "She could not but flatter herself, she answered, that it was from lowness of spirits and temporary dejection.   A young creature, she said, so very considerate as you naturally were, and fallen so low, must have enough of that.   Should they lose you, which God forbid! the scene would then indeed be sadly changed; for then those who now most resented would be most grieved; all your fine qualities would rise to their remembrance, and your unhappy error would be quite forgotten.

"She wished you would put yourself into your cousin's

protection entirely, and have nothing more to say to Mr. Belford."

And I would recommend it to your most serious consideration, my dear Miss Clary, whether now, as your cousin (who is your trustee for your grandfather's estate) is come, you should not give over all thoughts of Mr. Lovelace's intimate friend for your executor; more especially as that gentleman's interfering in the concerns of your family, should the sad event take place (which my heart aches but to think of), might be attended with those consequences which you are so desirous in other cases to obviate and prevent. And suppose, my dear young lady, you were to write one letter more to each of your uncles, to let them know how ill you are? and to ask their advice, and offer to be governed by it, in relation to the disposition of your estate and effects? Methinks I wish you would.

I find they will send you up a large part of what has been received from that estate since it was yours; together with your current cash which you left behind you: and this by your Cousin Morden, for fear you should have contracted debts which may make you uneasy.

They seem to expect that you will wish to live at your grand-father's house, in a private manner, if your cousin prevail not upon you to go abroad for a year or two.

Friday Morning.

Betty was with me just now. She tells me that your Cousin Morden is so much displeased with them all that he has refused to lodge any more at your Uncle Antony's; and has even taken up with inconvenient lodgings till he is provided with others to his mind. This very much concerns them; and they repent their violent treatment of him: and the more as he is resolved, he says, to make you his sole executrix, and heir to all his fortune.

What noble fortunes still, my dearest young lady, await you! I am thoroughly convinced, if it please God to preserve your life and your health, that everybody will soon be reconciled to you, and that you will see many happy days.

Your mother wished me not to attend you as yet, because she hopes that I may give myself that pleasure soon with every-body's good liking, and even at their desire. Your Cousin Morden's reconciliation with them, which they are very desirous of, I am ready to hope will include theirs with you.

But if that should happen which I so much dread, and I not

with you, I should never forgive myself. Let me, therefore, my dearest young lady, desire you to command my attendance, if you find any danger, and if you wish me peace of mind; and no consideration shall withhold me.

I hear that Miss Howe has obtained leave from her mother to see you; and intends next week to go to town for that purpose; and (as it is believed) to buy clothes for her approaching nuptials.

Mr. Hickman's mother-in-law is lately dead. Her jointure of £600 a year is fallen in to him; and she has, moreover, as an acknowledgment of his good behaviour to her, left him all she was worth, which was very considerable, a few legacies excepted to her own relations.

These good men are uniformly good: indeed could not else *be* good; and never fare the worse for being so. All the world agrees he will make that fine young lady an excellent husband: and I am sorry they are not as much agreed in her making him an excellent wife. But I hope a woman of her principles would not encourage his address if, whether she at present love him or not, she thought she could *not* love him; or if she preferred any other man to him.

Mr. Pocock undertakes to deliver this; but fears it will be Saturday night first, if not Sunday morning.

May the Almighty protect and bless you! I long to see you —my dearest young lady, I long to see you; and to fold you once more to my fond heart. I dare to say happy days are coming. Be but cheerful. Give way to hope.

Whether for this world, or the other, you *must* be happy. Wish to live, however, were it only because you are so well fitted in mind to make every one happy who has the honour to know you. What signifies this transitory eclipse? You are as near perfection, by all I have heard, as any creature in this world can be: for here is your glory: you are brightened and purified, as I may say, by your sufferings! How I long to hear your whole sad, yet instructive story, from your own lips!

For Miss Howe's sake, who, in her new engagements, will so much want you; for your Cousin Morden's sake; for your mother's sake, if I must go no farther in your family; and yet I can say, for all their sakes; and for my sake, my dearest Miss Clary; let your resumed and accustomed magnanimity bear you up. You have many things to do which I know not the person who will if you leave us.

Join your prayers then to mine, that God will spare you to a world that wants you and your example; and, although your days may seem to have been numbered, who knows but that, with the good King Hezekiah, you may have them prolonged? Which God grant, if it be His blessed will, to the prayers of

Your JUDITH NORTON.

Letter XCIX—Mr. Belford to Robert Lovelace, Esq.

Monday, Sept. 4.

THE lady would not read the letter she had from Mrs. Norton till she had received the Communion, for fear it should contain anything that might disturb that happy calm which she had been endeavouring to obtain for it. And when that solemn office was over, she was so composed, she said, that she thought she could receive any news, however affecting, with tranquillity.

Nevertheless, in reading it, she was forced to leave off several times through weakness and a dimness in her sight, of which she complained; if I may say *complained*; for so easy and soft were her complaints that they could hardly be called such.

She was very much affected at divers parts of this letter. She wept several times, and sighed often. Mrs. Lovick told me that these were the gentle exclamations she broke out into as she read: *Her unkind, her cruel brother! How* unsisterly! *Poor dear woman!* seeming to speak of Mrs. Norton. *Her kind cousin! Oh, these flaming spirits!* And then reflecting upon herself more than once: *What a deep error is mine! What evils have I been the occasion of!*

When I was admitted to her presence, I have received, said she, a long and not very pleasing letter from my dear Mrs. Norton. It will soon be in your hands. I am advised against appointing you to the office you have so kindly accepted of: but you must resent nothing of these things. My choice will have an odd appearance to them: but it is now too late to alter it if I would.

I would fain write an answer to it, continued she: but I have no distinct sight, Mr. Belford, no steadiness of fingers. This mistiness, however, will perhaps be gone by and by. Then turning to Mrs. Lovick: I don't think I am dying yet—not *actually* dying, Mrs. Lovick—for I have no bodily pain—no numbnesses; no signs of immediate death, I think.—And my breath, which used of late to be so short, is now tolerable, my head clear, my intellects free—I think I cannot be dying yet—I shall have agonies, I doubt—life will not give up so blessedly easy, I fear—yet how merciful is the Almighty, to give His poor creature such a sweet serenity! 'Tis what I have prayed for! What encouragement, Mrs. Lovick, so near one's dissolution, to have it to hope that one's prayers are answered!

Mrs. Smith, as well as Mrs. Lovick, was with her. They were both in tears; nor had I, any more than they, power to say a word in answer: yet she spoke all this, as well as what follows, with a surprising composure of mind and countenance.

But, Mr. Belford, said she, assuming a still sprightlier air and accent, let me talk a little to you, while I am thus able to say what I have to say.

Mrs. Lovick, don't leave us [for the women were rising to go]—pray sit down; and do you, Mrs. Smith, sit down too. Dame Shelburne, take this key, and open that upper drawer. I will move to it.

She did, with trembling knees. Here, Mr. Belford, is my will. It is witnessed by three persons of Mr. Smith's acquaintance.

I dare to hope that my Cousin Morden will give you assistance, if you request it of him. My Cousin Morden continues his affection for me: but as I have not seen *him*, I leave all the trouble upon *you*, Mr. Belford. This deed may want *forms*; and it *does*, no doubt: but the less, as I have my grandfather's will almost by heart, and have *often enough* heard that canvassed. I will lay it by itself in this corner; putting it at the farther end of the drawer.

She then took up a parcel of letters, enclosed in one cover, sealed with three seals of black wax: This, said she, I sealed up last night. The cover, sir, will let you know what is to be done with what it encloses. This is the superscription [holding it close to her eyes, and rubbing them]: *As soon as I am certainly dead, this to be broke open by Mr. Belford.* Here, sir, I put it [placing it by the will]. These folded papers are letters and copies of letters, disposed according to their dates. Miss Howe will do with those as you and she shall think fit. If I receive any more, or more come when I cannot receive them, they may be put into this drawer [pulling out and pushing in the looking-glass drawer], to be given to Mr. Belford, be they from whom they will: you 'll be so kind as to observe that, Mrs. Lovick, and Dame Shelburne.

Here, sir, proceeded she, I put the keys of my apparel [putting them into the drawer with her papers]. All is in order, and the inventory upon them, and an account of what I have disposed of: so that nobody need to ask Mrs. Smith any questions.

There will be no immediate need to open or inspect the trunks which contain my wearing apparel. Mrs. Norton will open them, or order somebody to do it for her, in your presence, Mrs. Lovick; for so I have directed in my will. They may be sealed up now: I shall never more have occasion to open them.

She then, though I expostulated with her to the contrary, caused me to seal them up with my seal.

After this she locked the drawer where were her papers; first taking out her book of *Meditations*, as she called it; saying she should perhaps have use for that; and then desired me to take the key of that drawer; for she should have no further occasion for that neither.

All this in so composed and cheerful a manner that we were equally surprised and affected with it.

You can witness for me, Mrs. Smith, and so can you, Mrs. Lovick, proceeded she, if any one ask after my life and conversation since you have known me, that I have been very orderly; have kept good hours; and never have lain out of your house but when I was in prison; and then, you know, I could not help it.

O Lovelace! that thou hadst heard her, or seen her, unknown to herself, on this occasion! Not one of us could speak a word.

I shall leave the world in perfect charity, proceeded she. And turning towards the women: Don't be so much concerned for me, my good friends. This is all but needful preparation; and I shall be very happy.

Then again rubbing her eyes, which she said were misty, and looking more intently round upon each, particularly on me: God bless you all! said she; how kindly are you concerned for me! Who says I am friendless? Who says I am abandoned and among strangers? Good Mr. Belford, don't be so *generously* humane! Indeed [putting her handkerchief to her charming eyes] you will make me less happy than I am sure you wish me to be.

While we were thus solemnly engaged, a servant came with a letter from her Cousin Morden: Then, said she, he is not come *himself*!

She broke it open; but every line, she said, appeared two to her: so that, being unable to read it herself, she desired I would read it to her. I did so; and wished it were more consolatory to her: but she was all patient attention; tears, however, often trickling down her cheeks. By the date it was written yesterday; and this is the substance of it:

He tells her, "That the Thursday before he had procured a general meeting of her principal relations at her father's; though not without difficulty, her haughty brother opposing it, and, when met, rendering all his endeavours to reconcile them to her ineffectual. He censures him as the most ungovernable young man he ever knew. Some great sickness, he says, some heavy misfortune, is wanted to bring him to a knowledge of himself, and of what is due from him to others; and he wishes that he were not *her* brother, and *his* cousin. Nor does he spare her father and uncles for being so implicitly led by him."

He tells her, "That he parted with them all in high displeasure, and thought never more to darken any of their doors: that he declared as much to her two uncles, who came to him on Saturday to try to accommodate with him; and who found him preparing to go to London to attend her; and that, notwithstanding their pressing entreaties, he determined so to do, and not to go with them to Harlowe Place, or to either of their own houses; and accordingly dismissed them with such an answer.

"But that her noble letter, as he calls it, of Aug. 31,[1] being brought him about an hour after their departure, he thought it might affect them as much as it did him; and give them the exalted opinion of her virtue which was so well deserved; he therefore turned his horse's head back to her Uncle Antony's, instead of forward towards London.

"That accordingly arriving there, and finding her two uncles together, he read to them the affecting letter; which left none of the three a dry eye: that the absent, as is usual in such cases, bearing all the load, they accused her brother and sister; and besought him to put off his journey to town till he could carry with him the blessings which she had formerly in vain solicited for; and (as they hoped) the happy tidings of a general reconciliation.

"That not doubting but his visit would be the more welcome to her if these good ends could be obtained, he the more readily complied with their desires. But not being willing to subject himself to the possibility of receiving fresh insults from her brother, he had given her uncles a copy of her letter for the family to assemble upon; and desired to know, as soon as possible, the result of their deliberations.

"He tells her that he shall bring her up the accounts relating to the produce of her grandfather's estate, and adjust them with her; having actually in his hands due to her from it.

"He highly applauds the noble manner in which she resents your usage of her. It is impossible, he owns, that you can either deserve her or to be forgiven. But as you do justice to

[1] See Letter xxxvii.

her virtue, and offer to make her all the reparation now in your power; and as she is so very earnest with him not to resent that usage; and declares that you could not have been the author of her calamities but through a strange concurrence of unhappy causes; and as he is not at a loss to know how to place to a *proper account* that strange concurrence; he desires her not to be apprehensive of any vindictive measures from him."

Nevertheless (as may be expected) "he inveighs against you; as he finds that she gave you no advantage over her. But he forbears to enter further into this subject, he says, till he has the honour to see her; and the rather as she seems so much determined against you. However, he cannot but say that he thinks you a gallant man, and a man of sense; and that you have the reputation of being thought a generous man in every instance but where the sex is concerned. In *such*, he owns that you have taken inexcusable liberties. And he is sorry to say that there are very few young men of fortune but who allow themselves in the same. Both sexes, he observes, too much love to have each other in their power: yet he hardly ever knew man or woman who was very fond of power make a right use of it.

"If she be so absolutely determined against marrying you, as she declares she is, he hopes, he says, to prevail upon her to take (as soon as her health will permit) a little tour abroad with him, as what will probably establish it; since travelling is certainly the best physic for all those disorders which owe their rise to grief or disappointment. An absence of two or three years will endear her to every one on her return, and every one to her.

"He expresses his impatience to see her. He will set out, he says, the moment he knows the result of her family's determination; which, he doubts not, will be favourable. Nor will he wait long for that."

When I had read the letter through to the languishing lady: And so, my friends, said she, have I heard of a patient who actually died while five or six principal physicians were in a consultation, and not agreed upon what name to give to his distemper. The patient was an emperor: the Emperor Joseph, I think.

I asked if I should write to her cousin, as he knew not how ill she was, to hasten up.

By no means, she said; since, if he were not already set out, she was persuaded that she should be so low by the time he could receive my letter and come, that his presence would but discompose and hurry *her*, and afflict *him*.

I hope, however, she is not so very near her end. And without saying any more to her, when I retired I wrote to Colonel Morden that, if he expects to see his beloved cousin alive, he must lose no time in setting out. I sent this letter by his own servant.

Dr. H. sent away *his* letter to her father by a particular hand this morning.

Mrs. Walton, the milliner, has also just now acquainted Mrs. Smith that her husband had a letter brought by a special messenger from Parson Brand within this half-hour, enclosing the copy of one he had written to Mr. John Harlowe recanting his officious one.

And as all these, and the copy of the lady's letter to Col. Morden, will be with them pretty much at a time, the devil's in the family if they are not struck with a remorse that shall burst open the double-barred doors of their hearts.

Will engages to reach you with this (late as it will be) before you go to rest. He begs that I will testify for him the hour and the minute I shall give it him. It is just half an hour after ten.

I pretend to be (now by use) the swiftest shorthand writer in England, next to yourself. But were matter to arise every hour to write upon, and I had nothing else to do, I cannot write so fast as you expect. And let it be remembered that your servants cannot bring letters or messages before they are written or sent.

J. BELFORD.

Letter C—Dr. H. to James Harlow, senior, Esq.

London, Sept. 4.

SIR.—If I may judge of the hearts of other parents by my own, I cannot doubt but you will take it well to be informed that you have yet an opportunity to save yourself and family great future regret, by dispatching hither some one of it, with your last blessing and your lady's, to the most excellent of her sex.

I have some reason to believe, sir, that she has been represented to you in a very different light from the true one. And this it is that induces me to acquaint you that I think her, on the best grounds, absolutely irreproachable in all her conduct which has passed under my eye, or come to my ear; and that her very misfortunes are made glorious to her, and honourable to all

that are related to her, by the use she has made of them; and by
the patience and resignation with which she supports herself
in a painful, lingering, and dispiriting decay; and by the greatness of mind with which she views her approaching dissolution.
And all this from proper motives; from motives in which a
dying saint might glory.

She knows not that I write. I must indeed acknowledge
that I offered to do so some days ago, and that very pressingly:
nor did she refuse me from obstinacy—she seems not to know
what that is—but desired me to forbear for two days only, in
hopes that her newly arrived cousin, who, as she heard, was
soliciting for her, would be able to succeed in her favour.

I hope I shall not be thought an officious man on this occasion:
but if I am, I cannot help it; being driven to write by a kind of
parental and irresistible impulse.

But, sir, whatever you think fit to do, or permit to be done,
must be speedily done; for she cannot, I verily think, live a
week: and how long of that short space she may enjoy her
admirable intellects to take comfort in the favours you may
think proper to confer upon her, cannot be said. I am, sir,

> Your most humble servant,
>   R. H.

Letter CI—*Mr. Belford to William Morden, Esq.*

London, Sept. 4.

Sir,—The urgency of the case, and the opportunity by your
servant, will sufficiently apologize for this trouble from a
stranger to your person; who, however, is not a stranger to
your merit.

I understand you are employing your good offices with the
parents of Miss Clarissa Harlowe, and other relations, to reconcile
them to the most meritorious daughter and kinswoman that
ever family had to boast of.

Generously as this is intended by you, we *here* have too much
reason to think all your solicitudes on this head will be unnecessary: for it is the opinion of every one who has the honour of
being admitted to her presence, that she cannot live over three
days: so that if you wish to see her alive you must lose no time
to come up.

She knows not that I write. I had done it sooner if I had had
the least doubt that before now she would not have received

from you some news of the happy effects of your kind mediation in her behalf.   I am, sir,

Your most humble servant,

J. Belford.

Letter CII—Mr. Lovelace to John Belford, Esq.

[*In answer to Letter* xcix, *p.* 288]

Uxbridge, Tuesday Morn. between 4 and 5.

And can it be that this admirable creature will so soon leave this cursed world?   For cursed I shall think it, and more cursed myself, when she is gone.   O Jack! thou, who canst sit so cool and, like Addison's Angel, *direct*, and even *enjoy*, the storm that tears up my happiness by the roots, blame me not for my impatience, however unreasonable!   If thou knewest that already I feel the torments of the damned, in the remorse that wrings my heart on looking back upon my past actions by her, thou wouldst not be the devil thou art, to halloo on a worrying conscience which, without thy merciless aggravations, is altogether intolerable.

I know not what I write, nor what I would write.   When the company that used to delight me is as uneasy to me as my reflections are painful, and I can neither help nor divert myself, must not every servant about me partake in a perturbation so sincere?

Shall I give thee a faint picture of the horrible uneasiness with which my mind struggles?   And faint indeed it must be; for nothing but outrageous madness can exceed it; and *that* only in the apprehension of others; since, as to the sufferer, it is certain that actual distraction (take it out of its lucid intervals) must be an infinitely more happy state than the state of suspense and anxiety which often brings it on.

Forbidden to attend the dear creature, yet longing to see her, I would give the world to be admitted once more to her beloved presence.   I ride towards London three or four times a day, resolving pro and con twenty times in two or three miles; and at last ride back; and, in view of Uxbridge, loathing even the kind friend and hospitable house, turn my horse's head again towards the town, and resolve to gratify my humour, let her take it as she will; but, at the very entrance of it, after infinite canvassings, once more alter my mind, dreading to offend and shock her, lest by that means I should curtail a life so precious.

Yesterday, in particular, to give you an idea of the strength of that impatience, which I cannot avoid suffering to break out upon my servants, I had no sooner dispatched Will than I took horse to meet him on his return.

In order to give him time, I loitered about on the road, riding up *this* lane to the one highway, down *that* to the other, just as my horse pointed; all the way cursing my very being; and though so lately looking *down* upon all the world, wishing to change conditions with the poorest beggar that cried to me for charity as I rode by him—and throwing him money, in hopes to obtain by his prayers the blessing my heart pants after.

After I had sauntered about an hour or two (which seemed three or four tedious ones), fearing I had slipped the fellow, I inquired at every turnpike whether a servant in such a livery had not passed through in his return from London, on a full gallop; for woe had been to the dog had I met him on a sluggish trot! And lest I should miss him at one end of Kensington, as he might take either the Acton or Hammersmith Road; or at the other, as he might come through the Park, or not; how many score times did I ride backwards and forwards from the Palace to the Gore, making myself the subject of observation to all passengers, whether on horseback or on foot; who, no doubt, wondered to see a well-dressed and well-mounted man, some-times ambling, sometimes prancing (as the beast had more fire than his master) backwards and forwards in so short a compass!

Yet all this time, though longing to espy the fellow, did I dread to meet him, lest he should be charged with fatal tidings.

When at distance I saw any man galloping towards me, my resemblance-forming fancy immediately made it to be him; and then my heart bounded to my mouth, as if it would have choked me. But when the person's nearer approach undeceived me, how did I curse the varlet's delay, and thee, by turns; and how ready was I to draw my pistol at the stranger for having the impudence to gallop; which none but my messenger, I thought, had either right or reason to do! For all the business of the world, I am ready to imagine, should stand still on an occasion so melancholy and so interesting to me. Nay, for this week past I could cut the throat of any man or woman I see laugh, while I am in such dejection of mind.

I am now convinced that the wretches who fly from a heavy scene labour under ten times more distress in the intermediate suspense and apprehension, than they could have were they present at it, and to see and know the worst: so capable is fancy or imagination, the more immediate offspring of the soul, to outgo fact, let the subject be either joyous or grievous.

And hence, as I conceive, it is that all *pleasures* are greater in the *expectation*, or in the *reflection*, than in *fruition*; as all *pains*, which press heavy upon both parts of that unequal union by which frail mortality holds its precarious tenure, are ever most acute in the time of suffering: for how easy sit upon the *reflection* the heaviest misfortunes when surmounted!—But *most* easy, I confess, those in which body has more concern than soul. This, however, is a point of philosophy I have neither time nor head just now to weigh: so take it as it falls from a madman's pen.

Woe be to either of the wretches who shall bring me the fatal news that she is no more! For it is but too likely that a shriek-owl so hated will never hoot or scream again; unless the shock, that will probably disorder my whole frame on so sad an occasion (by *unsteadying* my hand), shall divert my aim from his head, heart, or bowels, if it turn not against my own.

But, surely, she will not, she cannot yet die! Such a matchless excellence,

———————whose mind
Contains a world, and seems for all things fram'd,

could not be lent to be so soon demanded back again!

But may it not be that thou, Belford, art in a plot with the dear creature (who will not let me attend her to convince myself), in order to work up my soul to the deepest remorse; and that, when she is convinced of the sincerity of my penitence, and when my mind is made such wax as to be fit to take what impression she pleases to give it, she will then raise me up with the joyful tidings of her returning health and acceptance of me?

What would I give to have it so! And when the happiness of *hundreds*, as well as the peace and reconciliation of several eminent families, depend upon *her* restoration and happiness, why should it not be so?

But let me presume it will. Let me indulge my former hope, however improbable—I *will*; and *enjoy* it, too. And let me tell thee how ecstatic my delight would be on the unravelling of such a plot as this!

Do, *dear* Belford, let it be so! And, O my dearest, and ever-dear Clarissa, keep me no longer in this cruel suspense; in which I suffer a thousand times more than ever I made thee suffer. Nor fear thou that I will resent, or recede, on an *éclaircissement* so desirable: for I will adore thee for ever, and, without reproaching thee for the pangs thou hast tortured me with, confess thee as much my superior in noble and generous contrivances as thou art in virtue and honour!

But, once more—should the worst happen—say not what that worst is—and I am gone from this hated island—gone for ever—and may eternal—but I am crazed already—and will therefore conclude myself,

Thine more than my own,

(And no great compliment neither)

R. L.

Letter CIII—Mr. Belford to Robert Lovelace, Esq.

Tuesday, 5 Sept., 9 in the Morn. at Mr. Smith's.

WHEN I read yours of this morning, I could not help pitying you for the account you give of the dreadful anxiety and suspense you labour under. I wish from my heart all were to end as you are so willing to hope: but it will not be; and your suspense, if the worst part of your torment, as you say it is, will soon be over; but, alas! in a way you wish not.

I attended the lady just now. She is extremely ill: yet is she aiming at an answer to her Norton's letter, which she began yesterday in her own chamber, and has written a good deal; but in a hand not like her own fine one, as Mrs. Lovick tells me, but much larger, and the lines crooked.

I have accepted of the offer of a room adjoining to the Widow Lovick's, till I see how matters go; but unknown to the lady; and I shall go home every night for a few hours. I would not lose a sentence that I could gain from lips so instructive, nor the opportunity of receiving any command from her, for an estate.

In this my new apartment I now write, and shall continue to write as occasions offer, that I may be the more circumstantial: but I depend upon the return of my letters, or copies of them, on demand, that I may have together all that relates to this affecting story; which I shall reperuse with melancholy pleasure to the end of my life.

I think I will send thee Brand's letter to Mr. John Harlowe, recanting his base surmises. It is a matchless piece of pedantry; and may perhaps a little divert thy deep chagrin: some time hence at least it may, if not now.

What wretched creatures are there in the world! What

strangely mixed characters! So sensible and so silly at the same time! What a *various*, what a *foolish* creature is man!

Three o'clock.

The lady has just finished her letter, and has entertained Mrs. Lovick, Mrs. Smith, and me with a noble discourse on the vanity and brevity of life, to which I cannot do justice in the repetition: and indeed I am so grieved for her that, ill as she is, my intellects are not half so clear as hers.

A few things which made the strongest impression upon me, as well from the sentiments themselves as from her manner of uttering them, I remember. She introduced them thus:

I am thinking, said she, what a gradual and happy death God Almighty (blessed be His Name!) affords me! Who would have thought that, suffering what I have suffered, and abandoned as I have been, with such a tender education as I have had, I should be so long a dying! But see how by little and little it has come to this. I was first taken off from the power of *walking*: then I took a *coach*. A coach grew too violent an exercise: then I took a *chair*. The prison was a large DEATH-STRIDE upon me —I should have *suffered longer else*! Next, I was unable to go to *church*; then to go *up* or *down stairs*; now hardly can move from one *room* to *another*; and a *less room* will soon hold me. My *eyes* begin to fail me, so that at times I cannot see to read distinctly; and now I can hardly *write*, or hold a pen. Next, I presume, I shall know nobody, nor be able to thank any of you: I therefore now once more thank you, Mrs. Lovick, and you, Mrs. Smith, and you, Mr. Belford, while I *can* thank you, for all your kindness to me. And thus by little and little, in such a gradual sensible death as I am blessed with, God *dies away in us*, as I may say, all human satisfactions, in order to subdue His poor creatures to Himself.

Thou mayst guess how affected we all were at this moving account of her progressive weakness. We heard it with wet eyes; for what with the women's example, and what with her moving eloquence, I could no more help it than they. But we were silent nevertheless; and she went on, applying herself to me.

O Mr. Belford! This is a poor transitory life in its best enjoyments. We flutter about here and there, with all our vanities about us, like painted butterflies, for a gay but a very short season, till at last we lay ourselves down in a quiescent state, and turn into vile worms: and who knows in what form, or to what condition, we shall rise again?

I wish you would permit me, a young creature, just turned of nineteen years of age, blooming and healthy as I was a few months ago, now nipped by the cold hand of death, to influence you, in *these my last hours*, to a life of regularity and repentance for any past evils you may have been guilty of. For, believe me, sir, that now, in this last stage, very few things will bear the test, or be passed as laudable, if *pardonable*, at our own bar, much less at a more tremendous one, in all we have done, or delighted in, even in a life not very offensive neither, as *we* may think! Ought we not then to study in our *full day*, before the dark hours approach, so to live, as may afford reflections that will soften the agony of the last moments when they come, and let in upon the departing soul a ray of Divine mercy to illuminate its passage into an awful eternity?

She was ready to faint, and, choosing to lie down, I withdrew; I need not say, with a melancholy heart: and when I was got to my new-taken apartment, my heart was still more affected by the sight of the solemn letter the admirable lady had so lately finished. It was communicated to me by Mrs. Lovick; who had it to copy for me; but it was not to be *delivered to me* till after her departure. However, I trespassed so far as to prevail upon the widow to let me take a copy of it; which I did directly in character.

I send it enclosed. If thou canst read it, and thy heart not bleed at thy eyes, thy remorse can hardly be so deep as thou hast inclined me to think it is.

Letter CIV—*Miss Clarissa Harlowe to Mrs. Norton*
[*In answer to Letter XCVIII*] [1]

MY DEAREST MRS. NORTON,—I am afraid I shall not be able to write all that is upon my mind to say to you upon the subject of your last. Yet I will try.

As to my friends, and as to the sad breakfasting, I cannot help being afflicted for *them*. What, alas! has not my mother, in particular, suffered by my rashness! Yet to allow so much for a son!—so little for a daughter! But all now will soon be over, as to me. I hope they will bury all their resentments in my grave.

As to your advice in relation to Mr. Belford, let me only say

---

[1] Begun on Monday, Sept. 4, and by piecemeal finished on Tuesday; but not sent till the Thursday following.

that the unhappy reprobation I have met with, and my short
time, must be my apology now. I wish I *could* have written to
my mother and my uncles, as you advise. And yet favours
come *so* slowly from them!

The granting of one request only now remains as a desirable
one from them; which nevertheless, when granted, I shall not be
sensible of. It is that they will be pleased to permit my remains
to be laid with those of my ancestors—placed at the feet of my
dear grandfather—as I have mentioned in my will. This, however, as they please. For, after all, this vile body ought not so
much to engage my cares. It is a weakness—but let it be
called a *natural* weakness, and I shall be excused; especially
when a reverential gratitude shall be known to be the foundation
of it. You know, my dear woman, how my grandfather loved
me. And you know how much I honoured him, and that from
my very infancy to the hour of his death How often since have
I wished that he had not loved *me* so well!

I wish not now, at the writing of this, to see even my Cousin
Morden. O my blessed woman! My dear maternal friend!
I am entering upon a better tour than to France or Italy either!
or even than to settle at my once beloved Dairy-house! All
these prospects and pleasures, which used to be so agreeable to
me in health, how poor seem they to me now!

Indeed, indeed, my dear Mamma Norton, I shall be happy!
I *know* I shall! I have charming forebodings of happiness
already! Tell all my dear friends, for their comfort, that
I shall! Who would not bear the punishments I have borne,
to have the prospects and assurances I rejoice in! Assurances
I might *not have had,* were my own wishes to have been granted
to me!

Neither do I want to see even *you,* my dear Mrs. Norton.
Nevertheless I must, in justice to my own gratitude, declare
that there *was* a time, could you have been permitted to come,
without incurring displeasure from those whose esteem it is
necessary for you to cultivate and preserve, that your presence
and comfortings would have been balm to my wounded mind.
But were you now, even by consent, and with reconciliatory
tidings, to come, it would but add to your grief; and the sight
of one I so dearly love, so happily fraught with good news,
might but draw me back to wishes I have had great struggles
to get above. And let me tell you for your comfort that I have
not left undone anything that ought to be done, either respecting
mind or *person*; no, not to the minutest preparation: so that

nothing is left for *you* to do for me. Every one has her direction as to the last offices. And my desk, that I now write upon—O my dearest Mrs. Norton, all is provided! All is ready! And all will be as decent as it should be!

And pray let my Miss Howe know that by the time you will receive this, and she *your* signification of the contents of it, it will, in all probability, be too late for *her* to do me the inestimable favour, as I should once have thought it, to see me. *God will have no rivals in the hearts of those He sanctifies.* By various methods He deadens all other sensations, or rather absorbs them all in the love of Him.

I shall, nevertheless, love *you*, my Mamma Norton, and my Miss Howe, whose love to me *has passed the love of women*, to my latest hour! But yet, I am now above the quick sense of those pleasures which once most delighted me: and once more I say that I do not wish to see objects so dear to me which might bring me back again into sense, and rival my *supreme love.*

.   .   .   .   .   .

Twice have I been forced to leave off. I *wished* that my last writing might be to you, or to Miss Howe, if it might not be to my dearest Ma——

Mamma, I would have wrote—is the word distinct? My eyes are *so* misty! If, when I apply to you, I break off in half-words, do you supply them—the kindest are *your* due. Be sure take the kindest to fill up chasms with, if any chasms there be——

.   .   .   .   .   .

Another breaking off! But the new day seems to rise upon me with healing in its wings. I have gotten, I think, a recruit of strength: spirits, I bless God, I have not of late wanted.

Let my dearest Miss Howe purchase her wedding garments—and may all temporal blessings attend the charming preparation! Blessings *will,* I make no question, notwithstanding the little cloudinesses that Mr. Hickman encounters with now and then, which are but prognostics of a future golden day to him: for her heart is good, and her head not wrong. But great merit is coy, and that coyness has not always its foundation in pride: but, if it should *seem* to be pride, take off the skin-deep covering, and, in her, it is noble diffidence, and a love that wants but to be assured!

Tell Mr. Hickman I write this, and write it, as I believe, with my last pen; and bid him *bear* a little at first, and *forbear;* and all the future will be crowning gratitude and rewarding love: for Miss Howe has great sense, fine judgment, and exalted generosity; and can such a one be ungrateful or easy under those obligations which his assiduity and obligingness (when he shall be so happy as to call her his) will lay her under to him?

As for me, never bride was so ready as I am. My wedding garments are bought. And though not fine and gaudy to the sight, though not adorned with jewels and set off with gold and silver (for I have no beholders' eyes to wish to glitter in), yet will they be the easiest, the *happiest* suit, that ever bridal maiden wore, for they are such as carry with them a security against all those anxieties, pains, and perturbations which sometimes succeed to the most promising outsettings.

And now, my dear Mrs. Norton, do I wish for no other.

Oh, hasten, good God, if it be Thy blessed will, the happy moment that I am to be decked out in this all-quieting garb! And sustain, comfort, bless, and protect with the all-shadowing wing of Thy mercy, my dear parents, my uncles, my brother, my sister, my Cousin Morden, my ever dear and ever kind Miss Howe, my good Mrs. Norton, and every deserving person to whom *they* wish well! is the ardent prayer, first and last, of every beginning hour, as the clock tells it me (hours now are days, nay years) of

Your now not sorrowing or afflicted, but happy
CLARISSA HARLOWE.

Letter CV—Mr. Lovelace to John Belford, Esq.

Wedn. Morn. Sept. 6, half an hour after Three.

I AM *not* the savage which you and my worst enemies think me. My soul is *too much* penetrated by the contents of the letter which you enclosed in your last to say one word more to it than that my heart has bled over it from every vein! I will fly from the subject—but what other can I choose that will not be as grievous, and lead into the same?

I could quarrel with all the world; with thee, as well as the rest; obliging as thou supposest thyself for writing to me hourly. How daredst thou (though unknown to her) to presume to take an apartment under the same roof with her? I cannot bear to think that thou shouldst be seen at all hours passing to and repassing from her apartments, while *I*, who have so much reason to call her mine, and once was preferred by her to all the world, am forced to keep aloof, and hardly dare to enter the *city* where she is!

If there be anything in Brand's letter that will divert me, hasten it to me. But nothing now will ever divert me, will ever again give me joy or pleasure! I can neither eat, drink, nor sleep. I am sick of all the world.

Surely it will be better when *all is over*—when I know the *worst* the Fates can do against me. Yet how shall I bear that *worst?* O Belford, Belford! write it not to me; but, if it *must* happen, get somebody else to write; for I shall curse the pen, the hand, the head, and the heart employed in communicating to me the fatal tidings. But what is this saying, when already I curse the whole world except her—myself most?

In fine, I am a most miserable being. Life is a burden to me. I would not bear it upon these terms for one week more, let what would be my lot; for already is there a hell begun in my own mind. Never more mention to me, let *her* or who will say it, the *prison*—I cannot bear it. May damnation seize quick the accursed woman who could set death upon taking that *large stride*, as the dear creature calls it! I had no hand in it! But her relations, her implacable relations, have done the business. All else would have been got over. Never persuade me but it would. The *fire of youth*, and the *violence of passion*, would have pleaded for me to good purpose with an individual of a sex which loves to be addressed with passionate ardour, even to tumult, had it not been for that cruelty and unforgivingness which (the object and the penitence considered) have no example, and have aggravated the heinousness of my faults.

Unable to rest, though I went not to bed till two, I dispatch this ere the day dawn—who knows what this night, this dismal night, may have produced!

I must after my messenger. I have told the varlet I will meet him, perhaps at Knightsbridge, perhaps in Piccadilly; and I trust not myself with pistols, not only on his account, but my own: for pistols are *too ready* a mischief.

I hope thou hast a letter ready for him. He goes to thy lodgings first: for surely thou wilt not presume to take thy rest in an apartment near hers. If he miss thee there, he flies to Smith's, and brings me word whether in being, or not.

I shall look for him through the air as I ride, as well as on horseback; for if the prince of it serve *me* as well as I have served *him*, he will bring the dog by his ears, like another

Habakkuk, to my saddle-bow, with the tidings that my heart pants after.

Nothing but the excruciating pangs the condemned soul feels, at its entrance into the eternity of the torments we are taught to fear, can exceed what I *now* feel, and *have* felt for almost this week past; and mayest thou have a spice of those if thou hast not a letter ready written for

Thy Lovelace.

Letter CVI—Mr. Belford to Robert Lovelace, Esq.

Tuesday, Sept. 5, Six o'clock.

THE lady remains exceedingly weak and ill. Her intellects, nevertheless, continue clear and strong, and her piety and patience are without example. Every one thinks this night will be her last. What a shocking thing is that to say of such an excellence! She will not, however, send away her letter to her Norton as yet. She endeavoured in vain to superscribe it: so desired me to do it. Her fingers will not hold her pen with the requisite steadiness. She has, I fear, written and read her last!

Eight o'clock.

She is somewhat better than she was. The doctor has been here, and thinks she will hold out yet a day or two. He has ordered her, as for some time past, only some little cordials to take when ready to faint. She seemed disappointed when he told her she might yet live two or three days; and said she longed for dismission! Life was not so easily extinguished, she saw, as some imagine. *Death from grief* was, she believed, *the slowest of deaths*. But God's will must be done! Her only prayer was now for submission to it: for she doubted not but by the Divine goodness she should be a happy creature as soon as she could be divested of these *rags of mortality*.

Of her own accord she mentioned you; which, till then, she had avoided to do. She asked, with great serenity, where you were?

I told her where; and your motives for being so near; and read to her a few lines of yours of this morning, in which you mention your wishes to see her, your sincere affliction, and your resolution not to approach her without her consent.

I would have read more; but she said: Enough, Mr. Belford; enough! Poor man! Does his conscience begin to find him!

Then need not anybody to wish him a greater punishment! May it work upon him to a happy purpose!

I took the liberty to say that, as she was in such a frame that nothing now seemed capable of discomposing her, I could wish that you might have the benefit of her exhortations, which, I dared to say, while you were so seriously affected, would have a greater force upon you than a thousand sermons; and how happy you would think yourself if you could but receive her forgiveness on your knees.

How can you think of such a thing, Mr. Belford? said she, with some emotion. My composure is owing, next to the Divine goodness blessing my earnest supplications for it, to the *not* seeing him. Yet let him know that I now again repeat that I forgive him. And may God Almighty, clasping her fingers and lifting up her eyes, forgive him too; and perfect his repentance, and sanctify it to him! Tell him I say so! And tell him that if I could not say so with my whole heart I should be very uneasy, and think that my hopes of mercy to myself were but weakly founded; and that I had still, in any harboured resentments, some hankerings after a life which he has been the cause of shortening.

The divine creature then turning aside her head: Poor man, said she! I once could have loved him. This is saying more than ever I could say of any other man out of my own family! Would he have permitted me to have been a humble instrument to have made him good. I think I could have made him happy! But tell him not this if he be *really* penitent—it may too much affect him!—There she paused.

Admirable creature! Heavenly forgiver! Then resuming: But pray tell him that if I could know that my death might be a means to reclaim and save him, it would be an inexpressible satisfaction to me!

But let me not, however, be made uneasy with the apprehension of seeing him. I cannot *bear* to see him!

Just as she had done speaking, the minister, who had so often attended her, sent up his name; and was admitted.

Being apprehensive that it would be with difficulty that you could prevail upon that impetuous spirit of yours not to invade her in her dying hours, and of the agonies into which a surprise of this nature would throw her; I thought this gentleman's visit afforded a proper opportunity to renew the subject; and (having asked her leave) acquainted him with the topic we had been upon.

The good man urged that some condescensions were usually

expected on these solemn occasions, from pious souls like hers, however satisfied with *themselves*, for the sake of showing the *world*, and for *example's sake*, that all resentments against those who had most injured them were subdued: and if she would vouchsafe to a heart so truly penitent as I had represented Mr. Lovelace's to be, that *personal* pardon which I had been pleading for, there would be no room to suppose the least lurking resentment remained; and it might have very happy effects upon the gentleman.

I have no lurking resentment, sir, said she. This is not a time for resentment: and you will be the readier to believe me, when I can assure you (looking at me) that even what I have most rejoiced in, the truly friendly love that has so long subsisted between my Miss Howe and her Clarissa, although to my last gasp it will be the dearest to me of all that is dear in this life, has already abated in its fervour; has already given place to supremer fervours: and shall the remembrance of Mr. Lovelace's *personal* insults, which, I bless God, never corrupted that *mind* which *her* friendship so much delighted, be stronger in these hours with me than the remembrance of a love as pure as the human heart ever boasted? Tell, therefore, the *world*, if you please, and (if, Mr. Belford, you think what I said to you before not strong enough) tell the poor man that I not only forgive him, but have *such* earnest wishes for the good of his soul, and that from considerations of its immortality, that could my penitence avail for more sins than my own, my last tear should fall for him by whom I die!

Our eyes and hands expressed for us both what our lips could not utter.

Say not then, proceeded she, nor let it be said, that my resentments are unsubdued! And yet these eyes, lifted up to heaven as witness to the truth of what I have said, shall never, if I can help it, behold him more! For do you not consider, sirs, how short my time is; what much more important subjects I have to employ it upon; and how unable I should be (so weak as I am) to contend even with the avowed penitence of a person in strong health, governed by passions unabated, and always violent? And now I hope you will never urge me more on this subject.

The minister said it were pity ever to urge this plea again.

You see, Lovelace, that I did not forget the office of a friend, in endeavouring to prevail upon her to give you your last forgiveness personally. And I hope, as she is so near her end, you will not invade her in her last hours; since she must be extremely discomposed at such an interview; and it might make her leave the world the sooner for it.

This reminds me of an expression which she used on your barbarous hunting her at Smith's, on her return to her lodgings; and that with a serenity unexampled (as Mrs. Lovick told me, considering the occasion, and the trouble given her by it, and her indisposition at the time): He will not let me die decently, said the angelic sufferer! He will not let me enter into my Maker's presence with the composure that is required in entering into the drawing-room of an earthly prince!

I cannot, however, forbear to wish that the heavenly creature could have prevailed upon herself, in these her last hours, to see you; and that for *my* sake, as well as *yours*: for although I am determined never to be guilty of the crimes which till within these few past weeks have blackened my former life; and for which, at present, I most heartily hate myself; yet should I be less apprehensive of a relapse if (wrought upon by the solemnity which such an interview must have been attended with) you had become a reformed man: for no devil do I fear but one in your shape.

. . . .

It is now eleven o'clock at night. The lady, who retired to rest an hour ago, is, as Mrs. Lovick tells me, in a sweet slumber.

I will close here. I hope I shall find her the better for it in the morning. Yet, alas! how frail is hope! How frail is life; when we are apt to build so much on every shadowy relief; although in such a desperate case as this, sitting down to reflect, we *must* know that it is *but* shadowy!

I will enclose Brand's horrid pedantry. And for once am beforehand with thy ravenous impatience.

Letter CVII—Mr. Brand to Mr. John Walton

Sat. Night, Sept. 2.

DEAR MR. WALTON,—I am obliged to you for the very *hand-somely penned* (and *elegantly written*) letter which you have sent me on purpose to do *justice* to the *character* of the *younger* Miss Harlowe: and yet I must tell you that I had reason, *before that came*, to *think* (and to *know* indeed) that we were *all wrong*: and so I had employed the *greatest part* of this *week* in drawing up an *apologetical letter* to my worthy *patron* Mr. John Harlowe, in order to set all *matters right* between *me* and *them*, and (*as far as I could*) between *them* and *miss*. So it required little more than *connexion* and *transcribing* when I received *yours*; and it will be with Mr. Harlowe aforesaid *to-morrow morning*; and this, and the copy of that, will be with you on *Monday morning*.

You cannot imagine how sorry I am that *you*, and Mrs. Walton, and Mrs. Barker, and *I myself*, should have taken matters up so lightly (judging, alas-a-day! by appearance and conjecture) where *character* and *reputation* are concerned. Horace says truly:

> Et semel emissum volat irrevocabile verbum.

That is, *Words once spoken cannot be recalled*: but (Mr. Walton) they may be *contradicted* by *other* words; and we may confess ourselves guilty of a *mistake*; and express our *concern* for being *mistaken*; and resolve to make our *mistake* a *warning* to us for the *future*: and this is all that *can be done*; and what every *worthy mind will do*; and what nobody can be *readier to do* than *we four undesigning offenders* (as I see by *your letter*, on *your part*; and as you will see by the *enclosed copy*, on *mine*); which, if it be received as I *think it ought* (and as I *believe it will*), must give me a *speedy* opportunity to see you, when I *visit the lady*; to whom (as you will see in it) I expect to be sent up with the *olive-branch*.

The matter in which we all *erred* must be owned to be *very nice*; and (Mr. Belford's *character considered*) *appearances* ran very strong *against the lady*: but all that this serveth to show is, *that in doubtful matters the wisest people may be mistaken*; for so saith the *poet*:

> Fallitur in dubiis hominum solertia rebus.

If you have an *opportunity*, you may (as if *from yourself*, and *unknown to me*) show the enclosed to Mr. Belford, who (you tell me) *resenteth* the matter very heinously; but not to let him *see*, or *hear read*, those words *that relate to him* in the paragraph at the *bottom of the second page*, beginning [*But yet I do insist upon it*] to the *end* of that paragraph; for one would not make one's self *enemies*, you know: and I have *reason to think* that this Mr. *Belford* is as *passionate* and *fierce* a man as Mr. Lovelace. What pity it is the lady could find no *worthier a protector*! You may paste those lines over with *blue or black paper* before he seeth it; and if he insisteth upon taking a copy of my letter (for he, or anybody that *seeth it* or *heareth it read*, will, no doubt, be glad to have by them the copy of a letter so full of the *senti-ments* of the *noblest writers* of *antiquity*, and *so well adapted*, as

I will be bold to say they are, to the *point in hand*; I say, if he insisteth upon taking a copy), let him give you the *strongest assurances* not to suffer it to be *printed* on *any account*; and I make the same request to you, that *you* will not: for if anything be to be made of a *man's works*, who but the *author* should have the *advantage*? And if the *Spectators*, the *Tatlers*, the *Examiners*, the *Guardians*, and other of our polite papers, make such a *strutting* with a *single verse* or so, by way of *motto*, in the *front* of *each day's* paper; and if other *authors* pride themselves in *finding out* and *embellishing* the *title-pages* of their *books* with a *verse* or *adage* from the *classical writers*; what a figure would *such a letter as the enclosed* make, so full fraught with *admirable precepts* and *à-propos quotations* from the *best authority*?

I have been told that a *certain noble lord*, who once sat himself down to write a *pamphlet* in behalf of a *great minister*, after taking *infinite pains* to *no purpose* to find a *Latin motto*, gave commission to a friend of *his* to offer to *any one* who could help him to a *suitable one*, but of one or two lines, a *hamper of claret*. Accordingly, his lordship had a *motto found him* from *Juvenal*; which he *unhappily mistaking* (not knowing *Juvenal* was a *poet*), printed as a prose *sentence* in his *title-page*.

If, then, *one* or *two* lines were of so much worth (a *hamper of claret!* no *less!*), of what *inestimable value* would *such a letter as mine* be deemed? And who knoweth but that this noble p—r (who is now [1] living), if he should happen to see *this letter* shining with such *a glorious string of jewels*, might give the *writer a scarf*, in order to have him *always at hand*, or be a *means* (some way or other) to bring him into *notice*? And I will be bold to say (*bad* as the *world* is) a man of *sound learning* wanteth nothing but an *initiation* to make his *fortune*.

I hope (my good friend) that the lady will not *die*: I shall be much *grieved* if she doth; and the more because of mine *unhappy misrepresentation*: so will *you* for the *same cause*: so will her *parents* and *friends*. They are very *rich* and *very worthy* gentlefolks.

But let me tell you, *by the by*, that they had carried the matter against her *so far*, that I believe in my heart they were glad to *justify themselves* by *my report*; and would have been *less pleased* had I made a *more favourable one*: and yet in *their hearts* they *dote* upon her. But now they are all (as I hear) inclined to be *friends with her* and *forgive her*; her *brother* as well as *the rest*.

---

[1] i.e. at the time this letter was written.

But their *cousin*, Colonel Morden, *a very fine gentleman*, hath had such *high words* with them, and they with him, that they know not how to *stoop*, lest it should look like being frighted into an *accommodation*. Hence it is that *I* have taken the greater liberty to *press the reconciliation*; and I hope in *such good season* that they will all be *pleased* with it: for can they have a *better handle* to save their *pride* all round than by my *mediation*? And let me tell you (inter nos, *betwixt ourselves*), *very proud they all are*.

By this *honest means* (for by *dishonest ones* I would not be *Archbishop of Canterbury*) I hope to please everybody; to be *forgiven*, in the *first place*, by *the lady* (whom, being a *lover of learning* and *learned men*, I shall have great *opportunities* of *obliging*—for, when she departed from her father's house, I had but just the honour of her *notice*, and she seemed *highly pleased* with my *conversation*); and *next*, to be *thanked* and *respected* by her *parents* and *all her family*; as I am (I bless God for it) by my *dear friend* Mr. John Harlowe: who indeed is a man that professeth a *great esteem* for *men of erudition*; and who (with *singular delight*, I know) will run over with me the *authorities* I have *quoted*, and *wonder* at my *memory*, and the *happy knack* I have of recommending *mine own sense of things* in the words of the *greatest sages of antiquity*.

Excuse me, my good friend, for this *seeming vanity*. The great Cicero (you must have heard, I suppose) had a *much greater* spice of it, and wrote a *long letter begging* and *praying* to be *flattered*: but if I say *less of myself* than other people (who know me) *say of me*, I think I keep a *medium* between *vanity* and *false modesty*; the latter of which oftentimes gives itself the *lie*, when it is *declaring off* the *compliments* that *everybody* gives it as its due: a hypocrisy, as well as folly, that (I hope) I shall for ever scorn to be guilty of.

I have *another reason* (as I may tell to you, my *old schoolfellow*) to make me wish for this *fine lady's recovery* and *health*; and that is (by some distant intimations), I have heard from Mr. John Harlowe that it is *very likely* (because of the *slur* she hath received) that she will choose to *live privately* and *penitently*—and will probably (when she cometh into her *estate*) keep a *chaplain* to direct her in her *devotions* and *penitence*. If she doth, who can stand a *better chance* than *myself*? And as I find (by *your* account, as well as by *everybody's*) that she is innocent as to *intention*, and is resolved never to think of Mr. *Lovelace more*, who knoweth *what* (in time) *may happen*? And yet it must be after Mr. *Lovelace's death* (which may possibly sooner happen than he *thinketh* of, by means of his *detestable courses*): for, after all, a man who is of *public utility* ought not (for the *finest woman* in the world) to lay his *throat* at the *mercy* of a man who boggleth at nothing.

I beseech you, let not this hint *go farther* than to *yourself*, your *spouse*, and Mrs. *Barker*. I know I may trust my *life* in *your hands* and *theirs*. There have been (let me tell ye) *unlikelier* things come to pass, and that with *rich widows* (some of *quality* truly!), whose choice in their *first marriages* hath (perhaps) been guided by *motives of convenience*, or *mere corporalities*, as I may say; but who by their *second* have had for their view the *corporal* and *spiritual* mingled; which is the most eligible (no doubt) to *substances* composed *of both*, as *men* and *women* are.

Nor think (sir) that should such a thing come to pass, *either* would be *disgraced*; since *the lady*, in *me*, would marry a *gentleman* and a *scholar*: and as to *mine own honour*, as the *slur* would bring her *high fortunes* down to an *equivalence* with my *mean ones* (if *fortune* only, and not *merit*, be considered), so hath not the *life* of *this lady* been *so tainted* (either by *length of time* or *naughtiness of practice*) as to put her on a *foot* with the *cast Abigails*, that too, too often (God knoweth) are thought good enough for a *young clergyman*; who perhaps is drawn in by a *poor benefice*; and (if the *wicked one* be not quite *worn out*) groweth poorer and poorer upon it, by an *increase of family* he knoweth not whether *is most his*, or his *noble* (*ignoble*, I should say) *patron's*.

But all this *apart* and *in confidence*.

I know you made at school but a small progress in *languages*. So I have restrained myself from *many illustrations* from the *classics* that I could have filled this letter with (as I have done the enclosed one): and, being at a *distance*, I cannot *explain* them to you, as I *do to my friend* Mr. John Harlowe; who (after all) is obliged to *me* for pointing out to *him* many *beauties* of the *authors I quote* which otherwise would lie concealed from *him*, as they must from every *common observer*. But this (too) *inter nos*—for he would not take it well to *have it known*—*Jays* (you know, old schoolfellow, *jays*, you know) *will strut in peacocks' feathers*.

But whither am I running? I never know where to end when I get upon *learned topics*. And albeit I cannot compliment *you* with the *name of a learned man*, yet are you *a sensible man*; and (*as such*) must have *pleasure* in *learned men*, and in *their writings*.

In this confidence (Mr. Walton), with my *kind respects* to the good ladies (your *spouse* and *sister*), and in hopes, for the *young lady's sake,* soon to follow this long, long epistle *in person,* I conclude myself

Your loving and faithful friend,

ELIAS BRAND.

You will perhaps, Mr. Walton, wonder at the meaning of the *lines drawn under many of the words and sentences* (UNDER-SCORING we call it); and were my letters to be printed, those would be put in a *different character.* Now, you must know, sir, that *we learned men* do this to point out to the readers who are not *so learned* where the *jet of our arguments lieth,* and the *emphasis* they are to lay upon *those words;* whereby they will take in readily our *sense* and *cogency.* Some *pragmatical* people have said that an author who doth a *great deal of this,* either calleth his readers *fools,* or tacitly condemneth *his own style,* as supposing his meaning would be *dark* without it, or that all his *force* lay in *words.* But all of those with whom I have conversed in the learned way *think as I think.* And to give a very *pretty,* though *familiar illustration,* I have considered a page distinguished by *different characters* as a *verdant field* overspread with *butter-flowers* and *daisies* and other summer flowers. These the poets liken to *enamelling*—have you not read in the poets of *enamelled meads,* and so forth?

Letter CVIII—Mr. Brand to John Harlowe, Esq.

Sat. Night, Sept. 2.

WORTHY SIR,—I am under no *small concern* that I should (unhappily) be the *occasion* (I am sure I *intended* nothing like it) of *widening differences* by *light misreport,* when it is the *duty* of one of *my function* (and no less consisting with my *inclination*) to *heal* and *reconcile.*

I have received two letters to set me *right:* one from a *particular acquaintance* (whom I set to inquire of Mr. Belford's character); and that came on Tuesday last, informing me that your *unhappy niece* was greatly injured in the account I had had of her (for I had told *him* of it, and that with very *great concern,* I am sure, apprehending it to be *true*). So I *then* set about writing to you, to *acknowledge* the *error:* and had gone a good way in it, when the second letter came (a very *handsome one* it is, both in *style* and *penmanship*) from my friend Mr.

Walton (though I am sure it cannot be *his inditing*) expressing his
sorrow, and his wife's, and his sister-in-law's likewise, for having
been the cause of *misleading me*, in the account I gave of the
said *young lady*; whom they *now say* (upon *further inquiry*) they
find to be the *most unblamable* and *most prudent*, and (it seems)
the most *pious* young lady that ever (once) committed a *great
error*; as (to be sure) *hers was* in leaving such *worthy parents* and
relations for so *vile a man* as Mr. Lovelace: but what shall we
say?   Why, the divine Virgil tells us:

> Improbe amor, quid non mortalia pectora cogis?

For *my part*, I was but too much afraid (for we have *great
opportunities*, you are sensible, sir, at the *university*, of knowing
human nature from *books*, the *calm result* of the *wise men's
wisdom*, as I may say

> (Haurit aquam cribro, qui discere vult sine libro)

uninterrupted by the *noise* and *vanities* that will mingle with
personal conversation, which (in the *turbulent world*) is not to be
enjoyed but over a *bottle*, where you have a *hundred foolish things*
pass to *one that deserveth to be remembered*; I was but too much
afraid, *I say*) that so *great a slip* might be attended with *still
greater* and *worse*: for *your* Horace, and *my* Horace, the most
charming writer that ever lived among the *Pagans* (for the
lyric kind of poetry, I mean; for, to be sure, *Homer* and *Virgil*
would *otherwise* be *first* named in *their way*), well observeth (and
who understood *human nature* better than he?):

> Nec vera virtus, cum semel excidit,
> Curat reponi deterioribus.

And *Ovid* no less wisely observes:

> Et mala sunt vicina bonis.   Errore sub illo
> Pro vitio virtus crimina sæpe tulit.

Who that can draw *knowledge* from its *fountain-head*, the
works of the *sages of antiquity* (improved by the *comments* of
the *moderns*), but would *prefer* to all others the *silent quiet life*
which *contemplative men* lead in the *seats of learning*, were they
not called out (according to their *dedication*) to the *service* and
instruction of the world?

Now, sir, *another* favourite poet of mine (and not the *less a
favourite* for being a *Christian*) telleth us that it is the custom of

some, when in a *fault*, to throw the blame **upon** the backs of *others*:

> ——Hominum quoque mos est,
> Quæ nos cunque premunt, alieno imponere tergo.
>
> MANT.

But I, though (in this case) *misled* (*well-intendedly*, nevertheless, both in the *misleaders* and *misled*, and therefore entitled to lay hold of that plea, if *anybody* is so entitled), will not, however, be classed among such *extenuators*; but (contrarily) will always keep in mind that verse which *comforteth in mistake* as well as *instructeth*; and which I quoted in my last letter;

> Errare est hominis, sed non persistere——

And will own that I was very *rash* to take up with *conjectures* and *consequences* drawn from *probabilities*, where (especially) the *character* of so *fine a lady* was concerned.

> Credere fallaci gravis est dementia famæ.
>
> MANT.

Notwithstanding, Miss Clarissa Harlowe (I must be bold to say) is the *only young lady* that ever I heard of (or indeed read of) that, *having made such a false step*, so *soon* (of *her own accord*, as I may say) *recovered* herself, and conquered her *love of the deceiver* (a great conquest indeed!); and who flieth him, and resolveth to *die* rather than to be his; which now to her never-dying *honour* (I am well assured) is the case—and, in *justice* to her, I am now ready to take to myself (with no small vexation) that of Ovid:

> Heu! patior telis vulnera facta meis.

But yet I do insist upon it, that all *that part* of my *information* which I took upon mine own *personal inquiry*, which is what relates to Mr. *Belford* and *his character*, is *literally true*; for there is not anywhere to be met with a man of a more *libertine character* as to *women*, Mr. *Lovelace* excepted, than he bears.

And so, sir, I must desire of you that you will not let *any blame* lie upon my *intention*; since you see how ready I am to *accuse myself* of too lightly giving ear to a *rash information* (not knowing it so to be, however): for I depended the more upon it, as the *people I had it from* are very *sober*, and live in the *fear of God*: and indeed when I wait upon you, you will see by their letter that they must be *conscientious* good people: wherefore, sir, let me be entitled, from *all your good family*, to that of my last-named poet:

Aspera confesso verba remitte reo.

And now, sir (what is much more becoming of my *function*), let me, instead of appearing with the *face of an accuser* and a *rash censurer* (which in my *heart* I have not *deserved* to be thought), assume the character of *a reconciler*; and propose (by way of *penance* to myself for my *fault*) to be sent up as a *messenger of peace* to the *pious young lady*; for they write me word *absolutely* (and, I believe in my heart, *truly*), that the *doctors* have *given her over*, and that she *cannot live*. Alas! alas! what a sad thing would that be, if the *poor bough* that was only designed (as I *very well know* and am *fully assured*) *to be bent, should be broken*!

Let it not, dear sir, seem to the *world* that there was anything in your *resentments* (which, while meant for *reclaiming*, were just and fit) that has the *appearance* of *violence*, and *fierce wrath*, and *inexorability* (as it would look to some, if carried to extremity, after *repentance*, and *contrition*, and *humiliation* on the *fair offender's* side): for all this while (it seems) she has been a *second Magdalen* in her *penitence*, and yet not so bad as a *Magdalen* in her *faults* (faulty, nevertheless, as she has been once, the Lord knoweth!

Nam vitiis nemo sine nascitur: optimus ille est,
Qui minimis urgetur——

saith HORACE).

Now, sir, if I may be named for this *blessed* employment (for *Blessed is the peacemaker!*), I will hasten to London; and (as I know Miss had always a *great regard* to the *function* I have the honour to be of) I have no doubt of making myself acceptable to her, and to bring her, by *sound arguments* and *good advice*, into a *liking of life*, which must be the *first step* to her *recovery*: for, when the *mind* is *made easy*, the *body* will not *long suffer*; and the *love of life* is a *natural passion* that is soon *revived* when fortune turns about and smiles:

Vivere quisque diu, quamvis et egenus et æger,
Optat——

OVID.

And the sweet Lucan truly observes:

————Fatis debentibus annos
Mors invita subit——

And now, sir, let me tell you what shall be the *tenor* of my
pleadings with her, and *comfortings* of her, as she is, as I may say,
a *learned lady*; and as I can *explain* to her *those sentences* which
she cannot so readily *construe herself*: and this in order to
convince *you* (did you not already *know* my *qualifications*) how
well qualified I *am* for the *Christian office* to which I commend
myself.

I will, IN THE FIRST PLACE, put her in mind of the *common
course of things* in this *sublunary world*, in which *joy* and *sorrow*,
sorrow and *joy*, succeed one another by *turns*; in order to convince
her that her griefs have been but according to *that* common
course of things:

> Gaudia post luctus veniunt, post gaudia luctus.

SECONDLY, I will remind her of her own notable description
of *sorrow*, when she was once called upon to distinguish wherein
sorrow, *grief*, and *melancholy* differed from each other; which she
did *impromptu*, by their *effects*, in a truly admirable manner, to
the high satisfaction of every one: I myself could not, by *study*,
have distinguished *better*, nor more *concisely*: SORROW, said she,
wears; GRIEF *tears*; but MELANCHOLY *soothes*.

My inference to her shall be, that since a happy reconciliation
will take place, grief will be banished; sorrow dismissed; and
only sweet *melancholy* remain to *soothe* and *indulge* her *contrite
heart*, and show to all the world the penitent sense she hath of
her great error.

THIRDLY, That her *joys*,[1] when restored to health and favour,
will be the greater, the deeper her griefs were.

> Gaudia, quæ multo parta, labore placent.

FOURTHLY, That having *really* been guilty of a *great error*, she
should not take *impatiently* the *correction* and *anger* with which
she hath been treated.

> Leniter, ex merito quicquid patiare, ferundum est.

FIFTHLY, That *virtue* must be established by *patience*; as saith
Prudentius:

> Hæc virtus vidua est, quam non patientia firmat.

---

[1] *Joy*, let me here observe, my dear sir, by way of note, is not absolutely
inconsistent with *melancholy*; a *soft gentle joy*, not a *rapid*, not a *rampant
joy*, however; but such a *joy* as shall lift her *temporarily* out of her *soothing
melancholy*, and then *let her down gently* into it again; for *melancholy*, to
be sure, her *reflection* will generally make to be her state.

SIXTHLY, That, in the words of Horace, she may *expect better times* than (of late) she had *reason* to look for:

> Grata superveniet, quæ non sperabitur, hora.

SEVENTHLY, That she is really now in *a way* to be *happy*, since, according to *Ovid*, she *can count up all her woe*:

> Felix, qui patitur quæ numerare potest.

And those comforting lines:

> Estque serena dies post longos gratior imbres,
> Et post triste malum gratior ipsa salus.

EIGHTHLY, That, in the words of Mantuan, her *parents* and *uncles* could not *help loving her* all the time they were *angry at her*:

> Æqua tamen semper mens est, et amica voluntas,
> Sit licet in natos facies austera parentum.

NINTHLY, That the *ills she hath met with* may be turned (by the *good use* to be made of them) to her *everlasting benefit*; for that:

> Cum furit atque ferit, Deus olim parcere quærit.

TENTHLY, That she will be able to give a *fine lesson* (a *very* fine lesson) to all the *young ladies* of her *acquaintance*, of the *vanity* of being *lifted up* in *prosperity*, and the *weakness* of being *cast down* in *adversity*; since no one is so *high* as to be above being *humbled*; so *low* as to *need to despair*: for which purpose the advice of *Ausonius*:

> Dum fortuna juvat, caveto tolli:
> Dum fortuna tonat, caveto mergi.

I shall tell her that Lucan saith well when he calleth *adversity* the *element of patience*:

> ——Gaudet patientia duris.

That

> Fortunam superat virtus, prudentia famam.

That while weak souls are *crushed* by *fortune*, the *brave mind* maketh the fickle deity afraid of it:

> Fortuna fortes metuit, ignavos premit.

ELEVENTHLY, That if she take the advice of *Horace*:

> Fortiaque adversis opponite pectora rebus,

it will delight her *hereafter* (as *Virgil* says) to *revolve her past troubles*:

> ——Forsan et hæc olim meminisse juvabit.

And, to the same purpose, *Juvenal*, speaking of the *prating joy* of mariners, after all their *dangers are over*:

> Gaudent securi narrare pericula nautæ.

Which suiting the case so well, you 'll forgive me, sir, for *popping down* in *English metre*, as the *translative impulse* (pardon a new word, and yet we *scholars* are not fond of *authenticating new* words) came upon me *uncalled for*:

> The seaman, safe on shore, with joy doth tell
> What cruel dangers him at sea befell.

With *these*, sir, and a *hundred more* wise *adages*, which I have always at my *finger-ends*, will I (when reduced to *form* and *method*) entertain miss; and as she is a *well-read* and (I might say, but for this *one* great error) a *wise* young lady, I make no doubt but I shall *prevail* upon her, if not by *mine own arguments*, by those of *wits* and *capacities* that have a *congeniality* (as I may say) to *her own*, to take heart:

> ——Nor of the laws of fate complain,
> Since, though it has been cloudy, now 't clears up again.——

Oh! what *wisdom* is there in these *noble classical authors*! A *wise man* will (upon searching into them) always find that they speak *his* sense of *men* and *things*. Hence it is that they so readily occur to *my memory* on every occasion. Though this may look like *vanity*, it is too true to be omitted: and I see not why a man may not *know those things of himself* which *everybody* seeth and *saith of him*; who, nevertheless, perhaps know not *half so much as he* in other matters.

I know but of *one objection*, sir, that can lie against my going; and that will arise from your kind *care* and *concern* for the *safety of my person*, in case that *fierce* and *terrible man*, the wicked Mr. Lovelace (of whom every one standeth in fear), should come across me, as he may be resolved to try once more to *gain a footing* in *miss's affections*: but I will trust in *Providence* for *my safety*, while I shall be engaged in a *cause so worthy of my function*; and the *more* trust in it, as he is a *learned man*, as I am told.

Strange, too, that so *vile a rake* (I hope he will never see this!) should be a *learned man*; that is to say, that a *learned man* should find *leisure* to be a *rake*. Although possibly a *learned man* may be a *sly sinner*, and take opportunities *as they come in his way*— which, however, I do assure you, I *never did*.

I repeat, that as he is a *learned man*, I shall *vest myself*, as I may say, in *classical armour*; beginning *meekly* with him (for, sir, *bravery* and *meekness* are qualities *very consistent with each other*, and in no persons so shiningly *exert* themselves as in the *Christian priesthood*; beginning *meekly* with him, I say) from Ovid:

Corpora magnanimo satis est prostrâsse leoni:

so that, if I should not be safe behind the *shield* of *mine own prudence*, I certainly should behind the *shields* of the *ever-admirable classics*: of *Horace* particularly; who, being a *rake* (and a *jovial rake* too) himself, must have great weight with all *learned rakes*.

And who knoweth but I may be able to bring even this *Goliath in wickedness*, although in *person* but a *little David* myself (armed with the *slings* and *stones* of the *ancient sages*), to a due sense of his errors? And what a victory would that be!

I could here, sir, pursuing the allegory of David and Goliath, give you some of the *stones* (*hard arguments* may be called *stones*, since they *knock down a pertinacious opponent*) which I could *pelt him with*, were he to be wroth with me; and this in order to take from you, sir, all apprehensions for my *life* or my *bones*; but I forbear them till you demand them of me, when I have the honour to attend you in person.

And now (my dear sir) what remains but that, having shown you (what yet, I believe, you did not doubt) how *well qualified* I am to attend the lady with the *olive-branch*, I beg of you to dispatch me with it *out of hand*. For if she be so *very ill*, and if she should not live to receive the grace which (to my knowledge) all the *worthy family* design her, how much will that grieve you all! And then, sir, of what avail will be the *eulogies* you shall all, peradventure, join to give to her memory? For, as Martial wisely observeth:

——Post cineres gloria sera venit.

Then, as *Ausonius* layeth it down with *equal propriety*, that *those favours which are speedily conferred are the most graceful and obliging*——

And to the same purpose Ovid:

Gratia ab officio, quod mora tardat, abest.

And, sir, whatever you do, let the *lady's pardon* be as *ample*, and as *cheerfully given*, as she can *wish for it*; that I may be able to tell her that it hath your *hands*, your *countenances*, and your *whole hearts* with it—for, as the Latin verse hath it (and I presume to think I have not weakened its sense by my humble advice):

> Dat bene, dat multum, qui dat cum munere vultum.

And now, sir, when I survey this long letter [1] (albeit I see it enamelled, as a *beautiful meadow* is enamelled by the *spring* or *summer flowers*, very glorious to behold!), I begin to be afraid that I may have tired you; and the more likely as I have written without that *method* or *order* which I think constituteth the *beauty* of *good writing*: which *method* or *order*, nevertheless, may be the *better excused* in a *familiar epistle* (as this may be called), you pardoning, sir, the *familiarity* of the *word*: but yet not altogether *here*, I must needs own; because this is *a letter*, and *not a letter*, as I may say; but a kind of *short* and *pithy discourse*, touching upon *various* and *sundry topics*, every one of which might be a *fit theme* to enlarge upon, even to volumes: if this *epistolary discourse* (then let me call it) should be pleasing to you (as I am inclined to think it will, because of the *sentiments* and *aphorisms* of the *wisest of the ancients*, which *glitter through it* like so many dazzling *sunbeams*), I will (at my leisure) work it up into a *methodical discourse*, and perhaps may one day print it, with a *dedication* to my *honoured patron* (if, sir, I have *your* leave), *singly* at first (but not till I have thrown out anonymously two or three *smaller things*, by the success of which I shall have made myself of *some account* in the *commonwealth of letters*), and afterwards in my *works*—not for the *vanity* of the thing (however), I will say, but for the *use* it may be of to the *public*; for (as one well observeth), *though glory always followeth virtue, yet it should be considered only as its shadow.*

> Contemnit laudem virtus, licet usque sequatur
> Gloria virtutem, corpus ut umbra suum.

A very pretty saying, and worthy of all men's admiration!

And now (*most worthy sir*, my very good friend and patron), referring the whole to *yours*, and to your *two brothers'*, and to *young Mr. Harlowe's* consideration, and to the wise consideration of good *Madam Harlowe*, and her excellent daughter *Miss*

---

[1] And here, by way of note, permit me to say that no *sermon* I ever composed cost me half the *pains* that this letter hath done—but I know your great *appetite* after, as well as *admiration* of, the *ancient wisdom*, which you so justly prefer to the *modern*—and indeed I join with you to think that the *modern* is only *borrowed* (as the *moon* doth its light from the *sun*); at least, that we *excel* them in nothing; and that our *best cogitations* may be found, generally speaking, more *elegantly* dressed and expressed by *them*.

Arabella Harlowe; I take the liberty to subscribe myself, what I *truly am*, and *ever shall delight to be*, in *all cases*, and at *all times*,

Your and their most ready and obedient,

as well as faithful servant,

ELIAS BRAND.

Letter CIX—*Mr. Lovelace to John Belford, Esq.*

[*In answer to Letter CVI*]

Wedn. Morn. Sept. 6.

AND is she somewhat better? Blessings upon thee without number or measure! Let her still be better and better! *Tell* me so at least, if she be *not* so: for thou knowest not what a joy that poor temporary reprieve, that she will hold out yet a day or two, gave me.

But who told this hard-hearted and death-pronouncing doctor that she will hold it no longer? By what warrant says he this? What presumption in these parading solemn fellows of a college, which will be my contempt to the latest hour of my life, if this brother of it (eminent as he is deemed to be) cannot work an ordinary miracle in *her* favour, or rather in *mine*!

Let me tell thee, Belford, that already he deserves the *utmost* contempt, for suffering this charming clock to run down so low. What must be his art if it could not wind it up in a quarter of the time he has attended her, when, at his first visits, the springs and wheels of life and motion were so good that they seemed only to want common care and oiling!

I am obliged to you for endeavouring to engage her to see me. 'Twas acting like a friend. If she *had* vouchsafed me that favour, she should have seen at her feet the most abject adorer that ever kneeled to justly offended beauty.

What she bid you, and what she *forbid* you, to tell me (the latter for *tender* considerations); that she forgives me; and that, could she have made me a *good* man, she could have made me a *happy* one! That she even *loved me*! At such a moment to own that *she once loved me*! Never *before* loved any man! That she prays for me! That her last tear should be shed for me, could she by it save a soul doomed, without *her*, to perdition! —O Belford, Belford! I cannot bear it!—What a dog, what a devil have I been to a goodness so superlative! Why does she not inveigh against me? Why does she not execrate me?

Oh, the triumphant subduer! Ever above me! And now to leave me so infinitely below her!

Marry and repair, at any time; this, wretch that I was! was my plea to myself. To give her a lowering sensibility; to bring her down from among the stars which her beamy head was surrounded by, that my wife, so greatly above me, might not despise me; this was one of my reptile motives, owing to my *more* reptile envy, and to my consciousness of inferiority to her! Yet she, from step to step, from distress to distress, to maintain her superiority; and, like the sun, to break out upon me with the greater refulgence for the clouds that I had contrived to cast about her!—And now to escape me thus! No power left me to repair her wrongs! No alleviation to my self-reproach! No dividing of blame with her!

Tell her, oh, tell her, Belford, that her prayers and wishes, her superlatively generous prayers and wishes, shall *not* be vain: that I *can*, and *do*, repent—and *long* have repented. Tell her of my frequent deep remorses—it was impossible that such remorses should not at last produce *effectual* remorse. Yet she must not leave me—she must live, if she would wish to have my contrition perfect—for what can despair produce?

   .   .   .   .

I will do everything you would have me do, in the return of your letters. You have infinitely obliged me by this last, and by pressing for an admission for me, though it succeeded not.

Once more, how could I be such a villain to so divine a creature! yet love her all the time as never man loved woman! Curse upon my *contriving genius*! Curse upon my *intriguing head*, and upon my *seconding heart*! To sport with the fame, with the honour, with the *life* of such an angel of a woman! Oh, my damned incredulity! that, believing her to *be* a woman, I must hope to *find* her a woman! On my incredulity that there could be such virtue (virtue for *virtue's* sake) in the sex, founded I my hope of succeeding with her.

But say not, Jack, that she must leave us yet. If she recover, and if I can but re-obtain her favour, then indeed will life be life to me. The world never *saw* such a husband as I will make. I will have no will but hers. She shall conduct me in all my steps. She shall open and direct my prospects, and turn every motion of my heart as she pleases.

You tell me in your letter that at eleven o'clock she had sweet rest; and my servant acquaints me from Mrs. Smith that she has had a good night.   What hope does this fill me with!   I have given the fellow five guineas for his good news, to be divided between him and his fellow-servant.

Dear, dear Jack! confirm this to me in thy next—for *Heaven's* sake do!   Tell the doctor I will make him a present of a thousand guineas if he recover her.   Ask if a consultation be necessary.

Adieu, dear Belford!   Confirm, I beseech thee, the hopes that now with sovereign gladness have taken possession of a heart that, next to hers, is

Thine.

Letter CX—*Mr. Belford to Robert Lovelace, Esq.*

Wedn. Morn. Eight o'clock (6 *Sept.*).

YOUR servant arrived here before I was stirring.   I sent him to Smith's to inquire how the lady was; and ordered him to call upon me when he came back.   I was pleased to hear she had had tolerable rest.   As soon as I had dispatched him with the letter I had written overnight, I went to attend her.

I found her up and dressed; in a white satin night-gown. Ever elegant; but now more so than I had seen her for a week past: her aspect serenely cheerful.

She mentioned the increased dimness of her eyes, and the tremor which had invaded her limbs.   If this be dying, said she, there is nothing at all shocking in it.   My body hardly sensible of pain, my mind at ease, my intellects clear and perfect as ever. What a good and gracious God have I!   For this is what I always prayed for.

I told her it was not so serene with you.

There is not the same reason for it, replied she.   'Tis a choice comfort, Mr. Belford, at the winding-up of our short story, to be able to say I have rather *suffered* injuries *myself* than *offered* them to *others*.   I bless God, though I have been unhappy, as the *world* deems it, and once I thought more so than at present I think I ought to have done; since my calamities were to work out for me my everlasting happiness; yet have I not wilfully made any one creature so.   I have no reason to grieve for anything but for the sorrow I have given my friends.

But pray, Mr. Belford, remember me in the best manner to my Cousin Morden; and desire him to comfort them, and to tell them that all would have been the same had they accepted of my true penitence, as I wish and as I trust the Almighty has done.

I was called down: it was to Harry, who was just returned from Miss Howe's, to whom he carried the lady's letter. The stupid fellow, being bid to make haste with it, and return as soon as possible, stayed not till Miss Howe had it, she being at the distance of five miles, although Mrs. Howe would have had him stay, and sent a man and horse purposely with it to her daughter.

Wednesday Morning, 10 *o'clock.*

The poor lady is just recovered from a fainting fit, which has left her at death's door. Her late tranquillity and freedom from pain seemed but a *lightening*, as Mrs. Lovick and Mrs. Smith call it.

By my faith, Lovelace, I had rather part with all the friends I have in the world than with this lady. I never knew what a virtuous, a holy friendship, as I may call mine to her, was before. But to be so *new* to it, and to be obliged to forego it so soon, what an affliction! Yet, thank Heaven, I lose her not by *my own* fault!—But 'twould be barbarous not to spare thee now.

She has sent for the divine who visited her before, to pray with her.

Letter CXI—*Mr. Lovelace to John Belford, Esq.*

Kensington, Wednesday Noon.

LIKE Æsop's traveller, thou blowest hot and cold, life and death, in the same breath, with a view, no doubt, to distract me. How familiarly dost thou use the words *dying, dimness, tremor*! Never did any mortal ring so many changes on so few bells. Thy true father, I dare swear, was a butcher or an undertaker, by the delight thou seemest to take in scenes of death and horror. Thy barbarous reflection that thou losest her not by thy own fault is never to be forgiven. Thou hast but one way to atone for the torments thou givest me, and that is by sending me word that she is better, and will recover. Whether it be true or not, let me be told so, and I will go abroad rejoicing and believing it, and my wishes and imagination shall make out all the rest.

If she live but one year, that I may acquit myself *to* myself (no matter for the world!) that her death is not owing to me, I will compound for the rest.

Will neither vows nor prayers save her? I never prayed in my life, put all the years of it together, as I have done for this fortnight past: and I have most sincerely repented of all my baseness to her—and will nothing do?

But after all, if she recover not, *this* reflection must be my comfort; and it is *truth*: that her *departure* will be owing rather to wilfulness, to downright *female* wilfulness, than to any other cause.

It is difficult for people who pursue the dictates of a violent resentment to stop where first they designed to stop.

I have the charity to believe that even James and Arabella Harlowe, at first, intended no more by the confederacy they formed against this their angel sister, than to disgrace and keep her down, lest (sordid wretches!) their uncles should follow the example her grandfather had set, to *their* detriment.

So this lady, as I suppose, intended only at first to vex and plague me; and, finding she could do it to purpose, her desire of revenge insensibly became stronger in her than the desire of life; and now she is willing to die, as an event which she thinks will cut my heart-strings asunder. And still the *more* to be revenged, puts on the Christian and forgives me.

But I'll have none of her forgiveness! My own heart tells me I do not deserve it; and I cannot bear it! And what is it but a mere *verbal* forgiveness, as ostentatiously as cruelly given, with a view to magnify herself and wound me deeper? A little, dear, specious—but let me stop, lest I blaspheme!

.   .   .   .   .   .

Reading over the above, I am ashamed of my ramblings: but what wouldst have me do? Seest thou not that I am but seeking to run out of myself, in hope to lose myself; yet that I am unable to do either?

If *ever* thou lovedst but half so fervently as I love—but of that thy heavy soul is not capable.

Send me word by thy next, I conjure thee, in the names of all her kindred saints and angels, that she is living, and likely to live! If thou sendest ill news, thou wilt be answerable for the consequence, whether it be fatal to the messenger or to

Thy LOVELACE.

Letter CXII—Mr. Belford to Robert Lovelace, Esq.

Wednesday, 11 o'clock.

DR. H. has just been here. He tarried with me till the minister had done praying by the lady; and then we were both admitted. Mr. Goddard, who came while the doctor and the clergyman were with her, went away with them when they went. They took a solemn and everlasting leave of her, as I have no scruple to say; blessing her, and being blessed by her; and wishing (when it came to be their lot) for an exit as happy as hers is likely to be.

She had again earnestly requested of the doctor his opinion how long it was *now* probable that she could continue: and he told her that he apprehended she would hardly see to-morrow night. She said she should number the hours with greater pleasure than ever she numbered any in her life on the most joyful occasion.

How unlike poor Belton's last hours, hers! See the infinite difference in the effects, on the same awful and affecting occasion, between a good and a bad conscience!

This moment a man is come from Miss Howe with a letter. Perhaps I shall be able to send you the contents.

.   .   .   .

She endeavoured several times with earnestness, but in vain, to read the letter of her dear friend. The writing, she said, was too fine for her grosser sight, and the lines staggered under her eye. And, indeed, she trembled so she could not hold the paper: and at last desired Mrs. Lovick to read it to her, the messenger waiting for an answer.

Thou wilt see, in Miss Howe's letter, how different the expression of the same impatience and passionate love is, when dictated by the gentler mind of a woman, from that which results from a mind so boisterous and knotty as thine. For Mrs. Lovick will transcribe it; and I shall send it—to be read in this place, if thou wilt.

Miss Howe to Miss Clarissa Harlowe

Tuesday, Sept. 5.

O MY DEAREST FRIEND!—What will become of your poor Anna Howe! I see by your writing, as well as read by your own account (which, were you not very, *very* ill, you would have touched more tenderly), how it is with you! Why have I thus long delayed to attend you! Could I think that the comfortings of a faithful friend were as nothing to a gentle mind in distress, that I could be prevailed upon to forbear visiting you so much as *once* in all this time! I, as well as everybody else, to desert and abandon my dear creature to strangers! What will become of me if you be as bad as my apprehensions make you!

I will set out this moment, little as the encouragement is that you give me to do so! My mother is willing I should! Why, oh, why, was she not *before* willing!

Yet she persuades me too (lest I should be fatally affected were I to find my fears too well justified) to wait the return of this messenger, who rides our swiftest horse. God speed him with good news to me—else—but, O my dearest, dearest friend, what else? One line from your hand by him! Send me but *one* line to bid me attend you! I will set out the moment, the very moment I receive it. I am now actually ready to do so! And if you love me, as I love you, the sight of me will revive you to my hopes. But why, why, when I can think this, did I not go up sooner?

Blessed Heaven! deny not to my prayers, my friend, my admonisher, my adviser, at a time so critical to myself!

But methinks your style and sentiments are too well connected, too full of life and vigour, to give cause for so much despair as the staggering pen seems to forebode.

I am sorry I was not at home [I *must* add thus much, though the servant is ready mounted at the door] when Mr. Belford's servant came with your affecting letter. I was at Miss Lloyd's. My mamma sent it to me; and I came home that instant. But he was gone. He would not stay, it seems. Yet I wanted to ask him a hundred thousand questions. But why delay I thus my messenger? I have a multitude of things to say to you—to advise with you about. You shall direct me in everything. I will obey the holding up of your finger. But, if *you* leave me, what is the world, or anything in it, to

Your ANNA HOWE?

The effect this letter had on the lady, who is so near the end which the fair writer so much apprehends and deplores, obliged Mrs. Lovick to make many breaks in reading it, and many changes of voice.

This *is* a friend, said the divine lady (taking the letter in her hand and kissing it), worth wishing to live for. O my dear Anna Howe! How uninterruptedly sweet and noble has been our friendship! But we shall one day meet (and this hope must comfort us both) never to part again! Then, divested of the shades of body, shall we be all light and all mind. Then how unalloyed, how perfect, will be our friendship! Our love then will have one and the same adorable object, and we shall enjoy it and each other to all eternity!

She said her dear friend was so earnest for a line or two that she would fain write, if she could: and she tried; but to no purpose. She could dictate, however, she believed; and desired Mrs. Lovick would take pen and paper. Which she did, and then she dictated to *her*. I would have withdrawn; but at her desire stayed.

She wandered a good deal at first. She took notice that she did. And when she got into a little train, not pleasing herself, she apologized to Mrs. Lovick for making her begin again and again; and said that third time should go, let it be as it would.

She dictated the farewell part without hesitation; and when she came to the blessing and subscription, she took the pen, and dropping on her knees, supported by Mrs. Lovick, wrote the conclusion; but Mrs. Lovick was forced to guide her hand.

You will find the sense surprisingly entire, her weakness considered.

I made the messenger wait while I transcribed it. I have endeavoured to imitate the subscriptive part; and in the letter made pauses where, to the best of my remembrance, she paused. In nothing that relates to this admirable lady can I be too minute.

Wedn. near 3 *o'clock.*

My dearest Miss Howe,—You must not be surprised—nor grieved—that Mrs. Lovick writes for me. Although I cannot obey you, and write with my *pen*, yet my *heart* writes by hers— accept it so—it is the nearest to obedience I can!

And now, what *ought* I to say? What *can* I say?—But why should you not know the truth? since soon you must—very soon.

Know then, and let your tears be those, if of pity, of *joyful* pity! for I permit you to shed a few, to embalm, as I may say, a fallen blossom—know then, that the good doctor, and the pious clergyman, and the worthy apothecary, have just now— with joint benedictions—taken their last leave of me: and the former bids me hope—do, my dearest, let me say *hope*—hope for my enlargement before to-morrow sunset.

Adieu, therefore, my dearest friend!—Be this *your* consolation, as it is *mine*, that in God's good time we shall meet in a blessed eternity, never more to part!—Once more, then, adieu—and be happy!—which a generous nature cannot be, unless—to its power—it makes others so too.

God for ever bless you! prays, dropped on my bended knees, although supported upon them,

Your obliged, grateful, affectionate,

CL. HARLOWE.

When I had transcribed and sealed this letter, by her direction, I gave it to the messenger myself; who told me that Miss Howe waited for nothing but his return to set out for London.

Thy servant is just come; so I will close here. Thou art a merciless master. The two fellows are *battered* to death by thee, to use a female word; and all female words, though we are not sure of their derivation, have very significant meanings. I believe, in their hearts, they wish the angel in the heaven that is ready to receive her, and thee at thy proper place, that there might be an end of their *flurries*—another word of the same gender.

What a letter hast thou sent me! Poor Lovelace! is all the answer I will return.

[*Five o'clock.*] Colonel Morden is this moment arrived.

Letter CXIII—*Mr. Belford.* [*In continuation*]

Eight in the Evening.

I HAD but just time in my former to tell you that Colonel Morden was arrived. He was on horseback, attended by two servants, and alighted at the door just as the clock struck five. Mrs. Smith was then below in her back shop, weeping, her husband with her, who was as much affected as she; Mrs. Lovick having left them a little before, in tears likewise; for they had been bemoaning one another; joining in opinion that the admirable lady would not live the night over. She had told them it was *her* opinion too, from some numbnesses, which she called the forerunners of death, and from an increased inclination to doze.

The colonel, as Mrs. Smith told me afterwards, asked with great impatience, the moment he alighted, How Miss Harlowe was? She answered, Alive; but, she feared, drawing on apace. Good God! said he, with his hands and eyes lifted up. Can I see her? My name is Morden. I have the honour to be nearly related to her. Step up, pray; and let her know [she is sensible, I hope] that I am here. Who is with her?

Nobody but her nurse, and Mrs. Lovick, a widow gentlewoman, who is as careful of her as if she were her mother.

And *more* careful too, interrupted he, or she is not careful at all——

Except a gentleman be with her, one Mr. Belford, continued Mrs. Smith, who has been the best friend she has had.

If Mr. Belford be with her, surely I may—but, pray step up and let Mr. Belford know that I shall take it for a favour to speak with him first.

Mrs. Smith came up to me in my new apartment. I had but just dispatched your servant, and was asking her nurse if I might be again admitted; who answered that she was dozing in the elbow-chair, having refused to lie down, saying she should soon, she hoped, lie down for good.

The colonel, who is really a fine gentleman, received me with great politeness. After the first compliments, My kinswoman, sir, said he, is more obliged to you than to any of her own family. For my part, I have been endeavouring to move so many rocks in her favour; and, little thinking the dear creature so very bad, have neglected to attend her, as I ought to have done the moment I arrived; and *would*, had I known how ill she was, and what a task I should have had with the family. But, sir, your friend has been excessively to blame; and you being so *intimately* his friend has made her fare the worse for your civilities to her. But are there no hopes of her recovery?

The doctors have left her, with the melancholy declaration that there are none.

Has she had good attendance, sir? A skilful physician? I hear these good folks have been very civil and obliging to her——

Who could be otherwise? said Mrs. Smith, weeping. She is the sweetest lady in the world!

The character, said the colonel, lifting up his eyes and one hand, that she has from every living creature! Good God! How could your accursed friend——

And how could her cruel parents? interrupted I. We may as easily account for *him* as for *them*.

Too true! returned he, the vileness of the profligates of our sex considered, whenever they can get any of the other into their power.

I satisfied him about the care that had been taken of her; and told him of the friendly and even *paternal* attendance she had had from Dr. H. and Mr. Goddard.

He was impatient to attend her, having not seen her, as he said, since she was twelve years old; and that then she gave promises of being one of the finest women in England.

She *was* so, replied I, a very few months ago: and, though emaciated, she will appear to you to have confirmed those promises: for her features are so regular and exact, her proportion so fine, and her manner so inimitably graceful that, were she only skin and bone, she must be a beauty.

Mrs. Smith, at his request, stepped up, and brought us down word that Mrs. Lovick and her nurse were with her; and that she was in so sound a sleep, leaning upon the former in her elbow-chair, that she neither heard her enter the room nor go out. The colonel begged, if not improper, that he might see her, though sleeping. He said that his impatience would not let him stay till she awaked. Yet he would not have her disturbed; and should be glad to contemplate her sweet features, when she saw not him; and asked if she thought he could not go in and come out without disturbing her?

She believed he might, she answered; for her chair's back was towards the door.

He said he would take care to withdraw if she awoke, that his sudden appearance might not surprise her.

Mrs. Smith, stepping up before us, bid Mrs. Lovick and the nurse not stir when we entered: and then we went up softly together.

We beheld the lady in a charming attitude. Dressed, as I told you before, in her virgin white, she was sitting in her elbow-chair, Mrs. Lovick close by her in another chair, with her left arm round her neck, supporting it, as it were; for, it seems, the lady had bid her do so, saying she had been a mother to her, and she would delight herself in thinking she was in her mamma's arms; for she found herself drowsy; perhaps, she said, for the last time she should ever be so.

One faded cheek rested upon the good woman's bosom, the kindly warmth of which had overspread it with a faint, but charming flush; the other paler and hollow, as if already iced over by death. Her hands, white as the lily, with her meandering veins more transparently blue than ever I had seen even hers (veins so soon, alas! to be choked up by the congealment of that purple stream which already so languidly creeps rather than flows through them!); her hands hanging lifelessly, one before her, the other grasped by the right hand of the kind widow, whose tears bedewed the sweet face which her motherly bosom supported, though unfelt by the fair sleeper; and either insensibly to the good woman, or what she would not disturb her to wipe off, or to change her posture: her aspect was sweetly calm and serene; and though she started now and then, yet her sleep seemed easy; her breath indeed short and quick; but tolerably free, and not like that of a dying person.

In this heart-moving attitude she appeared to us when we approached her, and came to have her lovely face before us.

The colonel, sighing often, gazed upon her with his arms folded, and with the most profound and affectionate attention; till at last, on her starting, and fetching her breath with greater difficulty than before, he retired to a screen that was drawn before her *house*, as she calls it, which, as I have heretofore observed, stands under one of the windows. This screen was placed there at the time she found herself obliged to take to her chamber; and in the depth of our concern, and the fullness of other discourse at our first interview, I had forgotten to apprise the colonel of what he would probably see.

Retiring thither, he drew out his handkerchief, and, overwhelmed with grief, seemed unable to speak: but, on casting his eye behind the screen, he soon broke silence; for, struck with the shape of the coffin, he lifted up a purplish-coloured cloth that was spread over it, and, starting back, Good God! said he, what's here?

Mrs. Smith standing next him: Why, said he, with great emotion, is my cousin suffered to indulge her sad reflections with such an object before her?

Alas! sir, replied the good woman, who should control her? We are all strangers about her, in a manner: and yet we have expostulated with her upon this sad occasion.

I ought, said I (stepping softly up to him, the lady again falling into a doze), to have apprised you of this. I was here when it was brought in, and never was so shocked in my life. But she had none of her friends about her, and no reason to hope for any of them to come near her; and, assured she should not recover, she was resolved to leave as little as possible, especially as to what related to her person, to her executor. But it is not a shocking object to her, though it be to everybody else.

Curse upon the hard-heartedness of those, said he, who occasioned her to make so sad a provision for herself! What must her reflections have been all the time she was thinking of it, and giving orders about it? And what must they be every time she turns her head towards it? These uncommon geniuses—but indeed she *should* have been controlled in it had I been here.

The lady fetched a profound sigh, and, starting, it broke off our talk; and the colonel then withdrew farther behind the screen, that his sudden appearance might not surprise her.

Where am I? said she. How drowsy I am! How long have I dozed? Don't go, sir (for I was retiring). I am very stupid, and shall be more and more so, I suppose.

She then offered to raise herself; but, being ready to faint through weakness, was forced to sit down again, reclining her head on her chair-back; and, after a few moments: I believe now, my good friends, said she, all your kind trouble will soon be over. I have slept, but am not refreshed, and my fingers' ends seem numbed—have no feeling! (holding them up). 'Tis time to send the letter to my good Norton.

Shall I, madam, send my servant post with it?

Oh, no, sir, I thank you. It will reach the dear woman too soon (as she will think) by the post.

I told her this was not post day.

Is it Wednesday still? said she. Bless me! I know not how the time goes: but very tediously, 'tis plain. And now I think I must soon take to my bed. All will be most conveniently and with least trouble over there—will it not, Mrs. Lovick?— I think, sir, turning to me, I have left nothing to these last incapacitating hours. Nothing either to say or to do. I bless God, I have not. If I *had*, how unhappy should I be! Can you, sir, remind me of anything necessary to be done or said to make your office easy?

If, madam, your Cousin Morden should come, you would be glad to see him, I presume?

I am too weak to wish to see my cousin now. It would but discompose me, and him too. Yet, if he come while I *can* see, I *will* see him, were it but to thank him for former favours, and for his present kind intentions to me. Has anybody been here from him?

He has called, and will be here, madam, in half an hour; but he feared to surprise you.

Nothing can surprise me now, except my mamma were to favour me with her last blessing in person. That would be a welcome surprise to me, even yet. But did my cousin come purposely to town to see me?

Yes, madam. I took the liberty to let him know, by a line last Monday, how ill you were.

You are very kind, sir. I am and have been greatly obliged to you. But I think I shall be pained to see him now, because he will be concerned to see me. And yet, as I am not so ill as I shall presently be, the sooner he comes the better. But if he come, what shall I do about that screen? He will chide me, very probably; and I cannot bear chiding now. Perhaps [leaning upon Mrs. Lovick and Mrs. Smith] I can walk into the next apartment to receive him.

She motioned to rise; but was ready to faint again, and forced to sit still.

The colonel was in a perfect agitation behind the screen to hear this discourse; and twice, unseen by his cousin, was coming from it towards her; but retreated, for fear of surprising her too much.

I stepped to him and favoured his retreat; she only saying: Are you going, Mr. Belford? Are you sent for down? Is my cousin come? For she heard somebody step softly across the room, and thought it to be me; her hearing being more perfect than her sight.

I told her I believed he was; and she said: We must make the best of it, Mrs. Lovick and Mrs. Smith. I shall otherwise most grievously shock my poor cousin: for he loved me dearly once. Pray give me a few of the doctor's last drops in water, to keep up my spirits for this one interview; and that is all, I believe, that can concern me now.

The colonel (who heard all this) sent in his name; and I, pretending to go down to him, introduced the afflicted gentleman; she having first ordered the screen to be put as close to the window as possible, that he might not see what was behind it; while he, having heard what she had said about it, was determined to take no notice of it.

He folded the angel in his arms as she sat, dropping down on one knee; for, supporting herself upon the two elbows of the chair, she attempted to rise, but could not. Excuse, my dear cousin, said she, excuse me, that I cannot stand up. I did not expect this favour now. But I am glad of this opportunity to thank you for all your generous goodness to me.

I never, my best-beloved and dearest cousin, said he (with eyes running over), shall forgive myself that I did not attend you sooner. Little did I think you were so ill; nor do any of your friends believe it. If they did——

If they did, repeated she, interrupting him, I should have had more compassion from them. I am sure I should. But pray, sir, how did you leave them? Are *you* reconciled to them? If you are not, I beg, if you love your poor Clarissa, that you will: for every widened difference augments but my fault; since *that* is the foundation of all.

I had been expecting to hear from them in your favour, my dear cousin, said he, for some hours, when this gentleman's letter arrived, which hastened me up: but I have the account of your grandfather's estate to make up with you, and have bills and drafts upon their banker for the sums due to you; which they desire you may receive, lest you should have occasion for money. And this is such an earnest of an approaching reconciliation that I dare to answer for all the rest being according to your wishes, if——

Ah! sir, interrupted she, with frequent breaks and pauses, I wish I wish—this does not rather show that, were I to live, they would have nothing more to say to me. I never had any pride in being independent of them: all my actions, when I might have made myself *more* independent, show this—but what avail these reflections now? I only beg, sir, that you, and *this* gentleman—to whom I am exceedingly obliged—will adjust those matters—according to the will I have written. Mr. Belford will excuse me; but it was in truth more necessity than choice that made me think of giving him the trouble he so kindly accepts. Had I had the happiness to see you, my cousin, sooner—or to know that you still honoured me with your regard—I should not have had the assurance to ask this favour of *him*. But, though the friend of Mr. Lovelace, he is a man of honour, and he will make peace rather than break it. And, my dear cousin, let me beg of you to contribute your part to it— and remember that, while I have nearer relations than my Cousin Morden, dear as you are, and always were to me, you have no title to avenge my wrongs upon him who has been the occasion of them. But I wrote to you my mind on this subject, and my reasons; and hope I need not further urge them.

I must do Mr. Lovelace so much justice, answered he, wiping his eyes, as to witness how sincerely he repents him of his ungrateful baseness to you, and how ready he is to make you all the amends in his power. He owns *his* wickedness, and *your* merit. If he did not, I could not pass it over, though you *have* nearer relations: for, my dear cousin, did not your grandfather leave me in trust for you? And should I think myself concerned for your fortune, and not for your honour? But, since he is so desirous to do you justice, I have the less to say; and you may make yourself entirely easy on that account.

I thank you, thank you, sir, said she: all is now as I wished. But I am very faint, very weak. I am sorry I cannot hold up; that I cannot better deserve the honour of this visit: but it will not be. And saying this, she sunk down in her chair, and was silent.

Hereupon we both withdrew, leaving word that we would be at the Bedford Head, if anything extraordinary happened.

We bespoke a little repast, having neither of us dined; and while it was getting ready, you may guess at the subject of our discourse. Both joined in lamentation for the lady's desperate state: admired her manifold excellences: severely condemned you and her friends. Yet, to bring him into better opinion of you, I read to him some passages from your last letters, which showed your concern for the wrongs you had done her, and your deep remorse: and he said it was a dreadful thing to labour under the sense of a guilt so irremediable.

We procured Mr. Goddard (Dr. H. not being at home) once more to visit her, and to call upon us in his return. He was so good as to do so; but he tarried with her not five minutes; and told us that she was drawing on apace; that he feared she would not live till morning; and that she wished to see Colonel Morden directly.

The colonel made excuses where none were needed; and though our little refection was just brought in, he went away immediately.

I could not touch a morsel; and took pen and ink to amuse myself, and oblige you; knowing how impatient you would be for a few lines: for, from what I have recited, you will see it was impossible I could withdraw to write when your servant came at half an hour after five, or have an opportunity for it till now; and *this* is accidental: and yet your poor fellow was afraid to go away with the verbal message I sent; importing, as no doubt he told you, that the colonel was with us, the lady excessively ill, and that I could not stir to write a line.

Ten o'clock.

The colonel sent to me afterwards, to tell me that the lady having been in convulsions, he was so much disordered that he could not possibly attend me.

I have sent every half-hour to know how she does: and just now I have the pleasure to hear that her convulsions have left her; and that she is gone to rest in a much quieter way than could be expected.

Her poor cousin is very much indisposed; yet will not stir out of the house while she is in such a way; but intends to lie down on a couch, having refused any other accommodation.

Letter CXIV—Mr. Belford. [*In continuation*]

Soho, Six o'clock, Sept. 7.

THE lady is still alive. The colonel having just sent his servant to let me know that she inquired after me about an hour ago, I am dressing to attend her. Joel begs of me to dispatch him back, though but with one line to gratify your present impatience. He expects, he says, to find you at Knightsbridge, let him make what haste he can back; and if he has not a line or two to pacify you, he is afraid you will pistol him; for he apprehends that you are hardly yourself. I therefore dispatch this; and will have another ready as soon as I can, with particulars. But you must have a little patience; for how can I withdraw every half-hour to write, if I am admitted to the lady's presence, or if I am with the colonel?

Smith's, Eight in the Morning.

The lady is in a slumber. Mrs. Lovick, who sat up with her, says she had a better night than was expected; for although she slept little, she seemed easy; and the easier for the pious frame she was in; all her waking moments being taken up in devotion, or in an ejaculatory silence; her hands and eyes often lifted up, and her lips moving with a fervour worthy of these her last hours.

Ten o'clock.

The colonel being earnest to see his cousin as soon as she awoke, we were both admitted. We observed in her, as soon as we entered, strong symptoms of her approaching dissolution, notwithstanding what the women had flattered us with from her last night's tranquillity. The colonel and I, each loath to say what we thought, looked upon one another with melancholy countenances.

The colonel told her he should send a servant to her Uncle Antony's for some papers he had left there; and asked if she had any commands that way?

She thought not, she said, speaking more inwardly than she did the day before. She had indeed a letter ready to be sent to her good Norton; and there was a request intimated in it: but it was time enough if the request were signified to those

whom it concerned when all was over. However, it might be
sent then by the servant who was going that way. And she
caused it to be given to the colonel for that purpose.

Her breath being very short, she desired another pillow.
Having two before, this made her in a manner sit up in her
bed; and she spoke then with more distinctness; and, seeing us
greatly concerned, forgot her own stutterings to comfort us;
and a charming lecture she gave us, though a brief one, upon
the happiness of a timely preparation, and upon the hazards of
a late repentance, when the mind, as she observed, was so much
weakened, as well as the body, as to render a poor soul hardly
able to contend with its natural infirmities.

I beseech ye, my good friends, proceeded she, mourn not
for one who mourns not, nor has cause to mourn, for herself.
On the contrary, rejoice with me, that all my worldly troubles
are so near their end. Believe me, sirs, that I would not, if
I might, choose to live, although the pleasantest part of my life
were to come over again: and yet *eighteen years of it*, out of
nineteen, have been *very* pleasant. To be so much exposed to
temptation, and to be so liable to fail in the trial, who would not
rejoice that all her dangers are over! All I wished was pardon
and blessing from my dear parents. Easy as my departure
seems to promise to be, it would have been still easier had I had
that pleasure. BUT GOD ALMIGHTY WOULD NOT LET ME DEPEND
FOR COMFORT UPON ANY BUT HIMSELF.

She then repeated her request, in the most earnest manner, to
her *cousin*, that he would not *heighten* her fault by seeking to
avenge her death; to *me*, that I would endeavour to make up
all breaches, and use the power I had with my friend to prevent
all future mischiefs *from* him, as well as that which this trust
might give me to prevent any *to* him.

She made some excuses to her *cousin*, for having not been able
to alter her will, to join him in the executorship with me; and to
me, for the trouble she had given, and yet should give me.

She had fatigued herself so much (growing sensibly weaker)
that she sunk her head upon her pillows, ready to faint; and we
withdrew to the window, looking upon one another; but could
not tell what to say; and yet both seemed inclinable to speak:
but the motion passed over in silence. Our eyes only spoke;
and that in a manner neither's were used to; mine, at least, not
till I knew this admirable creature.

The colonel withdrew to dismiss his messenger, and send away
the letter to Mrs. Norton. I took the opportunity to retire

likewise; and to write thus far. And Joel returning to take it, I now close here.

Eleven o'clock.

Letter CXV—*Mr. Belford.* [*In continuation*]

THE colonel tells me that he has written to Mr. John Harlowe, by his servant, "That they might spare themselves the trouble of debating about a reconciliation; for that his dear cousin would probably be no more before they could resolve."

He asked me after his cousin's means of subsisting; and whether she had accepted of any favour from *me*: he was sure, he said, she would not from *you*.

I acquainted him with the truth of her parting with some of her apparel.

This wrung his heart; and bitterly did he exclaim as well against you as against her implacable relations.

He wished he had not come to England at all, or had come sooner; and hoped I would apprise him of the whole mournful story at a proper season. He added that he had thoughts, when he came over, of fixing here for the remainder of his days: but now, as it was impossible his cousin could recover, he would go abroad again, and resettle himself at Florence or Leghorn.

.   .   .   .

The lady has been giving orders, with great presence of mind, about her body; directing her nurse and the maid of the house to put her into her coffin as soon as she is cold. Mr. Belford, she said, would know the rest by her will.

.   .   .   .

She has just now given from her bosom, where she always wore it, a miniature picture set in gold of Miss Howe: she gave it to Mrs. Lovick, desiring her to fold it up in white paper, and direct it, *To Charles Hickman, Esq.*, and to give it to me, when she was departed, for that gentleman.

She looked upon the picture before she gave it her. *Sweet and ever-amiable friend—companion—sister—lover!* said she— and kissed it four several times, once at each tender appellation.

.   .   .   .

Your other servant is come. Well may you be impatient! Well may you!—But do you think I can leave off in the middle of a conversation to run and set down what offers, and send it away piecemeal as I write? If I *could*, must I not lose one half while I put down the other?

This event is nearly as interesting to *me* as it is to *you*. If you are more grieved than I, there can be but one reason for it; and that's at your heart! I had rather lose all the friends I have in the world (yourself in the number) than this divine lady; and shall be unhappy whenever I think of her sufferings, and of her merit; though I have nothing to reproach myself by reason of the former.

I say not this, just now, so much to reflect upon you, as to express my own grief; though your conscience, I suppose, will make you think otherwise.

Your poor fellow, who says that he begs for *his life* in desiring to be dispatched back with a letter, tears this from me—else perhaps (for I am just sent for down) a quarter of an hour would make you—not *easy* indeed—but *certain*—and that, in a *state* like yours, to a *mind* like yours, is a relief.

Thursday Afternoon, 4 o'clock.

Letter CXVI—*Mr. Belford to Richard Mowbray, Esq.*

Thursday Afternoon.

DEAR MOWBRAY,—I am glad to hear you are in town. Throw yourself the moment this comes to your hand (if possible with Tourville) in the way of the man who least of all men deserves the love of a worthy heart; but most that of thine and Tourville: else the news I shall most probably send him within an hour or two will make annihilation the greatest blessing he has to wish for.

You will find him between Piccadilly and Kensington, most probably on horseback, riding backwards and forwards in a crazy way; a waiter possibly, if so, watching for his servant's return to him from me.

.   .   .   .

His man Will is just come to me. He will carry this to you in his way back, and be your director. Hie away in a coach or anyhow. Your being with him may save either his or a servant's life. See the blessed effects of triumphant libertinism! Sooner or later it comes home to us, and all concludes in gall and bitterness! Adieu.

J. BELFORD.

Letter CXVII—Mr. Lovelace to John Belford, Esq.

CURSE upon the colonel, and curse upon the writer of the last letter I received, and upon all the world! Thou to pretend to be as much interested in my Clarissa's fate as myself! 'Tis well for one of us that this was not said to me, instead of written. Living or dying, she is mine—and only mine. Have I not earned her dearly? Is not damnation likely to be the purchase to me, though a happy eternity will be hers?

An eternal separation! O God! O God! How can I bear that thought! But yet there is life! Yet, therefore, hope—enlarge my hope, and thou shalt be my good genius, and I will forgive thee everything.

For this last time—but it must not, shall not be the *last*—let me hear, the moment thou receivest this—what I *am* to be—for at present I am

The most miserable of men.

Rose, at Knightsbridge, 5 o'clock.

My fellow tells me that thou art sending Mowbray and Tourville to me. I want them not. My soul 's sick of them, and of all the world; but most of myself. Yet, as they send me word they will come to me immediately, I will wait for them, and for thy next. O Belford! let it not be—— But hasten it, hasten it, be it what it may!

Letter CXVIII—Mr. Belford to Robert Lovelace, Esq.

Seven o'clock, Thursday Evening, Sept. 7.

I HAVE only to say at present: Thou wilt do well to take a tour to Paris; or wherever else thy destiny shall lead thee!!!——

JOHN BELFORD.

Letter CXIX—Mr. Mowbray to John Belford, Esq.

Uxbridge, Sept. 7, between 11 and 12 at Night.

DEAR JACK,—I send, by poor Lovelace's desire, for *particulars* of the fatal breviate thou sentest him this night. He cannot bear to set pen to paper; yet wants to know every minute passage of Miss Harlowe's departure. Yet why he should, I cannot see; for if she is gone, she is gone; and who can help it?

I never heard of such a woman in my life. What great matters has she suffered, that grief should kill her thus?

I wish the poor fellow had never known her. From first to

last, what trouble has she cost him! The charming fellow has
been half lost to us ever since he pursued her. And what is
there in one woman more than another, for matter of that?

It was well we were with him when your note came. You
showed your true friendship in your foresight. Why, Jack, the
poor fellow was quite beside himself—mad as any man ever was
in Bedlam.

Will brought him the letter just after we had joined him at
the Bohemia Head; where he had left word at the Rose at
Knightsbridge he should be; for he had been sauntering up and
down, backwards and forwards, expecting us and his fellow.
Will, as soon as he delivered it, got out of his way; and when he
opened it, never was such a piece of scenery. He trembled like
a devil at receiving it: fumbled at the seal, his fingers in a palsy,
like Tom Doleman's; his hand shake, shake, shake, that he tore
the letter in two before he could come at the contents: and,
when he had read them, off went his hat to one corner of the
room, his wig to the other. Damnation seize the world! and
a whole volley of such-like *execratious* wishes; running up and
down the room, and throwing up the sash, and pulling it down,
and smiting his forehead with his double fist with such force
as would have felled an ox, and stamping and tearing, that the
landlord ran in, and faster ran out again. And this was the
distraction scene for some time.

In vain was all Jemmy or I could say to him. I offered once
to take hold of his hands, because he was going to do himself a
mischief, as I believed, looking about for his pistols, which he had
laid upon the table, but which Will, unseen, had taken out with
him [a faithful, honest dog, that Will; I shall for ever love the
fellow for it], and he hit me a damned dowse of the chops as
made my nose bleed. 'Twas well 'twas he; for I hardly knew
how to take it.

Jemmy raved at him, and told him how wicked it was in him
to be so brutish to abuse a friend, and run mad for a woman.
And then he said he was sorry for it; and then Will ventured in
with water and a towel; and the dog rejoiced, as I could see by
his looks, that I *had it* rather than he.

And so, by degrees, we brought him a little to his reason, and
he promised to behave more like a man. And so I forgave him:
and we rode on in the dark to *here* at Doleman's. And we all
tried to shame him out of his mad ungovernable foolishness: for
we told him as how she was but a woman, and an obstinate,
perverse woman too; and how could he help it?

And you know, Jack (as we told him, moreover), that it was a shame to manhood, for a man who had served twenty and twenty women as bad or worse, let him have served Miss Harlowe never so bad, should give himself such *obstropulous* airs because she would die: and we advised him never to attempt a woman proud of her character and *virtue*, as they call it, any more: for why? The conquest did not pay trouble; and what was there in one woman more than another? Hey, you know, Jack! And thus we comforted him and advised him.

But yet his damned addled pate runs upon this lady as much now she's dead as it did when she was living. For, I suppose, Jack, it is no joke: she is certainly and *bona fide* dead: I'n't she? If not, thou deservest to be doubly damned for thy fooling, I tell thee that. So he will have me write for particulars of her *departure*.

He won't bear the word *dead* on any account. A squeamish puppy! How love unmans and softens! And such a *noble* fellow as this too! Rot him for an idiot and an oaf! I have no patience with the foolish *duncical* dog—upon my soul I have not!

So send the account, and let him howl over it, as I suppose he will.

But he must and shall go abroad: and in a month or two Jemmy, and you, and I will join him, and he'll soon get the better of this chicken-hearted folly, never fear; and will then be ashamed of himself: and then we'll not spare him; though *now*, poor fellow, it were pity to *lay him on so thick* as he deserves. And do thou, till then, spare all reflections upon him; for, it seems, thou hast *worked him* unmercifully.

I was willing to give thee some account of the hand we have had with the tearing fellow, who had certainly been a lost man, had we not been with him; or he would have killed somebody or other. I have no doubt of it. And *now* he is but very middling; sits grinning like a man in straw; curses and swears, and is confounded gloomy; and creeps into holes and corners, like an old hedgehog hunted for his grease.

And so, adieu, Jack. Tourville and all of us wish for thee; for no one has the influence upon him that thou hast.

R. MOWBRAY.

As I promised him that I would write for the particulars abovesaid, I write this after all are gone to bed; and the fellow is to set out with it by daybreak.

Letter CXX—Mr. Belford to Robert Lovelace, Esq.

Thursday Night.

I MAY as well try to write; since, were I to go to bed, I shall not sleep. I never had such a weight of grief upon my mind in my life as upon the demise of this admirable woman; whose soul is now rejoicing in the regions of light.

You may be glad to know the particulars of her happy exit. I will try to proceed; for all is hush and still; the family retired; but not one of them, and least of all her poor cousin, I dare say, to rest.

At four o'clock, as I mentioned in my last, I was sent for down; and, as thou usedst to like my descriptions, I will give thee the woeful scene that presented itself to me as I approached the bed.

The colonel was the first that took my attention, kneeling on the side of the bed, the lady's right hand in both his, which his face covered, bathing it with his tears; although she had been comforting him, as the women since told me, in elevated strains but broken accents.

On the other side of the bed sat the good widow; her face overwhelmed with tears, leaning her head against the bed's head in a most disconsolate manner; and turning her face to me, as soon as she saw me, O Mr. Belford, cried she, with folded hands—the dear lady—— A heavy sob permitted her not to say more.

Mrs. Smith, with clasped fingers and uplifted eyes, as if imploring help from the only Power which could give it, was kneeling down at the bed's feet, tears in large drops trickling down her cheeks.

Her nurse was kneeling between the widow and Mrs. Smith, her arms extended. In one hand she held an ineffectual cordial, which she had just been offering to her dying mistress; her face was swollen with weeping (though used to such scenes as this), and she turned her eyes towards me, as if she called upon me by them to join in the helpless sorrow; a fresh stream bursting from them as I approached the bed.

The maid of the house, with her face upon her folded arms, as she stood leaning against the wainscot, more audibly expressed her grief than any of the others.

The lady had been silent a few minutes, and speechless, as they thought, moving her lips without uttering a word; one hand, as I said, in her cousin's. But when Mrs. Lovick on my approach pronounced my name, O Mr. Belford, said she, with a faint inward voice, but very distinct nevertheless—Now!—Now! (in broken periods she spoke)—I bless God for His mercies to His poor creature—all will soon be over—a few—a very few moments—will end this strife—and I shall be happy!

Comfort here, sir—turning her head to the colonel—comfort my cousin—see!—the blam—able kindness—he would not wish me to be happy—so *soon*!

Here she stopped for two or three minutes, earnestly looking upon him: then resuming: My dearest cousin, said she, be comforted—what is dying but the common lot?—The mortal frame may *seem* to labour—but that is all!—It is not so hard to die as I believed it to be!—The preparation is the difficulty—I bless God I have had time for that—the rest is worse to beholders than to me!—I am all blessed hope—hope itself.

She *looked* what she said, a sweet smile beaming over her countenance.

After a short silence: Once more, my dear cousin, said she, but still in broken accents, commend me most dutifully to my father and mother—— There she stopped. And then proceeding: To my sister, to my brother, to my uncles—and tell them I bless them with my parting breath—for all their goodness to me—even for their displeasure I bless them—most happy has been to me my punishment *here*! Happy indeed!

She was silent for a few moments, lifting up her eyes, and the hand her cousin held not between his. Then: *O Death!* said she, *where is thy sting?* [the words I remember to have heard in the Burial Service read over my uncle and poor Belton.] And after a pause: *It is good for me that I was afflicted!* Words of Scripture, I suppose.

Then turning towards us, who were lost in speechless sorrow: O dear, *dear* gentlemen, said she, you know not what *foretastes* —what *assurances*——And there she again stopped, and looked up, as if in a thankful rapture, sweetly smiling.

Then turning her head towards me: Do *you*, sir, tell your friend that I forgive him!—And I pray to God to forgive him! Again pausing, and lifting up her eyes, as if praying that He would: Let him know how happily I die.—And that such as my own, I wish to be his last hour.

She was again silent for a few moments: and then resuming: My sight fails me!—Your voices only—for we both applauded her Christian, her divine frame, though in accents as broken as her own]; and the voice of grief is alike in all. Is not this Mr. Morden's hand? pressing one of his with that he had just

let go.   Which is Mr. Belford's? holding out the other.   I gave
her mine.   God Almighty bless you both, said she, and make
you both—in your last hour—for you *must* come to this—happy
as I am.

She paused again, her breath growing shorter; and, after a
few minutes: And now, my dearest cousin, give me your hand
—nearer—still nearer—drawing it towards her; and she pressed
it with her dying lips—God protect you, dear, dear sir—and
once more receive my best and most grateful thanks—and tell
my dear Miss Howe—and vouchsafe to see and to tell my worthy
Norton—she will be one day, I fear not, though now lowly in her
fortunes, a saint in heaven—tell them both that I remember
them with thankful blessings in my last moments!—and pray
God to give them happiness *here* for many, many years, for the
sake of their friends and lovers; and a heavenly crown *hereafter*;
and such assurances of it as I have, through the all-satisfying
merits of my blessed Redeemer.

Her sweet voice and broken periods methinks still fill my ears,
and never will be out of my memory.

After a short silence, in a more broken and faint accent: And
you, Mr. Belford, pressing my hand, may God preserve you,
and make you sensible of all your errors—you see, in me, how
all ends—may *you* be——And down sunk her head upon her
pillow, she fainting away, and drawing from us her hands.

We thought she was then gone; and each gave way to a
violent burst of grief.

But soon showing signs of returning life, our attention was
again engaged; and I besought her, when a little recovered, to
complete in my favour her half-pronounced blessing.   She waved
her hand to us both, and bowed her head six several times, as
we have since recollected, as if distinguishing every person
present; not forgetting the nurse and the maid-servant; the
latter having approached the bed, weeping, as if crowding in
for the divine lady's last blessing; and she spoke faltering and
inwardly: Bless—bless—bless—you all—and now—and now
[holding up her almost lifeless hands for the last time]—come—
O come—blessed Lord—Jesus!

And with these words, the last but half-pronounced, expired:
such a smile, such a charming serenity overspreading her sweet
face at the instant, as seemed to manifest her eternal happiness
already begun.

O Lovelace!——But I can write no more!

I resume my pen to add a few lines.

While warm, though pulseless, we pressed each her hand with our lips; and then retired into the next room.

We looked at each other with intent to speak: but, as if one motion governed, as one cause affected both, we turned away silent.

The colonel sighed as if his heart would burst: at last, his face and hands uplifted, his back towards me: Good Heaven! said he to himself, support me! And is it thus, O flower of nature!—Then pausing: And must we no more—*never more*!—My blessed, blessed cousin! uttering some other words, which his sighs made inarticulate: and then, as if recollecting himself: Forgive me, sir! Excuse me, Mr. Belford! And sliding by me: Anon I hope to see you, sir. And downstairs he went, and out of the house, leaving me a statue.

When I recovered I was ready to repine at what I *then* called an unequal dispensation; forgetting her happy preparation, and still happier departure; and that she had but drawn a common lot; triumphing in it, and leaving behind her every one less assured of happiness, though equally certain that the lot would one day be their own.

She departed exactly at 40 minutes after 6 o'clock, as by her watch on the table.

And thus died Miss CLARISSA HARLOWE, in the blossom of her youth and beauty: and who, her tender years considered, has not left behind her her superior in extensive knowledge and watchful prudence; nor hardly her equal for unblemished virtue, exemplary piety, sweetness of manners, discreet generosity, and true Christian charity: and these all set off by the most graceful modesty and humility; yet on all proper occasions manifesting a noble presence of mind and true magnanimity: so that she may be said to have been not only an ornament to her sex but to human nature.

A better pen than mine may do her fuller justice. Thine, I mean, O Lovelace! For well dost thou know how much she excelled in the graces both of mind and person, natural and acquired, all that is woman. And thou also canst best account for the causes of her immature death, through those calamities which in so short a space of time, from the highest pitch of felicity (every one in a manner adoring her), brought her to an exit so happy for herself, but that it was so *early*, so much to be deplored by all who had the honour of her acquaintance.

This task, then, I leave to thee: but now I can write no more, only that I am a sympathizer in every part of thy distress, except (and yet it is cruel to say it) in that which arises from thy guilt.

One o'clock, Friday Morning.

Letter CXXI—*Mr. Belford to Robert Lovelace, Esq.*

Nine, Friday Morn.

I HAVE no opportunity to write at length, having necessary orders to give on the melancholy occasion. Joel, who got to me by six in the morning, and whom I dispatched instantly back with the letter I had ready from last night, gives me but an indifferent account of the state of your mind. I wonder not at it; but time (and nothing else can) will make it easier to you: if (that is to say) you have compounded with your conscience; else it may be heavier every day than other.

.   .   .   .

Tourville tells me what a way you are in. I hope you will not think of coming hither. The lady in her will desires you may not see her. Four copies are making of it. It is a long one; for she gives her reasons for all she wills. I will write to you more particularly as soon as possibly I can.

.   .   .   .

Three letters are just brought by a servant in livery, directed *To Miss Clarissa Harlowe.* I will send copies of them to you. The contents are enough to make one mad. How would this poor lady have rejoiced to receive them. And yet, if she had, she would not have been enabled to say, as she nobly did,[1] *that God would not let her depend for comfort upon any but Himself.* And indeed for some days past she had seemed to have got above all worldly considerations—her *fervent love, even for her Miss Howe,* as she acknowledged, having given way to *supremer fervours.*[2]

Letter CXXII—*Mrs. Norton to Miss Clarissa Harlowe*

Wednesday, Sept. 6.

AT length, my best-beloved Miss Clary, everything is in the wished train: for all your relations are unanimous in your favour. Even your brother and sister are with the foremost to be reconciled to you.

[1] See p. 339.   [2] See p. 307.

I knew it must end thus! By patience and persevering sweetness, what a triumph have you gained!

This happy change is owing to letters received from your physician, from your Cousin Morden, and from Mr. Brand.

Colonel Morden will be with you no doubt before this can reach you, with his pocket-book filled with money-bills, that nothing may be wanting to make you easy.

And *now*, all our hopes, all our prayers are that this good news may restore you to spirits and health; and that (so long withheld) it may not come too late.

I know how much your dutiful heart will be raised with the joyful tidings I write you, and still shall more particularly tell you of when I have the happiness to see you: which will be by next Saturday at farthest; perhaps on Friday afternoon, by the time you can receive this.

For this day, being sent for by the general voice, I was received by every one with great goodness and condescension, and *entreated* (for that was the word they were pleased to use, when I needed *no* entreaty, I am sure) to hasten up to you, and to assure you of all their affectionate regards to you: and your father bid me say all the kind things that were in my *heart* to say, in order to comfort and raise you up; and they would hold themselves bound to make them good.

How agreeable is this commission to your Norton! My heart will overflow with kind speeches, never fear! I am already meditating what I shall say to cheer and raise you up, in the names of every one dear and near to you. And sorry I am that I cannot this moment set out, as I might instead of writing, would they favour my eager impatience with their chariot; but as it was not offered, it would be presumption to have asked for it: and to-morrow a hired chaise and pair will be ready; but at what hour I know not.

How I long once more to fold my dear precious young lady to my fond, my *more* than fond, my *maternal* bosom!

Your sister will write to you, and send her letter, with this, by a particular hand.

I must not let them see what I write, because of my wish about the chariot.

Your Uncle Harlowe will also write, and (I doubt not) in the kindest terms: for they are all extremely alarmed and troubled at the dangerous way your doctor represents you to be in; as well as delighted with the character he gives you. Would to Heaven the good gentleman had written *sooner*! And yet he writes that you know not he has *now* written. But it is all our confidence, and our consolation, that he would not have written at all had he thought it too late.

They will prescribe no conditions to you, my dear young lady; but will leave all to your own duty and discretion. Only your brother and sister declare they will never yield to call Mr. Lovelace brother: nor will your father, I believe, be easily brought to think of him for a son.

I am to bring you down with me as soon as your health and inclination will permit. You will be received with open arms. Every one longs to see you. All the servants please themselves that they shall be permitted to kiss your hands. The pert Betty's note is already changed; and she now runs over in your just praises. What friends does prosperity make! What enemies adversity! It always was, and always will be so, in every state of life, from the throne to the cottage. But let all be forgotten now on this jubilee change: and may you, my dearest miss, be capable of rejoicing in this good news; as I know you *will* rejoice, if capable of anything.

God preserve you to our happy meeting! And I will, if I may say so, weary Heaven with my incessant prayers to preserve and restore you afterwards!

I need not say how much I am, my dear young lady,
　　　　　Your ever affectionate and devoted
　　　　　　　　　JUDITH NORTON.

An unhappy delay as to the chaise will make it Saturday morning before I can fold you to my fond heart.

Letter CXXIII—Miss Arab. Harlowe to Miss Cl. Harlowe
　　　　　　　　　Wedn. Morning, Sept. 6.

DEAR SISTER,—We have just heard that you are exceedingly ill. We all loved you as never young creature was loved: you are sensible of that, Sister Clary. And you have been very naughty—but we could not be angry always.

We are indeed more afflicted with the news of your being so very ill than I can express: for I see not but, after this separation (as we understand that your misfortune has been greater than your fault, and that, however unhappy, you have demeaned yourself like the good young creature you used to be), we shall love you better, if possible, than ever.

Take comfort, therefore, Sister Clary; and don't be too much cast down—whatever your mortifications may be from such noble prospects overclouded, and from the reflections you will have from *within*, on your faulty step, and from the sullying of such a charming character by it, you will receive none from *any of us*: and, as an earnest of your papa's and mamma's favour and reconciliation, they assure you by me of their blessing and hourly prayers.

If it will be any comfort to you, and my mother finds this letter is received as we expect (which we shall know by the good effect it will have upon your health), she will herself go to town to you. Meantime, the good woman you so dearly love will be hastened up to you; and she writes by this opportunity, to acquaint you of it, and of all our returning love.

I hope you'll rejoice at this good news. Pray let us hear that you do. Your next grateful letter on this occasion, especially if it gives us the pleasure of hearing you are better upon this news, will be received with the same (if not greater) delight, that we *used* to have in all your prettily penned epistles. Adieu, my dear Clary! I am

Your loving sister, and true friend,
ARABELLA HARLOWE.

Letter CXXIV—To his dear Niece Miss Clarissa Harlowe

Wedn. Sept. 6.

WE were greatly grieved, my beloved Miss Clary, at your fault; but we are still more, if possible, to hear you are so very ill; and we are sorry things have been carried so far.

We know your talents, my dear, and how movingly you could write, whenever you pleased; so that nobody could ever deny you anything; and, believing you depended on your pen, and little thinking you were so ill, and that you had lived so regular a life, and were so truly penitent, are much troubled, every one of us, your brother and all, for being so severe. Forgive my part in it, my dearest Clary. I am your *second papa*, you know. And you *used* to love me.

I hope you'll soon be able to come down, and, after a while, when your indulgent parents can spare you, that you will come to me for a whole month, and rejoice my heart, as you used to do. But if, through illness, you cannot so soon come down as we wish, I will go up to you: for I long to see you. I never more longed to see you in my life; and you was always the darling of my heart, you know.

My brother Antony desires his hearty commendations to you, and joins with me in the tenderest assurance, that all shall be well, and, if possible, better than ever; for we now have been so long without you that we know the miss of you, and even hunger and thirst, as I may say, to see you, and to take you once more to our hearts: whence indeed you was never banished so far as our concern for the unhappy step made *us* think and *you* believe you were. Your sister and brother both talk of seeing you in town: so does my dear sister, your indulgent mother.

God restore your health, if it be His will: else I know not what will become of

> Your truly loving uncle, and second papa,
>   JOHN HARLOWE.

Letter CXXV—*Mr. Belford to Robert Lovelace, Esq.*

Friday Night, Sept. 8, past Ten.

I WILL now take up the account of our proceedings from my letter of last night, which contained the dying words of this incomparable lady.

As soon as we had seen the last scene closed (so blessedly for herself!), we left the body to the care of the good women, who, according to the orders she had given them that very night, removed her into that last house which she had displayed so much fortitude in providing.

In the morning, between seven and eight o'clock, according to appointment, the colonel came to me here. He was very much indisposed. We went together, accompanied by Mrs. Lovick and Mrs. Smith, into the deceased's chamber. We could not help taking a view of the lovely corpse, and admiring the charming serenity of her noble aspect. The women declared they never saw death so lovely before; and that she looked as if in an easy slumber, the colour having not quite left her cheeks and lips.

I unlocked the drawer, in which (as I mentioned in a former) [1] she had deposited her papers. I told you in mine of Monday last that she had the night before sealed up with three black seals a parcel inscribed, *As soon as I am certainly dead, this to be broke open by Mr. Belford.* I accused myself for not having done it overnight. But really I was then incapable of anything.

I broke it open accordingly, and found in it no less than eleven

[1] See p. 289.

letters, each sealed with her own seal and black wax, one of which was directed to me.

I will enclose a copy of it.

To John Belford, Esq.

Sunday Evening, Sept. 3.

SIR,—I take this last and solemn occasion to repeat to you my thanks for all your kindness to me at a time when I most needed countenance and protection.

A few considerations I beg leave, as *now* at your perusal of this, from the dead, to press upon you, with all the warmth of a sincere friendship.

By the time you will see this, you will have had an instance, I humbly trust, of the comfortable importance of a pacified conscience, in the last hours of one who, *to* the last hour, will wish your eternal welfare.

The great Duke of Luxemburgh, as I have heard, on his death-bed, declared that he would then much rather have had it to reflect upon, that he had administered a cup of cold water to a worthy poor creature in distress, than that he had won so many battles as he had triumphed for. And, as one well observes, All the sentiments of worldly grandeur vanish at that unavoidable moment which decides the destiny of men.

If, then, sir, at the tremendous hour, it be thus with the conquerors of armies, and the subduers of nations, let me in very few words (many are not needed) ask, What, at that period, must be the reflections of those (if *capable* of reflection) who have lived a life of sense and offence; whose study and whose pride most ingloriously have been to seduce the innocent, and to ruin the weak, the unguarded, and the friendless; made still more friendless by *their* base seductions? O Mr. Belford, weigh, ponder, and reflect upon it, now that in, health, and in vigour of mind and body, the reflections will most avail you—what an ungrateful, what an unmanly, what a meaner than reptile pride is this!

In the next place, sir, let me beg of you, for *my sake*, who AM, or, as *now* you will best read it, *have been*, driven to the necessity of applying to you to be the executor of my will, that you will bear, according to that generosity which I think to be in you, with all my friends, and particularly with my brother (who is really a worthy young man, but perhaps a little too headstrong in his first resentments and conceptions of things), if anything, by reason of this trust, should fall out disagreeably; and that you will study to make peace, and to reconcile all parties; and more especially that you, who seem to have a great influence upon your *still more* headstrong friend, will interpose, if occasion be, to prevent *further* mischief—for surely, sir, that violent spirit may sit down satisfied with the evils he has already wrought; and, particularly, with the wrongs, the heinous and ignoble wrongs, he has in me done to my family, wounded in the tenderest part of its honour.

For your compliance with this request I have already your repeated promise. I claim the observance of it, therefore, as a debt from you: and though I hope I need not doubt it, yet was I willing, on this solemn, this *last* occasion, thus earnestly to re-enforce it.

I have another request to make to you: it is only that you will be pleased, by a particular messenger, to forward the enclosed letters as directed.

And now, sir, having the presumption to think that a useful member is lost to society by means of the unhappy step which has brought my life so soon to its period, let me hope that I may be a humble instrument, in the hands of Providence, to reform a man of your abilities; and then I shall think that loss will be more abundantly repaired to the world, while it will be, by God's goodness, my gain: and I shall have this further hope, that once more I shall have an opportunity, in a blessed eternity, to thank you, as I now repeatedly do, for the good you have done to, and the trouble you will have taken for, sir,

Your obliged servant,
CLARISSA HARLOWE.

The other letters are directed to her father, to her mother, one to her two uncles, to her brother, to her sister, to her Aunt Hervey, to her Cousin Morden, to Miss Howe, to Mrs. Norton, and lastly one to you, in performance of her promise *that a letter should be sent you when she arrived at her father's house*!——I will withhold this last till I can be assured that you will be fitter to receive it than Tourville tells me you are at present.

Copies of all these are sealed up, and entitled, *Copies of my ten posthumous letters, for* J. Belford, *Esq.*; and put in among the bundle of papers left to my direction, which I have not yet had leisure to open.

No wonder, while able, that she was always writing, since thus only of late could she employ that time which heretofore, from the long days she made, caused so many beautiful works to spring from her fingers. It is my opinion that there never was a woman so young who wrote so much and with such celerity. Her thoughts keeping pace, as I have seen, with her pen, she hardly ever stopped or hesitated; and very seldom blotted out, or altered. It was a natural talent she was mistress of, among many other extraordinary ones.

I gave the colonel his letter, and ordered Harry instantly to get ready to carry the others.

Meantime (retiring into the next apartment) we opened the will. We were both so much affected in perusing it, that at one time the colonel, breaking off, gave it to me to read on; at another, I gave it back to him to proceed with; neither of us being able to read it through without such tokens of sensibility as affected the voice of each.

Mrs. Lovick, Mrs. Smith, and her nurse were still more touched, when we read those articles in which they are respectively remembered: but I will avoid mentioning the particulars (except in what relates to the thread of my narration), as in proper time I shall send you a copy of it.

The colonel told me he was ready to account with me for the money and bills he had brought up from Harlowe Place; which would enable me, as he said, directly to execute the legacy parts of the will; and he would needs at that instant force into my hands a paper relating to that subject. I put it in my pocket-book without looking into it; telling him that, as I hoped he would do all in his power to promote a literal performance of the will, I must beg his advice and assistance in the execution of it.

Her request to be buried with her ancestors made a letter of the following import necessary, which I prevailed upon the colonel to write; being unwilling myself (so *early* at least) to appear officious in the eye of a family which probably wishes not any communication with me.

To James Harlowe, jun., Esq.

Sir,—The letter which the bearer of this brings with him will, I presume, make it unnecessary to acquaint you and my cousins with the death of the most excellent of women. But I am requested by her executor, who will soon send you a copy of her last will, to acquaint her father (which I choose to do by your means) that in it she earnestly desires to be laid in the family vault, at the feet of her grandfather.

If her father will not admit of it, she has directed her body to be buried in the churchyard of the parish where she died.

I need not tell you that a speedy answer to this is necessary.

Her beatification commenced yesterday afternoon, exactly at forty minutes after six.

I can write no more, than that I am

Yours, etc.

WM. MORDEN.

Friday Morn. Sept. 8.

By the time this was written, and by the colonel's leave transcribed, Harry came booted and spurred, his horse at the door; and I delivered him the letters to the family, with those to Mrs. Norton and Miss Howe (eight in all), together with the above of the colonel to Mr. James Harlowe; and gave him orders to make the utmost dispatch with them.

The colonel and I have bespoke mourning for ourselves and servants.

Letter CXXVI—Mr. Belford to Robert Lovelace, Esq.

Sat. Ten o'clock.

POOR Mrs. Norton is come. She was set down at the door; and would have gone upstairs directly. But Mrs. Smith and Mrs. Lovick being together and in tears, and the former hinting too suddenly to the truly venerable woman the fatal news, she sunk down at her feet in fits; so that they were forced to breathe a vein to bring her to herself, and to a capacity of exclamation: and then she ran on to Mrs. Lovick and to me, who entered just as she recovered, in praise of the lady, in lamentations for her, and invectives against you: but yet so circumscribed were her invectives that I could observe in them the woman well educated, and in her lamentations the passion christianized, as I may say.

She was impatient to see the corpse. The women went up with her. But they owned that they were too much affected themselves on this occasion to describe her extremely affecting behaviour.

With trembling impatience she pushed aside the coffin-lid. She bathed the face with her tears, and kissed her cheeks and forehead, as if she were living. It was *she* indeed, she said! Her sweet young lady! Her very self! Nor had death, which changed all things, a power to alter her lovely features! She admired the serenity of her aspect. She no doubt was happy, she said, as she had written to her she should be: but how many miserable creatures had she left behind her! The good woman lamenting that she herself had lived to be one of them.

It was with difficulty they prevailed upon her to quit the corpse; and when they went into the next apartment, I joined them, and acquainted her with the kind legacy her beloved young lady had left her: but this rather augmented than diminished her concern. She ought, she said, to have attended her in person. What was the world to her, wringing her hands, now the child of her bosom, and of her heart, was no more? Her principal consolation, however, was that she should not long survive her. She hoped, she said, that she did not sin in wishing she might not.

It was easy to observe, by the similitude of sentiments shown in this and other particulars, that the divine lady owed to this excellent woman many of her good notions.

I thought it would divert the poor gentlewoman, and not altogether unsuitably, if I were to put her upon furnishing mourning for herself; as it would rouse her, by a seasonable and necessary employment, from that dismal lethargy of grief which generally succeeds the too violent anguish with which a gentle nature is accustomed to be torn upon the first communication of the unexpected loss of a dear friend. I gave her therefore the thirty guineas bequeathed to her and to her son for mourning; the only mourning which the testatrix has mentioned: and desired her to lose no time in preparing her own, as I doubted not that she would accompany the corpse, if it were permitted to be carried down.

The colonel proposes to attend the hearse, if his kindred give him not fresh cause of displeasure; and will take with him a copy of the will. And being intent to give the family some favourable impressions of me, he desired me to permit him to take with him the copy of the posthumous letter to me: which I readily granted.

He is so kind as to promise me a minute account of all that shall pass on the melancholy occasion. And we have begun a friendship and settled a correspondence, which but *one incident* can possibly happen to interrupt to the end of our lives. And that I hope will not happen.

But what must be the grief, the remorse, that will seize upon the hearts of this hitherto inexorable family, on the receiving of the posthumous letters, and that of the colonel apprising them of what has happened!

I have given requisite orders to an undertaker, on the supposition that the body will be permitted to be carried down; and the women intend to fill the coffin with aromatic herbs.

The colonel has obliged me to take the bills and drafts which he brought up with him, for the considerable sums accrued since the grandfather's death from the lady's estate.

I could have shown to Mrs. Norton the copies of the two letters which she missed by coming up. But her grief wants not the heightenings which the reading of them would have given her.

· · · · · · ·

I have been dipping into the copies of the posthumous latters to the family, which Harry has carried down. Well may I call this lady divine. They are all calculated to give comfort rather than reproach, though their cruelty to her merited nothing *but* reproach. But were I in any of their places, how much rather had I that she had quitted scores with me by the most severe recriminations, than that she should thus nobly triumph over me by a generosity that has no example!

I will enclose some of them, which I desire you to return as soon as you can.

Letter CXXVII—To the Ever-honoured Jas. Harlowe, sen., Esq.

MOST DEAR SIR!—With exulting confidence now does your emboldened daughter come into your awful presence by these lines, who dared not but upon this occasion to look up to you with hopes of favour and forgiveness; since, when this comes to your hands, it will be out of her power ever to offend you more.

And now let me bless you, my honoured papa, and bless you, as I write, upon my knees, for all the benefits I have received from your indulgence: for your fond love to me in the days of my prattling innocence: for the virtuous education you gave me: and, for the crown of all, the happy end, which, through Divine grace, by means of that virtuous education, I hope, by the time you will receive this, I shall have made. And let me beg of you, dear venerable sir, to blot from your remembrance, if possible, the last unhappy eight months; and then I shall hope to be remembered with advantage for the pleasure you had the goodness to take in your Clarissa.

Still on her knees, let your poor penitent implore your forgiveness of all her faults and follies; more especially of that fatal error which threw her out of your protection.

When you know, sir, that I have never been faulty in my will:

that ever since my calamity became irretrievable, I have been in a state of preparation: that I have the strongest assurances that the Almighty has accepted my unfeigned repentance; and that by this time you will (as I humbly presume to hope) have been the means of adding one to the number of the blessed; you will have reason for joy rather than sorrow. Since, had I escaped the snares by which I was entangled, I might have wanted those exercises which I look upon now as so many mercies dispensed to wean me betimes from a world that presented itself to me with prospects too alluring: and in that case (too easily satisfied with *worldly* felicity) I might not have attained to that blessedness in which now, on your reading of this, I humbly presume (through the Divine goodness) I am rejoicing.

That the Almighty, in His own good time, will bring you, sir, and my ever-honoured mother, after a series of earthly felicities, of which may my unhappy fault be the only interruption (and very grievous I know that must have been), to rejoice in the same blessed state, is the repeated prayer of, sir,

Your now happy daughter,
CLARISSA HARLOWE.

Letter CXXVIII—To the Ever-honoured Mrs. Harlowe

HONOURED MADAM,—The last time I had the boldness to write to you, it was with all the consciousness of a self-convicted criminal, supplicating her offended judge for mercy and pardon. I now, by these lines, approach you with more assurance; but nevertheless with the highest degree of reverence, gratitude, and duty. The reason of my assurance, my letter to my papa will give: and as I humbly on my knees implored *his* pardon, so now, in the same dutiful manner, do I supplicate yours, for the grief and trouble I have given you.

Every vein of my heart has bled for an unhappy rashness: which (although involuntary as to the act) from the moment it was committed carried with it its own punishment; and was accompanied with a true and sincere penitence.

God, who has been a witness of my distresses, knows that, great as they have been, the greatest of all was the distress that I knew I must have given to you, madam, and to my father, by a step that had so very ugly an appearance in your eyes and his; and indeed in the eyes of all my family: a step so unworthy of *your* daughter, and of the education you had given her!

But HE, I presume to hope, has forgiven me; and at the instant this will reach your hands, I humbly trust I shall be rejoicing in the blessed fruits of His forgiveness. And be this your comfort, my ever-honoured mamma, that the principal end of your pious care for me is attained, though not in the way so much hoped for.

May the grief which my fatal error has given to you both, be the only grief that shall ever annoy you in this world! May you, madam, long live to sweeten the cares, and heighten the comforts, of my papa! May my sister's continued and, if possible, augmented duty, happily make up to you the loss you have sustained in me! And whenever my brother and she change their single state, may it be with such satisfaction to you both as may make you forget my offence; and remember me only in those days in which you took pleasure in me: and, at last, may a happy meeting with your forgiven penitent, in the eternal mansions, augment the bliss of her who, purified by sufferings, already, when this salutes your hands, presumes she shall be

The happy, and for ever happy
CLARISSA HARLOWE.

Letter CXXIX—To James Harlowe, jun., Esq.

SIR,—There was but one time, but one occasion, after the rash step I was precipitated upon, that I could hope to be excused looking up to you in the character of a brother and a friend. And NOW is that time, and THIS the occasion. Now, at reading this, will you pity your late unhappy sister! Now will you forgive her faults, both supposed and real! And NOW will you afford to her *memory* that kind concern which you refused to her before!

I write, my brother, in the first place, to beg your pardon for the offence my unhappy step gave to you, and to the rest of a family so dear to me.

Virgin purity should not so behave as to be suspected: yet, when you come to know all my story, you will find further room for pity, if not for *more* than pity, for your late unhappy sister! Oh, that passion had not been deaf! That misconception would have given way to inquiry! That your rigorous heart, if it could not itself be softened (moderating the power you had obtained over every one), had permitted other hearts more indulgently to expand!

But I write not to give pain. I had rather you snould think me faulty still, than take to yourself the consequence that will follow from acquitting me.

Abandoning, therefore, a subject which I had not intended to touch upon (for I hope, at the writing of this, I am above the spirit of recrimination), let me tell you, sir, that my next motive for writing to youi n this last and most solemn manner is, to beg of you to forego any active resentments (which may endanger a life so precious to all your friends) against the man to whose elaborate baseness I owe my worldly ruin.

For ought an innocent man to run an *equal* risk with a guilty one? A *more* than equal risk, as the guilty one has been long inured to acts of violence, and is skilled in the arts of offence?

You would not arrogate to yourself God's province, who has said: *Vengeance is Mine, and I will repay it.* If you would, I tremble for the consequence: for will it not be suitable to the Divine justice to punish the *presumptuous* innocent (as you would be in this case) in the *very* error, and that by the hand of the *self-defending* guilty—reserving *him* for a future day of vengeance for his accumulated crimes?

Leave, then, the poor wretch to the Divine justice. Let your sister's fault die with her. At least, let it not be revived in blood. Life is a short stage where longest. A little time hence, the now green head will be grey, if it lives this little time: and if Heaven will afford him time for repentance, why should not *you*?

Then think, my brother, what will be the consequence to your dear parents, if the guilty wretch who has occasioned to them the loss of a daughter should likewise deprive them of their best hope, and only son, more worth in the family account than several daughters?

Would you add, my brother, to those distresses which you hold your sister so inexcusable for having (although from involuntary and undesigned causes) given?

Seek not, then, I beseech you, to extend the evil consequences of your sister's error. His conscience, when it shall please God to touch it, will be sharper than your sword.

I have still another motive for writing to you in this solemn manner: it is to entreat you to watch over your passions. The principal fault I know you to be guilty of, is the violence of your temper when you think yourself in the right; which you would oftener be, but for that very violence.

You have several times brought your life into danger by it.

Is not the man guilty of a high degree of injustice who is more apt to *give* contradiction than able to *bear* it?   How often, with you, has impetuosity brought on abasement?   A consequence too natural.

Let me then caution you, dear sir, against a warmth of temper, an impetuosity when moved, and you so *ready* to be moved, that may hurry you into unforeseen difficulties; and which it is in some measure a sin not to endeavour to restrain. God enable you to do it for the sake of your own peace and safety, as well present as future!   And for the sake of your family and friends, who all see your fault, but are tender of speaking to you of it.

As for me, my brother, my punishment has been seasonable. God gave me grace to make a right use of my sufferings.   I early repented.   I never loved the man half so much as I hated his actions, when I saw what he was capable of.   I gave up my *whole* heart to a better hope.   God blessed my penitence and my reliance upon Him.   And now I presume to say: I AM HAPPY.

May Heaven preserve you in safety, health, and honour, and long continue your life for a comfort and stay to your honoured parents: and may you in the change of your single state, meet with a wife as agreeable to every one else as to yourself, and be happy in a hopeful race, and not have one Clarissa among them, to embitter your comforts when she should give you *most* comfort.   But may my example be of use to warn the dear creatures whom once I hoped to live to see and to cherish, of the evils with which this deceitful world abounds, are the prayers of

Your affectionate sister,

CLARISSA HARLOWE.

Letter CXXX—*To Miss Harlowe*

Now may you, my dear Arabella, unrestrained by the severity of your virtue, let fall a pitying tear on the past faults and sufferings of your late unhappy sister; since, *now*, she can never offend you more.   The Divine mercy, which first inspired her with repentance (an *early* repentance it was; since it preceded her sufferings) for an error which she offers not to extenuate, although perhaps it were capable of some extenuation, has *now*, at the instant that you are reading this, as I humbly hope, blessed her with the fruits of it.

Thus already, even while she writes, in imagination, purified and exalted, she the more fearlessly writes to her sister; and NOW is assured of pardon for all those little occasions of displeasure

which her frowarder youth might give you; and for the disgrace
which her fall has fastened upon you and upon her family.

May you, my sister, continue to bless those dear and honoured
relations, whose indulgence so well deserves your utmost gratitude, with those cheerful instances of duty and obedience which
have hitherto been so acceptable to *them* and praiseworthy in
you! And may you, when a suitable proposal shall offer, fill up
more worthily that chasm which the loss they have sustained in
me has made in their family!

Thus, my Arabella! my only sister! and for many happy years,
my friend! most fervently prays that sister, whose affection for
you no acts of unkindness, no misconstruction of her conduct
could cancel! And who NOW, made perfect (as she hopes)
through sufferings, styles herself,

The happy
CLARISSA HARLOWE.

Letter CXXXI—To John and Antony Harlowe, Esqrs.

HONOURED SIRS,—When these lines reach your hands, your late
unhappy niece will have known the end of all her troubles; and,
as she humbly hopes, will be rejoicing in the mercies of a gracious
God, who has declared that He will forgive the truly penitent
of heart.

I write, therefore, my dear uncles, and to you both in one
letter (since your fraternal love has made you both but as one
person), to give you comfort, and not distress; for, however sharp
my afflictions have been, they have been but of short duration;
and I am betimes (happily as I hope) arrived at the end of a
painful journey.

At the same time I write to thank you both for all your kind
indulgence to me, and to beg your forgiveness of my last, my
only great fault to you and to my family.

The ways of Providence are unsearchable. Various are the
means made use of by it, to bring poor sinners to a sense of their
duty. Some are drawn by love, others are driven by terrors,
to their Divine refuge. I had for eighteen years out of nineteen
rejoiced in the favour and affection of every one. No trouble
came near my heart. I seemed to be one of those designed to be
drawn by the silken cords of love. But perhaps I was too apt
to value myself upon the love and favour of every one: the merit
of the good I delighted to do, and of the inclinations which were
given me, and which I could not *help* having, I was, perhaps,

too ready to attribute to myself; and now, being led to account for the cause of my temporary calamities, find I had a secret pride to be punished for, which I had not fathomed: and it was necessary perhaps that some sore and terrible misfortunes should befall me, in order to mortify that my pride and that my vanity.

Temptations were accordingly sent. I shrunk in the day of trial. My discretion, which had been so cried up, was found wanting when it came to be weighed in an equal balance. I was betrayed, fell, and became the byword of my companions, and a disgrace to my family, which had prided itself in me perhaps too much. But as my fault was not that of a culpable will, when my pride was sufficiently mortified, I was not suffered (although surrounded by dangers, and entangled in snares) to be totally lost: but purified by sufferings, I was fitted for the change I have NOW, at the time you will receive this, so newly, and, as I humbly hope, so happily experienced.

Rejoice with me, then, dear sirs, that I have weathered so great a storm. Nor let it be matter of concern that I am cut off in the bloom of youth. "There is no inquisition in the grave," says the wise man, "whether we lived ten or a hundred years; and the day of death is better than the day of our birth."

Once more, dear sirs, accept my grateful thanks for all your goodness to me, from my early childhood to the day, the unhappy day, of my error! Forgive that error! And God give us a happy meeting in a blessed eternity, prays

Your most dutiful and obliged kinswoman,
CLARISSA HARLOWE.

Mr. Belford gives the lady's posthumous letters to Mrs. Hervey, Miss Howe, and Mrs. Norton, at length likewise: but, although every letter varies in style as well as matter from the others ; yet, as they are written on the same subject, and are pretty long, it is thought proper to abstract them.

That to her Aunt Hervey is written in the same pious and generous strain with those preceding, seeking to give comfort rather than distress. "The Almighty, I hope, says she, has received and blessed my penitence, and I am happy. Could I have been more than so at the end of what is called a *happy* life of twenty, or thirty, or forty years to come? And what are twenty, or thirty, or forty years to look back upon? In half of any of these periods, what friends might I not have mourned for? what temptations from worldly prosperity might I not have encountered with? And in such a case, immersed in earthly pleasures, how little likelihood that, in my last stage, I should have been blessed with such a preparation and resignation as I have now been blessed with?"

She proceeds as follows: "Thus much, madam, of comfort to you and to myself from this dispensation. As to my dear parents, I hope they will console themselves, that they have still many blessings left, which ought to balance the troubles my error has given them: that, unhappy as I have been to be the interrupter of their felicities, they never, till this my fault, knew any *heavy evil*: that afflictions patiently borne may be turned into blessings: that uninterrupted happiness is not to be expected in this life: that, after all, they have not, as I humbly presume to hope, the probability of the everlasting perdition of their child to deplore: and that, in short, when my story comes to be fully known, they will have the comfort to find that my sufferings redound more to my honour than to my disgrace.

"These considerations will, I hope, make their temporary loss of but *one* child out of *three* (unhappily circumstanced too as she was) matter of greater consolation than affliction. And the rather, as we may hope for a happy meeting once more, never to be separated either by time or offences."

She concludes this letter with an address to her cousin Dolly Hervey, whom she calls her amiable cousin; and thankfully remembers for the part she took in her afflictions. "O my dear cousin, let your worthy heart be guarded against those delusions which have been fatal to my worldly happiness! That pity, which you bestowed upon *me*, demonstrates a gentleness of nature which may possibly subject you to misfortunes, if your eye be permitted to mislead your judgment. But a strict observance of your filial duty, my dearest cousin, and the precepts of so prudent a mother as you have the happiness to have (enforced by so sad an example in your own family as I have set), will, I make no doubt, with the Divine assistance, be your guard and security."

The posthumous letter to Miss Howe is extremely tender and affectionate. She pathetically calls upon her "to rejoice that all her Clarissa's troubles are now at an end; that the state of temptation and trial, of doubt and uncertainty, is now over with her; and that she has happily escaped the snares that were laid for her soul: the rather to rejoice, as that her misfortunes were of such a nature, that it was impossible she could be tolerably happy in this life."

She "thankfully acknowledges the favours she had received from Mrs. Howe and Mr. Hickman; and expresses her concern for the trouble she has occasioned to the former, as well as to her; and prays that all the earthly blessings they used to wish to each other, may singly devolve upon *her*."

She beseeches her "that she will not suspend the day which shall supply to herself the friend she will have lost in her, and give to herself a still nearer and dearer relation."

She tells her "that her choice (a choice made with the approbation of all her friends) has fallen upon a sincere, an honest, a virtuous, and what is more than all, a *pious* man; a man who, although he admires her person, is still more in love with the graces of her mind. And as those graces are improvable with every added year of life, which will impair the transitory ones of person, what a firm basis, infers she, has Mr. Hickman chosen to build his love upon!"

She prays "that God will bless them together: and that the remembrance of her, and of what she has suffered, may not interrupt their mutual happiness; she desires them to think of nothing but what she *now is*; and that a time will come when they shall meet again, never to be divided."

"To the Divine protection, meantime, she commits her; and charges her, by the love that has always subsisted between them, that she will not mourn too heavily for her; and again calls upon her, after a gentle tear, which she will allow her to let fall in memory of their uninterrupted friendship, to rejoice that she is so early released; and that she is purified by her sufferings, and is made, as she assuredly trusts, by God's goodness, eternally happy."

The posthumous letters to Mr. LOVELACE *and Mr.* MORDEN *will be inserted hereafter: as will also the substance of that written to Mrs.* NORTON.

Letter CXXXII—Mr. Belford to Robert Lovelace, Esq.

Sat. Afternoon, Sept. 9.

I UNDERSTAND that thou breathest nothing but revenge against *me*, for treating thee with so much freedom; and against the accursed woman and her infernal crew. I am not at all concerned for thy menaces against myself. It is my design to make thee *feel*. It gives me pleasure to find my intention answered. And I congratulate thee that thou hast not lost that sense.

As to the cursed crew, well do they deserve the fire *here* that thou threatenest them with, and the fire here*after* that seems to await them.   But I have this moment received news which will, in all likelihood, save thee the guilt of punishing the old wretch for her share of wickedness as thy *agent*.   But if that happens to her which is likely to happen, wilt thou not tremble for what may befall the *principal*?

Not to keep thee longer in suspense; last night, it seems, the infamous woman got so heartily intoxicated with her beloved liquor, arrack punch, at the expense of Colonel Salter, that, mistaking her way, she fell down a pair of stairs and broke her leg: and now, after a dreadful night, she lies foaming, raving, roaring, in a burning fever, that wants not any other fire to scorch her into a feeling more exquisite and durable than any thy vengeance could give her.

The wretch has requested me to come to her: and lest I should refuse a common messenger, sent her vile associate Sally Martin; who not finding me at Soho, came hither; another part of her business being to procure the divine lady's pardon for the old creature's wickedness to her.

This devil incarnate Sally declares that she never was so shocked in her life as when I told her the lady was dead.

She took out her salts to keep her from fainting; and when a little recovered, she accused herself for her part of the injuries the lady had sustained; as she said Polly Horton would do for hers; and shedding tears, declared that the world never produced such another woman.   She called her the ornament and glory of her sex; acknowledged that her ruin was owing more to *their instigations* than even (savage as thou art) to *thy own vileness*; since thou wert inclined to have done her justice more than once, had they not kept up thy profligate spirit to its height.

This wretch would fain have been admitted to a sight of the corpse.   But I refused her request with execrations.

She could forgive herself, she said, for everything but her insults upon the admirable lady at Rowland's: since all the rest was but in pursuit of a *livelihood*, to which she had been reduced, as she boasted, from better expectations, and which hundreds follow as well as she.   I did not ask her, *By whom reduced?*

At going away, she told me that the old monster's bruises are of more dangerous consequence than the fracture: that a mortification is apprehended: and that the vile wretch has so much compunction of heart, on recollecting her treatment of Miss Harlowe, and is so much set upon procuring her forgiveness, that she is sure the news she has to carry her will hasten her end.

All these things I leave upon thy reflection.

Letter CXXXIII—Mr. Belford to Robert Lovelace, Esq.

Sat. Night.

YOUR servant gives me a dreadful account of your raving unmanageableness. I wonder not at it. But as nothing violent is lasting, I dare say that your habitual gaiety of heart will quickly get the better of your frenzy: and the rather do I judge so, as your fits are of the raving kind (suitable to your natural impetuosity), and not of that melancholy species which seizes slower souls.

For this reason I will proceed in writing to you, that my narrative may not be broken by your discomposure; and that the contents of it may *find you*, and help you to reflection, when you shall be restored.

Harry is returned from carrying the posthumous letters to the family and to Miss Howe; and that of the colonel which acquaints James Harlowe with his sister's death, and with her desire to be interred near her grandfather.

Harry was not admitted into the presence of any of the family. They were all assembled together, it seems, at Harlowe Place, on occasion of the colonel's letter which informed them of the lady's dangerous way [1]; and were comforting themselves, as Harry was told, with hopes that Mr. Morden had made the worst of her state, in order to quicken their resolutions.

It is easy then to judge what must be their grief and surprise on receiving the fatal news which the letters Harry sent in to them communicated.

He stayed there long enough to find the whole house in confusion; the servants running different ways; lamenting and wringing their hands as they ran; the female servants particularly; as if somebody (poor Mrs. Harlowe, no doubt; and perhaps Mrs. Hervey too) were in fits.

Every one was in such disorder that he could get no commands, nor obtain any notice of himself. The servants seemed more inclined to execrate than welcome him. O master! O young man! cried three or four together, what dismal tidings have you brought! They helped him, at the very first word, to his horse;

[1] See p. 340.

which with great civility they had put up on his arrival: and he went to an inn; and pursued on foot his way to Mrs. Norton's; and finding her come to town, left the letter he carried down for her with her son (a fine youth); who, when he heard the fatal news, burst out into a flood of tears—first lamenting the lady's death, and then crying out, What—what would become of his poor mother? How would she support herself, when she should find on her arrival in town, that the dear lady, who was so deservedly the darling of her heart, was no more!

He proceeded to Miss Howe's with the letter for her. That lady, he was told, had just given orders for a young man, a tenant's son, to post to London, to bring her news of her dear friend's condition, and whether she should herself be encouraged, by an account of her being still alive, to make her a visit; everything being ordered to be in readiness for her going up, on his return with the news she wished and prayed for with the utmost impatience. And Harry was just in time to prevent the man's setting out.

He had the precaution to desire to speak with Miss Howe's woman or maid, and communicated to her the fatal tidings, that she might break them to her young lady. The maid was herself so affected, that her old lady (who, Harry said, seemed to be *everywhere at once*) came to see what ailed her; and was herself so struck with the communication that she was forced to sit down in a chair: O the sweet creature! said she. And is it come to this! O my poor Nancy! How shall I be able to break the matter to my Nancy!

Mr. Hickman was in the house. He hastened in to comfort the old lady—but he could not restrain his own tears. He feared, he said, when he was last in town, that this sad event would *soon* happen: but little thought it would be so *very* soon! But she is happy, I am sure, said the good gentleman.

Mrs. Howe, when a little recovered, went up, in order to break the news to her daughter. She took the letter, and her salts in her hand. And they had occasion for the latter. For the housekeeper soon came hurrying down into the kitchen, her face overspread with tears. Her young mistress had fainted away, she said. Nor did she wonder at it. Never did there live a lady more deserving of general admiration and lamentation than Miss Clarissa Harlowe! And never was there a stronger friendship dissolved by death than between her young lady and her.

She hurried with a lighted wax candle, and with feathers, to

burn under the nose of her young mistress; which showed that
she continued in fits.

Mr. Hickman afterwards, with his usual humanity, directed
that Harry should be taken care of all night; it being then the
close of day. He asked him after my health. He expressed
himself excessively afflicted, as well for the death of the most
excellent of women, as for the just grief of the lady whom he so
passionately loves. But he called the departed lady an angel of
light. We dreaded, said he (tell your master), to read the letter
sent. But we needed not. 'Tis a blessed letter, written by a
blessed hand! But the consolation she aims to give will for the
present heighten the sense we all shall have of the loss of so
excellent a creature! Tell Mr. Belford that I thank God I am
not the man who had the unmerited honour to call himself
her brother.

I know how terribly this *great* catastrophe (as I may call it,
since so many persons are interested in it) affects *thee*. I should
have been glad to have had particulars of the distress which the
first communication of it must have given to the *Harlowes*. Yet
who but must pity the unhappy mother?

The answer which James Harlowe returned to Colonel
Morden's letter of notification of his sister's death, and to her
request as to interment, will give a faint idea of what their
concern must be. Here follows a copy of it.

To William Morden, Esq.

Saturday, Sept. 9.

DEAR COUSIN,—I cannot find words to express what we all suffer
on the most mournful news that ever was communicated to us.

My sister Arabella (but, alas! I have now no *other* sister) was
preparing to follow Mrs. Norton up; and I had resolved to escort
her, and to have looked in upon the dear creature.

God be merciful to us all! To what purpose did the doctor
write if she was so near her end? Why, as everybody says, did
he not send sooner? or why at all?

The most admirable young creature that ever swerved!—not
one friend to be with her! Alas! sir, I fear my mother will
never get over this shock—she has been in hourly fits ever since
she received the fatal news. My poor father has the gout
thrown into his stomach; and Heaven knows—O cousin, O sir!—
I meant nothing but the honour of the family; yet have I all the

weight thrown upon me [O this cursed Lovelace! may I perish if he escape the deserved vengeance![1]].

We had begun to please ourselves that we should soon see her here. Good Heaven! that her next entrance into this house, after she abandoned us so precipitately, should be in a coffin!

We can have nothing to do with her executor (another strange step of the dear creature's!)—he cannot expect we will—nor, if he be a gentleman, will he think of acting. Do you, therefore, be pleased, sir, to order an undertaker to convey the body down to us.

My mother says she shall be for ever unhappy, if she may not in death see the dear creature whom she could not see in life: be so kind, therefore, as to direct the lid to be only half screwed down, that (if my poor mother cannot be prevailed upon to dispense with so shocking a spectacle) she may be obliged. She was the darling of her heart!

If we know her will in relation to the funeral, it shall be punctually complied with: as shall everything in it that is fit or reasonable to be performed; and this without the intervention of strangers.

Will you not, dear sir, favour us with your presence at this melancholy time? Pray do; and pity and excuse, with the generosity which is natural to the brave and the wise, what passed at our last meeting. Every one's respects attend you. And I am, sir,

Your inexpressibly afflicted cousin and servant,
JA. HARLOWE, jun.

Everything that is fit or reasonable to be performed [repeated I to the colonel, from the above letter, on his reading it to me]: that is everything which she has directed, that *can* be performed. I hope, colonel, that I shall have no contention with them. I wish no more for *their* acquaintance than they do for *mine*. But you, sir, must be the mediator between them and me; for I shall insist upon a literal performance in every article.

The colonel was so kind as to declare that he would support me in my resolution.

---

[1] The words thus enclosed [ ] were omitted in the transcript to Mr. Lovelace.

Letter CXXXIV—Mr. Belford to Robert Lovelace, Esq.

Sunday Morn. 8 o'clock, Sept. 10.

I STAYED at Smith's till I saw the last of all that is mortal of the divine lady.

As she has directed rings by her will to several persons, with her hair to be set in crystal, the afflicted Mrs. Norton cut off, before the coffin was closed, four charming ringlets; one of which the colonel took for a locket, which, he says, he will cause to be made, and wear next his heart in memory of his beloved cousin.

Between four and five in the morning the corpse was put into the hearse; the coffin before being filled, as intended, with flowers and aromatic herbs, and proper care taken to prevent the corpse suffering (to the eye) from the jolting of the hearse.

Poor Mrs. Norton is extremely ill. I gave particular directions to Mrs. Smith's maid (whom I have ordered to attend the good woman in a mourning chariot) to take care of her. The colonel, who rides with his servants within view of the hearse, says that he will see my orders in relation to her enforced.

When the hearse moved off, and was out of sight, I locked up the lady's chamber, into which all that had belonged to her was removed.

I expect to hear from the colonel as soon as he is got down, by a servant of his own.

Letter CXXXV—Mr. Mowbray to John Belford, Esq.

Uxbridge, Sunday Morn. 9 o'clock.

DEAR JACK,—I send you enclosed a letter from Mr. Lovelace; which, though written in the cursed algebra, I know to be such a one as will show what a *queer* way he is in; for he read it to us with the air of a tragedian. You will see by it what the mad fellow had intended to do, if we had not all of us interposed. He was actually setting out with a surgeon of this place, to have the lady opened and embalmed. Rot me if it be not my full persuasion that, if he had, her heart would have been found to be either iron or marble.

We have got Lord M. to him. His lordship is also much afflicted at the lady's death. His sisters and nieces, he says, will be ready to break their hearts. What a rout 's here about a woman! For after all she was no more.

We have taken a pailful of black bull's blood from him; and this has lowered him a little. But he threatens Colonel Morden, he threatens you for your cursed reflections [cursed reflections indeed, Jack!], and curses all the world and himself, still.

Last night his mourning (which is full as deep as for a wife) was brought home, and his fellows' mourning too. And though eight o'clock, he would put it on, and make them attend him in theirs.

Everybody blames him on this lady's account. But I see not for why. She was a *vixen* in her virtue. What a pretty fellow has she ruined—Hey, Jack!—and her relations are ten times more to blame than he. I will prove this to the teeth of them all. If *they* could use her ill, why should they expect *him* to use her well? You, or I, or Tourville, in his shoes, would have done as he has done. *Are not all the girls forewarned?* "Has he done by her as that caitiff *Miles* did to the farmer's daughter, whom he tricked up to town (a pretty girl also, just such another as Bob's Rosebud!) under a notion of waiting on a lady. *Drilled* her on, pretending the lady was abroad. Drank her light-hearted; then carried her to a play; then it was too late, you know, to see the pretended lady: then to a bagnio: ruined her, as they call it, and all the same day. Kept her on (an ugly dog too!) a fortnight or three weeks; then left her to the mercy of the people of the bagnio (never paying for anything); who stripped her of all her clothes, and because she would not *take on*, threw her into prison; where she died in want, and in despair!" A true story, thou knowest, Jack. This fellow deserved to be damned. But has our Bob been such a villain as this? And would he not have *married* this flinty-hearted lady?—*So he is justified very evidently.*

Why then should such cursed *qualms* take him? Who would have thought he had been such *poor blood?* Now [rot the puppy!] to see him sit silent in a corner, when he has tired himself with his mock-majesty, and with his argumentation (who so fond of *arguing* as he?), and teaching his shadow to make mouths against the wainscot—the devil fetch me, if I have patience with him!

But he has had no rest for these ten days: that's the thing! You must write to him; and prithee coax him, Jack, and send him what he writes for, and give him all his way: there will be no bearing him else. And get the lady buried as fast as you can; and don't let him know where.

This letter should have gone yesterday. We told him it did. But were in hopes he would not have inquired after it again. But he raves *as he has not* any answer.

What he *vouchsafed* to read of other of your letters has given my lord such a curiosity as makes him desire you to continue your accounts. Pray do: but not in your hellish *Arabic*; and we will let the poor fellow only into what we think fitting for his present way.

I live a cursed dull poking life here. With what I so lately saw of poor Belton, and what I now see of this charming fellow, I shall be as crazy as he soon, or as dull as thou, Jack; so must seek for better company in town than either of you. I have been forced to read sometimes to divert me; and you know I hate reading. It presently sets me into a fit of drowsiness, and then I yawn and stretch like a devil.

Yet in Dryden's *Palemon and Arcite* have I just now met with a passage that has in it much of our Bob's case. These are some of the lines.

Mr. Mowbray then recites some lines from that poem describing a distracted man, and runs the parallel; and then priding himself in his performance, says:

Let me tell you, that had I begun to write as early as you and Lovelace, I might have cut as good a figure as either of you. Why not? But boy or man I ever hated a book. 'Tis a folly to lie. I loved *action*, my boy. I hated *droning*; and have led in former days more boys from their book, than ever my master made to profit by it. Kicking and cuffing, and orchard-robbing, were my early glory.

But I am tired of writing. I never wrote such a long letter in my life. My wrists and my fingers and thumb ache damnably. The pen is a hundredweight at least. And my eyes are ready to drop out of my head upon the paper. The cramp but this minute in my fingers. Rot the goose and the goose-quill! I will write no more long letters for a twelvemonth to come. Yet one word: we think the mad fellow coming to. Adieu.

Letter CXXXVI—Mr. Lovelace to John Belford, Esq.

Uxbridge, Sat. Sept. 9.

Jack,—I think it absolutely right that my ever-dear and beloved lady should be opened and embalmed. It must be done out of hand—this very afternoon. Your acquaintance Tomkins, and old Anderson of this place, whom I will bring with me, shall be the surgeons. I have talked to the latter about it.

I will see everything done with that decorum which the case, and the sacred person of my beloved, require.

Everything that can be done to preserve the charmer from

decay shall also be done.   And when she *will* descend to her
original dust, or cannot be kept longer, I will then have her
laid in my family vault, between my own father and mother.
Myself, as I am in my *soul*, so in *person*, chief mourner.   But
her *heart*, to which I have such unquestionable pretensions, in
which once I had so large a share, and which I will prize above
my own, I *will* have.   I will keep it in spirits.   It shall never be
out of my sight.   And all the charges of *sepulture* too shall be
mine.

Surely nobody will dispute my right to her.   Whose was she
living?—Whose is she dead, but mine? Her cursed parents, whose
barbarity to her, no doubt, was the *true* cause of her death, have
long since renounced her.   She left *them* for *me*.   She chose *me*
therefore: and I was her husband.   What though I treated her
like a villain?   Do I not pay for it now?   Would she not have
been mine had I not?   Nobody will dispute but she would.
And has she not forgiven me?   I am then in *statu quo prius* with
her—am I not?—as if I had never offended?   Whose then can
she be but mine?

I will free you from your executorship and all your cares.

Take notice, Belford, that I do hereby actually discharge you,
and everybody, from all cares and troubles relating to her.
And as to her last testament, I will execute it myself.

There were no articles between us, no settlements; and she is
mine, as you see I have proved to a demonstration: nor could
she dispose of herself but as I pleased.   Damnation seize me,
then, if I make not good my right against all opposers!

Her bowels, if her friends are very solicitous about them, and
very humble and sorrowful (and none have they of their own),
shall be sent down to them—to be laid with *her* ancestors—
unless she has ordered otherwise.   For, except that she shall
not be committed to the unworthy earth, so long as she can be
kept out of it, her will shall be performed in everything.

I send in the meantime for a lock of her hair.

I charge you stir not in any part of her will but by my express
direction.   I will order everything myself.   For am I not her
husband?   And being forgiven by her, am I not the chosen of
her heart?   What else signifies her forgiveness?

The two insufferable wretches you have sent me plague me to
death, and would treat me like a babe in strings.   Damn the
fellows, what can they mean by it?   Yet that crippled monkey
Doleman joins with them.   And, as I hear them whisper, they
have sent for Lord M.—to *control* me, I suppose.

What can they mean by this usage? Sure all the world is run mad but myself. They treat me as they ought every one of themselves to be treated. The whole world is but one great Bedlam! God confound it, and everything in it, since now my beloved Clarissa Lovelace—no more Harlowe—curse upon that name, and every one called by it.

What I write to you for is:

1. To forbid you intermeddling with anything relating to her. To forbid Morden intermeddling also. If I remember right, he has threatened me, and cursed me, and used me ill—and let him be gone from her, if he would avoid my resentments.

2. To send me a lock of her hair instantly by the bearer.

3. To engage Tomkins to have everything ready for the opening and embalming. I shall bring Anderson with me.

4. To get her will and everything ready for my perusal and consideration.

I will have possession of her dear heart this very night; and let Tomkins provide a proper receptacle and spirits, till I can get a golden one made for it.

I will take her papers. And as no one can do her memory justice equal to myself, and I will not spare myself, who can better show the world what she was, and what a villain he that could use her ill? And the world shall also see what implacable and unworthy parents she had.

All shall be set forth in words at length. No mincing of the matter. Names undisguised as well as facts. For as I shall make the worst figure in it myself, and have a right to treat myself as nobody else shall, who will control me? Who dare call me to account?

Let me know if the damned mother be yet the subject of the devil's own vengeance—if the old wretch be dead or alive? Some exemplary mischief I must yet do. My revenge shall sweep away that devil, and all my opposers of the cruel Harlowe family, from the face of the earth. Whole hecatombs ought to be offered up to the manes of my Clarissa Lovelace.

Although her will may in some respects cross mine, yet I expect to be observed. I will be the interpreter of hers.

Next to mine, hers shall be observed; for she is my wife; and shall be to all eternity. I will never have another.

Adieu, Jack! I am preparing to be with you. I charge you, as you value my life or your own, do not oppose me in anything relating to my Clarissa Lovelace.

My temper is entirely altered. I know not what it is to laugh, or smile, or be pleasant. I am grown choleric and impatient, and will not be controlled.

I write this in characters as I used to do, that nobody but you should know what I write. For never was any man plagued with impertinents as I am.

R. LOVELACE.

In a separate paper enclosed in the above

Let me tell thee, in characters still, that I am in a dreadful way just now. My brain is all boiling like a cauldron over a fiery furnace. What a devil is the matter with me, I wonder! I never was so strange in my life.

In truth, Jack, I have been a most execrable villain. And when I consider all my actions to this angel of a woman, and in her the piety, the charity, the wit, the beauty I have *helped* to destroy, and the good to the world I have thereby been a means of frustrating, I can pronounce damnation upon myself. How then can I expect mercy anywhere else!

I believe I shall have no patience with you when I see you. Your damned stings and reflections have almost turned my brain.

But here Lord M., they tell me, is come! Damn him, and those who sent for him!

I know not what I have written. But her dear heart and a lock of her hair I will have, let who will be the gainsayers! For is she not mine? Whose else can she be? She has no father nor mother, no sister, no brother; no relations but me. And my beloved is mine; and I am hers: and that's enough—but oh!

> She's out! The damp of death has quench'd her quite!
> Those spicy doors, her lips, are shut, close lock'd,
> Which never gale of life shall open more!

And is it so? Is it *indeed* so? Good God! Good God!—But they will not let me write on. I must go down to this officious peer—who the devil sent for him?

Letter CXXXVII—Mr. Belford to Richard Mowbray, Esq.

Sunday, Sept. 10, 4 in the Afternoon.

I HAVE yours, with our unhappy friend's enclosed. I am glad my lord is with him. As I presume that his frenzy will be but of short continuance, I most earnestly wish that on his recovery he could be prevailed upon to go abroad. Mr. Morden, who is inconsolable, has seen by the will (as indeed he suspected before he read it) that the case is more than a common seduction; and has dropped hints already that he looks upon himself, on that account, as freed from his promises made to the dying lady, which were that he would not seek to avenge her death.

You must make the recovery of his health the motive for urging him on this head; for if you hint at his own safety, he will not stir, but rather seek the colonel.

As to the lock of hair, you may easily pacify him (as you once saw the angel) with hair near the colour, if he be intent upon it.

At my lord's desire I will write on, and in my common hand; that you may judge what is, and what is not, fit to read to Mr. Lovelace at present. But as I shall not forbear reflections as I go along, in hopes to reach his heart on his recovery, I think it best to direct myself to him still; and that as if he were not disordered.

As I shall not have leisure to take copies, and yet am willing to have the whole subject before me, for my own future contemplation, I must insist upon a return of my letters some time hence. Mr. Lovelace knows that this is one of my conditions; and has hitherto complied with it.

Thy letter, Mowbray, is an inimitable performance. Thou art a strange, impenetrable creature. But let me most earnestly conjure thee, and the idle flutterer Tourville, from what ye have seen of poor Belton's exit; from our friend Lovelace's frenzy, and the occasion of it; and from the terrible condition in which the wretched Sinclair lies; to set about an immediate change of life and manners. For my own part, I am determined, be your resolutions what they may, to take the advice I give.

As witness

J. BELFORD.

Letter CXXXVIII—Mr. Belford to Robert Lovelace, Esq.

O LOVELACE! I have a scene to paint in relation to the wretched Sinclair, that, if I do it justice, will make thee seriously ponder and reflect, or nothing can. I will lead to it in order; and that in my usual hand, that thy compeers may be able to read it as well as thyself.

When I had written the preceding letter; not knowing what to do with myself; recollecting, and in vain wishing for that delightful and improving conversation, which I had now for ever lost; I thought I had as good begin the task which I had for some time past *resolved* to begin; that is to say, to go to church;

and see if I could not reap some benefit from what I should hear there. Accordingly, I determined to go to hear the celebrated preacher at St. James's Church. But, as if the devil (for so I was then ready to conclude) thought himself concerned to prevent my intention, a visit was made me just as I was dressed, which took me off from my purpose.

From whom should this visit be, but from Sally Martin, accompanied by Mrs. Carter, the sister of the infamous Sinclair; the same, I suppose I need not tell you, who keeps the bagnio near Bloomsbury.

These told me that the surgeon, apothecary, and physician had all given the wretched woman over; but that she said she could not die, nor be at rest, till she saw me: and they besought me to accompany them in the coach they came in, if I had one spark of charity, of *Christian* charity, as they called it, left.

I was very loath to be diverted from my purpose by a request so unwelcome, and from people so abhorred; but at last went, and we got thither by ten: where a scene so shocking presented itself to me, that the death of poor desponding Belton is not, I think, to be compared with it.

The old wretch had once put her leg out by her rage and violence, and had been crying, scolding, cursing, ever since the preceding evening, that the surgeon had told her it was impossible to save her; and that a mortification had begun to show itself; insomuch that purely in compassion to their own *ears*, they had been forced to send for another surgeon, purposely to tell her, though against his judgment, and (being a friend of the other) to seem to convince *him* that he mistook her case; and that, if she would be patient, she might recover. But, nevertheless, her apprehensions of death, and her antipathy to the thoughts of dying, were so strong that their imposture had not the intended effect, and she was raving, crying, cursing, and even howling, more like a wolf than a human creature, when I came; so that as I went upstairs I said: Surely this noise, this howling, cannot be from the unhappy woman! Sally said it was; and assured me that it was nothing to the noise she had made all night; and stepping into her room before me, Dear *Madam* Sinclair, said she, forbear this noise. It is more like that of a bull than a woman! Here comes Mr. Belford; and you 'll frighten him away if you bellow at this rate.

There were no less than eight of her cursed daughters surrounding her bed when I entered; one of her partners, Polly Horton, at their head; and now Sally, her other partner, and

Madam Carter, as they called her (for they are all *madams* with one another), made the number ten: all in shocking dishabille, and without stays, except Sally, Carter, and Polly; who, not daring to leave her, had not been in bed all night.

The other seven seemed to have been but just up, risen perhaps from their customers in the fore house, and their nocturnal orgies, with faces, three or four of them, that had run, the paint lying in streaky seams not half blowzed off, discovering coarse wrinkled skins: the hair of some of them of divers colours, obliged to the blacklead comb where black was affected; the artificial jet, however, yielding apace to the natural brindle: that of others plastered with oil and powder; the oil predominating: but every one's hanging about her ears and neck in broken curls or ragged ends; and each at my entrance taken with one motion, stroking their matted locks with both hands under their coifs, mobs, or pinners, every one of which was awry. They were all slip-shoed; stockingless some; only under-petti-coated all; their gowns, made to cover straddling hoops, hanging trollopy, and tangling about their heels; but hastily wrapped round them as soon as I came upstairs. And half of them (unpadded, shoulder-bent, pallid-lipped, limber-jointed wretches) appearing, from a blooming nineteen or twenty perhaps over night, haggard well-worn strumpets of thirty-eight or forty.

I am the more particular in describing to thee the appearance these creatures made in my eyes when I came into the room because I believe thou never sawest any of them, much less a group of them, thus unprepared for being seen.[1]   I, for my part, never did before; nor had I now, but upon this occasion, been thus *favoured*. If thou *hadst*, I believe thou wouldst hate a profligate woman, as one of Swift's Yahoos, or Virgil's obscene harpies, squirting their ordure upon the Trojan trenchers; since the persons of such in their retirements are as filthy as their minds—hate them as much as I do; and as much as I admire, and next to adore, a truly virtuous and elegant woman: for to me it is evident, that as a neat and clean woman must be an angel of a creature, so a sluttish one is the impurest animal in nature.

But these were the veterans, the chosen band; for now and then flitted in, to the number of half a dozen or more, by turns, subordinate sinners, undergraduates, younger then some of the

---

[1] Whoever has seen Dean Swift's Lady's Dressing-room will think this description of Mr. Belford not only more *natural* but more *decent painting*, as well as better justified by the *design*, and by the *use* that may be made of it.

chosen phalanx, but not less obscene in their appearance, though indeed not so much beholden to the plastering fucus; yet unpropped by stays, squalid, loose in attire, sluggish-haired, under-petticoated only as the former, eyes half opened, winking and pinking, mispatched, yawning, stretching, as if from the unworn-off effects of the midnight revel; all armed in succession with supplies of cordials (of which every one present was either taster or partaker), under the direction of the busier Dorcas, who frequently popped in, to see her slops duly given and taken.

But when I approached the *old wretch*, what a spectacle presented itself to my eyes!

Her misfortune had not at all sunk, but rather, as I thought, increased her flesh; rage and violence perhaps swelling her muscular features. Behold her, then, spreading the whole tumbled bed with her huge quaggy carcass: her mill-post arms held up; her broad hands clenched with violence; her big eyes, goggling and flaming-red as we may suppose those of a salamander; her matted grizzly hair, made irreverent by her wickedness (her clouted head-dress being half off), spread about her fat ears and brawny neck; her livid lips parched, and working violently; her broad chin in convulsive motion; her wide mouth, by reason of the contraction of her forehead (which seemed to be half lost in its own frightful furrows), splitting her face, as it were, into two parts; and her huge tongue hideously rolling in it; heaving, puffing, as if for breath; her bellows-shaped and various-coloured breasts ascending by turns to her chin, and descending out of sight, with the violence of her gaspings.

This was the spectacle, as recollection has enabled me to describe it, that this wretch made to my eye when I approached her bedside, surrounded, as I said, by her suffragans and daughters, who surveyed her with scowling frighted attention, which one might easily see had more in it of horror and self-concern (and *self-condemnation* too) than of love or pity; as who should say: See! what we ourselves must one day be!

As soon as she saw me, her naturally big voice, more hoarsened by her ravings, broke upon me: O Mr. Belford! O sir! see what I am come to! See what I am brought to! To have such a cursed crew about me, and not one of them to take care of me! But to let me tumble downstairs so distant from the room I went from! so distant from the room I meant to go to! Cursed, cursed be every careless devil! May this or worse be their fate, every one of them!

And then she cursed and swore more vehemently, and the more, as two or three of them were excusing themselves on the score of their being at that time as unable to help themselves as she.

As soon as she had cleared the passage of her throat by the oaths and curses which her wild impatience made her utter, she began in a more hollow and whining strain to bemoan herself. And here, said she—Heaven grant me patience! [clenching and unclenching her hands]—am I to die thus miserably—of a broken leg in my old age!—snatched away by means of my own intemperance! Self-do! Self-undone! No time for my affairs! No time to repent! And in a few hours (Oh!—Oh!—with another long-howling O—h!—U—gh—o! a kind of screaming key terminating it), who knows, who can tell *where* I shall be! O! that indeed I never, never had had a being!

What could one say to such a wretch as this, whose whole life had been spent in the most diffusive wickedness, and who no doubt has numbers of souls to answer for? Yet I told her she must be patient: that her violence made her worse: and that, if she would compose herself, she might get into a frame more proper for her present circumstances.

Who, I? interrupted she: *I* get into a better frame! *I*, who can neither cry nor pray! Yet already feel the torments of the damned! What mercy can I expect? What hope is left for me?—Then, that sweet creature! That incomparable Miss Harlowe! She, it seems, is dead and gone! O that cursed man! Had it not been for *him*! I had never had this, the most crying of all my sins, to answer for!

And then she set up another howl.

And *is* she dead?—indeed dead? proceeded she, when her howl was over. O what an angel have I been the means of destroying! For though it was that wicked man's fault that ever she was in my house, yet it was mine, and yours, and yours, and yours, devils as we all were (turning to Sally, to Polly, and to one or two more), that he did not do her justice! And that, *that* is my curse, and will one day be yours!

And then again she howled.

I still advised patience. I said that if her time were to be so short as she apprehended, the more ought she to endeavour to compose herself: and then she would at least die with more ease to herself—and satisfaction to her friends, I was *going* to say—but the word *die* put her into a violent raving, and thus she broke in upon me:

Die, did you say, sir? *Die! I will not*, I *cannot* die! I know not *how* to die! *Die*, sir! And *must* I then die? Leave this world? I cannot bear it! And who brought *you* hither, sir (her eyes striking fire at me), who brought you hither to tell me I must *die*, sir? I cannot, I will not leave this world. Let others die who wish for another! who expect a better! I have had my plagues in this; but would compound for all future hopes, so as I may be nothing after this!

And then she howled and bellowed by turns.

By my faith, Lovelace, I trembled in every joint; and looking upon *her* who spoke this, and roared thus, and upon the *company* round me, I more than once thought myself to be in one of the infernal mansions.

Yet will I proceed and try for thy good if I can shock thee but half as much with my descriptions as I was shocked by what I saw and heard.

Sally! Polly! Sister Carter! said she, did you not tell me I might *recover*? Did not the *surgeon* tell me I might?

And so you *may*, cried Sally; Monsieur Garon says you may, if you'll be patient. But, as I have often told you this blessed morning, you are readier to take despair from your own fears than comfort from all the hope we can give you.

Yet, cried the wretch, interrupting, does not Mr. Belford (and to *him* you have told the truth, though you won't to *me*; does not he) tell me I shall *die*? I cannot bear it! I cannot bear the *thoughts* of dying!

And then, but that half a dozen at once endeavoured to keep down her violent hands, would she have beaten herself; as it seems she had often attempted to do from the time the surgeon popped out the word *mortification* to her.

Well, but to what purpose, said I (turning aside to her sister, and to Sally and Polly), are these hopes given her, if the gentlemen of the faculty give her over? You should let her know the worst, and then she *must* submit; for there is no running away from death. If she has any matters to settle, put her upon settling them; and do not, by telling her she will live, when there is no room to expect it, take from her the opportunity of doing needful things. Do the surgeons actually give her over?

They do, whispered they. Her gross habit, they say, gives no hopes. We have sent for both surgeons, whom we expect every minute.

Both the surgeons (who are French, for Mrs. Sinclair has heard Tourville launch out in the praise of French surgeons) came in while we were thus talking. I retired to the farther end of the room, and threw up a window for a little air, being half poisoned by the effluvia arising from so many contaminated carcasses; which gave me no imperfect idea of the stench of jails, which, corrupting the ambient air, gives what is called the prison distemper.

I came back to the bedside when the surgeons had inspected the fracture; and asked them if there were any expectation of her life?

One of them whispered me there was none: that she had a strong fever upon her, which alone, in such a habit, would probably *do the business*; and that the mortification had visibly gained upon her since they were there six hours ago.

Will amputation save her? Her affairs and her mind want settling. A few days added to her life may be of service to her in both respects.

They told me the fracture was high in her leg; that the knee was greatly bruised; that the mortification, in all probability, had spread half-way of the *femur*: and then, getting me between them (three or four of the women joining us, and listening with their mouths open, and all the signs of *ignorant wonder* in *their* faces, as there appeared of *self-sufficiency* in those of the *artists*), did they by turns fill my ears with an anatomical description of the leg and thigh, running over with terms of art; of the *tarsus*, the *metatarsus*, the *tibia*, the *fibula*, the *patella*, the *os tali*, the *os tibiæ*, the *tibialis posticus* and *tibialis anticus*, up to the *os femoris*, to the *acetabulum* of the *os ischion*, the *great trochanter*, *glutæus*, *triceps*, *lividus*, and *little rotators*; in short, of all the muscles, cartilages, and bones that constitute the leg and thigh from the great toe to the hip; as if they would show me that all their science had penetrated their heads no farther than their mouths; while Sally lifted up her hands with a Laud bless me! Are all surgeons so learned! But at last both the gentlemen declared that, if she and her friends would consent to amputation, they would *whip off her leg in a moment*.

Mrs. Carter asked to what purpose, if the operation would not save her?

Very true, they said; but it might be a satisfaction to the patient's friends, that all was done that could be done.

And so the poor wretch was to be lanced and quartered, as I may say, for an experiment only! And, without any hope of benefit for the operation, was to pay the surgeons for tormenting her!

I cannot but say I have a mean opinion of both these gentle-men, who, though they make a figure, it seems, in their way of living, and boast not only French extraction but a Paris educa-tion, never will make any in their practice.

How unlike my honest English friend Tomkins, a plain, serious, intelligent man, whose art lies deeper than in words; who always avoids parade and jargon; and endeavours to make every one as much a judge of what he is about as himself!

All the time that the surgeons run on with their anatomical process the wretched woman most frightfully roared and bellowed; which the gentlemen (who showed themselves to be of the class of those who are not affected with the evils they do not *feel*) took no other notice of than by raising *their* voices to be *heard*, as she raised *hers*—being evidently more solicitous to increase their acquaintance, and to propagate the notion of their skill, than to attend to the clamours of the poor wretch whom they were called in to relieve; though by this very means, like the dog and the shadow in the fable, they lost both aims with me; for I never was deceived in one rule, which I made early; to wit, *that the stillest water is the deepest*, while the bubbling stream only betrays shallowness; and that stones and pebbles lie there so near the surface, to point out the best place to ford a river dry-shod.

As nobody cared to tell the unhappy wretch what every one apprehended must follow, and what the surgeons convinced me soon would, I undertook to be the denouncer of her doom. Accordingly, the operators being withdrawn, I sat down by the bedside, and said: Come, Mrs. Sinclair, let me advise you to forbear these ravings at the carelessness of those who, I find, at the time, could take no care of themselves; and since the accident *has* happened, and cannot be remedied, to resolve to make the best of the matter: for all this violence but enrages the malady, and you will probably fall into a delirium if you give way to it, which will deprive you of that reason which you ought to make the best of, for the time it may be lent you.

She turned her head towards me, and hearing me speak with a determined *voice*, and seeing me assume as determined an *air*, became more calm and attentive.

I went on, telling her that I was glad, from the hints she had given, to find her concerned for her past misspent life, and par-ticularly for the part she had had in the ruin of the most excellent woman on earth: that if she would compose herself, and patiently submit to the consequence of an evil she had brought upon her-

self, it might possibly be happy for her yet. Meantime, continued I, tell me, with temper and calmness, why you was so
desirous to see me?

She seemed to be in great confusion of thought, and turned
her head this way and that; and at last, after much hesitation,
said: Alas for me! I hardly know *what* I wanted with you.
When I awoke from my intemperate trance, and found what
a cursed way I was in, my conscience smote me, and I was for
catching, like a drowning wretch, at every straw. I wanted to
see everybody and anybody but those I did see; everybody
who I thought could give me comfort. Yet could I expect
none from *you* neither; for you had declared yourself my enemy,
although I had never done you harm: for what, Jackey, in her
old tone, whining through her nose, was Miss Harlowe to you?
But *she* is happy! But oh! what will become of *me*? Yet tell
me (for the surgeons have told *you* the truth, no doubt), tell me,
shall I do well again? May I recover? If I *may*, I will begin a
new course of life: as I hope to be saved, I will. I'll renounce
you all—every one of you [looking round her], and scrape all
I can together, and live a life of penitence; and when I die, leave
it all to charitable uses—I will, by my soul—every doit of it to
charity. But this once, lifting up her rolling eyes, and folded
hands (with a wry-mouthed earnestness, in which every muscle
and feature of her face bore its part), this one time—good God
of heaven and earth—but this once! this once! repeating those
words five or six times, spare Thy poor creature, and every hour
of my life shall be passed in penitence and atonement: upon
my soul it shall!

Less vehement! a little less vehement! said I—it is not for
me, who have led so free a life, as you but too well know, to talk
to you in a reproaching strain, and to set before you the iniquity
you have lived in, and the many souls you have helped to
destroy. But as you are in so penitent a way, if I might advise,
you should send for a good clergyman, the purity of whose life
and manners may make all these things come from him with a
better grace than they can from me.

How, sir! What, sir! interrupting me; send for a parson!
Then you indeed think I shall die! Then you think there is no
room for hope!—A parson, sir!—Who sends for a parson while
there is any hope left? The sight of a parson would be death
immediate to me! I cannot, cannot die! Never tell me of it!
What! die! What! cut off in the midst of my sins!

And then she began again to rave.

I cannot bear, said I, rising from my seat with a stern air, to see a reasonable creature behave so outrageously! Will this vehemence, think you, mend the matter? Will it avail you anything? Will it not rather shorten the life you are so desirous to have lengthened, and deprive you of the only opportunity you can ever have to settle your affairs for both worlds? Death is but the common lot: and if it will be *yours* soon, looking at *her*, it will be also *yours*, and *yours*, and *yours*, speaking with a raised voice, and turning to every trembling devil round her [for they all shook at my forcible application], and *mine* also. And you have reason to be thankful, turning again to her, that you did not perish in that act of intemperance which brought you to this: for it might have been your neck, as *well* as your leg; and then you had not had the opportunity you now have for repentance. And, the Lord have mercy upon you! into what a state might you have awoke?

Then did the poor wretch set up an inarticulate frightful howl, such a one as I never before heard uttered, as if already pangs infernal had taken hold of her; and seeing every one half-frighted, and me motioning to withdraw, O pity me, pity me, Mr. Belford, cried she, her words interrupted by groans—I find you think I shall die! And *what* I may be, and *where*, in a very few hours—who can tell?

I told her it was in vain to flatter her: it was my opinion she would not recover.

I was going to re-advise her to calm her spirits, and endeavour to resign herself, and to make the best of the opportunity yet left her; but this declaration set her into a most outrageous raving. She would have torn her hair, and beaten her breast, had not some of the wretches held her hands by force, while others kept her as steady as they could, lest she should again put out her new-set leg: so that, seeing her thus incapable of advice, and in a perfect frenzy, I told Sally Martin that there was no bearing the room; and that their best way was to send for a minister to pray by her, and to reason with her, as soon as she should be capable of it.

And so I left them; and never was so sensible of the benefit of fresh air as I was the moment I entered the street.

Nor is it to be wondered at, when it is considered that, to the various ill smells that will be always found in a close sick-bed-room (for generally when the physician comes the air is shut out), *this* of Mrs. Sinclair was the more particularly offensive, as to the scent of plasters, salves, and ointments were added the

stenches of spirituous liquors, burnt and unburnt, of all deno-
minations: for one or other of the creatures, under pretence of
colics, gripes, or qualms, were continually calling for supplies
of these all the time I was there. And yet this is thought to
be a genteel house of the sort: and all the prostitutes in it are
prostitutes of price, and their visitors people of note.

O Lovelace! what lives do most of us rakes and libertines
lead! What company do we keep! And, for *such* company,
what society renounce, or endeavour to make like these!

What woman, nice in her person, and of purity in her mind
and manners, did she know what miry wallowers the generality
of men of our class are in themselves, and constantly trough and
sty with, but would detest the thoughts of associating with such
filthy sensualists, whose favourite taste carries them to mingle
with the dregs of stews, brothels, and common sewers?

Yet, to such a choice are many worthy women betrayed, by
that false and inconsiderate notion, raised and propagated, no
doubt, by the author of all delusion, *that a reformed rake makes
the best husband.* We rakes, indeed, are bold enough to suppose
that women in general are as much rakes in their *hearts* as the
libertines some of them suffer themselves to be taken with are
in their *practice.* A supposition, therefore, which it behoves
persons of true honour of that sex to discountenance, by
rejecting the address of every man whose character will not
stand the test of that virtue which is the glory of a woman: and
indeed, I may say, of a man too: why should it not?

How, indeed, can it be, if this point be duly weighed, that a
man who thinks *alike of all the sex,* and knows it to be in the
power of a wife to do him the greatest dishonour man can
receive, and doubts not her *will* to do it, if *opportunity offer,* and
importunity be not wanting: that *such* a one, from *principle,*
should be a good husband to *any* woman? And, indeed, little
do innocents think, what a *total revolution* of manners, what a
change of fixed habits, nay, what a *conquest of a bad nature,* and
what a portion of *Divine* GRACE is required to make a man a
good husband, a *worthy father,* and *true friend,* from *principle;*
especially when it is considered that it is not in a man's *own
power* to reform when he will. *This* (to say nothing of my own
experience) thou, Lovelace, hast found in the progress of thy
attempts upon the divine Miss Harlowe. For whose remorses
could be deeper, or more frequent, yet more transient, than
thine?

Now, Lovelace, let me know if the word *grace* can be read

from my pen without a sneer from thee and thy associates? I own that once it sounded oddly in *my* ears. But I shall never forget what a grave man once said on this very word—that with him it was a rake's *shibboleth*.[1] He had always hopes of one who could bear the mention of it without ridiculing it; and ever gave him up for an abandoned man who made a jest of it or of him who used it.

Don't be disgusted that I mingle such grave reflections as these with my narratives. It becomes me, in my present way of thinking, to do so, when I see, in Miss Harlowe, how all human excellence, and in poor Belton, how all inhuman libertinism, and am near seeing in this abandoned woman, how all diabolical profligacy, end. And glad should I be for your own sake, for your splendid family's sake, and for the sake of all your intimates and acquaintance, that you were labouring under the same impressions, that so *we*, who have been companions in (and promoters of one another's) wickedness, might join in a general atonement to the utmost of our power.

I came home reflecting upon all these things, more edifying to me than any sermon I could have heard preached: and I shall conclude this long letter with observing, that although I left the wretched howler in a high frenzy fit, which was excessively shocking to the bystanders; yet her frenzy must be the happiest part of her dreadful condition: for when she is *herself*, as it is called, what must be her reflections upon her past profligate life, throughout which it has been her constant delight and business, devil-like, to make others as wicked as herself! What must her terrors be (a hell already begun in her mind!) on looking forward to the dreadful state she is now upon the verge of! But I drop my trembling pen.

To have done with so shocking a subject at once, we shall take notice that Mr. Belford, in a future letter, writes that the miserable woman, to the surprise of the operators themselves (through hourly increasing tortures of body and mind), held out so long as till Thursday, Sept. 21. And then died in such agonies as terrified into a transitory penitence all the wretches about her.

Letter CXXXIX—Colonel Morden to John Belford, Esq.
Sunday Night, Sept. 10.

DEAR SIR,—According to my promise, I send you an account of matters here. Poor Mrs. Norton was so very ill upon the road, that, slowly as the hearse moved, and the chariot followed,

[1] See Judges xii, 6.

I was afraid we should not have got her to St. Albans. We put up there as I had intended. I was in hopes that she would have been better for the stop: but I was forced to leave her behind me. I ordered the servant-maid you were so considerately kind as to send down with her, to be very careful of her; and left the chariot to attend her. She deserves all the regard that can be paid her; not only upon my cousin's account, but on her own—she is an excellent woman.

When we were within five miles of Harlowe Place, I put on a hand-gallop. I ordered the hearse to proceed more slowly still, the cross-road we were in being rough; and having more time before us than I wanted; for I wished not the hearse to be in till near dusk.

I got to Harlowe Place about four o'clock. You may believe I found a mournful house. You desire me to be very minute.

At my entrance into the court, they were all in motion. Every servant whom I saw had swelled eyes, and looked with so much concern, that at first I apprehended some new disaster had happened in the family.

Mr. John and Mr. Antony Harlowe and Mrs. Hervey were there. They all helped on one another's grief, as they had before done each other's hardness of heart.

My Cousin James met me at the entrance of the hall. His countenance expressed a fixed concern; and he desired me to excuse his behaviour the last time I was there.

My Cousin Arabella came to me full of tears and grief.

O cousin! said she, hanging upon my arm, I dare not ask you any questions!

About the approach of the hearse, I suppose she meant.

I myself was full of grief; and without going farther or speaking, sat down in the hall in the first chair.

The brother sat down on one hand of me, the sister on the other. Both were silent. The latter in tears.

Mr. Antony Harlowe came to me soon after. His face was overspread with all the appearance of woe. He requested me to walk into the parlour; where, as he said, were all his fellow-mourners.

I attended him in. My Cousins James and Arabella followed me.

A perfect concert of grief, as I may say, broke out the moment I entered the parlour.

My Cousin Harlowe, the dear creature's father, as soon as he saw me, said: O cousin, cousin, of all our family, you are the only one who have nothing to reproach yourself with! *You* are a happy man!

The poor mother, bowing her head to me in speechless grief, sat with her handkerchief held to her eyes with one hand. The other hand was held by her Sister Hervey between both hers; Mrs. Hervey weeping upon it.

Near the window sat Mr. John Harlowe, his face and his body turned from the sorrowing company; his eyes red and swelled.

My Cousin Antony, at his re-entering the parlour, went towards Mrs. Harlowe: Don't—dear sister! said he. Then towards my Cousin Harlowe: Don't—dear brother! Don't thus give way. And without being able to say another word, went to a corner of the parlour, and, wanting himself the comfort he would fain have given, sunk into a chair, and audibly sobbed.

Miss Arabella followed her Uncle Antony, as he walked in before me; and seemed as if she would have spoken to the pierced mother some words of comfort. But she was unable to utter them, and got behind her mother's chair; and inclining her face over it on the unhappy lady's shoulder, seemed to claim the consolation that indulgent parent used, but then was unable to afford her.

Young Mr. Harlowe, with all his vehemence of spirit, was now subdued. His self-reproaching conscience, no doubt, was the cause of it.

And what, sir, must their thoughts be, which, at that moment, in a manner deprived them of all motion, and turned their speech into sighs and groans! How to be pitied, how greatly to be pitied, all of them! But how much to be cursed that abhorred Lovelace, who, as it seems, by arts uncommon, and a villainy without example, has been the sole author of a woe so complicated and extensive! God judge me, as——But I stop—the man (the *man* can I say?) is your friend! He already suffers, you tell me, in his intellect. Restore him, Heaven, to that—if I find the matter come out as I *apprehend* it will—indeed her own hint of his usage of her, as in her will, is enough—nor think, my beloved cousin, thou darling of my heart! that thy gentle spirit, breathing charity and forgiveness to the vilest of men, shall avail him!

But once more I stop — forgive me, sir! Who could behold such a scene, who could recollect it in order to describe it (as minutely as you wished me to relate how this unhappy family were affected on this sad occasion), every one of the mourners nearly related to himself, and not be exasperated against the author of all?

As I was the only person (grieved as I was myself) from whom any of them, at that instant, could derive comfort: Let us not, said I, my dear cousin, approaching the inconsolable mother, give way to a grief which, however just, can now avail us nothing. We hurt ourselves, and cannot recall the dear creature for whom we mourn. Nor would you wish it, if you knew with what assurances of eternal happiness she left the world. She is happy, madam! Depend upon it, she is happy! And comfort yourselves with that assurance.

O cousin, cousin! cried the unhappy mother, withdrawing her hand from that of her Sister Hervey, and pressing mine with it, you know not what a child I have lost! Then in a lower voice, And *how* lost!—That it is that makes the loss insupportable.

They all joined in a kind of melancholy chorus, and each accused him and herself, and some of them one another. But the eyes of all, in turn, were cast upon my Cousin James as the person who had kept up the general resentment against so sweet a creature. While he was hardly able to bear his own remorse: nor Miss Harlowe hers; she breaking out into words: How tauntingly did I write to her! How barbarously did I insult her! Yet how patiently did she take it! Who would have thought that she had been so near her end! O brother, brother! but for *you*!—but for *you*——!

Double not upon me, said he, my own woes! I have everything before me that has passed! I thought only to reclaim a dear creature that had erred! I intended not to break her tender heart! But it was the villainous Lovelace who did that —not any of us! Yet, cousin, did she not attribute all to *me*? I fear she did! Tell me only, did she name *me*, did she *speak* of me, in her last hours? I hope she, who could forgive the greatest villain on earth, and plead that he may be safe from our vengeance, I *hope* she could forgive *me*.

She died blessing you all; and justified rather than condemned your severity to her.

Then they set up another general lamentation. We see, said her father, enough we see, in her heart-piercing letters to us, what a happy frame she was in a few days before her death. But did it hold to the last? Had she no repinings? Had the dear child no heart-burnings?

None at all! I never saw, and never shall see, so blessed a *departure*: and no wonder; for I never heard of such a *preparation.* Every hour for weeks together was taken up in it. Let this be our comfort; we need only to wish for so happy an end for ourselves, and for those who are nearest to our hearts. We may any of us be grieved for acts of unkindness to her: but had all happened that once she wished for, she could not have made a happier, perhaps not so happy, an end.

Dear soul! and Dear sweet soul! the father, uncles, sister, my Cousin Hervey, cried out all at once in accents of anguish inexpressibly affecting.

We must for ever be disturbed for those acts of unkindness to so sweet a child! cried the unhappy mother. Indeed, indeed (softly to her Sister Hervey), I have been too passive, much too passive, in this case! The temporary quiet I have been so studious all my life to preserve has cost me everlasting disquiet!——

There she stopped.

Dear sister! was all Mrs. Hervey could say.

I have done but half my duty to the dearest and most meritorious of children! resumed the sorrowing mother. Nay, *not* half! How have we hardened our hearts against her!——

Again her tears denied passage to her words.

My *dearest, dearest sister!* again was all Mrs. Hervey could say.

Would to Heaven, proceeded, exclaiming, the poor mother, I had but *once* seen her! Then turning to my Cousin James and his sister: O my son! O my Arabella! If WE were to receive as little mercy——

And there again she stopped, her tears interrupting her further speech: every one, all the time, remaining silent; their countenances showing a grief in their hearts too big for expression.

Now you see, Mr. Belford, that my dearest cousin could be allowed all her merit!——*What a dreadful thing is after-reflection upon a conduct so perverse and unnatural !*

O this cursed friend of yours, Mr. Belford! This detested Lovelace! To him, to him is owing——

Pardon me, sir. I will lay down my pen till I have recovered my temper.

One in the morning.

In vain, sir, have I endeavoured to compose myself to rest. You wished me to be very particular, and I cannot help it. This melancholy subject fills my whole mind. I will proceed, though it be midnight.

About six o'clock the hearse came to the outward gate. The

parish church is at some distance; but the wind setting fair, the afflicted family were struck, just before it came, into a fresh fit of grief, on hearing the funeral bell tolled in a very solemn manner. A respect, as it proved, and as they all guessed, paid to the memory of the dear deceased out of officious love, as the hearse passed near the church.

Judge, when their grief was so great in expectation of it, what it must be when it arrived.

A servant came in to acquaint us with what its lumbering heavy noise up the paved inner courtyard apprised us of before.

He spoke not. He could not speak. He looked, bowed, and withdrew.

I stepped out. No one else could then stir. Her brother, however, soon followed me.

When I came to the door I beheld a sight very affecting.

You have heard, sir, how universally my dear cousin was beloved. By the poor and middling sort especially, no young lady was ever so much beloved. And with reason: she was the common patroness of all the honest poor in her neighbourhood.

It is natural for us in every deep and sincere grief to interest all we know in what is so concerning to ourselves. The servants of the family, it seems, had told *their* friends, and those *theirs*, that though, living, their dear young lady could not be received nor looked upon, her body was permitted to be brought home. The space of time was so confined, that those who knew when she died, must easily guess *near the time* the hearse was to come. A hearse, passing through country villages, and from London, however slenderly attended (for the chariot, as I have said, waited upon poor Mrs. Norton), takes every one's attention. Nor was it hard to guess whose *this* must be, though not adorned by escutcheons, when the cross-roads to Harlowe Place were taken, as soon as it came within six miles of it: so that the hearse, and the solemn tolling of the bell, had drawn together at least fifty of the neighbouring men, women, and children, and some of good appearance. Not a soul of them, it seems, with a dry eye; and each lamenting the death of this admired lady, *who*, as I am told, *never stirred out, but somebody was the better for her.*

These, when the coffin was taken out of the hearse, crowding about it, hindered, for a few moments, its being carried in; the young people struggling who should bear it; and yet with respectful *whisperings*, rather than clamorous *contention*. A mark of veneration I had never before seen paid, upon any occasion, in all my travels, from the underbred many, from whom noise is generally inseparable in all their emulations.

At last, six maidens were permitted to carry it in by the six handles.

The corpse was thus borne, with the most solemn respect, into the hall, and placed for the present upon two stools there. The plates, and emblems, and inscription, set every one gazing upon it and admiring it. The more, when they were told that all was of her own ordering. They wished to be permitted a sight of the corpse; but rather mentioned this as their *wish* than as their *hope*. When they had all satisfied their curiosity, and remarked upon the emblems, they dispersed with blessings upon her memory, and with tears and lamentations; pronouncing her to be happy; and inferring, that were *she* not so, what would become of them? While others ran over with repetitions of the good she delighted to do. Nor were there wanting those among them who heaped curses upon the man who was the author of her fall.

The servants of the family then got about the coffin. They could not before: and that afforded a new scene of sorrow: but a silent one; for they spoke only by their eyes, and by sighs, looking upon the lid, and upon one another, by turns, with hands lifted up. The presence of their young master possibly might awe them, and cause their grief to be expressed only in dumb show.

As for Mr. James Harlowe (who accompanied me, but withdrew when he saw the crowd), he stood looking upon the lid, when the people had left it, with a fixed attention: yet, I dare say, knew not a symbol or letter upon it at that moment, had the question been asked him. In a profound reverie he stood, his arms folded, his head on one side, and marks of stupefaction imprinted upon every feature.

But when the corpse was carried into the lesser parlour, adjoining to the hall, which she used to call *her* parlour, and put upon a table in the middle of the room, and the father and mother, the two uncles, her Aunt Hervey, and her sister came in, joining her brother and me, with trembling feet, and eager woe, the scene was still more affecting. Their sorrow was heightened, no doubt, by the remembrance of their unforgiving severity: and now seeing before them the receptacle that contained the glory of their family, who so lately was driven thence by their indiscreet violence; never, never more to be restored to them! no wonder that their grief was more than common grief.

They would have withheld the mother, it seems, from coming in: but when they could not, though undetermined before, they all bore her company, led on by an impulse they could not resist. The poor lady but just cast her eye upon the coffin, and then snatched it away, retiring with passionate grief towards the window; yet addressing herself, with clasped hands, as if to her beloved daughter: O my child, my child! cried she; thou pride of my hope! Why was I not permitted to speak pardon and peace to thee!—O forgive thy cruel mother!

Her son (his heart then softened, as his eyes showed) besought her to withdraw: and her woman looking in at that moment, he called her to assist him in conducting her lady into the middle parlour: and then returning, met his father going out at the door, who also had but just cast his eye on the coffin, and yielded to my entreaties to withdraw.

His grief was too deep for utterance, till he saw his son coming in; and then, fetching a heavy groan, Never, said he, was sorrow like my sorrow! O son! son! in a reproaching accent, his face turned from him.

I attended him through the middle parlour, endeavouring to console him. His lady was there in agonies. She took his eye. He made a motion towards her: O my dear, said he—but turning short, his eyes as full as his heart, he hastened through to the great parlour: and when there he desired me to leave him to himself.

The uncles and the sister looked and turned away, looked and turned away, very often, upon the emblems, in silent sorrow. Mrs. Hervey would have read to them the inscription. These words she did read: *Here the wicked cease from troubling*——but could read no further. Her tears fell in large drops upon the plate she was contemplating; and yet she was desirous of gratifying a curiosity that mingled impatience with her grief because she could *not* gratify it, although she often wiped her eyes as they flowed.

Judge you, Mr. Belford (for you have great humanity), how *I* must be affected. Yet was I forced to try to comfort them all.

But here I will close this letter, in order to send it to you in the morning early. Nevertheless, I will begin another, upon supposition that my doleful prolixity will not be disagreeable to you. Indeed, I am altogether indisposed for rest, as I mentioned before. So can do nothing but write. I have also more melancholy scenes to paint. My pen, if I may so say, is untired. These scenes are fresh upon my memory: and I myself, perhaps, may owe to you the favour of a review of them, with such other papers as you shall think proper to oblige me with, *when heavy grief has given way to milder melancholy.*

My servant, in his way to you with this letter, shall call at St. Albans upon the good woman, that he may inform you how she does. Miss Arabella asked me after her, when I withdrew to my chamber; to which she complacently accompanied me. She was much concerned at the bad way we left her in; and said her mother would be more so.

No wonder that the dear departed, who foresaw the remorse that would fall to the lot of this unhappy family when they came to have the news of her death confirmed to them, was so grieved for their apprehended grief, and *endeavoured to comfort them by her posthumous letters.* But it was still a greater generosity in her to try to excuse them to me, as she did when we were alone together a few hours before she died; and to aggravate more than (as far as I can find) she ought to have done, the only error she was ever guilty of. The more freely, however, perhaps (exalted creature!) that I might think the better of her friends, although at her own expense. I am, dear sir,

Your faithful and obedient servant,

WM. MORDEN.

Letter CXL—*Colonel Morden.* [*In continuation*]

WHEN the unhappy mourners were all retired, I directed the lid of the coffin to be unscrewed, and caused some fresh aromatics and flowers to be put into it.

The corpse was very little altered, notwithstanding the journey. The sweet smile remained.

The maids who brought the flowers were ambitious of strewing them about it: they poured forth fresh lamentations over her; each wishing she had been so happy as to have been allowed to attend her in London. One of them particularly, who is, it seems, my Cousin Arabella's personal servant, was more clamorous in her grief than any of the rest; and the moment she turned her back, all the others allowed she had reason for it. I inquired afterwards about her, and found that this creature was set over my dear cousin when she was confined to her chamber by indiscreet severity.

Good Heaven! that they should treat, and suffer thus to be treated, a young lady who was qualified to give laws to all her family!

When my cousins were told that the lid was unscrewed, they pressed in again, all but the mournful father and mother, as if by consent. Mrs. Hervey kissed her pale lips. Flower of the world! was all she could say; and gave place to Miss Arabella; who, kissing the forehead of *her* whom she had so cruelly treated, could only say to my Cousin James (looking upon the corpse, and upon him): O brother! While he, taking the fair lifeless hand, kissed it, and retreated with precipitation.

Her two uncles were speechless. They seemed to wait each other's example, whether to look upon the corpse or not. I ordered the lid to be replaced; and then they pressed forward, as the others again did, to take a last farewell of the casket which so lately contained so rich a jewel.

Then it was that the grief of each found fluent expression; and the fair corpse was addressed to, with all the tenderness that the sincerest love and warmest admiration could inspire; each according to their different degrees of relationship, as if none of them had before looked upon her. She was their *very* niece! both uncles said. The injured saint! her Uncle Harlowe. The same smiling sister! Arabella. The dear creature! all of them. The same benignity of countenance! The same sweet composure! The same natural dignity! *She* was questionless happy! That sweet smile betokened *her* being so; *themselves* most unhappy! And then, once more, the brother took the lifeless hand, and vowed revenge upon it, on the cursed author of all this distress.

The unhappy parents proposed to take one last view and farewell of their once darling daughter. The father was got to the parlour door, after the inconsolable mother: but neither of them were able to enter it. The mother said she must once more see the child of her heart, or she should never enjoy herself. But they both agreed to refer their melancholy curiosity till the next day; and hand in hand retired inconsolable, and speechless both, their faces overspread with woe, and turned from each other, as unable each to behold the distress of the other.

When all were withdrawn I retired, and sent for my Cousin James, and acquainted him with his sister's request in relation to the discourse to be pronounced at her interment; telling him how necessary it was that the minister, whoever he were, should have the earliest notice given him that the case would admit. He lamented the death of the Reverend Doctor Lewen, who, as he said, was a great admirer of his sister, as she was of him, and would have been the fittest of all men for that office.

He spoke with great asperity of Mr. Brand, upon whose light inquiry after his sister's character in town he was willing to lay some of the blame due to himself.

Mr. Melvill, Doctor Lewen's assistant, must, he said, be the man; and he praised him for his abilities, his elocution, and unexceptionable manners; and promised to engage him early in the morning.

He called out his sister, and she was of his opinion. So I left this upon them.

They both, with no little warmth, hinted their disapprobation of you, sir, for their sister's executor, on the score of your intimate friendship with the author of her ruin.

You must not resent anything I shall communicate to you of what they say on this occasion: depending that you will not, I shall write with the greater freedom.

I told them how much my dear cousin was obliged to your friendship and humanity: the injunctions she had laid you under, and your own inclination to observe them. I said that you were a man of honour: that you were desirous of consulting me, because you would not willingly give offence to any of them; and that I was very fond of cultivating your favour and correspondence.

They said there was no need of an executor out of their family; and they hoped that you would relinquish so *unnecessary* a trust, as they called it. My Cousin James declared that he would write to you as soon as the funeral was over, to desire that you would do so, upon proper assurances that all that the will prescribed should be performed.

I said you were a man of resolution: that I thought he would hardly succeed; for that you made a point of honour of it.

I then showed them their sister's posthumous letter to you; in which she confesses her obligations to you, and regard for you, and for your future welfare.[1] You may believe, sir, they were extremely affected with the perusal of it.

They were surprised that I had given up to you the produce of her grandfather's estate since his death. I told them plainly that they must thank themselves if anything disagreeable to them occurred from their sister's device; deserted, and thrown into the hands of strangers, as she had been.

They said they would report all I had said to their father and mother; adding that, great as their trouble was, they found they had more still to come. But if Mr. Belford *were to be* the

[1] See pp. 354–5.

executor of her will, contrary to their hopes, they besought me to take the trouble of transacting everything with you; that a friend of the man to whom they owed all their calamity might not appear to them.

They were extremely moved at the text their sister had chosen for the subject of the funeral discourse.[1] I had extracted from the will that article, supposing it probable that I might not so soon have an opportunity to show them the will itself, as would otherwise have been necessary on account of the interment: which cannot be delayed.

Monday Morning, between Eight and Nine.

The unhappy family are preparing for a mournful meeting at breakfast. Mr. James Harlowe, who has had as little rest as I, has written to Mr. Melvill, who has promised to draw up a brief eulogium on the deceased. Miss Howe is expected here by and by, to see, for the last time, her beloved friend.

Miss Howe, by her messenger, desires she may not be taken any notice of. She shall not tarry six minutes, was the word. Her desire will be easily granted her.

Her servant, who brought the request, if it were denied, was to return and meet her; for she was ready to set out in her chariot when he got on horseback.

If he met her not with the refusal, he was to stay here till she came. I am, sir,

Your faithful humble servant,
WILLIAM MORDEN.

Letter CXLI—Colonel Morden. [*In continuation*]

Monday Afternoon, Sept. 11.

SIR,—We are such bad company here to one another, that it is some relief to retire and write.

I was summoned to breakfast about half an hour after nine. Slowly did the mournful congress meet. Each, lifelessly and spiritless, took our places, with swollen eyes, inquiring, without expecting any tolerable account, how each had rested.

The sorrowing mother gave for answer that she should never more know what rest was.

By the time we were well seated, the bell ringing, the outward gate opening, a chariot rattling over the pavement of the courtyard, put them into emotion.

[1] See p. 427.

I left them; and was just time enough to give Miss Howe my hand, as she alighted: her maid in tears remaining in the chariot.

I think you told me, sir, you never saw Miss Howe. She is a fine graceful young lady. A fixed melancholy on her whole aspect, overclouded a vivacity and fire which, nevertheless, darted now and then through the awful gloom. I shall ever respect her for her love to my dear cousin.

Never did I think, said she, as she gave me her hand, to enter more these doors: but, living or dead, my *Clarissa* brings me after her anywhither!

She entered with me the little parlour; and seeing the coffin, withdrew her hand from mine, and with impatience pushed aside the lid. As impatiently she removed the face-cloth. In a wild air, she clasped her uplifted hands together; and now looked upon the corpse, now up to Heaven, as if appealing to that. Her bosom heaved and fluttered discernible through her handkerchief, and at last she broke silence: O sir!—see you not here!—see you not here—the glory of her sex? Thus by the most villainous of yours—*thus*—laid low!

O my blessed friend! said she—my sweet companion!—my lovely monitress!—kissing her lips at every tender appellation. And is this all!—is it all, of my CLARISSA's story!

Then, after a short pause, and a profound sigh, she turned to me, and then to her breathless friend. But *is* she, *can* she be, really dead! O no! She only sleeps. Awake, my beloved friend! My sweet, clay-cold friend, awake! Let thy Anna Howe revive thee; by her warm breath revive thee, my dear creature! And, kissing her again, Let my warm lips animate thy cold ones!

Then, sighing again, as from the bottom of her heart, and with an air, as if disappointed that she answered not: And can such perfection end thus!—And art thou really and indeed flown from thine Anna Howe! O my unkind CLARISSA!

She was silent a few moments, and then, seeming to recover herself, she turned to me: Forgive, forgive, Mr. Morden, this wild frenzy! I am not myself! I never shall be! You knew not the excellence, no, not *half* the excellence, that is thus laid low! Repeating, This cannot, surely, be all of my CLARISSA's story!

Again pausing, One tear, my beloved friend, didst thou allow me! But this *dumb* sorrow! O for a tear to ease my full-swollen heart, that is just bursting!

But why, sir, why, Mr. Morden, was she sent *hither?* Why

not to *me?* She has no father, no mother, no relations; no, not *one!* They had all renounced her. I was her sympathizing friend—and had not I the best right to my dear creature's remains? And must names, without nature, be preferred to such a love as mine?

Again she kissed her lips, each cheek, her forehead—and sighed as if her heart would break.

But why, why, said she, was I withheld from seeing my dearest, dear friend, before she commenced angel? Delaying still, and *too easily persuaded* to delay, the friendly visit my heart panted after; what pain will this reflection give me!—O my blessed friend! Who knows, who knows, had I come in time, what my cordial comfortings might have done for thee!

But—looking round her, as if she apprehended seeing some of the family—one more kiss, my angel, my friend, my ever-to-be-regretted, lost companion! And let me fly this hated house, which I never loved but for thy sake! Adieu, then, my dearest CLARISSA! *Thou* art happy, I doubt not, as thou assuredst me in thy last letter! O may we meet, and rejoice together, where no villainous *Lovelaces,* no hard-hearted *relations,* will ever shock our innocence, or ruffle our felicity!

Again she was silent, unable to go, though seeming to intend it; struggling, as it were, with her grief, and heaving with anguish. At last, happily, a flood of tears gushed from her eyes. Now!—now! said she, shall I—shall I—be easier. But for this kindly relief, my heart would have burst asunder. More, many more tears than these are due to my CLARISSA, whose counsel has done for me what mine could not do for her! But why, looking earnestly upon her, her hands clasped and lifted up—but why do I thus lament the HAPPY? And that thou art so, is my comfort. It is, it is, my dear creature! kissing her again.

Excuse me, sir (turning to me, who was as much moved as herself); I loved the dear creature, as never woman loved another. Excuse my frantic grief. How has the glory of her sex fallen a victim to villainy and to hard-heartedness!

Madam, said I, they all have it! Now indeed they have it——

And let them have it! I should belie my love for the friend of my heart, were I to pity them! But how unhappy am I (looking upon her) that I saw her not before these eyes were shut, before these lips were for ever closed! O sir, you know not the wisdom that continually flowed from these lips when she spoke!—nor what a friend I have lost!

Then, surveying the lid, she seemed to take in at once the

meaning of the emblems: and this gave her so much fresh grief, that though she several times wiped her eyes, she was unable to read the inscription and texts: turning therefore to me: Favour me, sir, I pray you, by a line, with the description of these emblems, and with these texts: and if I might be allowed a lock of the dear creature's hair——

I told her that her executor would order both; and would also send her a copy of her last will; in which she would find the most grateful remembrances of her love for her, whom she calls *the sister of her heart*.

Justly, said she, does she call me so; for we had but one heart, but one soul, between us: and now my better half is torn from me,—*what shall I do?*

But looking round her, on a servant's stepping by the door, as if again she had apprehended it was some of the family: Once more, said she, a solemn, an everlasting adieu! Alas! for *me*, a solemn, an everlasting adieu!

Then again embracing her face with both her hands, and kissing it, and afterwards the hands of the dear deceased, first one, then the other, she gave me her hand; and, quitting the room with precipitation, rushed into her chariot; and, when there, with profound sighs, and a fresh burst of tears, unable to speak, she bowed her head to me, and was driven away.

The inconsolable company saw how much I had been moved, on my return to them. Mr. James Harlowe had been telling them what had passed between him and me: and, finding myself unfit for company, and observing that they broke off talk at my coming in, I thought it proper to leave them to their consultations.

And here I will put an end to this letter; for indeed, sir, the very recollection of this affecting scene has left me nearly as unable to proceed as I was, just after it, to converse with my cousins. I am, sir, with great truth,

Your most obedient humble servant,
WILLIAM MORDEN.

Letter CXLII—Colonel Morden. [*In continuation*]

Tuesday Morning, Sept. 12.

THE good Mrs. Norton is arrived, a little amended in her spirits: owing to the very posthumous letters, as I may call them, which you, Mr. Belford, as well as I, apprehended would have had fatal effects upon her.

I cannot but attribute this to the right turn of her mind. It seems she has been inured to afflictions; and has lived in a constant hope of a *better* life, and, having no acts of unkindness to the dear deceased to reproach herself with, is most considerately resolved to exert her *utmost* fortitude in order to comfort the sorrowing mother.

O Mr. Belford, how does the character of my dear departed cousin rise upon me from every mouth! Had she been my own child, or my sister!—But do you think that the man who occasioned this great, this extended ruin——But I forbear.

The will is not to be looked into till the funeral rites are performed. Preparations are making for the solemnity; and the servants as well as principals of all the branches of the family are put into close mourning.

I have seen Mr. Melvill. He is a serious and sensible man. I have given him particulars to go upon in the discourse he is to pronounce at the funeral: but had the less need to do this, as I find he is extremely well acquainted with the whole unhappy story; and was a personal admirer of my dear cousin, and a sincere lamenter of her misfortunes and death. The reverend Dr. Lewen, who is but very lately dead, was his particular friend, and had once intended to recommend him to her favour and notice.

.   .   .   .

I am just returned from attending the afflicted parents, in an effort they made to see the corpse of their beloved child. They had requested my company, and that of the good Mrs. Norton. A last leave, the mother said, she *must* take!

An *effort*, however, it was, and no more. The moment they came in sight of the coffin, before the lid could be put aside, O my dear, said the father, retreating, I cannot, I find I cannot, bear it! Had I—had I—had I never been hard-hearted! Then turning round to his lady, he had but just time to catch her in his arms, and prevent her sinking on the floor. O my dearest life! said he, this is too much!—too much indeed! Let us—let us retire. Mrs. Norton, who (attracted by the awful receptacle) had but just left the good lady, hastened to her. Dear, dear woman, cried the unhappy parent, flinging her arms about her neck, bear me—bear me hence! O my child! my child! my own Clarissa Harlowe! thou pride of my life so lately!— never, never more must I behold thee!

I supported the unhappy father, Mrs. Norton the sinking mother, into the next parlour. She threw herself on a settee there: he into an elbow-chair by her: the good woman at her feet, her arms clasped round her waist. The two mothers, as I may call them, of my beloved cousin, thus tenderly engaged! What a variety of distress in these woeful scenes!

The unhappy father, in endeavouring to comfort his lady, loaded himself. Would to God, my dear, said he, would to God I had no more to charge myself with than you have!—You relented!—you would have prevailed upon *me* to relent!

The greater my fault, said she, when I knew that displeasure was carried too high, to acquiesce as I did! What a barbarous parent was I, to let two angry children make me forget that I was mother to a third—to *such* a third!

Mrs. Norton used arguments and prayers to comfort her. O my dear Norton, answered the unhappy lady, you was the dear creature's *more natural* mother! Would to Heaven I had no more to answer for than *you have*!

Thus the unhappy pair unavailingly recriminated, till my Cousin Hervey entered, and, with Mrs. Norton, conducted up to her own chamber the inconsolable mother. The two uncles, and Mr. Hervey, came in at the same time, and prevailed upon the afflicted father to retire with them to his—both giving up all thoughts of ever seeing more the child whose death was so deservedly regretted by them.

Time only, Mr. Belford, can combat with advantage such a heavy deprivation as this. Advice will not do, while the loss is recent. Nature will have way given to it (and so it ought) till sorrow has in a manner exhausted itself; and then reason and religion will come in seasonably with their powerful aids, to raise the drooping heart.

I see here no face that is the same I saw at my first arrival. Proud and haughty every countenance then, unyielding to entreaty: now, how greatly are they humbled! The utmost distress is apparent in every protracted feature, and in every bursting muscle, of each disconsolate mourner. Their eyes, which so lately flashed anger and resentment, now are turned to every one that approaches them, as if imploring pity! *Could ever wilful hard-heartedness be more severely punished?*

The following lines of Juvenal are, upon the whole, applicable to this house and family: and I have revolved them many times since Sunday evening:

> Humani generis mores tibi nôsse volenti
> Sufficit una domus: paucos consumere dies, et
> Dicere te miserum, postquam illinc veneris, aude.

Let me add that Mrs. Norton has communicated to the family the posthumous letter sent her.   This letter affords a foundation for *future* consolation to them; but at *present* it has new-pointed their grief, by making them reflect on their cruelty to so excellent a daughter, niece, and sister.[1]   I am, dear sir,

Your faithful humble servant,

WM. MORDEN.

Letter CXLIII—Colonel Morden.   [*In continuation*]

Thursday Night, Sept. 14.

WE are just returned from the solemnization of the last mournful rite.   My Cousin James and his sister, Mr. and Mrs. Hervey, and *their* daughter, a young lady whose affection for my departed cousin shall ever bind me to her, my Cousins John and Antony Harlowe, myself, and some other more distant relations of the

---

[1] This letter contains in substance: "Her thanks to the good woman for her care of her in her infancy; for her good instructions, and the excellent example she had set her; with self-accusations of a vanity and presumption which lay lurking in her heart unknown to herself, till her calamities (obliging her to look into herself) brought them to light.

"She expatiates upon the benefit of afflictions to a mind modest, fearful, and diffident.

"She comforts her on her early death; having finished, as she says, her *probatory course*, at so early a time of life, when many are not ripened by the sunshine of Divine grace for a better, till they are fifty, sixty, or seventy years of age.

"I hope, *she says*, that my father will grant the request I have made to him in my last will, to let you pass the remainder of your days at my *Dairy-house*, as it used to be called, where once I promised myself to be happy in you.   Your discretion, prudence, and economy, my dear good woman, proceeds she, will make your presiding over the concerns of that house as beneficial to them as it can be convenient to you.   For *your* sake, my dear Mrs. Norton, I hope they will make you this offer.   And, if they do, I hope you will accept of it for *theirs*."

She remembers herself to her foster-brother in a very kind manner; and charges her, for his sake, that she will not take too much to heart what has befallen her.

She concludes as follows:

"Remember me, in the last place, to all my kind well-wishers of your acquaintance, and to those whom I used to call *My poor*.   They will be *God's poor*, if they trust in Him.   I have taken such care, that I hope they will not be losers by my death.   Bid them therefore rejoice, and do you also, my reverend comforter and sustainer (as well in my darker as in my fairer days), likewise rejoice, that I am so soon delivered from the evils that were before me, and that I am NOW, when this comes to your hand, as I humbly trust, exulting in the mercies of a gracious God, who has conducted me through the greatest trials in safety, and put so happy an end to all my temptations and distresses; and who, I most humbly trust, will, in His own good time, give us a joyful meeting in the regions of eternal blessedness."

names of Fuller and Allinson (who, to testify their respect to the memory of the dear deceased, had put themselves in mourning), self-invited, attended it.

The father and mother would have joined in these last honours, had they been able: but they were both very much indisposed; and continue to be so.

The inconsolable mother told Mrs. Norton that the two mothers of the sweetest child in the world ought not, on this occasion, to be separated. She therefore desired her to stay with *her*.

The whole solemnity was performed with great decency and order. The distance from Harlowe Place to the church is about half a mile. All the way the corpse was attended by great numbers of people of all conditions.

It was nine when it entered the church; every corner of which was crowded. Such a profound, such a silent respect did I never see paid at the funeral of princes. An attentive sadness overspread the face of all.

The eulogy pronounced by Mr. Melvill was a very pathetic one. He wiped his own eyes often, and made everybody present still oftener wipe theirs.

The auditors were most particularly affected when he told them that the solemn text was her own choice.

He enumerated her fine qualities, naming with honour their late worthy pastor for his authority.

Every enumerated excellence was witnessed to in different parts of the church in respectful whispers by different persons, as of their own knowledge, as I have been since informed.

When he pointed to the pew where (doing credit to religion by her example) she used to sit or kneel, the whole auditory, as one person, turned to the pew with the most respectful solemnity, as if she had been herself there.

When the gentleman attributed condescension and mingled dignity to her, a buzzing approbation was given to the attribute throughout the church; and a poor neat woman under my pew added "that she was indeed all graciousness, and would speak to anybody."

Many eyes ran over when he mentioned her charities, her well-judged charities. And her reward was decreed from every mouth, with sighs and sobs from some, and these words from others, "The poor will dearly miss her."

The *cheerful giver*, whom God is said *to love*, was allowed to be *her*: and a young lady, I am told, said it was Miss Clarissa

Harlowe's care to find out the unhappy, upon a sudden distress, before the sighing heart was overwhelmed by it.

She had a set of poor people, chosen for their remarkable honesty and ineffectual industry. These voluntarily paid their last attendance on their benefactress; and mingling in the church as they could crowd near the aisle where the corpse was on stands, it was the less wonder that her praises from the preacher met with such general and such grateful whispers of approbation.

Some it seems there were who, knowing her unhappy story, remarked upon the dejected looks of the brother, and the drowned eyes of the sister: "O what would they now give, they'd warrant, had they not been so hard-hearted!" Others pursued, as I may say, the severe father and unhappy mother into their chambers at home: "They answered for their relenting, now that it was too late! What must be their grief! No *wonder* they could not be present!"

Several expressed their astonishment, as people do every hour, "that a man could live whom such perfections could not engage to be just to her"; to be *humane*, I may say. And who, her rank and fortune considered, could be so disregardful of his own *interest*, had he had no other motive to be just!

The good divine, led by his text, just touched upon the unhappy step that was the cause of her untimely fate. He attributed it to the state of things below, in which there could not be absolute perfection. He very politely touched upon the noble disdain she showed (though earnestly solicited by a whole splendid family) to join interests with a man whom she found unworthy of her esteem and confidence; and who courted her with the utmost earnestness to accept of him.

What he most insisted upon was the happy end she made; and thence drew consolation to her relations, and instruction to the auditory.

In a word, his performance was such as heightened the reputa- which he had before in a very eminent degree obtained.

When the corpse was to be carried down into the vault (a very spacious one, within the church) there was great crowding to see the coffin-lid, and the devices upon it. Particularly two gentle-men, muffled up in cloaks, pressed forward. These, it seems, were Mr. Mullins and Mr. Wyerley; both of them professed admirers of my dear cousin.

When they came near the coffin, and cast their eyes upon the lid, "In that little space, said Mr. Mullins, is included all human excellence!" And then Mr. Wyerley, unable to contain himself, was forced to quit the church; and we hear is very ill.

It is said that Mr. Solmes was in a remote part of the church, wrapped round in a horseman's coat: and that he shed tears several times. But I saw him not.

Another gentleman was there incognito, in a pew near the entrance of the vault, who had not been taken notice of, but for his great emotion when he looked over his pew at the time the coffin was carried down to its last place. This was Miss Howe's worthy Mr. Hickman.

My Cousins John and Antony, and their nephew James, chose not to descend into the vault among their departed ancestors.

Miss Harlowe was extremely affected. Her *conscience*, as well as her love, was concerned on the occasion. She would go down with the corpse of her dear, her only sister, she said: but her brother would not permit it. And her overwhelmed eye pursued the coffin till she could see no more of it: and then she threw herself on the seat, and was near fainting away.

I accompanied it down, that I might not only satisfy myself, but you, sir, her executor, that it was deposited, as she had directed, at the feet of her grandfather.

Mr. Melvill came down, contemplated the lid, and shed a few tears over it. I was so well satisfied with his discourse and behaviour that I presented him on the solemn spot with a ring of some value; and thanked him for his performance.

And here I left the remains of my beloved cousin; having bespoken my own place by the side of her coffin.

On my return to Harlowe Place, I contented myself with sending my compliments to the sorrowing parents, and retired to my chamber. Nor am I ashamed to own that I could not help giving way to a repeated fit of humanity, as soon as I entered it I am,

Sir,
Your most faithful and obedient servant,
WM. MORDEN.

P.S. You will have a letter from my Cousin James, who hopes to prevail upon you to relinquish the executorship. It has not my encouragement.

Letter CXLIV—Mr. Belford to William Morden, Esq.

Saturday, Sept. 16.

DEAR SIR,—I once had thoughts to go down privately, in order, disguised, to see the last solemnity performed. But there was no need to give myself this melancholy trouble, since your last letter so naturally describes all that passed, that I have every scene before my eyes.

You crowd me, sir, methinks, into the silent slow procession— now with the sacred bier do I enter the awful porch: now measure I, with solemn paces, the venerable aisle: now, ambitious of a relationship to her, placed in a near pew to the eye-attracting coffin, do I listen to the moving eulogy: now, through the buzz of gaping, eye-swollen crowds, do I descend into the clammy vault, as a true executor, to see that part of her will performed with my own eyes. There, with a soul filled with musing, do I number the surrounding monuments of mortality, and contemplate the present stillness of so many once busy vanities, crowded all into one poor vaulted nook, as if the living grudged room for the corpses of those for which, when animated, the earth, the air, and the waters, could hardly find room. Then seeing her placed at the feet of him whose earthly delight she was; and who, as I find, ascribes to the pleasure she gave him the prolongation of his own life [1]; sighing, and with averted face, I quit the solemn mansion, the symbolic coffin, and, for ever, the glory of her sex; and ascend with those who, in a few years, after a very short blaze of life, will fill up other spaces of the same vault, which now (while they mourn only for her, whom they jointly persecuted) they press with their feet.

Nor do your affecting descriptions permit me *here* to stop: but, ascended, I mingle my tears and my praises with those of the numerous spectators. I accompany the afflicted mourners back to their uncomfortable mansion; and make one in the general concert of unavailing woe; till retiring, as I imagine, as *they* retire, like them, in reality, I give up to new scenes of solitary and sleepless grief; reflecting upon the perfections I have seen the end of; and having no relief but from an indignation, which makes me approve of the resentments of others against the *unhappy man*, and those *equally unhappy relations of hers*, to whom the irreparable loss is owing.

Forgive me, sir, these reflections; and permit me, with this, to send you what you declined receiving till the funeral was over.

[1] See vol. i, p. 21.

He gives him then an account of the money and effects which he sends him down by this opportunity, for the legatees at Harlowe Place, and in its neighbourhood ; which he desires him to dispose of according to the will.

He also sends him an account of other steps he has taken in pursuance of the will ; and desires to know if Mr. Harlowe expects the discharge of the funeral expenses from the effects in his hands ; and the reimbursement of the sums advanced to the testatrix since her grandfather's death.

These expeditious proceedings, *says he,* will convince Mr. James Harlowe that I am resolved to see the will completely executed; and yet, by my manner of doing it, that I desire not to give unnecessary mortifications to the family, since everything that relates to them shall pass through your hands.

Letter CXLV—*Mr. James Harlowe to John Belford, Esq.*

Harlowe Place, Friday Night, Sept. 15.

SIR,—I hope from the character my worthy Cousin Morden gives you, that you will excuse the application I make to you, to oblige a whole family in an affair that much concerns their peace, and cannot equally concern anybody else. You will immediately judge, sir, that this is the executorship of which my sister has given you the trouble by her last will.

We shall all think ourselves extremely obliged to you, if you please to relinquish this trust to our own family; the reasons which follow pleading for our expectation of this favour from you :

First, because she never would have had the thought of troubling you, sir, if she had believed any of her near relations would have taken it upon themselves.

Secondly, I understand that she recommends to you in the will to trust to the honour of any of our family, for the performance of such of the articles as are of a domestic nature. We are, *any* of us, and *all* of us, if you request it, willing to stake our honours upon this occasion: and all you can desire, as a man of honour, is that the trust be executed.

We are the more concerned, sir, to wish you to decline this office, because of your short and accidental knowledge of the dear testatrix, and long and intimate acquaintance with the man to whom *she* owed her ruin, and *we* the greatest loss and disappointment (her manifold excellences considered) that ever befell a family.

You will allow due weight, I dare say, to this plea, if you make our case your own: and so much the readier, when I assure you that your interfering in this matter so much against our inclinations (excuse, sir, my plain-dealing) will very probably occasion an opposition in some points, where otherwise there might be none.

What, therefore, I propose is, not that my father should assume this trust: he is too much afflicted to undertake it—nor yet myself—I might be thought too much concerned in interest: but that it may be allowed to devolve upon my two uncles; whose known honour, and whose affection to the dear deceased, nobody ever doubted: and they will treat with you, sir, through my Cousin Morden, as to the points they will undertake to perform.

The trouble you have already had will well entitle you to the legacy she bequeaths you, together with the reimbursement of all the charges you have been at, and allowance of the legacies you have discharged, although you should not have qualified yourself to act as an executor; as I presume you have not *yet* done; nor will *now* do.

Your compliance, sir, will oblige a family (who have already distress enough upon them) in the circumstance that occasions this application to you; and more particularly, sir,

Your most humble servant,
JAMES HARLOWE, jun.

I send this by one of my servants, who will attend your dispatch.

Letter CXLVI—Mr. Belford to James Harlowe, jun., Esq.

Saturday, Sept. 16.

SIR,—You will excuse my plain-dealing in turn: for I must observe that if I had *not* the just opinion I have of the sacred nature of the office I have undertaken, some passages in the letter you have favoured me with would convince me that I ought not to excuse myself from acting in it.

I need name only one of them. You are pleased to say that your uncles, if the trust be relinquished to them, will *treat with me*, through Colonel Morden, *as to the points they will undertake to perform.*

Permit me, sir, to say that it is the *duty* of an executor to see *every point* performed that *can* be performed. Nor will I leave the performance of mine to any other persons, especially where a qualifying is so directly intimated, and where all the branches of your family have shown themselves, with respect to the incomparable lady, to have but one mind.

You are pleased to urge that she recommends to me the leaving to the honour of any of your family such of the articles as are of a *domestic nature*. But admitting this to be so, does it not imply that the *other* articles are still to obtain my care? But even these, you will find by the will, she gives not up; and to that I refer you.

I am sorry for the hints you give of an *opposition*, where, as you say, there might be none, if I did not interfere. I see not, sir, why your animosity against a man who cannot be defended, should be carried to such a height against one who never gave you offence: and this only because he is acquainted with that man. I will not say all I might say on this occasion.

As to the legacy to myself, I assure you, sir, that neither my circumstances nor my temper will put me upon being a gainer by the executorship. I shall take pleasure to tread in the steps of the admirable testatrix in all I may; and rather will increase than diminish her poor's fund.

With regard to the trouble that may attend the execution of the trust, I shall not, in honour to her memory, value ten times more than this can give me. I have indeed two other executorships on my hands; but they sit light upon me. And *survivors cannot better or more charitably bestow their time*.

I conceive that every article but that relating to the poor's fund (such is the excellence of the disposition of the most excellent of women) may be performed in two months' time, at furthest.

Occasions of litigation or offence shall not proceed from me. You need only apply to Colonel Morden, who shall command me in everything that the will allows me to oblige your family in. I do assure you that I am as unwilling to obtrude myself upon it, as any of it can wish.

I own that I have not yet proved the will; nor shall I do it till next week at soonest, that you may have time for amicable objections, if such you think fit to make through the colonel's mediation. But let me observe to you, sir, "That an executor's power, in such instances as I have exercised it, is the same before the probate as after it. He can even, without taking *that* out, *commence* an action, although he cannot *declare* upon it: and these acts of administration make him liable to actions himself." I am, therefore, very proper in the steps I have taken in part of the execution of this sacred trust; and want not *allowance* on the occasion.

Permit me to add, that when you have perused the will, and coolly considered everything, it is my hope that you will yourself be of opinion that there can be no room for dispute or opposition: and that if your family will join to expedite the execution, it will be the most natural and easy way of shutting up the whole affair, and to have done with a man so causelessly, as to his *own* particular, the object of your dislike, as is, sir,

Your very humble servant (notwithstanding),

John Belford.

THE WILL

To which the following preamble, written on a separate paper, was stitched with black silk

To my Executor

"I hope I may be excused for expatiating, in divers parts of this solemn last act, upon subjects of importance. For I have heard of so many instances of confusion and disagreement in families, and so much doubt and difficulty, for want of absolute clearness in the testaments of departed persons, that I have often concluded (were there to be no other reasons but those which respect the peace of surviving friends) that this last act, as to its designation and operation, ought not to be the last in its composition or making; but should be the result of cool deliberation; and (as is more *frequently* than *justly* said) of a *sound mind* and *memory*; which too seldom are to be met with but in *sound health*. All pretences of insanity of mind are likewise prevented, when a testator gives reasons for what he wills; all cavils about words are obviated; the obliged are assured; and they enjoy the benefit for whom the benefit was intended. Hence have I for some time past employed myself in penning down heads of such a disposition; which, as reasons offered, I have altered and added to; so that I never was absolutely destitute of a *will*, had I been taken off ever so suddenly. These minutes and imperfect sketches enabled me, as God has graciously given me time and sedateness, to digest them into the form in which they appear."

I, Clarissa Harlowe, now, by strange melancholy accidents, lodging in the Parish of St. Paul, Covent Garden, being of sound and perfect mind and memory, as I hope these presents, drawn up by myself, and written with my own hand, will testify; do [this second day of September [1]], in the year of our Lord ——,[2] make and publish this my last will and testament, in manner and form following:

In the first place, I desire that my body may lie unburied three days after my decease, or till the pleasure of my father be known concerning it. But the occasion of my death not admitting of doubt, I will not, on any account, that it be opened; and it is my desire that it shall not be touched but by those of my own sex.

I have always earnestly requested that my body might be deposited in the family vault with those of my ancestors. If it might be granted, I could now wish that it might be placed at the feet of my dear and honoured grandfather. But as I have, by one very unhappy step, been thought to disgrace my whole lineage, and therefore this last honour may be refused to my corpse; in this case, my desire is that it may be interred in the churchyard belonging to the parish in which I shall die; and that in the most private manner, between the hours of eleven and twelve at night; attended only by Mrs. Lovick, and Mr. and Mrs. Smith, and their maidservant.

But it is my desire that the same fees and dues may be paid which are usually paid for those who are laid in the best ground, as it is called, or even in the chancel. And I bequeath five pounds to be given, at the discretion of the churchwardens, to twenty poor people, the Sunday after my interment; and this whether I shall be buried here or elsewhere.

I have already given verbal directions, that after I am dead (and laid out in the manner I have ordered), I may be put into my coffin as soon as possible: it is my desire that I may not be unnecessarily exposed to the view of anybody; except any of my relations should vouchsafe, for the last time, to look upon me.

And I could wish, if it might be avoided without making ill-will between Mr. Lovelace and my executor, that the former might not be permitted to see my corpse. But if, as he is a man very uncontrollable, and as I am nobody's, he insist upon viewing *her dead* whom he once before saw in a manner dead, let his gay curiosity be gratified. Let him behold and triumph over the wretched remains of one who has been made a victim to his barbarous perfidy: but let some good person, as by my

---

[1] A blank at the writing was left for this date, and filled up on this day. See p. 264.

[2] The date of the year is left blank for particular reasons.

desire, give him a paper, whilst he is viewing the ghastly spectacle, containing these few words only: "Gay, cruel heart!
behold here the remains of the once ruined, yet now happy,
Clarissa Harlowe! See what thou thyself must quickly be;
—and REPENT!"—

Yet, to show that I die in perfect charity with *all the world*,
I do most sincerely forgive Mr. Lovelace the wrongs he has
done me.

If my father can pardon the error of his unworthy child, so
far as to suffer her corpse to be deposited at the feet of her
grandfather, as above requested, I could wish (my misfortunes
being so notorious) that a short discourse might be pronounced
over my remains before they are interred. The subject of the
discourse I shall determine before I conclude this writing.

So much written about what deserves not the least consideration,
and about what will be nothing when this writing comes to be opened
and read, will be excused, when my present unhappy circumstances
and absence from all my natural friends are considered.

And *now*, with regard to the worldly matters which I shall die
possessed of, as well as to those which of right appertain to me,
either by the will of my said grandfather, or otherwise; thus
do I dispose of them.

In the first place, I give and bequeath all the real estates in
or to which I have any claim or title by the said will, to my
ever-honoured father, James Harlowe, Esq.; and that rather
than to my brother and sister, to whom I had once thoughts of
devising them, because, if they survive my father, those estates
will assuredly vest in them, or one of them, by virtue of his
favour and indulgence, as the circumstances of things with
regard to marriage-settlements, or otherwise, may require; or as
they may respectively merit by the continuance of their duty.

The house, late my grandfather's, called *The Grove*, and by
him, in honour of me, and of some of my voluntary employments,
my Dairy-house, and the furniture thereof as it now stands (the
pictures and large iron chest of old plate excepted), I also bequeath to my said father; only begging it as a favour that he will
be pleased to permit my dear Mrs. Norton to pass the remainder
of her days in that house; and to have and enjoy the apartments
in it known by the name of *The Housekeeper's Apartments*, with
the furniture in them; and which (plain and neat) was bought for
me by my grandfather, who delighted to call me his housekeeper;
and which therefore in his lifetime I used as such: the office to
go with the apartments. And I am the more earnest in this

recommendation, as I had once thought to have been very happy there with the good woman; and because I think her prudent management will be as beneficial to my father as his favour can be convenient to her.

But with regard to what has accrued from that estate since my grandfather's death, and to the sum of nine hundred and seventy pounds, which proved to be the moiety of the money that my said grandfather had by him at his death, and which moiety he bequeathed to me for my sole and separate use [as he did the other moiety in like manner to my sister [1]]; and which sum (that I might convince my brother and sister that I wished not for an independence upon my father's pleasure) I gave into my father's hands, together with the management and produce of the whole estate devised to me—these sums, however considerable when put together, I hope I may be allowed to dispose of absolutely, as my love and my gratitude (not confined wholly to my own family, which is very wealthy in all its branches) may warrant: and which therefore I shall dispose of in the manner hereafter mentioned. But it is my will and express direction that my father's account of the above-mentioned produce may be taken and established absolutely (and without contravention or question), as he shall be pleased to give it to my Cousin Morden, or to whom else he shall choose to give it; so as that the said account be not subject to litigation, or to the control of my executor, or of any other person.

My father, of his love and bounty, was pleased to allow me the same quarterly sums that he allowed my sister for apparel and other requisites; and (pleased with me then) used to say that those sums should not be deducted from the estate and effects bequeathed to me by my grandfather: but having *mortally* offended him (as I fear it may be said) by one unhappy step, it may be expected that he will reimburse himself those sums. It is therefore my will and direction that he shall be allowed to pay and satisfy himself for all such quarterly or other sums which he was so good as to advance me from the time of my grandfather's death; and that his account of such sums shall likewise be taken without questioning: the money, however, which I left behind me in my escritoire, being to be taken in part of those disbursements.

My grandfather, who, in his goodness and favour to me, knew no bounds, was pleased to bequeath to me all the family pictures at his late house, some of which are very masterly performances;

[1] See vol. i, p. 55.

with command that if I died unmarried, or if married and had no descendants, they should then go to that son of his (if more than one should be then living) whom I should think would set most value by them. Now, as I know that my honoured uncle, John Harlowe, Esq., was pleased to express some concern that they were not left to him, as eldest son; and as he has a gallery where they may be placed to advantage; and as I have reason to believe that he will bequeath them to my father, if he survive him; who, no doubt, will leave them to my brother; I therefore bequeath all the said family pictures to my said uncle, Joseph Harlowe. In these pictures, however, I include not one of my own, drawn when I was about fourteen years of age; which I shall hereafter in another article bequeath.

My said honoured grandfather having a great fondness for the old family plate, which he would never permit to be changed, having lived, as he used to say, to see a great deal of it come into request again in the revolution of fashions; and having left the same to me, with a command to keep it entire; and with power at my death to bequeath it to whomsoever I pleased that I thought would forward his desire; which was, as he expresses it, that it should be kept *to the end of time*; this family plate, which is deposited in a large iron chest, in the strong-room at his late dwelling-house, I bequeath entire to my honoured uncle, Antony Harlowe, Esq., with the same injunctions which were laid on me; not doubting but he will confirm and strengthen them by his own last will.

I bequeath to my ever valued friend Mrs. Judith Norton, to whose piety and care, seconding the piety and care of my ever honoured and excellent mother, I owe, morally speaking, the qualifications which, for eighteen years of my life, made me beloved and respected, the full sum of six hundred pounds, to be paid her within three months after my death.

I bequeath also to the same good woman thirty guineas, for mourning for her and for her son, my foster-brother.

To Mrs. Dorothy Hervey, the only sister of my honoured mother, I bequeath the sum of fifty guineas, for a ring; and I beg of her to accept of my thankful acknowledgments for all her goodness to me from my infancy; and particularly for her patience with me, in the several altercations that happened between my brother and sister and me, before my unhappy departure from Harlowe Place.

To my kind and much valued cousin, Miss Dolly Hervey, daughter of my Aunt Hervey, I bequeath my watch and equipage, and my best Mechlin and Brussels head-dresses and ruffles; also my gown and petticoat of flowered silver of my own work; which having been made up but a few days before I was confined to my chamber, I never wore.

To the same young lady I bequeath likewise my harpsichord, my chamber-organ, and all my music-books.

As my sister has a very pretty library; and as my beloved Miss Howe has also her late father's, as well as her own; I bequeath all my books in general, with the cases they are in, to my said cousin, Dolly Hervey. As they are not ill-chosen for a woman's library, I know that she will take the greater pleasure in them (when her friendly grief is mellowed by time into a remembrance more sweet than painful) because they were mine; and because there are observations in many of them of my own writing; and some very judicious ones, written by the truly reverend Dr. Lewen.

I also bequeath to the same young lady twenty-five guineas for a ring, to be worn in remembrance of her true friend.

If I live not to see my worthy cousin, William Morden, Esq., I desire my humble and grateful thanks may be given to him for his favours and goodness to me; and particularly for his endeavours to reconcile my other friends to me at a time when I was doubtful whether he would forgive me himself. As he is in great circumstances, I will only beg of him to accept of two or three trifles, in remembrance of a kinswoman who always honoured *him* as much as he loved *her*. Particularly, of that piece of flowers which my Uncle Robert, his father, was very earnest to obtain, in order to carry it abroad with him.

I desire him likewise to accept of the little miniature picture set in gold, which his worthy father made me sit for to the famous Italian master whom he brought over with him; and which he presented to me, that I might bestow it, as he was pleased to say, upon the man whom I should be one day most inclined to favour.

To the same gentleman I also bequeath my rose-diamond ring, which was a present from his good father to me; and will be the more valuable to him on that account.

I humbly request Mrs. Annabella Howe, the mother of my dear Miss Howe, to accept of my respectful thanks for all her favours and goodness to me, when I was so frequently a visitor to her beloved daughter; and of a ring of twenty-five guineas price.

My picture at full length, which is in my late grandfather's closet (excepted in an article above from the family pictures), drawn when I was near fourteen years of age; about which time my dear Miss Howe and I began to know, to distinguish, and to love one another so dearly—I cannot express how dearly— I bequeath to that sister of my heart; of whose friendship, as well in adversity as prosperity, when I was deprived of all other comfort and comforters, I have had such instances, as that our love can only be exceeded in that state of perfection, in which I hope to rejoice with her hereafter, to all eternity.

I bequeath also to the same dear friend my best diamond ring, which, with other jewels, is in the private drawer of my escritoire: as also all my finished and framed pieces of needlework; the flower-piece excepted, which I have already bequeathed to my Cousin Morden.

These pieces have all been taken down, as I have heard [1]; and my relations will have no heart to put them up again: but if my good mother chooses to keep back any one piece (the above capital piece, as it is called, excepted), not knowing but some time hence she may bear the sight of it; I except that also from this general bequest; and direct it to be presented to her.

My whole-length picture in the Vandyke taste,[2] that used to hang in my own parlour, as I was permitted to call it, I bequeath to my Aunt Hervey, except my mother shall think fit to keep it herself.

I bequeath to the worthy Charles Hickman, Esq., the locket, with the miniature picture of the lady he best loves, which I have constantly worn, and shall continue to wear near my heart till the approach of my last hour.[3] It must be the most acceptable present that can be made him, next to the *hand* of the dear original. "And, O my dear Miss Howe, let it not be long before you permit his claim to the *latter*—for indeed you know not the value of a virtuous mind in that sex; and how preferable such a mind is to one distinguished by the more dazzling flights of unruly wit; although the latter were to be joined by that specious outward appearance which too, too often attracts the hasty eye and susceptible heart."

Permit me, my dear friends, this solemn apostrophe, in this last solemn act, to a young lady so deservedly dear to me!

I make it my earnest request to my dear Miss Howe, that she will not put herself into mourning for me. But I desire her acceptance of a ring with my hair; and that Mr. Hickman will also accept of the like; each of the value of twenty-five guineas.

[1] Vol. ii, p. 170.   [2] Ibid.   [3] See p. 340 of this volume.

I bequeath to Lady Betty Lawrance, and to her sister, Lady Sarah Sadleir, and to the Right Honourable Lord M., and to their worthy nieces, Miss Charlotte and Miss Martha Montague, each an enamelled ring, with a cipher Cl. H. with my hair in crystal, and round the inside of each, the day, month, and year of my death; each ring, with brilliants, to cost twenty guineas. And this as a small token of the grateful sense I have of the honour of their good opinions and kind wishes in my favour; and of their truly noble offer to me of a very considerable annual provision, when they apprehended me to be entirely destitute of any.

To the reverend and learned Dr. Arthur Lewen, by whose instructions I have been equally delighted and benefited, I bequeath twenty guineas for a ring. If it should please God to call him to Himself before he can receive this small bequest, it is my will that his worthy daughter may have the benefit of it.

In token of the grateful sense I have of the civilities paid me by Mrs. and Miss Howe's domestics, from time to time in my visits there, I bequeath thirty guineas to be divided among them, as their dear young mistress shall think proper.

To each of my worthy companions and friends, Miss Biddy Lloyd, Miss Fanny Alston, Miss Rachel Biddulph, and Miss Cartwright Campbell, I bequeath five guineas for a ring.

To my late maidservant, Hannah Burton, an honest, faithful creature, who loved *me*, reverenced my *mother*, and respected my *sister*, and never sought to do anything unbecoming of her character, I bequeath the sum of fifty pounds, to be paid within one month after my decease, she labouring under ill-health: and if that ill-health continue, I commend her for further assistance to my good Mrs. Norton, to be put upon my poor's fund, hereafter to be mentioned.

To the coachman, groom, and two footmen, and five maids, at Harlowe Place, I bequeath ten pounds each; to the helper five pounds.

To my sister's maid, Betty Barnes, I bequeath ten pounds, to show that I resent not former disobligations; which I believe were owing more to the insolence of office, and to natural pertness, than to personal ill-will.

All my wearing apparel, of whatever sort, that I have not been obliged to part with, or which is not already bequeathed (my linen excepted), I desire Mrs. Norton will accept of.

The trunks and boxes in which my clothes are sealed up,

I desire may not be opened, but in presence of Mrs. Norton (or of someone deputed by her) and of Mrs. Lovick.

To the worthy Mrs. Lovick above-mentioned, from whom I have received great civilities, and even maternal kindnesses; and to Mrs. Smith (with whom I lodge), from whom *also* I have received great kindnesses; I bequeath all my linen, and all my unsold laces; to be divided equally between them, as they shall agree; or, in case of disagreement, the same to be sold, and the money arising to be equally shared by them.

And I bequeath to the same two good women, as a further token of my thankful acknowledgments of their kind love and compassionate concern for me, the sum of twenty guineas each.

To Mr. Smith, the husband of Mrs. Smith above-named, I bequeath the sum of ten guineas, in acknowledgment of his civilities to me.

To Katharine, the honest maidservant of Mrs. Smith, to whom (having no servant of my own) I have been troublesome, I bequeath five guineas; and ten guineas more, in lieu of a suit of my wearing apparel, which once, with some linen, I thought of leaving to her. With this she may purchase what may be more suitable to her liking and degree.

To the honest and careful widow, Anne Shelburne, my nurse, over and above her wages, and the customary perquisites that may belong to her, I bequeath the sum of ten guineas. Hers is a careful and (to persons of such humanity and tenderness) a melancholy employment, attended in the latter part of life with great watching and fatigue, which is hardly ever enough considered.

The few books I have at my present lodgings I desire Mrs. Lovick to accept of; and that she be permitted, if she please, to take a copy of my book of *Meditations*, as I used to call it; being extracts from the best of books; which she seemed to approve of, although suited particularly to my own case. As for the book itself, perhaps my good Mrs. Norton will be glad to have it, as it is written all with my own hand.

In the middle drawer of my escritoire at Harlowe Place are many letters and copies of letters, put up according to their dates, which I have written or received in a course of years (ever since I learned to write), from and to my grandfather, my father and mother, my uncles, my brother and sister, on occasional little absences; my late Uncle Morden, my Cousin Morden; Mrs. Norton, and Miss Howe, and other of my companions and friends before my confinement at my father's: as also from the three reverend gentlemen, Dr. Blome, Mr. Arnold, and Mr. Tompkins, now with God, and the very reverend Dr. Lewen, on serious subjects. As these letters exhibit a correspondence that no person of my sex need to be ashamed of, allowing for the time of life when mine were written; and as many excellent things are contained in those written to me; and as Miss Howe, to whom most of them have been communicated, wished formerly to have them, if she survived me: for these reasons, I bequeath them to my said dear friend Miss Anna Howe; and the rather, as she had for some years past a very considerable share in the correspondence.

I do hereby make, constitute, and ordain John Belford, of Edgware in the County of Middlesex, Esq., the sole executor of this my last will and testament; having previously obtained his leave so to do. I have given the reasons which induced me to ask this gentleman to take upon him this trouble to Miss Howe. I therefore refer to her on this subject.

But I do most earnestly beg of him, the said Mr. Belford, that, in the execution of this trust, he will (as he has repeatedly promised) studiously endeavour to promote peace with, and suppress resentments in, every one; so as that all further mischiefs may be prevented, as well *from* as *to* his friend. And in order to this, I beseech him to cultivate the friendship of my worthy Cousin Morden; who, as I presume to hope (when he understands it to be my dying request), will give him his advice and assistance in every article where it may be necessary; and who will perhaps be so good as to interpose with my relations, if any difficulty should arise about carrying any of the articles of this my last will into execution, and to soften them into the wished-for condescension: for it is my earnest request to Mr. Belford, that he will not seek by law, or by any sort of violence, either by word or deed, to extort the performance from *them.* If there be any articles of a merely domestic nature that my relations shall think unfit to be carried into execution; such articles I leave entirely to my said Cousin Morden and Mr. Belford to vary, or totally dispense with, as they shall agree upon the matter; or, if they two differ in opinion, they will be pleased to be determined by a third person, to be chosen by them both.

Having been pressed by Miss Howe and her mother to collect the particulars of my sad story, and given expectation that I would, in order to do my character justice with all my friends and companions: but not having time before me for the painful

task, it has been a pleasure to me to find, by extracts kindly
communicated to me by my said executor, that I may safely
trust my fame to the justice done me by Mr. Lovelace, in his
letters to him my said executor. And as Mr. Belford has
engaged to contribute what is in his power towards a compile-
ment to be made of all that relates to my story, and knows my
whole mind in this respect; it is my desire that he will cause two
copies to be made of this collection; one to remain with Miss
Howe, the other with himself; and that he will show or lend his
copy, if required, to my Aunt Hervey, for the satisfaction of any
of my family; but under such restrictions as the said Mr. Belford
shall think fit to impose; that neither any other person's safety
may be endangered, nor his own honour suffer, by the
communication.

I bequeath to my said executor the sum of one hundred
guineas, as a grateful, though insufficient acknowledgment of
the trouble he will be at in the execution of the trust he has so
kindly undertaken. I desire him likewise to accept of twenty
guineas for a ring. And that he will reimburse himself for all
the charges and expenses which he shall be at in the execution
of this trust.

In the worthy Dr. H. I have found a physician, a father, and
a friend. I beg of him, as a testimony of my gratitude, to
accept of twenty guineas for a ring.

I have the same obligations to the kind and skilful Mr. Goddard, who attended me as my apothecary. His very moderate
bill I have discharged down to yesterday. I have always
thought it incumbent upon testators to shorten all they can the
trouble of their executors. I know I underrate the value of
Mr. Goddard's attendances, when over and above what may
accrue from yesterday, to the hour that will finish all, I desire
fifteen guineas for a ring may be presented to him.

To the Reverend Mr. ——, who frequently attended me, and
prayed by me in my last stages, I also bequeath fifteen guineas
for a ring.

There are a set of honest indigent people, whom I used to call
My Poor, and to whom Mrs. Norton conveys relief each month
(or at shorter periods), in proportion to their necessities, from a
sum I deposited in her hands, and from time to time recruited,
as means accrued to me; but now nearly, if not wholly expended:
now, that my fault may be as little aggravated as possible by the
sufferings of the worthy people whom Heaven gave me a heart
to relieve; and as the produce of my grandfather's estate

(including the moiety of the sums he had by him, and was pleased to give me, at his death, as above mentioned), together with what I shall further appropriate to the same use in the subsequent articles, will, as I hope, more than answer all my legacies and bequests; it is my will and desire that the remainder, be it little or much, shall become a fund to be appropriated, and I hereby direct that it be appropriated, to the like purposes with the sums which I put into Mrs. Norton's hands, as aforesaid—and this under the direction and management of the said Mrs. Norton, who knows my whole mind in this particular. And in case of her death, or of her desire to be acquitted of the management thereof, it is my earnest request to my dear Miss Howe, that she will take it upon herself, and at her own death, that she will transfer what shall remain undisposed of at the *time*, to such persons, and with such limitations, restrictions, and provisos as she shall think will best answer my intention. For, as to the management and distribution of all or any part of it, while in Mrs. Norton's hands, or her own, I will that it be entirely discretional, and without account, either to my executor or any other person.

Although Mrs. Norton, as I have hinted, knows my whole mind in this respect; yet it may be proper to mention, in this last solemn act, that my intention is, that this fund be entirely set apart and appropriated to relieve temporarily, from the interest thereof (as I dare say it will be put out to the best advantage), or even from the principal, if need be, the honest, industrious, labouring poor only; when sickness, lameness, unforeseen losses, or other accidents disable them from following their lawful callings; or to assist such honest people of large families as shall have a child of good inclinations to put out to service, trade, or husbandry.

It has always been a rule with me, in my little donations, to endeavour to aid and set forward the sober and industrious poor. Small helps, if seasonably afforded, will do for such; and so the fund may be of more extensive benefit; an ocean of wealth will not be sufficient for the idle and dissolute: whom, therefore, since they will be always in want, it will be no charity to relieve, if worthier creatures would by relieving the others be deprived of such assistance as may set the wheels of their industry going, and put them in a sphere of useful action.

But it is my express will and direction, that let this fund come out to be ever so considerable, it shall be applied only in support of the *temporary exigencies* of the persons I have described; and that no one family or person receive from it, at one time, or in one year, more than the sum of twenty pounds.

It is my will and desire, that the set of jewels which was my grandmother's, and presented to me, soon after her death, by my grandfather, be valued; and the worth of them paid to my executor, if any of my family choose to have them; or otherwise, that they be sold, and go to the augmentation of my poor's fund. But if they may be deemed an equivalent for the sums my father was pleased to advance to me since the death of my grandfather, I desire that they may be given up to him.

I presume that the diamond necklace, solitaire, and buckles, which were properly my own, presented by my mother's uncle, Sir Josias Brookland, will not be purchased by any one of my family, for a too obvious reason: in this case I desire that they may be sent to my executor; and that he will dispose of them to the best advantage; and apply the money to the uses of my will.

In the beginning of this tedious writing, I referred to the latter part of it the naming of the subject of the discourse which I wished might be delivered at my funeral, if permitted to be interred with my ancestors: I think the following will be suitable to my case. I hope the alterations of the words *her* and *she*, for *him* and *he*, may be allowable.

"Let not *her* that is deceived trust in vanity; for vanity shall be *her* recompense. *She* shall be accomplished before *her* time; and *her* branch shall not be green. *She* shall shake off *her* unripe grape as the vine, and shall cast off *her* flower as the olive." [1]

But if I am to be interred in town, let only the usual Burial Service be read over my corpse.

If my body be permitted to be carried down, I bequeath ten pounds to be given to the poor of the parish, at the discretion of the churchwardens, within a fortnight after my interment.

If any necessary matter be omitted in this my will; or if anything appear doubtful or contradictory, as possibly may be the case; since, besides my inexperience in these matters, I am now, at this time, very weak and ill; having put off the finishing hand a little too long, in hopes of obtaining the last forgiveness of my honoured friends; in which case I should have acknowledged the favour with a suitable warmth of duty, and filled up some blanks which I left to the very last,[2] in a more agreeable manner to myself than now I have been enabled to do—in case of such omissions and imperfections. I desire that my Cousin

[1] Job xv, 31, 32, 33. [2] See p. 264.

Morden will be so good as to join with Mr. Belford in considering them, and in comparing them with what I have more explicitly written; and if, after *that*, any doubt remain, that they will be pleased to apply to Miss Howe, who knows my whole heart: and I desire that the construction of these three may be established: and I hereby establish it, provided it be unanimous, and direct it to be put in force, as if I had so written and determined myself.

And now, O my blessed REDEEMER, do I, with a lively faith, humbly lay hold of Thy meritorious death and sufferings; hoping to be washed clean in Thy precious blood from all my sins: in the bare hope of the happy consequences of which, how light do those sufferings seem (grievous as they were at the time) which, I confidently trust, will be a means, by Thy grace, to work out for me a more exceeding and eternal weight of glory!

CLARISSA HARLOWE.

Signed, sealed, published, and declared, the day and year above written, by the said Clarissa Harlowe, as her last will and testament; contained in seven sheets of paper, all written with her own hand, and every sheet signed and sealed by herself, in the presence of us,

John Williams,
Arthur Bedall,
Elizabeth Swanton.

Letter CXLVII—Colonel Morden to John Belford, Esq.

Sat. Sept. 16.

I HAVE been employed in a most melancholy task: in reading the will of the dear deceased.

The unhappy mother and Mrs. Norton chose to be absent on the affecting occasion. But Mrs. Harlowe made it her earnest request that every article of it should be fulfilled.

They were all extremely touched with the preamble.

The first words of the will: "I, Clarissa Harlowe, now, by strange melancholy accidents, lodging," etc., drew tears from some, sighs from all.

The directions for her funeral, in case she were or were not permitted to be carried down; the mention of her orders having been given for the manner of her being laid out, and the presence of mind visible throughout the whole, obtained their admiration, expressed by hands and eyes lifted up, and by falling tears.

When I read the direction, "That her body was not to be viewed, except any of her relations should *vouchsafe for the last time to look upon her*"; they turned away, and turned to me, three or four times alternately. Mrs. Hervey and Miss Arabella sobbed; the uncles wiped their eyes; the brother looked down; the father wrung his hands.

I was obliged to stop at the words "That she was *nobody's*."

But when I came to the address to be made to the accursed man, "if he were not to be diverted from seeing *her* dead, whom ONCE before he had seen in a manner dead"—execration, and either vows or wishes of revenge, filled every mouth.

These were still more fervently renewed when they came to hear read her forgiveness of even this man.

You remember, sir, on our first reading of the will in town, the observations I made on the foul play which it is evident the excellent creature met with from this abandoned man, and what I said upon the occasion. I am not used to repeat things of that nature.

The dear creature's noble contempt of the *nothing*, as she as nobly calls it, about which she had been giving such particular directions, to wit, her body; and her apologizing for the particularity of those directions from the circumstances she was in, had the same, and as strong an effect upon me, as when I first read the animated paragraph; and, pointed by my eye (by turns cast upon them all), affected them all.

When the article was read which bequeathed to the father the grandfather's estate, and the reason assigned for it (so generous and so dutiful), the father could sit no longer; but withdrew, wiping his eyes, and lifting up his spread hands at Mr. James Harlowe; who arose to attend him to the door, as Arabella likewise did—all he could say: O son! son!—O girl! girl! as if he reproached them for the parts they had acted, and put him upon acting.

But yet, on some occasions, this brother and sister showed themselves to be true will-disputants.

Let tongue and eyes express what they will, Mr. Belford, the first reading of a will, where a person dies worth anything considerable, generally affords a true test of the relations' love to the deceased.

The clothes, the thirty guineas for mourning to Mrs. Norton, with the recommendation of the good woman for housekeeper at *The Grove*, were thought sufficient, had the article of £600, which was called monstrous, been omitted. Some other passages in the will were called *flights, and such whimsies as distinguish people of imagination from those of judgment.*

My Cousin Dolly Hervey was grudged the library. Miss Harlowe said that as she and her sister never bought the same books, she would take that to herself, and would *make it up* to her Cousin Dolly *one way or other.*

I intend, Mr. Belford, to save you the trouble of interposing —the library *shall* be my Cousin Dolly's.

Mrs. Hervey could hardly keep her seat. On *this* occasion, however, she only said that her late dear and *ever* dear niece was *too good* to her and *hers.* But, *at another time,* she declared, with tears, that she could not forgive herself for a letter she wrote [1] [looking at Miss Arabella, whom, it seems, unknown to anybody, she had consulted before she wrote it], and which, she said, must have wounded a spirit that now, she saw, had been too deeply wounded before.

O my aunt, said Arabella, no more of that! Who would have thought that the dear creature had been such a penitent?

Mr. John and Mr. Antony Harlowe were so much affected with the articles in their favour (bequeathed to them without a word or hint of reproach or recrimination) that they broke out into self-accusations; and lamented that their sweet niece, as they called her, was now got above all grateful acknowledgment and returns.

Indeed, the mutual upbraidings and grief of all present, upon those articles in which every one was remembered for good, so often interrupted me, that the reading took up above six hours. But curses upon the accursed man were a refuge to which they often resorted, to exonerate themselves.

How wounding a thing, Mr. Belford, is a generous and well-distinguished forgiveness! What revenge can be more effectual, and more noble, were revenge intended, and were it wished to strike remorse into a guilty or ungrateful heart! But my dear cousin's motives were all duty and love. She seems indeed to have been, as much as a mortal could be, LOVE itself. Love sublimed by a purity, by a true delicacy, that hardly any woman before her could boast of. O Mr. Belford, what an example would she have given in every station of life (as wife, mother, mistress, friend), had her lot fallen upon a man blessed with a mind like her own!

The £600 bequeathed to Mrs. Norton, the library to Miss Hervey, and the remembrances to Miss Howe, were not the only

[1] See vol. ii, pp. 162 et seq.

articles grudged. Yet to what purpose did they regret the pecuniary bequests, when the poor's fund, and not themselves, would have had the benefit, had not those legacies been bequeathed?

But enough passed to convince me that my cousin was absolutely right in her choice of an executor out of the family. Had she chosen one in it, I dare say that her will would have been no more regarded than if it had been the will of a dead king; than that of Louis XIV in particular; so flagrantly broken through by his nephew, the Duke of Orleans, before he was cold. The only will of that monarch, perhaps, which was ever disputed.

But little does Mr. James Harlowe think, that while he is grasping at hundreds, he will, most probably, lose thousands, if he be my survivor. A man of a spirit so selfish and narrow shall not be my heir.

You will better conceive, Mr. Belford, than I can express, how much they were touched at the hint that the dear creature had been obliged to part with some of her clothes.

Silent reproach seized every one of them, when I came to the passage where she mentions that she deferred filling up some blanks in hopes of receiving their last blessing and forgiveness.

I will only add, that they could not bear to hear read the concluding part, so solemnly addressed to her Redeemer. They all arose from their seats, and crowded out of the apartment we were in: and then, as I afterwards found, separated, in order to seek that consolation in solitary retirement which, though they could not hope for from their own reflections, yet, at the time, they had less reason to expect in each other's company. I am,

Sir,

Your faithful and obedient servant,

WM. MORDEN.

Letter CXLVIII—Mr. Belford to the Right Honourable Lord M.

London, Sept. 14.

MY LORD,—I am very apprehensive that the affair between Mr. Lovelace and the late excellent Miss Clarissa Harlowe will be attended with further bad consequences, notwithstanding her dying injunctions to the contrary. I would therefore humbly propose that your lordship and his other relations will forward the purpose your kinsman lately had to go abroad; where I hope he will stay till all is blown over. But as he will not stir, if he know the true motives of your wishes, the avowed inducement, as I hinted once to Mr. Mowbray, may be such as respects his own health both of person and mind. To Mr. Mowbray and Mr. Tourville all countries are alike; and they perhaps will accompany him.

I am glad to hear that he is in a way of recovery: but this the rather induces me to press the matter. And I think no time should be lost.

Your lordship has heard that I have the honour to be the executor of this admirable lady's last will. I transcribe from it the following paragraph.

He then transcribes the article which so gratefully mentions this nobleman, and the ladies of his family, in relation to the rings she bequeaths them, about which he desires their commands.

Letter CXLIX—Miss Montague to John Belford, Esq.

M. Hall, Friday, Sept. 15.

SIR,—My lord having the gout in his right hand, his lordship, and Lady Sarah, and Lady Betty, have commanded me to inform you that, before your letter came, Mr. Lovelace was preparing for a foreign tour. We shall endeavour to hasten him away on the motives you suggest.

We are all extremely affected with the dear lady's death. Lady Betty and Lady Sarah have been indisposed ever since they heard of it. They had pleased themselves, as had my sister and self, with the hopes of cultivating her acquaintance and friendship after he was gone abroad, upon her own terms. Her kind remembrance of each of us has renewed, though it could not heighten, our regrets for so irreparable a loss. We shall order Mr. Finch, our goldsmith, to wait on you. He has our directions about the rings. They will be long, long worn in memory of the dear testatrix.

Everybody is assured that you will do all in your power to prevent *further* ill consequences from this melancholy affair. My lord desires his compliments to you. I am, sir,

Your humble servant,

CH. MONTAGUE.

THIS collection having run into a much greater length than was wished, it is thought proper to omit several letters that passed between Colonel Morden, Miss Howe, Mr. Belford, and Mr. Hickman, in relation to the execution of the lady's will, etc.

It is, however, necessary to observe on this subject, that the unhappy mother, being supported by the two uncles, influenced the afflicted father to overrule all his son's objections, and to direct a literal observation of the will; and at the same time to give up all the sums which he was empowered by it to reimburse himself; as also to take upon himself to defray the funeral expenses.

Mr. Belford so much obliged Miss Howe by his steadiness, equity, and dispatch, and by his readiness to contribute to the directed collection, that she voluntarily entered into a correspondence with him, as the representative of her beloved friend. In the course of which he communicated to her (in confidence) the letters which passed between him and Mr. Lovelace, and, by Colonel Morden's consent, those which passed between that gentleman and himself.

He sent with the first parcel of letters which he had transcribed out of shorthand for Miss Howe, a letter to Mr. Hickman, dated the 16th of September, in which he expresses himself as follows:

"But I ought, sir, in this parcel to have kept out one letter. It is that which relates to the interview between yourself and Mr. Lovelace, at Mr. Dormer's.[1]   In which Mr. Lovelace treats you with an air of levity, which neither your *person*, your *character*, nor your *commission*, deserved; but which was his *usual way of treating every one whose business he was not pleased with.* I hope, sir, you have too much greatness of mind to be disturbed at the contents of this letter, should Miss Howe communicate them to you; and the rather as it is impossible that you should suffer with her on that account."

Mr. Belford then excuses Mr. Lovelace as a good-natured man with all his faults; and gives instances of his still greater freedoms with himself.

To this Mr. Hickman answers, in his letter of the 18th:

"As to Mr. Lovelace's treatment of me in the letter you are pleased to mention, I shall not be concerned at it, whatever it be.   I went to him prepared to expect odd behaviour from him; and was not disappointed.   I argue to myself, in all such cases as this, as Miss Howe, from her ever dear friend, argues, *That if the reflections thrown upon me* are just, *I ought not only to forgive them, but to endeavour to profit by them*: if unjust, *that I ought to despise them, and the reflector too ; since it would be inexcusable to strengthen by anger an enemy whose malice might be disarmed by contempt.*   And, moreover, I should be almost sorry to find

[1] See vol. iii, Letter cxviii.

myself spoken well of by a man who could treat, as he treated, a lady who was an ornament to her sex and to human nature.

"I thank you, however, sir, for your consideration for me in this particular; and for your whole letter, which gives me so desirable an instance of the friendship which you assured me of when I was last in town; and which I as cordially embrace as wish to cultivate."

Miss Howe, in hers of the 20th, acknowledging the receipt of the letters, and papers, and legacies, sent with Mr. Belford's letter to Mr. Hickman, assures him, "That no use shall be made of his communications, but what he shall approve of."

He had mentioned with compassion the distresses of the Harlowe family—"Persons of a *pitiful nature*, says she, *may* pity them. I am not one of those. You, I think, pity the infernal man likewise; while I from my heart grudge him his frenzy, because it deprives him of that remorse which, I hope, on his recovery, will never leave him. At times, sir, let me tell you that I hate your whole sex for his sake; even men of unblamable characters, whom at those times I cannot but look upon as persons I have not yet *found out*.

"If my dear creature's personal jewels be sent up to you for sale, I desire that I may be the purchaser of them, at the *highest* price—of the necklace and solitaire particularly.

"Oh, what tears did the perusal of my beloved's will cost me!—But I must not touch upon the heart-piercing subject. I can neither take it up, nor quit it, but with execration of the man whom all the world must execrate."

Mr. Belford, in his answer, promises that she shall be the purchaser of the jewels, if they come into his hands.

He acquaints her that the family had given Colonel Morden the keys of all that belonged to the dear departed: that the unhappy mother had (as the will allows) ordered a piece of needlework to be set aside for her, and had desired Mrs. Norton to get the little book of *Meditations* transcribed, and to let her have the original, as it was all of her dear daughter's handwriting; and as it might, when she could bear to look into it, administer consolation to herself. And that she had likewise reserved for herself her picture in the Vandyke taste.

Mr. Belford sends with this letter to Miss Howe the lady's memorandum-book; and promises to send her copies of the several posthumous letters. He tells her that Mr. Lovelace being upon the recovery, he had enclosed the posthumous letter directed for him to Lord M., that his lordship might give it to him, or not, as he should find he could bear it. The following is a copy of that letter:

To Mr. Lovelace

Thursday, Aug. 24.

I TOLD you, in the letter I wrote to you on *Tuesday* last,[1] that you should have another sent you when I had got to *my father's house.*

I presume to say that I am *now*, at your receiving of this, arrived there; and I invite you to follow me, as soon as you can be *prepared* for so great a journey.

Not to allegorize further—my fate is *now*, at your perusal of this, accomplished. My doom is unalterably fixed: and I am either a miserable or a happy being to all eternity. If *happy*, I owe it solely to the Divine mercy: if *miserable*, to your un-deserved cruelty.—And consider now, for your own sake, gay, cruel, fluttering, unhappy man! consider whether the barbarous and perfidious treatment I have met with from you was worthy of the hazard of your immortal soul; since your wicked views were not to be effected but by the wilful breach of the most solemn vows that ever were made by man; and those aided by a violence and baseness unworthy of a human creature.

In time then, once more, I wish you to consider your ways. Your golden dream cannot long last. Your present course can yield you pleasure no longer than you can keep off thought or reflection. A hardened insensibility is the only foundation on which your inward tranquillity is built. When once a dangerous sickness seizes you; when once effectual remorse breaks in upon you; how dreadful will be your condition! How poor a triumph will you then find it, to have been able, by a series of black perjuries, and studied baseness, under the name of gallantry or intrigue, to betray poor inexperienced young creatures, who perhaps knew nothing but their duty till they knew you!—Not one good action in the hour of languishing to recollect, not one worthy intention to revolve, it will be all reproach and horror;

---

[1] See p. 157 of this volume. The reader may observe, by the date of this letter, that it was written within two days of the allegorical one, to which it refers; and while the lady was labouring under the increased illness occasioned by the hurries and terrors into which Mr. Lovelace had thrown her, in order to avoid the visit he was so earnest to make her at Smith's—so early written, perhaps, that she might not be surprised by death into a seeming breach of her word.

High as her Christian spirit soars in this letter, the reader has seen, in Letter cvi and in other places, that that exalted spirit carried her to still more divine elevations, as she drew nearer to her end.

and you will wish to have it in your power to compound for annihilation.

Reflect, sir, that I can have no other motive, in what I write, than your good, and the safety of other innocent creatures, who may be drawn in by your wicked arts and perjuries. You have not, in my wishes for your future welfare, the wishes of a suppliant wife, endeavouring for her *own* sake, as well as for *yours*, to induce you to reform those ways. They are wholly as disinterested as undeserved. But I should mistrust my own penitence, were I capable of wishing to recompense evil for evil—if, black as your offences have been against me, I could not forgive as I wish to be forgiven.

I repeat, therefore, that I *do* forgive you. And may the Almighty forgive you too! Nor have I, at the writing of this, any other essential regrets than what are occasioned by the grief I have given to parents, who till I knew you were the most indulgent of parents; by the scandal given to the other branches of my family; by the disreputation brought upon my sex; and by the offence given to virtue in my fall.

As to myself, you have only robbed me of what once were my favourite expectations in the transient life I shall have quitted when you receive this. You have only been the cause that I have been cut off in the bloom of youth, and of curtailing a life that might have been agreeable to myself, or otherwise, as had suited the designs and ends of Providence. I have reason to be thankful for being taken away from the evil of supporting my part of a yoke with a man so *unhappy*; I will only say that, in all probability, every hour I had lived with him might have brought with it some new trouble. And I am (indeed through sharp afflictions and distresses) indebted to you, *secondarily*, as I humbly presume to hope, for so many years of glory, as might have proved years of danger, temptation, and anguish, had they been added to my mortal life.

So, sir, though no thanks to your *intention*, you have done me *real service*; and in return I wish you happy. But such has been your life hitherto, that you can have no time to lose in setting about your repentance. Repentance to such as have lived only carelessly, and in the omission of their regular duties, and who never aimed to draw any poor creatures into evil, is not so easy a task, nor so much in our own power, as some imagine. How difficult a grace then to be obtained, where the guilt is premeditated, wilful, and complicated!

To say I once respected you with a preference, is what I ought to blush to own, since, at the very time, I was far from thinking you even a moral man; though I little thought that you, or indeed that any man breathing, could be—what you have proved yourself to be. But indeed, sir, I have long been greatly above you: for from my heart I have despised you, and all your ways, ever since I saw what manner of man you were.

Nor is it to be wondered that I should be able so to do, when that preference was not grounded on ignoble motives. For I was weak enough, and presumptuous enough, to hope to be a means in the hand of Providence to reclaim a man whom I thought worthy of the attempt.

Nor have I yet, as you will see by the pains I take, on this solemn occasion, to awaken you out of your sensual dream, given over all hopes of this nature.

Hear me, therefore, O Lovelace! as one speaking from the dead—Lose no time. Set about your repentance instantly. Be no longer the instrument of Satan, to draw poor souls into those subtile snares, which at last shall entangle your own feet. Seek not to multiply your offences, till they become beyond the *power*, as I may say, of the Divine mercy to forgive; since *justice*, no less than *mercy*, is an attribute of the Almighty.

Tremble and reform, when you read what is *the portion of the wicked man from God*. Thus it is written:

"The triumphing of the wicked is short, and the joy of the hypocrite but for a moment. He is cast into a net by his own feet—he walketh upon a snare. Terrors shall make him afraid on every side, and shall drive him to his feet. His strength shall be hunger-bitten, and destruction shall be ready at his side. The first-born of death shall devour his strength. His remembrance shall perish from the earth; and he shall have no name in the streets. He shall be chased out of the world. He shall have neither son nor nephew among his people. They that have seen him shall say, Where is he? He shall fly away as a dream: he shall be chased away as a vision of the night. His meat is the gall of asps within him. He shall flee from the iron weapon, and the bow of steel shall strike him through. A fire not blown shall consume him. The heaven shall reveal his iniquity, and the earth shall rise up against him. The worm shall feed sweetly on him. He shall be no more remembered. This is the fate of him that knoweth not God."

Whenever you shall be inclined to consult the sacred oracles, from whence the above threatenings are extracted, you will find doctrines and texts which a truly penitent and contrite heart may lay hold of for its consolation.

May yours, Mr. Lovelace, become such! And may you be enabled to escape the fate denounced against the abandoned man, and be entitled to the mercies of a long-suffering and gracious God, is the sincere prayer of

CLARISSA HARLOWE.

Letter CL—Mr. Lovelace to John Belford, Esq.

M. Hall, Thursday, Sept. 14.

EVER since the fatal seventh of this month, I have been lost to myself, and to all the joys of life. I might have gone farther back than that fatal seventh; which, for the future, I will never see anniversarily revolve but in sables; only till that cursed day I had some gleams of hope now and then darting in upon me.

They tell me of an odd letter I wrote to you.[1] I remember I did write. But very little of the contents of what I wrote do I remember.

I have been in a cursed way. Methinks something has been working strangely retributive. I never was such a fool as to disbelieve a Providence: yet am I not for resolving into judgments everything that seems to wear an avenging face. Yet if we must be punished either here or hereafter for our misdeeds, better *here*, say I, than *hereafter*. Have I not then an interest to think my punishment already not only begun, but completed; since what I have suffered, and do suffer, passes all description?

To give but one instance of the *retributive*—here I, who was the barbarous cause of the loss of senses for a week together to the most inimitable of women, have been punished with the loss of my own—preparative to—who knows what? When, Oh, when, shall I know a joyful hour?

I am kept excessively low; and excessively low I *am*. This sweet creature's posthumous letter sticks close to me. All her excellences rise up hourly to my remembrance.

Yet dare I not indulge in these melancholy reflections. I find my head strangely working again. Pen, begone!

Friday, Sept. 15.

I resume, in a sprightly vein, I hope—Mowbray and Tourville have just now——

But what of Mowbray and Tourville! What's the world? What's anybody in it?

[1] See his delirious letter, No. cxxxvi.

Yet they are highly exasperated against thee, for the last letter thou wrotest to them [1]—such an unfriendly, such a merciless——

But it won't do! I must again lay down my pen. O Belford! Belford! I am still, I am still most miserably absent from myself! Shall never, never more be what I was!

.   .   .   .

Saturday, Sunday, nothing done. Incapable of anything.

Monday, Sept. 18.

Heavy, damnably heavy, and sick at soul, by Jupiter! I must come into their expedient. I must see what change of climate will do.

You tell these fellows, and you tell me, of repenting and reforming: but I can do neither. He who *can*, must not have the *extinction* of a Clarissa Harlowe to answer for. Harlowe!—Curse upon the name!—and curse upon myself for not changing it, as I might have done! Yet have I no need of urging a curse upon myself—I have it effectually.

"To say I once respected you with a preference." [2]—In what stiff language does maidenly modesty on these nice occasions express itself!—*To say I once loved you*, is the English; and there is truth and ease in the expression. "To say I once loved you," then let it be, "is what I ought to blush to own."

And dost thou own it, excellent creature? and dost thou then own it?—What music in these words from such an angel! What would I give that my Clarissa were in being, and *could* and *would* own that she loved me?

"But indeed, sir, I have long been greatly above you."

Long, my blessed charmer!—Long indeed, for you have been *ever* greatly above me, and above your sex, and above all the world.

"That preference was not grounded on ignoble motives."

What a wretch was I, to be so distinguished by her, and yet to be so unworthy of her hope to reclaim me!

Then, how generous her motives! Not for her *own* sake merely, not altogether for *mine*, did she hope to reclaim me; but equally for the sake of innocents who might otherwise be ruined by me.

And now, *why* did she write this letter, and *why* direct it to be given me when an event the most deplorable had taken place, but for my good, and with a view to the safety of innocents she

[1] This letter appears not.   [2] See p. 436.

knew not?—And *when* was this letter written? Was it not at the time, at the very time, that I had been pursuing her, as I may say, from place to place; when her soul was bowed down by calamity and persecution; and herself was denied all forgiveness from relations the most implacable?

Exalted creature!—And couldst thou, at *such a time*, and *so early*, and in *such circumstances*, have so far subdued thy own just resentments, as to wish happiness to the principal author of all thy distresses? Wish happiness to him who had robbed thee "of all thy favourite expectations in this life"? To him who had been the cause "that thou wert cut off in the bloom of youth"?

Heavenly aspirer! What a frame must thou be in, to be able to use the word ONLY in mentioning these important deprivations!—And as this was before thou puttedst off mortality, may I not presume that thou now,

> ——with pitying eye,
> Not derogating from thy perfect bliss,
> Survey'st all heav'n around, and wishest for me?

"Consider my ways."—Dear life of my life! Of what avail is consideration now, when I have lost the dear creature for whose sake alone it was worth while to *have* consideration? Lost her beyond retrieving—swallowed up by the greedy grave —for *ever* lost her—that, *that's* the sting—matchless woman! how does this reflection wound me!

"Your golden dream cannot long last."—Divine prophetess! my golden dream is *already* over. "Thought and reflection *are* no longer to be kept off."—No *longer continues* that "hardened insensibility" thou chargest upon me. "Remorse *has* broken in upon me." "Dreadful *is* my condition!" "It *is* all reproach and horror with me!"—A thousand vultures in turn are preying upon my heart!

But no more of these fruitless reflections—since I am incapable of writing anything else; since my pen will slide into this gloomy subject, whether I will or not; I will once more quit it; nor will I again resume it till I can be more *its master*, and my own.

All I took pen to write for is, however, unwritten. It was, in few words, to wish you to proceed with your communications, as usual. And why should you not? Since, in her ever-to-be-lamented death, I know everything shocking and grievous. Acquaint me, then, with all thou knowest which I do *not* know: how her relations, her cruel relations, take it; and whether, now, the barbed dart of after-reflection sticks not in their hearts, as in mine, up to the very feathers.

. . . .

I will soon quit this kingdom. For now my Clarissa is no more, what is there in it (in the world indeed) worth living for? But should I not first, by some masterly mischief, avenge her and myself upon her cursed family?

The accursed woman, they tell me, has broken her leg. Why was it not her neck?—All, all, but what is owing to her relations, is the fault of that woman, and of her hell-born nymphs. *The greater the virtue, the nobler the triumph*, was a sentence for ever in their mouths. I have had it several times in my head to set fire to the execrable house; and to watch at the doors and windows, that not a devil in it escape the consuming flames. Had the house stood by itself, I had certainly done it.

But, it seems, the old wretch is in the way to be rewarded, without my help. A shocking letter is received of somebody's in relation to her—yours, I suppose—too shocking for me, they say, to see at present.[1]

They govern me as a child in strings: yet did I suffer so much in my fever, that I am willing to bear with them till I can get tolerably well.

At present I can neither eat, drink, nor sleep. Yet are my disorders nothing to what they were: for, Jack, my brain was on fire day and night: and had it not been of the *asbestos* kind, it had all been consumed.

I had no distinct ideas, but of dark and confused misery: *it was all remorse and horror* indeed! Thoughts of hanging, drowning, shooting; then rage, violence, mischief, and despair took their turns with me. My lucid intervals still worse, giving me to reflect upon what I *was* the hour before, and what I was likely to be the next, and perhaps for life—the sport of enemies! the laughter of fools! and the hanging-sleeved, go-carted property of hired slaves; who were perhaps to find their account in manacling, and (abhorred thought!) in personally abusing me by blows and stripes!

Who can bear such reflections as these? To be made to *fear* only, to such a one as me, and to fear *such wretches* too! What a thing was this, but *remotely* to apprehend! And yet for a man to be in such a state as to render it necessary for his dearest friends to suffer this to be done for his own sake, and in order

[1] See Letter cxxxviii.

to prevent further mischief!—There is no thinking of these things!

I will *not* think of them, therefore: but will either get a train of cheerful ideas, or hang myself, by to-morrow morning.

——To be a dog, and dead,
Were paradise, to such a life as mine.

Letter CLI—*Mr. Lovelace to John Belford, Esq.*

Wedn. Sept. 20.

I WRITE to demand back again my last letter. I own it was my mind at the different times I wrote it; and, whatever ailed me, I could not *help* writing it. Such a gloomy impulse came upon me, and increased as I wrote, that, for my soul, I could not forbear running into the miserable.

'Tis strange, very strange, that a man's conscience should be able to force his fingers to write whether he will or not; and to run him into a subject he more than once, at the very time, resolved not to think of.

Nor is it less strange that (no new reason occurring) he should, in a day or two more, so totally change his mind; have his mind, I should rather say, so wholly illuminated by gay hopes and rising prospects, as to be ashamed of what he had written.

For, on reperusal of a copy of my letter, which fell into my hands by accident, in the handwriting of my Cousin Charlotte, who, unknown to me, had transcribed it, I find it to be such a letter as an enemy would rejoice to see.

This I know, that were I to have continued but one week more in the way I was in when I wrote the latter part of it, I should have been confined, and in straw, the next: for I now recollect that all my distemper was returning upon me with irresistible violence—and that in spite of water-gruel and soupe-maigre.

I own that I am still excessively grieved at the disappointment this admirable woman made it so much her whimsical choice to give me. But, since it has thus fallen out; since she was determined to leave the world; and since she actually ceases *to be*; ought I, who have such a share of life and health in hand, to indulge gloomy reflections upon an event that is past; and *being* past, cannot be recalled? Have I not had a specimen of what will be my case if I do?

For, Belford ('tis a folly to deny it), I have been, to use an old word, quite *bestraught*.

Why, why did my mother bring me up to bear no control? Why was I so educated, *as that to my very tutors it was a request that*

I should not know what contradiction or disappointment was?
Ought she not to have known what cruelty there was in her
kindness?

What a punishment, to have my first very great disappointment touch my intellect! And intellects once touched——
but that I cannot bear to think of—only thus far; the very
repentance and amendment wished me so heartily by my kind
and cross dear have been invalidated and postponed, who knows
for how long?—the *amendment* at least:—can a madman be
capable of either?

Once touched, therefore, I must endeavour to banish those
gloomy reflections, which might *otherwise* have brought on the
right turn of mind; and this, to express myself in Lord M.'s
style, that my wits may not be sent a *wool-gathering*.

For, let me moreover own to thee, that Dr. Hale, who was my
good *Astolfo* [you read *Ariosto*, Jack], and has brought me back
my *wit-jar*, had much ado, by starving diet, by profuse phle-
botomy, by flaying blisters, eyelet-hole cupping, a dark room, a
midnight solitude in a midday sun, to effect my recovery. And
now, for my comfort, he tells me that I may still have returns
upon full moons—horrible! most horrible!—and must be as
careful of myself at both equinoctials as Cæsar was warned
to be of the Ides of March.

How my heart sickens at looking back upon what I was!
Denied the sun, and all comfort: *all* my visitors low-born, tiptoe
attendants: even those tiptoe slaves never approaching me but
periodically, armed with gallipots, boluses, and cephalic draughts;
delivering their orders to me in hated whispers; and answering
other curtain-holding impertinents, inquiring how I was, and
how I took their execrable potions, whisperingly too! What a
cursed still-life was this! Nothing active in me, or about me,
but the worm that never dies.

Again I hasten from the recollection of scenes which *will*, at
times, obtrude themselves upon me.

Adieu, Belford!

But return me my last letter—and build nothing upon its
contents. I *must*, I *will*, I have *already*, overcome these fruitless
gloominesses. Every hour my constitution rises stronger and
stronger to befriend me; and, except a tributary sigh now and
then to the memory of my heart's beloved, it gives me hope that
I shall quickly be what I was—life, spirit, gaiety, and once more
the plague of a sex that has been my plague, and will be every
man's plague at one time or other of his life.

I repeat my desire, however, that you will write to me as usual. I hope you have good store of particulars by you to communicate, when I can better bear to hear of the dispositions that were made for all that was mortal of my beloved Clarissa.

But it will be the joy of my heart to be told that her implacable friends are plagued with remorse. Such things as those you may *now* send me: for company in misery is some relief; especially when a man can think those he hates as miserable as himself.

Once more adieu, Jack!

Letter CLII—Mr. Lovelace to John Belford, Esq.

I AM preparing to leave this kingdom. Mowbray and Tourville promise to give me their company in a month or two.

I'll give thee my route.

I shall first to Paris; and, for amusement and diversion's sake, try to renew some of my old friendships: thence to some of the German courts: thence, perhaps, to Vienna: thence descend through Bavaria and the Tyrol to Venice, where I shall keep the carnival: thence to Florence and Turin: thence again over Mount Cenis to France: and, when I return again to Paris, shall expect to see my friend Belford, who by that time, I doubt not, will be all crusted and bearded over with penitence, self-denial, and mortification; a very anchorite, only an itinerant one, journeying over in hope to cover a multitude of his own sins, by proselyting his old companion.

But let me tell thee, Jack, if stock rises on, as it has done since I wrote my last letter, I am afraid thou wilt find a difficult task in succeeding, should such be thy purpose.

Nor, I verily think, can thy own penitence and reformation hold. Strong habits are not so easily rooted out. Old Satan has had too much benefit from thy faithful services, for a series of years, to let thee so easily get out of his clutches. He knows what will do with thee. A fine, strapping Bona Roba, in the Chartres taste, but well-limbed, clear-complexioned, and Turkish-eyed; thou the first man with her, or made to believe so, which is the same thing; how will thy frosty face shine upon such an object! How will thy tristful visage be illumined by it! A composition will be made between thee and the grand tempter: thou wilt promise to do him suit and service till old age and inability come. And then will he, in all probability, be sure of thee for ever. For wert thou to outlive thy present reigning appetites, he will trump up some other darling sin, or make a now secondary one darling, in order to keep thee firmly attached to his infernal interests. Thou wilt continue resolving to amend, but never amending, till, grown old before thou art aware (*a dozen years after thou art old with everybody else*), thy for-time-built tenement having lasted its allotted period, he claps down upon thy grizzled head the universal trapdoor: and then all will be over with thee in his own way.

Thou wilt think these hints uncharacteristic from me. But yet I cannot help warning thee of the danger thou art actually in; which is the greater, as thou seemest not to know it. A few words more, therefore, on this subject.

Thou hast made good resolutions. If thou keepest them not, thou wilt never be able to keep any. But, nevertheless, the devil and thy time of life are against thee: and six to one thou failest. Were it only that thou hast *resolved*, six to one thou failest. And if thou dost, thou wilt become the scoff of men, and the triumph of devils. Then how will I laugh at thee! For this warning is not from principle. Perhaps I wish it were: *but I never lied to man, and hardly ever said truth to woman.* The first is *what all free-livers cannot say*: the second, *what every one can.*

I am mad again, by Jupiter! But, thank my stars, not gloomily so! Farewell, farewell, farewell, for the third or fourth time, concludes

Thy LOVELACE.

I believe Charlotte and you are in private league together. Letters, I find, have passed between her, and you, and Lord M. I have been kept strangely in the dark of late; but will soon break upon you all, as the sun upon a midnight thief.

Remember that you never sent me the copy of my beloved's will.

Letter CLIII—*Mr. Belford to Robert Lovelace, Esq.*

Friday, Sept. 22.

JUST as I was sitting down to answer yours of the 14th to the 18th, in order to give you all the consolation in my power, came your revoking letter of Wednesday.

I am really concerned, and disappointed, that your first was so soon followed by one so contrary to it.

The shocking letter you mention, which your friends withhold from you, is indeed from me. They may now, I see, show you anything. Ask them, then, for that letter, if you think it worth while to read aught about the true mother of your mind.

I will suppose that thou hast just read the letter thou callest shocking, and which I *intended* to be so. And let me ask what thou thinkest of it? Dost thou not tremble at the horrors the vilest of women labours with, on the apprehensions of death and future judgment? How sit the reflections that must have been raised by the perusal of this letter upon thy yet unclosed eyelet-holes? Will not some serious thoughts mingle with thy melilot, and tear off the callus of thy mind, as that may flay the leather from thy back, and as thy epispastics may strip the parchment from thy plotting head? If not, then indeed is thy conscience seared, and no hopes will lie for thee.

Mr. Belford then gives an account of the wretched Sinclair's terrible exit, which he had just then received.

If this move thee not, I have news to acquaint thee with, of another dismal catastrophe that is but within this hour come to my ear, of another of thy blessed agents. Thy TOMLINSON!— Dying, and, in all probability, before this can reach thee, dead, in Maidstone Jail. As thou sayst in thy first letter, *something strangely retributive seems to be working.*

This his case. He was at the head of a gang of smugglers, endeavouring to carry off run goods, landed last Tuesday, when a party of dragoons came up with them in the evening. Some of his comrades fled. M'Donald being surrounded, attempted to fight his way through, and wounded his man; but having received a shot in his neck, and being cut deeply in the head by a broadsword, he fell from his horse, was taken, and carried to Maidstone Jail: and there my informant left him, just dying, and assured of hanging if he recover.

Absolutely destitute, he got a kinsman of his to apply to me, and, if in town, to the rest of the confraternity, for something, not to *support* him was the word (for he expected not to live till the fellow returned), but to bury him.

I never employed him but once, and then he ruined my project. I now thank Heaven that he did. But I sent him five guineas, and promised him more, as from you, and Mowbray, and Tour-ville, if he live a few days, or to take his trial. And I put it upon you to make further inquiry of him, and to give him what you think fit.

His messenger tells me that he is very penitent; that he weeps continually. He cries out that he has been the vilest of men: yet palliates that his necessities made him worse than he should otherwise have been [*an excuse which none of us can plead*]: but that what touches him most of all is a vile imposture he was put upon, to serve a certain gentleman of fortune, to the ruin of the most excellent woman that ever lived; and who, he had heard, was dead of grief.

Let me consider, Lovelace—*Whose turn can be next?* I wish it may not be thine. But since thou givest me one piece of advice (which I should indeed have thought out of character, hadst thou not taken pains to convince me that it proceeds not from *principle*), I will give thee another: and that is, *prosecute, as fast as thou canst, thy intended tour.* Change of scene, and of climate, may establish thy health: while this gross air, and the approach of winter, may thicken thy blood; and, with the help of a conscience that is upon the struggle with thee, and like a cunning wrestler watches its opportunity to give thee another fall, may make thee miserable for thy life.

I return your revoked letter. Don't destroy it, however. The same dialect may one day come in fashion with you again.

As to the family at Harlowe Place, I have most affecting letters from Colonel Morden relating to their grief and compunction. But are you, to whom the occasion is owing, entitled to rejoice in their distress?

I should be sorry if I could not say, that what you have warned me of in *sport* makes me tremble in *earnest*. I hope (for this is a serious subject with me, though nothing can be so with you) that I never shall deserve, by my apostasy, to be the scoff of men, and the triumph of devils.

All that you say of the difficulty of conquering rooted habits, is but too true. Those, and time of life, are indeed too much against me: but, when I reflect upon the ends (some untimely) of those of our companions whom we have formerly lost; upon Belton's miserable exit; upon the howls and screams of Sinclair, which are still in my ears; and now upon your miserable Tomlinson; and compare their ends with the happy and desirable end of the inimitable Miss Harlowe; I hope I have reason to think my footing morally secure. Your caution, nevertheless, will be of use, however you might design it: and since I know my weak side, I will endeavour to fortify myself in that quarter by marriage, as soon as I can make myself worthy of the confidence and esteem of some virtuous woman; and, by this means, become the subject of your envy, rather than of your scoffs.

I have already begun my retributory purposes, as I may call them. I have settled an annual sum for life upon poor John Loftus, whom I disabled while he was endeavouring to protect his young mistress from my lawless attempts. I rejoice that I succeeded not in that; as I do in recollecting many others of the like sort in which I miscarried.

Poor Farley, who had become a bankrupt, I have set up again; but have declared that the annual allowance I make her shall cease, if I hear she returns to her former courses: and I have made her accountable for her conduct to the good widow Lovick; whom I have taken, at a handsome salary, for my housekeeper at Edgware (for I have let the house at Watford); and she is to dispense the quarterly allotment to her, as she merits.

This good woman shall have other matters of the like nature under her care, as we grow better acquainted: and I make no doubt that she will answer my expectations, and that I shall be both confirmed and improved by her conversation: for she shall generally sit at my own table.

The undeserved sufferings of Miss Clarissa Harlowe, her exalted merit, her exemplary preparation, and her happy end, will be standing subjects with us.

She shall read *to* me, when I have no company; write *for* me, out of books, passages she shall recommend. Her years (turned of fifty), and her good character, will secure me from scandal; and I have great pleasure in reflecting that I shall be better myself for making her happy.

Then, whenever I am in danger, I will read some of the admirable lady's papers: whenever I would abhor my former ways, I will read some of thine, and copies of my own.

The consequence of all this will be, that I shall be the delight of my own relations of both sexes, who were wont to look upon me as a lost man. I shall have good order in my own family, because I shall give a good example myself. I shall be visited and respected, not perhaps by Lovelace, by Mowbray, and by Tourville, because they cannot see me upon the *old* terms, and will not, perhaps, see me upon the *new*, but by the best and worthiest gentlemen, clergy as well as laity, all around me. I shall look upon my past follies with contempt; upon my old companions with pity. Oaths and curses shall be for ever banished from my mouth: in their place shall succeed conversation becoming a rational being and a gentleman. And instead of acts of *offence*, subjecting me perpetually to acts of *defence*, will I endeavour to atone for my past evils, by doing all the good in my power, and by becoming a universal benefactor to the extent of that power.

Now tell me, Lovelace, upon this faint sketch of what I hope to *do*, and to *be*, if this be not a scheme infinitely preferable to the wild, the pernicious, the dangerous ones, both to body and soul, which we have pursued?

I wish I could make my sketch as amiable to you as it appears to me. I wish it with all my soul: for I always loved you. It has been my misfortune that I did: for this led me into infinite riots and follies, of which otherwise, I verily think, I should not have been guilty.

You have a great deal more to answer for than I have, were it only in the temporal ruin of this admirable woman. Let me now, while yet you have youth, and health, and intellect, prevail upon you: for I am afraid, very much afraid, that such is the enormity of this single wickedness, in depriving the world of such a shining light, that if you do not quickly reform, it will be out of your power to reform at all; and that Providence, which has already given you the fates of your agents Sinclair and Tomlinson to take warning by, will not let the principal offender escape, if he slight the warning.

You will, perhaps, laugh at me for these serious reflections. Do, if you will. I had rather you should laugh at me for continuing in this way of thinking and acting, than triumph over me, as you threaten, on my swerving from purposes I have determined upon with such good reason, and induced and warned by such examples.

And so much for this subject at present.

I should be glad to know when you intend to set out. I have too much concern for your welfare, not to wish you in a thinner air and more certain climate.

What have Tourville and Mowbray to do, that they cannot set out with you? They will not covet my company, I dare say; and I shall not be able to endure theirs when you are gone: take them, therefore, with you.

I will not, however, forswear making you a visit at Paris, at your return from Germany and Italy: but hardly with the hope of reclaiming you, if due reflection upon what I have set before you, and upon what you have written in your two last, will not by that time have done it.

I suppose I shall see you before you go. Once more, I wish you were gone. This heavy island air cannot do for you what that of the Continent will.

I do not think I ought to communicate with you, as I used to do, on this side the Channel: let me then hear from you on the opposite shore, and you shall command the pen, as you please; and, honestly, the power, of

J. BELFORD.

Letter CLIV—Mr. Lovelace to John Belford, Esq.

Tuesday, Sept. 26.

FATE, I believe, in my conscience, spins threads for tragedies, on purpose for thee to weave with. Thy Watford uncle, poor Belton, the fair inimitable [exalted creature! and is she to be found in such a list!], the accursed woman, and Tomlinson, seem to have been all doomed to give thee a theme for the dismal and the horrible! And, by my soul, *thou dost work it going*, as Lord M. would phrase it.

That's the horrid thing: a man cannot begin to *think*, but *causes* for thought crowd in upon him: the gloomy takes place, and mirth and gaiety abandon his heart for ever!

Poor M'Donald!—I am really sorry for the fellow. He was a useful, faithful, solemn varlet, who could act incomparably any part given him, and knew not what a blush was. He really took honest pains for me in the last affair; which has cost him and me so dearly in reflection. Often gravelled, as we both were, yet was he never daunted. Poor M'Donald! I must once more say —for carrying on a solemn piece of roguery, he had no equal.

I was so solicitous to know if he were really as bad as thou hast a knack of painting everybody whom thou singlest out to exercise thy murdering pen upon, that I dispatched a man and horse to Maidstone, as soon as I had thine; and had word brought me that he died in two hours after he had received thy five guineas. And all thou wrotest of his concern in relation to the ever dear Miss Harlowe, it seems, was true.

I can't help it, Belford!—I have only to add that it is happy that the poor fellow lived not to be hanged; as it seems he would have been: for who knows, as he had got into such a penitential strain, what might have been in his dying speech?

When a man has not *great* good to comfort himself with, it is right to make the best of the *little* that may offer. There never was any discomfort happened to mortal man, but some little ray of consolation would dart in, if the wretch was not so much a wretch as to *draw*, instead of *undraw*, the curtain, to keep it out.

And so much, at this time, and for ever, for poor Capt. Tomlinson, as I called him.

Your solicitude to get me out of this heavy changeable

climate exactly tallies with everybody's here. They all believe that travelling will establish me. Yet I think I am quite well. Only these plaguy *news* and *fulls*, and the *equinoctials*, fright me a little when I think of them; and that is always: for the whole family are continually ringing these changes in my ears, and are more sedulously intent than I can well account for, to get me out of the kingdom.

But wilt thou write often when I am gone? Wilt thou then piece the thread where thou brokest it off? Wilt thou give me the particulars of *their* distress, who were my *auxiliaries* in bringing on the event that affects me?—Nay, *principals* rather: since, say what thou wilt, what did I do worth a woman's breaking her heart for?

Faith and troth, Jack, I have had very hard usage, as I have often said:—to have such a plaguy ill name given me, pointed at, screamed out upon, run away from, as a mad dog would be: all my own friends ready to renounce me!

Yet I think I deserve it all: for have I not been as ready to give up myself as others are to condemn me?

What madness, what folly this! Who will take the part of a man that condemns himself? Who *can*? He that pleads guilty to an indictment leaves no room for aught but the sentence. Out upon me for an impolitic wretch! I have not the art of the least artful of any of our Christian princes, who every day are guilty of ten times worse breaches of faith; and yet, issuing out a manifesto, they wipe their mouths, and go on from infraction to infraction, from robbery to robbery; commit devastation upon devastation; and destroy—for their *glory*! And are rewarded with the names of *conquerors*, and are dubbed *Le Grand*; praised, and even deified, by orators and poets, for their butcheries and depredations.

While I, a poor, single, harmless prowler; at least *comparatively* harmless; in order to satisfy my hunger, steal but one poor lamb; and every mouth is opened, every hand is lifted up against me.

Nay, as I have just now heard, I am to be *manifestoed* against, though no prince: for Miss Howe threatens to have the case published to the whole world.

I have a good mind not to oppose it; and to write an answer to it, as soon as it comes forth, and exculpate myself, by throwing all the fault upon the *old ones*. And this I have to plead, supposing all that my worst enemies can allege against me were true—That I am not answerable for all the extravagant consequences that this affair has been attended with; and which could not possibly be foreseen.

And this I will prove demonstrably by a case which, but a few hours ago, I put to Lord M. and the two Misses Montague. This it is:

Suppose *A*, a miser, had hid a parcel of gold in a *secret place*, in order to keep it there till he could lend it out at extravagant interest.

Suppose *B* in such great want of this treasure as to be unable to *live without it*.

And suppose *A*, the *miser*, has such an opinion of *B*, the *wanter*, that he would rather lend it to him than to any mortal living; but yet, though he has *no other* use in the world for it, insists upon very unconscionable terms.

B would gladly pay *common* interest for it; but would be undone (in *his own* opinion, at least, and that is everything to him) if he complied with the miser's terms; since he would be sure to be soon thrown into *jail* for the debt, and made a *prisoner for life*. Wherefore guessing (being an arch, penetrating fellow) where the *sweet hoard* lies, he *searches* for it, when the miser is in a *profound sleep*, finds it, and runs away with it.

[*B*, in this case, can be only a *thief*, that's plain, Jack.]

Here Miss Montague put in very smartly. A thief, sir, said she, that steals what is and ought to be dearer to me than life, deserves less to be forgiven than he who murders me.

But what is this, Cousin Charlotte, said I, that is dearer to you than your life? Your *honour*, you'll say—I will not talk to a lady (*I never did*) in a way she cannot answer me. But in the instance for which I put my case (allowing all you attribute to the phantom), what honour is lost, where the *will* is not violated, and the person cannot help it? But, with respect to the case put, how knew we, till the theft *was committed*, that the miser did actually set so romantic a value upon the treasure?

Both my cousins were silent; and my lord, because he could not answer me, cursed me; and I proceeded.

Well, then, the result is that *B* can only be a thief; that's plain. To pursue, therefore, my case:

Suppose this same miserly *A*, on awaking, and searching for, and finding his treasure gone, takes it so much to heart that he starves himself;

Who but himself is to blame for that? Would either equity, law, or conscience, hang *B* for a murder?

And now to apply, said I——

None of your applications, cried my cousins, both in a breath. None of your applications, and be d—ned to you, the passionate peer.

Well, then, returned I, I am to conclude it to be a case so plain, that it needs none; looking at the two girls, who tried for a blush apiece. And I hold myself, of consequence, acquitted of the *death*.

Not so, cried my lord [peers are judges, thou knowest, Jack, in the last resort]: for if, by committing an unlawful act, a capital crime is the consequence, you are answerable for both.

Say you so, my good lord? But will you take upon you to say, supposing (as in the present case) a rape (saving your presence, Cousin Charlotte, saving your presence, Cousin Patty); is death the *natural* consequence of a rape? Did you ever hear, my lord, or did you, ladies, that it was? And if not the *natural* consequence, and a lady will destroy herself, whether by a lingering death, as of grief; or by the dagger, as Lucretia did; is there more than one fault the *man's*? Is not the other *hers*? Were it not so, let me tell you, my dears, chucking each of my blushing cousins under the chin, we either have had no men so wicked as young Tarquin was, or no women so virtuous as Lucretia, in the space of—how many thousand years, my lord? And so Lucretia is recorded as a single wonder!

You may believe I was cried out upon. People who cannot answer will rave: and this they all did. But I insisted upon it to them, and so I do to you, Jack, that I ought to be acquitted of everything but a common theft, a private larceny, as the lawyers call it, in this point. And were my life to be a forfeit to the law, it would not be for murder.

Besides, as I told them, there was a circumstance strongly in my favour in this case: for I would have been glad, with all my soul, to have purchased my forgiveness by a compliance with the terms I first boggled at. And this, you all know, I offered; and my lord, and Lady Betty, and Lady Sarah, and my two cousins, and all my cousins' cousins, to the fourteenth genera-tion, would have been bound for me. But it would not do: the sweet miser would break her heart, and die; and how could I help it?

Upon the whole, Jack, had not the lady died, would there

have been half so much said of it, as there is? Was I the cause
of her death, or could I help it? And have there not been, in a
million of cases like this, nine hundred and ninety-nine thousand
that have not ended as this has ended? How hard, then, is my
fate! Upon my soul, I won't bear it as I have done; but,
instead of taking guilt to myself, claim pity. And this (since
yesterday cannot be recalled) is the only course I can pursue to
make myself easy. Proceed anon.

Letter CLV—*Mr. Lovelace to John Belford, Esq.*

BUT what a pretty scheme of life hast thou drawn out for
thyself and thy old widow! By my soul, Jack, I am mightily
taken with it. There is but one thing wanting in it; and that
will come of course: only to be in the commission, and one of the
quorum. Thou art already provided with a clerk, as good as
thou 'lt want, in the widow Lovick; for thou understandest
law, and the conscience: a good Lord Chancellor between ye!
I should take prodigious pleasure to hear thee decide in a
bastard case, upon thy new notions and old remembrances.

But raillery apart [all gloom at heart, by Jupiter! although the
pen and the countenance assume airs of levity!]: If, after all,
thou canst so easily repent and reform, as thou thinkest thou
canst: if thou canst thus shake off thy old sins and thy old habits:
and if thy old master will so readily dismiss so tried and so
faithful a servant, and permit thee thus calmly to enjoy thy new
system; no room for scandal; all temptation ceasing: and if at
last (thy reformation warranted and approved by time) thou
marriest, and livest honest—why, Belford, I cannot but say, that
if all these IF's come to pass, thou standest a good chance to
be a happy man!

All I think, as I told thee in my last, is that the devil knows
his own interest too well to let thee off so easily. Thou thyself
tellest me that we cannot repent when we will. And indeed
I found it so: for in my lucid intervals I made good resolutions:
but as health turned its blithe side to me, and opened my
prospects of recovery, all my old inclinations and appetites
returned; and this letter, perhaps, will be a thorough conviction
to thee that I *am* as wild a fellow as ever, or in the way to be so.

Thou askest me, very seriously, if, upon the faint sketch thou
hast drawn, thy new scheme be not infinitely preferable to any
of those which we have so long pursued? Why, Jack—let me
reflect—why, Belford—I can't say—I can't say—but it is. To

speak out—it is really, as Biddy in the play says, a good comfortable scheme.

But when thou tellest me that it was thy misfortune to love me, because thy value for me made thee a wickeder man than otherwise thou wouldst have been; I desire thee to revolve this assertion: and I am persuaded that thou wilt not find thyself in so right a train as thou imaginest.

No false colourings, no glosses, does a true penitent aim at. Debasement, diffidence, mortification, contrition, are all near of kin, Jack; and inseparable from a repentant spirit. If thou knowest not this, thou art not got three steps (out of threescore) towards repentance and amendment. And let me remind thee, before the grand accuser comes in to do it, that thou wert ever above being a passive follower in iniquity. Though thou hadst not so good an invention as he to whom thou writest, thou hadst as active a heart for mischief as ever I met with in man.

Then for improving a hint, thou wert always a true Englishman. I never started a roguery that did not come out of *thy* forge in a manner ready anvilled and hammered for execution, when I have sometimes been at a loss to make anything of it myself.

What indeed made me appear to be more wicked than thee was, that I being a handsome fellow, and thou an ugly one, when we had started a game, and hunted it down, the poor frightened puss generally threw herself into *my* paws, rather than into *thine*: and then, disappointed, hast thou wiped thy blubber-lips, and marched off to start a new game, calling me a wicked fellow all the while.

In short, Belford, thou wert an excellent *starter* and *setter*. The old women were not afraid for their daughters when they saw such a face as thine. But, when *I* came, whip, was the key turned upon their girls. And yet all signified nothing; for love, upon occasion, will draw an elephant through a keyhole. But for thy HEART, Belford, who ever doubted the wickedness of *that*?

Nor even in this affair, that sticks most upon me, which my conscience makes such a handle of against me, art thou so innocent as thou fanciest thyself. Thou wilt stare at this: but it is true; and I will convince thee of it in an instant.

Thou sayst thou wouldst have saved the lady from the ruin she met with. Thou art a pretty fellow for this: for *how* wouldst thou have saved her? What methods didst thou *take* to save her?

Thou knewest my designs all along. Hadst thou a mind to

make thyself a good title to the merit to which thou now pre-
tendest to lay claim, thou shouldst, like a true knight-errant,
have sought to set the lady free from the enchanted castle.
Thou shouldst have apprised her of her danger; have stolen in,
when the giant was out of the way; or, hadst thou had the true
spirit of chivalry upon thee, and nothing else would have done,
have killed the giant; and then something wouldst thou have had
to brag of.

"Oh, but the giant was my friend: he reposed a confidence in
me: and I should have betrayed my friend, and his confidence!"
This thou wouldst have pleaded, no doubt.   But try this plea
upon thy present principles, and thou wilt see what a caitiff
thou wert to let it have weight with thee, upon an occasion where
a breach of confidence is more excusable than to keep the
secret.   Did not the lady herself once put this very point home
upon thee?   And didst thou not on that occasion heavily
blame thyself? [1]

Thou canst not pretend, and I know thou wilt not, that thou
wert afraid of thy life by taking such a measure: for a braver
fellow lives not, nor a more fearless, than Jack Belford.   I
remember several instances, and thou canst not forget them,
where thou hast ventured thy bones, thy neck, thy life, against
numbers, in a cause of roguery; and hadst thou had a spark of
that virtue which now thou art willing to flatter thyself thou
hast, thou wouldst surely have run a risk to save an innocence
and a virtue that it became every man to protect and espouse.
This is the truth of the case, greatly as it makes against myself.
But I hate a hypocrite from my soul.

I believe I should have killed thee at the *time*, if I could, hadst
thou betrayed me thus.   But I am sure *now*, that I would have
thanked thee for it with all my heart; and thought thee more a
father, and a friend, than my real father, and my best friend.
And it was natural for thee to think, with so exalted a merit as
this lady had, that this would have been the case, when consideration took place of passion; or, rather, when that damned
fondness for intrigue ceased, which never was my pride so
much as it is now, upon reflection, my curse.

Set about defending thyself, and I will probe thee still deeper,
and convict thee still more effectually, that thou hast more
guilt than merit even in this affair.   And as to all the others,
in which we were accustomed to hunt in couples, thou wert
always the forwardest whelp, and more ready, by far, to run

[1] See vol. iii, pp. 463, 466.

away with me, than I with thee. Yet canst thou now compose thy horse-muscles, and cry out, How much more hast thou, Lovelace, to answer for, than I have! Saying *nothing*, neither, when thou sayst this, were it *true*:—for thou wilt not be tried, when the time comes, by *comparison*.

In short, thou mayst, at this rate, so miserably deceive thyself, that notwithstanding all thy self-denial and mortification, when thou closest thy eyes, thou mayst perhaps open them in a place where thou thoughtest least to be.

However, consult thy old woman on this subject. I shall be thought to be out of character if I go on in this strain. But really, as to a title to merit in this affair, I do assure thee, Jack, that thou less deservest praise than a horse-pond: and I wish I had the sousing of thee.

. . . .

I am actually now employed in taking leave of my friends in the country. I had once thoughts of taking Tomlinson, as I called him, with me: but his destiny has frustrated that intention.

Next Monday I think to see you in town; and then you, and I, and Mowbray, and Tourville, will laugh off that evening together. They will both accompany me (as I expect *you* will) to Dover, if not across the water. I must leave you and them good friends. They take extremely amiss the treatment you have given them in your last letters. They say you strike at their understandings. I laugh at them; and tell them, that those people who have *least* are the most apt to be angry when it is called in question.

Make up all the papers and narratives you can spare me against the time. The will particularly I expect to take with me. Who knows but that those things, which will help to secure *you* in the way you are got into, may convert *me*?

Thou talkest of a wife, Jack: what thinkest thou of our Charlotte? Her family and fortune, I doubt, according to thy scheme, are a little too high. Will those be an objection? Charlotte is a smart girl. For piety (thy present turn) I cannot say much: yet she is as serious as most of her sex at her time of life—would flaunt it a little, I believe, too, like the rest of them, were her reputation under covert.

But it won't do neither, now I think of it:—Thou art so homely, and so awkward a creature! Hast such a boatswain-like air! People would think she had picked thee up in Wapping or

Rotherhithe; or in going to see some new ship launched, or to view the docks at Chatham or Portsmouth. So gaudy and so clumsy! Thy tawdriness won't do with Charlotte! So sit thee down contented, Belford: although I think, in a whimsical way, as *now*, I mentioned Charlotte to thee once before.[1]

Yet would I fain secure thy morals too, if matrimony will do it.—Let me see!—Now I have it.

Has not the widow Lovick a daughter, or a niece? It is not every girl of *fortune* and *family* that will go to prayers with thee *once or twice a day*. But since thou art for taking a wife to mortify with, what if thou marriest the widow herself? She will then have a double concern in thy conversion. You and she may *tête-à-tête* pass many a comfortable winter's evening together, comparing *experiences*, as the good folks call them.

I am serious, Jack, faith I am. And I would have thee take it into thy wise consideration.

R. L.

Mr. Belford returns a very serious answer to the preceding letter; *which appears not.*

In it he most heartily wishes that he had withstood Mr. Lovelace, whatever had been the consequence, in designs so elaborately base and ungrateful, and so long and steadily pursued, against a lady whose merit and innocence entitled her to the protection of every man who had the least pretences to the title of a *gentleman*; and who deserved to be even *the public care.*

He most severely censures himself for his false notions of honour to his friend, on this head; and recollects what the divine lady, as he calls her, said to him on this very subject, as related by himself in his letter to Lovelace, No. cxi, vol. iii, to which Lovelace also (both *instigator* and *accuser*) refers, and to his own regret and shame on the occasion. He distinguishes, however, between an irreparable injury intended to a CLARISSA, and to one designed to *such* of the sex as contribute by their weakness and indiscretion to their own fall, and thereby entitle themselves to a large share of the guilt which accompanies the crime.

He offers not, he says, to palliate or extenuate the crimes he himself has been guilty of: but laments, for Mr. Lovelace's own sake, that he gives him, with so ludicrous and unconcerned an air, such solemn and useful lessons and warnings. Nevertheless, he resolves to make it his whole endeavour, he tells him, to

[1] See p. 237.

render them efficacious to himself: and should think himself but too happy, if he shall be enabled to set him such an example, as may be a means to bring about the reformation of a man so dear to him as he has always been, from the first of their acquaintance; and who is capable of thinking so rightly and deeply; though at present to such little purpose, as makes his very knowledge add to his condemnation.

Letter CLVI—Mr. Belford to Colonel Morden

Thursday, Sept. 21.

GIVE me leave, dear sir, to address myself to you in a very serious and solemn manner on a subject that I must not, cannot, dispense with; as I promised the divine lady that I would do everything in my power to prevent that further mischief of which she was so very apprehensive.

I will not content myself with distant hints. It is with very great concern that I have just now heard of a declaration which you are said to have made to your relations at Harlowe Place, that you will not rest till you have avenged your cousin's wrongs upon Mr. Lovelace.

Far be it from me to offer to defend the unhappy man, or even *unduly* to extenuate his crime: but yet I must say that the family, by their persecutions of the dear lady at first, and by their implacableness afterwards, ought, *at least*, to *share* the blame with him. There is even great reason to believe that a lady of such a religious turn, her virtue neither to be surprised nor corrupted, her will inviolate, would have got over a *mere personal* injury; especially as he would have done all that was in his power to repair it; and as, from the application of all his family in his favour, and other circumstances attending his sincere and voluntary offer, the lady might have condescended, with greater glory to herself, than if he had never offended.

When I have the pleasure of seeing you next, I will acquaint you, sir, with all the circumstances of this melancholy story; from which you will see that Mr. Lovelace was extremely ill-treated at first, by the whole family, this admirable lady excepted. This exception, I know, heightens his crime: but as his principal intention was but to try her virtue; and that he became so earnest a suppliant to her for marriage; and as he has suffered so deplorably in the loss of his reason, for not having it in his power to repair her wrongs; I presume to hope that much is to be pleaded against such a resolution as you are said to have made.

I will read to you at the same time some passages from letters of his; two of which (one but this moment received) will convince you that the unhappy man, who is but now recovering his intellects, needs no greater punishment than what he has from his own reflections.

I have just now read over the *copies* of the dear lady's posthumous letters. I send them all to you, except that directed for Mr. Lovelace; which I reserve till I have the pleasure of seeing you. Let me entreat you to read once more *that* written to yourself; and *that* to her brother [1]; which latter I now send you; as they are in point to the present subject.

I think, sir, they are unanswerable. Such, at least, is the effect they have upon me, that I hope I shall never be provoked to draw my sword again in a private quarrel.

To the weight these must needs have upon you, let me add that the unhappy man has given no *new* occasion of offence since your visit to him at Lord M.'s, when you were so well satisfied of his intention to atone for his crimes, that you yourself urged to your dear cousin *her* forgiveness of him.

Let me *also* (though I presume to hope there is no need, when you coolly consider everything) remind you of your own promise to your departing cousin; relying upon which, her last moments were the easier.

Reflect, my dear Colonel Morden, that the highest injury was to *her*: her family all have a share in the *cause*: *she* forgives it: why should we not endeavour to imitate what we admire?

You asked me, sir, when in town, if a brave man could be a premeditatedly base one? *Generally speaking*, I believe bravery and baseness are incompatible. But Mr. Lovelace's character, in the instance before us, affords a proof of the truth of the common observation, that there is no general rule but has its exceptions: for England, I believe, as gallant a nation as it is deemed to be, has not in it a braver spirit than his; nor a man who has greater skill at his weapons; nor more *calmness* with his skill.

I mention not this with a thought that it can affect Colonel Morden; who, if he be not withheld by SUPERIOR MOTIVES, as well as influenced by those I have reminded him of, will tell me that this skill, and this bravery, will make him the more worthy of being called upon by him.

[1] See Letter cxxix.

To these SUPERIOR motives then I refer myself: and with the greater confidence, as a pursuit ending in blood would not, at *this time*, have the plea lie for it with *anybody*, which sudden passion might have with *some*: but would be construed by *all* to be a cool and deliberate act of revenge for an evil absolutely irretrievable: an act of which a brave and noble spirit (such as is the gentleman's to whom I now write) is not capable.

Excuse me, sir, for the sake of my executorial duty and promise, keeping in eye the dear lady's *personal injunctions*, as well as *written will*, enforced by *letters posthumous*. Every article of which (solicitous as we *both* are to see it truly performed) she would have dispensed with, rather than further mischief should happen on her account.   I am,

Dear sir,
Your affectionate and faithful servant,
J. BELFORD.

The following is the posthumous letter to Colonel Morden, referred to in the above.

Letter CLVII—Superscribed: To my beloved Cousin, William Morden, Esq.   To be delivered after my death.

MY DEAREST COUSIN,—As it is uncertain, from my present weak state, whether, if living, I may be in a condition to receive as I ought the favour you intend me of a visit, when you come to London, I take this opportunity to return you, while able, the humble acknowledgments of a grateful heart, for all your goodness to me from childhood till now: and more particularly for your present kind interposition in my favour.   God Almighty for ever bless you, dear sir, for the kindness you endeavoured to procure for me.

One principal end of my writing to you in this solemn manner, is to beg of you, which I do with the utmost earnestness, that when you come to hear the particulars of my story, you will not suffer *active* resentment to take place in your generous breast on my account.

Remember, my dear cousin, that vengeance is God's province, and He has undertaken to repay it; nor will you, I hope, invade that province:—especially as there is no necessity for you to attempt to vindicate my fame; since the offender himself (before he is called upon) has stood forth, and offered to do me all the justice that you could have extorted from him, had I lived: and when your own person may be endangered by running an *equal* risk with a *guilty man*.

Duelling, sir, I need not tell *you*, who have adorned a public character, is not only a usurpation of the Divine prerogative; but it is an insult upon magistracy and good government. 'Tis an impious act. 'Tis an attempt to take away a life that ought not to depend upon a private sword: an act, the consequence of which is to hurry a soul (all its sins upon its head) into perdition; endangering that of the poor triumpher—since neither intend to give to the other that *chance*, as I may call it, for the Divine mercy, in an opportunity for repentance, which each presumes to hope for himself.

Seek not then, I beseech you, sir, to aggravate my fault by a pursuit of blood, which must necessarily be deemed a consequence of that fault. Give not the unhappy man the merit (were you assuredly to be the victor) of falling by your hand. At present he is the perfidious, the ungrateful deceiver; but will not the forfeiture of his life, and the probable loss of his soul, be a dreadful expiation for having made me miserable for *a few months* only, and through that misery, by the Divine favour, happy to all eternity?

In such a case, my cousin, where shall the evil stop? And who shall avenge on you? And who on your avenger?

Let the poor man's conscience, then, dear sir, avenge me. He will one day find punishment more than enough from that. Leave him to the chance of repentance. If the Almighty will give him time for it, why should you deny it him? Let him still be the guilty aggressor; and let no one say, Clarissa Harlowe is now amply revenged in his fall; or, in the case of yours (which Heaven avert!), that her fault, instead of being buried in her grave, is perpetuated, and aggravated, by a loss far greater than that of herself.

Often, sir, has the *more* guilty been the vanquisher of the *less*. An Earl of Shrewsbury, in the reign of Charles II, as I have read, endeavouring to revenge the greatest injury that man can do to man, met with his death at Barn Elms, from the hand of the ignoble duke who had vilely dishonoured him. Nor can it be thought an unequal dispensation, were it *generally* to happen that the usurper of the Divine prerogative should be punished for his presumption by the man whom he sought to destroy, and who, however previously criminal, is put, in this case, upon a necessary act of self-defence.

May Heaven protect you, sir, in all your ways; and, once more

I pray, reward you for all your kindness to me: a kindness so worthy of *your* heart, and so exceedingly grateful to *mine*: that of seeking to make peace, and to reconcile parents to a once beloved child; uncles to a niece late their favourite; and a brother and sister to a sister whom once they thought not unworthy of that tender relation. A kindness so greatly preferable to the vengeance of the murdering sword.

Be a comforter, dear sir, to my honoured parents, as you have been to me: and may we, through the Divine goodness to us both, meet in that blessed eternity, into which, as I humbly trust, I shall have entered when you read this.

So prays, and to her latest hour will pray, my dear Cousin Morden, my friend, my guardian, but *not* my avenger—[dear sir! remember that!]

Your ever affectionate and obliged
CLARISSA HARLOWE.

Letter CLVIII—Colonel Morden to John Belford, Esq.

Sat. Sept. 23.

DEAR SIR,—I am very sorry that anything you have heard I have said should give you uneasiness.

I am obliged to you for the letters you have communicated to me; and still further for your promise to favour me with others occasionally.

All that relates to my dear cousin I shall be glad to see, be it from whom it will.

I leave to your own discretion, what may or may not be proper for Miss Howe to see from a pen so free as mine.

I admire her spirit. Were she a *man*, do you think, sir, *she*, at *this time*, would have your advice to take upon such a subject as that upon which you write?

Fear not, however, that your communications shall put me upon any measures that otherwise I should not have taken. The wickedness, sir, is of such a nature as admits not of aggravation.

Yet I do assure you that I have not made any resolutions that will be a tie upon me.

I have indeed expressed myself with vehemence upon the occasion. Who could forbear to do so? But it is not my way to resolve in matters of moment, till opportunity brings the execution of my purposes within my reach. We shall see by what manner of spirit this young man will be acted, on his recovery. If he continue to brave and defy a family, which he has so irreparably injured—if——But resolutions depending upon future contingencies are best left to future determination, as I just now hinted.

Meantime, I will own that I think my cousin's arguments unanswerable. No *good* man but must be influenced by them. But, alas! sir, who *is* good?

As to your arguments; I hope you will believe me, when I assure you, as I now do, that your opinion, and your reasoning, have, and will always have, great and deserved weight with me: and that I respect you still more than I did, if possible, for your expostulations in support of my cousin's pious injunctions to me. They come from *you*, sir, with the greatest propriety, as her executor and representative; and likewise as you are a man of humanity, and a well-wisher to both parties.

I am not exempt from violent passions, sir, any more than your friend; but then I hope they are only capable of being raised by other people's insolence, and not by my own arrogance. If ever I am stimulated by my imperfections and my resentments to act against my judgment, and my cousin's injunctions, some such reflections as these that follow will run away with my reason. Indeed, they are always present with me.

In the first place; my own disappointment: who came over with the hope of passing the remainder of my days in the conversation of a kinswoman so beloved; and to whom I had a double relation as her cousin and trustee.

Then I reflect, too—too often perhaps for my engagements to her in her last hours—that the dear creature could only forgive for *herself*. She, no doubt, is happy: but who shall forgive for a *whole family*, in all its branches made miserable for their lives?

That the more faulty her friends were as to *her*, the more enormous his ingratitude, and the more inexcusable—What! Sir, was it not enough that she suffered what she did *for him*, but the barbarian must make her suffer for her sufferings for *his sake?* —Passion makes me express this weakly: passion refuses the aid of expression sometimes, where the propriety of a resentment *prima facie* declares expression to be needless. I leave it to *you*, sir, to give this reflection its due force.

That the author of this diffusive mischief perpetrated it premeditatedly, wantonly, in the gaiety of his heart. To *try* my cousin, say you, sir? To try the virtue of a Clarissa, sir! Had she then given him any cause to doubt her virtue? It could *not* be. If he avers that she did, I am indeed called upon——But I will have patience.

That he carried her, as now it appears, to a vile brothel, purposely to put her out of all human resource; himself out of the reach of all humane remorse: and that, finding her proof against all the common arts of delusion, base and unmanly arts were there used to effect his wicked purposes. *Once dead*, the injured saint, in her will, says, *he has seen her*.

That I could not know this when I saw him at M. Hall: that, the object of his attempts considered, I could not suppose there was such a monster breathing as he: that it was natural for me to impute her refusal of him rather to transitory resentment, to consciousness of human frailty, and mingled doubts of the sincerity of his offers, than to villainies which had given the irreversible blow, and had at that instant brought her down to the gates of death, which in a very few days enclosed her.

That he is a man of defiance: a man who thinks to awe every one by his insolent darings, and by his pretensions to superior courage and skill.

That, disgrace as he is to his name, and to the character of a gentleman, the man would not want merit who, in vindication of the *dishonoured* distinction, should expunge and blot him out of the worthy list.

That the injured family has a son who, however unworthy of such a sister, is of a temper vehement, unbridled, fierce; unequal, therefore (as he has once indeed been found), to a contention with this man: the loss of which son, by a violent death, on such an occasion, and by a hand so justly hated, would complete the misery of the whole family: and who, nevertheless, resolves to call him to account, if I do not: his very *misbehaviour* perhaps to such a sister stimulating his perverse heart to do her memory the *more signal* justice; though the attempt might be fatal to himself.

Then, sir, to be a witness, as I am every hour, to the calamity and distress of a family to which I am related; every one of whom, however averse to an alliance with him while it had *not* taken place, would no doubt have been soon reconciled to the admirable creature, had the man (to whom, for his family and fortunes, it was not a disgrace to be allied) done her but common justice!

To see them hang their pensive heads; mope about, shunning one another; though formerly never used to meet but to rejoice in each other; afflicting themselves with reflections, that the last time they respectively saw the dear creature, it was here, or there, at such a place, in such an attitude; and could they have thought that it would have been the *last*?

Every one of them reviving instances of her excellences that will for a long time make their very blessings a curse to them!

Her closet, her chamber, her cabinet, given up to me to disfurnish, in order to answer (now *too late* obliging!) the legacies bequeathed; unable themselves to enter them; and even making use of less convenient back stairs, that they may avoid passing by the doors of her apartment!

Her parlour locked up; the walks, the retirements, the summer-house in which she delighted, and in which she used to pursue her charming works; *that*, in particular, from which she went to the fatal interview; shunned, or hurried by, or over!

Her perfections, nevertheless, called up to remembrance, and enumerated: incidents and graces, unheeded before, or passed over in the group of her numberless perfections, now brought into notice, and dwelt upon!

The very servants allowed to expatiate upon these praiseful topics to their principals! Even eloquent in their praises—the distressed principals listening and weeping! Then to see them break in upon the zealous applauders, by their impatience and remorse, and throw abroad their helpless hands, and exclaim; then again to see them listen to hear more of her praises, and weep again—they even encouraging the servants to repeat how they used to be stopped by strangers to ask after her, and by those who knew her, to be told of some new instances to her honour—how aggravating all this!

In *dreams* they see her, and *desire* to see her: always an angel, and accompanied by angels: always clad in robes of light: always endeavouring to comfort *them*, who declare that they shall never more know comfort!

What an example she set! How she indited! How she drew! How she wrought! How she talked! How she sang! How she played! Her voice music! Her accent harmony!

Her conversation how instructive! how sought after! The delight of persons of all ages, of both sexes, of all ranks! Yet how humble, how condescending! Never were dignity and humility so illustriously mingled!

At other times, how generous, how noble, how charitable, how judicious in her charities! In every action laudable! In every attitude attractive! In every appearance, whether full-dressed, or in the housewife's more humble garb, equally elegant, and equally lovely! *Like* or *resembling* Miss Clarissa Harlowe, they now remember to be a praise denoting the highest degree of excellence, with every one, whatever person, action, or rank, spoken of.

The desirable daughter; the obliging kinswoman; the affec-tionate sister (all envy now subsided!); the faithful, the warm friend; the affable, the kind, the benevolent mistress!—Not one fault remembered! All their severities called cruelties: mutually accusing each other; each him and herself; and all to raise *her* character, and torment themselves.

Such, sir, was the angel of whom the vilest of men has deprived the world! You, sir, who know more of the barbarous machina-tions and practices of this strange man, can help me to still more inflaming reasons, were they needed, why a man *not perfect* may stand excused to the generality of the world, if he should pursue his vengeance; and the rather, as through an absence of six years (high as just report, and the promises of her early youth from childhood, had raised her in his esteem) he could not till now know one half of her excellences—till now! that we have lost, for ever lost, the admirable creature!

But I will force myself from the subject, after I have repeated that I have not yet made any resolutions that can bind me. Whenever I do, I shall be glad they may be such as may merit the honour of your approbation.

I send you back the copies of the posthumous letters. I see the humanity of your purpose in the transmission of them to me; and I thank you most heartily for it. I presume that it is owing to the same laudable consideration that you kept back the copy of that to the wicked man himself.

I intend to wait upon Miss Howe in person with the diamond ring, and such other of the effects bequeathed to her as are here. I am, sir,

Your most faithful and obliged servant,

WM. MORDEN.

Mr. Belford, in his answer to this letter, further enforces the lady's dying injunctions; and rejoices that the colonel has made no vindictive resolutions; and hopes everything from his prudence and consideration, and from his promise given to the dying lady.

He refers to the seeing him in town on account of the dreadful ends of two of the greatest criminals in his cousin's affair. "This, *says he,* together with Mr. Lovelace's disorder of mind, looks as if Providence had already taken the punishment of these unhappy wretches into its own hands."

He desires the colonel will give him a day's notice of his coming to town, lest otherwise he may be absent at the time.

This he does, though he tells him not the reason, with a view to prevent a meeting between him and Mr. Lovelace ; who might be in town (as he apprehends) about the same time, in his way to go abroad.

Letter CLIX—Colonel Morden to John Belford, Esq.

Tuesday, Sept. 26.

DEAR SIR,—I cannot help congratulating myself, as well as you, that we have already got through with the family every article of the will, where *they* have any concern.

You left me a discretional power in many instances; and, in pursuance of it, I have had my dear cousin's personal jewels valued; and will account to you for them, at the highest price, when I come to town, as well as for other matters that you were pleased to entrust to my management.

These jewels I have presented to my Cousin Dolly Hervey, in acknowledgment of her love to the dear departed. I have told Miss Howe of this; and she is as well pleased with what I have done as if she had been the purchaser of them herself. As that young lady has jewels of her own, she could only have wished to purchase these because they were her beloved friend's.

The grandmother's jewels are also valued; and the money will be paid me for you, to be carried to the uses of the will.

Mrs. Norton is preparing, by general consent, to enter upon her office as housekeeper at *The Grove*. But it is my opinion that she will not be long on this side heaven.

I waited upon Miss Howe myself, as I told you I would, with what was bequeathed to her and her mother. You will not be displeased, perhaps, if I make a few observations with regard to that young lady, so dear to my beloved cousin, as you have not a personal acquaintance with her.

There never was a firmer and nobler friendship in women than that between my dear cousin and Miss Howe, to which this wretched man has given a period.

Friendship, generally speaking, Mr. Belford, is too fervent a flame for female minds to manage: a light that but in few of their hands burns steady, and often hurries the sex into flight and absurdity. Like other extremes, it is hardly ever durable. Marriage, which is the highest state of friendship, generally absorbs the most vehement friendships of female to female; and that whether the wedlock be happy or not.

What female mind is capable of two fervent friendships at the same time?

This I mention as a *general observation*: but the friendship that subsisted between these two ladies affords a remarkable exception to it: which I account for from those qualities and attainments in *both*, which, were they more common, would furnish more exceptions still in favour of the sex.

Both had an *enlarged*, and even a *liberal* education: both had minds thirsting after virtuous knowledge. Great readers both: great writers—[and *early familiar writing* I take to be one of the greatest openers and improvers of the mind that man or woman can be employed in]. Both generous. High in fortune; therefore above that dependence each on the other that frequently destroys the familiarity which is the cement of friendship. Both excelling in *different ways*, in which neither sought to envy the other. Both blessed with clear and distinguishing faculties; with solid sense; and from their first intimacy [*I have many of my lights, sir, from Mrs. Norton*], each seeing something in the other to *fear*, as well as to *love*; yet making it an indispensable condition of their friendship each to tell the other of her failings; and to be thankful for the freedom taken. One by nature *gentle*; the other *made so* by her *love* and *admiration* of her exalted friend—impossible that there could be a friendship better calculated for duration.

I must, however, take the liberty to blame Miss Howe for her behaviour to Mr. Hickman. And I infer from it that even women of sense are not to be trusted with power.

By the way, I am sure I need not desire you not to communicate to this fervent young lady the liberties I take with her character.

I dare say my cousin could not approve of Miss Howe's behaviour to this gentleman: a behaviour which is talked of *by as many as know Mr. Hickman and her*. Can a *wise* young lady be easy under such censure? She *must* know it.

Mr. Hickman is really a very worthy man. Everybody speaks well of him. But he is gentle-dispositioned, and he adores Miss Howe; and love admits not of an air of even *due dignity* to the object of it. Yet will Mr. Hickman hardly ever get back the reins he has yielded up; unless she, by carrying too far the power of which she seems at present too sensible, should, when she has no favours to confer which he has not a right to demand, provoke him to throw off the too heavy yoke. And should he do so, and then treat her with negligence, Miss Howe, of all the women

I know, will be the least able to support herself under it. She will then be *more* unhappy than she ever made him: for a man who is uneasy at home can divert himself abroad; which a woman cannot so easily do without scandal.

Permit me to take further notice as to Miss Howe, that it is very obvious to me that she has, by her haughty behaviour to this worthy man, involved herself in one difficulty, from which she knows not how to extricate herself with that grace which accompanies all her actions. She intends to have Mr. Hickman. I believe she does not dislike him. And it will cost her no small pains to descend from the elevation she has climbed to.

Another inconvenience she will suffer from her having taught everybody (for she is above disguise) to think, by her treatment of Mr. Hickman, *much more meanly of him than he deserves to be thought of*. And must *she* not suffer dishonour in *his* dishonour?

Mrs. Howe is much disturbed at her daughter's behaviour to the gentleman. He is very deservedly a favourite of hers. But [*another* failing in Miss Howe!] her mother has not all the authority with her that a mother ought to have. Miss Howe is indeed a woman of fine sense; but it requires a high degree of good understanding, as well as a sweet and gentle disposition of mind, and great discretion, in a child, when grown up, to let it be seen that she mingles *reverence* with her *love*, to a parent who has talents visibly inferior to her own.

Miss Howe is *open, generous, noble*. The mother has not any of her fine qualities. Parents, in order to preserve their children's veneration for them, should take great care not to let them see anything in their conduct, or behaviour, or principles, which they themselves would not approve of in others.

Mr. Hickman has, however, this consideration to comfort himself with; that the same vivacity by which *he* suffers, makes Miss Howe's own *mother*, at times, *equally sensible*. And as he sees enough of this beforehand, he will have more reason to blame himself than the lady, should she prove as lively a wife as she was a mistress, for having continued his addresses, and married her against such threatening appearances.

There is also another circumstance which good-natured men who engage with even lively women, may look forward to with pleasure; a circumstance which generally lowers the spirits of the ladies, and *domesticates* them, as I may call it: and which, as it will bring those of Mr. Hickman and Miss Howe nearer to a par, that worthy gentleman will have *double* reason, when it happens, to congratulate himself upon it.

But, after all, I see that there is something so charmingly brilliant and frank in Miss Howe's disposition, although at present visibly overclouded by grief, that it is impossible not to love her, even for her failings. She *may*, and I hope she *will*, make Mr. Hickman an obliging wife. And if she do, she will have an additional merit with me; since she cannot be apprehensive of check or control; and may, therefore, by her *generosity* and *prudence*, lay an obligation upon her husband, by the performance of what is no more than her *duty*.

Her mother both *loves* and *fears* her. Yet is Mrs. Howe also a woman of vivacity, and ready enough, I dare say, to cry out when she is pained. But, alas! she has, as I hinted above, *weakened her authority* by the *narrowness of her mind*.

Yet once she praised her daughter to me with so much *warmth* for the generosity of her spirit, that had I not known the old lady's character, I should have thought her generous *herself*. And yet I have always observed that people even of narrow tempers are ready to praise generous ones: and *thus* have I accounted for it: that such persons generally find it to their purpose, that all the world should be open-minded but themselves.

The old lady applied herself to me, to urge to the young one the contents of the will, in order to hasten her to fix a day for her marriage: but desired that I would not let Miss Howe know that she did.

I took the liberty upon it to tell Miss Howe that I hoped that *her* part of a will, so soon, and so punctually, in almost all its other articles, fulfilled, would not be the only one that would be slighted.

Her answer was, she would consider of it: and made me a curtsy with such an air, as showed me that she thought me more out of my sphere than I could allow her to think me, had I been permitted to argue the point with her.

I found Miss Howe and her own servant-maid in deep mourning. This, it seems, had occasioned a great debate at first between her mother and her. Her mother had the words of the will on her side; and Mr. Hickman's interest in her view; her daughter having said that she would wear it for six months at least. But the young lady carried her point. "Strange, said she, if I, who shall mourn the heavy, the irreparable loss to the last hour of my life, should not show my concern to the world for a few months!"

Mr. Hickman, for his part, was so far from uttering an opposing word on this occasion, that on the very day that Miss Howe put on hers, he waited on her in a new suit of mourning, as for a near relation. His servants and equipage made the same respectful appearance.

Whether the mother was consulted by him in it, I cannot say; but the daughter knew nothing of it till she saw him in it. She looked at him with surprise, and asked him for whom he mourned?

The dear, and ever dear Miss Harlowe, he said.

She was at a loss, it seems. At last, All the world ought to mourn for my Clarissa, said she; but whom, man (that was her whimsical address to him), thinkest thou to oblige by this appearance?

It is more than *appearance,* madam. I love not my own sister, worthy as she is, better than I loved Miss Clarissa Harlowe. I oblige *myself* by it. And if I disoblige not you, that is all I wish.

She surveyed him, I am told, from head to foot. She knew not, at first, whether to be angry or pleased. At length, "I thought at first, said she, that you might have a bolder and freer motive—but (as my mamma says) you *may* be a well-meaning man, though generally a little wrong-headed—however, as the world is censorious, and may think us nearer of kin than I would have it supposed, I must take care that I am not seen abroad in your company."

But let me add, Mr. Belford, that if this compliment of Mr. Hickman (or this *more* than compliment, as I may well call it, since the worthy man speaks not of my dear cousin without emotion) does not produce a short day, I shall think Miss Howe has less generosity in her temper than I am willing to allow her.

You will excuse me, Mr. Belford, for the particularities which you invited and encouraged.

Having now seen everything that relates to the will of my dear cousin brought to a desirable issue, I will set about making my own. I shall follow the dear creature's example, and give my reasons for every article, that there may be no room for after-contention.

What but a fear of death, a fear unworthy of a creature who knows that he must one day as surely die as he was born, can hinder any one from making such a disposition?

I hope soon to pay my respects to you in town. Meantime I am, with great respect, dear sir,

Your faithful and affectionate humble servant,

WM. MORDEN.

Letter CLX—Mr. Belford to Miss Howe

Thursday, Sept. 28.

MADAM,—I do myself the honour to send you with this, according to my promise,[1] copies of the posthumous letters written by your exalted friend.

These will be accompanied with other letters, particularly a copy of one from Mr. Lovelace, begun to be written on the 14th, and continued down to the 18th.[2] You will see by it, madam, the dreadful anguish that his spirits labour with, and his deep remorse.

Mr. Lovelace sent for this letter back. I complied; but I first took a copy of it. As I have not told him that I have done so, you will be pleased to forbear communicating of it to anybody but Mr. Hickman. That gentleman's perusal of it will be the same as if nobody but yourself saw it.

One of the letters of Colonel Morden which I enclose, you will observe, madam, is only a copy.[3] The true reason for which, as I will ingenuously acknowledge, is, some free but respectful animadversions which the colonel has made upon your declining to carry into execution your part of your dear friend's last requests. I have, therefore, in respect to that worthy gentleman (having a caution from *him* on that head), omitted those parts.

Will you allow me, madam, however, to tell you, that I myself could not have believed that my inimitable testatrix's own Miss Howe would have been the most backward in performing such a part of her dear friend's last will as is entirely in her own power to perform—especially when that performance would make *one of the most deserving men in England happy;* and whom, I presume, she *proposes* to honour with her hand?

Excuse me, madam. I have a most sincere veneration for you; and would not disoblige you for the world.

I will not presume to make remarks on the letters I send you; nor upon the informations I have to give you of the dreadful end of two unhappy wretches who were the greatest criminals in the affair of your adorable friend. These are the infamous *Sinclair*, and a person whom you have read of, no doubt, in the letters of the charming innocent, by the name of Captain *Tomlinson.*

The wretched woman died in the extremest tortures and despondency: the man from wounds got in defending himself in

¹ See p. 434.   ² See pp. 438–42.   ³ Viz. the preceding.

carrying on a contraband trade, both accusing themselves, in their last hours, for the parts they had acted against the most excellent of women, as of the crime that gave them the deepest remorse.

Give me leave to say, madam, that if your *compassion* be not excited for the poor man who suffers so greatly from his own anguish of mind, as you will observe by his letter he does; and for the unhappy family, whose remorse, as you will see by Colonel Morden's, is so deep; your *terror* must. And yet I shall not wonder, if the just sense of the irreparable loss you have sustained hardens a heart against pity, which, on a less extraordinary occasion, would want its *principal grace*, if it were not compassionate.

I am, madam, with the greatest respect and gratitude,
Your most obliged and faithful humble servant,
J. BELFORD.

Letter CLXI—Miss Howe to John Belford, Esq.

Sat. Sept. 30.

SIR,—I little thought I ever could have owed so much obligation to any man as you have laid me under. And yet what you have sent me has almost broken my heart and ruined my eyes.

I am surprised, though agreeably, that you have so soon, and so well, got over that part of the trust you have engaged in which relates to the family.

It may be presumed, from the exits you mention of two of the infernal man's accomplices, that the thunderbolt will not stop short of the principal. Indeed I have some pleasure to think it seems rolling along towards the devoted head that has plotted all the mischief. But let me, however, say, that although I think Mr. Morden not altogether in the wrong in his reasons for resentment, as he is the dear creature's kinsman and trustee, yet I think you very much in the right in endeavouring to dissuade him from it, as you are her executor, and act in pursuance of her earnest request.

But what a letter is that of the infernal man! I cannot observe upon it. Neither can I, for very different reasons, upon my dear creature's posthumous letters; particularly on that to him. O Mr. Belford! what numberless perfections died, when my Clarissa drew her last breath!

If decency be observed in his letters; for I have not yet had patience to read above two or three of them (besides this horrid one, which I return you enclosed); I may some time hence be curious to look, by *their* means, into the hearts of wretches which, though they must be the abhorrence of virtuous minds, will, when laid open (as I presume they are in them), afford a *proper warning* to those who read them, and teach them to *detest men of such profligate characters*.

If your reformation be sincere, you will not be offended that I do not except you on this occasion—and thus have I helped you to a criterion to try yourself by.

By this letter of the wicked man it is apparent that there are still wickeder women. But see what a guilty commerce with the devils of your sex will bring those to whose morals ye have ruined! For these women were once innocent: it was *man* that made them otherwise. The first bad man, perhaps, threw them upon worse men: those upon still worse; till they commenced devils incarnate—*the height of wickedness, or of shame, is not arrived at all at once,* as I have somewhere heard observed.

But this man, this monster rather, for *him* to curse these women, and to curse the dear creature's family (implacable as the latter were), in order to lighten a burden he voluntarily took up, and groans under, is *meanness* added to *wickedness*: and in vain will he one day find his low plea of sharing with *her friends,* and with *those common wretches,* a guilt which will be adjudged him *as all his own*; though *they* too may meet with their punishment, as it is evidently begun; in the *first,* in their ineffectual reproaches of one another; in the *second*—as you have told me.

This letter of the abandoned wretch I have not shown to anybody; not even to Mr. Hickman: for, sir, I must tell you, I do not as *yet* think it the same thing as only seeing it myself.

Mr. Hickman, like the rest of his sex, would grow upon indulgence. One distinction from me would make him pay two to himself. Insolent creepers, or encroachers, all of you! To show any of you a *favour* to-day, you would expect it as a *right* to-morrow.

I am, as you see, very open and sincere with you; and design in another letter to be still more so, in answer to your call, and Colonel Morden's call, upon me, in a point that concerns me to explain myself upon to my beloved creature's executor, and to the colonel, as her *only tender* and *only worthy* relation.

I cannot but highly applaud Colonel Morden for his generosity to Miss Dolly Hervey.

O that he had arrived time enough to save my inimitable friend from the machinations of the vilest of men, and from the envy and malice of the most selfish and implacable of brothers and sisters!

ANNA HOWE.

Letter CLXII—Miss Howe to John Belford, Esq.

Monday, Oct. 2.

WHEN you question me, sir, as you do, and on a subject so affecting to me, in the character of the representative of my best beloved friend, and have in every particular hitherto acted up to that character, you are entitled to my regard: especially as you are joined in your questioning of me by a gentleman whom I look upon as the dearest and nearest (because worthiest) relation of my dear friend: and who, it seems, has been so severe a censurer of my conduct, that your politeness will not permit you to send me his letter, with others of his; but a copy only, in which the passages reflecting upon me are omitted.

I presume, however, that what is meant by this alarming freedom of the colonel, is no more than what you both have already hinted to me; as if you thought I were not inclined to pay so much regard to my beloved creature's last will, in my own case, as I would have others pay to it. A charge that I ought not to be quite silent under.

You have observed, no doubt, that I have seemed to value myself upon the freedom I take in declaring my sentiments without reserve upon every subject that I pretend to touch upon: and I can hardly question that I have, or shall, in your opinion, by my unceremonious treatment of you upon so short an acquaintance, run into the error of those who, wanting to be thought above hypocrisy and flattery, fall into rusticity, if not ill manners; a common fault with such who, not caring to correct constitutional failings, seek to gloss them over by some *nominal* virtue; when all the time, perhaps, these failings are entirely owing to native arrogance; or, at least, to a contracted rust, that they will not, because it would give them pain, submit to have filed off.

You see, sir, that I can, however, be as free with myself as with you: and, by what I am going to write, you will find me still more free: and yet I am aware that such of my sex as will not assume some little dignity, and exact respect from yours, will render themselves cheap; and perhaps, for their modesty and diffidence, be repaid with scorn and insult.

But the scorn I will endeavour not to deserve; and the insult I will not bear.

In some of the dear creature's papers which you have had in your possession, and must again have in order to get transcribed, you will find several friendly but severe reprehensions of me, on account of a natural, or, at least, a *habitual,* warmth of temper, which she was pleased to impute to me.

I was thinking to give you her charge against me in her own words, from one of her letters delivered to *me* with her own hands, on taking leave of me, on the last visit she honoured me with. But I will supply that charge by confession of more than it imports; to wit, "That I am haughty, uncontrollable, and violent in my temper"; this *I say*; "Impatient of contradiction," *was my beloved's charge* [from anybody but her dear self, she should have said]; "and aim not at that affability, that gentleness next to meekness, which, in the letter I was going to communicate, she tells me are the peculiar and indispensable characteristics of a real fine lady; who, she is pleased to say, should appear to be gall-less as a dove; and never should know what warmth or high spirit is, but in the cause of religion or virtue; or in cases where her own honour, the honour of a friend, or that of an innocent person, is concerned."

Now, sir, as I must needs plead guilty to this indictment, do you think I ought not to resolve upon a single life?—I, who have such an opinion of your sex that I think there is not one man in a hundred whom a woman of sense and spirit can either *honour* or *obey,* though you make us promise *both,* in that solemn form of words which unites or rather *binds* us to you in marriage?

When I look round upon all the married people of my acquaintance, and see how *they* live, and what *they* bear who live *best,* I am confirmed in my dislike to the state.

Well do your sex contrive to bring us up fools and idiots, in order to make us bear the yoke you lay upon our shoulders; and that we may not despise you from our hearts (as we certainly should if we were brought up as you are) for your *ignorance,* as much as you often make us do (as it is) for your *insolence.*

These, sir, are some of my notions. And, with these notions, let me repeat my question, *Do you think I ought to marry at all ?*

If I marry either a sordid or an imperious wretch, can I, do you think, live with him? And ought a man of a contrary character, for the sake of either of our reputations, to be plagued with me?

Long did I stand out against all the offers made me, and

against all the persuasions of my mother; and, to tell you the truth, the *longer*, and with the *more* obstinacy, as the person my choice would have first fallen upon was neither approved by my mother, nor by my dear friend. This riveted me to my pride, and to my opposition: for although I was convinced, after a while, that my choice would neither have been prudent nor happy; and that the specious wretch was not what he had made me believe he was; yet could I not easily think of any other man: and indeed, from the detection of him, took a settled aversion to the whole sex.

At last Mr. Hickman offered himself; a man worthy of a better choice. He had the good fortune [*he thinks it so*] to be agreeable (and to make his proposals agreeable) to my mother.

As to myself; I own that, were I to have chosen a brother, Mr. Hickman should have been the man; virtuous, sober, sincere, friendly, as he is. But I wished not to marry: nor knew I the man in the world whom I could think deserving of my beloved friend. But neither of our parents would let us live single.

The accursed Lovelace was proposed warmly to *her* at one time; and, while she was yet but indifferent to him, they by ungenerous usage of him (for then, sir, he was not known to be Beelzebub himself), and by endeavouring to force her inclinations in favour first of one worthless man, then of another, *in antipathy to him*, through her foolish brother's caprice, turned that indifference (from the natural generosity of her soul) into a regard which she never otherwise would have had for a man of his character.

Mr. Hickman was proposed *to me*. I refused him again and again. He persisted: my mother his advocate. My mother made my beloved friend his advocate too. I told him my dislike of all men: of him: of matrimony. Still he persisted. I used him with tyranny—led indeed partly by my temper, partly by design; hoping thereby to get rid of him; till the poor man (his character unexceptionably uniform) still persisting, made himself a merit with me by his patience. This brought down my pride [I never, sir, was accounted very ungenerous, nor quite ungrateful], and gave me, at one time, an inferiority in my own opinion to him; which lasted just long enough for my friends to prevail upon me to promise him encouragement, and to receive his addresses.

Having so done, when the weather-glass of my pride got up again, I found I had gone too far to recede. My mother and my friend both held me to it. Yet I tried him; I vexed him in a hundred ways; and not so much neither with *design* to vex him, as to make him hate me, and decline his suit.

He bore this, however; and got nothing but my pity: yet still my mother and my friend, having obtained my promise (made, however, not to *him*, but to *them*), and being well assured that I valued no man *more* than Mr. Hickman (who never once disobliged me in word, or deed, or look, except by his foolish perseverance), insisted upon the performance.

While my dear friend was in her unhappy uncertainty, I could not think of marriage: and now, what encouragement have I? She, my monitress, my guide, my counsel, gone, for ever gone! by whose advice and instructions I hoped to acquit myself tolerably in the state into which I could not avoid entering. For, sir, my mother is so partially Mr. Hickman's friend, that I am sure, should any difference arise, she would always censure me, and acquit him; even were he ungenerous enough to remember me in his day.

This, sir, being my situation, consider how difficult it is for me to think of marriage. Whenever we approve, we can find a hundred good reasons to justify our approbation. Whenever we dislike, we can find a thousand to justify our dislike. Everything in the latter case is an impediment: every shadow a bugbear. Thus can I enumerate and swell, perhaps, only *imaginary* grievances: "I must go whither he would have me to go: visit whom he would have me to visit: well as I love to write (though now, alas! my grand inducement to write is over), it must be to whom he pleases": and *Mrs. Hickman* (who, as *Miss Howe*, cannot do wrong) would hardly ever be able to do right. Thus, the tables turned upon me, I am reminded of my vowed obedience; *madame'd up* perhaps to matrimonial perfection, and all the wedded warfare practised comfortably over between us (for I shall not be passive under insolent treatment), till we become curses to each other, a byword to our neighbours, and the jest of our own servants.

But there must be *bear* and *forbear*, methinks some wise body will tell me: but why must I be teased into a state where that *must* be necessarily the case; when now I can do as I please, and wish only to be let alone to do as best pleases me? And what, in effect, does my mother say? "Anna Howe, you now do everything that pleases you: you now have nobody to control you: you go and you come; you dress and you undress; you rise and you go to rest; just as you think best: but you must be happier still, child!"

As how, madam?

"Why, you must marry, my dear, and have none of these options; but, in everything, do as your husband commands you."

This is very hard, you will own, sir, for such a one as me to think of. And yet, engaged to enter into that state, as I am, how can I help myself? My mother presses me; my friend, my beloved friend, writing as from the dead, presses me; and you and Mr. Morden, as executors of her will, remind me; the man is not afraid of me [I am sure, were I the man, I should not have half his courage]; and I think I ought to conclude to punish him (the only effectual way I have to do it) for his perverse adherence and persecution, *with the grant of his own wishes*; a punishment which many others who enjoy theirs very commonly experience.

Let me then assure you, sir, that when I can find, in the words of my charming friend in her will, writing of her Cousin Hervey, that my grief for her is *mellowed by time into a remembrance more sweet than painful*, that I may not be utterly unworthy of the passion a man of some merit has for me, I will answer the request of my dear friend, so often repeated, and so earnestly pressed; and Mr. Hickman shall find, if he continue to deserve my gratitude, that my endeavours shall not be wanting to make him amends for the patience he has had, and must still a little while longer have with me: and then will it be his own fault (I hope not mine), if our marriage answer not those happy *prognostics*, *which filled her* generous *presaging mind*, upon this view, as she once, for *my* encouragement, and to induce me to encourage him, told me.

Thus, sir, have I, in a very free manner, accounted to you, as to the executor of my beloved friend, for all that relates to you, as such, to know; and even for more than I needed to do, against myself: only that you will find as much against me in some of *her* letters; and so, *losing* nothing, I *gain* the character of *ingenuity* with you.

And thus much for the double reprimand, on my delaying my part of the performance of my dear friend's will.

And now, while you are admonishing me on this subject, let me remind you of one great article relating to yourself: it is furnished me by my dear creature's posthumous letter to you—I hope you will not forget that the most benevolent of her sex expresses herself as earnestly concerned for your thorough reformation, as she does for my marrying. You'll see to it, then, that her wishes are as completely answered in that particular, as you are desirous they should be in all others.

I have, I own, disobeyed her in one article; and that is, where she desires that I will not put myself into mourning. I could not help it.

I send this and mine of Saturday last together: and will not add another word, after I have told you that I think myself

Your obliged servant,

A. HOWE.

Letter CLXIII—Mr. Belford to Miss Howe

Thursday Night, Oct. 5.

I RETURN you, madam, my most respectful thanks for your condescending hint, in relation to the pious wishes of your exalted friend for my thorough reformation.

I will only say that it shall be my earnest and unwearied endeavour to make those generous wishes effectual: and I hope for the Divine blessing upon such my endeavours, or else I know they will be in vain.

I cannot, madam, express how much I think myself obliged to you for your further condescension, in writing to me so frankly the state of your past and present mind, in relation to the single and matrimonial life. If the lady by whom, as the executor of her inimitable friend, I am thus honoured, *has* failings, never were failings so lovely in woman!—How much more lovely, indeed, than the virtues of many of her sex!

I might have ventured into the hands of such a lady the colonel's original letter entire. That worthy gentleman exceedingly admires you; and his caution was the effect of his politeness only, and of his regard for you.

I send you, madam, a letter from Lord M. to myself; and the copies of three others written in consequence of that. These will acquaint you with Mr. Lovelace's departure from England, and with other particulars which you will be curious to know.

Be pleased to keep to yourself such of the contents as your own prudence will suggest to you ought not to be seen by anybody else.

I am, madam, with the profoundest and most grateful respect,

Your faithful and obliged humble servant,

JOHN BELFORD.

Letter CLXIV—Lord M. to John Belford, Esq.

M. Hall, Friday, Sept. 29.

DEAR SIR,—My kinsman Lovelace is now setting out for London; proposing to see you, and then to go to Dover, and so embark. God send him well out of the kingdom!

On Monday he will be with you, I believe. Pray let me be favoured with an account of all your conversations; for Mr. Mowbray and Mr. Tourville are to be there too; and whether you think he is grown quite his own man again. What I mostly write for is to wish you to keep Colonel Morden and him asunder; and so I give you notice of his going to town. I should be very loath there should be any mischief between them, as you gave me notice that the colonel threatened my nephew. But my kinsman would not bear that; so nobody let him know that he did. But I hope there is no fear: for the colonel does not, as I hear, threaten now. For his own sake I am glad of that; for there is not such a man in the world as my kinsman is said to be at all the weapons—as well he was not; he would not be so daring.

We shall all here miss the wild fellow. To be sure, there is no man better company when he pleases.

Pray, do you never travel thirty or forty mile? I should be glad to see you here at M. Hall. It will be charity when my kinsman is gone; for we suppose you will be his chief correspondent: although he has promised to write to my nieces often. But he is very apt to forget his promises; to us his relations particularly. God preserve us all; Amen! prays

Your very humble servant,

M.

Letter CLXV—Mr. Belford to Lord M.

London, Tuesday Night, Oct. 3.

MY LORD,—I obey your lordship's commands with great pleasure.

Yesterday in the afternoon Mr. Lovelace made me a visit at my lodgings. As I was in expectation of one from Colonel Morden about the same time, I thought proper to carry him to a tavern which neither of us frequented (on pretence of a half-appointment); ordering notice to be sent me thither, if the colonel came: and Mr. Lovelace sent to Mowbray, and Tourville, and Mr. Doleman of Uxbridge (who came to town to take leave of him), to let them know where to find us.

Mr. Lovelace is *too well* recovered, I was going to say. I never saw him more gay, lively, and handsome. We had a good deal of bluster about some parts of the trust I have engaged in; and upon freedoms I had treated him with; in which he would have it that I had exceeded our agreed-on limits: but on the arrival of our three old companions, and a nephew of Mr. Doleman's (who had a good while been desirous to pass an hour with Mr. Lovelace), it blew off for the present.

Mr. Mowbray and Mr. Tourville had also taken some exceptions at the freedoms of my pen; and Mr. Lovelace, after his way, took upon him to reconcile us; and did it at the expense of all three; and with such an infinite run of humour and raillery, that we had nothing to do but to laugh at what he said, and at one another. I can deal tolerably with him at my pen; but in conversation he has no equal. In short, it was his day. He was glad, he said, to find himself alive; and his two friends, clapping and rubbing their hands twenty times in an hour, declared that now once more he was all himself; the charmingest fellow in the world; and they would follow him to the farthest part of the globe.

I threw a bur upon his coat now and then; but none would stick.

Your lordship knows that there are many things which occasion a roar of applause in conversation, when the heart is *open*, and men are *resolved* to be merry, which will neither bear repeating, nor thinking of afterwards. Common things, in the mouth of a man we admire, and whose wit has passed upon us for sterling, become, in a gay hour, *uncommon*. We watch every turn of such a one's countenance, and are resolved to laugh when he smiles, even before he utters what we are expecting to flow from his lips.

Mr. Doleman and his nephew took leave of us by twelve. Mowbray and Tourville grew very noisy by one; and were carried off by two. Wine never moves Mr. Lovelace, notwithstanding a vivacity which generally helps on over-gay spirits. As to myself, the little part I had taken in their gaiety kept me unconcerned.

The clock struck three before I could get him into any serious or attentive way—so natural to him is gaiety of heart; and such strong hold had the liveliness of the evening taken of him. His conversation, you know, my lord, when his heart is free, runs off to the bottom without any dregs.

But after that hour, and when we thought of parting, he

became a little more serious: and then he told me his designs, and gave me a plan of his intended tour; wishing heartily that I could have accompanied him.

We parted about four; he not a little dissatisfied with me; for we had some talk about subjects which, he said, he loved not to think of; to wit, Miss Harlowe's will; my executorship; papers I had in confidence communicated to that admirable lady (with no unfriendly design, I assure your lordship); and he insisting upon, and I refusing, the return of the letters he had written to me, from the time that he had made his first addresses to her.

He would see me once again, he said; and it would be upon very ill terms if I complied not with his request. Which I bid him not expect. But, that I might not deny him everything, I told him that I would give him a copy of the will; though I was sure, I said, when he read it, he would wish he had never seen it.

I had a message from him about eleven this morning, desiring me to name a place at which to dine with him, and Mowbray, and Tourville, for the last time: and soon after, another from Colonel Morden, inviting me to pass the evening with him at the Bedford Head in Covent Garden. And, that I might keep them at distance from one another, I appointed Mr. Lovelace at the Eagle in Suffolk Street.

There I met him, and the two others. We began where we left off at our last parting; and were very high with each other. But, at last, all was made up, and he offered to forget and forgive everything, on condition that I would correspond with him while abroad, and continue the series which had been broken through by his illness; and particularly give him, as I had offered, a copy of the lady's will.

I promised him: and he then fell to rallying me on my gravity, and on my reformation schemes, as he called them. As we walked about the room expecting dinner to be brought in, he laid his hand upon my shoulder; then pushed me from him with a curse; walking round me, and surveying me from head to foot; then calling for the observation of the others, he turned round upon his heel, and, with one of his peculiar wild airs, "Ha, ha, ha, ha, burst he out, that these sour-faced proselytes should take it into their heads that they cannot be pious without forfeiting both their good nature and good manners!—Why, Jack, turning me about, prithee look up, man! Dost thou not know that religion, if it has taken proper hold of the heart, is the most cheerful *countenance-maker* in the world? I have heard my beloved Miss Harlowe say so: and she knew, or nobody did.

And was not *her* aspect a benign proof of the observation? But by these wamblings in thy cursed gizzard, and thy awkward grimaces, I see thou 'rt but a novice in it yet!—Ah, Belford, Belford, thou hast a confounded parcel of briers and thorns to trample over barefoot, before religion will illumine these gloomy features!"

I give your lordship this account, in answer to your desire to know if I think him the man he was?

In our conversation at dinner, he was balancing whether he should set out the next morning, or the morning after. But finding he had nothing to do, and Colonel Morden being in town (which, however, I told him not of), I turned the scale; and he agreed upon setting out to-morrow morning; they to see him embark; and I promised to accompany them for a morning's ride (as they proposed their horses); but said that I must return in the afternoon.

With much reluctance they let me go to my evening's appointment: they little thought with whom: for Mr. Lovelace had put it as a case of honour to all of us, whether, as he had been told that Mr. Morden and Mr. James Harlowe had thrown out menaces against him, he ought to leave the kingdom till he had thrown himself in their way.

Mowbray gave his opinion that he ought to leave it like a man of honour, as he was; and if he did not take those gentlemen to task for their opprobrious speeches, that, at least, he should be seen by them in public before he went away; else they might give themselves airs, as if he had left the kingdom in fear of them.

To this he himself so much inclined, that it was with difficulty I persuaded him that, as they had neither of them proceeded to a *direct* and *formal challenge*; as they knew he had not made himself difficult of access; and as he had already done the family injury enough; and it was Miss Harlowe's earnest desire that he would be content with that; he had no reason, from any point of honour, to delay his journey; especially as he had so just a motive for his going as the establishment of his health; and as he might return the sooner, if he saw occasion for it.

I found the colonel in a very solemn way. We had a good deal of discourse upon the subject of certain letters which had passed between us in relation to Miss Harlowe's will, and to her family.

He has some accounts to settle with his banker; which, he says, will be adjusted to-morrow; and on Thursday he proposes to go down again, to take leave of his friends; and then intends to set out directly for Italy.

I wish Mr. Lovelace could have been prevailed upon to take any other tour than that of France and Italy. I did propose Madrid to him; but he laughed at me, and told me that the proposal was in character from a *mule*; and from one who was become as grave as a Spaniard of the *old cut*, at *ninety*.

I expressed to the colonel my apprehensions that his cousin's dying injunctions would not have the force upon him that were to be wished.

"They have *great force* upon me, Mr. Belford, said he; or *one world* would not have held Mr. Lovelace and me thus long. But my intention is to go to Florence; not to lay my bones there, as upon my cousin's death I told you I thought to do; but to settle all my affairs in those parts, and then to come over, and reside upon a little paternal estate in Kent, which is strangely gone to ruin in my absence. Indeed, were I to meet Mr. Lovelace, either here or abroad, I might not be answerable for the consequence."

He would have engaged me for to-morrow. But having promised to attend Mr. Lovelace on his journey, as I have mentioned, I said I was obliged to go out of town, and was uncertain as to the time of my return in the evening. And so I am to see him on Thursday morning at my own lodgings.

I will do myself the honour to write again to your lordship to-morrow night. Meantime, I am, my lord,

Your lordship's, etc.

Letter CLXVI—Mr. Belford to Lord M.

Wedn. Night, Oct. 4.

My Lord,—I am just returned from attending Mr. Lovelace as far as Gad's Hill, near Rochester. He was exceeding gay all the way. Mowbray and Tourville are gone on with him. They will see him embark, and under sail; and promise to follow him in a month or two; for they say there is no living without him, now he is once more himself.

He and I parted with great and even solemn tokens of affection; but yet not without gay intermixtures, as I will acquaint your lordship.

Taking me aside, and clasping his arms about me, "Adieu, dear Belford! said he. May you proceed in the course you have entered upon!—Whatever airs I give myself, this charming creature has fast hold of me *here* [clapping his hand upon his heart]; and I must either appear what you see me, or be what I so lately was. O the divine creature!" lifting up his eyes——

"But if I live to come to England, and you remain fixed in your present way, and can give me encouragement, I hope rather to follow your *example*, than to ridicule you for it. This will [for I had given him a copy of it] I will make the companion of my solitary hours. You have told me part of its melancholy contents; and that, and her posthumous letter, shall be my study; and they will prepare me for being your disciple, if you hold on.

"*You*, Jack, may marry, continued he; and I have a wife in my eye for you. Only thou 'rt such an awkward mortal" [he saw me affected, and thought to make me smile]: "but we don't make ourselves, except it be worse by our dress. Thou art in mourning now, as well as I: but if ever thy ridiculous turn lead thee again to be beau-brocade, I will *bedizen* thee, as the girls say, on my return, to my own fancy, and according to thy own *natural appearance*—thou shalt doctor my soul, and I will doctor thy body: thou shalt see what a clever fellow I will make of thee.

"As for *me*, I never *will*, I never *can*, marry. That I will not take a few liberties, and that I will not try to start some of my former game, I won't promise—habits are not easily shaken off—but they shall be by way of weaning. So *return* and *reform* shall go together.

"And now, thou sorrowful monkey, what aileth thee?" [I do love him, my lord.]

"Adieu!—and once more adieu!—embracing me. And when thou thinkest thou hast made thyself an interest *out yonder* (looking up), then put in a word for thy Lovelace."

Joining company, he recommended to me to write often; and promised to let me quickly hear from him; and that he would write to your lordship, and to all his family round; for he said that you had all been more kind to him than he had deserved.

And so we parted.

I hope, my lord, for all your noble family's sake, that we shall see him soon return, and reform, as he promises.

I return your lordship my humble thanks for the honour of your invitation to M. Hall. The first letter I receive from Mr. Lovelace shall give me the opportunity of embracing it. I am, my lord,

Your most faithful and obedient servant,

J. BELFORD.

Letter CLXVII—Mr. Belford to Lord M.

Thursday Morning, Oct. 5.

IT may be some satisfaction to your lordship to have a brief account of what has just now passed between Colonel Morden and me.

We had a good deal of discourse about the Harlowe family, and those parts of the lady's will which still remain unexecuted; after which the colonel addressed himself to me in a manner which gave me some surprise.

He flattered himself, he said, from my present happy turn, and from my good constitution, that I should live a great many years. It was, therefore, his request that I would consent to be *his* executor; since it was impossible for him to make a better choice, or pursue a better example than his cousin had set.

His heart, he said, was in it: there were some things in his cousin's will and *his* analogous; and he had named one person with me, with whom he was sure I would not refuse to be joined; and to whom he intended to apply for his consent, when he had obtained mine.[1] [Intimating, as far as I could gather, that it was Mr. Hickman, son of Sir Charles Hickman; to whom I know your lordship is not a stranger: for he said, every one who was dear to his beloved cousin must be so to him: and he knew that the gentleman whom he had thoughts of, would have, besides my advice and assistance, the advice of one of the most sensible ladies in England.]

He took my hand, seeing me under some surprise: You must not hesitate, much less deny me, Mr. Belford. Indeed you must not. Two things I will assure you of: that I have, as I hope, made everything so clear that you cannot have any litigation: and that I have done so justly, and I hope it will be thought so generously, by all my relations, that a mind like yours will rather have pleasure than pain in the execution of this trust. And this is what I think every honest man, who hopes to find an honest man for his executor, should do.

I told him that I was greatly obliged to him for his good opinion of me: that it was so much every man's *duty* to be an honest man, that it could not be interpreted as vanity to say that I had no doubt to be found so. But if I accepted of this trust, it must be on condition——

---

[1] What is between crotchets, thus [ ], Mr. Belford omitted in the transcription of this letter to Miss Howe.

I could name no condition, he said, interrupting me, which he would refuse to comply with.

This condition, I told him, was, that as there was as great a probability of his being *my* survivor, as I *his*, he would permit me to name *him* for mine; and, in that case, a week should not pass before I made my will.

With all his heart, he said; and the readier, as he had no apprehensions of suddenly dying; for what he had done and requested was really the effect of the satisfaction he had taken in the part I had already acted as his cousin's executor; and in my ability, he was pleased to add: as well as in pursuance of his cousin's advice in the preamble to her will; to wit, "That this was a work which should be set about in full health, both of body and mind."

I told him that I was pleased to hear him say that he was not in any apprehension of suddenly dying; as this gave me assurance that he had laid aside all thoughts of acting contrary to the dying request of his beloved cousin.

Does it argue, said he, smiling, that if I were to pursue a vengeance so justifiable in my own opinion, it must be in apprehension of falling by Mr. Lovelace's hand? I will assure you that I have no fears of that sort. But I know this is an ungrateful subject to you. Mr. Lovelace is your friend; and I will allow that a *good* man may have a friendship for a *bad one,* so far as to wish him well, without countenancing him in his evil.

I will assure you, added he, that I have not yet made any resolutions either way. I have told you what force my cousin's repeated requests have with me. Hitherto they have withheld me——But let us quit this subject.

This, sir [giving me a sealed-up parcel], is my will. It is witnessed. I made no doubt of prevailing upon you to do me the requested favour. I have a duplicate to leave with the other gentleman; and an attested copy, which I shall deposit at my banker's. At my return, which will be in six or eight months at furthest, I will allow you to make an exchange of yours, if you will have it so. I have only now to take leave of my relations in the country. And so, God protect you, Mr. Belford! You will soon hear of me again.

He then very solemnly embraced me, as I did him: and we parted.

I heartily congratulate your lordship on the narrow escape each gentleman has had from the other: for I apprehend that they could not have met without fatal consequences.

Time, I hope, which subdues all things, will subdue their resentments. I am, my lord,

Your lordship's most faithful and obedient servant,

J. BELFORD.

Several other letters passed between Miss Howe and Mr. Belford, relating to the disposition of the papers and letters ; to the poor's fund ; and to other articles of the lady's will: wherein the method of proceeding in each case was adjusted. After which the papers were returned to Mr. Belford, that he might order the two directed copies of them to be taken.

In one of these letters Mr. Belford requests Miss Howe to give the character of the friend she so dearly loved : "a task, he imagines, that will be as agreeable to herself as worthy of her pen."

"I am more especially curious to know, *says he*, what was that particular disposition of her time, which I find mentioned in a letter which I have just dipped into, where her sister is enviously reproaching her on that score.[1] This information may perhaps enable me, *says he*, to account for what has often surprised me; how, at so tender an age, this admirable lady became mistress of such extraordinary and such various qualifications."

Letter CLXVIII—Miss Howe to John Belford, Esq.

Thursday, Oct. 12.

SIR,—I am incapable of doing justice to the character of my beloved friend; and that not only from want of talents, but from grief; which, I think, rather increases than diminishes by time; and which will not let me sit down to a task that requires so much thought, and a greater degree of accuracy than I ever believed myself mistress of.

And yet I so well approve of your motion, that I will throw into your hands a few materials, that may serve by way of supplement, as I may say, to those you will be able to collect from the papers themselves; from Col. Morden's letters to you, particularly that of Sept. 23[2]; and from the letters of the detestable wretch himself, who, I find, has done her justice, although to his own condemnation: all these together will enable *you*, who seem to be so great an admirer of her virtues, to perform the task; and, I think, better than any person I know. But I make it my request, that if you do anything in this way, you

[1] See vol. i, p. 213.   [2] See Letter clviii of this volume.

will let me see it. If I find it not to my mind, I will add or diminish, as justice shall require.

She was a wonderful creature from her *infancy*: but I suppose you intend to give a character of her at those years when she was qualified to be an example to other young ladies, rather than a history of her life.

Perhaps, nevertheless, you will choose to give a description of her person: and, as you knew not the dear creature when her heart was easy, I will tell you what yet, in part, you can confirm:

That her shape was so fine, her proportion so exact, her features so regular, her complexion so lovely, and her whole person and manner so distinguishedly charming, that she could not move without being admired and followed by the eyes of every one, though strangers, who never saw her before. Colonel Morden's letter, above referred to, will confirm this.

In her dress she was elegant beyond imitation; and generally led the fashion to all the ladies round her, without seeming to intend it, and without being proud of doing so.[1]

She was rather tall than of a middling stature; and had a dignity in her aspect and air, that bespoke the mind that animated every feature.

This *native* dignity, as I may call it, induced some superficial persons, who knew not how to account for the reverence which involuntarily filled their hearts on her appearance, to impute pride to her. But these were such as knew that they should have been proud of any *one* of her perfections: judging, therefore, by their own narrowness, they thought it impossible that the lady who possessed *so many*, should not think herself superior to them all.

Indeed, I have heard her noble aspect found fault with, as indicating pride and superiority. But people awed and controlled, though but by their own consciousness of inferiority, will find fault, right or wrong, with those of whose rectitude of mind and manners their own culpable hearts give them to be afraid. But, in the bad sense of the word, Miss Clarissa Harlowe knew not what pride was.

You may, if you touch upon this subject, throw in these sentences of hers, spoken at different times, and on different occasions:

"Persons of accidental or shadowy merit may be proud: but inborn worth must be always as much above conceit as annoyance.

[1] See p. 97 of this volume.

"Who can be better, or more worthy, than they should be? And, who shall be proud of talents they give not to themselves?

"The darkest and most contemptible ignorance is that of not knowing oneself; and that all we have, and all we excel in, is the gift of God.

"All human excellence is but comparative—there are persons who excel us as much as we fancy we excel the meanest.

"In the general scale of beings, the lowest is as useful, and as much a link of the great chain, as the highest.

"The grace that makes every other grace amiable is HUMILITY.

"There is but one pride pardonable; that of being above doing a base or dishonourable action."

Such were the sentiments by which this admirable young lady endeavoured to conduct herself, and to regulate her conduct to others.

And, in truth, never were affability and complacency (*graciousness*, some have called it) more eminent in any person, man or woman, than in her, to those who put it in her power to oblige them: insomuch that the benefited has sometimes not known *which* to prefer—the grace bestowed, or the manner in which it was conferred.

It has been observed, that what was said of Henry IV of France might be said of her manner of refusing a request: that she generally sent from her presence the person refused nearly as well satisfied as if she had granted it.

Then she had such a sacred regard to truth. You cannot, sir, expatiate too much upon this topic. I dare say that in all her letters, in all the letters of the wretch, her veracity will not once be found impeachable, although her calamities were so heavy, the horrid man's wiles so subtle, and her struggles to free herself from them so active.

Her charity was so great, that she always chose to defend or acquit where the fault was not so flagrant that it became a piece of justice to condemn it: and was always an advocate for an absent person, whose discretion was called in question, without having given *manifest* proofs of indiscretion.

Once I remember, in a large circle of ladies, every one of which [I among the rest] having censured a generally reported indiscretion in a young lady—Come, my Miss Howe, said she [for we had agreed to take each other to task when either thought the other gave occasion for it; and when by blaming each other we intended a *general* reprehension, which, as she used to say, it would appear arrogant or assuming to level *more properly*], let

me be Miss Fanny Darlington.　Then removing out of the circle,
and standing up, Here I stand, unworthy of a seat with the rest
of the company till I have cleared myself.　And now, suppose
me to be her, let *me* hear your charge, and do *you* hear what the
poor culprit can say to it in her own defence.　And then answering the *conjectural* and *unproved* circumstances, by circumstances
as *fairly* to be supposed *favourable*, she brought off triumphantly
the censured lady; and so much to every one's satisfaction that
she was led to her chair, and voted a double rank in the circle—
as the reinstated Miss Fanny Darlington, and as Miss Clarissa
Harlowe.

"Very few persons, she used to say, would be condemned, or
even accused, in the circles of ladies, were they present: it is
generous, therefore, nay, it is but just, said she, to take the part
of the absent, if not flagrantly culpable."

But though *wisdom* was her *birthright*, as I may say, yet she
had not lived years enow to pretend to so much *experience* as to
exempt her from the necessity of sometimes altering her opinion
both of persons and things: but, when she found herself obliged
to do this, she took care that the particular instance of mistaken
worthiness in the person should not narrow or contract her
almost universal charity into general doubt or jealousy.　An
instance of what I mean occurs to my memory.

Being upbraided, by a severe censurer, with a person's proving
base whom she had frequently defended, and by whose baseness
my beloved friend was a sufferer: "You, madam, said she, had
more penetration than such a young creature as I can pretend
to have.　But although human depravity may, I doubt, oftener
justify those who judge harshly, than human rectitude can those
who judge favourably, yet will I not part with my charity.
Nevertheless, for the future, I will endeavour, in cases where the
judgment of my elders is against me, to make mine consistent
with caution and prudence."

Indeed, when she was convinced of *any* error or mistake (however seemingly derogatory to her judgment and sagacity), no one
was ever so acknowledging, so ingenuous, as she.　"It was a
merit, she used to say, next in degree to that of having avoided
error, frankly to own an error.　And that the offering at an
excuse in a blamable matter was the undoubted mark of a
disingenuous, if not of a perverse mind."

But I ought to add, on this head [of her great charity where
character was concerned, and where there was *room* for charity],
that she was always deservedly severe in her reprehensions of a

wilful and *studied* vileness. How could she then forgive the wretch by whose *premeditated* villainy she was entangled?

You must everywhere insist upon it, that had it not been for the stupid persecutions of her relations, she never would have been in the power of that horrid Lovelace. And yet, on several occasions, she acknowledged frankly, that were *person*, and *address*, and *alliance*, to be *allowably* the principal attractives in the choice of a lover, it would not have been difficult for her eye to mislead her heart.

When she was last with me (three happy weeks together!), in every visit the wretch made her, he left her more dissatisfied with him than in the former. And yet his behaviour before her was too specious to have been very exceptionable to a woman who had a less share of that charming delicacy, and of that penetration, which so much distinguished her.

In obedience to the commands of her gloomy father, on his allowing her to be my guest, for *that* last time [as it most unhappily proved!], she never would see him out of my company; and would often say, when he was gone, "O my Nancy! this is not THE man." At other times, "Gay, giddy creature, he has always something to be forgiven for!" At others, "This man will much sooner excite one's fears than attract one's love." And then would she repeat, "This is not THE man. All that the world says of him cannot be untrue. But what title have I to call him to account, who intend not to have him?"

In short, had she been left to a judgment and discretion, which nobody ever questioned who had *either*, she would soon have discovered enough of him to cause her to discard him for ever.

She was an admirable mistress of all the graces of elocution. The hand she wrote, for the neat and free cut of her letters (like her mind, solid, and above all *flourish*), for its fairness, evenness, and swiftness, distinguished her as much as the correctness of her orthography, and even punctuation, from the generality of her own sex, and left her none, among the most accurate of the other, who excelled her.

And here you may, if you please, take occasion to throw in one hint for the benefit of such of our sex as are too careless in their orthography [a consciousness of a defect in which generally keeps them from writing]. She was used to say, "It was a proof that a woman understood the derivation as well as sense of the words she used, and that she stopped not at *sound*, when she spelt accurately."

On this head you may take notice, that it was always matter

of surprise to her that the sex are generally so averse as they are to writing; since the pen, next to the needle, of all employments, is the most proper, and best adapted to their geniuses; and this as well for improvement as amusement: "Who sees not, would she say, that those women who take delight in writing, excel the men in all the graces of the familiar style? The gentleness of their minds, the delicacy of their sentiments (improved by the manner of their education), and the liveliness of their imaginations, qualify them to a high degree of preference for this employment: while men of learning, as they are called (that is to say, of *mere* learning), aiming to get above that natural ease and freedom which distinguish this (and indeed every other) kind of writing, when they think they have best succeeded, are got above, or rather *beneath*, all natural beauty."

Then, stiffened and starched [let *me* add] into dry and indelectable affectation, *one sort* of these scholars assume a style as rough as frequently are their manners: they spangle over their productions with *metaphors*: they rumble into *bombast*: the *sublime*, with them, lying in *words* and not in *sentiment*, they fancy themselves most exalted when least understood; and down they sit, fully satisfied with their own performances, and call them MASCULINE. While a *second* sort, aiming at *wit*, that wicked misleader, forfeit all title to *judgment*. And a *third*, sinking into the *classical pits*, there poke and scramble about, never seeking to show genius of their own; all their lives spent in commonplace *quotation*; fit only to write *notes* and *comments* upon other people's *texts*; all their pride, that they know those beauties of two thousand years old in *another* tongue, which they can only *admire*, but not *imitate*, in their own.

And these, truly, must be learned men, and despisers of our *insipid* sex!

But I need not mention the exceptions which my beloved friend always made [and to which I subscribe] in favour of men of sound learning, true taste, and extensive abilities: nor, in particular, her respect even to reverence for gentlemen of the cloth; which, I dare say, will appear in every paragraph of her letters wherever any of the clergy are mentioned. Indeed the pious Dr. Lewen, the worthy Dr. Blome, the ingenious Mr. Arnold, and Mr. Tompkins, gentlemen whom she names, in one article of her will, as learned divines with whom she held an *early* correspondence, well deserved her respect; since to their conversation and correspondence she owed many of her valuable acquirements.

Nor were the little slights she would now and then (following, as I must own, my lead) put upon such *mere* scholars [and her stupid and pedantic brother was one of those who deserved those slights] as despised not only *our sex*, but all such as had not had their opportunities of being acquainted with the *parts of speech* [I cannot speak low enough of such] and with the dead languages, owing to that contempt which some affect for what they have not been able to master; for she had an admirable facility in learning languages, and read with great ease both Italian and French. She had begun to apply herself to Latin; and having such a critical knowledge of her own tongue, and such a foundation from the two others, would soon have made herself an adept in it.

But, notwithstanding all her acquirements, she was an excellent ECONOMIST and HOUSEWIFE. And these qualifications, you must take notice, she was particularly fond of inculcating upon all her reading and writing companions of the sex: for it was a maxim with her, "That a woman who neglects the *useful* and the *elegant*, which distinguish *her own sex*, for the sake of obtaining the learning which is supposed more peculiar to the *other*, incurs more *contempt* by what she *foregoes*, than she gains *credit* by what she *acquires*."

"All that a woman *can* learn, she used to say [expatiating on this maxim], above the useful knowledge proper to her sex, *let her learn*. This will show that she is a good housewife of her time; and that she has not a narrow or confined genius. But then let her not give up for these, those *more necessary*, and therefore not *meaner*, employments which will qualify her to be a *good mistress* of a family, a *good wife*, and a *good mother*: for what can be more disgraceful to a woman, than either, through negligence of *dress*, to be found to be a *learned slattern*; or, through ignorance of *household management*, to be known to be a stranger to domestic economy?"

Then would she instance to me two particular ladies; one of which, while she was fond of giving *her* opinion, in the company of her husband, and of his learned friends, upon doubtful or difficult passages in Virgil or Horace, knew not how to put on her clothes with that necessary grace and propriety which should preserve to her the love of her husband, and the respect of every other person: while the other, affecting to be thought as learned as men, could find no better way to assert her pretensions than by despising her own sex, and by dismissing that characteristic delicacy, the loss of which no attainment can supply.

She would have it indeed, sometimes, from the frequent ill use learned women make of that respectable acquirement, that it was no great matter whether the sex aimed at anything but excelling in the knowledge of the beauties and graces of their mother-tongue: and once she said that this was field enough for a woman; and an ampler was but endangering her family usefulness. But I, who think our sex inferior in nothing to the other but in want of opportunities, of which the narrow-minded mortals industriously seek to deprive us, lest we should surpass them as much in what they chiefly value themselves upon, as we do in all the graces of a fine imagination, could never agree with her in *that*. And yet I was entirely of her opinion that those women who were solicitous to obtain that knowledge or learning which they supposed would add to their significance in sensible company, and in their attainment of it imagined themselves above all domestic usefulness, deservedly incurred the contempt which they hardly ever failed to meet with.

Perhaps you will not think it amiss further to observe on this head, as it will show that *precept* and *example* always went hand in hand with her, that her dairy at her grandfather's was the delight of every one who saw it; and she of all who saw her in it.

Her grandfather, in honour of her dexterity, and of her skill in all the parts of the dairy management, as well as of the elegance of the offices allotted for that use, would have his seat, before known by the name of *The Grove*, to be called *The Dairy-house*.[1] She had an easy, convenient, and graceful habit made on purpose, which she put on when she employed herself in these works; and it was noted of her, that in *the same hour* that she appeared to be a most elegant dairymaid, she was, when called to a change of dress, the finest lady that ever graced a circle.

Her grandfather, father, mother, uncles, aunt, and even her brother and sister, made her frequent visits there, and were delighted with her silent ease and unaffected behaviour in her works; for she always out of modesty chose rather the *operative* than the *directive* part, that she might not discourage the servant whose proper business it was.

Each was fond of taking a regale from her hands in her *Dairy-house*. Her mother and Aunt Hervey generally admired her in silence, that they might not give uneasiness to her sister; a spiteful, perverse, unimitating thing, who usually looked upon her all the time with speechless envy. Now and then, however, the pouting creature would suffer extorted and sparing praise to

[1] See vol. i, p. 4.

burst open her lips; though looking at the same time like Saul meditating the pointed javelin at the heart of David, the glory of his kingdom. And now, methinks, I see my angel-friend (too superior to take notice of her gloom) courting her acceptance of the milk-white curd from hands more pure than that.

Her skill and dexterity in every branch of family management, seem to be the only excellence of her innumerable ones which she owed to her family: whose narrowness, immensely rich, and immensely carking, put them upon indulging her in the turn she took to this part of knowledge; while her elder sister affected dress without being graceful in it; and the fine lady, which she could never be; and which her sister was without studying for it, or seeming to know she was so.

It was usual with the one sister, when company was expected, to be half the morning dressing; while the other would give directions for the whole business and entertainment of the day; and then go up to her dressing-room, and, before she could well be missed [*having all her things in admirable order*], come down fit to receive company, and with all that graceful ease and tranquillity as if she had nothing else to think of.

Long after *her* [hours perhaps of previous preparation having passed], down would come rustling and bustling the tawdry and awkward Bella, disordering more her native disorderliness at the sight of her serene sister, by her sullen envy, to see herself so much surpassed with such little pains, and in a sixth part of the time.

Yet was this admirable creature mistress of all these domestic qualifications without the least intermixture of narrowness. She knew how to distinguish between *frugality*, a necessary virtue, and *niggardliness*, an odious vice: and used to say, "That to define generosity, it must be called the happy medium betwixt parsimony and profusion."

She was the most graceful *reader* I ever knew. She added, by her melodious voice, graces to those she found in the parts of books she read out to her friends; and gave grace and significance to others where they were not. She had no tone, no whine. Her accent was always admirably placed. The emphasis she always forcibly laid as the subject required. No buskin elevation, no tragedy-pomp, could mislead her; and yet poetry was poetry *indeed* when she read it.

But if her voice was melodious when she *read*, it was all harmony when she *sang*. And the delight she gave by that, and by her skill and great compass, was heightened by the ease and gracefulness of her air and manner, and by the alacrity with which she obliged.

Nevertheless, she generally chose rather to hear others sing or play, than either to play or sing herself.

She delighted to give praise where deserved: yet she always bestowed it in such a manner as gave not the least suspicion that she laid out for a return of it to herself, though so universally allowed to be her due.

She had a talent of saying uncommon things in such an easy manner that everybody thought they could have said the same; and which yet required both genius and observation to say them.

Even severe things appeared gentle, though they lost not their force, from the sweetness of her air and utterance, and the apparent benevolence of her purpose.

We form the truest judgment of persons by their behaviour on the *most familiar* occasions. I will give an instance or two of the correction she favoured me with on such a one.

When *very young*, I was guilty of the fault of those who want to be courted to sing. She cured me of it, at the first of our happy intimacy, by her own *example*; and by the following correctives, occasionally, yet privately enforced:

"Well, my dear, shall we take you at your word? Shall we suppose that you sing but indifferently? Is not, however, the *act of obliging* (the company so worthy!) preferable to the *talent of singing*? And shall not young ladies endeavour to make up for their defects in *one part* of education, by their excellence in *another*?"

Again, "You must convince us, by attempting to sing, that you *cannot* sing; and then we will rid you, not only of *present*, but of *future* importunity." An indulgence, however, let me add, that but *tolerable* singers do not always wish to meet with.

Again, "I know you will favour us by and by; and what do you by your excuses but raise our expectations, and enhance your own difficulties?"

At another time, "Has not this accomplishment been a part of your *education*, my Nancy? How then, for *your own* honour, can we allow of your excuses?"

And I once pleading a cold, the usual pretence of those who love to be entreated: "Sing, however, my dear, *as well as you can*. The greater the difficulty to you, the higher the compliment to the company. Do you think you are among those who know not how to make allowances? You *should* sing, my love, lest there should be anybody present who may think your excuses owing to affectation."

At another time, when I had *truly* observed that a young lady present sang better than I; and that, therefore, I chose not to sing before that lady—"Fie! said she (drawing me on one side), is not this pride, my Nancy? Does it not look as if your principal motive to oblige was to obtain applause? A generous mind will not scruple to give advantage to a *person of merit,* though not always to *her own* advantage. And yet she will have a high merit *in doing that.* Supposing this excelling person absent, who, my dear, if your example spread, shall sing after *you?* You know every one *else* must be but as a foil to you. Indeed I must have you as much superior to other ladies in these *smaller* points as you are in *greater*." So she was pleased to say to shame me.

She was as much above reserve as disguise. So communicative, that no young lady could be in her company half an hour and not carry away instruction with her, whatever was the topic. Yet all sweetly insinuated; nothing given with the air of prescription: so that while she seemed to ask a question for information sake, she dropped in the needful instruction, and left the instructed unable to decide whether the thought (which being started, she, the instructed, could improve) came primarily from herself, or from the sweet instructress.

She had a pretty hand at drawing, which she obtained with a very little instruction. Her time was too much taken up to allow, though to so fine an art, the attention which was necessary to make her greatly excel in it: and she used to say, "That she was afraid of aiming at *too many things,* for fear she should not be tolerable at *anything.*"

For her years, and her opportunities, she was an extraordinary judge of painting. In this, as in everything else, *nature* was her *art,* her *art* was *nature.* She even prettily performed in it. Her grandfather, for this reason, bequeathed to her all the family pictures. Charming was her fancy: alike sweet and easy was every touch of her pencil and her pen. Yet her judgment exceeded her performance. She did not practise enough to excel in the executive part. She could not in everything excel. But, upon the whole, she knew what every subject required, according to the nature of it: in other words, was an absolute mistress of the *should-be.*

To give a familiar instance for the sake of young ladies; she (untaught) observed, *when but a child,* that the sun, moon, and stars never appeared at once; and were, therefore, never to be in one piece: that bears, tigers, lions, were not natives of an English climate, and should not, therefore, have place in an English landscape: that these ravagers of the forest consorted not with lambs, kids, or fawns; nor kites, hawks, and vultures with doves, partridges, and pheasants.

And, alas! she knew, before she was nineteen years of age, by fatal experience she knew! that all these beasts and birds of prey were outdone in treacherous cruelty by MAN! Vile, barbarous, plotting, destructive man! who, infinitely less excusable than those, destroys through wantonness and sport what those only destroy through hunger and necessity!

The mere pretenders to those branches of science which she aimed at acquiring, she knew how to detect; and all from nature. *Propriety*, another word for nature, was (as I have hinted) her law, as it is the foundation of all true judgment. But, nevertheless, she was always uneasy, if what she said exposed those pretenders to knowledge, even in their *absence*, to the ridicule of lively spirits.

Let the *modern* ladies, who have not any one of her excellent qualities; whose whole time, in the short days they generally make, and in the inverted night and day, where they make them longer, is wholly spent in dress, visits, cards, plays, operas, and musical entertainments; wonder at what I have written, and shall further write: and let them look upon it as an incredible thing, that when, at a maturer age, they cannot boast one of her perfections, there should have been a lady so young who had so many.

These must be such as know not how she employed her time; and cannot form the least idea of what may be done in those hours in which they lie *enveloped with the shades of death*, as she used to call sleep.

But before I come to mention the distribution she usually made of her time, let me say a few words upon another subject, in which she excelled all the young ladies I ever knew.

This was her skill in almost all sorts of fine needleworks: of which, however, I shall say the less, since possibly you will find it mentioned in some of the letters.

That piece which she bequeaths to her Cousin Morden is indeed a capital piece; a performance so admirable that that gentleman's father, who resided chiefly abroad, was (as is mentioned in her will) very desirous to obtain it, in order to carry it to Italy with him, to show the curious of *other* countries (as he used to say), for the honour of *his own*, that the cloistered confinement was not necessary to make English women excel in any of those fine arts upon which nuns and recluses value themselves.

Her quickness at these sort of works was astonishing; and a great encouragement to herself to prosecute them.

Mr. Morden's father would have been continually making her presents, would she have permitted him to do so: and he used to call them, and so did her grandfather, tributes due to a merit so sovereign, and not presents.

As to her diversions, the accomplishments and acquirements she was mistress of will show what they must have been. She was far from being fond of *cards*, the fashionable foible of modern ladies: nor, as will be easily perceived from what I have said, and more from what I shall further say, had she much time for play. She never, therefore, promoted their being called for; and often insensibly diverted the company from them, by starting some entertaining subject, when she could do it without incurring the imputation of particularity.

Indeed very few of her intimates would propose cards, if they could engage her to read, to talk, to touch the keys, or to sing, when any new book or new piece of music came down. But when company was so numerous that conversation could not take that agreeable turn which it oftenest does among four or five friends of like years and inclinations, and it became in a manner necessary to detach off some of it, to make the rest better company, she would not refuse to play, if, upon casting-in, it fell to her lot. And then she showed that her disrelish to cards was the effect of choice only; and that she was an easy mistress of every genteel game played with them. But then she always declared against playing high. "Except for trifles, she used to say, she would not submit to *chance* what she was already sure of."

At other times, "She should make her friends a very ill compliment, she said, if she supposed they would wish to be possessed of what of right belonged to her; and she should be very unworthy, if she desired to make herself a title to what was theirs.

"High gaming, in short, she used to say, was a sordid vice; an immorality; the child of avarice; and a direct breach of that commandment which forbids us to covet what is our neighbour's."

She was exceedingly charitable; the only one of her family that knew the meaning of the word: and this with regard both to the souls and the bodies of those who were the well-chosen objects of her benevolence. She kept a list of these, whom she used to call *her Poor*, entering one upon it, as another was provided for, by death, or any other way: but always made a reserve, nevertheless, for unforeseen cases, and for accidental distresses. And it must be owned that in the prudent distribution of them she had neither example nor equal.

The aged, the blind, the lame, the widow, the orphan, the unsuccessful industrious, were particularly the objects of it; and the contributing to the schooling of some, to the putting out to trades and husbandry the children of others of the labouring or needy poor, and setting them forward at the expiration of their servitude, were her great delights; as was the giving good books to others, and, when she had opportunity, the instructing the poorer sort of her honest neighbours, and father's tenants, in the use of them. "That charity, she used to say, which provides for the *morals*, as well as for the *bodily wants* of the poor, gives a double benefit to the *public*, as it adds to the number of the *hopeful* what it takes from that of the *profligate*. And can there be, in the eyes of that God, she was wont to say, who requires nothing so much from us as acts of beneficence to one another, a charity more worthy?"

Her Uncle Antony, when he came to settle in England with his vast fortune obtained in the Indies, used to say, "This girl by her charities will bring down a blessing upon us all." And it must be owned they trusted pretty much to this presumption.

But I need not say more on this head; nor perhaps was it necessary to say so much; since the charitable bequests in her will sufficiently set forth her excellence in this branch of duty.

She was extremely moderate in her diet. "*Quantity* in food," she used to say, "was more to be regarded than *quality*: that a full meal was the great enemy both to study and industry: that a well-built house required but little repairs."

By this moderation in her diet she enjoyed, with a delicate frame of body, a fine state of health; was always serene, lively; cheerful, of course. And I never knew but of one illness she had; and that was by a violent cold caught in an open chaise, by a sudden storm of hail and rain, in a place where was no shelter; and which threw her into a fever, attended with dangerous symptoms, that no doubt were lightened by her temperance; but which gave her friends, who *then* knew her value, infinite apprehensions for her.[1]

---

[1] In her commonplace-book she has the following note upon the recollection of this illness in the time of her distress :

"In a dangerous illness with which I was visited a few years before I

In all her readings, and in her conversations upon them, she was fonder of finding beauties than blemishes, and chose to applaud both authors and books, where she could find the least room for it. Yet she used to lament that certain writers of the first class, who were capable of exalting virtue, and of putting vice out of countenance, too generally employed themselves in works of *imagination only*, upon subjects *merely speculative, disinteresting,* and *unedifying*; from which no useful moral or example could be drawn.

But she was a severe censurer of pieces of a *light* or *indecent* turn, which had a tendency to corrupt the morals of youth, to convey polluted images, or to wound religion, whether in itself, or through the sides of its professors, and this, whoever were the authors, and how admirable soever the execution. She often pitied the celebrated Dr. Swift for so employing his admirable pen that a pure eye was afraid of looking into his works, and a pure ear of hearing anything quoted from them. "Such authors, she used to say, were not *honest* to their own talents, nor grateful to the God who gave them." Nor would she, on these occasions, admit their beauties as a palliation; on the contrary, she held it an aggravation of their crime, that they, who were so capable of *mending the heart*, should in any places show a *corrupt one* in themselves; which must weaken the influences of their good works; and pull down with one hand what they built up with the other.

All she said, and all she did, was accompanied with a natural ease and dignity, which set her above affectation, or the suspicion of it; insomuch that that degrading fault, so generally imputed to a learned woman, was never laid to her charge. For, with all her excellences, she was forwarder to *hear* than *speak*; and hence no doubt derived no small part of her improvement.

Although she was well read in the English, French, and Italian poets, and had read the best translations of the Latin classics; yet seldom did she quote or repeat from them, either in her letters or

---

had the unhappiness to know this ungrateful man! [would to Heaven I had died in it!], my bed was surrounded by my dear relations—father, mother, brother, sister, and my two uncles, weeping, kneeling round me, then put up their vows to Heaven for my recovery, and I, fearing that I should drag down with me to my grave, one or other of my sorrowing friends, wished and prayed to recover for *their* sakes.—Alas! how shall parents in such cases know what to wish for! How happy for them, and for me, had I then been denied to their prayers! But now am I eased of that care. All those dear relations are living still—but not one of them (such, as they think, has been the heinousness of my error!) but, far from being grieved, would rejoice to hear of my death."

conversation, though exceedingly happy in a tenacious memory; principally through modesty, and to avoid the imputation of that *affectation* which I have just mentioned.

Mr. Wyerley once said of her, she had such a fund of knowledge of her own, and made naturally such fine observations upon persons and things, being capable, *by the* EGG [that was his familiar expression], *of judging of the* BIRD, that she had seldom either room or necessity for foreign assistances.

But it was plain, from her whole conduct and behaviour, that she had not so good an opinion of herself, however deserved; since, whenever she was urged to give her sentiments on any subject, although all she thought fit to say was clear and intelligible, yet she seemed in haste to have done speaking. Her reason for it, I know, was twofold; that she might not lose the benefit of other people's sentiments, by engrossing the conversation; and lest, as were her words, she should be praised into *loquaciousness*, and so forfeit the good opinion which a person always maintains with her friends, who knows when she has said enough. It was, finally, a rule with her, "to leave her hearers wishing her to say more, rather than to give them cause to show, by their *inattention*, an uneasiness that she had said so much."

You are curious to know the particular distribution of her time; which you suppose will help you to account for what you own yourself surprised at; to wit, how so young a lady could make herself mistress of so many accomplishments.

I will premise that she was from infancy inured to rise early in a morning, by an excellent, and, as I may say, a *learned* woman, Mrs. Norton, to whose care, wisdom, and example she was beholden for the groundwork of her taste and acquirements, which meeting with such assistances from the divines I have named, and with such a genius, made it the less wonder that she surpassed most of her age and sex.

Her sex, did I say? What honour to the *other* does this imply! when one might challenge the proudest pedant of them all, to say he has been *disciplined* into greater improvement than she had made from the mere force of genius and application. But it is demonstrable to all who know how to make observations on their acquaintance of both sexes, arrogant as some are of their superficialities, that a lady at eighteen, take the world through, is more prudent and conversable than a man at twenty-five. I can prove this by nineteen instances out of twenty in my own knowledge. Yet how do these poor boasters value themselves upon the advantages their education gives them! Who has not

seen some one of them, just come from the university, disdainfully smile at a mistaken or ill-pronounced *word* from a lady,
when her *sense* has been clear, and her sentiments just; and when
he could not himself utter a single sentence fit to be repeated, but
what he borrowed from the authors he had been obliged to
study, as a painful exercise to slow and creeping parts? But
how I digress!

This excellent young lady used to say, "It was incredible to
think what might be done by *early rising*, and by *long days* well
filled up."

It may be added, that had she calculated according to the
practice of *too many*, she had actually lived more years at *sixteen*
than *they* had at *twenty-six*.

She was of opinion, "That no one could spend their time
properly who did not live by some rule: who did not appropriate
the hours, as near as might be, to particular purposes and
employments."

In conformity to this self-set lesson, the usual distribution of
the twenty-four hours, when left to her own choice, was as
follows:

For REST *she allotted* SIX *hours only.*

She thought herself not so well, and so clear in her intellects
[so *much alive*, she used to say], if she exceeded this proportion.
If she slept not, she chose to rise sooner. And in winter had her
fire laid, and a taper ready burning to light it; not loving to give
trouble to servants, "whose harder work, and later hours of
going to bed, she used to say, required consideration."

I have blamed her for her greater regard to them than to
herself: but this was her answer: "I have my choice: *who* can
wish for more? Why should I oppress others to gratify myself?
You see what *freewill* enables one to do; while *imposition* would
make a light burden heavy."

Her first THREE *morning hours*

were generally passed in her study, and in her closet duties:
and were occasionally augmented by those she saved from rest:
and in these passed her epistolary amusements.

Two *hours she generally allotted to domestic management.*

These at different times of the day, as occasions required; all
the housekeeper's bills, in ease of her mother, passing through

her hands. For she was a perfect mistress of the four principal rules of arithmetic.

FIVE *hours to her needle, drawings, music, etc.*

In these she included the assistance and inspection she gave to her own servants, and to her sister's servants, in the needle-work required for the family: for her sister, as I have above hinted, is a MODERN. In these she also included Dr. Lewen's conversation visits; with whom likewise she held a correspond-ence by letters. That reverend gentleman delighted himself and her twice or thrice a week, if his health permitted, with these visits: and she always preferred his company to any other engagement.

Two *hours she allotted to her two first meals.*

But if conversation, or the desire of friends, or the falling-in of company or guests, required it to be otherwise, she never scrupled to oblige; and would, on such occasions, *borrow*, as she called it, from other distributions. And as she found it very hard not to exceed in this appropriation, she put down

ONE *hour more to dinner-time conversation,*

to be added or subtracted, as occasions offered, or the desire of her friends required: and yet found it difficult, as she often said, to keep this account even; especially if Dr. Lewen obliged them with his company at their table: which, however, he seldom did; for, being a valetudinarian, and in a regimen, he generally made his visits in the afternoon.

ONE *hour to visits to the neighbouring poor ;*

to a select number of whom, and to their children, she used to give brief instructions, and good books: and as this happened not every day, and seldom above twice a week, she had two or three hours at a time to bestow in this benevolent employment.

The remaining FOUR *hours*

were occasionally allotted to supper, to conversation, or to reading after supper to the family. This allotment she called *her fund,* upon which she used to draw to satisfy her other debits: and in this she included visits received and returned, shows, spectacles, etc., which, in a *country life,* not occurring every day, she used to think a great allowance, no less than *two* days in *six*, for amusements only: and she was wont to say that it was hard if she could not steal time out of this fund for an excursion of even two or three days in a month.

If it be said that her relations, or the young neighbouring ladies, had but little of her time, it will be considered that besides these four hours in the twenty-four, great part of the time she was employed in her needleworks she used to converse as she worked: and it was a custom she had introduced among her acquaintance, that the young ladies in their visits used frequently, in a neighbourly way (in the winter evenings especially), to bring their work with them; and one of half a dozen of her select acquaintance used by turns to read to the rest as they were at work.

This was her usual method, when at her own command, for *six* days in the week.

The SEVENTH DAY

she kept as it ought to be kept: and as some part of it was frequently employed in works of mercy, the hour she allotted to visiting the neighbouring poor was occasionally supplied from this day, and added to her fund.

But I must observe, that when in her grandfather's lifetime she was three or four weeks at a time his housekeeper and guest, as also at either of her uncles, her usual distribution of time was varied: but still she had an eye to it as nearly as circumstances would admit.

When I had the happiness of having her for my guest, for a fortnight or so, she likewise dispensed with her rules in mere indulgence to my foibles, and idler habits; for I also (though I had the benefit of an example I so much admired) am too much of a *modern*.   Yet, as to *morning risings*, I had corrected myself by such a precedent, in the summer time; and can witness to the benefit I found by it in my health; as also to the many useful things I was enabled by that means with ease and pleasure to perform.   And in her account-book I have found this memorandum since her ever-to-be-lamented death: "From *such a day* to *such a day*, all holidays, at my dear Miss Howe's."   At her return: "Account resumed, *such a day*," naming it; and then she proceeded regularly, as before.

Once a week she used to reckon with herself; when, if within the 144 hours, contained in the six days, she had made her account even, she noted it accordingly: if otherwise, she carried the debit to the next week's account; as thus: *Debtor to the article of benevolent visits*, so many hours. And so of the rest.

But it was always an especial part of her care that, whether visiting or visited, she showed in all companies an entire ease, satisfaction, and cheerfulness, as if she kept no such particular account, and as if she did not make herself answerable to herself for her occasional exceedings.

This method, which to others will appear perplexing and unnecessary, her *early hours*, and *custom*, had made easy and pleasant to her.

And indeed, as I used to tell her, greatly as I admired her in all her methods, I could not bring myself to this, might I have had the world for my reward.

I had indeed too much impatience in my temper, to observe such a regularity in accounting between me and myself. I satisfied myself in a *lump account*, as I may call it, if I had nothing greatly wrong to reproach myself with, when I looked back on a past week, as she had taught me to do.

For she used indulgently to say, "I do not think ALL I do necessary for another to do: nor even for myself: but when it is more pleasant to me to keep such an account than to let it alone, why may I not proceed in my supererogatories? There can be no harm in it. It keeps up my attention to accounts; which one day may be of use to me in more material instances. Those who will not keep a *strict* account, seldom long keep *any*. I neglect not more useful employments for it. And it teaches me to be covetous of time; the only thing of which we can be *allowably* covetous; since we live but once in this world; and when gone, are gone from it for ever."

She always reconciled the necessity under which these *interventions*, as she called them, laid her, of now and then breaking into some of her appropriations; saying, "There was good sense, and good manners too, in the common lesson, *When at Rome, do as they do at Rome*: and that to be easy of persuasion, in matters where one could oblige without endangering virtue, or worthy habits, was an apostolical excellence; since, if a person conformed with a view of making herself an interest in her friend's affections, in order to be heeded in greater points, it was imitating his example, who *became all things to all men, that he might gain some*." Nor is it to be doubted, had life been spared her, that the sweetness of her temper, and her cheerful piety, would have made virtue and religion appear so lovely that her example would have had no small influence upon the minds and manners of those who would have had the honour of conversing with her.

O Mr. Belford! I can write no further on this subject. For, looking into the account-book for other particulars, I met with a most affecting memorandum; which, being written on the extreme edge of the paper, with a fine pen, and in the dear creature's smallest hand, I saw not before. This it is; written, I suppose, at some calamitous period *after* the day named in it. Help me to a curse to blast the monster who gave occasion for it!

APRIL 10. *The account concluded!—*
And with it all my worldly hopes and prospects ! ! !

.   .   .   .

I take up my pen; but not to apologize for my execration. Once more I pray to God to avenge me of him!—*Me* I say—for mine is the loss—hers the gain.

O sir! you *did* not, you *could* not know her as I knew her! Never was such an excellence!—So warm, yet so cool a friend!—So much what I wish to be, but never shall be!—For, alas! my stay, my adviser, my monitress, my directress, is gone! for ever gone!

She honoured me with the title of *the sister of her heart*: but I was only so in the love I bore her (a love beyond a sister's—infinitely beyond *her* sister's!); in the hatred I have to every mean and sordid action; and in my love of virtue; for, otherwise, I am of a high and haughty temper, as I have acknowledged heretofore, and very violent in my passions.

In short, she was the nearest perfection of any creature I ever knew. She never preached to me lessons which she practised not herself. She lived the life she taught. All humility, meekness, self-accusing, others-acquitting, though the *shadow* of the fault was hardly hers, the *substance* theirs whose only honour was their relation to her.

To lose such a friend, such a guide—if ever my violence was justifiable, it is upon this recollection! For she only lived to make me sensible of my failings, but not long enough to enable me to conquer them; as I was resolved to endeavour to do.

Once more then let me execrate—— But now violence and passion again predominate!—And how can it be otherwise?

But I force myself from the subject, having lost the purpose for which I resumed my pen.

A. HOWE.

Letter CLXIX—Mr. Lovelace to John Belford, Esq.

Paris, Octob. 14.

——Timor et minæ
Scandunt eodem quo dominus: neque
Decedit ærata triremi, et
Post equitem sedet atra cura.

IN a language so expressive as the English, I hate the pedantry of tagging or prefacing what I write with Latin scraps; and ever was a censurer of the motto-mongers among our weekly and daily scribblers. But these verses of Horace are so applicable to my case that, whether on shipboard, whether in my post-chaise, or in my inn at night, I am not able to put them out of my head. Dryden once, I thought, said well in these bouncing lines:

Man makes his Fate according to his mind.
The weak, low spirit Fortune makes her slave;
But she 's a drudge, when hector'd by the brave.
If Fate weave common thread, I 'll change the doom,
And with new purple weave a nobler loom.

And in these:

Let Fortune empty her whole quiver on me,
I have a soul, that, like an ample shield,
Can take in all, and verge enough for more.
Fate was not mine: nor am I Fate's——
Souls know no conquerors——

But in the first-quoted lines, considering them closely, there is nothing but blustering absurdity: in the other, the poet says not truth; for CONSCIENCE is the conqueror of souls: at least it is the conqueror of mine: and who ever thought it a narrow one?

But this is occasioned partly by poring over the affecting will, and posthumous letter. What an army of texts has she drawn up in array against me in the latter! But yet, Jack, do they not show me that, two or three thousand years ago, there were as wicked fellows as myself? They do—and that 's some consolation.

But the generosity of her mind displayed in both is what stings me most. And the more still, as it is now out of my power any way in the world to be even with her.

I ought to have written to you sooner. But I loitered two days at Calais, for an answer to a letter I wrote to engage my former travelling valet, De la Tour; an ingenious, ready fellow, as you have heard me say. I *have* engaged him, and he is now with me.

I shall make no stay here; but intend for some of the Electoral Courts. That of Bavaria, I think, will engage me longest. Perhaps I may step out of my way (if I can be out of my way anywhere) to those of Dresden and Berlin: and it is not impossible that you may have one letter from me at Vienna. And then perhaps I may fall down into Italy by the Tyrol; and so, taking Turin in my way, return to Paris; where I hope to see Mowbray and Tourville: nor do I despair of you.

This a good deal differs from the plan I gave you. But you may expect to hear from me as I move; and whether I shall pursue this route, or the other.

I have my former lodgings in the Rue St. Antoine: which I shall hold, notwithstanding my tour: so they will be ready to accommodate any two of you, if you come hither before my return: and for this I have conditioned.

I write to Charlotte; and that is writing to all my relations at once.

Do thou, Jack, inform me duly of everything that passes: particularly, how thou proceedest in thy reformation scheme: how Mowbray and Tourville go on in my absence: whether thou hast any chance for a wife [I am the more solicitous on this head, because thou seemest to think that thy mortification will not be complete, nor thy reformation secure, till thou art shackled]: how the Harlowes proceed in their penitentials: if Miss Howe be married, or near being so: how honest Doleman goes on with his empiric, now he has dismissed his regulars, or they him; and if any likelihood of his perfect recovery. Be sure be very minute: for every trifling occurrence relating to those we value becomes interesting when we are at a distance from them. Finally, prepare thou to piece thy broken thread, if thou wouldst oblige

Thy LOVELACE.

Letter CLXX—*Mr. Belford to Robert Lovelace, Esq.*

London, Oct. 25.

I WRITE to show you that I am incapable of slighting even the minutest requests of an absent and distant friend. Yet you may believe that there cannot be any great alterations in the little time that you have been out of England, with respect to the subjects of your inquiry. Nevertheless I will answer to each, for the reason above given; and for the reason you mention, that even trifles and chit-chat are agreeable from friend to friend, and of friends, and even of those to whom we give the importance of deeming them our *foes*.

First, then, as to my reformation scheme, as you call it, I hope I go on very well. I wish you had entered upon the like, and could say so too. You would then find infinitely more peace of mind than you are likely ever otherwise to be acquainted with. When I look back upon the sweep that has been made among us in the two or three past years, and forward upon what may still happen, I hardly think myself secure; though of late I have been guided by other lights than those of sense and appetite, which have hurried so many of our confraternity into worldly ruin, if not into eternal perdition.

I am very earnest in my wishes to be admitted into the nuptial state. But I think I ought to pass some time as a probationary, till, by steadiness in my good resolutions, I can convince some woman, whom I could love and honour, and whose worthy example might confirm my morals, that there is *one* libertine who had the grace to reform, before age or disease put it out of his power to sin on.

The Harlowes continue inconsolable; and I dare say will to the end of their lives.

Miss Howe is not yet married; but I have reason to think will soon. I have the honour of corresponding with her; and the more I know of her, the more I admire the nobleness of her mind. She must be conscious that she is superior to half *our* sex, and to most of *her own*; which may make her give way to a temper naturally hasty and impatient; but, if she meet with condescension in her man [and who would not veil to a superiority so visible, if it be not exacted with arrogance?], I dare say she will make an excellent wife.

As to Doleman, the poor man goes on trying and hoping with his empiric. I cannot but say that, as the latter is a sensible and judicious man, and not rash, opinionative, or over-sanguine, I have great hopes (little as I think of quacks and nostrum-mongers in general) that he will do him good, if his case will admit of it. My reasons are—That the man pays a *regular* and *constant* attendance upon him: watches, with his own eye, every change and new symptom of his patient's malady: varies his applications as the indications vary: fetters not himself to rules laid down by the fathers of the art, who lived many hundred years ago, when diseases, and the causes of them, were different, as the modes of living were different from what they are now, as well as climates and accidents: that he is to have his reward, not in daily fees, but (after the first five guineas for medicines) in proportion as the patient himself shall find amendment.

As to Mowbray and Tourville; what novelties can be expected, in so short a time, from men who have not sense enough to strike out or pursue new lights, either good or bad? Now, especially, that you are gone, who were the soul of all enterprise, and in particular *their* soul. Besides, I see them but seldom. I suppose they'll be at Paris before you can return from Germany; for they cannot live without you: and you gave them such a specimen of your recovered volatility, in the last evening's conversation, as equally delighted *them,* and concerned *me.*

I wish, with all my heart, that thou wouldst bend thy course towards the Pyrenean. I should then (if thou writest to thy Cousin Montague an account of what is most observable in thy tour) put in for a copy of thy letters. I wonder thou wilt not; since then thy subjects would be as new to thyself as to

Thy BELFORD.

Letter CLXXI—Mr. Lovelace to John Belford, Esq.

Paris, Oct. 16–27.

I FOLLOW my last of the $\frac{14}{25}$th, on occasion of a letter just now come to hand from Joseph Leman. The fellow is conscience-ridden, Jack; and tells me "that he cannot rest either day or night for the mischiefs which he fears he has been, and may still further be the means of doing." He wishes, "if it please God, and if it please *me,* that he had never seen my Honour's face."

And what is the cause of his present concern, as to his own particular? What but "the *slights* and *contempts* which he receives from every one of the Harlowes; from those particularly, he says, whom he has endeavoured to serve as faithfully as his engagements to *me* would let him serve them? And I always made him believe, he tells me (*poor weak soul as he was from his cradle!*), that serving me was serving both, *in the long run.* But this, and the death of his dear young lady, is a grief, he declares, that he shall never *claw off,* were he to live to the age of *Matthew-Salem*: althoff, and howsomever, he is sure that he shall not live *a month to an end*; being strangely pined, and his *stomach* nothing like what it was: and Mrs. Betty being also (now she *has got his love*) very *cross and slighting*: but, thank his God for punishing her! she is in a poor way *hersell.*

"But the chief occasion of troubling my Honour now, is not

his own griefs only, *althoff* they are very great; but to prevent future mischiefs to me: for he can assure me that Colonel Morden has set out from them all, with a full resolution to *have his will of me*: and he is well assured that he said, and swore to it, *as how* he was resolved that he would either have my Honour's heart's blood, or I should have his; or *some such-like sad threatenings*: and that all the family rejoice in it, and hope I shall *come short home.*"

This is the substance of Joseph's letter; and I have one from Mowbray, which has a hint to the same effect. And I recollect now that you was very importunate with me to go to Madrid, rather than to France and Italy, the last evening we passed together.

What I desire of you is, by the first dispatch, to let me faithfully know all that you know on this head.

I can't bear to be threatened, Jack. Nor shall any man, unquestioned, give himself airs in my absence, if I know it, that shall make me look mean in anybody's eyes: that shall give my friends *pain* for me: that shall put them upon wishing me to change my intentions, or my plan, to avoid him. Upon such despicable terms as these, think you that I could bear to live?

But why, if such were his purpose, did he not let me know it before I left England? Was he unable to work himself up to a resolution till he knew me to be out of the kingdom?

As soon as I can inform myself where to direct to him, I will write to know his purpose; for I cannot bear suspense in such a case as this: that solemn act, were it even to be marriage or hanging, which must be done to-morrow, I had rather should be done to-day. My mind tires and sickens with impatience on ruminating upon scenes that can afford neither variety nor certainty. To dwell twenty days in expectation of an event that may be decided in a quarter of an hour is grievous.

If he come to Paris, although I should be on my tour, he will very easily find out my *lodgings*: for I every day see someone or other of my countrymen, and divers of them have I entertained *here*. I go frequently to the opera and to the play, and appear at court, and at all public places. And, on my quitting this city, will leave a direction whither my letters from England, or elsewhere, shall from time to time be forwarded. Were I sure that his intention is what Joseph Leman tells me it is, I would stay here, or shorten his course to me, let him be where he would.

I cannot get off my regrets on account of this dear lady for the blood of me. If the colonel and I are to meet, as he has done me no injury, and loves the memory of his cousin, we shall engage with the same sentiments as to the object of our dispute: and that, you know, is no very common case.

In short, I am as much convinced that I have done wrong as he can be; and regret it as much. But I will not bear to be threatened by any man in the world, however conscious I may be of having deserved blame.

Adieu, Belford! be sincere with me. No palliation, as thou valuest

Thy LOVELACE.

Letter CLXXII—Mr. Belford to Robert Lovelace, Esq.

London, Oct. 26.

I CANNOT think, my dear Lovelace, that Colonel Morden has either threatened you in those gross terms mentioned by the vile, hypocritical, and ignorant Joseph Leman, or intends to follow you. They are the words of people of that fellow's class, and not of a gentleman: not of Colonel Morden, I am sure. You'll observe that Joseph pretends not to say that he heard him speak them.

I have been very solicitous to sound the colonel, for your sake, and for his own, and for the sake of the injunctions of the excellent lady to me, as well as to him, on that subject. He is (and you will not wonder that he should be) extremely affected; and owns that he has expressed himself in terms of resentment on the occasion. Once he said to me, that had his beloved cousin's case been that of a *common seduction*, her own credulity or weakness contributing to her fall, he could have forgiven you. But, in so many words, he assured me that he had not taken any resolutions; nor had he declared himself to the family in such a way as should bind him to resent; on the contrary, he has owned that his cousin's injunctions have hitherto had the force upon him which I could wish they should have.

He went abroad in a week after you. When he took his leave of me, he told me that his design was to go to Florence; and that he would settle his affairs there; and then return to England, and here pass the remainder of his days.

I was indeed apprehensive that if you and he were to meet, something unhappy might fall out: and as I knew that you proposed to take Italy, and very likely Florence, in your return to France, I was very solicitous to prevail upon you to take the Court of Spain into your plan. I am still so. And if you are not to be prevailed upon to do that, let me entreat you to avoid Florence or Leghorn in your return, since you have visited both heretofore. At least, let not the proposal of a meeting come from you.

It would be matter of serious reflection to me, if the *very fellow*, this *Joseph Leman*, who gave you such an opportunity to turn all the artillery of his masters against themselves, and to play them upon one another to favour your plotting purposes, should be the instrument in the devil's hand (unwittingly too) to avenge them all upon *you*: for should you even get the better of the colonel, would the mischief end there? It would but add remorse to your present remorse; since the interview *must* end in death; for he would not, I am confident, take his life at your hand. The Harlowes would, moreover, prosecute you in a legal way. You hate *them*; and *they* would be gainers by *his* death: rejoicers in *yours*—and have you not done mischief enough already?

Let *me*, therefore (and through me all your friends), have the satisfaction to hear that you are resolved to avoid this gentleman. Time will subdue all things. Nobody doubts your bravery. Nor will it be known that your plan is changed through persuasion.

Young Harlowe talks of calling you to account. This is a plain evidence that Mr. Morden has not taken the quarrel upon himself for their family.

I am in no apprehension of anybody but Colonel Morden. I know it will not be a means to prevail upon you to oblige me, if I say that I am well assured that this gentleman is a skilful swordsman; and that he is as cool and sedate as skilful. But yet I will add, that if I had a value for my life, he should be the last man, except yourself, with whom I would choose to have a contention.

I have, as you required, been very candid and sincere with you. I have not aimed at palliation. If you seek not Colonel Morden, it is my opinion he will not seek you: for he is a man of principle. But if you seek him, I believe he will not shun you.

Let me re-urge [it is the effect of my love for you!] that you know your own guilt in this affair, and should not be again an aggressor. It would be pity that so brave a man as the colonel should drop, were you and he to meet: and, on the other hand, it would be dreadful that you should be sent to your account unprepared for it, and pursuing a fresh violence. Moreover, seest thou not, in the deaths of two of thy principal agents, *the handwriting upon the wall against thee?*

My zeal on this occasion may make me guilty of repetition. Indeed I know not how to quit the subject. But if what I have written, added to your own remorse and consciousness, cannot prevail, all that I might further urge would be ineffectual.

Adieu, therefore! Mayst thou repent of the past! and may no new violences add to thy heavy reflections, and overwhelm thy future hopes! are the wishes of

Thy true friend,
JOHN BELFORD.

Letter CLXXIII—Mr. Lovelace to John Belford, Esq.

Munich, Nov. 11–22.

I RECEIVED yours this moment, just as I was setting out for Vienna.

As to going to Madrid, or one single step out of the way, to avoid Colonel Morden, let me perish if I do! You cannot think me so mean a wretch.

And so you own that he *has* threatened me; but not in gross and ungentlemanly terms, you say. If he has threatened me like a gentleman, I will resent his threats like a gentleman. But he has not done as a man of honour, if he has threatened me at all behind my back. I would scorn to threaten any man to whom I *knew* how to address myself either personally, or by pen and ink.

As to what you mention of my guilt; of the handwriting on the wall; of a legal prosecution, if he meet his fate from my hand; of his skill, coolness, courage, and such-like poltroon stuff; what can you mean by it? Surely you cannot believe that such insinuations as those will weaken either my hands or my heart. No more of this sort of nonsense, I beseech you, in any of your future letters.

He had not taken any resolutions, you say, when you saw him. He *must* and *will* take resolutions, one way or other, very quickly; for I wrote to him yesterday, without waiting for this or your answer to my last. I could not avoid it. I could not (as I told you in that) live in suspense. I have directed my letter to Florence. Nor could I suffer my friends to live in suspense as to my safety. But I have couched it in such moderate terms, that he has fairly his option. He will be the challenger, if he take it in the sense in which he may so handsomely avoid taking it. And if he does, it will demonstrate that malice and revenge were the predominant passions with him; and that he was determined but to settle his affairs, and then *take his resolutions,* as you phrase it — yet, if we are to meet [for I know what *my* option would be, in *his* case, on *such a letter,* complaisant as it is], I wish *he* had a worse, *I* a better cause. It would be sweet revenge to him, were I to fall by his hand. But what should I be the better for killing him?

I will enclose the copy of the letter I sent him.

.   .   .   .

On reperusing yours in a cooler moment, I cannot but thank you for your friendly love and good intentions. My value for you, from the first hour of our acquaintance till now, I have never found misplaced; regarding at least your *intention:* thou must, however, own a good deal of blunder of the over-do and under-do kind, with respect to the part thou actedst between me and the beloved of my heart. But thou art really an honest fellow, and a sincere and warm friend. I could almost wish I had not written to Florence till I had received thy letter now before me. But it is gone. Let it go. If he wish peace, and to avoid violence, he will have a fair opportunity to embrace the one, and shun the other. If not—he must take his fate.

But be this as it may, you may contrive to let young Harlowe know [he is a menacer too!] that I shall be in England in March next at farthest.

This of Bavaria is a gallant and polite court. Nevertheless, being uncertain whether my letter may meet with the colonel at Florence, I shall quit it, and set out, as I intended, for Vienna; taking care to have any letter or message from him conveyed to me there: which will soon bring me back hither, or to any other place to which I shall be invited.

As I write to Charlotte, I have nothing more to add, after compliments to all friends, than that I am

Wholly yours,
LOVELACE.

Mr. Lovelace to William Morden, Esq.

[Enclosed in the above]

Munich, Nov. 10–21.

SIR,—I have heard, with a great deal of surprise, that you have thought fit to throw out some menacing expressions against me.

I should have been very glad that you had thought I had punishment enough in my own mind, for the wrongs I have done to the most excellent of women; and that it had been possible for two persons, so ardently joining in one love (especially as I was desirous, to the utmost of my power, to repair those wrongs), to have lived, if not on amicable terms, in such a way, as not to put either to the pain of hearing of threatenings thrown out in absence, which either ought to be despised for, if he had not spirit to take notice of them.

Now, sir, if what I have heard be owing only to warmth of temper, or to sudden passion, while the loss of all other losses the most deplorable to me was recent, I not only excuse but commend you for it. But if you are really *determined* to meet me on any other account [which, I own to you, is not however what I wish], it would be very blamable, and very unworthy of the character I desire to maintain, as well with you as with every other gentleman, to give you a difficulty in doing it.

Being uncertain when this letter may meet you, I shall set out to-morrow for Vienna; where any letter directed to the post-house in that city, or to Baron Windisgratz's (at the Favorita), to whom I have commendations, will come to hand.

Meantime, believing you to be a man too generous to make a wrong construction of what I am going to declare, and knowing the value which the dearest of all creatures had for you, and your relation to her, I will not scruple to assure you that the most acceptable return will be, that Colonel Morden chooses to be upon an amicable, rather than upon any other footing, with

His sincere admirer, and humble servant,

R. LOVELACE.

Letter CLXXIV—Mr. Lovelace to John Belford, Esq.

Lintz, { Nov. 28.
{ Dec. 9.

I AM now on my way to Trent, in order to meet Colonel Morden, in pursuance of his answer to my letter enclosed in my last. I had been at Pressburgh, and had intended to visit some other cities of Hungary: but having obliged myself to return first to Vienna, I there met with his letter: which follows:

Munich, { Nov. 21.
{ Dec. 2.

SIR,—Your letter was at Florence four days before I arrived there.

That I might not appear unworthy of your favour, I set out for this city the very next morning. I knew not but that the politeness of this court might have engaged, beyond his intention, a gentleman who has only his pleasures to pursue.

But being disappointed in my hope of finding you here, it becomes me to acquaint you that I have such a desire to stand well in the opinion of a man of your spirit, that I cannot hesitate a moment upon the option, which I am sure Mr. Lovelace in my situation (thus called upon) would make.

I own, sir, that I have, on all occasions, spoken of your treatment of my ever dear cousin as it deserved. It would have been very surprising if I had not. And it behoves me (now you have given me so noble an opportunity of explaining myself) to convince you, that no words fell from my lips, of you, merely because you were absent. I acquaint you, therefore, that I will attend your appointment; and would, were it to the farthest part of the globe.

I shall stay some days at this court; and if you please to direct for me at M. Klienfurt's in this city, whether I remain here or not, your commands will come safely and speedily to the hands of, sir,

Your most humble servant,

WM. MORDEN.

So you see, Belford, that the colonel, by his ready, his even eagerly expressed acceptance of the offered interview, *was determined*. And is it not much better to bring such a point as this to an issue, than to give pain to friends for my safety, or continue in suspense myself; as I must do, if I imagined that another had aught against me?

This was my reply:

Vienna, { Nov. 25.
 { Dec. 6.

SIR,—I have this moment the favour of yours. I will suspend a tour I was going to take into Hungary, and instantly set out for Munich: and, if I find you not there, will proceed to Trent. This city, being on the confines of Italy, will be most convenient, as I presume, to you, in your return to Tuscany; and I shall hope to meet you in it on the $\frac{3}{14}$th of December.

I shall bring with me only a French valet and an English footman. Other particulars may be adjusted when I have the honour to see you. Till when, I am, sir,

Your most obedient servant,

R. LOVELACE.

Now, Jack, I have no manner of apprehension of the event of

this meeting. And I think I may say he seeks me; not I him. And so let him take the consequence.

What is infinitely nearer to my heart is my ingratitude to the most excellent of women—my *premeditated* ingratitude! Yet all the while enabled to distinguish and to adore her excellences, in spite of the mean opinion of the sex which I had imbibed from early manhood.

But this lady has asserted the worthiness of her sex, and most gloriously has she exalted it with me now. Yet, surely, as I have said and written a hundred times, there cannot be such another woman.

But as my loss in her departure is the greatest of any man's, and as she was nearer to me than to any other person in the world, and once she herself *wished to be so*, what an insolence in any man breathing to pretend to avenge her on *me*! Happy! happy! thrice happy! had I known how to value, as I ought to have valued, the glory of such a preference!

I will not aggravate to myself this aggravation of the colonel's pretending to call me to account for my treatment of a lady so much *my own*, lest, in the approaching interview, my heart should relent for one so nearly related to her, and who means honour and justice to her memory; and I should thereby give him advantages which otherwise he cannot have. For I know that I shall be inclined to trust to my skill, to save a man who was so much and so justly valued by her; and shall be loath to give way to my resentment, as a threatened man. And in this respect only am I sorry for his skill, and his courage, lest I should be obliged, in my own defence, to add a chalk to a score that is already too long.

.   .   .   .

Indeed, indeed, Belford, I am, and shall be, to my latest hour, the most miserable of beings. Such exalted generosity!—Why didst thou put into my craving hands the copy of her will? Why sentest thou to me the posthumous letter? What though I was earnest to see the will? Thou knewest what they *both* were [*I* did not]; and that it would be cruel to oblige me.

The meeting of twenty Colonel Mordens, were there twenty to meet in turn, would be nothing to me; would not give me a moment's concern, as to my own safety: but my reflections upon my vile ingratitude to so superior an excellence will ever be my curse.

Had she been a Miss Howe to me, and treated me as if I were

a Hickman, I had had a call for revenge; and policy (when I had intended to be a husband) might have justified my attempts to humble her. But a *meek and gentle temper* was hers, though a *true heroine*, whenever honour or virtue called for an exertion of spirit.

Nothing but my cursed devices stood in the way of my happiness. Rememberest thou not how repeatedly, from the *first*, I poured cold water upon her rising flame, by meanly and ungratefully turning upon her the *injunctions* which *virgin delicacy*, and *filial duty*, induced her to lay me under, before I got her into my power? [1]

Did she not tell me, and did I not *know it*, if she had *not* told me, *that she could not be guilty of affectation or tyranny to the man whom she intended to marry?* [2] I knew, as she once upbraided me, that from the time I had got her from her father's house, *I had a plain path before me.*[3] True did she say, and I triumphed in the discovery, that from that time *I had held her soul in suspense a hundred times.*[4] My ipecacuanha trial alone was enough to convince an infidel that she had a mind in which love and tenderness would have presided, had I permitted the charming buds to put forth and blow.[5]

She *would have had no reserves*, as once she told me, *had I not given her cause of doubt.*[6] And did she not own to thee, *that once she could have loved me ; and, could she have made me good, would have made me happy?* [7] O Belford! here was love; a love of the noblest kind! A love, as she hints in her posthumous letter,[8] that extended to the soul; and which she not only avowed in her dying hours, but contrived to let me know it after death, in that letter filled with warnings and exhortations, which had for their sole end my eternal welfare!

The cursed women, indeed, endeavoured to excite my vengeance, and my pride, by preaching to me eternally *her doubts*, her *want of* love, and *her contempt of me*. And my pride was, at times, too much excited by their vile insinuations. But had it even been as they said; well might she, who had been used to be

[1] See vol. ii, pp. 27–8. See also ibid., Letters x, xxxviii, xxxix, and many other places.

[2] See vol. iii, p. 118. It may be observed further, that all Clarissa's occasional lectures to Miss Howe, on that young lady's treatment of Mr. Hickman, prove that she was herself above affectation and tyranny. See, more particularly, the advice she gives to that friend of her heart, Letter lxxiv of this volume: "O my dear," says she in that letter, p.198, "that it had been *my* lot (as I was not permitted to live single) to have met with a man by whom I could have acted generously and unreservedly!" etc. etc.

[3] Vol. iii, pp. 76, 113.   [4] Vol. iii, p. 119.
[5] Vol. ii, Letters cxii, cxiii.   [6] Vol. iii, p. 139.
[7] See p. 306 of this vol.   [8] See pp. 435–8 of this vol.

courted and admired by every desiring eye, and worshipped by every respectful heart—well might *such* a woman be allowed to draw back, when she found herself kept in suspense, *as to the great question of all*, by a designing and intriguing spirit; pretending awe and distance, as reasons for reining-in a fervour which, if real, cannot be reined-in. Divine creature! Her very doubts, her reserves (so justly doubting) would have been my assurance, and my glory! And what other trial needed her virtue? What other needed a purity so angelic (blessed with such a *command of her passions in the bloom of youth*), had I not been a villain—and a wanton, a conceited, a proud fool, as well as a villain?

These reflections sharpened, rather than their edge by time abated, accompany me in whatever I do, and wherever I go; and mingle with all my diversions and amusements. And yet I go into gay and splendid company. I have made new acquaintance in the different courts I have visited. I am both esteemed and sought after by persons of rank and merit. I visit the colleges, the churches, the palaces. I frequent the theatre: am present at every public exhibition; and see all that is worth seeing, that I had not seen before, in the cabinets of the curious: am sometimes admitted to the toilette of an eminent toast, and make one with distinction at the assemblies of others—yet can think of nothing, nor of anybody, with delight, but of my CLARISSA. Nor have I seen one woman with advantage to herself, but as she resembles in stature, air, complexion, voice, or in some feature, that charmer, that *only* charmer, of my soul.

What greater punishment than to have these astonishing perfections, which she was mistress of, strike my remembrance with such force, when I have nothing left me but the remorse of having deprived myself and the world of such a blessing? Now and then, indeed, am I capable of a gleam of comfort, arising (not ungenerously) from the moral certainty which I have of her everlasting happiness, in spite of all the machinations and devices which I set on foot to ensnare her virtue, and to bring down so pure a mind to my own level.

> For can I be, at *worst* [Avert that worst,
> O Thou SUPREME, who only canst avert it!]
> So much a wretch, so very far abandon'd,
> But that I must, ev'n in the horrid'st gloom,
> Reap intervenient joy, at least some respite
> From pain and anguish, in *her* bliss.—

If I find myself thus miserable abroad, I will soon return to England, and follow your example, I think—turn hermit, or some plaguy thing or other, and see what a constant course of penitence and mortification will do for me. There is no living at this rate—d——n me if there be!

If any mishap should befall me, you'll have the particulars of it from De la Tour. He indeed knows but little of English: but every modern tongue is yours. He is a trusty and ingenious fellow: and, if anything happen, will have some other papers, which I shall have ready sealed up, for you to transmit to Lord M. And since thou art so expert and so ready at executorships, prithee, Belford, accept of the office for me, as well as for my Clarissa—CLARISSA LOVELACE let me call her.

By all that's good, I am bewitched to her memory. Her very name, with mine joined to it, ravishes my soul, and is more delightful to me than the sweetest music.

Had I carried her [I must still recriminate] to any other place than to that accursed woman's—for the potion was her invention and mixture; and all the persisted-in violence was at her instigation, and at that of her wretched daughters, *who have now amply revenged upon me their own ruin, which they lay at my door*—

But this looks so like the confession of a thief at the gallows, that possibly thou wilt be apt to think I am intimidated in prospect of the approaching interview. But far otherwise. On the contrary, most cheerfully do I go to meet the colonel; and I would tear my heart out of my breast with my own hands, were it capable of fear or concern on that account.

Thus much only I know, that if I should kill him [which I will not do if I can help it], I shall be far from being easy in my mind; *that* shall I never more be. But as the meeting is evidently of his own seeking, against an option fairly given to the contrary, and I cannot avoid it, I'll think of that hereafter. It is but repenting and mortifying for all at once: for I am as sure of victory as I am that I now live, let him be ever so skilful a swordsman; since, besides that I am no unfleshed novice, this is a sport that, when provoked to it, I love as well as my food. And, moreover, I shall be as *calm and undisturbed* as the bishop at his prayers: while he, as is evident by his letter, must be actuated by revenge and passion.

Doubt not, therefore, Jack, that I shall give a good account of this affair. Meantime, I remain

Yours most affectionately, etc.

LOVELACE.

To-morrow is to be the day that will, in all probability, send either one or two ghosts to attend the manes of my CLARISSA.

I arrived here yesterday; and inquiring for an English gentleman of the name of Morden, soon found out the colonel's lodgings. He had been in town two days; and left his name at every probable place.

He was gone to ride out; and I left *my* name, and where to be found: and in the evening he made me a visit.

He was plaguy gloomy. That was not I. But yet he told me that I had acted like a man of true spirit in my first letter; and with honour, in giving him so readily this meeting. He wished I had in other respects; and then we might have seen each other upon better terms than now we did.

I said there was no recalling what was passed; and that I wished some things had not been done, as well as he.

To recriminate now, he said, would be as exasperating as unavailable. And as I had so cheerfully given him this opportunity, words should give place to business. *Your* choice, Mr. Lovelace, of time, of place, of weapon, shall be *my* choice.

The two latter be yours, Mr. Morden. The time to-morrow, or next day, as you please.

Next day, then, Mr. Lovelace; and we'll ride out to-morrow to fix the place.

Agreed, sir.

Well, now, Mr. Lovelace, do you choose the weapon.

I said I believed we might be upon an equal foot with the single rapier; but, if he thought otherwise, I had no objection to a pistol.

I will only say, replied he, that the chances may be more equal by the sword, because we can neither of us be to seek in that: and you would stand, says he, a worse chance, as I apprehend, with a pistol: and yet I have brought two; that you may take your choice of either: for, added he, I never missed a mark at pistol-distance, since I knew how to hold a pistol.

I told him that he spoke like himself: that I was expert enough that way, to embrace it, if he chose it; though not so sure of my mark as he pretended to be. Yet the devil's in 't, colonel, if I, who have slit a bullet in two upon a knife's edge, hit not my man. So I have no objection to a pistol, if it be *your* choice. No man, I'll venture to say, has a steadier hand or eye than I have.

They may both be of use to you, sir, at the sword, as well as at the pistol: the sword, therefore, be the thing, if you please.

With all my heart.

We parted with a solemn sort of ceremonious civility: and this day I called upon him; and we rode out together to fix upon the place: and both being of one mind, and hating to put off for the morrow what could be done to-day, would have decided it then: but De la Tour, and the colonel's valet, who attended us, being unavoidably let into the secret, joined to beg we would have with us a surgeon from Brixen, whom La Tour had fallen in with there, and who had told him he was to ride next morning to bleed a person in a fever, at a lone cottage, which, by the surgeon's description, was not far from the place where we then were, if it were not that very cottage within sight of us.

They undertook so to manage it that the surgeon should know nothing of the matter till his assistance was called in. And La Tour being, as I assured the colonel, a ready contriving fellow [whom I ordered to obey him as myself, were the chance to be in *his* favour], we both agreed to defer the decision till to-morrow, and to leave the whole about the surgeon to the management of our two valets; enjoining them absolute secrecy: and so rode back again by different ways.

We fixed upon a little lone valley for the spot—ten to-morrow morning the time—and single rapier the sword. Yet I repeatedly told him that I valued myself so much upon my skill in that weapon that I would wish him to choose any other.

He said it was a gentleman's weapon; and he who understood it not, wanted a qualification that he ought to suffer for not having: but that, as to him, one weapon was as good as another throughout all the instruments of offence.

So, Jack, you see I take no advantage of him: but my devil must deceive me if he take not his life or his death at my hands before eleven to-morrow morning.

His valet and mine are to be present; but both strictly enjoined to be impartial and inactive: and, in return for my civility of the like nature, he commanded *his* to be assisting to me, if he fell.

We are to ride thither, and to dismount when at the place; and his footman and mine are to wait at an appointed distance, with a chaise to carry off to the borders of the Venetian territories the survivor, if one drop; or to assist either or both, as occasion may demand.

And thus, Belford, is the matter settled.

A shower of rain has left me nothing else to do: and therefore

I write this letter; though I might as well have deferred it till to-morrow twelve o'clock, when I doubt not to be able to write again, to assure you how much I am

Yours, etc.

LOVELACE.

Letter CLXXVI—Translation of a Letter from F. J. De la Tour to John Belford, Esq., near Soho Square, London

Trent, Dec. 18. *N.S.*

SIR,—I have melancholy news to inform you of, by order of the Chevalier Lovelace. He showed me his letter to you before he sealed it; signifying that he was to meet the Chevalier Morden on the 15th. Wherefore, as the occasion of the meeting is so well known to you, I shall say nothing of it here.

I had taken care to have ready, within a little distance, a surgeon and his assistant, to whom, under an oath of secrecy, I had revealed the matter (though I did not own it to the two gentlemen); so that they were prepared with bandages, and all things proper. For well was I acquainted with the bravery and skill of my chevalier; and had heard the character of the other; and knew the animosity of both. A post-chaise was ready, with each of their footmen, at a little distance.

The two chevaliers came exactly at their time: they were attended by Monsieur Margate (the colonel's gentleman) and myself. They had given orders overnight, and now repeated them in each other's presence, that we should observe a strict impartiality between them: and that, if one fell, each of us should look upon himself, as to any needful help or retreat, as the servant of the survivor, and take his commands accordingly.

After a few compliments, both the gentlemen, with the greatest presence of mind that I ever beheld in men, stripped to their shirts, and drew.

They parried with equal judgment several passes. My chevalier drew the first blood, making a desperate push, which, by a sudden turn of his antagonist, missed going clear through him, and wounded him on the fleshy part of the ribs of his right side; which part the sword tore out, being on the extremity of the body: but, before my chevalier could recover himself, the colonel, in return, pushed him into the inside of the left arm, near the shoulder: and the sword (raking his breast as it passed), being followed by a great effusion of blood, the colonel said, Sir, I believe you have enough.

My chevalier swore by G—d he was not hurt: 'twas a pin's point: and so made another pass at his antagonist; which he, with a surprising dexterity, received under his arm, and run my dear chevalier into the body; who immediately fell, saying, The luck is yours, sir—Oh, my beloved Clarissa!—Now art thou—— Inwardly he spoke three or four words more. His sword dropped from his hand. Mr. Morden threw his down, and ran to him, saying in French, Ah, monsieur, you are a dead man!— Call to God for mercy!

We gave the signal agreed upon to the footmen; and they to the surgeons; who instantly came up.

Colonel Morden, I found, was too well used to the bloody work; for he was as cool as if nothing so extraordinary had happened, assisting the surgeons, though his own wound bled much. But my dear chevalier fainted away two or three times running, and vomited blood besides.

However, they stopped the bleeding for the present; and we helped him into the voiture; and then the colonel suffered his own wound to be dressed; and appeared concerned that my chevalier was between whiles (when he could speak and struggle) extremely outrageous. Poor gentleman! he had made quite sure of victory!

The colonel, against the surgeons' advice, would mount on horseback to pass into the Venetian territories; and generously gave me a purse of gold to pay the surgeons; desiring me to make a present to the footman; and to accept of the remainder as a mark of his satisfaction in my conduct; and in my care and tenderness of my master.

The surgeons told him that my chevalier could not live over the day.

When the colonel took leave of him, Mr. Lovelace said, You have well revenged the dear creature.

I have, sir, said Mr. Morden: and perhaps shall be sorry that you called upon me to this work, while I was balancing whether to obey or disobey the dear angel.

There is a fate in it! replied my chevalier—a cursed fate!—or this could not have been! But be ye all witnesses that I have provoked my destiny, and acknowledge that I fall by a man of honour.

Sir, said the colonel, with the piety of a confessor (wringing Mr. Lovelace's hand), snatch these few fleeting moments, and commend yourself to God.

And so he rode off.

The voiture proceeded slowly with my chevalier; yet the motion set both his wounds bleeding afresh; and it was with difficulty they again stopped the blood.

We brought him alive to the nearest cottage; and he gave orders to me to dispatch to you the packet I herewith send sealed up; and bid me write to you the particulars of this most unhappy affair: and give you thanks, in his name, for all your favours and friendship to him.

Contrary to all expectation, he lived over the night: but *suffered much*, as well from his *impatience* and *disappointment* as from his *wounds*; for he seemed *very unwilling to die.*

He was delirious at times in the two last hours; and then several times cried out, as if he had seen some frightful spectre, Take her away! take her away! but named nobody. And sometimes praised some lady (that Clarissa, I suppose, whom he had invoked when he received his death's wound), calling her, Sweet Excellence! Divine Creature! Fair Sufferer! And once he said, Look down, Blessed Spirit, look down!——And there stopped; his lips, however, moving.

At nine in the morning he was seized with convulsions, and fainted away; and it was a quarter of an hour before he came out of them.

His few last words I must not omit, as they show an ultimate composure; which may administer some consolation to his honourable friends.

Blessed—said he, addressing himself no doubt to Heaven; for his dying eyes were lifted up. A strong convulsion prevented him for a few moments saying more, but recovering, he again, with great fervour (lifting up his eyes and his spread hands), pronounced the word *blessed*. Then, in a seeming ejaculation, he spoke inwardly, so as not to be understood: at last, he distinctly pronounced these three words,

LET THIS EXPIATE!

And then, his head sinking on his pillow, he expired, at about half an hour after ten.

He little thought, poor gentleman! his end so near: so had given no direction about his body. I have caused it to be embowelled, and deposited in a vault, till I have orders from England.

This is a favour that was procured with difficulty; and would have been refused, had he not been an Englishman of rank: a nation with reason respected in every Austrian Government.

For he had refused ghostly attendance, and the Sacraments in the Catholic way.   May his soul be happy, I pray God!

I have had some trouble also, on account of the manner of his death, from the magistracy here: who have taken the requisite informations in the affair.   And it has cost me some money. Of which, and of my dear chevalier's effects, I will give you a faithful account in my next.   And so, waiting at this place your commands, I am, sir,

Your most faithful and obedient servant,
F. J. DE LA TOUR.

CONCLUSION

Supposed to be written by Mr. Belford

WHAT remains to be mentioned for the satisfaction of such of the readers as may be presumed to have interested themselves in the fortunes of those other principals in the story, who survived Mr. Lovelace, will be found summarily related as follows:

The news of Mr. LOVELACE's unhappy end was received with as much grief by his own relations, as it was with exultation by the Harlowe family and by Miss Howe. His own family were most to be pitied, because, being sincere admirers of the inimitable lady, they were greatly grieved for the injustice done her; and now had the *additional* mortification of losing the only male of it by a violent death.

That his fate was deserved, was still a heightening of their calamity, as they had, for that very reason, and his unpreparedness for it, but too much ground for apprehension with regard to his future happiness. While the other family, from their unforgiving spirit, and even the noble young lady abovementioned, from her lively resentments, found his death some little, some temporary, alleviation of the heavy loss they had sustained, principally through his means.

Temporary alleviation, we repeat, as to the Harlowe family; for THEY were far from being happy or easy in their reflections upon their own conduct. And still the less, as the inconsolable mother rested not till she had procured, by means of Colonel Morden, large extracts from some of the letters that compose this history, which convinced them all that the very correspondence which Clarissa, while with them, renewed with Mr. Lovelace, was renewed for *their sakes* more than for *her own*: that she had given him no encouragement contrary to her duty, and to that prudence for which she was so early noted: that had they trusted to a discretion which they owned she had never brought into question, she would have extricated them and herself (as she once proposed [1] to her mother) from all difficulties as to Lovelace: that she, if any woman ever could, would have given a glorious instance of a passion conquered, or at least kept under, by

[1] See vol. i, p. 83.

reason, and by piety, the man being too immoral to be implicitly beloved.

The unhappy parents and uncles, from the perusal of these extracts, too evidently for their peace, saw that it was entirely owing to the avarice, the ambition, the envy of her implacable brother and sister, and to the senseless confederacy entered into by the whole family, to compel her to give her hand to a man she must despise, or she had not been a CLARISSA, and to their consequent persecutions of her, that she ever thought of quitting her father's house. And that even when she first entertained such a thought, it was with intent, if possible, to procure for herself a private asylum with Mrs. Howe, or at some other place of safety (but not with Mr. Lovelace, nor with any of the ladies of his family, though invited by the latter), from whence she might propose terms which ought to have been complied with, and which were entirely consistent with her duty—that though she found herself disappointed of the hoped-for refuge and protection, she intended not, by meeting Mr. Lovelace, to put herself into his power; all that she aimed at by taking that step being to endeavour to pacify so fierce a spirit, lest he should (as he indeed was determined to do) pay a visit to her friends, which might have been attended with fatal consequences; but was spirited away by him in such a manner as made her an object of pity rather than of blame.

These extracts further convinced them all that it was to her unaffected regret that she found that marriage was not in her power afterwards for a long time; and at last, but on one occasion, when their unnatural cruelty to her (on a new application she had made to her Aunt Hervey, to procure mercy and pardon) rendered her incapable of receiving his proffered hand; and so obliged her to suspend the day; intending only to suspend it till recovered.

They saw, with equal abhorrence of Lovelace, and of their own cruelty, and with the highest admiration of her, that the majesty of her virtue had awed the most daring spirit in the world, so that he durst not attempt to carry his base designs into execution till, by wicked potions, he had made her senses the previous sacrifice.

But how did they in a manner adore her memory! How did they recriminate upon each other! when they found that she had not only preserved herself from repeated outrage, by the most glorious and intrepid behaviour, in defiance, and to the utter confusion of all his libertine notions; but had the fortitude, constantly, and with a noble disdain, to reject him. Whom?

Why, the man she once could have loved, kneeling for pardon, and begging to be permitted to make her the best reparation then in his power to make her; that is to say, by marriage. His fortunes high and unbroken. She his prisoner at the time in a vile house: rejected by all her friends; upon repeated application to them, for mercy and forgiveness, rejected — mercy and forgiveness, and a last blessing, afterwards imploring; and that as much to lighten their future remorses, as for the comfort of her own pious heart—yet, though savagely refused, on a supposition that she was not so near her end as was represented, departed, forgiving and blessing them all.

Then they recollected that her posthumous letters, instead of reproaches, were filled with comfortings: that she had in her last will, in their own way, laid obligations upon them all; obligations which they neither deserved nor expected; as if she thought to repair the injustice which self-partiality made some of them conclude done to them by her grandfather in his will.

These intelligences and recollections were perpetual subjects of recrimination to them: heightened their anguish for the loss of a child who was the glory of their family; and not seldom made them shun each other (at the times they were accustomed to meet together in the family way), that they might avoid the mutual reproaches of eyes that spoke when tongues were silent— their stings also sharpened by time; what an unhappy family was this family! Well might Colonel Morden, in the words of Juvenal, challenge all other miserable families to produce such a growing distress as the Harlowe family (a few months before so happy!) were able to produce:

> Humani generis mores tibi nôsse volenti
> Sufficit una domus: paucos consumere dies, et
> Dicere te miserum, postquam illinc veneris, aude.

Mrs. HARLOWE lived about two years and a half after the lamented death of her CLARISSA.

Mr. HARLOWE had the additional affliction to survive his lady about half a year; *her* death, by new-pointing his former anguish and remorse, hastening his own.

Both, in their last hours, however, comforted themselves that they should be restored to their BLESSED daughter, as they always (from the time that they were acquainted with the above particulars of her story, and with her happy *exit*) called her.

They both lived, however, to see their son *James* and their daughter *Arabella* married: but not to take joy in either of their nuptials.

Mr. JAMES HARLOWE married a woman of family, an orphan; and is obliged, at a very great expense, to support her claim to estates which were his principal inducement to make his addresses to her; but which, to this day, he has not recovered; nor is likely to recover; having very powerful adversaries to contend with, and a title to assert, which admits of litigation; and he not blessed with so much patience as is necessary to persons embarrassed in law.

What is further observable with regard to him is, that the match was entirely of his own head, against the advice of his father, mother, and uncles, who warned him of marrying in this lady a lawsuit for life. His ungenerous behaviour to his wife, for what she cannot help, and for what is as much *her* misfortune as *his*, has occasioned such estrangements between them (she being a woman of spirit) as, were the lawsuits determined, and even more favourably than probably they will be, must make him unhappy to the end of his life. He attributes all his misfortunes, when he opens himself to the *few* friends he has, *to his vile and cruel treatment of his angelic sister*. He confesses these misfortunes to be just, without having temper to acquiesce in the acknowledged justice. One month in every year he puts on mourning, and that month commences with him on the 7th of September, during which he shuts himself up from all company. Finally, he is looked upon, and often calls himself,

THE MOST MISERABLE OF BEINGS.

ARABELLA'S fortune became a temptation to a man of quality to make his addresses to her: his title an inducement with her to approve of him. Brothers and sisters, when they are not friends, are generally the sharpest enemies to each other. He thought too much was done for her in the settlements. She thought not enough. And for some years past they have so heartily hated each other, that if either know a joy, it is in being told of some new misfortune or displeasure that happens to the other. Indeed, before they came to an open rupture, they were continually loading each other, by way of exonerating themselves (*to the additional disquiet of the whole family*), with the *principal* guilt of their implacable behaviour and sordid cruelty to their admirable sister. May the reports that are spread of this lady's further unhappiness from her lord's free life; a fault she *justly* thought so odious in Mr. Lovelace (though that would not have been an insuperable objection with her to his addresses); and of his public slights and contempt of her, and even sometimes of his *personal abuses,* which are said to be owing to her impatient spirit and violent passions; be utterly groundless. For, what a heart must that be, which would wish she might be as great a torment to herself as she had aimed to be to her sister! Especially as she regrets to this hour, and declares that she shall *to the last of her life,* her cruel treatment of that sister; and (as well as her brother) is but too ready to attribute to *that* her own unhappiness.

Mr. ANTONY and Mr. JOHN HARLOWE are still [at the writing of this] living: but often declare that, with their beloved niece, they lost all the joy of their lives: and lament, without reserve, in all companies, the unnatural part they were induced to take against her.

Mr. SOLMES is also still living, if a man of his cast may be said to live; for his general behaviour and sordid manners are such as justify the aversion the excellent lady had to him. He has, moreover, found his addresses rejected by several women of far inferior fortunes (great as his own are) to those of the lady to whom he was encouraged to aspire.

Mr. MOWBRAY and Mr. TOURVILLE having lost the man in whose conversation they so much delighted; shocked and awakened by the several unhappy catastrophes before their eyes; and having always rather *ductile* than *dictating* hearts; took their friend Belford's advice: converted the remainder of their fortunes into annuities for life; and retired, the one into Yorkshire, the other into Nottinghamshire, of which counties they are natives: their friend Belford managing their concerns for them, and corresponding with them, and having more and more hopes, every time he sees them (which is once or twice a year, when they come to town), that they will become more and more worthy of their names and families.

As those sisters in iniquity, SALLY MARTIN and POLLY HORTON, had abilities and education superior to what creatures of their cast generally can boast of; and as their histories are nowhere given in the preceding papers, in which they are frequently mentioned; it cannot fail of gratifying the reader's curiosity, *as well* as answering the *good ends* designed by the publication of this work, to give a brief account of their parentage and manner of training-up, preparative to the vile courses they fell into, and of what became of them after the dreadful exit of the infamous Sinclair.

SALLY MARTIN was the daughter of a substantial mercer at the court end of the town; to whom her mother, a grocer's daughter in the city, brought a handsome fortune; and both having a gay turn, and being fond of the fashions which it was their business to promote; and which the wives and daughters of the uppermost tradesmen (especially in that quarter of the town) generally affect to follow; it was no wonder that they brought up their daughter accordingly: nor that she, who was a very sprightly and ready-witted girl, and reckoned very pretty and very genteel, should every year improve upon such examples.

She early found herself mistress of herself. All she did was right; all she said was admired. Early, very early, did she dismiss blushes from her cheek. She could not blush, because she could not doubt: and silence, whatever were the subject, was as much a stranger to her as diffidence.

She never was left out of any party of pleasure after she had passed her ninth year; and, in honour of her prattling vein, was considered as a principal person in the frequent treats and entertainments which her parents, fond of luxurious living, gave with a view to increase their acquaintance for the sake of their business; not duly reflecting that the part they suffered her to take in what made for their interest, would probably be a means to quicken the appetites and ruin the morals of that daughter, for whose sake, as an only child, they were solicitous to obtain wealth.

The CHILD so much a woman, what must the WOMAN be?

At fifteen or sixteen she affected, both in dress and manners, to ape such of the quality as were most apish. The richest silks in her father's shop were not too rich for her. At all public diversions she was the leader, instead of the led, of all her female kindred and acquaintance; though they were a third older than herself. She would bustle herself into a place, and make room for her more bashful companions, through the frowns of the first possessors, at a crowded theatre; leaving every one near her amazed at her self-consequence, wondering she had no servant to keep place for her; whisperingly inquiring who she was; and then sitting down admiring her fortitude.

She officiously made herself of consequence to the most noted players; who, as one of their patronesses, applied to her for her interest on their benefit nights. She knew the *Christian*, as well as *sur*name, of every pretty fellow who frequented public places; and affected to speak of them by their former.

Those who had not obeyed the call her eyes always made upon all of them for notice at her entrance, or before she took her seat, were spoken of with haughtiness as Jacks or Toms; while her favourites, with an affectedly endearing familiarity, and a prettiness of accent, were Jackeys and Tommys; and if they stood very high in her graces, dear devils and agreeable toads.

She sat in judgment, and an inexorable judge she was, upon the actions and conduct of every man and woman of quality and fashion, as they became the subjects of conversation. She was deeply learned in the scandalous chronicle: she made every character, every praise, and every censure serve to exalt herself. *She should scorn to do so or so!* or, *That was ever her way*; and *Just what she did, or liked to do*; and judging herself by the vileness of the most vile of her sex, she wiped her mouth, and sat down satisfied with her own virtue.

She had her chair to attend her wherever she went, and found people among her *betters*, as her pride stooped to call some of the most insignificant people in the world, to encourage her visits.

She was practised in all the arts of the card-table: a true Spartan girl; and had even courage, occasionally, to wrangle off a detection. Late hours (turning night into day, and day into night) were the almost unavoidable consequence of her frequent play. Her parents pleased themselves that their Sally had a charming constitution: and as long as she suffered not in her health, they were regardless of her morals.

The needle she hated: and made the constant subjects of her ridicule the fine works that used to employ, and to keep out of idleness, luxury, and extravagance, and at *home* (were they to have been of no other service), the women of the last age, when there were no Vauxhalls, Ranelaghs, Marybones, and such-like places of diversion, to dress out for and gad after.

And as to family management, her parents had not required any knowledge of that sort from her; and she considered it as a qualification only necessary for hirelings and the low-born, and as utterly unworthy of the attention of a modern fine lady.

Although her father had great business, yet, living in so high and expensive a way, he pretended not to give her a fortune answerable to it. Neither he nor his wife having set out with any notion of frugality could think of retrenching. Nor did their daughter desire that they should retrench. They thought glare or ostentation reputable. They called it living *genteelly*. And as they lifted their heads above their neighbours, they supposed their credit concerned to go forward rather than backward in outward appearances. They flattered themselves, and they flattered their girl, and she was *entirely* of their opinion, that she had charms and wit enough to attract some man of rank; of *fortune* at least: and yet this daughter of a mercer-father and grocer-mother could not bear the thoughts of a creeping cit; encouraging herself with the few instances (*comparatively* few), which she had always in her head as *common ones*, of girls much inferior to herself in station, talents, education, and even fortune, who had succeeded—as she doubted not to succeed. Handsome settlements, and a chariot, that tempting gewgaw to the vanity of the middling class of females, were the least that she proposed to herself. But all this while, neither her parents nor herself considered that she had appetites indulged to struggle with, and a turn of education given her, as well as a warm constitution, unguarded by sound principles, and unbenefited by example, which made her much better qualified for a mistress than a wife.

Her twentieth year, to her own equal wonder and regret, passed over her head, and she had not had one offer that her pride would permit her to accept of. A girl from fifteen to eighteen, her beauty then beginning to blossom, will, as a new thing, attract the eyes of men: but if she make her face cheap at public places, she will find that *new* faces will draw more attention than *fine* faces constantly seen. Policy, therefore, if nothing else were considered, would induce a young beauty, if she could tame her vanity, just to show herself, and to be talked of, and then withdrawing, as if from discretion (and discreet it will be to do so), expect to be *sought after*, rather than to be thought to *seek for*; only reviving now and then the memory of herself, at the public places in turn, if she find herself likely to be forgotten; and then she will be new again. But this observation ought young ladies always to have in their heads, that they can hardly ever expect to gratify their vanity, and at the same time gain the admiration of men worthy of making partners for life. They may, in short, have many admirers at public places, but not one lover.

Sally Martin knew nothing of this doctrine. Her beauty was in its bloom, and yet she found herself neglected. "Sally Martin, the mercer's daughter: she never fails being here," was the answer, and the accompanying observation, made to every questioner, Who is that lady?

At last her destiny approached. It was at a masquerade that she first saw the gay, the handsome Lovelace, who was just returned from his travels. She was immediately struck with his figure, and with the brilliant things that she heard fall from his lips as he happened to sit near her. He, who was not then looking out for a wife, was taken with Sally's smartness, and with an air that at the same time showed her to be equally genteel and self-significant; and signs of approbation mutually passing, he found no difficulty in acquainting himself where to visit her next day. And yet it was some mortification to a person of her self-consequence, and gay appearance, to submit to be known by so fine a young gentleman as no more than a mercer's daughter. So natural is it for a girl brought up as Sally was, to be occasionally ashamed of those whose folly had set her above herself.

But whatever it might be to Sally, it was no disappointment to Mr. Lovelace, to find his mistress of no higher degree; because he hoped to reduce her soon to the lowest condition that an unhappy woman can fall into.

But when Miss Martin had informed herself that her lover was the nephew and presumptive heir of Lord M., she thought him the very man for whom she had been so long and so impatiently looking out; and for whom it was worth her while to spread her toils. And here it may not be amiss to observe, that it is very probable that Mr. Lovelace had Sally Martin in his thoughts, and perhaps two or three more whose hopes of marriage from him had led them to their ruin, when he drew the following whimsical picture, in a letter to his friend Belford not inserted in the preceding collection.

"Methinks, says he, I see a young couple in courtship, having each a design upon the other: the girl plays off: she is very happy as she is: she cannot be happier: she will not change her single state: the man, I will suppose, is one who does not *confess* that he desires not that she *should*: she holds ready a net under her apron, he another under his coat; each intending to throw it over the other's neck; she over his, when her pride is gratified, and she thinks she can be sure of him; he over hers, when the watched-for yielding moment has carried consent *too far*. And suppose he happens to be the more dexterous of the two, and whips his net over her before she can cast hers over him; how, I would fain know, can she be justly entitled to cry out upon cruelty, barbarity, deception, sacrifices, and all the rest of the exclamatory nonsense with which the pretty fools, in such a case, are wont to din the ears of their conquerors? Is it not just, thinkest thou, when she makes her appeals to gods and men, that both gods and men should laugh at her, and hitting her in the teeth with her own felonious intentions, bid her sit down patiently under her deserved disappointment?"

In short, Sally's parents, as well as herself, encouraged Mr. Lovelace's visits. They thought they might trust to a discretion in her which she herself was too wise to doubt. Pride they knew she had; and that, in these cases, is often called discretion.— Lord help the sex, says Lovelace, if they had not pride!—Nor did they suspect danger from that specious air of sincerity, and gentleness of manners, which he could assume or lay aside whenever he pleased.

The second masquerade, which was no more than their third meeting abroad, completed her ruin from so practised, though so young a deceiver; and that before she well knew she was in danger: for, having prevailed on her to go off with him about twelve o'clock to his Aunt Forbes's, a lady of honour and fortune, to whom he had given reason to expect her *future niece* [the only hint of marriage he ever gave her], he carried her to the house of the wicked woman who bears the name of Sinclair in these papers: and there, by promises which she understood in the favourable sense (for where a woman loves, she seldom doubts enough for her own safety), obtained an easy conquest over a virtue that was little more than nominal.

He found it not difficult to induce her to proceed in the guilty commerce, till the effects of it became too apparent to be hid. Her parents then (in the first fury of their disappointment, and vexation for being deprived of all hopes of such a son-in-law) turned her out of doors.

Her disgrace thus published, she became hardened; and, protected by her seducer, whose favourite mistress she then was, she was so incensed against her parents for an indignity so little suiting with her pride, and the head they had always given her, that she refused to return to them, when, repenting of their passionate treatment of her, they would have been reconciled to her: and, becoming the favourite daughter of her Mother Sinclair, at the persuasions of that abandoned woman, she practised to bring on an abortion, which she effected, though she was so far gone that it had like to have cost her her life.

Thus, unchastity her first crime, murder her next, her conscience became seared; and, young as she was, and fond of her deceiver, soon grew indelicate enough, having so thorough-paced a schoolmistress, to do all she could to promote the pleasures of the man who had ruined her; scrupling not, with a spirit truly diabolical, to endeavour to draw in others to follow her example. And it is hardly to be believed what mischiefs of this sort she was the means of effecting; woman confiding in and daring woman; and she a creature of specious appearance and great art.

A still viler wickedness, if possible, remains to be said of Sally Martin.

Her father dying, her mother, in hopes to *reclaim* her, as she called it, proposed to her to quit the house of the infamous Sinclair, and to retire with her into the country, where her disgrace, and her then wicked way of life, would not be known; and there so to live as to save appearances; the only virtue she had ever taught her; besides that of endeavouring rather to delude than to be deluded.

To this Sally consented; but with no other intention, as she often owned (and gloried in it), than to cheat her mother of the greatest part of her substance, in revenge for consenting to her being turned out of doors long before, and by way of reprisal for having persuaded her father, as she would have it, to cut her off, in his last will, from any share in his fortune.

This unnatural wickedness, in half a year's time, she brought about; and then the serpent retired to her obscene den with her spoils, laughing at what she had done; even after it had broken her mother's heart, as it did in a few months' time: a severe, but just punishment for the unprincipled education she had given her.

It ought to be added that this was an iniquity of which neither Mr. Lovelace, nor any of his friends, could bear to hear her boast; and always checked her for it whenever she did; condemning it with one voice: and it is certain that this and other instances of her complicated wickedness turned early Lovelace's heart against her; and, had she not been subservient to him in his other pursuits, he would not have endured her: for, speaking of her, he would say, Let not any one reproach *us*, Jack: *there is no wickedness like the wickedness of a woman.*[1]

A bad education was the preparative, it must be confessed: and for this Sally Martin had reason to thank her parents, as they had reason to thank themselves, for what followed: but had she not met with a Lovelace, she had avoided a Sinclair; and might have gone on at the common rate of wives so educated; and been the mother of children turned out to take their chance in the world, as she was; so many lumps of soft wax, fit to take any impression that the first accident gave them; neither happy, nor

[1] Ecclus. xxv, 19.

making happy; everything but useful, and well off, if not extremely miserable.

POLLY HORTON was the daughter of a gentlewoman well descended; whose husband, a man of family and of honour, was a captain in the Guards.

He died when Polly was about nine years of age, leaving her to the care of her mother, a lively young lady of about twenty-six; with a genteel provision for both.

Her mother was extremely fond of her Polly; but had it not in *herself* to manifest the true, the genuine fondness of a parent, by a strict and guarded education; dressing out, and visiting, and being visited by the gay of her own sex, and casting out her eye abroad, as one very ready to try her fortune again in the married state.

This induced those airs, and a love to those diversions, which make a young widow, of so lively a turn, the unfittest tutoress in the world, even to her own daughter.

Mrs. Horton herself having had an early turn to music, and that sort of reading which is but an earlier debauchery for young minds, preparative to the grosser at riper years, to wit, romances and novels, songs and plays, and those without distinction, moral or immoral, she indulged her daughter in the same taste; and at those hours when they could not take part in the more active and lively amusements and *kill-times*, as some call them, used to employ miss to read to her; happy enough, in her own imagination that, while she was diverting her own ears, and sometimes, as the piece was, corrupting her own heart, and her child's too, she was teaching miss to read, and improve her mind; for it was the boast of every tea-table half-hour, *That Miss Horton, in propriety, accent, and emphasis, surpassed all the young ladies of her age*: and, at other times, complimenting the pleased mother, *Bless me, madam, with what a surprising grace Miss Horton reads! She enters into the very spirit of her subject. This she could have from nobody but you!* An intended praise; but, as the subjects were, would have been a severe *satire* in the mouth of an enemy! While the fond, the inconsiderate mother, with a delighted air, would cry, *Why, I cannot but say Miss Horton does credit to her tutoress!* And then a *Come hither, my best love!* and, with a kiss of approbation, *What a pleasure to your dear papa, had he lived to see your improvements, my charmer!* Concluding with a sigh of satisfaction; her eyes turning round upon the circle, to take in all the silent applauses of theirs! But little thought the fond, the foolish mother, what the plant would be which was springing up from these seeds! Little imagined she that her own ruin, as well as her child's, was to be the consequence of this fine education; and that, in the same ill-fated hour, the honour both of mother and daughter was to become a sacrifice to the intriguing invader.

This the laughing girl, when abandoned to her evil destiny, and in company with her sister Sally and others, each recounting their settings-out, their progress, and their fall, frequently related to be her education and manner of training-up.

This, and to see a succession of humble servants buzzing about a mother, who took too much pride in addresses of that kind, what a beginning, what an example, to a constitution of tinder, so prepared to receive the spark struck from the steely forehead and flinty heart of such a libertine as at last it was their fortune to be encountered by!

In short, as miss grew up under the influences of such a directress, and of books so light and frothy, with the inflaming additions of music, concerts, operas, plays, assemblies, balls, drums, routs, and the rest of the rabble of amusements of the modern life, it is no wonder that, like early fruit, she was soon ripened to the hand of the insidious gatherer.

At fifteen she owned she was ready to fancy herself the heroine of every novel and of every comedy she read, so well did she enter into the *spirit* of her subject: she glowed to become the object of some hero's flame; and perfectly longed to begin an intrigue, and even to be *run away with* by some enterprising lover: yet had neither *confinement* nor *check* to apprehend from her indiscreet mother: which she thought absolutely necessary to constitute a Parthenissa!

Nevertheless, with all these fine modern qualities, did she complete her nineteenth year before she met with any address of consequence: one half of her admirers being afraid, because of her gay turn and but middling fortune, to make serious applications for her favour; while others were kept at distance by the superior airs she assumed; and a third sort, not sufficiently penetrating the foibles either of mother or daughter, were kept off by the supposed watchful care of the former.

But when the man of intrepidity and intrigue was found, never was heroine so soon subdued, never goddess so early stripped of her celestials! For, at the opera, a diversion at which neither she nor her mother ever missed to be present, she beheld the specious Lovelace; beheld him invested with all the airs of heroic insult, resenting a slight affront offered to his Sally Martin by two gentlemen who had known her in her more hopeful state, one of whom Mr. Lovelace obliged to sneak away with a broken head, given with the pommel of his sword, the other with a bloody nose; neither of them well supporting that readiness of offence which, it seems, was a part of their *known* characters to be guilty of.

The gallantry of this action drawing every bystander on the side of the hero, *Oh, the brave man!* cried Polly Horton aloud to her mother, in a kind of rapture. *How needful the protection of the brave to the fair!* with a softness in her voice, which she had taught herself, to suit her fancied *high* condition of life.

A speech so much in his favour could not but take the notice of a man who was but too sensible of the advantages which his fine person and noble air gave him over the gentler hearts, who was always watching every female eye, and who had his ear continually turned to every affected voice; for that was one of his indications of a proper subject to be attempted—*Affectation of every sort,* he used to say, *is a certain sign of a wrong-turned head; of a faulty judgment: and upon such a basis I seldom build in vain.*

He instantly resolved to be acquainted with a young creature who seemed so strongly prejudiced in his favour. Never man had a readier invention for all sorts of mischief. He gave his Sally her cue. He called her *sister* in their hearing. And Sally whisperingly gave the young lady and her mother, in her own way, the particulars of the affront she had received; making herself an angel of light, to cast the brighter ray upon the character of her heroic brother. She particularly praised his known and approved courage; and mingled with her praises of him such circumstances relating to his birth, his fortune, and endowments, as left him nothing to do but to fall in love with the enamoured Polly.

Mr. Lovelace presently saw what turn to give to his professions. *So brave a man! yet of manners so gentle!* hit the young lady's taste: nor could she suspect the heart that such an aspect covered. *This was the man! the very man!* she whispered to her mother: and, when the opera was over, his servant procuring a coach, he undertook, with his specious sister, to set them down at their own lodgings, though situated a quite different way from his: and there were they prevailed upon to alight, and partake of a slight repast.

Sally pressed them to return the favour to her at her Aunt Forbes's, and hoped it would be before her brother went to his own seat.

They promised her, and named their evening.

A splendid entertainment was provided. The guests came, having in the interim found all that was said of his name, and family, and fortune, to be true. Persons of so little strictness in their own morals took it not into their heads to be very inquisitive after his.

Music and dancing had their share in the entertainment: these opened their hearts, already half-opened by love: the *Aunt* Forbes, and the lover's sister, *kept* them open by their own example: the hero sang, vowed, promised: their gratitude was moved, their delights were augmented, their hopes increased, their confidence was engaged, all their appetites up in arms; the rich wines co-operating, beat quite off their guard, and not *thought* enough remaining so much as for suspicion—miss, detached from her mother by Sally, soon fell a sacrifice to the successful intriguer.

The widow herself, half intoxicated, and raised as she was with artful mixtures, and inflamed by love, unexpectedly tendered by one of the libertines, his constant companions (to whom an *opportunity* was contrived to be given to be alone with her, and that closely followed by *importunity*), fell into her daughter's error. The consequences of which, in length of time, becoming apparent, grief, shame, remorse, seized her heart (her own indiscretion not allowing her to arraign her daughter's), and she survived not her delivery; leaving Polly with child likewise: who, when delivered, being too fond of the gay deluder to renounce his company, even when she found herself deluded, fell into a course of extravagance and dissoluteness; ran through her fortune in a very little time; and, as a high preferment, at last, with Sally, was admitted a quarter-partner with the detestable Sinclair.

All that is necessary to add to the history of these unhappy women will be comprised in a very little compass.

After the death of the profligate Sinclair, they kept on the infamous trade with too much success; till an accident happened in the house—a gentleman of family killed in it in a fray, contending with another for a new-vamped face. Sally was accused of holding the gentleman's arm, while his more favoured adversary ran him through the heart, and then made off. And she being tried for her life, narrowly escaped.

This accident obliged them to break up housekeeping; and not having been frugal enough of their ill-gotten gains (lavishing upon one what they got by another), they were compelled, for subsistence sake, to enter themselves as under-managers at such another house as their own had been. In which service, soon after, Sally died of a fever and surfeit got by a debauch: and the other, about a month after, by a violent cold, occasioned through carelessness in a salivation.

Happier scenes open for the remaining characters; for it might be descending too low to mention the untimely ends of *Dorcas*, and of *William*, Mr. Lovelace's wicked servant; and the pining and consumptive ones of *Betty Barnes* and *Joseph Leman*, unmarried both, and in less than a year after the happy death of their excellent young lady.

The good Mrs. NORTON passed the small remainder of her life as happily as she wished, in her beloved foster-daughter's Dairy-house, as it used to be called: *as she wished*, we repeat; for she had too strong aspirations after another life to be greatly attached to this.

She laid out the greatest part of her time in doing good by her advice, and by the prudent management of the fund committed to her direction. Having lived an exemplary life from her youth upwards; and seen her son happily settled in the world; she departed with ease and calmness, without pang or agony, like a tired traveller, falling into a sweet slumber: her last words expressing her hope of being restored to the child of her bosom; and to her own excellent father and mother, to whose care and pains she owed that good education to which she was indebted for all her other blessings.

The poor's fund, which was committed to her care, she resigned, a week before her death, into the hands of Mrs. Hickman, according to the direction of the will, and all the accounts and disbursements with it; which she had kept with such an exactness, that that lady declares that she will follow her method, and only wishes to discharge the trust as well.

Miss HOWE was not to be persuaded to quit her mourning for her dear friend until six months were fully expired: and then she made Mr. HICKMAN one of the happiest men in the world. A woman of her fine sense and understanding, married to a man of virtue and good nature (who had no *past capital errors* to reflect upon, and to abate his joys, and whose behaviour to *Mrs. Hickman* is as affectionate as it was respectful to *Miss Howe*), could not do otherwise. They are already blessed with two fine children; a daughter, to whom, by joint consent, they have given the name of her beloved friend; and a son, who bears that of his father.

She has allotted to Mr. Hickman, who takes delight in doing good (and that as much for its own sake as to oblige her), *his part* of the management of the poor's fund; to be accountable for it, as she pleasantly says, to *her*. She has appropriated every Thursday morning for *her part* of that management; and takes so much delight in the task, that she declares it to be one of the most agreeable of her amusements. And the more agreeable, as she teaches every one whom she benefits *to bless the memory of her departed friend ;* to whom she attributes the merit of all *her own* charities, as well as the honour of those which she dispenses in pursuance of her will.

She has declared that this fund shall never fail while she lives. She has even engaged her mother to contribute annually to it. And Mr. Hickman has appropriated twenty pounds a year to the same. In consideration of which she allows him to recommend four objects yearly to partake of it. *Allows* is her style; for she assumes the whole prerogative of dispensing this charity; the *only* prerogative she *does* or has *occasion* to assume. In every other case there is but *one will* between them; and that is generally *his* or *hers*, as either speaks first, upon any subject, be it what it will. Mrs. HICKMAN, she sometimes as pleasantly as generously tells him, must not *quite* forget that she was once Miss HOWE, because if he had not loved her as such, and with all her foibles, she had never been MRS. HICKMAN. Nevertheless she seriously, on all occasions, and that to others as well as to himself, confesses that she owes him *unreturnable* obligations for his patience *with* her in HER day, and for his generous behaviour *to* her in HIS.

And still the more highly does she esteem and love him, as she reflects upon his past kindness to her beloved friend; and on that dear friend's good opinion of him. Nor is it less grateful to her that the worthy man joins most sincerely with her in all those respectful and affectionate recollections which make the memory of the departed precious to survivors.

Mr. BELFORD was not so destitute of humanity and affection as to be unconcerned at the unhappy fate of his most intimate friend. But when he reflects upon the untimely ends of several of his companions, but just mentioned in the preceding history [1]: on the shocking despondency and death of his poor friend *Belton*; on the signal justice which overtook the wicked *Tomlinson*; on the dreadful exit of the infamous *Sinclair*; on the deep remorses of his more valued friend; and, on the other hand, on the example

[1] See pp. 37, and 447, of this volume.

set him by the most excellent of her sex, and on her blessed preparation and happy departure; and when he considers, as he often does with awe and terror, that his *wicked habits* were so *rooted* in his depraved heart, that all *these warnings*, and this *lovely example*, seemed to be *but necessary* to enable him to subdue them, and to reform; and that such awakening calls are *hardly ever afforded to men of his cast*, or (if they *are*) but seldom attended with such happy effects in the prime of youth, and in the full vigour of constitution—when he reflects upon all these things, he adores the Mercy which through these calls has snatched him as a *brand out of the fire*: and thinks himself obliged to make it his endeavour to find out, and to reform, any of those who may have been endangered by his means; as well as to repair, to the utmost of his power, any damage or mischiefs which he may have occasioned to others.

With regard to the trust with which he was honoured by the inimitable lady, he had the pleasure of acquitting himself of it in a very few months, to everybody's satisfaction; even to that of the unhappy family; who sent him their thanks on the occasion. Nor was he, at delivering up his accounts, contented without resigning the legacy bequeathed to him to the uses of the will: so that the poor's fund, as it is called, is become a very considerable sum; and will be a lasting bank for relief of objects who *best deserve* relief.

There was but one earthly blessing which remained for Mr. Belford to wish for, in order, morally speaking, to secure to him all his other blessings; and that was the greatest of all worldly ones, a virtuous and prudent wife. So free a liver as he had been, he did not think that he could be worthy of such a one, till, upon an impartial examination of himself, he found the pleasure he had in his new resolutions so great, and his abhorrence of his former courses so sincere, that he was the less apprehensive of a deviation.

Upon this presumption, having also kept in his mind some encouraging hints from Mr. Lovelace; and having been so happy as to have it in his power to oblige Lord M., and that whole noble family, by some services grateful to them (the request for which from his unhappy friend was brought over, among other papers, with the dead body, by De la Tour), he besought that nobleman's leave to make his addresses to Miss CHARLOTTE MONTAGUE, the eldest of his lordship's two nieces: and making at the same time such proposals of settlements as were not objected to, his lordship was pleased to use his powerful interest in his favour. And his worthy niece having no engagement, she had the goodness to honour Mr. Belford with her hand; and thereby made him as completely happy as a man *can be*, who has enormities to reflect upon, which are out of his power to atone for, by reason of the death of *some* of the injured parties, and the *irreclaimableness* of *others*.

"Happy is the man who, in time of health and strength, sees and reforms the error of his ways! But how much more happy is he who has no capital and wilful errors to repent of! How *unmixed* and *sincere* must the joys of such a one come to him!"

Lord M. added bountifully in his lifetime, as did also the two ladies his sisters, to the fortune of their worthy niece. And as Mr. Belford has been blessed with a son by her, his lordship at his death [which happened just three years after the untimely one of his unhappy nephew] was pleased to devise to that son, and to his descendants for ever (and in case of his death unmarried, to any other children of his niece), his Hertfordshire estate (*designed for Mr. Lovelace*), which he made up to the value of a moiety of his real estates; bequeathing also a moiety of his personal to the same lady.

Miss PATTY MONTAGUE, a fine young lady [to whom her noble uncle, at his death, devised the other moiety of his real and personal estates, including his seat in Berkshire], lives at present with her excellent sister Mrs. Belford; to whom she removed upon Lord M.'s death: but, in all probability, will soon be the lady of a worthy baronet of ancient family, fine qualities, and ample fortunes, just returned from his travels, with a character superior to the *very* good one he set out with: a case that very seldom happens, although the *end of travel is improvement*.

Colonel MORDEN, who, with so many virtues and accomplishments, cannot be unhappy, in several letters to the executor, with whom he corresponds from Florence [having, since his unhappy affair with Mr. Lovelace, changed his purpose of coming so soon to reside in England as he had intended], declares, that although he thought himself obliged either to accept of what he took to be a challenge, as such; or tamely to acknowledge that he gave up all resentment of his cousin's wrongs; and in a manner to beg pardon for having spoken freely of Mr. Lovelace behind his back; and although at *the time* he owns he was not sorry to be called upon, as he was, to take either the one course or the other; yet now, coolly reflecting upon his beloved cousin's reasonings against duelling; and upon the price it had too probably cost the unhappy man; he wishes he had more fully considered those words in his cousin's posthumous letter: "If God will allow him time for repentance, why should you deny it him?"[1]

To conclude: The worthy widow LOVICK continues to live with Mr. Belford; and by her prudent behaviour, piety, and usefulness, has endeared herself to her lady, and to the whole family.

[1] Several worthy persons have wished that the heinous practice of duelling had been more forcibly discouraged, by way of note, at the conclusion of a work designed to recommend the *highest and most important doctrines of Christianity*. It is humbly presumed that those persons have not sufficiently attended to what is already done on that subject in vol. i, Letter lv. and in this volume, Letters cxxix, clvi, clvii, clviii.

POSTSCRIPT
Referred to in the Preface

IN WHICH

Several objections that have been made, as well to the Catastrophe, as to different parts of the preceding history, are briefly considered.

THE foregoing work having been published at three different periods of time, the author, in the course of its publication, was favoured with many anonymous letters, in which the writers differently expressed their wishes with regard to the apprehended catastrophe.

Most of those directed to him by the gentler sex, turned in favour of what they called a fortunate ending. Some of the fair writers, enamoured, as they declared, with the character of the heroine, were warmly solicitous to have her made happy: and others, likewise of their mind, insisted that poetical justice required that it should be so. And when, says one ingenious lady, whose undoubted motive was good-nature and humanity, it must be concluded, that it is in an author's power to make his piece end as he pleases, why should he not give pleasure rather than pain to the reader whom he has interested in favour of his principal characters?

Others, and some gentlemen, declared against tragedies in general, and in favour of comedies, almost in the words of Lovelace, who was supported in his taste by all the women at Mrs. Sinclair's, and by Sinclair herself. "I have too much feeling," said he.[1] "There is enough in the world to make our hearts sad, without carrying grief into our diversions, and making the distresses of others our own."

And how was this happy ending to be brought about? Why, by this very easy and trite expedient; to wit, be reforming Lovelace, and marrying him to Clarissa—not, however, abating her one of her trials, nor any of her sufferings (for the sake of the sport her distresses would give to the tender-hearted reader as she went along) the last outrage excepted: that indeed, partly in compliment to Lovelace himself, and partly for delicacy-sake, they were willing to spare her.

[1] See vol. ii, p. 339.

But whatever were the fate of his work, the author was resolved to take a different method. He always thought, that sudden conversions, such especially as were left to the candour of the reader to suppose and make out, had neither art, nor nature, nor even probability, in them; and that they were moreover of very bad example. To have a Lovelace for a series of years glory in his wickedness, and think that he had nothing to do, but as an act of grace and favour to hold out his hand to receive that of the best of women, whenever he pleased, and to have it thought, that marriage would be a sufficient amends for all his enormities to others, as well as to her; he could not bear that. Nor is reformation, as he has shewn in another piece, to be secured by a fine face; by a passion that has sense for its object; nor by the goodness of a wife's heart, nor even example, if the heart of the husband be not graciously touched by the divine finger.

It will be seen by this time that the author had a great end in view. He has lived to see scepticism and infidelity openly avowed, and even endeavoured to be propagated from the press: the great doctrines of the gospel brought into question: those of self-denial and mortification blotted out of the catalogue of Christian virtues: and a taste even to wantonness for out-door pleasure and luxury, to the general exclusion of domestic as well as public virtue, industriously promoted among all ranks and degrees of people.

In this general depravity, when even the pulpit has lost great part of its weight, and the clergy are considered as a body of interested men, the author thought he should be able to answer it to his own heart, be the success what it would, if he threw in his mite towards introducing a reformation so much wanted. And he imagined, that in an age given up to diversion and entertainment, he could steal in, as may be said, and investigate the great doctrines of Christianity under the fashionable guise of an amusement; he should be most likely to serve his purpose; remembering that of the poet:

> A verse may find him who a sermon flies,
> And turn delight into a sacrifice.

He was resolved therefore to attempt something that never yet had been done. He considered that the tragic poets have as seldom made their heroes true objects of pity, as the comic theirs laudable ones of imitation: and still more rarely have made them in their deaths look forward to a future hope. And thus, when they die, they seem totally to perish. Death, in such instances, must appear terrible. It must be considered as the greatest evil. But why is death set in shocking lights, when it is the universal lot?

He has indeed thought fit to paint the death of the wicked, as terrible as he could paint it. But he has endeavoured to draw that of the good in such an amiable manner, that the very Balaams of the world should not forbear to wish that their latter end might be like that of the heroine.

And after all, what is the poetical justice so much contended for by some, as the generality of writers have managed it, but another sort of dispensation than that with which God, by revelation, teaches us, He has thought fit to exercise mankind; whom placing here only in a state of probation, He hath so intermingled good and evil, as to necessitate us to look forward for a more equal dispensation of both?

The author of the history (or rather dramatic narrative) of Clarissa, is therefore well justified by the Christian system, in deferring to extricate suffering virtue to the time in which it will meet with the completion of its reward.

But not absolutely to shelter the conduct observed in it under the sanction of religion (an authority perhaps not of the greatest weight with some of our modern critics) it must be observed, that the author is justified in its catastrophe by the greatest master of reason, and best judge of composition, that ever lived. The learned reader knows we must mean ARISTOTLE; whose sentiments in this matter we shall beg leave to deliver in the words of a very amiable writer of our country.

[Richardson here quotes from Addison, *The Spectator*, Nos. 40 and 548. See the Everyman's Library edition: vol. i, pp. 120–1, line 20; vol. iv, pp. 226–9, line 10.]

Mr. Addison, as we have seen above, tells us, that Aristotle, in considering the tragedies that were written in either of the kinds, observes, that those which ended unhappily had always pleased the people, and carried away the prize, in the public disputes of the stage, from those that ended happily. And we shall take leave to add, that this preference was given at a time when the entertainments of the stage were committed to the care of the magistrates; when the prizes contended for were given by the state; when, of consequence, the emulation among writers was ardent; and when learning was at the highest pitch of glory in that renowned commonwealth.

It cannot be supposed, that the Athenians, in this their

highest age of taste and politeness, were less humane, less tender-hearted, than we of the present. But they were not afraid of being moved, nor ashamed of shewing themselves to be so, at the distresses they saw well painted and represented. In short, they were of the opinion, with the wisest of men, that it was better to go to the house of mourning than to the house of mirth; and had fortune enough to trust themselves with their own generous grief, because they found their hearts mended by it.

Thus also Horace, and the politest Romans in the Augustan age, wished to be affected:

Ac ne forte putes me, quae facere ipse recusem,
Cum recte tractant alii, laudare maligne;
Ille per extentum funem mihi posse videtur
Ire poeta, meum qui pectus inaniter angit,
Irritat, mulcet; falsis terroribus implet,
Ut magus; & modo me Thebis, modo ponit Athenis.

Thus Englished by Mr. Pope:

Yet, lest you think I rally more than teach.
Or praise malignly *Arts* I cannot reach;
Let me, for once, presume t'instruct the times
To know the *Poet* from the *Man of Rhymes*.
'Tis he who gives my breast a thousand pains:
Can make me *feel* each passion that he feigns;
Enrage—compose—with more than magic art,
With *pity* and with *terror* tear my heart;
And snatch me o'er the earth, or thro' the air,
To Thebes, to Athens, when he will, and where.

Our fair readers are also desired to attend to what a celebrated critic [1] of a neighbouring nation says on the nature and design of tragedy, from the rules laid down by the same great ancient.

"Tragedy", says he, "makes man modest, by representing the great masters of the earth humbled; and it makes him tender and merciful, by shewing him the strange accidents of life, and the unforeseen disgraces to which the most important persons are subject.

"But because man is naturally timorous and compassionate, he may fall into other extremes. Too much fear may shake his

---

[1] Rapin, on Aristotle's *Poetics*.

constancy of mind, and too much compassion may enfeeble his equity. 'Tis the business of tragedy to regulate these two weaknesses. It prepares and arms him against disgraces, by shewing them so frequent in the most considerable persons; and he will cease to fear extraordinary accidents, when he sees them happen to the highest part of mankind. And still more efficacious, we may add, the example will be, when he sees them happen to the best.

"But as the end of tragedy is to teach men not to fear too weakly common misfortunes, it proposes also to teach them to spare their compassion for objects that deserve it. For there is an injustice in being moved at the afflictions of those who deserve to be miserable. We may see, without pity, Clytemnestra slain by her son Orestes in Aeschylus, because she had murdered Agamemnon, her husband; yet we cannot see Hippolytus die by the plot of his stepmother Phaedra, in Euripides, without compassion, because he died not, but for being chaste and virtuous."

These are the great authorities so favourable to the stories that end unhappily. And we beg leave to reinforce this inference from them, that if the temporary sufferings of the virtuous and the good can be accounted for and justified on pagan principles, many more and infinitely stronger reasons will occur to a Christian reader in behalf of what are called unhappy catastrophes, from the consideration of the doctrine of future rewards; which is everywhere strongly enforced in the history of Clarissa.

Of this (to give one instance) an ingenious modern, distinguished by his rank, but much more for his excellent defence of some of the most important doctrines of Christianity, appears convinced in the conclusion of a pathetic monody, lately published; in which, after he had deplored, as a man without hope (expressing ourselves in the Scripture phrase) the loss of an excellent wife; he thus consoles himself:

Yet, O my soul! thy rising murmurs stay,
Nor dare th' All-wise Disposer to arraign,
    Or against his supreme decree
        With impious grief complain.
That all thy full-blown joys at once should fade,
Was his most righteous Will: And be that Will obey'd.
    Would thy fond love his grace to her controul,
And in these low abodes of sin and pain
        Her pure, exalted soul,
Unjustly, for thy partial good detain?

No—rather strive thy grov'ling mind to raise
   Up to that unclouded blaze,
That heav'nly radiance of eternal light,
In which enthron'd she now with pity sees,
   How frail, how insecure, how slight,
     Is ev'ry mortal bliss.

But of infinitely greater weight than all that has been above produced on this subject, are the words of the psalmist:

"As for me," says he,[1] "my feet were almost gone; my steps had well nigh slipt: for I was envious at the foolish, when I saw the prosperity of the wicked. For their strength is firm: they are not in trouble as other men; neither are they plagued like other men.—Their eyes stand out with fatness: they have more than their heart could wish.—Verily I have cleansed mine heart in vain, and washed my hands in innocence: For all the day long have I been plagued, and chastened every morning.—When I thought to know this, it was too painful for me. Until I went into the sanctuary of God; then understood I their end.—Thou shalt guide me with thy counsel, and afterwards receive me to glory."

This is the psalmist's comfort and dependence. And shall man, presuming to alter the common course of nature, and, so far as he is able, to elude the tenure by which frail mortality indispensably holds, imagine, that he can make a better dispensation; and by calling it poetical justice, indirectly reflect on the divine?

The more pains have been taken to obviate the objections arising from the notion of poetical justice, as the doctrine built upon it had obtained general credit among us; and as it must be confessed to have the appearance of humanity and good nature for its supports. And yet the writer of the history of Clarissa is humbly of opinion, that he might have been excused referring to them for the vindication of his catastrophe, even by those who are advocates for the contrary opinion; since the notion of poetical justice, founded on the modern rules, has hardly ever been more strictly observed in works of this nature, than in the present performance.

For, is not Mr. Lovelace, who could persevere in his villainous views, against the strongest and most frequent convictions and remorses that ever were sent to awaken and reclaim a wicked man—is not this great, this wilful transgressor, condignly punished, and his punishment brought on through the intelligence of the very Joseph Leman whom he had corrupted [2]; and

---

[1] Psalm lxxiii.   [2] See vol. iv, p. 514.

by means of the very woman whom he had debauched [1]—is not Mr. Belton, who has an uncle's hastened death to answer for [2]— are not the whole Harlowe family—is not the vile Tomlinson— are not the infamous Sinclair and her wretched partners—and even the wicked servants, who, with their eyes open, contributed their parts to the carrying on of the vile schemes of their respective principals—are they not all likewise exemplarily punished?

On the other hand, is not Miss Howe, for her noble friendship to the exalted lady in calamities—is not Mr. Hickman, for his unexceptionable morals, and integrity of life—is not the repentant and not ungenerous Belford—is not the worthy Norton —made signally happy?

And who that are in earnest in their profession of Christianity, but will rather envy than regret the triumphant death of CLARISSA; whose piety, from her early childhood, whose diffusive charity; whose steady virtue; whose Christian humility; whose forgiving spirit; whose meekness, and resignation, Heaven *only* could reward? [3]

We shall now, according to the expectation given in the preface to this edition, proceed to take brief notice of such other objections as have come to our knowledge: for, as is there said: "This work being addressed to the public as an history of life and manners, those parts of it which are proposed to carry with them the force of example, ought to be as unobjectionable as is consistent with the design of the whole, and with human nature."

Several persons have censured the heroine as too cold in her love, too haughty, and even sometimes provoking. But we may presume to say, that this objection has arisen from want of attention to the story, to the character of Clarissa, and to her particular situation.

It was not intended that she should be in love, but in liking only, if that expression may be admitted. It is meant to be everywhere inculcated in the story, for example sake, that she never would have married Mr. Lovelace, because of his immoralities, had she been left to herself; and that her ruin was principally owing to the persecutions of her friends.

What is too generally called love, ought (perhaps as generally)

---

[1] See vol. iv, p. 525.   [2] Ibid. p. 169.
[3] And here it may not be amiss to remind the reader, that so early in the work as vol. i, pp. 419-20, the dispensations of Providence are justified by herself. And thus she ends her reflections—"I shall not live always—may my closing scene be happy!"
She had her wish. It *was* happy.

to be called by another name. Cupidity, or Paphian stimulus, as some women, even of condition, have acted, are not words too harsh to be substituted on the occasion, however grating they may be to delicate ears. But, take the word "love" in the gentlest and most honourable sense, it would have been thought by some highly improbable, that Clarissa should have been able to shew such a command of her persons, as makes so distinguishing a part of her character, had she been as violently in love, as certain warm and fierce spirits would have had her to be. A few observations are thrown in by way of note in the present edition, at proper places, to obviate this objection, or rather to bespeak the attention of hasty readers to what lies obviously before them. For thus the heroine anticipates this very objection, expostulating with Miss Howe on her contemptuous treatment of Mr. Hickman; which (far from being guilty of the same fault herself) she did on all occasions, and declares she would do, whenever Miss Howe forgot herself, although she had not a day to live:

"O my dear," says she, "that it had been my lot (as I was not permitted to live single) to have met with a man, by whom I could have acted generously and unreservedly!

"Mr. Lovelace, it is now plain, in order to have a pretence against me, taxed my behaviour to him with stiffness and distance. You, at one time, thought me guilty of some degree of prudery. Difficult situations should be allowed for; which often make seeming occasions for censure unavoidable. I deserved not blame from him, who made mine difficult. And you, my dear, had I had any other man to deal with than Mr. Lovelace, or had he had but half the merit which Mr. Hickman has, would have found, that my doctrine on this subject, should have governed my whole practice."

It has been thought, by some worthy and ingenious persons, that if Lovelace had been drawn an infidel or scoffer, his character, according to the taste of the present worse than sceptical age, would have been more natural. It is, however, too well known, that there are very many persons, of his cast, whose actions discredit their belief. And are not the very devils, in Scripture, said to believe and tremble?

But the reader must have observed, that great and, it is hoped, good use, has been made throughout the work, by drawing Lovelace an infidel only in practice; and this as well in the arguments of his friend Belford, as in his own frequent remarks, when touched with temporary compunction, and in his last scenes;

which could not have been made had either of them been painted as sentimental unbelievers. Not to say, that Clarissa, whose great objection to Mr. Wyerly was, that he was a scoffer, must have been inexcusable had she known Lovelace to be so, and had given the least attention to his addresses. On the contrary, thus she comforts herself, when she thinks she must be his: This one consolation, however, remains: he is not an infidel, an unbeliever. Had he been an infidel, there would have been no room at all for hope of him; but (priding himself as he does in his fertile invention) he would have been utterly abandoned, irreclaimable, and a savage. And it must be observed, that scoffers are too witty in their own opinion (in other words, value themselves too much upon their profligacy) to aim at concealing it.

Besides, had Lovelace added ribald jests upon religion to his other liberties, the freedoms which would then have passed between him and his friend, must have been of a nature truly infernal. And this farther hint was meant to be given, by way of inference, that the man who allowed himself in those liberties either of speech or action, which Lovelace thought shameful, was so far a worse man than Lovelace. For this reason he is everywhere made to treat jests on sacred things and subjects, even down to the mythology of the pagans, among pagans, as undoubted marks of the ill-breeding of the jesters; obscene images and talk, as liberties too shameful for even rakes to allow themselves in; and injustice to creditors, and in matters of *Meum* and *Tuum*, as what it was beneath him to be guilty of.

Some have objected to the meekness, to the tameness, as they will have it to be, of Mr. Hickman's character. And yet Lovelace owns that he rose upon him with great spirit in the interview between them; once, when he thought a reflection was but implied on Miss Howe; and another time, when he imagined himself treated contemptuously.[1] Miss Howe, it must be owned (though not to the credit of her own character) treats him ludicrously on several occasions. But so she does her mother. And perhaps a lady of her lively turn would have treated as whimsically any man but a Lovelace. Mr. Belford speaks of him with honour and respect.[2] So does Colonel Morden. [3] And so does Clarissa on every occasion. And all that Miss Howe herself says of him, tends more to his reputation than discredit,[4] as Clarissa indeed tells her.[5]

---

[1] Vol. ii, p. 495.
[2] Vol. iv, pp. 13–14.
[3] Ibid., p. 469.

[4] Vol. ii, pp. 116–17.
[5] Vol. i, pp. 278–9.

And as to Lovelace's treatment of him, the reader must have observed, that it was his way to treat every man with contempt, partly by way of self-exaltation, and partly to gratify the natural gaiety of his disposition. He says himself to Belford [1]: "Thou knowest I love him not, Jack; and whom we love not, we cannot allow a merit to; perhaps not the merit they should be granted."

"Modest and diffident men," writes Belford, to Lovelace, in praise of Mr Hickman, "wear not soon off those little precisenesses, which the confident, if ever they had them, presently get over."

But, as Miss Howe treats her mother as freely as she does her lover; so does Mr. Lovelace take still greater liberties with Mr. Belford, than he does with Mr. Hickman, with respect to his person, air, and address, as Mr. Belford himself hints to Mr. Hickman.[2] And yet he is not so readily believed to the discredit of Mr. Belford, by the ladies in general, as he is when he disparages Mr. Hickman. Whence can this partiality arise?

Mr. Belford had been a rake: but was in a way of reformation.

Mr. Hickman had always been a good man.

And Lovelace confidently says, *that the women love a man whose regard for them is founded in the knowledge of them.*[3]

Nevertheless, it must be owned, that it was not proposed to draw Mr. Hickman, as the man of whom the ladies in general were likely to be very fond. Had it been so, *goodness of heart,* and *gentleness of manners, great assiduity,* and *inviolable* and *modest* love, would not of themselves have been supposed sufficient recommendations He would not have been allowed the least share of *preciseness* or *formality,* although those defects might have been imputed to his reverence for the object of his passion. But in his character it was designed to shew, that the same man could not be everything; and so intimate to ladies, that in choosing companions for life, they should rather prefer the honest heart of a Hickman, which would be all their own, than to risk the chance of sharing, perhaps with scores (and some of those probably the most profligate of the sex), the volatile mischievous one of a Lovelace: in short, that they should choose, if they wished for durable happiness, for rectitude of mind, and not for speciousness of person or address: nor make a jest of a good man in favour of a bad one, who would make a jest of them and of their whole sex.

Two letters, however, by way of accommodation, are inserted

[1] Vol. iii, p. 485.   [3] Vol. iii, p. 81.
[2] Vol. iv, p. 443.

in this edition, which perhaps will give Mr. Hickman's character from heightening with such ladies as love spirit in a man; and had rather suffer by it, than not meet with it:

> "Women, born to be controul'd,
> Stoop to the forward and the bold."

Says Waller—and Lovelace too!

Some have wished that the story had been told in the usual narrative way of telling stories designed to amuse and divert, and not in letters written by the respective persons whose history is given in them. The author thinks he ought not to prescribe to the taste of others; but imagined himself at liberty to follow his own. He perhaps mistrusted his talents for the narrative kind of writing. He had the good fortune to succeed in the epistolary way once before. A story in which so many persons were concerned either principally or collaterally, and of characters and dispositions so various, carried on with tolerable connection and perspicuity, in a series of letters from different persons, without the aid of digressions and episodes foreign to the principal end and design, he thought had novelty to be pleaded for it: and that, in the present age, he supposed would not be a slight recommendation.

Besides what has been said above, and in the Preface, on this head, the following opinion of an ingenious and candid foreigner, on this manner of writing, may not be improperly inserted here.

"The method which the author has pursued in the History of Clarissa, is the same as in the Life of Pamela: both are related in familiar letters by the parties themselves, at the very time in which the events happened: and this method has given the author great advantages, which he could not have drawn from any other species of narration. The minute particulars of events, the sentiments and conversation of the parties, are, upon this plan, exhibited with all the warmth and spirit that the passion supposed to be predominant at the very time could produce, and with all the distinguishing characteristics which memory can supply in a history of recent transactions.

"Romances in general, and Marivaux's amongst others, are wholly improbable; because they suppose the history to be written after the series of events is closed by the catastrophe: a circumstance which implies a strength of memory beyond all example and probability in the persons concerned, enabling them, at the distance of several years, to relate all the particulars of a transient conversation: or rather, it implies a yet more improbable confidence and familiarity between all these persons and the author.

"There is, however, one difficulty attending the epistolary method; for it is necessary that all the characters should have an uncommon taste for this kind of conversation, and that they should suffer no event, not even a remarkable conversation to pass, without immediately committing it to writing. But for the preservation of the letters once written, the author has provided with great judgment, so as to render this circumstance highly probable." [1]

It is presumed that what this gentleman says of the difficulties attending a story thus given in the epistolary manner of writing, will not be found to reach the history before us. It is very well accounted for in it, how the two principal female characters came to take so great a delight in writing, Their subjects are not merely subjects of amusement; but greatly interesting to both: yet many ladies there are who now laudably correspond, when at distance from each other, on occasions that far less affect their mutual welfare and friendships, than those treated of by these ladies. The two principal gentlemen had motives of gaiety and vainglory for their inducements. It will generally be found, that persons who have talents for familiar writing, as these correspondents are presumed to have, will not forbear amusing themselves with their pens, on less arduous occasions than what offer to these. These four (whose stories have a connection with each other) out of the great number of characters which are introduced in this history, are only eminent in the epistolary way: the rest appear but as occasional writers, and as drawn in rather by necessity than choice, from the different relations in which they stand with the four principal persons.

The length of the piece has been objected to by some, who looked upon it as a mere novel or romance; and yet of these there are not wanting works of equal length.

They were of opinion that the story moved too slowly, particularly in the first and second volumes, which are chiefly taken up with the altercations between Clarissa and several persons of her family.

---

[1] This quotation is translated from a *Critique on the History of Clarissa*, written in French, and published at Amsterdam. The whole Critique, rendered into English, was inserted in the *Gentleman's Magazine* of June and August 1749. The author has done great honour in it to the History of Clarissa; and as there are remarks published with it, which answer several objections made to different passages in the story by that candid foreigner, the reader is referred to the aforesaid magazine for both.

But is it not true, that those altercations are the foundation of the whole, and therefore a necessary part of the work? The letters and conversations, where the story makes the slowest progress, are presumed to be characteristic. They give occasion likewise to suggest many interesting personalities, in which a good deal of the instruction essential to a work of this nature is conveyed. And it will, moreover, be remembered, that the author, at his first setting out, apprised the reader, that the story (interesting as it is generally allowed to be) was to be principally looked upon as the vehicle to the instruction.

To all which we may add, that there was frequently a necessity to be very circumstantial and minute, in order to preserve and maintain that air of probability, which is necessary to be maintained in a story designed to represent real life; and which is rendered extremely busy and active by the plots and contrivances formed and carried on by one of the principal characters.

Some there are, and ladies too! who have supposed that the excellencies of the heroine are carried to an improbable, and even to an impracticable height, in this history. But the education of Clarissa from early childhood ought to be considered as one of her very great advantages; as, indeed, the foundation of all her excellencies; and, it is hoped for the sake of the doctrine designed to be inculcated by it, that [it] will.

She had a pious, a well-read, a not meanly descended woman for her nurse, who with her milk, as Mrs. Harlowe says,[1] gave her that nurture which no other nurse could give her. She was very early happy in the conversation-visits of her learned and worthy Dr. Lewen, and in her correspondencies, not with him only, but with other divines mentioned in her last will. Her mother was, upon the whole, a good woman, who did credit to her birth and her fortune; and both delighted in her for those improvements and attainments, which gave her, and them in her, a distinction that caused it to be said, that when she was out of the family, it was considered but as a common family.[2] She was moreover a country lady, and, as we have seen in Miss Howe's character of her,[3] took great delight in rural and household employments; though qualified to adorn the brightest circle.

It must be confessed, that we are not to look for Clarissas among the constant frequenters of Ranelagh and Vauxhall, nor among those who may be called 'Daughters of the Card-table'.

[1] Vol. ii, p. 289.

[2] See vol. iv, p. 174. See also her mother's praises of her to Mrs. Norton, vol. i, p. 192.

[3] See vol. iv, pp. 496–8.

If we do, the character of our heroine may then indeed be justly thought not only improbable, but unattainable. But we have neither room in this place, nor inclination, to pursue a subject so invidious. We quit it therefore, after we have repeated, that we know there are some, and we hope there are many, in the British dominions [or they are hardly anywhere in the European world] who, as far as occasion has called upon them to exert the like humble and modest yet steady and useful virtues, have reached the perfections of a Clarissa.

Having thus briefly taken notice of the most material objections that have been made to different parts of this history, it is hoped we may be allowed to add, that had we thought ourselves at liberty to give copies of some of the many letters that have been written on the other side of the question, that is to say, in approbation of the catastrophe, and of the general conduct and execution of the work, by some of the most eminent judges of composition in every branch of literature; most of what has been written in this postscript [might] have been spared.

But as the principal objection with many has lain against the length of the piece, we shall add to what we have said above on that subject, in the words of one of those eminent writers: "That, if, in the history before us, it shall be found, that the spirit is duly diffused throughout; that the characters are various and natural; well distinguished and uniformly supported and maintained: if there be a variety of incidents sufficient to excite attention, and those so conducted, as to keep the reader always awake! the length then must add proportionably to the pleasure that every person of taste receives from a well-drawn picture of nature. But where the contrary of all these qualities shock the understanding, the extravagant performance will be judged tedious, though no longer than a fairy-tale."

CONTENTS OF VOLUME IV

567

CONTENTS OF VOLUME IV